MODERN
SPANISH DRAMATISTS

MODERN
SPANISH DRAMATISTS

A Bio-Bibliographical Sourcebook

Edited by
MARY PARKER

GREENWOOD PRESS
Westport, Connecticut • London

Library of Congress Cataloging-in-Publication Data

Modern Spanish dramatists : a bio-bibliographical sourcebook / edited by Mary Parker.
　　p.　cm.
　　Includes bibliographical references and index.
　　ISBN 0–313–30578–1 (alk. paper)
　　　　1. Spanish drama—20th century—History and criticism.　2. Spanish drama—19th
century—History and criticism.　3. Spanish drama—18th century—History and criticism.　4.
Spanish drama—20th century—Bio-bibliography.　5. Spanish drama—19th
century—Bio-bibliography.　6. Spanish drama—18th century—Bio-bibliography.　I. Parker,
Mary
PQ6051.M53　2002
822.009—dc21　　　　00–052143
[B]

British Library Cataloguing in Publication Data is available.

First published in 2002

Greenwood Press, 88 Post Road West, Westport, CT 06881
An imprint of Greenwood Publishing Group, Inc.
www.greenwood.com

Printed in the United States of America

The paper used in this book complies with the
Permanent Paper Standard issued by the National
Information Standards Organization (Z39.48–1984).

10　9　8　7　6　5　4　3　2　1

CONTENTS

Contents

PREFACE

Modern Spanish Dramatists contains entries on thirty-three dramatists who wrote from 1700 to 1999. When we began the present book, Spanish was fashionable and the language of choice in academe. Yet the existing sources and specialized studies circulated solely among subscribers to professional scholarly publications; materials in English needed to catch up with the enthusiastic and growing interest in the artistic creations of Spain and other countries. Of course, major dramatists are featured in dictionaries, and generally these same names are covered within studies that span the whole literary history of Spanish drama and literature. That realization and the small but increasing number of English translations of modern classics inspired us to make available to the contemporary English speaker a larger picture of the changing modern Spanish drama. Not to publish it on time offered others the opportunity to develop the idea in similar publications.

Each of the thirty-three entries is divided into the following sections: Biography, Dramaturgy: Major Works and Themes, Critics' Response, Awards and Distinctions, Notes (where applicable), and Bibliography. Dramaturgy contains evaluative and analytical commentary on the literary and historical contexts; the principal texts; dominant themes, structure, styles, and techniques; edition(s), date(s) of publication, staging(s), and opening night performance, if recorded; and reception of the play. Critics' Response examines the scholarship and critical interpretations the plays have elicited, including the contributor's original analysis and interpretation of one major play. The Bibliography at the end of each entry lists the major short and full-length plays, well-received editions and translations, and the central books and articles on the specific dramatist and on the major play chosen by each contributing author. The General Bibliography, Index, and About the Contributors sections conclude the book.

The entries in *Modern Spanish Dramatists* follow an alphabetical format. Our scope and format facilitate the appreciation of each author and his or her art. Both the scope and format help to sketch a larger image of the authors, their writings, and the stage than the one portrayed in existing English-oriented encyclopedias, histories of literature, one-theme or one-author collected essays.

The total range of dramatists spans from Arniches to Zorrilla. It includes writers who have been translated, anthologized, and studied for centuries as Spanish classic authors; major names who—not without disagreement—are considered the classical writers of today (Ramón de la Cruz, Duque de Rivas, Zorrilla, Benavente, Buero Vallejo, J. E. Hartzenbusch, Lorca, Sastre, and most recently, Arrabal); well-known writers such as Pérez Galdós, Salinas, and Unamuno, whose theater remains mainly known to specialists, Martínez de la Rosa, Aub, and Casona; and prolific playwrights whose proven box office successes and strong popularity have always been questioned, their fame disputed, discounted, denied, or diminished, not always for artistic reasons. Uninterrupted interest in their plays continues to be strong. The book also treats some disdained and little known, but significant, plays that mark a particular dramatist's artistic and/or ideological evolution. Among these dramatists are Echegaray, García Gutiérrez, Jardiel Poncela, and even Benavente. A number of emerging and promising dramatists who have been successful on the Spanish stage have become drama critics, television scriptwriters, play-text or play-act authors, professors, directors, and producers. Those who have shown the most talent as dramatists are seen in academic and theatrical circles as talent who are on their way to joining or changing the canon.

As a unit, the thirty-three entries in the book highlight the trends, movements, and historical situations to which modern and postmodern dramatists have been responsive.[1] They apply the various theories of interpretation that informed conventional thought and current methods of reading and interpreting plays—the themes, styles, and techniques through which the *modern Spanish* dramatists expressed their attitudes, experiences, dreams, and concerns. The contributors' original views suggest new approaches to commenting or judging the dramatists. Their opinions and the plays they treat sometimes project changing ideologies, opinions, and attitudes toward history, the theater, and modernity.

Here are a few examples: It is an error to consider Echegaray a lesser dramatist who wrote modern melodrama. A reassessment of the playwright shows that in the context of their time his plays do not represent the typical melodrama of the Restoration. It is fundamental to note his use of the immersion technique and to mark the difference that exists between melodrama and the melodramatic. Martínez de la Rosa "is not a hot headed rebel or an overthrower of accepted eighteenth-century forms." Duque de Rivas's *Don Alvaro* illuminates his unique perspective on Spanish nationalism. Galdós's feminism relates to his way of life. His liberal creed represents a continuation of the progressive ideology of the Enlightenment. However, when his teachings are examined closely, they appear less than altruistic. The "new women," "new couple," "new world" he wants and advocates are also *realidad*—more self-serving concepts than a reformer's idealistic dreams. The strong, unconventional female protagonists glorified as models in Galdós's novels and dramas were created for, or inspired by, the married women in his multiple unorthodox unions. Alejandro Casona, a promoter of the Spanish classic drama and known mostly for a couple of plays, authored works on a wide range of issues, including the violation of taboos treated as society's system of oppression. A balanced analysis of Alfonso Paso's dramaturgy consistently shows that critics and writers hostile to the Franco regime disparage Paso's evolution from an early writer and would-be reformer to a dramatist whose later comedies they strongly condemn for their blatant ideological conformism. Concha Romero's feminist approach to historical women adds the long-missing feminine perspective. There is renewed interest and a newfound significance in the local color, humor, and mordant sociopolitical satire inherent to the short theatrical forms called *Teatro Menor.* These deceivingly trivial subgenre pieces, *interludes, sainetes, tonadillas* (short sung pieces) by Ramón de la Cruz, Arniches, and the highly stylized *esperpentos* of Valle Inclán, reflect standpoints, issues, and disagreements on the methods used to carry out the commonly perceived need for cultural renovation and renewal. Their longevity confirms the assertion that, in each century, dramatists weight the reconfiguration of the national popular play and the restoration of the classics as the means to take the stage and the state from slumber to modernity.

Worthwhile dramatists whose plays are in any of the other languages of Spain—Guimera, Rusiñol, Sirera, and Bonet i Jornet, for example—will be missed. The double language limitation and lack of or hard-to-find English or Spanish editions or translations make them and others who are significant in their particular geographical areas basically unknown to bilingual specialists and stages even in Spain. In faraway places, they, like their predecessors, remain known, sometimes by choice, as Catalonian or, separately, as Valencian, and Galician celebrities. Belbel is translating, directing, and producing Bonet i Jornet. Happily, since this project began, Catalán authors, who do not write in Spanish, have been the subject of studies published as books, monographs, and articles in books or professional journals in Spain, England, and the United States.[2]

Among this volume's authors are academics, literary critics, editors, and publishers of journals dedicated to the theater. They also introduce, actively promote, perform, translate, stage, or host them in their colleges and universities. Their contributions ensure the value of this book to other specialists in Spanish and other drama and literature. The specialized reader will find that along with the new paths for understanding the works, political change appears central to our knowledge of recently surfaced, published, or staged plays whose heroes are radical social agitators. Recent history is the framework for the drama that Aub, Arrabal, Buero Vallejo, Sastre, and many of their contemporaries wrote during the dictatorship period and made known in exile or, in Spain, after Franco's death. In such plays, dramatists go from criticism and antagonism to radicalism and social activism. Radical social agitators as heroes no longer seem relevant or artistically fashionable today, but the plays they wrote remain significant among those who adhere to the world view of the writers or know them personally. These rebels created models meant to be a strong force in society, influential living voices that would make art and life one. As Susan Polansky points out, Salinas found such force lacking in both moral stimulus and profound spiritual orientation. The hope is that easy access to the life, writing career, and source materials on a number of modern Spanish dramatists will nurture enthusiasm and interest in their lives and work. As a reference book, this volume is meant to attract attention and stimulate curiosity and to give English-speaking audiences a helpful guide to reading and understanding a distinguished group of modern Spanish dramatists.

The Introduction that follows highlights trends that will help to define and trace modernity, its forces, voices, and influence. It explores their effects on the dramatists, their plays, the culture, and the stage. In addition, the Introduction touches on salient issues, contrasting comments, ideas, and further information on dramatists or plays that are central to the balanced picture we endeavor to present.

NOTES

1. Ignacio Armestoy Egiguren, "La literatura dramática española en la encrucijada de la posmodernidad," *Insula* 601–602 (1997): 2–5.

2. See the special issue of *Estreno* entitled *Homage to Catalán Theater* 24.2 (1998).

ACKNOWLEDGMENTS

The idea for this project was met with enthusiastic approval from all of my collaborators. The need for a book such as ours was first recognized by Dr. James T. Sabin and the Greenwood Press. To him I offer my deepest-felt "Thank you." Thanks also to Dr. George F. Butler, who wrote constructive remarks and made suggestions. My warm and very special thanks to my husband for his unending support. I am indebted to Glenn D. Tiffert who, with my husband, introduced me to computers and solved my many PC crises. My thanks also go to Robert Sheehan and his late wife Gela who was kind and understanding of Bob's lively interest and hard work in the draft of a long chapter that does not appear in the book, owing to the need to reduce the length of the original volume. Bob, I will not forget your advice, our scholarly discussions, arguments, the openness with which we challenged each other, nor our humorous digressions. I owe special thanks to Martha Halsey and David Gies, for their kindness and help in getting the project started, and to María Delgado, for the names of the UK contributors.

To all of my collaborators, I appreciate all of your hard work. If we have succeeded in our purpose, the reader will find the fruits of our efforts *dulce e utile*.

INTRODUCTION: MODERN SPANISH DRAMATISTS

Mary Parker

The word *modern* in our volume's title will stir curiosity, perhaps even controversy. Its concept and terms are topics of endless contention among playwrights, theater professionals, drama historians, strict linguists, critics, and audiences. It is helpful, and fitting, to recall known notions, voices, and definitions intended to capture its evolving nature and unsettling spirit.

Modernity has been described as the transient, as fugitive, as contingent aesthetic curiosities—one half of what art is; the other is the eternal and the immutable.[1] Earlier, with irony, the Theologian Benito Jerónimo Feijoo (1676–1764) determines the indescribable, essential quality of artistic creations, "talent," in his *El no sé qué*, the translation of the well-known French expression. He also addresses the modern artistic contingencies of the Age of Reason in *La razón de la Moda*. While investigating the transcendental value of art as a way to truth and discovery during *modernism*, Valle-Inclán held *La lámpara maravillosa* [The Magic Lantern] and discovered that the creative spirit is timeless— "El alma creadora está fuera del tiempo"—and that the same eternal quality of the spirit is the very essence of artistic creation.[2]

Modern drama exhibits a constant search for the new, the old, the physical, the essential, the contingent, and the permanent. That search illuminates the quality and distinctive connection that dramatists of any present time have with their artistic and literary past. It portrays modernity as an ambitious aesthetic project aimed at artistic regeneration on the basis that values would emerge from the theater's honest representation of historical and immediate reality. The dramatists' struggle for permanence and change can be seen in terms of Bloom's affirmation that "poets wrestle with their precursors so as to clear imaginative space for themselves."[3] Harold Bloom's notion also aids understanding artistic change. It helps sort out the tangible from the intangible regarding data such as David T. Gies's finding that "throughout the nineteenth century it became almost *de rigueur* to begin a piece on the theater by bemoaning the terrible state to which the theater had sunk in the previous few years."[4] At its less evident level, it reveals the writer's determination to penetrate the secrets of mastery and survival, an attempt to transcend time, be like their masters, an example in life, an inspiration in death. At an immediate, practical level the dramatist's struggle for survival is a sustained commitment to effect cultural and social change. Plays expressing conflicts and clashes between cultural heritage and fashion, or between Spain's two dramatic traditions, typically define modern drama further as a cultural product as much as an instrument of it. Wilfried Floeck posits, correctly, that for modern Spanish dramatists commitment is "universal law, the conscience of the nation, the reason of artistic creation, the immediate political crisis, the ideological indoctrination of the reader, the aggressive criticism of society or plans for future utopias."[5] What that utopia became is—and perhaps it should be—a matter of contention.

Plays as well as nondramatic writings, plans, and manifestos reveal the basic stands and united commitment to modernize, reformulate, and reconceptualize the nation and the stage. A radical stance is to abandon Lope's *arte nuevo* tradition (the *new play* or *comedia nueva*) to follow the French neoclassic aesthetic fashionable in Europe. A moderate position, the most successful and far-reaching, is to continue the popular tradition; maintain the best plays; and rewrite, "improve," and adapt them to the neoclassic artistic mold in fashion. A notable example of the compromised position is García de la Huerta's adaptation of *La judia de Toledo* [The Jewess from Toledo]. It was immediately hailed, and remains, the most artful, successful, controversial neoclassic tragedy, for in the spirit of the age, it wrongs the reputation of a Spanish king and/or his court by forcing historical connections with the distant past. With the wrong and adulterous acts of a monarch, and the tragic consequence for his paramour, Huerta reconstructs a moral tragedy where he expresses the vision (many still hold today) of Spain's history as tragic history. A third stance, indicative of modernity's pervasive influence and changing nature, is to write as Azorin recommends, *Al margen de los clásicos*. Azorín's twentieth-century title in favor of leaving the classics at the margins[6] represents a moment of avid innovation—a time when both the ancient and the modern classic traditions seemed an obstacle to creativity or artistic freedom. Dramatists saw hope (some say it was false hope) for renewal, new freedom, energy and opportunity for innovation, experimentation, and success in the revolutionary avant-garde movements of Europe, particularly, in the aesthetics of surrealism. The persistent hope and commitment to modernity introduce recurring conflicts and divisions between circles that welcome influences from Europe, the East, or the United States and those that favor and insist on modernization from within, especially in periods defined by social revolt, political unrest, crisis, or confrontations. Stricken by the neoclassic fashion, enlightened dramatists enact their hard decision and determination to bring dead drama to life—also their ambition to leave an imprint of their own while dredging the classic past.

Along with the major political and cultural upheavals, social changes, and reactions that take place in 1688, 1810–1813, the 1820s, 1865, 1868, 1898, and 1936, drama takes its course against magical comedies and *autos* (sacramental plays) and in favor of earthy realism. With the migration to the cities for employment and abandonment of the farmland arrives the new unsung hero—the laboring farmer; the peasant (Saint Isidore the Farmer, the patron saint, becomes one ideal role model); the progressive, salaried middle-class individual; the ideological, working-class hero in Dicenta; the young, liberal and liberated, modern man, woman, and couple in Galdós, next to the new urban poor. They and the land workers in Gimera's plays—all are made examples of the assertive, modern, and ideologically progressive citizens. This baggage and hero take the stage from elegance to foppish dandyism, or *majismo*, which is well studied by René Andioc.[7] After him, Caro Baroja, Coulon, Varela, and Vilches have written on "Los majos."[8] It takes society from idealism to realism, from farming to industrialism, to Marxism and socialism; aesthetics from a continuing Iberianism/regionalism to neoclassicism, Romanticism, modernism, avant-gardism, aesthetic technicism, to neoprimitivism and simplicity of means in the year 2000. In short, when one examines the multifarious panorama of real life and art, it becomes clearer that choices or changes in modern drama are not fortuitous, that dramatists' choices and decisions are essentially ideological, expressing attitudes about life in the capital, in other cities, and in rural settings and, ultimately, about class and power, which underpin the structure of the society they see, avow, or reject. To assess the modernity of Spanish dramatists entails a side view of the drama of earlier times when the modern experiment began. To explore their significance further, bits of history and dramatic context are useful.

Renaissance influences sparked the first literary debates about ancient and modern attitudes toward literature and art. In the seventeenth century, Cervantes and Lope participated in the polemic going on in their century over how the work of art should be. They forcefully argued for and against imitating the artistic beauty of ancient classic models or creating an *arte nuevo* copying life. The polemic is between the secular and the worshipful artistic views—between awe, respect, and admiration versus the deification of art. The new attitude or idea attempts to free the curious imagination, to write drama that speaks for the spirit of the age, addresses its contemporaries or records them. The dramatists represented in this volume are combatants in favor of the new attitude. Plays by them—and others such as Iriarte, Cadalso, Cienfuegos Jovellanos, Moratín (the father and son), García de la Huerta, Zamora, Cañizares, Grimaldi, Rodríguez Rubí, Tamayo y Baus, N. Serra, Azorín, and Sanchiz Sinisterra—are expressions of an irrepressible sensibility and style deemed necessary for the modern nation, a free country, an equitable society, and the mass communal ideal that invaded and subjugated large parts of Europe. The Enlightenment's dream was to bring back high culture, to raise society's artistic, ethical, and moral levels. The opponents' dream was to recapture the prestige and defend what they posited as the unique, indomitable spirit of the nation and its plays. The struggle to effect their vision of the theater, the nation, and society is depicted in similar struggles, with different degrees of imagination and success.

For the most part, their tragedy, farce, comedy, or tragicomedy consistently mask, reveal, and ingenuously record living tragedy and human drama.

Eighteenth-century drama records a peculiar bitterness of strife that had been ravishing the country (and all of Europe) since the two previous centuries. Atheists, Protestants, Catholics, and Calvinists assail one another over issues involving the interrelationship of the monarchy, the kingdom, and the church, the nature of authority, and scopes of freedom. A new form of individualism is depicted in rebellions of wronged proud town's folk against the lesser nobility, or between lower and high nobility against the king. The monarchs side with the common people, who have just cause. In return the king has their total loyalty and unending support. A deeply felt need to modernize and "save" Spain from itself, its theater, and the ideas and beliefs it portrays delineates, with precision, events, issues, themes, and techniques that map the roads to modernity. Arguably, Percy Shelley's dictum "Poets are the unacknowledged legislators of the world"[9] is a fitting characterization of many Spanish dramatists of the three centuries that concern us.

Eighteenth-century Spanish writers—intellectual, religious, and political leaders—looked beyond their boundaries and saw a much different world: developments in science, philosophy, theology, and social and moral ideology. They saw that the framework of the prosperous modern nation was a composite of democratic philosophy, a work ethic, empirical methodology, and strict moral and aesthetic principles. The modernizers who favored Europeanization sought to influence high arts, intellectual disciplines, and public spheres guided by the progressive social ideologies of Bacon, Newton, Locke, Adam Smith, and Hobbes (who believed that man needs to be governed). They were guided, also, by the strict neoclassic aesthetic and French philosophic thought, especially the doctrines espoused by Voltaire, Rousseau, and Diderot. Reason, peace, progress, and prosperity obsessed the heart and intellect of a few but influential leaders who laid down the foundations that would give Spain and its theater a modern outlook. Modernity became the axis and axiom in the fierce literary and culture wars of their radical reform movement. They fought for change and for control of the collective mind as a fundamental moral imperative; they pursued it with evangelical conviction, a didactic purpose, and a dogmatic stance. Their quest for progress and social uplift invigorates the tension that exists between leaders who favor openness and Europeanization and their opponents who insist on keeping a cultural independence from Europe. Not totally without reason, they felt that the European model and plans for radical reform and modernization posed a threat to Spain. They argued that by advancing it the reformers were betraying their own culture. They foresaw their larger goals were to change Spain's political power structure, to take away the Church's influence over the king on social issues, to increase theirs, to recover nobility's rights and privileges, and to turn the government and country into an autocratic, secular, modern power.

The social concept of privilege protecting the old proud lineage of Castile was being debated in Cervantes's time by unsung heroes of modern wars. The privilege given to inhabitants of old Castile, "el Castellano viejo," who populated the area, farmed the land, or fought to forge or free the country was extended to their descendants, not to heroes of recent wars. Drama records that reality. With disaffection, Cervantes, a warrior of modern wars, treats fear, anxiety, and boasting of pure, old Castilian blood as fiction and theater. *El retablo de las maravillas* [The Magical Little Theater] deals with two well-known motifs: "the world as theater" and "the emperor has no clothes." Neither is Spanish. But *El retablo* develops its theme of truth and deception or appearance, illusion and reality, in the context of a particular place and language of Spain. As a theatrical piece (metatheatrical in anachronic modern idiom), *El retablo* embraces the definition that "art is a lie that tells the truth." Lope places *purity of blood* at the core of honor, the theme of his success. A 1990s play entitled *Purasangre* will probably justify my digression. Its sardonic nominalism personalizes the treatment of the concept. Its theme underscores the essential relationship that connects the present drama of any age with its classic Spanish past. Anxiety over cultural contamination for ideological and political reasons is not always unfounded in any country. Strict Spanish national statesmen, writers, and political leaders in the 1600s and 1700s were distrustful of rulers born outside Spain who could threaten to turn the Spanish empire into one part of their dreamed great or universal empire. They were not pleased with being left out or being left with very little power in government to oppose what they viewed as the devastation of Spain's financial and human capital in foreign wars. A three-year war, in the nineteenth century (1810–1813), to regain independence from France, plus France's contribution to the wars for independence in Spain's New World colonies, probably confirmed their distrust and trepidations.

On the basis of a needed purpose, moral commitment, and artistic discipline, 1700 Spain made popular theater and its ideas the target and centerpiece of reform. Luzán,[10] the patriarch of neoclassicism, wrote his *Poética* to advance Horacio's neo-Aristotelian principles: Language and action must be believable, enjoyable, and beneficial; the neoclassic play respects the unities of place, time, and action, and it has a moral didactic purpose. Tragedy shows the actions of legendary kings, heroes, or noblemen whose fall, death, or defeats impart examples to rulers and high nobility. Comedy entertains but corrects the behavior of the citizenry. In their plays the flawed character repents, reforms, ends tragically, or is publicly ridiculed. Besides their underestimated drama, mostly based on contrary history, they write drama of biblical depth such as *Guzmán el Bueno* by Nicholás Fernández de Moratín. Like Isaac, Guzmán's moral duty or sacred obligation to God interplays the love-honor commitment with the conflict and drama of choice in the new historical time.

Jovellanos probably knew of Jeremy Collier or his book *English Stage*.[11] They coincide or share the common belief in the efficacy of the theater as an institution of social and moral reform. As spokesman for the prevailing attitude of the eighteenth century, Jovellanos summarizes the general sentiment when he writes that the theater is not only a source of diversion but an important instrument commonly used to deform the heart of the citizens.[12] Popular Spanish plays—in particular, the short popular pieces being represented—were, in their view, an impediment to the creation of the modern (moral, enlightened, and happier) citizen. Jovellanos favors reforming the Golden Age *comedia* to "correct" its defects and weaknesses in structure, moral laxity, and ideological misconceptions. When asked, Jovellanos formulated the reformers' dramatic ideal, which remains contentious to today. They wanted a theater that would "exalt virtue" and ignite the emotions that burned the human heart—a theater that diverts the mind from wanderings about truth and dogma that may lead to erroneous notions about doctrine or prevent the practice of virtue by exciting sinful passions and sentiments. Vice, in the theater, far from deserving protection, will warrant hate and censorship from the authorities. Government officials, in turn, should be humane and incorruptible citizens, full of virtue and patriotism, prudent and faithful heads of family, and loyal friends. In short, Jovellanos continues, they should be heroic and strong government officials, guardians of the public welfare, freedom, and rights of the citizens, protectors of the innocent, and the unrelenting persecutors of inequity (*Memorias* 460). As a dramatist, Jovellanos wrote several plays that advance the neoclassic, didactic, moral principle and artistic norm. He follows structural order, linear development, a simple plot; the nobility learns through tragically flawed characters who meet their due punishment. His drama aims to help form the new honorable man, the citizen who will make a better society.

El delincuente honrado [The Honorable Culprit], Jovellanos's best-known play, introduces the sentimental play, which was popular all over Europe, and a new sentiment toward crime and punishment. *El delincuente* reflects a social evolution inspired by the influential judicial tenets contained in *Dei delitti e delle pene*, which Cesare Beccaria penned in 1764.[13] Jovellanos warrants the modern system of criminal justice, adapting its ideas to a specific, immediate reality. When the characters, a husband and his wife, denounce absurd, cruel, and unjust laws, Jovellanos compares the different social and artistic contexts. They specifically underscore basic contradictions between the social law that requires gentlemen to live by the code of honor and the criminal law that imparts capital punishment on duelists. The contrasting attitude toward law and convention lends a new universal dimension to the honor theme, which distances *El delincuente* from a number of notable *comedia* precedents. Dramatists who carry on the *comedia* popular tradition today attack the influence of what dramatist Rodríguez Méndez, as historian of the theater, says is the influence of a liberal middle class that arrived in Spain in the 1850s with the Bourbon age.

García de la Huerta, Moratín, Iriarte, Nicholás Fernández de Moratín, and his son Leandro are all involved in the cultural warfare that radical reform, recuperation, and reconstruction signify. They write dramatic theory; put it into practice in plays corrective of society and aesthetics; and help form other neoclassic writers by providing them with concrete, perfectly structured, neoclassic models. The eighteenth-century audiences and critics considered the neoclassic comedies and tragedies well-constructed examples of the French neoclassic aesthetics—but too languid, dead, and inauthentic for the Spanish taste. That judgment determined the fate of, among other plays, *La petimetra* [The Primping Lady, 1762] by Nicolás de Moratín. *Lucrecia* (1773), and *Hormesinda* (1770), his tragedies debasing history based on legend, were judged academically perfect by his contemporaries. According to Martínez de la Rosa, *Hormesinda* failed because his friend Moratín chose the wrong subject and the wrong point of view. In their highly charged times the issues the plays treated were extremely sensitive. Later, Moratín wrote significant drama but failed to find a stage, so it could only be read. *El sí de las niñas* [The Maiden's Consent] (1806), by his son Leandro Fernández de Moratín, acclaimed a "perfect neoclassic jewel" by his contemporaries, satirizes the pretended ways of a new nobility, a society based on forced marriages. Moratín exposes the new ways that the impoverished nobility become enriched and the rich honorable commoners gain noble status as signs of social and moral decadence. No matter that the most punctilious neoclassicists maintained that humor and satire reduced the importance of the message, both styles define the most successful eighteenth-century stage. In numerous plays, ideology and aesthetic taste are transformed into extreme patterns used to attack the "imperfect" play (*comedia nueva*), the extremely popular short theater pieces, and to combat their inclement satirical humor. Since the neoclassics favored "imitation" over originality, adaptations and remakes throughout the century seem inevitable, even natural. Nevertheless, in practice, both sides also wrought controversial plays where they demonized each other by disregarding or emphasizing the pleasure principle. The images present in comedy, as well as its humor combating the dramatics of literary satire, substantiate the argument that their plays are primarily written in response to other plays.

In the mordant satire *La Comedia Nueva o el café*, [New Play or the Cafe] (1792) Leandro F. de Moratín caricatures competitors like Comella, Jovellanos, Trigueros, and other members of the popular drama club known as the *tertulia* of Olavide, in Seville. These defenders of the national theatrical vein gathered in that tavern to chat of the theater in general, critique each other's plays, or write collectively or individually. One product of the *tertulia* is *El no de las niñas* (a close translation is "The Maiden Says No"), an obvious reaction to *La Comedia Nueva*. Its author or authors chose to remain anonymous. But they must have been identified by their target and in their respective theatrical circles. The little-known response *El no de las niñas* (a freer translation, closer to its source of inspiration could be "The Maiden Does Not Consent) clearly parodies Moratín's enormously successful *El sí de las niñas* [The Maiden's Consent]. Moratín's influence reaches far, to the twentieth century. Benavente's urban comedies, epitomized in *Lo cursi*, are a reaction to the artificiality and affectation in bad modern copies of Moratín's comedy of manners and conventions of society. With light irony and gentle humor, Benavente scorns the dramatic fashion and modern plays representing "known people" who may be sitting in the audience as if they were like the ridiculous dramatic types, called *cursi* (tacky) since the nineteenth century. *Gente Conocida* makes currently staged theatrical imitations of upper middle-class citizens—Benavente's social group—bad, *cursi* theater, bad artistic models, and untrue representations of society. In another instance, Benavente draws from Moratín and borrows from *commedia d'll arte* to signal his criticism, artistic parallels, and the veiled cultural implications of *Bonds of Interest*, his celebrated play. Karl Shapiro puts this idea in perspective when he declares, "Ours is primarily an Age of Culture and only secondarily an Age of Art."[14] As said at the beginning, Spain's dramatic production is a product as much as it is an instrument of culture except, perhaps, for the few but notable exceptions of modernism. The extremely popular theater by Ramón de la Cruz, Jardiel Poncela, Arniches, Mihura, Muñiz, Sanchiz Sinisterra, and R. Méndez bears proof.

Ramón de la Cruz, a strong defender of popular theater in the literary and cultural wars of the Enlightenment, is the nemesis of Iriarte and Moratín, the apostles of the reconstruction movement. Rebecca Haidt underlines Cruz's significance. The reformers fought him as a major obstacle to their plan for progress, morality, and good taste. His interludes, *sainetes*, and *tonadillas* (short sung pieces) may be perceived as genuine expressions of the divide between the common, natural, sometimes low-life speech and the refined style, between *cosmopolitanism* and nativism. In this respect, Bloom's concept of "anxiety of influence" helps clarify common charges that in Spain there is a xenophobic attitude that results from its extreme nationalism and that its antagonism toward "imports" colors its reaction to foreign influences and plays.[15] In reality, Spain's "anxiety of influence" bears on what comes from outside, including cultures and languages from regions other than old Castile, "la España, castiza." Notably, dramatists inflect with bias, their representation of the conflict between attitudes and life in the capital, other urban centers, and the countryside through serious characters and caricatures of living artistic models. As it is in many countries, satire and irreverent humor are still common tools.

Emilio Palacios argues that popular theater of great historical consequence—artistically superior from regions other than Castile, Andalucía in particular—has been unjustly overlooked and long forgotten. In his Andalucian view, Cruz's distinct humor is "a crude antidote for the elevated style poetics of the sixteenth and seventeenth centuries."[16] And his theater is "the continuation of the still current rank ("rancias") esthetics of the *Arte Nuevo de hacer comedias en este tiempo*, with which Lope established popular dramatic art." The neoclassics who fostered the cultivated literary style both condemned and combatted the extreme mocking practice in these short, popular pieces, which they considered non-literary and in poor taste. The mocking technique used through distorted official language—Sayagués and Latin "*macaronico*" in the short and full-length popular plays—is also found in other literatures. The use of double meaning and euphemisms is itself a humorous joke today. *Pasos, sainetes, interludes*, many *comedias*, and Shaw's *Pygmalion*, the source of the musical *My Fair Lady*, are notable examples containing distorted syntax, language jokes imitating regional dialects, learned Italian, French, and less frequently English, affected speech, and neologisms. A balanced opinion is that Cruz's choice of types, the life styles that inspired his characters and move his pieces, place him not only in the tradition established by Rueda through Cervantes, to the twentieth century, but also with the burlesques that were fashionable in eighteenth-century Europe.

Heinrich Falk's assessment of the impact of the ideas, attitudes, and values of the Enlightenment on Spaniards, in terms of popular theatrical materials, is an important contribution to this field of study.[17] But it only represents one half of the equation. Joan Lynne Pataki Kasove narrows the gap significantly with *The "Comedia Lacrimosa,"* an "examination of the philosophical bases and dramatic techniques of the sentimental comedy in Spain."[18] Douglas McKay published the first comprehensive book on Arniches and the genre in the United States. Nancy Membrez did seminal work in her study of the genre, especially her doctoral studies on *theater by the hour*. The same stage battles and intense open debate over the theater for utilitarian ends continue in the nineteenth century and much of the twentieth. The aesthetic and the philosophical are dominated by overt and hidden political agendas. In high political crises, long dynastic fights over the crown, and a civil war in 1936, dramatists of these two centuries turn to black humor, hermetic language, direct confrontation, and iconoclastic rage. D. Gies sees its theater as the battleground and the stage as the forum from where Spanish political writers fought their allegorical cultural, ideological, and theatrical wars.[19] The dramatic force of these plays centers on the problem of legitimate succession; the abolition of the Salic Law, women's right to inherit the throne (French-born Isabel II); the rivalry between the aristocracy, the farmers, and the rising mercantile middle class; and the disintegration of the empire in the Americas. It is repeatedly said that crisis of the monarchy comes with the new anxiety of influence and threats of an actual exile and backslide to what Ermanno Caldera asserts is "a typical isolation," triggered by the country's antagonism and conflict with a powerful few who profess a cosmopolitan vocation.[20] Those few form the milieu that keep faith and hope in an enlightened society—a society that disavows its history and rejects heroic dreams as the ideal for the present or the future. It proposes instead a workforce that includes all privileged groups as the solution for economic prosperity.

The 1810 war crisis corroborated distrust and bred or solidified antiforeign sentiment. Often, the sentiment is misunderstood as xenophobic, mainly because there is a tendency to lose full sight of the importance of variations in lifetime experiences and individual contexts. In addition, Spanish dramatists, almost singularly, enact sentiment with hyperbole and heated rhetoric in a direct, often cathartic, way. In 1868 Enrique Zumel recorded the dethronement and exile of Queen Isabel II with his title *Oprimir no es gobernar* [To Oppress Is Not to Govern]. Adelardo López de Ayala, in *Numancia*, entreated Spaniards to put differences aside and to unite behind the enlightened King Carlos III and avoid civil war—or else they would fight their opponents to the death, like the citizens of Numancia, immortalized in seventeenth-century drama. In *Españoles sobre todo*, Eusebio Asquerino appeals to national sentiment in the fight for freedom from France. It asks Francoist reformers to join the nation's fight for freedom and independence—to be Spaniards Above All. Besides the flag-waving plays about heroic actions, like *Numancia*, which were intended to inspire nationalism and fire up lukewarm hearts, there are caricatures of Joseph Bonaparte, after Napoleon crowned him king of Spain; plays responding or reacting to them; and drama both recovering and/or further damaging the image of legendary kings (Pelayo, Charles I/V, Philip II), glorious battles, heroes, saints, and religious literary personalities, which the antiheroic, peace-loving Age of Reason had rejected, dishonored, or disdained. The indictment of unreasonableness, and the passions among powers in war are recorded in Goya's paintings and emblematic etchings about the Franco-Spanish war. *The Sleep of Reason* which awakens the monster of war in 1810 is an admonition. The real and symbolic meanings of his motto gain poignancy and fresh power in dramas by, among others, Sastre, Arrabal, Buero, and Recuerda, with reference to the 1936–1939 civil war. They expose the monsters and horrors of war, but, at the same time, they advocate violence and dramatize personal affinities with extreme positions and partisan disputes. Their antithetical texts and subtext at once incite and indict. Buero recalls Goya in an identical title that is more than a clinical study or biographical sketch of the painter. The point is the growing madness which each perceives during the wars they have witnessed. At the root of war reason lies dormant, which leads to suffering, isolation, and death. Several apparently pacifist plays are blowup plays that could only surface in the period of democracy. Many are dramas that are explosively nihilistic of the culture, and in these dramas the playwrights disavow the painter's admonition. But their dramatic renditions of powerful figures and social systems created a genealogy of monsters that may confirm the old motto in artistic terms.

Dissatisfied dramatists of the 1800s challenge the political system and the predominance of the inherited artistic norm. They experiment with the Romantic notions, develop new themes, and base their dramas on marginal history and society, thus spreading the seeds of the lachrymose play—but not without proving their ability within the neoclassic norm. Their drama bespeaks a loss of faith, disenchantment, and a belief in the power of the stars in the form of negative determinism. As Alvin Sherman indicates, *La fuerza del Sino* [The force of destiny], which Rivas dramatized, has deep social implications. That it leads to helplessness and results in ultimate rebellion is subversive but not unique. In the Romantic play, the social or the political dominates the artistic, rage over control, emotion over reason, despair over hope. Hartzenbusch and Echegaray, among respected moderate contemporaries, censured the closely designed Romantic imitations; others react and respond dramatically to them. As they saw it, the plays are philosophically (theologicaly) flawed, lack ethical standards, and have too many "imported" non-Christian components. Fernández

Espino speaks against *De la moral en el drama* [On Morality in Drama] (Gies 234). Artistically, Larra protested the lack of diligence and originality. He voiced the common view that the large and growing number of servile imitations of translated plays by Hugo, Byron, and Schiller were transforming Spain into "a translated country." Grimaldi's extremely successful *La pata de la cabra* [The Goat's Hoof] (1829) is full of folklore and magic lore. Mesonero Romanos responded in a newspaper column with the delightful caricature defining *Romanticism and the Romantics*. His targets are still recognizable "imitators" of the French and German artistic fashion Schlegel introduced. A parade of hilarious parodies of servile imitations of the new style followed.

Leading critics, who were dramatists and government officials and influential in literary circles, moved to rescue the stage that is repeatedly described, very much like the state, as sick, decaying, dead, or dying. Eugenio Ochoa, Rodríguez Rubí, and Agustín Durán concluded that government intervention and a new plan for theatrical reform and regeneration were needed. Plays by Nuñez de Arce treat an extreme materialism; Rubí gave successful impetus to a nascent genre, *high comedy*, to replace " 'the tipsy dishonest' boulevard comedies and their jokes" (Gies 318); Juan Lombai investigated and concluded that literary and economic poverty is *Causa principal de la decadencia del teatro en España* [Principal Cause of the Decline of the Theater in Spain, 1845], and E. Ochoa began his multivolume *Theatro Hespañol*. The series Ochoa and Mesonero Romanos published, unpublished manuscripts, and the well-known and little-known collections back Gies's affirmation revising the accepted view about the limited number of nineteenth-century Spanish dramas. He found "literally thousands of one- to four-act works destined to be performed, published, read and discussed in high and low circles" (3–4). Agustín Durán diagnosed the theatrical problem differently. He wielded the Enlightenment's idea that the theater is the measuring rod of a nation, "el termómetro de los pueblos," to defend Spain's concept of drama against the neoclassic attack that it was "too Spanish."

After a flirtation with English, French, and German Romanticism the dramatist of the century turned around. Changes in political climate, critics' response, peer pressure, public demand, and the success of others forced dramatists to reconnect with their Spanish historic context and classic drama. Echegaray, García Gutiérrez, Hartzenbusch, Larra, Martínez de la Rosa, Rivas, and Bretón took high comedy to new heights; Tamayo y Baus, Nuñez de Arce, and Zorrilla poured into the romantic mold and style successful drama about political, financial, and moral corruption, adaptations of popular classic Spanish legend, themes, and history-based drama.[21] Generally, critics are in agreement that the nineteenth-century stage triumphed when dramatists returned to their theatrical Spanish roots. The equally successful popular political caricatures, literary masks, and cartoons found followers in Jardiel Poncela, Arniches, Muñoz Seca, and especially Valle-Inclán, who modernized, developed, transformed, and elevated the style in the twentieth century. High-and lowbrow comedy, modern or modernized musicals (*zarzuelas* and operetta), melodrama, and parody are also important genres in nineteenth-century stage. Notwithstanding a strong opposition from advocates of a literary theater, their life and popularity extend to the next century, when theater regulars such as Manuel Martínez Espada blamed the *Decadencia del teatro español* [Decline of the Spanish Theater] (1900, 2) on the prevalence of poor translation and performance of imports and on the general lack of talent manifest in the new inane plays put on the stages of Spain's capital. The sole notable exception in his view was Benavente, his contemporary.

    The political attitude, national concerns, and artistic vision in 1898 define the first "regenerative, reform group" of the twentieth century.[22] Their motto is "Vieja España, patria nueva" [Old Spain, new nation]. The general sentiment is anthologized in the plays treated in this volume. The dialectic between art and society and between art and art in the first thirty years of the twentieth century is associated with the avant-garde—although its very existence has been questioned, defended, denied, and confirmed. Brian Morris underlines its manifestations,[23] and Drew Dougherty and Francisca Vilches de Frutos assessed the years between 1926 and 1931 as a period of transition. In several books of collected essays, they analyze, document, and discuss tradition and avant-garde in the Spanish drama of 1918–1931. General approaches associate early twentieth-century drama with the new European aesthetic currents and with the reenergized liberal, progressive movements, socialism, and the left side of politics. In numerous instances a relationship is established between the artistic and political ideology of Sartre, Burke, Lukács, Barthes, Marx, Althausser, and Burkheimer. Echoes of their concept of practical, didactic, negative action, critical detachment, and isolation, which resound in studies and criticism of the plays, certify their influence. E. Giménez Cavallero saw them preying on young and naive minds.[24] From the beginning of the century to the 1970s, dramatists incorporated controversial notions in highly committed plays of resistance, repression, and extreme patterns of action that fit into Harold Bloom's notion that to poets "[t]he Ethos is the daemon" and "resistance to their vision of the world and times" (Bloom 99). The regime's perception was that behind the theories of *garde* experimentation was an incursion on government for control. Censorship was a strict response, followed by exile. Azorín, who is regarded unsuccessful as a dramatist, nevertheless sets the picture when he voices the belief that art (not chaos) is the principal factor of the revolution "el arte es el principal factor de la revolución"). He and Baroja look for "la España de siempre" [the eternal Spain]. In fact, the whole debate is personalized by Azorín in prose. His *Fantasías y divagaciones de un caballero inactual* [Fantasies and Wanderings of an Old-Fashioned Gentleman][25] advocates throwing old artistic forms to the ground. The sentiment about Spain's prosperity is summarized in "[w]ords Azorín attributed to Doménech: those of us who wish and want Spain's redemption, do not want to see it prosperous without a link with its past . . . prosperous, but substantially the same."[26] In that spirit, men like Galdós, Unamuno, and Benavente wrote plays that are old and new, artistic and political, urban and farmland, cosmopolitan and local, emotional and cerebral. Galdós appropriates the hegemonic dramatic discourse in defense of women who violate the social code. The feminism in his plays, for personal convenience, advances the transformation of liberty into libertine conduct in drama. This brand of rebelliousness develops and gains force in later drama that desacralizes marriage, virtue, the family structure, and religious belief. It defends divorce, adultery, salacious conduct, and same-sex unions—all of which explain Galdós's growing popularity as a modern, influential author. Other dramatists absorbed and adapted modern artistic methods, types, and themes of Europe and the United States in successful drama. But their unpopular and wobbly positions on the nation's grave issues affected the significance of their dramaturgy. *Indecisive* and *ambiguous* also describe their reception and influence as writers.

Historical crises hastened commitment to rupture and continuity, when dramatists turned from civilian to war themes in 1936. Spain is tragically divided. In literary utopias of the past there is the Knight of Unity, as Salinas wrote. In life, the view is that Spain had lost its soul, its identity. Part of the individual is also lost. It is as if the personal self and the collective self have been mysteriously taken over and fused. A new victor-victim composite being in *El otro* [*y yo*] mirror each other. The new man lives in doubt, confused, deeply divided, as is the individual human heart, thought Unamuno. He looked into his heart, meditated about the war, about himself as citizen and writer, and decided to continue to fight his inner war, reuniting himself with his work like Cervantes and his Errant Knight. In current literary utopias, there are no siblings. Instead, betrayals and crime in families symbolizing raw passions among factions are present in domestic dramas and tragedies by Benavente and Lorca. They make a strong connection between word and fact, character and resolve, illusion and fantasy, fiction and reality. Lorca's *La casa de Bernarda Alba* is a metaphor of repression, as critics have pointed out. But it owes its survival to its powerful imagery and dramatic ending. The play investigates silence and provides a response, not a solution, to the problems of oppression, transgression, and sexuality. Bernarda's strict rule is as powerful as the willful nature of the youngest woman who betrays the family. Her ability to satisfy her sexual desire symbolically in a stable shatters the argument of extreme repression and absolute control. Her rebellion and death mark the causes, reasons, and effects of both conduct and the repressed atmosphere. Ultimate protest, despair, and madness emphasize the even more extreme control, unhealthy fear, mindlessness, and especially silence that befall the women who remain in the house. Unamuno distances the author from the man as literary and social critic. His modern adaptations of classic plays, characters, myths and themes like Phaedra, Medea, Don Juan, Cain and Abel, their allusion or association, encapsulate products of centuries of conceptions and representations of men and women in Western culture, rerooted in the Spanish society.

As cultural historian, Unamuno wrote in the introduction to his modern adaptation *El Moderno Don Juan* [The Modern Don Juan] that the meaning of an original fictional construct changes with time, and so each of its subsequent literary transformations is best understood, treated, or read in the literary context of its time. From the trickster, Don Juan is reinvented and changed to a good family man, back to his original type in countless parodies that include *Don Juan* in a bordello in the nineteenth century and a contemporary satire of Don Juan, either as a sexually ambiguous character or as a definition of maleness. In line with studies based on scientific approaches to personality types, dramatists emphasize Don Juan's cunning personality, ambiguous nature, adventurous, and predatory temperament from both political and inward points of view. There is an analogy to be made between their war and Don Juan's erotic transgressions. Sexual violence, death, rebellion, and his hellish feasting on his own flesh and bones give clear meaning to their civil war, as well as to present and future rewritings of the theater as an evolving cultural, ideological activity. Dramatically, Don Juan's repeated erotic transgressions or the artistic assaults on the source text coincide with Artaud's conception of the theater as an assault, a jarring violation of boundaries. For the 1898 Generation, life's conflicts parallel the dramatists' struggle to drive out the animal they carry inside—to cut loose and then capture the present-day spirit and themes. Political conflict and artistic dreams, failures, and disappointments are often symbolized or explained in the struggle between the dramatist and his source(s)—thus, Benavente's animalistic conception of *La comida de las fieras* [The Meal of the Beasts]. This play is sometimes listed as *La comedia de las fieras* and seen as a probable adaptation of Marquina's *La cena de las burlas* [The Roasting]. John Dowling's chapter covers Benavente's domestic tragedies.

Intellectuals make a further connection between art and their 1898 reality. It ties together the person and modern surrounding circumstances: mass culture, a spineless, incapable government and leaders, and humanity abandoned for questionable principles. "Dehumanization" was how Ortega and his generation saw art and life. Aub and Buero Vallejo treat physical and spiritual darkness through the theme of blindness. They warn about inhumanity, ignorance, and blindness to the truth in their milieu; ethical concerns and the search and discovery of the surrounding truth are at the core of their drama and tragedy, as Arie Vicente and Martha Halsey demonstrate. Well-studied influences during the century generally include Brecht, Annhui, Ibsen, Maeterlinck, Shaw, Pirandello, Miller, T. Williams, Albee, O'Neill, Beckett, Artaud, and Genette. Echoes of Kierkegaard, Sartre, Nietzsche, Darwin, and Freud are included as well. The writers adopt (sometimes volatilize) doctrine and adapt ideas, artistic fashion, and intellectual attitudes. The most committed blend modern dramaturgy, classicism, national dramatic tradition, world thought, and immediate concerns. The influence of O'Neill's theater may exist or may be argued in Lorca's women who inhabit *La casa de Bernarda Alba* and in Mediero's *Las hermanas de Buffalo Bill*. Dehumanization in various ways and degrees can be found in plays of the 1960s to 1990s, similar in content and texture to the latter title, which John Gabriele treats in this book. The closest to the American playwright's use of animalistic symbolism and expression of sexual and perverse exploration of women's sexuality is *Los gatos* [Cats] (1962) by Gómez Arcos; Albee's theater may have had its timely, indecorous influence on Arrabal, Sastre, and their contemporaries. In postwar years (the 1898 war, the civil war, and World War II despite Spain's neutrality) playwrights treat machismo as myth. They associate erotic desire with power; possession with domination, violence, and rebellion. Within the modern sociopolitical context, dreams of Spain regaining its political power—or the stage, artistic dominance—appear as impossible dreams, illusionist reality. Dreamers only wake to disillusionment and are condemned like the hero of the Romantic drama *Despertar en un sueño* by Rivas. The apparent oxymoron carries a long literary and dramatic history. For Unamuno's generation, their failed hopes in Spain's artistic, political, and spiritual regeneration are depicted in *Sombras de sueños* [Shadows of Dreams]. Dispondency and "the here and now" evince modern skepticism toward Reason, the spiritual and temporal laws, and brotherhood. Inhumanity, tragic doubts, fear, angst, and angry agnosticism dissolved into spiritual indifference and isolation in plays by Unamuno, Aub, and Buero Vallejo; open revolt in Sastre; irreverence, heresy, and blazing apostasies in Gomez Arcos, Nieva, and Arrabal. These attitudes sever art from science, religion, philosophy, and as Brecht advocates, society. Then the transformation of dream into reality is fulfilled in the repeated acts of assault and transgression on morality that feverish and later hyperactive drama depicts. Lorca dreams his fantasies in the form of self-delirium, as writer-director. He directs, coldly, his "teatro imposible"—having absolute power over texts where he reveals himself in his art. The dramatic transformation of his dream is *Público*. Its "impossible" subject hides an extraliterary, personal agenda that implies a modernizing function of the entire dramatic system. He abandons the continued artistic norm of the Romantics. His dream includes a new concept of truth and reality on the stage, with a new audience to sanction it and new tools, methods, and directing techniques. Instead of the symbolic, emotional landscapes, Lorca proposes emphasizing human truth, representing the mental, psychic, and outward nature. At this point Adorno, Bajtin, Derida, Facault, and Lacan dictate modern dramatic theory and practice. They also animate numerous analyses of plays he influenced.

Lorca, the canonized standard-bearer in the fight to modernize poetry and drama in the 1930s, wrote wishfully, some say prophetically, that what was "Impossible Theater" (silenced, hidden, hermetic theater, difficult to understand and stage) would no longer be so [Once Five Years Passed]. He was not too bad a prognosticator. Fully confident of his associations, creative power, and influence, Lorca speculated that his two unfinished plays introducing explicit homosexuality would make the theme an open literary topic and socially accepted behavior in five years, *Así que pasen cinco años*. And it is no wonder. The latest intellectual currents and creeds were advocating that instead of empathy or emotional attachment the public was to be shaken, to be strongly impacted by transgressions of the norm through neorealism, surrealism, raw naturalism, and the antiaesthetic style. (Breton's surrealist manifesto and poetry, Buñuel's cinema of the time and Dalí's obscene pictorial texts with a multiplaned viewpoint transgress the norm of representation and decorum.) Lorca took the pulse of his time and ethos with yet another play that gives a high-voltage jolt, even in print: Kristine Ibsen is "revolted" by crude, sexual images and violent scenes in L's *Viaje a la luna* where he juxtaposes traditional scenes—representative women in black mourning dress (reminiscent of the paradigmatic Bernarda Alba)—with imagery and words of "the very sexuality that their institutionalized religion holds taboo."[27] Likewise, the New York performance of *Público* caught me by surprise. I expected another play by Lorca! The winding structure or multiplane construction is needed to hold a manual for homosexuals, held as the modern recipe to reform the play, the theater, their kindred's, and the audience's attitude and lead to social change. Its production uses floodlights to create awareness and empathy in the audience. Existential and dramatic truth are rendered by what must be a proverbial garb or characteristic of the "pure" homosexual male. The atmospheric lighting emphasizes the dream quality meant to support the claim that it is a "surrealist" verse play. The character Lorca directs the young characters who are wearing the "toga virilis" to take off their metaphoric theatrical masks, express their true identity, and expose their true personality—go "public." Religious implications, masked as sentimental appeal to the public, can be equally offensive to Christians, the unaware, and misinformed viewers who do not wish to have any social agenda forced upon them. Lorca's prediction regarding his *impossible theater* did not happen in five years. But today it has a female equivalent in *Helénicas. Poemas para "El Público" Una pieza teatral* by Margarita Borja (Barcelona: Antropos, 1996); his two uncovered works are widely available in print and on the stage. His explicit manifesto *Público* is staged regularly; one growing field is gay literature and male and female gay textual literary criticism; naked truth is no longer a figure of speech. In our day their being "public" is defended, proposed, and associated with the modern ambition to exhibit the total personality; dramatists are fulfilling Lorca's dream by writing, directing, and producing other's and their own "impossible theater" in the open.

Before Lorca's plays surfaced, a number of plays hailed as wildly imaginative, creatively hermetic, or "surrealist" disguise identity, existential truth, and true social purpose with obtuse style, deep resentment, and outrage. When the new freedoms exploded, advocacy of alternative sexual preference and identity was unmasked; left-liberal and liberated dramatists challenged and turned morality and religion into taboos and vilified their values in plays that enact the sexual revolution and pushed the limits to extremes. Jaime Salom's play *Bartolomé de Las Casas, una hoguera al amanecer* [Las Casas, Bonfire at Dawn] (in Zatlin's translation) follows what Martha Halsey calls "history from below," not official history. In his 1992 prize-winning drama about the personal, illicit sexual motives of the historical figure, Salom is careful in his treatment of the character, theme, and story of the missionary's love for the Indian he took to the monarchs, to argue for the protection and rights of the slaves. The play cautiously brings to the fore Las Casas' intense homosexual nature. It was staged during Spain's 500th anniversary celebration of Columbus' landing in America, a time when revisionists in and out of Spain wrote plays demythologizing history. The strong theme, the fact that in Spain Las Casas is held responsible for the "black legend" of the country's presence in the New World, that for such an auspicious occasion Salom uses contrary history and legend to portray the unknown identity and intense struggle of the man remembered as champion of human rights, and his place in national history—all are fashionable ingredients that have contributed to Salom's resounding popular success. Dramatic revolt in the Spanish stage is the preferred tool used in the culture wars fought in the twentieth century to produce ideologies and wrapped agendas that would newly define its ideals, the modern play, and modern aesthetics.

Other modern playwrights who began their career at the beginning of the twentieth century, and continue writing today, are Sastre, Arrabal, Buero Vallejo, Rodríguez Méndez, Martín Recuerda, Martínez Mediero. They became known outside Spain during the Civil War with plays of protest (war theater, agit events, underground plays) denouncing the war, the dictatorship, and all the evils both entail, notably human sacrifice. Their drama, full of passion and fear of (real, imagined, or symbolic) political persecution and exile, attracted the attention of Hispanists from several countries who helped them become famous. These dramatists are struggling to overcome "The Realism Generation" and "Underground" labels. Their highly ideological, anarchic, or iconoclast drama attacking Spain's social and economic systems, the military, the monarchy and the cleric, and the Church played well in various countries including what was the Soviet Union. Champions of talent and of their cause from around the world applaud protagonists who fight the established order and tell the audiences to open their eyes. They also admire the courage and perseverance of heroes who risk their lives, search and find windows of understanding, or set out to escape from physical and mental prisons. Producers, professionals of the theater, critics, and academics make the plays known and promote their authors in Europe, Latin America, and the United States. Ironically, some of these dramatists are mostly moved by anticosmopolitanism and by a passionate protectionist anxiety over what makes their people and nation unique. They are dedicated to an aesthetic project and tradition that vies for the regeneration of the popular theater on the basis of a sincere representation of historical and current social reality.

Jaime Salom and Lauro Olmo also wrote, published, or staged highly political and socially committed plays between 1926 and 1936, between 1936 and 1939, and from the 1940s to the 1970s. Phyllis Zatlin's chapter on Jaime Salom lists the socially committed drama for which he is better known. Lauro Olmo, now dead, became a success with the portrayal of political rebels who survived the war and find themselves so destitute that they have to share *La camisa* [The Shirt] one of them owns. With the revisionist aesthetics in vogue, and attitudes in their favor, the "Generación Realista" and "Underground" find the labels *realistic* and *marginal* more agreeable. The decision to downplay strong ideological positions and the controversial stance associated with the new Liberal Left, which colored their portrayal of society, is a practical one. The political pertinence of the plays is over, and to a large degree, they had the expected effect. The actions and thinking of individuals portrayed with the technique of the excess percolated subtly in the audience's psyche. Furthermore, the opposition to old labels suggests that playwrights who want to join the newer generation of dramatists are ready to transcend their rebellious image, move on to other plays, focus on their artistic evolution, and experiment with what is being written now. Lastly, their objection implies a degree of abjuration or recanting— even, perhaps, some disagreement with much of what has been stressed as "social theater" or social *realism* in analyses and interpretations of the plays.

From the artistic point of view, it helps to keep in mind that there are two kinds of realism present in their plays: classic realism, which can be, at once, satirical, illusionist, and a recognizable copy of the surrounding universe (Olmo, Salom, Rodríguez Méndez); and absurd realism, which, as Harold Pinter has explained, can be one extreme form of realism in the theater (Arrabal, Sastre, Mediero). Absurdist plays contain apparently "idiotic" references to a senseless world of contemporary, everyday life, which Samuel Beckett made popular. This distinct brand of realism make some of us think of the transformations from the political to the artistic and entertaining in dramaturgy; of the changes across centuries from abstraction to reality, from allegoric personification to the cruel or poetic treatment of daily life by Lorca, Valle-Inclán, Gala, and Arrabal from the humorous short plays to the perplexed magic plays, to the rhetoric of rage and frustration over society's ways—and the obsession to justify it all.

In 1999, Arrabal saw first the long-awaited publication of his *Complete Works* in Spain. Then he saw himself honored as a dramatist of choice. Delighted, he yet recalls the drama and human tragedies of the civil war that made him a pariah. Fortune, he says, was slow in turning, late in giving him favors. To him the taste of victory is bittersweet. In a lecture honoring Lorca's hundredth birthday, the dramatist Arrabal, feigning the theatrical mask, mixed the tragic and the comic, conjured the spirit of dead writers, his "real heroes," and ventured that surely they would also be "amused by the irony of [his] vindication and new status." Finally, his theater reached its natural end: the public, in print or on the stage. The irony of his words demonstrates that Arrabal the man is committed to what his generation says is the unfinished project of modernity, whereas Arrabal the dramatist continues the avant-garde dialectic about revolutionary aesthetics and politics.[28]

In the last chapters of his *Reception and Renewal in Modern Spanish Theater: 1939–1963*, John London professes that in Spain avant-garde is Arrabal, and vice versa. He alone revolutionized the Spanish theater.[29] His absurdist, avant-garde plays contain commonly mentioned elements and influences, which Peter Podol discusses. Through elements learned in their dramatic idioms, Arrabal expresses his individual condemnation of Franco Spain, fascism in general, and of course, the Church. He is not alone. Both are the common target in the wide world of "isms," including "anti-isms." His dis-sensitizing plays speak best, as London says, to modern audiences outside Spain[30]—only those audiences that have learned to enjoy all sorts of iconoclastic novelties and stage scandals of surrealism. Peter Podol writes in his entry on Arrabal that this dramatist is "mellowing" with age. Lately, he is much harder on the playwright. The assessment is that Arrabal's "recent plays," specifically *Como Lirio entre espadas*, "show a lost of nerve and a lack of passion that make his theater much less compelling, and less fun to read." Floeck would agree fully. He perceives a lack of authenticity in plays published, staged, or written during postmodernity that leads to his affirmation that "the *avant-garde* experiment reached its high point with the post modernity of today as a result of convention not commitment" (*Escritura* 12). It appears that from his mature perspective the playwright feels comfortable with the contribution he has made as a committed, activist writer.

Without doubt, Arrabal and Sastre fulfilled the utilitarian artistic principle when they created a theater of the masses for the enjoyment of a designated sector of society and for the vicarious thrills of what is called the Liberal-Left elite. They, like other writers of Spain's turbulent years, before, throughout the civil war, and during Franco's dictatorship, would not make concessions to the public or authorities. During democracy, they decided to become famous as artists. The need to be read, represented, appreciated, celebrated, and paid for it, in their own country, probably motivated them to revise or rewrite scenes and dialogues that were responsible for their marginality, public rejection of their plays, and exile from the Spanish stage. From their more adult viewpoint, seeking self-fulfillment and success may no longer seem to them deplorable bourgeois ambitions. Nonetheless, commitment as the value that separates their modern from the postmodern play could be reexamined on the basis of apparency and reality.

It appears that since the 1980s ideological differences, political crises, and divisions no longer are the dramatists' mission, conflict, or struggle. Yet, in reality, only the very aggressive quality of "the criticism of society" and "plans for future utopias" have completely disappeared from the postmodern stage. Their commitment is the same. The quality of the discourse is not. Martínez Mediero continued to write, stage, and publish committed absurdist plays in the 1980s. In an interview with John Gabriele Mediero insists that the theater in the 1990s is as political as ever. In interviews and speaking engagements, Arrabal reassures his disappointed, doubting, or anxious admirers that, still, he and his contemporaries are primarily committed to the unfinished project of modernity. Alberto Miralles attributes the commonly perceived lack of authenticity in absurd and surrealist plays written, published, or staged during postmodernity to the fact that the committed dramatists have had to adapt, not without difficulty, to a life that for the younger writers is not new but natural.[31] In the new challenges they saw choice and opportunity. One was to recast a sharper artistic image, to concentrate on their future significance as playwrights. Accordingly, still in keeping with their commitment to the utilitarian principle, they revisited their favorite plays to lift unpalatable vulgarities and strong materials humored by a theater establishment that was largely dominated by a sociopolitical underground.

Today the plays they revisited are finding wider acceptance, more space on the stage, in libraries, and in bookstores. Fans are missing the outrage—that transient, fugitive, and contingent combatant quality that first grabbed attention and later gave them stature as prolific dramatists. In the meantime, by striving to gain wide popularity and official recognition as modern Spanish dramatists, they are also consciously struggling to secure a lasting life for their plays and a place for themselves with Spain's immortal writers. Thus, if the dramatists' extreme belligerence and iconoclasm faded somewhat with postmodernity, their determined attitude to enact their dream and realize their worldview and dramatic vision outlives the main force that drove their demon.

Remarkably, Sastre, long considered a classic for his literary plays, evoked the spirit of Edgar Allan Poe and reemerged after a long hiatus with another successful play staged in Madrid in 1997 and 1999: *Dónde estás Ulalume, dónde estás?* [Where Are You Ulalume, Where Are You?] Sastre, Belbel, and Arrabal were the 1999 national celebrities. Distrusting judges who do not accept the existing canon are optimistic about the future. They are looking through their long-lens telescopes and predicting the success of younger playwrights who are struggling to transform it, to create other galaxies to expand it, even to be the new canon of generations to come. Karl Shapiro offers a reasonable explanation that both skeptics and believers may want to endorse: ". . . [A]n author growing up in an age of doctrine and counter-doctrine, takes for granted that drama is just another form of strife in the world. It will not occur to him that he is exempt from service with both . . . the Radicals and the intransigents" (*Beyond Criticism* 53).

In effect, twentieth-century iconoclast and innovative dramatists turned the theater around and took drama in a completely opposite direction from what their eighteenth century predecessors dreamed. In their efforts to live in a world of their own creation, dramatists attacked values and beliefs that are generally associated with the Enlightenment and the Victorian Age. Vanguard dramatists and their postmodern heirs grapple with personal dilemmas—political, social, or religious—with their backs to the public. In place of order, moral didactic purpose, determined attitude, or artistic and social goals aimed to uplift the country, there is anarchy, chaos, search for absolute and complete freedom, amorality, sexual politics, and emphasis on the personal, the deconstructed body, style, and form. In exchange for the principle of decorum, audiences witness all kinds of experimentation. The most well-known modern dramatists burst taboos, invite scandal, and seek to inspire intense rupture of the limits of art, religion, and society. They seek artistic success and perform personal advocacy in the projection of the existential dilemma they choose to make public. Cases of kitsch, low-life, erotic scenes, and nudity, on the stage certify modernity, the sexual revolution, and its rhetoric.

At the same time, dissenting dramatists who also present rebellious heroes and heroines await revisiting. Their dissonant voices and nonconventional heroes and heroines espouse socially progressive, sometimes explosive ideas and revolutionary politics intended to revitalize and reconstruct both the country and the stage. Apparently there is a kind of pack mentality, a tacit agreement to look at modern drama with one eye. Peers and critics gloss over, overlook, underestimate, or misrepresent independently minded dramatists who either did not subscribe to or deserted the antiestablishment side of politics. Luis Riaza, Jacinto Grau, Calvo Sotelo, Mihura, Rodríguez Méndez, Paso, Gala, Jardiel Poncela, Buero Vallejo combat principles, values, fashion, and taste associated with their favorite target, the upper and middle classes. But they disagreed, abandoned, or refused to be pressured by the "No posibilista" motto; they decided they were writers first and opted to fight for change from within, on their own terms. To their apologists, their neglect or vocal opposition to their fame has to do more with their political affiliations or positions than with the intrinsic characteristics of their work.

Another impetuous group with an increased number of women playwrights began their careers between 1960 and 1990. Enrique Centeno called it *nuevo teatro español* [New Spanish Theater].[32] They are also known by the more defining term *postmodern*. Like modernism, postmodernism has been described as a state of being, not a movement that is easy to define ("un estado no un movimiento fácil de definirse"). Wilfried Floeck singles out Cabal and Belbel as postmodern writers.[33] Among the postmodern characteristics in the texts he studies are: "multiplicity of forms," "plurality," "heterogeneity." These terms are puzzling. The same qualities are found in the Spanish theater of all ages, except in the most strict neoclassic comedies and tragedies written in the eighteenth century. More solid information is the diagnosis of "postmodern texts typical to the decade of 1980–1990" based on the work of Leotard, E. Fisher, Hichte Schwind, and Habernas. Among the characteristics he traces in his investigation are a radical ideological and epistemological relativism; nonhistorical, nonideological, and nonpolitical thought; and the loss of faith in universal norms and truths that permeate today's theatrical world. In this world the protagonists have no psychological depth. They exist without identity as part of an unclear social mass, without understanding its meaning or how it functions (Floeck, "Escritura" 12). Pérez Rasilla, Oliva, Amestoy, and Floeck concur in the observation that the theatrical works of the democracy are uneventful, "sin circunstancia." Probably it is because, in addition to ethos changes, most postmodern dramatists, like most of the global society, are looking "in" at themselves, or after themselves, and less and less at the society they have no reason, will, or excuse to despise.

For the new group, writing is a craft. They hope to succeed in it and are challenging choice and opportunity in other ways. It should come as no surprise that dramatists portray disassociated, private individuals with no psychological depth whose comportment is sometimes automatic—images or beings who inhabit a world of virtual and mindless reality. Elinor Fuchs' study on modern world stage production puts us in the right perspective. She writes that play-wrights internalize and apply contemporary theories that give importance to stage arts, the visual, body language, acting over dialogue, performance over text, image and reflections over character.[34] From this perspective, their mo-dernity succeeds.

Postmodern dramatists are simply expressing their own reality. They are part of the modern society that the previous age vehemently acted to change. Without the grave civil conflicts, revolts, and confrontations their predecessors experi-enced, they are more inclined to forgive, to remain socially involved in a less ideologically proactive way. Among them are dramatists who outgrew or never embraced the post-Franco aesthetics nor the art form on the Left of the Republic whose names began to appear on the marquees. The 1960s to 1980s intellectuals, critics, and dramatists are involved in their daily activity and are better able to concentrate their attention on aesthetics and theatrical matters of individual con-cern, such as direction and production of their out-of-the-mainstream texts, gen-der politics in the theater, artistic mastery, and success. There is creative energy, diversity, and in some cases, movement toward upper aesthetic levels, although confusion over artistic systems, doctrines, and theories is dragging postmodern dramatists in many different directions.

Belbel, Cabal, Diosdado, Pedrero, and C. Romero have been gaining recog-nition increasingly as important dramatists on the national and international scenes. They coexist with their immediate predecessors, compete with them, and have garnered highly coveted prizes. The popularity of Spanish, easy travel, wide and instant communication, and the new cache of popular culture make it necessary to keep abreast of innovative theories, practice, dramatic fashion, writ-ing, performance, and stage techniques. To dare success they explore and some-times juggle different forms and modes of expression (drama, comedy, psychodrama, musicals, dramatic history, literary criticism, journalism, and teaching). They experiment and mix elements, themes, languages, and tech-niques taken from entertainment shows, televised series, soap operas, detective stories, cinema, and science fiction. Gómez-Arcos, who is in their midst, achieved multimedia success in *Pre-papá* [The Pregnant Dad] (1962; staged in 1965), which Hollywood made into a movie in the 1990s. His science fiction text (a man who gives birth) has international dimensions. It reverses natural male and female roles, blurs the representation of genre, and links the play to the politics of gender/genre, ideologies of the global village of today. Studies and analyses of these plays place a strong reliance on modern world linguistics, semiotics, formalism, structuralism, poststructuralism, and deconstruction. World extreme feminist and/or gay specialists in dramaturgy who also write for the stage utilize transgression in writing and analyzing plays critical and sub-versive of the culture. Their new approaches and forceful attitudes have led scholars to associations of the body of the text, the representation of the human body, and a body of modern hermetic plays. Investigations have revealed that several dramatic texts purposely written in an encoded language veil underlying truth and agenda.

Leonora Levi perceptively links modern language reconfiguration and experimentation with representations of gender and desire. She writes that filmic and fictional discourses concerning social, political, and religious taboos and their violation are using transgression, desire, and textual perversion "in a series of linguistic proxies set up to create the daring subterranean cultural spectacle that emerges."[35] Thus, the dialectic about language as artistic tool as communication changes to the polemics of genre and gender, the politics of sex, and artistic experimentation, which are the aesthetic ideologies of nations undergoing a series of critical changes in modernity.[36] Discourses declaring that gender/genre differences are purely a social invention are rarely used only to satisfy the required, cutting-edge transgression. I would suggest, therefore, that not just reconfiguration is implied. Reconceptualization is inherent in the linguistic changes and revisions that develop, in drama and cinema, during modernity and postmodernity. Levi's study unravels fictional discourses in which a series of daring dialectic transgressions perform a subversion, by which the body becomes a theater where natural identity is asserted or hypothesized by granting a voice to their sexually repressed otherness. Ramón Gómez de la Serna perceived half beings, *Medios Seres*. The disparity in quality, form, and style, in the various modern and postmodern texts of one given author, now is associated with a search for ways of communicating unsanctioned sexuality and artistic identity. Language experimentation is an effective metatheatrical device.

The novelist Juan Goytisolo's explanation for the postmodern emphasis on language technique and experimentation is the vast changes in Spain's artistic, social, and political climates. In the present-day capitalist world, "there are no virulent or daring themes. Language and only language can be subversive."[37]

El baile de los ardientes [The Dance of Ardent Men] (attributed to Nieva, then to Gala, now dead), *El niño de Belén* [The Child from Bethlehem], *Las hermanas de Buffalo Bill* [The Sisters of Buffalo Bill] (by Mediero), *La cereza mágica* [The Magic Cherry, about women's virginity "myth"], and *Color de agosto* [Color of August] (by Pedrero) display an association of eros and art. These dramatists utilize transgression in writing plays critical and subversive of the culture. Their language subverts social mores. Their themes and images concerning traditional morality and philosophical and literary discourse on gender/genre bending or on women's sexuality express social criticism and perform the transgression of cultural taboos. Cabal and Nieva are among the dramatists who constantly change the signs, symbols, and language they use to voice deep-seated resentment, anger, and indignation toward political and sexual repression. For some time, obscure texts by Nieva were praised for their artistic "neo-baroque" style. A reexamination disclosed that his themes and dramatic actions dilute, blur, or transgress social and cultural sexual limits, that his characters have a double presence; the crude, eschatological, obscure language he uses in hermetic coded texts is a disguised attempt to communicate and conceal.

On the political side of repression, Buero's socialist dramas attacking crime, censorship, and inordinate fear as enemies of freedom utilize sane artistic rhetoric to circumvent official censorship. Circumstances turn his young idealists, intensively critical, into activist rebels or distant and isolated Brechtian characters. When his heroes and heroines find themselves engaged in an uphill battle against values and the political philosophies of the world, they acquire the solidity of an aesthetic and the value of an ethic. Buero's modern themes of social and socialist concerns in the plays of the Franco and post-Franco years (a left socialist view of capitalism, multinationals, and foundations), political and financial corruption (money laundering), hedonism, excessive materialism, modern isolation, fascination with tech gadgets (they help maintain a level of contact when direct human communication is not possible), extramarital sex, irresponsible parenting, and dysfunctional and broken families create a mixed, unsettled world. That world gives a higher literary value and lends greater prestige to a theater that is at once traditional, classical, and modern—traditional because in *The Art of Getting Rich* [El arte de hacer fortuna] (1845), *A Vein of Gold* [El gran filón] (1874; by R. Rubí), *The Percentage* [El tanto por ciento] (by López de Ayala; premiered in May 1861), dramatists project moral problems in the money culture of the 1870s. Plays exposing an extreme preoccupation with moneymaking white-collar crime, economic corruption, and greed among leaders who are expected to be *The Upright Men* [Los hombres de bien] (by Tamayo y Baus; staged December 1870) underscore their moral and ethical concerns along with the capitalist consciousness of the upper middle class of the 1850s to 1878.

Buero's younger colleague José María Rodríguez Méndez aligns himself with all political reactions against means of distribution, but he voices his contempt for cosmopolitan dramatists who are in the sector of society that came to dominate Spain's progressive, popular movement, whose base, in his words, is still helplessly marginal.[38] As a strong defender of the autochthonous theater and "Iberismo" in politics, he probably saw himself alone, honoring a classic poet in *El pájaro solitario* [The Solitary Bird], a celebration of the spirit and style of Saint John of the Cross. With this verse play likely written years earlier Rodríguez Méndez captures the National Prize for Dramatic Literature in 1994. He and Martín Recuerda are the clearest manifestations of the intent to rejuvenate the Spanish dramatic tradition, upheld as a form of militant patriotism and the spread of national ideals very much discredited since the 1700s.

Rodríguez Méndez affirms that the "antination" sentiment of our time, which is present in symbolism, modernism, and vanguard, coincides with the doctrines of universalism that disturb the world today ("las doctrinas universalistas, actuales que conmueven hoy al mundo").[39] It is helpful to dwell on this point since the roles and effects of Europeanization and nationalism are the rationale for characterization of the country, its people and its culture in modern drama and since they occupy many in each century—most recently, John London. He typically anchors the argument of his book in Spain's excessive nationalism, declaring it the root of Spain's habitual censorship and "xenophobia." Few Spaniards, if any, would dispute that both were extreme during 1939–1963, the Franco years London investigates. He proclaims its "old-fashioned beliefs," and "the hypocritical value system" result in the outrageous adaptations of foreign plays, the stands on foreign culture, the perception of foreign theater in Spain, and the few-significant plays written, published, or produced during Franco's Spain (J. London, 146–177). Ignacio Amestoy, who was in that scenario, clarifies: During the ideological revolts, revolution, and war, the theater was the means to an end. It was the weapon most used by experts who make a profession of culture. The persons who inherited the Teatro Independiente were keeping the theater alive with plays "contaminated" by socialist and underground ideologies. And convinced that the time for theatrical renovation had come when the socialists gained power in 1982, they proceeded to act on those beliefs. Their aggressive cultural and political agendas, he says, caused a hemorrhage of talent; it created a void in the stage that affected the theater and it future.[40]

The dramatist Itziar Pascual seems to concur. His metonymic character Pereskoff scoffs at capable dramatists, their politics, and their servile dramatic imitations, which opponents generally deride as "translations." Moreover, what people of the theater of all time strongly reject is the poor quality, production choices, and the unjustifiable long runs of poor foreign productions that dominate and control the playhouses of Madrid and Barcelona. In their performance review columns and theater criticism, Mariano José de Larra, M. Martínez Espada, and A. Martínez Olmedilla, denounce the "invasion" of the Spanish stage by comic opera, servile imitations, and unsuccessful adaptations of foreign plays. D. Augusto Martínez Olmedilla, who writes on the Spanish theatrical life of the last 100 years, gives a native's perspective on what is known as the "Género éxotico" [Foreign Genre]. London agrees with him regarding quality, not on the reasons. Authenticity is what is valued and missing. Martínez Olmedilla writes that the production of foreign plays is "absurd. . . . The dilemmas . . . the dialogue, are not convincing. All sounds hollow, forced, bogus to us. Their total disregard for morality is alien to our temperament and sensibility."[41] Of opposing view is Ventura de la Vega, who portrayed a modern Don Juan in a humiliated *Hombre de mundo* [Man of the World] (1845). Vega was widely opposed and criticized as head of the Teatro Español and the Theater Bureau for favoring foreign, particularly French, plays, to the detriment of Spain's talent. Olmedilla quotes a writer and critic who satirizes the Royal Academy of the Language for electing Vega as one of its members and his taste for French creations: "Vega académico es/si tales sujetos premia,/pronto dará la Academia/ el Diccionario en Francés" (*Arriba el telón* 2).

It is a matter of balance. I have heard the same protest in other countries on that side of the Atlantic. Brien Morris, who first researched, argued, and studied much of what London develops, is more balanced and open-minded in his judgments and conclusions. The documents Morris published in the appendixes to *The Surrealist Adventure in Spain* show that a nucleus of authors, in Madrid and Barcelona, were not isolated. Their plays and other writings evince a broad contact with world figures in art and letters, open vistas to the real and sometimes subreal world of the stage.[42] London himself admits that "the presence of foreign culture reveals the cracks in the shell while at the same time anticipating a large-scale political turnabout and underlining the hypocrisy of the regime" (*Reception* 146). Regarding censorship, a critic's column reminds us (correctly) that there is not one source but all kinds of censorship: the censorship that authors impose on dissidents and opponents, the critics, market demands, public preference, personal censorship, and more. Momentous innovations and significant plays either ignored or generally critiqued and judged unfavorably suggest a spirit of intolerance born out of political activism typified by the argued "lack of general interest" in large numbers of suppressed important theatrical writings. Mihura's defenders credit him with the successful grotesque tragedy; Muñoz Seca, one almost forgotten sacrifice of the civil war, created the extremely avant-garde, onomatopoeic *astracán*, which almost volatilized an entire genre when the line between the popular and the populous was eliminated. A marked commitment to write propaganda texts to shift the culture, to eradicate its "old-fashioned beliefs," and artistic creation to reverse censorship over artistic concerns are methods used to deal with the opposition or silence it. These divisive forces also result in Spain's having very good dramatists but none of great significance in modern world theater. Publication and production choices, prizes, and distinctions might be other areas of activism and censorship.

One of the clearest uncovered examples of neglect due to political activism is the case of Ernesto F. Cavallero, a most notorious and noisy Spanish avant-garde writer who faced up to other modern avant-garde dramatists. He believed in modernizing the dramatic text but saw artistic suicide in extremely innovative but subliterary propaganda texts, anarchy of mind, and refusal to play by any social, official, or artistic rules. Arrabal's fiery, "Panic" avant-garde apostasies, crude expression, and new popularity manifest a bias favorable to writers and plays conveying the extreme political and social ideologies of Europe and modern-day Spain. The anarchists' case earns sympathy as they sound the cause of exile, freedom of the creative imagination, and aesthetic ideals. But while proposing a reconfiguration of text, character, and the structure of the dramatic language, they postulate a total and complete rejection of, and resistance to, all existing systems and cultural models. These committed dramatists dogmatically pursued a utilitarian agenda with an intransigent attitude toward dissenters that itself is a contradiction of the liberty and freedom they claim to be their goal. It may perhaps be a generational question and ethos, but most studies leave untouched crucial dramatic texts revising modernity. Language that ironically treats the libertine and subverts itself in action may help to understand modern structural and linguistic experimentation and discourse concerning new paradigms, myths, and taboos. The legacy of dissident writers is now being reassessed along with the Spanish vanguard.[43]

Here the histrionic angle of the discussion makes it useful to recall dramatists from different times who take a poke at political matters and other concerns. Gies (320) cites *El rico y el pobre* [The Rich and the Poor Man] (performed in 1855) by Francisco Botella y Andrés. In challenging subversive plays, his leading character exclaims tongue in cheek: "!Cielos! Si será algún demócrata perseguido por la justicia!" [Freely: Heavens! It must be the justice victimizing one of the subversive, anti-monarch democrats!]. Botella's play responds to defenders of socialism who write about instigating revolution against monarchism, oppression, and social inequality in plays such as *Juan barbudo*, by Sixto Cámara, and *Un día de revolución* [A Day of Revolution] (1855), by Fernando Garrido. His defense of left socialism/republicanism threatens, "When the ferocious communism ennobles poverty the harrowing masses will drag you to the abyss" [Cuando el feroz comunismo . . . enaltezca el pauperismo / la horda patibularia / le arrastrará a usted al abismo] (Geis 318). On control, censorship, and intellectual isolation, Mariano José de Larra bitingly wrote that the few pesetas he paid at the Spanish border allowed him to bring a whole library into his country.

If a silver lining can be found in the numerous tales of the terribly painful experience of exile, it is that, in the three centuries, exile enhanced opportunities for writers to become modern dramatists and, in some cases, internationally successful on the stage. I have mentioned Agustín Durán's defense of Spain's national theater. His influential *Discurso sobre el influjo que ha tenido la crítica moderna en la decadencia del teatro antiguo español* [Discourse on the Influence that Modern Criticism Has Had on the Decline of Old Spanish Theater] (1828) heightens the danger of transcultural (mis)understanding, which can still be valid everywhere today. I also see America widely misunderstood. It is time for more balance. Members of the most recent groups of dramatists, with a handful of playwrights of the generations in front of them, have come to realize that it is time to transcend topical fixation and abandon extremism. Artistic reality may dictate what Botella's character voices with intended irony and deflated spirit: "Pero en fin, todos hemos errado, y la revolución [of 1848] echó un velo sobre nuestras deplorables equivocaciones" [In the end we were all wrong, and the revolution drew a veil over our deplorable mistakes] (320–321).

One could reasonably ask why, when censorship is something of a dinosaur, there are fewer and fewer plays or dramatists who will matter beyond showtime. In fact, more and more drama critics and specialists insist that significant plays and dramatists are rare and good candidates for inclusion on lists of endangered species. Could it be also that, in terms of drama, modernity might have been creating a Frankenstein?

People who know the theater from inside aired dissatisfaction with modernity, its forces, and the mid–1990s stage. A top actress who has played more than 100 character roles in classic plays told an interviewer that in today's stage there is little appreciation or demand for professional classic players because "estamos en un mundo en el que el dinero y el cartel es lo que priva" [We are in a world where money and the billboard or the marquee is what counts].[44] Production choices affect all aspects of the theater, including the plays that are being written. In Spain, she said, "There exists the idea of the theater as industry and as a cultural enterprise" [Existe la idea del teatro como industria y la idea del teatro como una acción cultural]. Consequently, there is more demand for innovative plays and works that use the theater to effect social change. Everyone is aware that, increasingly, since the end of the eighteenth century in Spain and elsewhere, the greatest amount of theater demand and publicity go to market-based theater. Today they go to players who embody easy dramatic characters and to plays that side with extreme left positions on the controversial issues of divorce, drugs, prostitution, sexuality, nontraditional marriages, and so on. In order to keep the theaters full, producers and directors demand plays that advance a social agenda appealing to marginal groups of society, or defer to them. To be in demand, players are happy to act in roles that appeal to basic human instincts or identify with the loudest voices. Of course, the benefit principle applies to the theater, and dramatists should expect their plays to bring them artistic and economic success.

What should raise questions is the accepted premise that socially erosive acts and transgression make plays modern and easier to market or that, to be competitive and successful, women had to "be like the bad boys," who draw their material from the low life. A number of the so-called feminist, personal advocacy plays are populated by male and female characters who lose themselves in the freedoms they champion. We meet them in realistic places, caught up in hopeless situations and problematic relationships, desperately experimenting with all kinds of unions and alternative lifestyles. Women's "imitations" follow successful dramatic methods and models. Their creations are anxious, lonesome, and exploited characters who wait, hope, and resort to drugs and prostitution, believing they will not go beyond desire. They could, of course, be looking for their souls. But instead of the human condition, in these erotically charged plays, feminists utilize the newfound sexual freedoms in a limited social scope. It may be that in some cases women who began their theater careers acting those roles fell in love with the character or the dramatist who created it. Not surprisingly, a gap results between the subject and the reader or viewer. It may be a mentor's, eros's, or a mimetic influence, but characters and discourse strike the skeptic as fashion, mannerism, or a winning venue intended to please specific judges on demand.

Initially, Paloma Pedrero was hailed as a woman capable of using "daring" and "blunt language" in plays that express a "brave" feminist's point of view. Increasingly a popular dramatist in U.S. university circles and stages, she has seen her plays of the 1980s and 1990s. In a 1999 trip to Madrid, Candyce Leonard heard from various academic sources and in theatrical circles that "Paloma Pedrero is the undisputed best woman dramatist in Spain today." In other places, her preeminence is questioned, if not strongly challenged, by critics who admire the more essential, avant-garde Luisa Canillé, who writes in Catalán and Spanish. At their side are unconventional, independently minded playwrights who disregard the norm and express competing feminist, political, and artistic attitudes on a higher artistic plane. Their titles, which increasingly appear on marquees, represent diversity and change.

There are a few key dramatists whose plays address the creative process, the text, and the role the audience should play in the performance. Their characters often are able to dominate the situations they are in. If there is failure, or a mixed outcome, the plays exalt the resolute spirit or the world of the creative imagination, where artists believe freedom lies. Concha Romero, Carmen Resino, and J. L. Alonso de Santos independently challenge versions, visions, and revisions of fiction presented as reality in farces, comedies, and history-based drama. Several plays deal with a modern thematic, not peculiarly Spanish, which include prescribed, abused, and criminal drug addiction, feminist issues, women's issues, mental illness, incest, and child sexual abuse. Still, when they dwell on the base or the negative, there is artistic quality in these plays.

Concha Romero challenges contemporary feminists' viewpoint. As Caroline Harris points out, Romero recreates noble women who have become protagonists in a masculine world not by hating or imitating men, not by renouncing their femininity or their feminine vision and values but by finding a way to subvert the authority that limits their possibilities and self-affirmation. Two plays deal with legendary queens who each married the man she loved and changed history. The portrayal of Isabella I, the Catholic Spanish Queen, and of her daughter, Queen Joan of Castile, the mother of Charles I of Spain, from a revisionist point of view, earned her awards, honors, and distinction. She has a close nineteenth-century precedent in Rodríguez Rubí's high comedy also entitled *Isabel la Católica* in honor of Isabel II (by association with Isabel I of Castile), which earned the highest awards and applause from the monarch, the nobility, his peers, the critics, and the crowds. Likewise, in a fusion of myth, art, and life, Romero explores prevailing female themes and new modern myths. Instead of sisterhood, she braves a timeless rivalry and struggle between the world of artistic creation and intellectual activity in the myth of Aracne. Turned into a spider and condemned to weave for all of time the same tapestry in a metaphorical ceiling, Aracne–Romero reenacts the two archetypal powers in allegorical war and weaves scenes of human action for audiences' contemplation. The proverbial "glass ceiling"—which twentieth-century political feminists repeatedly hit, punctuated, and cracked—is lifted tastefully and artistically in this play. With the enduring example of Aracne, Romero pulls together the past and the present, the particular and the universal. The character's innate psychological depth and dramatic force dispel the usual modern liberal mythology surrounding sex/gender, the revolutionary politics in the theater of her particular moment. In her treatment the classic myth works against the artistic thematic fetish and against situations that would facilitate the creation or perpetuation of future myths. Concha Romero uses modern and postmodernist techniques such as the allegorical status of the text, its relationship with other fictional constructs, and metatheater but turns to classic tales of wisdom and artistic beauty for inspiration. An essential connection emerges between classic and modern drama. It is the transformation of a famous human action into art entertainment that discourages injustice and exalts the enduring spirit and instructs about human nature. The capacity to extract lasting victory from transitory defeat confirms the artistic viability and pertinence of the classics in modern times.

Carmen Resino develops current deeply disturbing issues: child sexual abuse in the Church. The power of conscience and the psychological effects of crime and sin make all the parties involved in wrongdoing feel they are *bajo sospecha* (suspects). There is black humor in her irony. Guilt and terror are about being charged with malfeasance of the parish property—not about abusing innocent souls, its priceless possessions. The play dramatizes an unsuspected world (a parish) where souls are lost, not found, where, as the actress Riaza puts it, "money is the only thing that counts." The priest's conscience, obviously warped, is pitted against innocent parishioners, especially the child who is mortified and afraid to talk. Angelino develops from a child to a young adult and from victim to a person who takes control. His exemplary dramatic role satisfies the moral requirement drama used to have. He lets his dark secret be known, and truth sets him free.

The postmodern tendency to address themes that are not peculiarly Spanish occurs at a time when there is a greater interest in viewing artistic creations from around the world in a global context. For the more adventurous dramatists, the global context presents greater freedoms and opportunity to create, remain competitive, or succeed. The implicit dilemma continues to be whether to faithfully imitate exemplary models; to follow fashion or bliss in their attempt to create the paradigm of the future; to revolutionize the theater of their time; or to reinvent and transcend the past. Globalization has its price. Changing theories, definitions, and approaches to the theater, in addition to language barriers, tend to emphasize economy in style, time, and resources; to minimize the primary roll of the dramatist and the text; and to heighten performance over the written and spoken dialogue. Increasingly, writing is considered equal, even second, to directing and producing.

In the theatrical world of the mid-1980s to 1990s, there was less and less demand for text-based plays or a clear story. The dramatist and play text are but contributing elements to the whole stage performance. Participants add their individual talent in writing, directing, acting, and staging. Even the audience is expected to contribute to the total theatrical experience. As a result, dramatists enter these areas and experiment with these forms of artistic expression. The most successful "diversify." They divide their newfound time lecturing, conducting drama seminars in universities, translating their plays into cinema and television movies, writing multimedia scripts, producing, and directing. The point Nieva, Cabal, Belbel, and Alonso de Santos make is that in their new roles as writers-directors-producers they fill a void. They stage controversial, not market-oriented, plays that otherwise would not be staged. As directors, Sastre argues, the dramatist eludes unavoidable disagreements, the predictable ego tensions authors and directors have over the text, in particular, texts that are deemed a commercial risk. With little time left, the busiest authors/impresarios forfeit the primary roll they used to have as writers. The end results are texts that read as scripts, almost no dialogue to be spoken on the stage. Opportune, they embraced modernity's limited dialogue fad. Like the theater of centuries ago, or silent movies, world directors for a while relied on stage arts, movement, gesture, location, and voice. I think of *The Fantastiks*, because any major theater of the twentieth century is definitely a global theater, enriched in some degree by the influence of theater and movie directors, producers, and writers such as Samuel Beckett, Harold Pinter, Heiner Müeller, Bernard-Maria Koltés, Thomas Bernhard, and and Peter Brook.

In Spain, dramatists, directors, and scene designers of the democratic regime who seek to entertain world audiences may long for the technical stage proficiency of London, Paris, New York, and Hollywood. However, for economic reasons and/or artistic fashion, personal choice, or expedience, dramatists who are also directors are obliged to rely more on stage techniques than on modern technology for important theatrical effects. They favor expressive acting techniques, undemanding plays, an action fit for a minimalist stage set, and little dialogue or, in extreme cases, no spoken dialogue at all. There are artistically ambitious experiments in the bare dramatic style by central dramatists such as Sanchiz Sinisterra, Ignasi Garcí, Sergi Belbel, and the widely considered, utmost exponent of the minimal aesthetic Luisa Canillé. Realistically, time and cost play a practical role. Of course, a more fitting aesthetic explanation is the lure of the style. Supposedly, the least amount of physicality stresses the essentiality that the dramatist seeks to project. A growing number of minimalist plays have drawn reaction. The witticism *"mini-mal"* was the headline of a respected first-night performance review column. The syllabic *mal* effectively renders the reviewer's judgment in the smallest metonymy possible. The reviewer critically assesses the disjointed, meager dialogue and the bare imagery, action, and stage props used in Belbel's play. In the characteristic manner David George traces, Belbel was energized; rewrote the play text, taking advantage of the criticism; published a full text-based play; and marked a turning point. A dramatist whose reaction represents the known alternative is José Luis Alonso de Santos. He bets modernity and success on the classic Spanish literary tradition.

J. L. Alonso de Santos epitomizes best the conflicting but sustained relation dramatists of any period have with their literary and dramatic past. In his quest to write unconventional modern drama and carve a place for himself, de Santos relies on the style, vision, humor, and attitude of Cervantes, the classic paradigm, who revolutionized the world of artistic creation, literary fashion, and tradition. In the popularly and critically successful *Fuera de quicio* [Mad—literally, Out of Mind], Alonso de Santos participates in the uninterrupted dialectic between modern and old stands and mind-sets. This play successfully recalls and then subverts old and current dramatic techniques. Mixed with the more universal preoccupations of traditional drama are the modern versions or reincarnations of emblematic historical figures conventionally treated as mad. Their shadow or symbolic presence in memories, characters, and dreams weigh heavily in the writer's consciousness. His artistic expression projects, visually, a wrestling with long-dead, idealized writers and the powerful influence they continue to have in life at the end of the twentieth century. Meanwhile, Alonso de Santos crosses the line of the existing norms, suggesting parallels between what is happening in the play, in the theatrical phenomenon, and beyond. It seems that the minimalist fashion—rewriting cultural history, overshadowing the character, the text, or the author—has him "out of his wits." In *Fuera de quicio* he steps into the world of nihilist idealism, which sought to obliterate the artistic past to coincide with "Iberistas" and/or Nietzsche, who in the *Twilight of the Idols* refused to regard the poetical past as primarily an obstacle to fresh creation.

Mad with the age of doctrine and counterdoctrine, Alonso de Santos confronts both forms of realism in the theater—agit events; testimonial, war, and propaganda theater; the absurdist vanguard play; and theater of the absurd—but continues to support social change from the left side of politics. What that means is to fight against the cultural supremacy in their society, to dismantle all coercion in what they portray as a world of absolutes influenced by religion. In creating fiction around madness, he may be thinking of plays like *Tararí* (opened on September 29, 1929) where madmen rise against the guardians to signify surrealists' hostility to reason or enthusiasm for unhindered thought. The leader of the rebels explains that "we have risen against reason and philosophy and we defend thought that is free from the shackles of logic, spontaneous thought without the slightest artificial elaboration" (qtd. in Morris, *The Surrealist Adventure* 146). The vague feeling of unreality by the author Andrés Alvarez seems to heed Alonso de Santos's play and its parallels with Cervantes, the master realist who, with humor, demolished literary genres, broke down the division between high art and popular art, and dramatically blurred frontiers between madness and sanity, fact and fiction, reality, imagination, and make-believe.

Likewise, with antics and tricks of his imagination de Santos expects to distract the mind or eliminate the certain wall of opposition to the social/political subject in which he rests the pertinence of his play. In a dialogue between himself and Spain's revered master (the analogue of a fictitious dialogue between Cervantes and Lope, which has been attributed to Montaigne), Santos mimics, parodies, and ties together past and present, art and life, appearance and reality, fact and fantasy. He mixes old and new realism, themes, and techniques of representation. The atmosphere of dreams, flashback, literary themes, and images emphasizes the fictional character of the text. Memory, references to live and dead emblematic writers, saints, playwrights, current heads of government, and politicians, visual and metatheatrical images, and language techniques add to the delusion of reality. He lashes his attack while dialoguing with Cervantes about their respective worlds. In the physical world, Alonso de Santos's play highlights modern-day life and entertainment (dramatic fashion; the abuse of prescribed drugs to treat mental illness; taste for cruelty, violence, and crime in the print and electronic media). His metatheatrical portrayal of life in the asylum, symbolizing the mindless world, exposes basic contradictions in systems, rituals, values, and beliefs, just as Mediero does with the bullfight and the bullfighter's dream in his erosive *El niño de Belén.*

Humor, madness, cruelty, and crime are joint in the awful parody exposing the scandalous milieu but aimed at dismantling, not benefitting, Christian life. With the cavalier attitude of postmodern times, Alonso de Santos equates the writings, mystical experience, and spiritual quests of enduring personalities with madness. Vulgar characters of an asylum who, in their dementia, believe they are venerated or idealized historical personalities (St. Theresa, the mother of Charles I, Queen Joan the Mad, St. Isidore) create confusion, debase religion, kill, and rebel. Surely, putting the memory of personalities and writers long dead, who helped to change history and shape the world in which they lived (the church, the palace, the throne, and the empire), in the mindless living originates a literary, cultural, and stage revolt. The modern compression and fusion of time reach back and beyond the confining dramatic space. The old and the new elements, ideas and ideologies, dead and living personalities form an amalgam in which art and life influence each other and fuse. The madness, confusion, and periodic awareness of danger, fear, happiness, and tragedy, which audiences experience as diversion, are contextual reality in the writer's mind.

There is irony in Alonso de Santos's use of classic Spanish modes that coincide with modern and postmodern artistic elements. There may be temptations to find influences of Ibsen and Pirandello in the conscious, subconscious reflections, shadows, or tricks of the mind. These virtual elements create textual and contextual parallels, engage the audience, and move it, with the play and the characters, between appearance and reality, the living and the dead, time present and time past, truth and make-believe. Alonso de Santos demeans inspiring images of confined or solitary historical individuals who disavowed authority, violated the rule, and changed the norm. From their cell, altar, throne, or prison, they overcame their enemies and survived death. To challenge fate and fame, he conjures the idealized models, challenges them, struggles with them, and his memories, as if to shake off their continuing psychic and artistic influence. Invulnerable, they reappear in dreams and revel in present-day live theater, electronically and chemically induced rebellious "acts" of madness. Perhaps the intoxication of national specificity, antinational pursuit of realism, and utilitarian truth are as valid as ever. The farce where a distorted portrayal of beliefs and rituals, marriage, elections, television viewing, and medicinal and illegal drugs equals madness is consistent with the timeless attitude and convention of combatant writers. It is also in agreement with avant-garde ideological formulations. Wilma Newberry saw it correctly. "The media of the left are shown to have as much mind destructive power as narcotics; indeed, they can be said to outdo religion as 'opium' of the masses."[45] She continues "that in *Fuera de quicio* there are many more intoxicants that were available in the age of Dionysus . . . and they do not tend to enhance human experience" ("Dionysus" 30). A skeptic of the usefulness of writing beyond the self, the dramatist de Santos projects his own wrestling with life and equates his and their social, religious, or artistic acts of rebellion with irony and subversive antics. At the core of Alonso de Santos's heretical attitude, irreverent humor, and toxic dramatic irony, there are personal truths. One is ambition. He seeks to "imitate" not the master's classic style or personal stories but the course of action that gave them the power and ability to cast a long shadow upon the world.

Alonso de Santos's successful, apparently no-sense play gives contemporary resonances to the uninterrupted dramatic debates about real and ideal artistic truth, originality, contingency, tradition, and modernity. The art-life debates dramatized with ambiguity in the polarities illusion—reality, truth, make-believe—in the seventeenth century extend their existence with this postmodern text. It includes autoreferential technique, repetition, coexisting forms, and aesthetics. Irony, crime and cruelty, recurrent psychedelic dreams, and induced "madness" make Alonso de Santos's unassailable ambiguity seem dated and modern at once. Its modern techniques—flashback, metadrama, and intertextual references—mirror images of age-old styles, methods, writing practices, and concerns passed on from Cervantes through Calderón to Jardiel to the 1990s. In effect, these devices disguise and reveal Cervantes's incontestable modernity, the jesting of avant-garde inventions, and the postmodern status of the play. Part of its postmodernity rests on the turn of tough social realism into a representation of reality that is self-consciously theatrical. A striking note is that in addition to the timeless notion that "art and life influence each other," his dramatic response to global theory confirms that art inspires other art—or responds to it.

Jerónimo López Mozo, who had been asking, "¿Dónde está el 'nuevo' teatro?" (Where is the new theatre?), answers his own question with a play entitled *El engaño a los ojos* [A Deception to the Eyes]. His intriguing "tromp l'oeil" title also dissuades readers/viewers from associating the play he wrote with the recent psychodrama by Alonso de Santos. Rather, his play and its immediate precedent belong to a literary genealogy. He includes a similar dialogue in which he communicates with Cervantes across time. In a short article David Herzenberger establishes that López Mozo traces his roots to Cervantes's *entremés* (interlude.)[46]

In his dramatic reproof *El engaño a los ojos*, López Mozo challenges the validity of the generally accepted designation "new" for drama written between the 1960s and 1999. Evidently, the dramatist's semantic arguments regarding "new" theater may be better satisfied with the term *modern* in the title of this book. It may also satisfy John London for whom Buero's *Historia de una escalera* and Sastre's *Escuadra hacia la muerte*, both canonical plays of the 1940s and 1950s, are nineteenth-century plays, not new theater, not even good theater.[47] Surely Lope and Cervantes would wink, smile, and show pacific feelings toward the combatants.

These postmodern rebels seek to subvert existing fads, mindless acts, and mental habits. They express their disagreements and talent in modern plays that

uphold the universality and timelessness of the old and modern classics, a tradition of realistic representation of reality so as to regenerate the spirit, not
necessarily old values and beliefs. Their renewed emphasis on artistic quality
carries with it a cultural rebellion insofar as these plays challenge the rift between arts and letters, encourage originality, and promote change in the theatrical scene. A parallel reaction took place with the short-lived *modernism* and
its drive to return to literary theater in 1898 when dramatists rejected the still
popular nineteenth-century melodrama, parody, popular arts theater, and the veritable realism of the day. To encourage men of letters, Benavente, leading the
shift, declared that "in Spain and in the world all great playwrights have been
poets."[48] Jesús Rubio Jiménez considers that efforts to renew the theater between
1915 and 1930 originated vanguard poetic texts.[49] E. Marquina, the Machado
brothers, and López Rubio are among the modernizers. Pérez de Ayala and Gala
revived the text-based play and penned celebrated vanguard poetic drama to
which the realists objected and derided as escapist. Idealism, dedication, and
personal or outside pressures and demands motivated committed dramatists to
write utilitarian, political plays, propaganda, testimonial, and true-to-life realistic
plays between 1898 and 1936 and from 1940 to 1970s. From Galdós onward,
there are sociological, psychological, and social(ist) plays with clear, veiled, and
apparent influences of Maeterlinck, Ibsen, especially Chekhov, and Miller, who
were successful and fashionable in the world stage.

Today, the dramatists committed to undo the existing culture are no longer
"marginal," nor should they be viewed as unbiased exponents of realism. The
more artful dramatists are still tempted by the vanguard. Belbel, one of Arrabal's
strongest admirers, is himself enjoying increasing popularity. He won The Critics' Award as Spain's most influential dramatist of 1992. Fermín Cabal and J. L.
Alonso de Santos shared the same prize in 1995. Belbel rewrites as he translates
his own plays into Spanish and French. He also translates into Spanish and
directs plays by Bonet i Jornet, for whom writing in Catalán remains a political
statement against central statecraft. Belbel's own translations and participation
in the stage productions of his male erotically charged *Caricies*[50] and revisited
Després de la Pluja earned him critical success. *Caricies*, performed in Paris,
captured the 1999 Moliere French Theater prize. There is discontent among
dramatists wishing to bring back to the stage its Spanish attitude and flavor.

Alonso de Santos, Belbel, Cabal, Nieva, and Pedrero validate the perception
that out of the dramatists most singled out, those who have a particular core
agenda that is realized not on the observance but on the transgression of the
norm are finding an easier and happier life in the theater—easier than their
immediate predecessors, successors, or even their contemporaries, who also
grew up in the post-Franco era or were born in the democratic period. Alberto
Miralles calls them "los alternativos."[51] Their first opportunity to stage a recommended, promising play is, generally, an opening-day performance in small,
out-of-the-way, alternative houses. Those who are beginning to break away began by imitating their mentors of favorite successful models. Not surprisingly,

their plays manifest that naturalism—that is, innate vulgarity. Bad language, strong acts for impact, remain high theatrical values. E. Centeno, a dramatist turned critic, singles out Miguel Romero Esteo in the group *nuevo teatro español* (New Spanish Theater) on the basis that with *Pasodoble* he introduced the most major innovation in the *esperpento* since Valle-Inclán. Centeno approvingly suggests that Esteo portrays, deconstructs, dances, and steps on regional social institutions. His extreme criticism of society is so crude that Centeno credits the play with being "por obseno, valiente" (*Escritura dramatica: La escena española* 211). Surely, a handful of the original seeds of modern drama developed, its roots evolved, and its artistic fruit is falling farther from the tree than was ever imagined. There is an irony. Both postmodern radicals Centeno and Esteo and the times are at odds with Valle-Inclán's transcendental thought that a maxim of aesthetic doctrine should be to love all things in a joyful communion with their essential beauty, then query the reasons and the norm.[52]

Coincidentally, modern antitheater theories, definitions, and approaches to dialogue and text are having their effect on drama. There is greater need, desire, challenge, or possibility to be competitive in a time when the antitheater movement increasingly regards performance over text, directing and producing over writing. The persistent wars within the theater culture itself again result in more demand for works that are a mixture of multiple ethnic or marginal elements, more demand for creative pieces with alternative artistic means of expression, patterns, and methods: song, dance, musicals, movies, and cinema clips, proposed as total theater in one-hour cabaret shows, and variety shows. One reads that this rich entertainment variety takes representation closer to the idea of a *total theater*. It is, perhaps, because when concert halls were losing audiences to drama and opera, Richard Wagner proposed the concept of a total theater. Cocteau developed the idea in France when failure forced him to abandon the marginal surrealist play. Rather, it seems that variety of means brings back the traditional stage. In the past, mixing daily concerns with artistic expressions of the culture, its symbols, and icons added richness and contributed to the enormous success and popularity that the old and the modernized *zarzuela* and the *comedia nueva* enjoy to this day. The situation is not dissimilar to the movement toward "re-teatralización" [retheatrically] of the stage to combat the dominion of the dramatic text over the spectacle on the stage. Its result, then and now, as Rubio Jiménez indicates, is the displacement of literature while all that concerns representation gains ground—hence the cultivation of pastiche, pantomime, and all experiments already and not yet mentioned (Rubio, *Modernismo y teatro* 58).

A theatrical production based on Picasso's cubist painting *Guernica* is a concrete example of the novel theater concept up to 2000.[53] The New York production of *Guernika*, on April 7 to May 14, was a response to the need and demand for fun, variety, and innovative popular shows. The 1969 play text and its author Jerónimo López Mozo are contributing elements to the total stage performance. The emphasis on visual and the tangible are influences of cinema and television, the newest viewing art and big theater competitor. The piece introduces animation as a new form of artistic imitation on the stage. The author has looked for reference in other art forms, making art in the museum a source of inspiration. The play text obliterates traditional spoken dramatic dialogue. Thus, it eliminates or minimizes the role of the character performer. The piece could be described as art imitating art or, more accurately here, as a theatrical collage that breathes new life into Picasso's painting denouncing the 1937 Spanish tragedy. The criteria for this experiment may be life in historical art, the problem of individual experience, and perception of events. *Guernika* brings to life the known visual static images in the painting, whereas the text's suggestive spelling communicates changes of vision, ideology, and artistic planes across time. The stress on performance introduces new ways of contemplating, responding, and representing art. In place of the painting's impassioned charge of dehumanized power, at best, the Disney-like production expresses a vision that complements and reinforces the theme of its pictorial source void of hurtful sentiment, as the audience may not be expected to add signification to the total theatrical experience. Rather, the performance instills awareness of the impending similar tragedy about to take place. Fused fiction and reality, time, space, and history evoke the power of fear, the other tragic aesthetic emotion. *Guernika* mostly seems designed to show that in the performance all art is organic, moves, lives on. On the stage, the collective fear of death as it appears in the pictorial source is also alive. As a play, *Guernika* represents an effort to enliven and renovate the stage with popular entertainment, a compromise that brings art to the people, moves art's boundaries, removes language barriers, speaks to world audiences by speaking the universal language of art. Its emphasis on stage arts, the visual, the tangible, and the various artistic languages aid those aspects of creativity in the theater that substantially had not changed. As artistic transgression, *Guernika* changes the definition of theater from *text and performance* to the more generalized modern concept of *arts and entertainment*. It is theater without spoken dialogue, the traditional character, drama, or transcendence. In *Guernika*, López Mozo lives up to the commitment of an artistic tradition devoted to represent social reality as a passionate concern for the specificity of his people and country. With the two simultaneous forms of cultural history expressing individual and collective memory, the show fulfills its role in the plan to carry out modernity's ambitious aesthetic project of artistic regeneration and renewal. In his hands, arts and letters, drama, and light entertainment fuse again; the *living art* or *visual art* concept gains new life, exposure, meaning, and a festive mood. At the heart of this postmodern representation of two cultural expressions is the celebration of the theater as popular entertainment. The expected, and welcomed, dramatic response may be found in plays that transmit a feeling of anxiety over certain modern trends—in plays that indicate that a shadow hovers over the theater, that dramatize personal fears of its death, its danger of extinction, and the struggle to keep it alive.

Unamuno dramatized his double struggle in such plays as *Sombra de Sueño* and *Domador de sombras* [Shadow of Sleep and Tamer of Shadows]. His wrestling to master, control, and influence modernity from the stage to outlive its difficult odds constitutes the forces that have motivated, inspired, and influenced dramatists of all ideological persuasions since the Enlightenment. The odds at the beginning of the new century were soccer, bullfighting, cinema, video movies, and television. As a defense or protection against the strong competing forces threatening the theater, dramatists relentlessly treat the issue and relate its downshift to entertainment habits and, as always, to the idiosyncracies of the characters in the play or of fictional audiences on the stage. An aura of symbolism and realism of the absurd encircles reconstructionist plays wrought by members of the theater group El astillero and first staged in alternative theaters known as *la cuarta pared.*[54] At the same time, dramatists wishing to speak to audiences inside and beyond borders follow the new artistic wave, experiment further, look for novel reference sources in painting and other artistic expressions and incorporate the newer artistic forms or elements as part of the dramatic text.

The next five dramatists, born between 1960 and 1970, have seen their plays produced and published with some degree of success or their talent acknowledged with coveted awards for drama. They are: Luisa Canillé (*Libración*), Juan Mayorga (*Cartas de Amor a Stalin. El sueño de Ginebra, El jardín desolado* [*The Scorched Garden*]), Antonio Onetti (*Purasangre*), Itziar Pascual Sánchez (*El domador de sombras*), and Margarita Sánchez Roldán. (*Sobre ascuas*, staged in 1997 and 1999). They are trying less fresh but valid and effective solutions to the age-old problem of how to create a new image and model that would shift, define, and lead the Spanish theater of the new millennium. The less cosmopolitan, less adventurous, experimental drama of the late 1990s stage wears a Janus mask in its march into the new century. The Janus image suggestive of the future involves dramatists who, on the eve of the year 2000, stood gazing back with a different outlook. Alonso de Santos, in parody and metatheatrically, stepped forward and on the borderline between modernity and postmodernity. Others were attempting the reconfiguration of the play, gathering the pieces of deconstruction, writing text-based drama. While theoreticians such as James Briton, Frank D'Angelo, and James Muffett are gaining popularity, emerging dramatists and defenders and detractors of the modernizing movements sound old voices declaring the theater sick or dying.

Ignacio Amestoy's assessment of the modern committed plays of the 1900s is that Spain still awaits "the splendid resurrection of the theater that was supposed to occur when the Franco era ended . . . the miracle they saw coming did not happen" [no ha llegado/la esperada resurrección esplendorosa del teatro español a la salida del franquismo . . . no ocurrió el deseado milagro].[55] Sanchiz Sinisterra in *El cerco de Leningrado* (staged in 1995) reviews, with sardonic humor, the past and present of the Marxist Left. Coincidentally, Jerónimo López Mozo declares, with irony, their illusionist deception. Yet another dramatist curiously enacts the exact intuitions found in performance reviews by Haro Tecglen. The theater critic's columns suggest that while the iconoclast *vanguard* elements in raw, blunt, and daring feminist plays of the 1980s and 1990s were provoking dialogue, they would generate a negative public reaction; inevitably, low audience numbers would speed the normal process of decay and evolution and eventually force change. By analogy for a dying circus—the Circus theater?—dramatist Itziar Pascual critiques the modern play and denounces its deception and effects. He satirizes its protest, claim of originality, and innovation (the transgender act/actor on the stage). His "action" heightens the source and status of the play, the players, the dramatists' fears, and struggle for survival. It is best to let the dramatist's words summarize and corroborate the preceding pages.

(I translate) Grock (a clown): Stop protesting . . .

Voice of Perezoff: Esteemed and respectable audience! / Prepare yourselves to contemplate what never has been seen before / impressing acrobatics from the deadly trapeze! / the unequaled cubist beauty of the bearded woman! The nobility and elegance of the new generation of artists! All of this plus magnificent awards, prizes, and gifts . . .

Grock (a clown): What do they hope to gain if they dedicate themselves to deceive the public. People are not fools: [they know what they see.] They know what a tiger is . . . / and a defrauded spectator never comes back.

The specter of the clown Grock: I could say: We are a ruined circus . . . / . . . We have a director who is a "ludopath" . . . / . . . What are we to do?

Grock: I don't know! I don't know. It is very easy to destroy, but to construct takes time.

(Stage direction: Exit Grock with his specter) (Itziar Pascual Sánchez, *El domador de sombras*, vi: 186–187)

Crock (un payaso): Déjate de protestar . . .

Voz de Perezoff: Estimado y respectable público! . . . / . . . Prepárense a contemplar lo nunca visto . . . / . . . las acrobacias más impresionantes desde el trapecio de la muerte! La inegualable belleza cubista de la mujer barbuda! La nobleza y elegancia de una nueva generación de artistas! Todo ello con magníficos premios obsequios y regalos . . . / . . .

Grock (un payaso): Qué esperan conseguir si se dedican a engañar al público. La gente no es tonta: sabe lo que es un tigre . . . / y un espectador defraudado no vuelve nunca al circo.

(El espectro del payaso Grock): Podría decir: Somos un circo arruinado. . . . / . . . Tenemos un director ludópata . . . / . . . Que le vamos a hacer?

Grock: No lo sé! No lo sé. Destruir es muy fácil, pero para construír se necesita tiempo.

Acotación: Grock sale de escena con su espectro)

There is no gloom. The dramatist is leading his generation to seize the moment. The play's final realization is a reflection of Pascual's artistic reality, critical stance, and attempt to bring body and spirit together so that truth and dead or dying dramatic art may continue to live. "Time is needed" to fight competition, to overcome the effects of modern theatrical experiments, the anarchists, the small crowd-pleasing plays that undermine and underestimate today's knowledgeable audiences. One discerns a sense of the dramatist's exhaustion from having wrestled, perhaps too long, against plays that have a nearly fatal mission.

Evidently, the early controversies that Cervantes and Lope loudly voiced and epitomized over dramatic theory and practice are still being debated. And the age-old battles over the nature, content, and purpose of art—the case for modernity—are still going on. Like it was then, today's monsters and giants in the literary and dramatic fields raise doubts, ask questions, and dream of viable answers. Today's attitudes and goals for the twenty-first century reveal some sure steps. With the movement toward recuperation, there is a beginning of what seems the *eternal return*, which countless dramatists treat. The hope for the future is for less mixing of the arts, more text-based theater productions, and more professional writers who will write exclusively for the theater.

A number of playwrights who close and open our two centuries treat the same thematic content, mix old ideals and tradition with modern concepts and attitudes. From a play written in a realistic style, they move to one in imaginative theatrical form. They favor simplicity of means, a theater of daily life, closeness, family relationships. In balance, the writers appear anxious but confident. Many plays continue to deal with ethical and social problems: prescribed, abused and criminal drug addiction, feminist issues, women's issues, mental illness, incest, and sexual abuse of the young. One still finds sexually liberated and still frustrated marginal heroes and heroines. Often they are psychiatric cases. Some have been committed or belong in institutions and rebel. Margarita Sánchez Roldán captures the mood best. *Sobre ascuas*, a monodrama, treats domestic violence, abandonment, fear, silent emotion, and open revolt. A sexually abused teenage woman is pregnant. A battered mother has abandoned her husband and child. On the eve of her seventeenth birthday Pepa enacts a debate with Antonio in which she asserts her selfhood. A lover of truth and clarity, she confronts him with reality. No longer afraid of him or his dying, she has "learned to start the fire" that will light the surrounding darkness. She has learned to spell her name and acts against his will. Deep fear will no longer force her to accept his control, disregard her sad past, or hide her illicit yearnings. While the victimizer releases insults and irritation, she admits to feeling the lure of the reckless desire that destroyed him, her, and their family. Dramatically, Pepa's decision and promise to raise her unborn child, whose father is also the grandfather, puts the theme of incest in today's amoral context. The decision to keep the baby, her willingness to continue cohabitation and social deception as a safe pathway to their future, and outlasting death push the limits on both sides of the social and ethical argument. Violence and abandonment turns a seven-year-old child into a surrogate wife who grows up as a guiltless, shameless young woman. On one level, the play records both a modern context and a feminist mind-set. Free choice, taking control, and assertiveness in opportunity make the case for women issues and modernity. On the large issues, it does not. Pepa chooses subversion over abasement and resignation to her seducer or to the feminist creed. She elects life over death, motherhood over abortion. At the same time, ignorance, mind, and spiritual darkness are at the center of reasoning in this condensed play. The exact time span, Antonio's terminal illness, his pain, black, burning fear, and anticipation of death operate a kind of poetic justice on the violator of women and the natural law. Lust may be killing him. It is at the root of all affliction in the situation. With ingenuity, Roldán associates it, the name "Pepa," and "papa," his bad heart and head and a dark, sick mentality. At the human level the "action," a clinical case, distances the doer from the act. Thus, while the play represents the dying and the budding outlooks, it also records contemporary amoral attitudes and ways to reason or rationalize unacceptable behavior. There is, however, a higher power that punctually exacts justice. Creatively, Roldán participates in the fashion of the breaking of taboos but only to rebel against artistic incest. She will bring to life her creation on her own terms. The open dialogue displays the dramatist's sense of confidence and control over the strong subject. There is a chilling aloofness in characterization. What happens to the characters and what they say are more important than how they are because the play seeks and elicits a mindful rather than an emotional reaction. An Ibsen-like door slam, in reverse—she stays, he goes—provides the liberating artistic end.

Also backed by the modernizing principle, other playwrights who close and open our two centuries mine Golden Age drama and adapt their artistic legacy to today's political reality, taste, values, and daily concerns. In the 1990s *La sombra de Tenorio* [Tenorio's Shadow] persists in Suárez and in Alonso de Santos's 1995 successful collaboration. Other titles suggest interpretations of everyday life and of previous well-known theatrical versions of it: *Horas de visita* [Visiting, or better, Dr's. Office Hours], by Mari Carrillo; *El brujo* [The Sorcerer], by Rafael Álvarez; and *Purasangre*, by Onetti. These dramatists mix the old Spanish thematic content, ideals, and tradition with modern concepts and attitudes. They may change a source play written in old realistic style to one in imaginative theatrical form, or vice versa. The published, produced, and/ or read dramatists of the late 1990s prefer to write a theater of daily life and close relationships that bring life, as it is lived, closer to the dream. Ernesto Caballero, in *Rosaura o el sueño es vida* [Rosaura Is Life and the Dream (1984)], treats Calderón's basic themes without the conflict, its poetry, or its transcendence. It and *La ultima cena* [The Last Supper] (1995) are expressive of the modern sentiment, inane realism, and prosaic point of view.

Five of the ten dramatists Gabriele and Leonard anthologized or made known in feature interviews of May 1996 and October 1996[56] have received awards of distinction in the last decade: Ernesto Caballero for *Nostalgia del agua*; Ignacio Moral for *Fugadas*; Antonio Plou for *Rey Sancho*; Rodrigo García for *Prometeo*; and Antonio Álamo for *El hombre que quería volar*, which has the title and elements from short stories by García Márquez. These dramatists verify further the constant, essential connection between the old and the new in modern drama. There is in these plays a consistency and a creative interest to express a coherent sense of personal as well as collective identity. Both consistency and interest in reconditioning their artistic legacy add perspective and provide a key to the concept and to the dynamics of modernity. One important tendency that emerges from the larger picture of modern Spanish drama—from the *autos* and the *comedias mágicas*, banned in the eighteenth century (1765 and 1778), to sociopolitical, historical farce, drama, or tragedy, to social comedy—is that the most major dramatists endeavor to offset coercion, repression, or restraint with freedom of the imagination, to balance that urge, or the requirement of a realistic portrayal and the sometimes irrepressible creative spirit. Noticeably, they associate themselves with their most honored and privileged predecessors, yet they seek to leave an imprint of their own in the new dramatic creation.

Nonetheless, it is still surprising to find Unamuno's *El domador de sombras* opening and closing our two centuries. He and Itziar Pascual, transitional dramatists who are a century apart, teach or explain that "with time we learn to tame our deamons." It seems that the eternal return concept dramatized in many plays had begun again. Theater fans are seeing with Unamuno *El pasado que vuelve.* His contemporaries, Azorín and Vicente Soriano Gandía, who welcomed the new artistic and social movements with optimism, dramatized a generation's hopes for the state and stage return to glory with the notion of circularity [el eterno retorno]. In identical titles they make transparent an absolute certainty that *Ayer será mañana* [Yesterday Will Be Tomorrow]. Their tomorrow is yesterday and today. And dramatists have yet to find a defining artistic method as modern, original, and successful as Lope's formula or as the syntheses present in the timeless works by Cervantes and Calderón. Their persistent, sometimes powerful influence is projected in conscious and subconscious images or in mental and physical forms that continue to attract audiences.

Their perpetual shadow disturbs the creative, revolutionary spirit of defenders and detractors still striving to create the new image that will be an example in life, an artistic model, and their lasting shadow. The physical, mental, and spiritual shadows, reflections, or specters that occur in the magic plays, in Sastre, Mediero, Rivas, Unamuno, Gala, Alonso de Santos, ghosts in Gómez Arcos and Pascual, ultimately project faith and fear in a struggle for fate and fame. Their plays record and confirm the constant preoccupation with self-expression, with the need for a core cultural identity (deeply disagreeing on what that identity is) and with portraying both profoundly affected by historical change. Recurrent titles, icons, visions, and revisions of political, literary, and dramatic reality refract the surrounding world, their major obstacle standing in the way to their dream.

El sueño de la vida [Life's Dream], *Sombras de sueño* [Shadow of Sleep], the Specter (of the character) Grock, the creative spirit in *El domador de sombras* [Tamer of Shadows], and the Attic prophecy contained in the title *Ayer será mañana* deflect, fuse, compress, reproduce, and reflect a long-extended poetic image of modern Spanish dramatists as "the mirrors of gigantic shadows which futurity casts upon the present."[57]

NOTES

1. Charles Baudelaire, *La Curiosités esthétique et autres ecrits sur l'art* (Paris: Hermann, 1968).

2. Robert Lima, Introduction, to *'La lampápara maravillosa' Valle-Inclán: Nueva valoración de su obra*, ed. Clara Luisa Barreito (University Park: Pennsylvania State University Press, 1988), 36.

3. Harold Bloom, *The Anxiety of Influence: A Theory of Poetry*, 2d ed. (New York: Oxford University Press, 1997), 5.

4. David Thatcher Gies, *The Theater in Nineteenth-Century Spain* (Cambridge: Cambridge University Press, 1994), 3.

5. Wilfried Floeck, "Escritura dramática y posmodernidad: El teatro actual entre realismo y vanguardia," *Insula* 601–602 1997: 12–14.

6. Paul Julian Smith's *Writing in the Margin: Spanish Literature of the Golden Age* (Oxford: Clarendon Press, 1988), is a striking title and concept.

7. René Andioc, *Teatro y sociedad en el Madrid del siglo XVIII* (Madrid: Castalia, 1976).

8. *Cuadernos Americanos* 299 (May 1975): 281–349.

9. Percy Shelley, *A Defense of Poetry*, ed., intro., and notes by Albert S. Cook (Boston: Ginn, 1891), 46.

10. Ignacio de Luzán is best known for his *Poetica* (1737). After his stay in Paris from 1747 to 1750, he wrote *Memorias literarias de Paris* (1751) and *Década epistolar sobre el estado de las letras en Francia* (1781) under the pseudonym Francisco Maria de Silva. He translated Diderot and Chaussée's *Le préjugé a la mode* as *La razón contra la moda* and made Diderot's ideas his own. In this last named work he applies the rules of the sentimental play he favors and prescribes: the classical unities of time, place, and action, the principle of verisimilitude, a simple plot, characters, language, and themes drawn from daily life, and a didactic moral purpose.

11. Jeremy Collier, *Short View of the Immorality and Profaneness of the English Stage*, 2d ed. (1698; rpt., New York: Ams Press, 1974), 1, 2. Collier, an Englishman, is credited with opening the door to literary reform in Europe. He attacked the "misbehavior of the stage with respect to Morality, and Religion. [T]he business of plays is to recommend Virtue and discountenance Vice." Intolerable is to him "their making their characters libertines and giving them success in their debauchery."

12. D. Gaspar Melchor de Jovellanos, *Memorias para el arreglo de la policía de los espectáculos y diversiones públicas y sobre su origen en España* [Document for Reforming the Policing of Spectacles and Public Entertainment and of Its Origin in Spain], in *Obras* [Works], *Nueva Biblioteca de autores españoles*, Vol. 46 (Madrid: Real Academica, 1951), 495.

13. Cesare Beccaria, *Dei delitti e delle pene* (Torino: Unione Tipografico-Editrice Torinese, 1911).

14. Karl Shapiro, *Beyond Criticism* (University of Nebraska Press, 1953), 3, and "Career of the Poem" on p. 53.

15. Most recently, John London, *Reception and Renewal in Modern Spanish Theatre, 1939–1963*, vol. 45 (Leeds: W. S. Maney and Sons, for the Modern Humanities Research Association, 1997), 178–235.

16. Emilio Palacios Fernández, *El teatro popular español del siglo XVIII* (Leida, Es-

paña: Milenio, 1998), 73. On the other hand, Josefina Pérez Teijón considers the neglect of the short humorous pieces unjustifiable. See her Introducción, Algunas observaciones sobre el teatro neoclásico con especial atención al saincte in her *Aportaciones al estudio de la literatura popular y burlesca del siglo XVIII* (Salamanca: Gráficos Cervantes, 1991), 11 n.1.

17. Heinrich Falk, "Enlightenment Ideas, Attitudes, and Values in the Teatro Menor of Luis Moncín," in *Studies in Eighteenth-Century Spanish Literature and Romanticism in Honor of John Clarkson Dowling*, ed. Douglas Barnette and Linda Jane Barnette (Newark, DE: Juan de la Cuesta Hispanic Monographs, 1985).

18. Joan Lynne Pataki Kasove, Preface, The *"Comedia Lacrimosa" and Spanish Romantic Drama (1773–1865)* (London: Tamesis, 1977), 11.

19. Gies, *The Theater in Nineteenth-Century Spain*, 36.

20. Ermanno Caldera, *Il dramma romantico in Spagna*, Instituto di Letteratura Spagnola E Ispano-Americana, Collona di studi diretta da Guido Mancini (Pisa, Italy: Universita di Piza, 1974).

21. See Charles Ganelín, *Rewriting Theatre: The Comedia and the Nineteenth-Century Refundiciones* (Lewisburg, PA: Bucknell University Press, 1994).

22. Diego Nuñez, "El legado regeneracionista" in *La democracia frustrada y la restauración, Revista de Libros*, ed., Manuel Pérez Ledesima, 22 (October 1998): 8.

23. C. Brian Morris, ed., *The Surrealist Adventure in Spain* (Ottawa, Canada: Doven House, 1991); see also his *Surrealism and Spain, 1920–1936* (Cambridge: Cambridge University Press, 1972).

24. The text in Spanish is: "El Surrealismo es hoy un caza incautos. Una morfina más, un estupefaciente que los zorros y las zorras dan a los niños de la burguesía para encanallarlos." Nigel Dennis, "Ernesto Giménez Cavallero y Surrealismo: A Reading of 'Yo, inspector de alcantarillas,' " in Morris, *The Surrealist Adventure in Spain*, 97, n.11.

25. Antonio Azorín, *Obras*, vol. 5 (Madrid: Aguilar, 1954), 42.

26. The quote in Spanish is: "Los que esperamos y deseamos la redención de España, no la queremos ver como un país próspero sin unión con el pasado; la queremos ver próspera, pero esencialmente la España de siempre." Antonio Azorín, "Desde la República del 73 al 98," in *Obras selectas* (Madrid: Biblioteca Nueva, 1962), 20. On the battles over modern art from Moratín to Galdós he wrote "Política, literatura, nación," 202–224, 227.

27. Kristine Ibsen "The Illusory Dream: García Lorca's *'Viaje a la luna'* [Trip to the moon],' " in Morris, *The Surrealist Adventure in Spain*, 224–239.

28. William M. Sherzer, *Juan Merce: Entre la ironía y la dialéctica* (Madrid: Editorial Fundamentos, 1982). Sherzer studies the device in the context of the Spanish contemporary novel.

29. London, *Reception and Renewal*. Chapters 6 and 7, 178–235, deal with Spanish dramatists.

30. Ibid., 146.

31. Alberto Miralles, *Approximación al teatro alternativo* (Madrid: Asociacón de Autores de Teatro, 1994), 16.

32. Enrique Centeno, *Escritura dramática La escena española actual. Crónica de una década: 1984–1994* (Madrid: Marco Gráfico, 1996), 211.

33. Floeck, "Escritura dramática y posmodernidad," 7, n.5.

34. Elinor Fuchs, "The Death of Character: Reflections on Theater after Modernism"

(Ph.D. diss., Graduate School and University Center of The City University of New York, 1995), 1, 2, 126ss.

35. Leonora Levi, "Transgression, Desire and Textual Power" (Ph.D. diss., Harvard University, 1992), 1–4.

36. Ibid., 2.

37. Juan Goytisolo's words are: "En el mundo capital actual no hay temas virulentos o audaces. El lenguage y sólo el lenguage puede ser subversivo." *Disidencias* (Barcelona: Seix Barral, 1977), 167.

38. José María Rodríguez Méndez, "El teatro como expresión social y cultural," in *La tabernera y las tinajas: Los inocentes de la Moncloa* (Madrid: Taurus, 1968), 92–95.

39. José María, Rodríguez Méndez, *Comentarios impertinentes sobre el teatro español*, Edcs de Bolsillo 199 (Barcelona: Península, 1972), 40.

40. "La literatura dramática en la encrucijada de la postmodernidad," *Insula* 601–602 (February 1997): 30.

41. Augusto Martínez Olmedilla, "Seiscientas cuarenta y cinco ilustraciones y ocho láminas" [Six Hundred and Forty-five Color Illustrations and Eight Photographs] in *Arriba el telón. Colección panorama de un siglo* (Madrid: Aguilar, 1961), 327. Anecdotes, details, and documents about the theater, performance, staging, costumes, actors, and actresses in the last 100 years.

42. Morris, *The Surrealist Adventure in Spain*; Morris, *Surrealism and Spain, 1920–1936*.

43. See Carmen Bassolas, *La ideología de los escritores. Literatura y política en "La Gaceta Literaria" 1927–1932* (Barcelona Fontanara, 1975); Guillermo Díaz-Plaja, *Memorias de una generación destruida 1920–1936* (Barcelona: Editora Delos-Ayurá, 1966). For a historical perspective on both sides of the issues debated in the plays, see Manuel Perez Ledesma, ed., *La democracia frustrada y la restauración* in *Revista de libros* 22 (October 1998); and Dennis, "Ernesto Giménez Cavallero and Surrealismo," 97.

44. Berta Riazza, "Encuentro con el mundo del teatro: Resistencia y pasión" [Encounter with the Theatrical World: Resistance and Passion], *Insula* 601–602 (1997): 19–22.

45. Wilma Newberry, "Dionysus Triumphant: José Luis Alonso de Santos's Metatheatrical Farce *Fuera de Quicio*," *Estreno Cuadernos del Teatro Español Contemporáneo* 21.1 (Spring 1995): 28–31. Also see Hazel Cazorla, "Miguel Medina Vicario *Los géneros literarios en la obra teatral de José Luis Alonso de Santos* Madrid: Ediciones Libertarias, 1993," *Reseña Estreno* 21.2 (1995): 56.

46. David K. Herzenberger, "El engaño a los ojos: The Theatrics of Theatrical History," *Estreno* 25.2 (otoño 1999): 20–22.

47. London, *Reception and Renewal*, 234. See also "Autarquía política e indigenismo teatral. La escena española y la cultura del franquismo vistas desde fuera." Review of John London's *Reception and Renewal* by Victor García Ruiz in *Insula* 625–626 (1999): 9.

48. Jesús Rubio Jiménez, *Modernismo y teatro poético en España (1900–1914): Una renovación necesaria. Cien años de azul (1888–1988)* (Granada: University of Granada Press, 1992), 28.

49. Jesús Rubio Jiménez, "El 'Teatro de Arte' (1908–1911): Un eslabón necesario entre el modernismo y las vanguardias," *Siglo XX/20th Century* 5.1–2 (1987–1988): 25–33.

50. There may be dramatic sources accepted or denied for this play. However, its title is surprisingly close to a nondramatic book. Brian Morris describes a "pseudo-scientific" male sexual pornography book entitled *The Science of the Caresses* found in a deceased psychiatrist's book collection. Morris traces its influences in plays by Domenechina and quotes one character who says that "psychoanalysis is a precious discovery for literature." In Morris's correct view, it is "a convenient façade behind which to pack pretentious displays of pseudo-medical knowledge." Morris, *The Surrealist Adventure in Spain*, 36–37, n.140.

51. Miralles, *Aproximación al teatro alternativo*, 16, 39.

52. Robert Lima, Introduction to "*La lampara maravillosa,*" *Valle-Inclan: Nueva valoración de su obra*, 36.

53. There are other *Guernica* plays by Fernando Arrabal, Ignacio Amestoy, and Francisco Torres Monreal with the subtitle *Variación escénica sobre temas de Picasso* (his own play, the painting, and Neruda's poetry).

54. The better-known founders of the group Astillero are Guillermo Heras, their director and mentor, Miguel González Cruz, and Juan Mayorga, who is credited with the idea of putting together a group of dramatists who were working on the same wavelength to share their artistic vision, interests, motivations, and ideals.

55. Amestoy Egiguren, "La literatura dramática española en la encrucijada de la posmodernidad," 3.

56. Candyce Leonard and John Gabriele, *Panorámica del teatro español actual* (Madrid: Espiral/Fundamentos, 1996); also see their *El teatro de la España democrata: Los noventa* (Madrid: Editorial Fundamentos, 1996).

57. Shelley, *A Defense of Poetry*, 45.

CARLOS ARNICHES Y BARRERA
(1866–1943)

Nancy J. Membrez

BIOGRAPHY

Carlos Arniches y Barrera was a native of Alicante, an ancient port city in southeastern Spain, but found fame and fortune, as did so many of his generation, in the capital city of Madrid. In Arniches's first phase of literary production, he premiered his play *Casa editorial* [Publishing House] in 1888, the first in a long series of one-act plays, alone and in collaboration, with music and without, in the popular genre of the time called the *género chico*, literally, "the little genre." The *género chico* was defined by its theatrical venue, the *teatro por horas* [theater by the hour] that worked on the "one hour/ one play/ one penny" success formula from 1867 until 1922. Some of these plays were musicals called *zarzuelas*, whose tunes are recognized even today by millions in Spain and Latin America.

In the course of his lifetime, Arniches had three principal collaborators—(in chronological order) Gonzalo Cantó, Celso Lucio, and Enrique García Alvarez—but as his lengthy list of works demonstrates (see appendices in McKay, Ríos, or Monleón), he also collaborated with playwrights Joaquín Abati, José López Silva, Carlos Fernández Shaw, and a host of others (for a grand total of twenty-four individuals) and with popular composers Ruperto Chapí, Tomás López Torregrosa, Jerónimo Jiménez, Vicente Lleó, Rafael Calleja, Joaquín Valverde, Quinito Valverde (Joaquín's son), José Serrano, Amadeo Vives, and others. He wrote 82 plays alone and 113 in collaboration, for a grand total of 195 plays, the majority in one-act, 111 of which were musical—an astounding number for any playwright.

It is hard for us to imagine nowadays the rapidity of one-act play turnover that this formula created, nor the unprecedented shuffling of collaborators and composers in the frenzied search for novelty and hilarity in the theater. The best comparison that might be made is to the dizzying arrangement and rearrangement of TV situation comedies in our era.

It is understandable that English-speaking audiences have never heard of Arniches. The idiomatic nature of the language he employed in his plays, a lexicon difficult if not impossible to translate, has precluded the translation of his plays to other languages. Another impediment to translation, particularly of the one-acts of his first phase, was the subject matter: the *cuadro de costumbres*, that is, the painting of popular customs viewed from the bourgeois perspective.

In the second phase of Arniches's literary production, a new element was introduced: the grotesque. Literary historians usually date this new direction from the premiere of *La señorita de Trevélez* in 1916, which he called a *farsa cómica*, a comic farce, the first in a series in the late teens and 1920s.

The Spanish Civil War (1936–1939) interrupted Arniches's life but not his literary production. He spent the war years in Buenos Aires, Argentina, premiering comedies, and returned to Madrid to pick up where he had left off, undisturbed by the new authoritarian regime. (See Sotomayor Sáez.) He died there in 1943, the last of his generation of playwrights. It is Arniches Spaniards remember (many with nostalgia) when the *género chico* is mentioned, due in part to his longevity and popularity with middle-class audiences (Monleón 38). His plays even returned briefly in the avant-garde café-theaters of the 1960s.

It is important to note that from the 1920s to the 1950s Arniches's later works resurface time and time again, not only on stage but in the movies as well. Spanish studios produced numerous silent versions of Arniches's plays in the 1920s, sound versions in the 1930s, and surprisingly, Mexican companies adapted his plays to their reality in the 1940s (Membrez, "Delírium" 171, 179). Reruns of the latter group are frequently seen on Spanish-language networks in the United States.

English-speaking film buffs might recognize two subtitled films based on Arniches's plays, *El bruto* (*Don Quintín el amargao*) [The Brute], directed by the transnational Luis Buñuel in 1953, and *Calle mayor* [Main Street], the prize-winning film adaptation of Arniches's play *La señorita de Trevélez* [Miss Trevélez], directed by Juan Antonio Bardem in 1956.

DRAMATURGY: MAJOR WORKS AND THEMES

In his lifetime, Arniches was a rich, applauded, and popular author, perhaps one of the more conservative of the playwrights writing in his era. His conservatism is borne out in his plays, which feature either middle-class characters or working-class characters (by dress and language) with pronounced bourgeois morals.

Since Arniches's works are far too numerous to describe here, I have chosen two representative works, one from his *género chico* period and one from his grotesque period.

The best-known play of his first phase is, disputably, *El santo de la Isidra* (1898), a slice of working-class life bursting with colorful idioms, phonetic representation of lower-class speech, and catchy music. In this *cuadro de costumbres*, a life portrait, in which stereotypes and musical characterization advance the action (*género chico* staples), an honorable working man finally works up the courage to defend his true love from her lazy, bullying boyfriend. In his study Douglas McKay explores this recurring theme in Arniches's plays at length, as well as providing short plot summaries for the majority of his plays.

A methodical writer, Arniches spent long hours in working-class taverns and cafés, collecting colloquial expressions and wordplays for his comedies. This is how Arniches described his direct method of observation to Wenceslao Fernández Flórez in 1917:

I go for walks in farflung neighborhoods, down streets that you, as a newcomer to Madrid, probably don't even know yet. I got to see the women workers leave the cigarette factory. . . . I go into some bar. . . . At first my presence arouses suspicion. Later, the bartenders themselves help me out. "Don Carlos—they say to me—today you are going to meet a real character. . . ." And they show him to me, and I talk to the other customers in the tavern. "This gentleman—the bartenders assure them—is a friend of mine." Invariably, they take me for a cityhall bureaucrat. I listen to them and I have a great time. If I could only bring to the stage all the colorful, original characters I meet! (120–121)

[Yo paseo frecuentemente por los barrios extremos, por calles que seguramente usted, que lleva en Madrid poco tiempo, no conocerá todavía, Voy a ver salir de la fábrica a las cigarreras . . . entro en alguna taberna. . . . Al principio, mi presencia extraña. Después, los mismos taberneros favorecen mis propósitos. "Don Carlos—me dicen—hoy va a conocer usted un tipo. . . ." Y me lo muestran, y charlo con sus parroquianos. "Este señor—les asegura—es un amigo mío." Invariablemente la clientela me toma por un empleado del Ayuntamiento. Les oigo y paso ratos felicísimos. ¡Si pudiese traer al teatro a muchos de esos sujetos, con toda su viva originalidad!]

Among critics there has been a controversy of some years standing as to whether Arniches simply made up the colloquial expressions he used or whether he imported them wholesale from his adventures in working-class Madrid. The clearest answer appears to be both. In sparse interviews, he and other playwrights of his generations admit to collecting and then stretching popular idioms in unimagined new ways, such as changing a noun to a verb or an adjective to a noun. Seco, Trinidad, and Senabre have written entire linguistic studies, even dictionaries, centered on this process. Yet verifying such word origins today is impossible because as fast as Arniches reinvented popular language, working-class Spaniards assimilated his neologisms and made them their own (Membrez, "(Re)invención" 79–84).

In the second phase, illustrious *sainetero* Carlos Arniches combined elements of the melodrama, the *sainete* and the *juguete cómico* [one-act comedy] in order to break with the *género chico*'s set molds and produce an original theatrical form: the *tragedia grotesca* (or *tragicomedia grotesca*) [the grotesque tragedy or grotesque tragicomedy]. While the *tragedia grotesca* owes a great debt to the *sainete*, it was not a *fin de fiesta* in the classical sense, nor a one-act play as understood in the nineteenth-century *teatro por horas'* heyday. It was not even written in verse. Yet it retained enough of the *sainete*'s spirit, if not its form, to be considered the *sainete*'s twentieth-century heir.

In the teens, with the theaters favoring double sessions that encouraged two- and three-act works, the stage was set for Arniches's innovation. As he himself explained it:

I had great successes; it was what the public demanded in those days, and I was in no hurry to improve myself, as much as I occasionally felt compelled to raise the quality of my work. And then one day the heyday of the multiact play arrived and I evolved spontaneously. ("Está en Buenos Aires" 13)

[Obtenía grandes éxitos; era lo que el público de entonces exigía, y yo no me apuraba por superarme, por más que muchas veces me acometieran deseos de elevar mi prod- ucción. Y vino el momento del género grande, y yo, espontáneamente evolucioné.]

Most literary historians consider *La señorita de Trevélez* (1916) Arniches's first *tragedia grotesca* [grotesque tragedy] because of its characteristic grotesque elements, particularly its main characters who are "tragic in their context, laugh- able on a larger scale" ["trágico(s) en su esfera, risible(s) en su proyección"] (Berenguer Carisomo 81). Others cite *¡Que viene mi marido!* [My Husband's Coming!] (1918), the first play actually subtitled a *tragedia grotesca* by its author. In any case, the grotesque element is crucial to Arniches's move to a longer comedy format, usually three acts, and the creation of what Manuel Ruiz Lagos has called the "anti-alta comedia" [anti-high comedy] (284).

The best-known play of his second phase, *La señorita de Trevélez* centers on the shenanigans of a group of idle provincials who enjoy pulling practical jokes at the expense of the hapless villagers. They set up their friend bachelor Nu- meriano Galán with old maid Flora de Trevélez and conspire to make them the butt of their latest caper. Disaster is narrowly averted when Galán reveals the truth to Flora's brother, but her only hope of marriage dies with the end of the heartless charade. Arniches announces the moral of the story when a character declares that smart alecs ["guasones"] are a national problem, and only education can put an end to their wasted, unproductive lives.

This moral, while proposing a social reform for the provincial idle rich, steers clear of another more radical solution that was being proposed in the Spanish press of that time period: the education of women, particularly of old maids ("las mujeres que sobran," leftover women) (Membrez, *Hemerography of Women in the Illustrated Spanish Weekly 1857–1938*, in progress). Flora de Trevélez's tragedy might have been mitigated if such an option had been pos- sible, but she was not offered this alternative. As an old maid she was to con- tinue to be a public embarrassment to her older (unmarried) brother. Interestingly, the play focuses on Galán grotesque dilemma, whereas the film *Calle mayor* emphasizes Flora de Trevélez's pathos.

These unique plays are grotesque because tragedy contains elements of com- edy, and vice versa. According to José Monleón:

Arniches constantly works with the idea of opposites; for this reason we speak of tragicomedy, not in the sense that Fernando Rojas (author of *La Celestina*) used it—by alternating happiness and misfortune—but by positing the simultaneity of the funny and the pathetic. (46)

[Arniches opera constantemente con este sentimiento de lo contrario; por eso se habla de tragicomedia, no en el sentido que le dio Fernando Rojas—de alternancia de lo feliz y lo desgraciado—sino en el de simultaneidad de lo risible y lo patético.]

Argentine Arturo Berenguer Carisomo asserts that the *tragedia grotesca* was the latest cultural projection of the grotesque in Spanish literature, citing forerunner Don Quixote among other fictional characters (79–80). Nevertheless, at the time of the *tragedia grotesca*'s debut, literary heavyweight Ramón Pérez de Ayala perceived the conscious introduction of the grotesque into theater as something new in Spanish letters and accorded Arniches a thorough—and astonishingly favorable—review. About *La señorita de Trevélez* he wrote:

Miss Trevélez is, at heart or by design, one of the most serious, most human and most captivating comedy of manners in recent Spanish theater, and as a result, a deeply sad comedy, even if it frequently makes us laugh. . . . In the future, when some curiosity-seeker rummages through old papers looking for the cause of the deep-seated spiritual malaise of our times, [i.e.] our cruelty engendered by boredom, our despicable insensitivity to love, justice, moral beauty, [and] spiritual elevation, few literary works will provide him so subtle, so penetrating, so honest, so true and so ingenious an example as *La señorita de Trevélez*. (223–231)

[*La señorita de Trevélez* es, en el fondo o intención, una de las comedias de costumbres más serias, más humanas y más cautivadoras de la reciente dramaturgia hispana, y, en consecuencia, una comedia hondamente triste, bien que con frecuencia provoque la risa. . . . Cuando, a la vuelta de los años, algún curioso de lo añejo quiera procurarse noticias de ese morbo radical del alma española de nuestros días, la crueldad engendrada por el tedio, la rastrera insensibilidad para el amor, para la justicia, para la belleza moral, para la elevación del espíritu, pocas obras literarias le darán ideal tan sutil, penetrativa, pudibunda, fiel e ingeniosa como *La señorita de Trevélez*.]

In a sense, Arniches fulfilled what novelista Armando Palacio Valdés had in mind when in 1881 he urged the *saineteros* to write about the middle class instead of choosing lower-class models.[1] Even when Arniches subtitled his plays "farsas cómicas" (Pérez de Ayala preferred calling them "farsas macabras" [macabre farces]), they were still *tragedias grotescas* by another name.

Nowadays, it is common to see the radical shift in Arniches's attitudes toward his models in the context of public cynicism toward a corrupt government and the disillusionment of the "disaster of 1898," the war between Spain and the United States over the Cuban question. In effect, this new consciousness qualifies him as a late bloomer of the Generation of 98. Enrique Llovet postulates:

Without beating around the bush, the grotesque tragicomedy expresses clearly and explicitly Arniches's participation in the pain of injustice and his suffering on behalf of

Spain. What bubbles up in the tragicomic text is a fierce protest against the *caciques*, the *chulos*, the presumptuous *señoritos*, the bosses, the haughty, the cruel, the fanatics, the bums, the unjust, the flagwavers, the envious, the filthy. These characters are not there just to make us laugh but to scold us from center stage. . . .

Arniches' journey, this leap of his from a photographic and almost naturalistic realism to a grotesque and *esperpentic* realism was carried out with such expressive mastery, that he salvaged all the emotional ferment of the *género chico* that had brought people back to the theater and, in addition, he incorporated the active current of the middle class with its painful dilemmas. (10–11)

[La tragicomedia grotesca expresa nítidamente, sin rodeos, de forma bien explícita, la participación de Arniches en el dolor por la injusticia y en el dolor por España. Lo que entra a borbotones en el texto de la tragicomedia es una feroz protesta contra los caciques, los chulos, los señoritos prepotentes, los mandones cerriles, los soberbios, los crueles, los fanáticos, los vagos, los injustos, los falsos patriotas, los envidiosos, los sucios. Que no están "ahí" solamente para hacer reír, sino para escarmentar desde la picota del escenario. . . .

Este viaje de Arniches, este avance desde un realismo fotográfico y casi naturalista a un realismo "grotesco" y "esperpéntico," se realiza con tal maestría expresiva, que se salvan todos los fermentos emocionales del género chico que han vuelto a llevar al pueblo al teatro y se incorpora, además, el activo río de la "clase media" con su doliente problemática.]

Increasingly, Arniches's ideas about the *tragedia grotesca* are seen as linked to Ramón María del Valle-Inclán's *esperpento* (*Luces de bohemia*, 1920) and Pedro Muñoz Seca's wild *astracán* (*La venganza de Don Mendo*, 1918), with a clear precedent in the *género chico*'s penchant for lower-class irony (present in Arniches's first phase) and especially in the theater parodies of Salvador María Granés and other nineteenth-century parodists.[2]

Surprisingly, Arniches did not create a school of followers. While there may have been grotesque characters and/or situations in other plays, aspiring playwrights did not rush to produce huge quantities of *tragedias grotescas*, as had happened previously with the *género chico* success formula. Of course, the theater crisis precipitated by the collapse of *the teatro por horas* had precluded this from happening in the 1920s and 1930s. Therefore, Arniches's achievement stands out even more. As Enrique Llovet concluded in 1969, Arniches's *tragedias grotescas* and *farsas cómicas*

achieve a double effect; they draw more serious and esteemed consideration to the literary virtues of the author's longer, denser works, and as a side effect this attention and appreciation is extended to include his earlier production of one-act plays, thus keeping his works from being forgotten, from falling into that oblivion that almost all other *zarzuelas* and *sainetes* have fallen. (11)

[logran un doble efecto; atraer sobre su autor una consideración más atenta y valorativa de las virtudes literarias, mucho más densas, de estas obras largas y, subsidiariamente, hace beneficiar a todo el periódo género chico de Arniches de una consideración y aprecio que salvan su labor de esa especie de vasto olvido, de esta caída en el anónimo que ha sufrido casi todo el resto de zarzuelas y saintes.]

In the long run, it is Arniches's multilayered plays of the *tragedia grotesca* that will assure his place in the early twentieth-century Spanish literary canon. Arniches himself said it best:

So, long live comedy! and let's laugh; at everything, even at those who censor us, and condemn us, although they may wrong us.

In the end, in 25 or 30 years, when we have fallen silent, Time will tell, and it will say with its clear, eternal voice who has done it best and who is worthy of being heard. . . . And Time will not be so *nouveau riche* as to deny remembrance of those of us who gladly brought a ray of noble pleasure into the soul of our contemporaries. ("Epílogo" 253)

[Conque, ¡viva lo cómico! y riamos; riamos de todo, hasta de los que nos censuran y condenan, aunque nos injurien.

A la postre, dentro de veinticinco o treinta años, cuando todos hayamos callado, hablará el tiempo, y él dirá con su eterna y clara voz quiénes han dicho lo mejor y más digno de ser oído. . . . Y el Tiempo no será tan cursi que niegue su recuerdo a los que llevaron con buena voluntad un rayo de noble alegría al alma de sus contemporáneos.]

CRITICS' RESPONSE

Literary criticism in any language on the works of Carlos Arniches has always been sparse. The plays themselves were reviewed in their time period in weekly illustrated magazines such as *Blanco y Negro, Mundo Gráfico,* and *Nuevo Mundo,* but these are largely unindexed, inaccessible, or unavailable. As painful as it is to admit, we must recognize that for many years literary critics and historians simply considered the *género chico*—and any author associated with it—to be too popular and therefore unworthy of serious academic attention, if not beneath contempt. I am pleased to report that this prejudice is gradually fading.

In Spanish, fundamental resources are the essays by major critics—José Monleón, José Bergamín, Pío Baroja, Francisco García Pavón, Francisco Nieva, and Lauro Olmo—published as preliminary studies to Monleón's edition of Arniches's plays. This valuable edition also includes a short autobiography by Arniches and a reprint of an essay by Ramón Pérez de Ayala, the first literary critic to appreciate Arniches's transition to the *tragedia grotesca*. It is one of the best critical editions of Arniches's plays.

In the 1940s Josefina Romo published a bibliography, which I attempted to supersede in my dissertation bibliography (1987) by indexing articles from the illustrated weeklies mentioned above.

Douglas McKay has published the lengthiest and most complete monograph in English for Twayne (1972) and is highly recommended for the monolingual speaker.

More recently, a group of scholars met for a week in 1993 in Alicante to honor Arniches and to discuss his works. The result was the book *Estudios sobre Carlos Arniches*, edited by Juan Antonio Ríos Carratalá, conference organizer and himself author of a valuable monographic study on Arniches. The book includes serious essays by Andrés Amorós, Serge Salaün, María Francisca Vilches de Frutos, Luis Iglesias Feijóo, Manfred Lentzen, Nancy J. Membrez, María Victoria Sotomayor, José A. Pérez Bowie, Pilar Nieva de la Paz, Josep Lluís Sirera, Javier Huerta, Ricardo de la Fuente, Carlos Serrano, Mariano de Paco, Nel Diago, Juan Antonio Ríos Carratalá, and Juan de Mata Moncho.

A subject search on WorldCat on-line will turn up a dozen Ph.D. dissertations at American and German universities. Some of these are written in English with Spanish examples.

AWARDS AND DISTINCTIONS

This category is not applicable, although there is a theater (now a cinema) named after him in Madrid and streets named after him in Madrid and Alicante. It is significant that Arniches has been so honored by the public while literary canonization has lagged behind.

NOTES

1. Armando Palacio Valdés, "El género flamenco," in his *La literatura en 1881: Obras completas* (Madrid: Aguilar, 1945), 1471–1473.
2. This is Alonso Zamora Vicente's thesis in *La realidad esperpéntica: Aproximación a Luces de bohemia* (Madrid: Gredos, 1969).

BIBLIOGRAPHY

A Listing of Editions and Translations

Arniches's complete works were published in 1948 by Aguilar but have not been reprinted. These volumes are usually obtainable through interlibrary loan. Several of his *tragedias grotescas* and some of the *sainetes rápidos* appear in inexpensive Austral editions.

No English translations are available.

Selected Works

Arniches y Barrera, Carlos. *Carlos Arniches: el alma popular.* Málaga: Litoral, 1994. A selection of his works.
"Epílogo." In *Los castizos*, by Antonio Casero. Madrid: Sáenz de Jubera Hermanos, 1911.
La pareja científica y otros sainetes. Ed. José Montero Padilla. Madrid: Anaya, 1964. A selection of *Del Madrid castizo.*

La señorita de Trevélez, La heroica villa, Los milagros del jornal. Ed. by José Monleón. Madrid: Taurus Ediciones, 1967.

La señorita de Trevélez y Es mi hombre. Ed. Enrique Llovet. Madrid: Salvat Editores, 1969.

Teatro completo. Madrid:Aguilar, 1948.

Critical Studies

Aragonés, Juan Emilio. *Carlos Arniches: conferencias pronunciadas con motivo del primer centenario de su nacimiento.* Alicante: Excmo. Ayuntamiento de Alicante, 1967.

Berenguer Carisomo, Arturo. *El teatro de Carlos Arniches.* Buenos Aires: El Ateneo Iberamericano, 1937.

"Está en Buenos Aires Carlos Arniches." *La Nación,* 10 enero 1937: 13.

Fernández Flórez, Wenceslao. "¿Dónde está Arniches?" *ABC,* 14 abril 1917. Rpt. in his *El país de papel.* Madrid: Talleres Poligráficos, 1929.

Jiménez, Fernando. *Arniches.* Madrid: Publicaciones Españolas, 1966.

López Estrada, Francisco. "Notas al habla de Madrid: El lenguaje en una obra de Carlos Arniches." *Cuadernos de Literatura Contemporánea* 9–10 (1943): 261–272.

Llovet, Enrique. "Prólogo." In his edition of Arniches's *La señorita de Trevélez y Es mi hombre.* Madrid: Salvat Editores, 1969.

McKay, Douglas R. *Carlos Arniches.* New York: Twayne Publishers, 1972.

Membrez, Nancy J. "Delírium tremens: Se encaran el cinematógrafo y el teatro 1896–1946." *Letras peninsulares* 7.1 (Spring 1994): 165–184.

———. "La (re)invención de Madrid en el teatro por horas: Tipomania y lenguaje." In *Estudios sobre Carlos Arniches,* Juan Antonio Ríos Carratalá. Alicante: Diputación de Alicante, 1994.

———. "The Teatro por horas: History, Dynamics and Comprehensive Bibliography of a Madrid Industry (1867–1922)." Ph.D. Diss., University of California, Santa Barbara, 1987.

Pérez de Ayala, Ramón. *Las máscaras.* Madrid: Editorial Saturnino Calleja, 1919. Review rpt. in Arniches's *Obras completas* and Monleón's edition.

Ramos, Vicente. *Vida y teatro de Carlos Arniches.* Madrid: Alfaguara, 1966.

Ríos Carratalá, Juan Antonio, ed. *Estudios sobre Carlos Arniches.* Alicante: Diputación de Alicante, 1994.

Ríos Carratalá, Juan Antonio, and Rosa María Monzó Seva. *Arniches:El escritor alicantino y la crítica.* Alicante: Caja de ahorros provincial de Alicante, 1990.

Romo Arregui, Josefina. "Carlos Arniches, bibliografía." *Cuadernos de Literatura Contemporánea* 9–10 (1943): 299–307.

Ruiz Lagos, Manuel. "Sobre Arniches: Sus arquetipos y su esencia dramática." *Segismundo* 2.4 (1966): 284.

Seco Reymundo, Manuel. *Arniches y el habla de Madrid.* Madrid:Alfaguara, 1970.

Senabre, Ricardo. "Creación y deformación en la lengua de Arniches." *Segismundo* 2.4 (1966): 247–278.

Sotomayor Sáez, María Victoria. *Teatro, público y poder: la obra dramática del último Arniches.* Madrid: Ediciones de la Torre, 1998.

Trinidad, Francisco. *Arniches: Un estudio del habla popular madrileña.* Madrid: Editorial Góngora, 1969. (Originally a Ph.D. dissertation at UCLA.)

FERNANDO ARRABAL
(1932–   )

Peter L. Podol

BIOGRAPHY

Fernando Arrabal, playwright, novelist, essayist, critic, poet, artist, and film-maker, was born in Melilla, Spanish Morocco, on August 11, 1932. When the Spanish Civil War broke out on July 17, 1936, his father, Fernando Arrabal Ruiz, was arrested by the Nationalists because of his leftist tendencies and was summarily sentenced to death. Arrabal was never to see him again. His mother, Carmen Terán González, whose politics were diametrically opposed to those of her husband, refused to allow the children to visit their incarcerated father, or even to speak about him. The family moved to Ciudad Rodrigo soon after the outbreak of the Civil War, where they resided with Arrabal's maternal grand-parents. Arrabal's only memory of those early years of relative harmony in Melilla is documented in his interview with Alain Schifres,[1] in which he recalls his father gently covering his legs with sand at the beach.

After the death of his grandfather, the young Arrabal and his immediate fam-ily moved to Madrid, where Arrabal grew up in a strict, conservative Catholic ambience, dominated by his mother, who never permitted his absent father to be mentioned and even excised his image from all accessible photos. Self-doubt, insecurities, and complexes, associated in part with his small stature and large head, emerged in the repressive atmosphere that permeated both his home and all of post–Civil War Spain. This period in his life, characterized by retributions against supporters of the Spanish Republic and harsh punishments and cruelty in the Church-run schools, in society, and even in the games that children played, is documented most tellingly by Arrabal in his *Letter to General Franco* (*Carta al General Franco*) (1972)[2] and in many of his early plays and novels.

Arrabal's resistance to his mother's attempts to shape his value system in accordance with her traditional beliefs began to manifest itself after his enroll-ment in a military academy in 1947. At about that time, he was introduced to the films of Charlie Chaplin, Laurel and Hardy, and others, as well as to the imaginative fantasies of Lewis Carroll, all of which he found more to his liking than his studies. The strength for full-fledged rebellion, however, came from a chance discovery. In 1949, Arrabal happened upon a collection of his father's letters and photographs and came to realize the full import of the impact of "the two Spains" on his family. He ceased speaking to his mother for five years, a period of intense psychological turmoil during which he searched for his father both figuratively and literally. His quest ended with the report that the elder Fernando Arrabal Ruiz, who was confined to a mental institution in Burgos after a suicide attempt, had escaped from that facility during the winter of 1942. At the time of his escape he was dressed only in pajamas, and the ground was covered with snow.

During the early 1950s, Arrabal abandoned his studies of law and his job in the paper industry. He spent hours reading such writers as Franz Kafka and Fyodor Dostoyevsky and wrote what was to be his first published play, *Picnic on the Battlefield*, in 1952. In 1955, funded by a grant from the Spanish government, he returned to France to study theater. Arriving ill with tuberculosis, he spent much of 1956 confined to a sanatorium; his long hours there afforded him ample time to write and also to develop what was to be a lifelong passion: chess. In 1958 he married Luce Moreau, a professor of Spanish literature at the Sorbonne, and he received a contract for the publication of all of his theater from Juillard in Paris. To date, his plays are written initially in Spanish, then translated to French with the assistance of his wife, for publication.

The decade of the 1960s was marked by several significant events and experiences, both political and artistic. In 1962, after a number of meetings with Roland Topor (an artist) and Alejandro Jodorowsky (a filmmaker) the Panic Movement was created.[3] Arrabal came to know and collaborate with virtually all of the leading writers, directors, and artists of the avant-garde in Paris. His contact with Andre Breton, the founder of Surrealism, and with three expatriate Argentine directors—Víctor García, Jerome Savary, and Jorge Lavelli—had a profound influence on his work. Despite hostile reviews, he attracted a following and emerged as France's most performed playwright. The play that is generally considered his masterpiece, *The Architect and the Emperor of Assyria* (1965) dates from this period and has been staged around the world, from the Old Vic in London to La Mama in New York City.

Arrabal's inclination for controversy and delight at provoking his audience both in the theater and in "real" life, characteristics that are both individual and reflective of that period, came into direct conflict with the repressive forces of the Franco dictatorship in 1967. While in Spain to promote one of his novels, he wrote a blasphemous inscription in a book that fell into the wrong hands. The irreverent statement resulted in his arrest in the middle of the night. He spent almost a month in prison and was spared a sentence of six years for blasphemy and for insulting the Spanish nation only because many of the world's luminaries of the arts protested his treatment and pressured the Spanish government into releasing him. That prison experience, coupled with his direct participation in the student rebellions in Paris in 1968, gave a new, more overtly political direction to his theater for a period of time. The 1960s and 1970s marked an expansion of Arrabal's artistic endeavors. Although theater has always remained the focus of his creative work, films, novels, essays, poetry, painting, chess columns for *L'Express*, photography, and directing all became part of his repertoire. After Franco's death in 1975, Arrabal, in contrast with other exiled writers, opted not to return to Spain until all political prisoners were freed. But by 1977 he began to make frequent visits. A number of his plays have been staged in his native land, although the response to much of his theater has been generally less positive in Spain than abroad. The play *Inquisición* (1980) became the first of his works to premiere in Spain rather than in France. As a prose writer, Arrabal received the prestigious Premio Nadal for the outstanding novel of 1982, *The Tower Struck by Lightning* [La torre herida por el rayo], and the Premio Espasa for the finest collection of essays of 1994, entitled *The Doubtful Light of Day* [La dudosa luz del día]. His latest essay, the *Letter to the King* [Carta al rey] (1995), provides a forum for his sociopolitical thoughts, highlighted by his idea of "selling the government" to finance social programs and support the arts.

In an interview conducted by this author in 1995, Arrabal, then sixty-three years of age, seemed more mellow, finding cause for optimism about the future of a world free from Communism. In the years following that comment, he has continued to produce a variety of works in a number of genres. No longer the "enfant terrible," he still sees the world with the wonderment of a child, and his creative energy and artistic production show no signs of abating.

DRAMATURGY: MAJOR WORKS AND THEMES

An overview of the theatrical production of Fernando Arrabal is complicated by the sheer volume of dramas that he has authored. In order to trace the evolution of his principal themes and his dramatic techniques, his nineteen-volume production will be divided into several periods; a representative play or plays from each period will be identified and considered briefly, and an in-depth analysis of *The Architect and the Emperor of Assyria* [El arquitecto y el emperador de Asiria] (1965) will conclude this brief study of Arrabal's contributions to Spanish and world theater.

The first period of Arrabal's theater is characterized by childlike characters whose amorality leads them to commit acts of cruelty and violence and who are generally crushed by the oppressive, incomprehensible world that surrounds them. Black humor, the grotesque, and the poetic all combine in these early plays, which were linked to the Absurdists by such critics as Martin Esslin.[4] Elements and techniques of the Absurd and the Surreal are indeed present, but Arrabal's mathematical sense of structure, affirmation of freedom, exploration of psychological forces, especially the nefarious influence of the mother figure (*The Two Executioners* [Los dos verdugos] [1956]), incorporation of games, conflation of the sociopolitical and the psychological, and penchant for circularity in form combine to produce a theater that, despite its connection to the ideology and techniques of the 1960s/1970s, is uniquely his. Outstanding plays of this period include *The Labyrinth* [El laberinto] (1956), inspired by Kafka and his novels *The Trial* and *Amerika; Fando and Lis* (1956); *Ceremony for an Assassinated Black* [Ceremonia por un negro asesinado] (1956); and especially *The Automobile Graveyard* [El cementerio de automóviles] (1957). The latter combines Arrabal's negative view of our mechanized contemporary world, captured by the title of the piece, with his account of the passion of Christ. Placing special emphasis on games, the metamorphosis of characters and theater as religious ceremony replete with elements of magic and mystery, this play emerges as the culminating work of Arrabal's first period, evincing an enriched artistic vocabulary on the part of the playwright. A subsequent staging of the work by Víctor García, which incorporated several other short plays as well, realized in 1966, demonstrated the close relationship between Antonin Artaud's concept of theater and Arrabal's.[5] Indeed, for some critics, Arrabal is the playwright who has best realized the possibilities for theater described by Artaud in his landmark work *The Theater and Its Double* (1938).

Arrabal's second period coincided with his development of the Panic Movement in 1962. The tenets of "Panic" describe a lifestyle rather than a type of theater or art. More of an antimovement than a serious expression of artistic or philosophical principles, "Panic" derives its name from the Greek god Pan and focuses on the interplay of chance and confusion in life and in art. Associated with the *happening*, "Panic" combined with the influence of Surrealism, alchemy, Grotowski, and Artaud to inspire some of Arrabal's finest dramas written during the 1960s. The first play linked with the ideas of "Panic" was his short work *Solemn Communion* [Primera comunión] (1963); but the full-length plays that stand out during this period are *The Grand Ceremonial* (1963) and *The Architect and the Emperor of Assyria* (1965).

Arrabal's third period of dramatic creation was inspired by his direct experiences with politics in Spain and France. His incarceration in Spain in 1967 and his participation in the May 1968 student rebellion in Paris gave rise to a series of plays that were more overtly political than any of his previous works. The transitional work inspired by these experiences was *The Red and Black Dawn* (1968), but the more highly developed *And They Will Put Handcuffs on the Flowers* [Y pondrán esposas en las flores] (1969) stands out as his most memorable work of political theater. It is a drama that is at once specific in its attack on the Franco regime, and what he sees as the complicity of the Church and the State in suppressing freedom in Spain, and universal in its protest of cruelty, hypocrisy, and totalitarianism throughout the world. The barriers between audience and performers are largely eliminated in Arrabal's conception of the work. And the use of stage space, shocking language and gestures, blasphemy, and the grotesque make *Handcuffs* a visceral experience for the audience and a work that has aroused both praise and outrage among theater critics.

Arrabal's dramaturgy during the 1970s, 1980s, and 1990s becomes increasingly difficult to categorize. Certainly the term "avant-garde" remains pertinent. The period coinciding with the final years of the Franco dictatorship saw the emergence of the themes of Spain and the playwright's exile in such significant works as *On the High Wire* [En la cuerda floja] (1974) and *The Tower of Babel* [La torre de Babel] (1975). Spain continues to occupy Arrabal's attention in *Inquisition* (1980), his first work to premiere in his native country since his departure in 1955. Farce, international politics, intriguing events from real life such as the mother who killed her gifted daughter (*The Red Madonna* [1988]), and even a work with a character named after an American Spanish professor (*The Bodybuilder's Book of Love* [1986], with a character named Phyllis, inspired by Professor Phyllis Zatlin of Rutgers University) figure among Arrabal's most memorable recent works.

His complete theater was finally published in Spanish in 1997 in two volumes edited by Francisco Torres Monreal. The theater season of 2000–2001 in Spain saw a major new production of *The Automobile Graveyard* tour the country, culminating with performances of the play in the National Theater in Madrid.

At this time, *The Architect and the Emperor of Assyria* appears to be the play for which Arrabal will best be remembered. A lengthy, two-character drama, it integrates a number of Arrabal's principal themes and techniques with such virtuosity that the play in performance proves to be an overwhelming experience for its audience. The structure is, again, circular; the work begins and ends with a plane crash that delivers one character to the desert island occupied by the other. But the roles are reversed; the primitive Architect of the opening has been transformed into the Emperor through an act of cannibalism that clearly alludes to the Transubstantiation. When an articulate Architect lands at the play's conclusion, the Emperor is rendered incapable of speech, and the cycle begins all over again. During the course of the play, the two characters assume a wide range of roles, and the metatheatrical scenes that constitute the essence of the play allow Arrabal to explore such themes as man's search for God, nature versus technology, the institution of war, sadomasochism and sexuality, man's need for love and the other, the role of the mother in man's psyche, and the quest to reconcile opposing forces in the human soul. Black humor, scatology, satire, parody, poetry, and an energized use of stage space all contribute to the impact of the play.

The Emperor's conflictive feelings about his mother, which climax in his confession of matricide and demand that the Architect kill him and devour him while dressed in his mother's clothes, emerge as the central, unifying motif in the second act of the drama. Various games intervene, but that motif proves to be inescapable and leads to the play's climax. Luis Arata correctly affirms the importance of metatheatrics when he comments: "In *L'Architecte et l'empereur d'Assyrie*, the game is never over; the Emperor remains constantly caught in his roles and the Architect keeps on learning how to play the games of the Emperor."[6]

The game of chess figures directly in the play as well. In one significant theater game, the Emperor feigns his own death and demands to be buried as the Bishop of Chess. The final reversal of roles and initiation of a new cycle of games that ends *The Architect* suggest a chess competition where each new game involves reversing the black and white pieces.

Another memorable sequence in the play involves the Emperor's attempt to prove the existence of God by playing pinball. It forms part of a lengthy monologue addressed to an absent Architect in the form of a scarecrow, climaxes inconclusively with respect to the deity, and culminates with the discovery at the end of Act I that the Architect is thousands of years old. The entire sequence constitutes a dazzling display of theatrics that ultimately serves to affirm the Emperor's underlying need for the Architect. Indeed, the two characters are inseparable; they are at once two diametrically opposed human beings, symbols of the decadence of civilization and the purity of nature, and components of a single, tortured psyche seeking wholeness and peace with itself. As Diana Taylor has perceptively noted in her excellent introduction to the Spanish text: "The interaction between the Architect and the Emperor is moreover analogous to the interaction between the self and the ego" [La interacción entre el Arquitecto y el Emperador es además análoga a la interacción entre el Self y el ego].[7] For José Ortega, "all of Arrabal's texts are characterized by their circularity and each one of his plays represents a return to the search and expression of his uniqueness, to a new cycle where the recurrent theme is defined by the polarity of destruction (alienation and repression) and creation (art)" [Todos los textos de Arrabal se caracterizan por su circularidad y cada una de sus piezas representa un retorno a la búsqueda y expresión de su mismidad, a un nuevo ciclo donde el tema recurrente viene definido por la polaridad de la destrucción (alienación y represión) y creación (arte)].[8] This statement about Arrabal's theater clearly captures a central direction in many of his works, but at the same time it serves to reaffirm the key position that *The Architect and the Emperor of Assyria* occupies among his works of dramatic literature.

CRITICS' RESPONSE

In the early years of his career, Arrabal's theater met with mostly hostile reviews. Ironically, the critics who denounced his dramas as blasphemous and pornographic helped him to acquire an audience. Countless reviews over the decades have ranged from high praise to condemnation, but many have certainly affirmed the intrigue of Arrabal's theater. Perhaps the most significant of the positive reviews was the one that Clive Barnes wrote of Tom O'Horgan's production of *The Architect and the Emperor of Assyria* on May 30, 1976, for the *New York Times*, which concluded as follows:

Mr. Arrabal, with his perceptions, absurdities, loves and understanding, is a playwright to be honored, treasured and understood. In this play he is saying something about the isolation, the solitariness and the need of 20th century man that, so far as I can see, no other playwright has quite gotten on stage before. A playwright reveals himself when in the electric instant of the moment he tells us the story of our lives. Mr. Arrabal does that with the grace of the fantastic and the gauchness of the real.

AWARDS AND DISTINCTIONS

Fernando Arrabal has received a number of major awards in France, Spain and elsewhere. The following constitute a few of the most significant of them:

1942, Spain: Prize for the supergifted (superdotado)

1959, USA: Ford Foundation Award

1965, France: Lugne Poe Theater Prize

1967, France: Grand Prize for Theater

1976, United States: Obie Award (for Off-Broadway theater in New York).

1983, France: Chëvalier des Arts et des Lettres

1984, Spain: Premio Nadal (for outstanding novel, awarded for *La torre herida por el rayo*)

1986, Spain: Gold Medal for Fine Arts (Bellas Artes)

1993, France: Theater Prize from the French Academy

1994, Italy: International Nabokov Prize for the novel

1994, Spain: Espasa Prize for Outstanding Essay (for *La dudosa luz del día*)

1995, Spain: Gold Medal from the city of Melilla

1996, France: Prize from the National Book Center

1997, United States: Medal from the Center of French Culture and Civilization (New York University)

1999, Italy: Alessandro Manzoni Poeotry Prize

2000, Spain: Teresa de Avila Prize

NOTES

1. Alain Schifres, *Entretiens avec Arrabal* (Paris: Editions Pierre Belfond, 1969), 15.

2. Fernando Arrabal, *Letter to General Franco* [Carta al General Franco] (Paris: Union Générale d'Editions, 1972). Other works that deal with this aspect of his life in fictional form include his first novel *Baal Babylon*, trans. Richard Howard (New York: Grove Press, 1961), and his film *Long Live Death* [Viva la muerte] (1971).

3. See Arrabal's essay "The Panic Man" [El hombre pánico] in the collection of plays *El cementerio de automóviles. Ciugrena. Los dos verdugos* (Madrid: Taurus, 1965), 31–44. Also consult Francisco Torres Monreal's Introduction to *Teatro pánico* (Madrid: Cátedra, 1986), 9–74, for a consideration of *Panic* and Arrabal's panic theater.

4. Martin Esslin, *The Theater of the Absurd* (New York: Anchor Banks, 1969). Arrabal has assiduously denied that categorization of his works. When his early play *The Tricycle* [Los hombres del triciclo] (1953) received only second prize in a playwrighting contest

in Barcelona, the author was puzzled by the explanation that his work was too derivative of Beckett. He had never heard of Samuel Beckett and thought that his play was being linked with Bécquer, the nineteenth-century Spanish romantic poet, a comparison that was certainly absurd. Later, Arrabal came to know and admire Beckett, even naming his son after that writer. Critics continue to note similarities between plays by Beckett such as *Waiting for Godot* and works by Arrabal such as *The Architect and the Emperor of Assyria*, especially in the circularity of their structures.

5. Artaud's "theater of cruelty" emphasized the idea of assaulting the senses of the audience, minimizing the importance of the dramatic text in favor of a "total theater" experience for the audience.

6. Luis Oscar Arata, *The Festive Play of Fernando Arrabal* (Lexington: University of Kentucky Press, 1982), 66.

7. Fernando Arrabal, *El cementerio de automóviles. El Arquitecto y el Emperador de Asiria*, ed. Diana Taylor (Madrid: Cátedra, 1984), 47.

8. José Ortega, "El sentido de la obra de Fernando Arrabal," *Estreno* 2.1 (1975): 13.

BIBLIOGRAPHY

Selected Editions and Translations

Spanish Editions

El cementerio de automóviles El Arquitecto y el emperador de Asiria. Ed. Diana Taylor. Madrid: Cátedra, 1984.
Inquisición. Ed. Angel Berenguer. Granada: Editorial Don Quijote, 1982.
Pic-Nic. El triciclo. El laberinto. Ed. Angel Berenguer. Madrid: Cátedra, 1977.
Y pondrán esposas en las flores. Ed. Peter Podol. Salamanca: Ediciones Almar, 1984.
Teatro completo. Volumen I. Preliminar de Angel Berenguer. Madrid: Cuspa Editorial, 1979. (Contains: *Pic-Nic, El triciclo, Fando y Lis, Ceremonia por un negro asesinado, El laberinto, Los dos verdugos, Oración, El cementerio de automóviles*)
Teatro Completo. 2 Volumes. Ed. Francisco Torres Monreal. Madrid: Espasa Calpe, 1997.
Teatro pánico. Ed. Francisco Torres Monreal. Madrid: Cátedra, 1986.

Selected English Translations

The Architect and the Emperor of Assyria. Trans. Everard D'Harnoncourt and Adele Shank. New York: Grove Press, 1969.
Garden of Delights. Trans. Helen Gary Bishop and Tom Bishop. New York: Grove Press, 1974.
Guernica and Other Plays. Trans. Barbara Wright. New York: Grove Press, 1967. (Contains: *Guernica, The Labryinth, Picnic on the Battlefield*)
And They Will Put Handcuffs on the Flowers. Trans. Charles Marowitz. New York: Grove Press, 1973.

Critical Studies

Arata, Luis Oscar. *The Festive Play of Fernando Arrabal.* Lexington: University of Kentucky Press, 1982.

Berenguer, Angel, y Joan Berenguer, eds. Madrid: *Fernando Arrabal*. Editorial Fundamentos, 1979.

Cantalapiedra, Fernando, and Francisco Torres Monreal. *El teatro de vanguardia de Fernando Arrabal*. Kassel: Edition Reichenberger, 1997.

Cassanelli, Rino. *El cosmos de Fernando Arrabal*. New York: Peter Lang, 1991.

De Long-Tonelli, Beverly. "Bicycles and Balloons in Arrabal's Dramatic Structure." *Modern Drama* 14 (1971): 205–209.

Diaz, Janet. "Theater and Theories of Fernando Arrabal." *Kentucky Romance Quarterly* 16 (1969): 143–154.

Donahue, Thomas John. *The Theater of Fernando Arrabal*. New York: New York University Press, 1980.

Essif, Lee. "La hamaca como 'objecto-espacio' social en *El cementerio de automóviles* de Fernando Arrabal." In *De lo particular a lo universal. El teatro español del siglo XX y su contexto*, ed. John Gabriele. Frankfurt am Main: Vervuert, 1994.

Glibota, Ante. *Arrabal Espace*. Paris: Studio di Val Cervo, 1994.

Green, Renee. "Arrabal's *The Architect*." *Romance Notes* 19.2 (1978): 140–145.

Knowles, Dorothy. "Ritual Theater: Fernando Arrabal and the Latin Americans." *Modern Language Review* 70.3 (1975): 526–538.

Kronik, John. "Arrabal and the Myth of Guernica." *Estreno* 2.1 (1975): 15–20.

Lyons, Charles. "The Psychological Base of Arrabal's *L'Architecte et l'Empereur d'Assyrie*." *French Review* 45.4 (1972): 123–136.

Orenstein, Gloria. *The Theater of the Marvelous*. New York: New York University Press, 1975.

Ortega, José. "El sentido de la obra de Fernando Arrabal." *Estreno* 2.1 (1975): 11–13.

Podol, Peter. *Fernando Arrabal*. Boston: Twayne Publishers, 1978.

———. "Spain: A Recurring Theme in the Theater of Fernando Arrabal." In *The Contemporary Spanish Theater: A Collection of Critical Essays* ed. Martha T. Halsey and Phyllis Zatlin. Lanham, MD: University Press of America, 1988. 131–145.

Polo de Bernabé, José. "El teatro de Fernando Arrabal: Vanguardia e ideología." *Anales de la Literatura Española Contemporánea* 6 (1981): 173–182.

Schifres, Alain. *Entretiens avec Arrabal*. Paris: Editions Pierre Belfond, 1969.

MAX AUB
(1903–1972)

Arie Vicente

BIOGRAPHY

No author in the Spanish literature of the first half of this century has represented the stormy history of Spain and Europe better than Max Aub, who, through his eventful life and intense work, can be considered a genuine testimony to those times. In this time of turmoil, he found himself at a crossroad. With a death sentence awaiting him in Spain because of his involvement in antifascist republican opposition, exiled to France where he was held prisoner in detention camps on the charge of communism, in danger of being exterminated in German concentration camps as a Jew, his origin, ideas, and life set him at the bull's-eye of all ideologies in power.

He was born in Paris on June 2, 1903, of a French mother and a German father. At the outbreak of World War I in 1914, the French authorities confiscated the German family's properties while his father, a sales representative, was on a business trip in Valencia. The fearful surrounding climate prompted the family to join his father in Valencia and settle there. After a transitional period in the Allianza Francesa, he pursued his secondary studies in the Escuela Moderna, the only secular school in the city, and got his *Bachillerato* degree (a nationally recognized examination administered by the state at the end of high school) at the Instituto de Valencia. These formative years, immersed in the great classics of French and Spanish literature—Molière, Racine, Victor Hugo, the Spanish Golden Age writers and Galdós—were of extreme significance to his sense of identity and his future intellectual life. Later, when asked about his origin and feeling of identity, he humorously answered that "one is from the place where one gets the Bachillerato." On the very year of his *Bachillerato*, at the age of twenty, his identity as a Spanish writer crystallized with his first drama, *Crime* [Crimen] (1923).

Max Aub's dramatic work extends over three distinct moments in the history of Europe: (1) In the post–World War I social and political optimism of the 1920s, he engages in deep psychological introspection with his avant-garde dramas, akin to Unamuno and Pirandello; (2) in the face of the rise of fascism and inspired by Marxist ideology, he becomes an active socialist and creates political dramas; (3) after the Spanish Civil War and until 1950, his work explores the victim's mind and sharpens his critical analysis of oppression.

In the first period, he combined his work as a sales representative with intense intellectual activity, through writing and contacts with European literary circles. His profession enabled him to further his observation and his knowledge of humankind: The world became his stage. The works of the 1920s belong to the aesthetics of the avant-garde, which prevailed at the time in the theater of Lorca and Casona and also reflected tendencies existing then in the French theater, specifically the satirical farce of Achard, Vitrac, and Jules Romains. Themes of human isolation and incommunicability, which will be characterized by the critic Soldevila as Aubian *par excellence*, are already present in his first drama, *Crime*. Smothered in thick silence made of doubts and the difficulty to express love, the characters wither and drift into crime. Crime becomes the grimacing and burlesque outcome of the discrepancy between the objectivity of the outer world and the subjective dimensions of the inner world of the individual in *the Jealous and His Beloved* [El celoso y su enamorada] (1925). The philosophical dilemma is made explicit and amplified in the two other plays, where characters "play their own role, disguise themselves, and lie," in the words of the skeptical protagonist, in *The Distrustful Prodigy* [El desconfiado prodigioso] (1924), who adds that "the world is a theater! And the truth is hidden." The attitude embodied in the same play by the main character asserts the strong will to preserve the Unamunian "I."

The Bottle [La botella] (1924) concludes that the only way to make sense out of this dilemma is to view as true not the objects themselves, as objective realism would assume, but their perception by the mind. This aesthetic and philosophical view was lined with political overtones in *The Bottle* and more clearly in his next play, *Mirror of Avarice* [Espejo de avarica] (first act finished in 1925; two acts added in 1934). In the latter, money, to which he refers by using the Quevedian title "Don Dinero," constitutes the historical mechanism that drives individuals and institutions as well. The main protagonist, a miser, is visited in his daydreams by the apparitions of the very institutions that control money: messengers of the Jesuits, Rockefeller, the Pirats, and Cooks and MacAndrews, respective incarnations of the Church, the Bank, the Army, and the Financial Interest—all "stemming from the troubled bourgeois mind of the miser" (*Teatro completo* 178). These ghosts will become real characters, taking active part in the plots in the future dramas.

The 1930s initiate a period of political commitment and action. History becomes his stage. A member of the PSOE (Partido Socialista Obrero Español— Spanish Socialist Party) since November 1929, he was later editor of the socialist newspaper *Verdad* and director of the liberal theater company of the University of Valencia. Like many of his contemporaries, he follows the evolution of communism in Russia and takes special interest in the social function of the arts.

His life, as well as his literary work reflects these preoccupations. The introduction to his drama *The War* [La guerra] (1935) mentions the influence of Erwin Piscator's political drama, and the play ends with the singing in crescendo of the international Communist Anthem. Also, as a director of the Pedagogic Programs (Misiones Pedagógicas), he directs his endeavors toward the emancipation of the working classes, their education, and their development of a class conciousness. Aub produced what he himself called a "theater of circumstances" (teatro de circunstancias) of eight short plays committed to the Republican cause that address the working-class struggles, the accusation and denunciation of fascist forces, and a call-up to mobilize Republican Spain in their war against Franco. The first theme appears in *The Story of the Miser* [Jácara del avaro] (1935), in which the witty and intelligent servant manages to switch positions with his master after having possession of his fortune through ingenious stratagems.

With the crucial elections of 1936 in Spain comes the accusation phase. In a speech directed to the assembly of people, the schoolteacher, in *The Water Does Not Belong to the Sky* [El agua no es del cielo] (1936), sharply points to the three main pillars of fascism—the Army, the Church, and the Bank. The six plays written during the war have great testimonial value and reflect militant commitment. Besides these dramas during the war, he held the official position of Cultural Attaché of the Spanish Embassy in Paris, which facilitated his contacts with intellectual milieux. As a representative of the Republican government, it was he who ordered Picasso's *Guernica*. He acted as a consultant for the production of Cervantes's *Numancia* with the famous actor and producer Jean-Louis Barrault. Later he wrote the script for the film *Sierra de Teruel* and participated in its direction with André Malraux.

The end of the war marks the beginning of the last period of Aub's dramatic creation. Franco's victory overturned Aub's life. In the crushing constraints of his short exile in Paris, before his imprisonment in French detention camps, he wrote *A Short While Ago* [De algún tiempo a esta parte] (1939), a heartrending monologue, described by Francisco Ruiz Ramón as "one of the masterpieces in contemporary western theater" (257). He perceives, with an extraordinary lucidity, the face of the Nazi monster, its rituals, and ministers—ordinary people from all walks of life who are caught in the collective frenzy. His confinement silenced his voice until 1942, the year when he escaped and fled to Mexico. However, the shock that is going to permeate his drama is the silence and indifference of the world witnessing this human tragedy. The years 1942 to 1950 are Aub's most productive years. He wrote six plays, which he collected under the title *Major Theater* [Teatro mayor]. From dictatorship to the tragedy of human condition, they all reflect on the need for political commitment when destructive forces exist: the role of the intellectual under dictatorship and the contrast between active and passive characters in *Conjugal Life* [La vida conyugal] (1942); the tragic fate of the Jewish people under Nazism in *San Juan* (1942); human kindness and solidarity against adversity in *The Abduction of*

Europe [El rapto de Europa] (1943); French opposition to the Spanish Republicans in *Death for Having Closed One's Eyes* [Morir por cerrar los ojos] (1944); contrast between intellectual ideals and the pragmatic military forces in *Heads and Tails* [Cara y cruz] (1944); and finally, the end of the European tragedy in *No* (1949).

By 1950 Aub had written practically all of his dramatic work with two monologues—*The Pope's Monologue* [Monólogo del Papa] (1948); *Speech at the Plaza de la Concordia* [Discurso de la Plaza de la Concordia] (1950); the four plays constituting *The Exile* ["Los trasterrados"]—*Drifting Off* [A la deriva] (1943); *Transit* [Tránsito] (1944); *The Harbor* [El puerto] (1944); *The Top Floor* [El último piso] (1944); his "plays of Franco Spain"—*The Guerrillas* [Los guerrilleros] (1944); *The Prison* [La cárcel] (1946); *Oblivion* [Un olvido] (1947); from his "secret police theater"—*The Anarchist* [Un anarquista] (1946); *The Marvelous Men* [Los excelentes varones] (1946); his "teatrillo"—*The Dead* [Los muertos] (1945); *One of Many* [Uno de tantos] (1946); *New Third Act* [Nuevo tercer acto] (1947); *She Does Not Know What She Carries Within Her* [Una no sabe lo que lleva dentro] (1947); *The Never-ending Comedy* [Comedia que no acaba] (1947); *Deseada* (1948); and finally the three "diversiones"—*An Acceptable Proposal* [Una proposición decente] (1946); *The Manager* [El director] (1948); *Short Melodrama* [Dramoncillo] (1948).

Two dramas deserve careful attention, *No* and *Speech at the Plaza de la Concordia*. *No* shows the last war refugees who arrive at the border that separates the American forces in Europe and the Soviet police. The refugees realize that they are rejected by both sides, because although both sides have opposing ideologies, they exhibit the same attitudes. Both systems fear losing their power to those fighters for freedom. In the second play, Aub takes up the same theme; but the main character, the Big Fool (el Gran Mentecato), the author's alter ego, assesses the cold war and the role of the writer in such a context. The harsh times in his life have passed, and he finds himself in a comfortable situation: "I have a beautiful house, some good pictures, and some good books" (*Teatro completo* 794). But when he asked why he maintains his attitude of defense of the oppressed, he replies: "because I am happy. And I see how the world is turning and where things are going. Because I am outraged at the sight of so much ignominy" 794). Like an obelisk, he stands in the middle of the Plaza of the Concordia, which ironically used to be the location where executions took place. He stands as a target for all opposing systems, which, in his view, share the same objectives but use different methods. The individual has been sacrificed to the interests of the nations. In the Plaza de la Concordia, the Big Fool points an accusing finger to the two powers present and cries out for the respect of human dignity. This was Aub's last dramatic expression of the convergence of History and his life. In this absurd world the committed playwright pulls down the curtain. During his Mexican years and until his death in 1972, Aub remained a very prolific writer, and he combined his teaching at the Universidad Nacional Autónoma de México (UNAM) with several cultural responsibilities. He directed the university's radio and television network and was actively involved in writing scripts and producing films, in collaboration, especially with his longtime friend Luis Buñuel.

DRAMATURGY: MAJOR WORKS AND THEMES

Aub's work as a playwright has long been neglected due to his exile, to the political conditions in Franco's Spain, and to the general veiling of issues pertaining to individual and collective collaboration with fascism in Europe. The reccurring preoccupation and dramatic tension in his major plays dwell in the struggle for freedom and dignity of the individual facing the oppressive forces of the State.

A Short While Ago (1939) is a play in which a woman, Emma, a Catholic of Jewish origin, finds herself confined in the attic room of her own house in Vienna after the Nazi government's confiscation of her property. In a long interior soliloquy she recollects her life, her happy childhood, her successful career, her quiet and fulfilling life with her family before the death of her son in the Spanish war, the ordeal of her husband in a concentration camp, and his death. Through her descriptions of the deep but almost imperceptible joy she sees in the eyes of the old man, or the symbolic gesture of the child throwing a stone on the Jewish store being destroyed by Nazi groups, the audience can visualize the spread of the Nazi cancer over the Austrian population. As Casimir Gandia has pointed out, "There is a theme that underlies all of Max Aub's work: the need to open one's eyes to historic events, the need to be alert" (64).

This same theme is explicitly mentioned in the title of another major play, *Death for Having Closed One's Eyes* (1944). This long play in six acts is composed of two distinct sections taking place in two opposite spaces: the home, which symbolizes the place for personal freedom and control of one's own life, and the detention camp, which stands for the negation of both. In the first section, in a Petainist France that has started arresting all the "foreigners"—Jews and foreign citizens—a couple, Julio, a Spanish shop owner, and María, the French woman he married, try to convince themselves that they will not be affected since they have never been involved in any political activity. However, the people around them, neighbors, concierge, are staring at them, like vultures waiting for their prey, ready to snatch their property and belongings. As in the previous play, the ordinary people, with their greed and racist joy at the others' misfortune, are shown to serve the cause of the collaboration with Nazism.

Julio's brother, a participant in the Spanish war, visits them and thus precipitates the events leading to the husband's imprisonment. The second part shows Julio's and Juan's nightmare in several successive detention camps and the role they assume in the camps: Julio remains a fighter for freedom, whereas his bourgeois brother becomes a police informer. Julio's wife takes on the struggle to free her husband and his brother. After enduring rape by the camp officer, she finally realizes that she has lost the battle and recognizes: "I have been blind, dead for having closed my eyes" [He vivido ciega, muerta, por cerrar los ojos] (570). María's symbolic function in the play becomes clear moments later when she perceives herself "Like France, torn apart by traitors, sold by misers, destroyed by cowards, mutilated by crows, shattered by some rotten old men, dead for having closed her eyes" (570). The new awareness gives her the strength to find a way to defend herself against the soldiers who are under orders to arrest her, and at top of her voice, she begins to sing the "Marseillaise." Such a rebellious act, which appeals to the French revolutionary values of justice and freedom, is taken up by all the prisoners with the effect of immobilizing the soldiers. The importance of this final scene has often been misjudged by literary critics. José Monleón dedicates a large part of *El teatro de Max Aub* (1971) to this play. His conclusion about the function of the French anthem is that it is a manifestation of the bourgeois character that took over the Revolutionary spirit. Contrary to this interpretation, I suggest that it bears a tremendous dramatic effect as well as the message of hope: The "Marseillaise" has become one of the universal anthems of freedom. Aub criticizes here the France that has betrayed these values and become chauvinist and nationalist. The same tension that exists between these two forces also animated the battlefield that Europe was in the first half of the twentieth century.

Moving away from all political and historical preoccupations, *Deseada* (1950) constitutes what Ricardo Doménech, in his essay preceding the 1967 edition of *Morir por cerrar los ojos*, called "an aesthetic week-end," a sentimental interlude, a melodramatic parenthesis in his work. However, the play is worth mentioning here because of its commercial success. The plot is organized around the conflict of a young woman and her mother and ends in their reconciliation. The mother's solitude and the daughter's suffering do not, in my opinion, reach the tragic levels of Lorca's theater, as was implied in Monleón's analysis. By writing this play, Aub has shown that he was able to write light commercial successes, had he so desired. This is, however, a form of theater art against which he stood firmly and strongly as being contrary to his concept of art as social commitment.

Aub's unanimously recognized masterpiece is *San Juan* (1943). The play is inspired by convergence of one autobiographical and one specific historical event. After his detention in France, Max Aub was transported in dramatic conditions on the boat *Sidi Aicha*, which brought him to a French detention camp in North Africa. Before World War II, news was circulating about several boats transporting Jews who were expelled by Nazi Germany and who went from country to country in a vain search for asylum. Aub created a classical tragedy in three acts, compressed in the intensity of one space the boat and one unit of time (a little more than twenty-four hours). In the first two acts the boat is anchored in a port, awaiting with anguish governmental decisions about their fate. The playwright introduces the main themes through children playing a pursue and capture game; and through the dramatization of the different reactions they show when they face losing their freedom—the active leader and his obedient followers, on the one hand, and on the other, one frightened victim and one who tries to drop out of the game—they mirror the world of adults. The young Leva, a Communist, believes with conviction that he can organize the escape, whereas, at the other end of the spectrum, Ephraim is paralyzed by fear. The third protagonist, Carlos, although he is going to share the collective fate of his companions, wants to remain "out of the game," refusing every self-deceiving comfort such as love, political ideas, and religion. He persists in his understanding of the situation: These people are on the boat because they are Jews, and nothing will save them from their tragic end. The end of the third act shows the rejected boat in the middle of the ocean, with hope gradually diminishing as the boat finally sinks, and Carlos, "(stretching out his arms, cries out the motto of his soccer team) Sport! Sport! Sport! Ra, ra, ra!" (*San Juan* [Barcelona: Anthropos, 1992], 105).

In addition to the most widespread interpretation of *San Juan* as the representation of the collective tragedy of a people, I propose that this tragedy and the whole situation are embodied by Carlos, who therefore is a focal character. He is the outsider *par excellence*, the crystallization of all the characteristics of the exiled, of the foreigner, the stranger, the other. He belongs nowhere. A handsome, strong, blond young man, born of a freethinker German family, raised as an agnostic, in the forefront of German society as the main player in the Sportverein, his soccer team, he possessed every asset to belong and succeed in his world. But this world fell apart when the Nazis uncovered his father's Jewish origin and expelled the whole family from Germany. With this shock, he loses his comfortable reliance on a promising life and understands that this was all self-deception. He then becomes the negator of all convictions. He rejects the militant Communist position—"Do you know what you are?; disgusting idealists" (44); love or pity—to his sister who declares her love for her fiance, he replies, "What do you love? his skeleton? his skull? his teeth?" (44); and religious convictions—"You will not convince me. You would have to be more than God to do so" (97). He no longer belongs to the German people, but he does not recognize himself in the Jewish population of the boat either. He finds himself in the absurd condition of the individual categorized by the others but unable to assume any identity for himself, except that of the "one who does not belong." By his experience and by his fate, this protagonist embodies the sense of the absurd that Camus describes in the following terms: "This exile is without recourse for he [the human being] is deprived of memories of a lost fatherland or of the hope of a promised land. A split between man and his life, the actor and the scene, this is exactly the sense of absurdity" (*Essais* [Paris: Editions Gallimard et Calmann-Lévy, 1965], 101; translation mine). It is also what makes Aub's plays both an invaluable testimony of life in a tragic age and real drama that offers deep insights into the human condition.

CRITICS' RESPONSE

Studies on Aub's dramaturgy have recognized Max Aub as one of the most important Spanish playwrights in the twentieth century. The task was difficult, particularly during the Franco regime, which negated the existence of the liberal Spain. Since the first work of the most prominent specialist on Max Aub, Ignacio Soldevila, major studies by Doménech (1967), Monleón (1971), and Ruiz Ramón (1975) have analyzed Aub's theater in terms of a classification into three distinct periods based on historical and literary movements: the avant-garde, the Spanish Civil War dramas, and the post–Civil War dramas. However, most studies constitute general introductions and surveys of Aub's theater. Thorough analyses of specific dramas are almost nonexistent to this day. Doménech's long essay published as the introduction to *Morir por cerrar los ojos* does not offer a detailed study of this play but rather a general overview of Aub's dramatic works, which was a challenge in those years. In this excellent presentation of Aub's dramatic work, Doménech considers the play *Pedro López García* as the key to understanding the transition between the first period of "irrational theater" and the second, the politically committed theater, and views this play as an important element for the study of the relationship between drama and society. The present study proposes a classification of Aub's dramatic work not in external terms such as historical and literary trends but rather following Aub's internal intellectual and political development, suggesting that the playwright's work was social and political since the beginning.

AWARDS AND DISTINCTIONS

A new platform for the study of Aub's work has been created around the University of Valencia, specially with Manuel Aznar Soler and the formation, in 1993, of a group dedicated to the research and study of the literature written in exile, the Grupo de Estudios del Exilio Literario (GEXEL). Max Aub's life and work represent a crossroads between several cultures, in constant flux. This very aspect of Aub's personality was one motivating force for the creation of the Max Aub Archives and Library that will hold and preserve his work in Segorbe, Spain. Honoring Aub's birthday, every June 2, young students from the schools around Segorbe meet to celebrate Aub's cultural day. Exhibitions are organized, and scholars are invited to select the recipients of the International Max Aub literary award. Such a celebration of his intellectual stature around the Town Hall in Segorbe shows that the sad and lonely speech of the "Gran Mentecato" has been heard and represents the most authentic hommage to be made to a playwright: Children as well as adults gather in the public space, which has become Aub's stage.

BIBLIOGRAPHY

Plays by Max Aub

Narciso. Barcelona: Imprenta Altés, 1928.

Teatro incompleto (El desconfiado prodigioso, Una botella, El celoso y su enamorada, Espejo de avaricia, Crimen). Madrid: Sociedad General Española de Librerías, 1931.

Pedro López García. In *Hora de España* 19 (July 1938).

San Juan

    a. México: Tezontle, 1943.

    b. In *Primer Acto* 52 (Mayo 1964): 22–41.

    c. Barcelona: Anthropos, 1992.

Morir por cerrar, los ojos

    a. México: Tezontle, 1944.

    b. Barcelona: Aymá, 1967.

La vida conyugal

    a. México: Tezontle, 1944.

    b. La Habana: Instituto del Libro, Teatro Español Actual, 1945.

El rapto de Europa. México: Tezontle, 1946.

Cara y cruz. México: Sociedad General de Autores Mexicanos, 1948.

De algún tiempo a esta parte. México: Tezontle, 1949.

Deseada. México: Tezontle, 1950.

No. México: Tezontle, 1952.

Tres monólogos y uno solo verdadero. México: Tezontle, 1956.

Obras en un acto. 2 vols. (1: *Crimen. El desconfiado prodigioso. Una botella. El celoso y su enamorada. Espejo de avaricia. Pedro López García. A la deriva. Tránsito. El puerto. La vuelta. Los guerrilleros. La cárcel. Un olvido*; 2: *Un anarquista. Los excelentes varones. Los muertos. Otros muertos. Uno de tantos. El último piso. Homenaje a Xavier Villaurrutia o Nuevo tercer acto. Una no sabe lo que lleva dentro. Comedia que no acaba. Jácara del avaro. Una proposición decente. Entremés del gran director. Dramoncillo.*) México: Universidad Nacional Autónoma de México, 1960.

Las vueltas. México: Joaquín Mortiz, 1964.

El cerco. México: Joaquín Mortiz, 1968.

Teatro completo. México: Aguilar, 1968.

Retrato de un general, visto de frente y vuelto hacia la izquierda. México: Joaquín Mortiz, 1969.

Los muertos. México: Joaquín Mortiz, 1971.

La guerra (selection) in Aznar Soler, Manuel. *Max Aub y la vanguardia teatral (Escritos sobre teatro, 1928–1938).* Barcelona: Universitat de Valencia, 1993.

Critical Studies

Aznar Soler, Manuel. *Max Aub y la vanguardia teatral (Escritos sobre teatro, 1928–1938).* Barcelona: Universitat de Valencia, 1993.

Borrás, Angel. "Max Aub: Monologues of Exile." *Estreno* 18.1 (1992): 17–19.

————. *El teatro del exilio de Max Aub*. Sevilla: Publicaciones de la Universidad de Sevilla, 1975.

Bosch, Rafael. "El teatro de Max Aub." *Hispanófila* 19 (septiembre 1963): 25–34.

Buero Vallejo, Antonio. "El teatro de Max Aub y su espera infinita." *Cuadernos Americanos* 187 (marzo–abril 1973): 64–70.

Cardiel Reyes, Raúl. "La tragedia del buque San Juan." *Cuadernos Americanos* 187 (marzo–abril 1973): 96–101.

Doménech, R. "Introducción al teatro de Max Aub." In *Morir por cerrar los ojos*. Barcelona: Aymá, 1967.

Embeita, María. "Max Aub y su generación" (interview). *Insula* 22.253 (1967): 11–12.

Gandía, Casimir. "Max Aub, nuestro vecino despierto." *Primer Acto* 185 (agosto–septiembre 1980): 64–66.

García Antón, Cecilia. "Max Aub. La epopeya del hombre trasterrado. Sobre *Morir por cerrar los ojos*." *Revista de Literatura* 55.109 (1993): 129–138.

García Lora, J. "Fabulación dramática del fabuloso Max Aub." *Insula* 222 (mayo 1965): 14.

Hoyo, A. "Prólogo." In *Teatro completo*. México: Aguilar, 1968.

Isasi Angulo, A. "El teatro de Max Aub." *Insula* 320–321 (julio–agosto 1973): n.p.

Kemp, Lois A. "The Plays of Max Aub. A Kaleidoscopic Approach to Theater." Ph.D. diss., University of Wisconsin, 1972.

López, Estela. *El teatro de Max Aub*. San Juan: Editorial Universitaria, Universidad de Puerto Rico, 1977.

Monleón, José. *El teatro de Max Aub*. Madrid: Taurus, 1971.

Moraleda, Pilar. "El teatro de Max Aub." *Cuadernos Hispanoamericanos* 411 (septiembre 1984): 148–156.

Morales, José Ricardo. "Max Aub. De *El búho* al destierro." *Primer Acto* 247 (enero–febrero 1993): 66–69.

Pérez Minik, D. "Max Aub: El teatro que es y no fue." *Insula* 320–321 (julio–agosto 1973): n.p.

Quinto, J. María de. "Informa apresurado sobre el teatro de Max Aub." *Primer Acto* 52 (mayo 1964): n.p.

Ruiz Ramón, Francisco. *Historia del teatro español del siglo XX*. Madrid: Ediciones Cátedra, 1975.

Soldevila Durante, Ignacio. "El español Max Aub." *La Torre* 33 (enero–marzo 1961): 103–120.

————. "Max Aub, dramaturgo." *Segismundo* 19–20 (1974): 140–192.

Szapiro, Francine. "Wien 38." *L'Arche* 363 (junio 1987): 11.

Vicente, Arie. "Max Aub." In *Lo judío en el teatro español contemporáneo*. Madrid: Editorial Pliegos, 1991.

"El exilio aubiano como referencia imaginaria en los monólogos de Max Aub." In *Entre Actos: diálogos sobre teatro español entre siglos*, ed. Martha Halsey and Phyllis Zatlin. University Park, PA: *Estreno*, 1999. 221–229.

Wright, Lucinda. "Max Aub and the Tragedy: A study of 'Cara y Cruz' and 'San Juan' " Ph.D. diss., University of North Carolina, 1986.

SERGI BELBEL
(1963–)

María M. Delgado and David George

BIOGRAPHY

Arguably the most lauded young playwright in the contemporary Spanish theater, as well as an accomplished director and translator, Sergi Belbel ranks
among the prominent figures in current Catalán language theater. Born in Terrassa on May 29, 1963, of Andalusian parents, Belbel had already written his
first play *Calidoscopios y faros de hoy* (1985) before he had completed his
undergraduate degree in Romance and French philology at Barcelona's Autonomous University. The play, begun in Catalán but completed in Spanish, was
staged in Madrid at the Centro Nacional de Nuevas Tendencias Escénicas and
immediately established Belbel as a dramatist of some originality and veritable
promise whose dramatic priorities seemed very different to those of the protest
dramatists of the Franco era.

In the years following this success, Belbel continued to produce work at a
prolific rate (at least one play a year and usually written in Catalán), all of which
received major stagings at important Catalán venues, including the Teatre Romea and El Mercat de les Flors, Barcelona's old flower market now converted
into a flexible performance space. In addition, a number of these plays, translated
by Belbel into Spanish, were staged in Madrid, largely at the Sala Olimpia and
the Centro Nacional del Nuevas Tendencias. These are arguably the city's most
adventurous theater houses, and are responsible for the promotion of innovative
or radical new work.

Belbel has subsequently explained that since it was his mother tongue, he had
never really questioned Spanish. Catalán, on the other hand, was a language he
felt he could manipulate, because he was more distant from it.[1] However, since
his parents moved to Catalonia before the great wave of emigration from Andalusia in the 1960s, Belbel never mixed much with Andalusian émigrés and
was integrated into Catalanist circles at an early age. His own facility with both
languages has enabled him to translate his own plays from Catalan to Spanish

on a regular basis, thus ensuring that his Catalan-language successes are rapidly presented on the main stages of Madrid.

Belbel began directing his own work in 1987, when he codirected *Minim.mal Show* with Miquel Górriz at the Institut del Teatre, but has increasingly staged the works of other dramatists. His production of Georges Perec's *L'augment*, initially presented at the Aula de Teatre at Barcelona's Autonomous University and then transferring to the Teatro Teixidors a mà-Teatreneu in Barcelona, was the first of such ventures. Since then he has directed the work of his Catalan contemporaries, most conspicuously Josep M. Benet i Jornet, as well as an earlier generation of Catalan dramatists like Àngel Guimerà. He has also directed Shakespeare, Molière, and Goldoni in translation, again at prominent Catalan venues like the Teatre Poliorama and the Teatre Grec.

Although recognized primarily as a playwright, and more recently a director, Belbel is also a lecturer in Dramatic Literature at Barcelona's Institut del Teatre, where he has worked since 1988. He is also an accomplished translator, translating not only his own work but also the plays of a number of classical and contemporary French dramatists—including Racine, Beckett, and Bernard-Marie Koltès—into both Catalan and Spanish. Of all contemporary Spanish dramatists, Belbel is perhaps the most widely translated. Productions of his plays have been staged in Portuguese, English, German, French, Galician, Italian, Finnish, and Swedish.

One of Belbel's plays, *Tàlem*, was performed on Catalan television in 1991. Belbel has recently followed in the steps of the dramatist Josep Benet i Jornet in writing a Catalan soap opera, *Secrets de família*, which he coauthored with the novelist Maria Mercè Roca. It ran to 190 half-hour episodes and was screened at prime viewing time. It attracted large audiences and has served to establish the reputations of a number of its actors and actresses. More recently Belbel collaborated with veteran Catalan filmmaker Ventura Pons on an acclaimed screen version of *Carícies*, seen at the 1998 Berlin Film Festival. Evoking Max Ophul's cinematic rendition of *La Ronde*, it conjured a materialist postmodernist Barcelona of fraught domestic encounters, numbing cruelty, and occasional glimmers of passion. A second collaboration has followed: *Morir (o no)*, in 1999.

DRAMATURGY: MAJOR WORKS AND THEMES

Belbel's first play, *A.G./V.W., Calidoscopios y faros de hoy* (originally published in Spanish, later in Catalan under the more explanatory title *André Gide/ Virginia Wolf: calidoscopis i fars d'avui*) is constructed around a juxtaposition of Virginia Woolf and Andre Gide and a contemporary couple and contains many of the thematic and stylistic features that characterize his work as a whole. It defies the reaffirmative tendencies of the classic realist play, in that it features precious little exposition, and the characters appear to have no past, in complete contrast to those of the well-made play. The result is that the readers/spectators feel disorientated, as Belbel creates a sense of a society of shifting alliances where anything is up for negotiation. Dehumanized action unfolds on a bare stage where any specified item is used in inventive allegorical manner—a technique visible in much of his subsequent work.

Like the rest of his plays, *A.G./V.W., Calidoscopios y faros de hoy/André Gide/Virginia Woolf: calidoscopis i fars d'avui* is meticulously crafted. Belbel delights in playing linguistic games, and his plays are a sophisticated elucidation on the torturous nature of language. Shifting, ambiguous, and evasive, Belbel's work acknowledges a clear debt to the Catalan avant-garde tradition and, in the wider European context, to absurdist dramatists like Beckett and Ionesco.

Despite the fact that all Belbel's work can be categorized as antinaturalistic, it is worth drawing attention to its stylistic range, from the complex *Tàlem* (1991) to the three monologues of *Elsa Schneider* (1987). What all the plays exhibit is a fascination with textuality—the authorial voice intervening conspicuously by quoting or alluding to a variety of filmic and literary references. A number of Belbel's plays overtly refer to other literary antecedents: One of the three monologues that make up *Elsa Schneider* recounts the troubled private life of the movie star Romy Schneider; *La nit del cigne* (*L'impossible silenci*) (1986) features a Chehkovian recital; *Tàlem* (1989) offers a playful reworking of the bedroom farce; *Carícies* (1991) provides a rewriting of Arthur Schnitzler's *La Ronde* for the fractured 1990s. Additionally, such postmodernist reflections on his texts' fictional status and their ambivalent relationship with other fictional constructs frequently manifest themselves through a specific use of metatheater, with the actors drawing attention to their roles as performers enacting a series of orchestrated actions for an audience's contemplation: This is visible both in *La nit del cigne* (*L'impossible silenci*), where an actor due to perform a Chekhovian piece first engages with the audience, requesting how he should begin, and in *Elsa Schneider*, where, in the third monologue, the actress playing the role of Romy Schneider betrays her confusion about how to execute her performance.

Not that all the plays can be reduced to intertextual reflections on the inherently artificial nature of theater. *En companyia d'abisme*, premiered at the Institut del Teatre in Barcelona in 1989, and often credited with consolidating Belbel's reputation as a major force in the Catalan theater, is a more introverted study of verbal coersion and the usurping potential of language. The action takes place in a stark "bare zone in the abyss" [zona abissal indefinida, completament buida][2] where two men whose relationship is frustratingly never properly defined meet unexpectedly, or so the text initially leads us to believe. Their ambiguous and evasive conversations become a battleground over which each man attempts to establish a dominant position over the other. In the absence of physical action (each character executes only three brief movements, although each inflicts damage on his still adversary), words become the primary weapon through which status and power are established. The meticulous body positions that Belbel details in his stage directions—excruciatingly difficult for an actor to maintain and grueling for an audience to watch—are far removed from the demands of the pseudonaturalistic play, yet they fulfill a central role in creating the tense stage environment in which the characters' mysterious interactions take place. From an atmosphere of eerie stillness, Belbel creates a devastating commentary on the pain inflicted by human beings on each other. As in Bernard-Marie Koltès *Dans la solitude des champs de coton*, a play that Belbel has translated into both Spanish and Catalan, the shifting nature of the dialogue works to comment on the unreliable nature of language and the manner in which it both facilitates and impedes communication.

Likewise, *Tàlem* (1990) offers a blistering exposition of the limitations of verbal language, significantly focusing on the game-playing that lies behind the most mundane interactions. The action unfolds in an empty room, bereft of doors or windows, where the only item of furniture is an enormous bed. This is the focus of the action as one of the play's two couples attempts to persuade the other to sleep in it. Through a series of short episodic scenes the characters lure themselves and each other into compromising (emotional and physical) positions. Transcending its literal significance, the bed becomes both a visual metaphor for the sexual undercurrent that is ever present in the play and a manifestation of the characters' deepest fears and hopes. As in *En companyia d'abisme*, desire exceeds the means through which it can be consummated, for circumstances conspire to ensure the bed remains unused. The play derives its energy from the inventive strategies employed (by both playwright and characters) simultaneously to aid and evade the use of the bed. As much a comment on the fragile and inherently deceptive nature of human relationships as a sophisticated and witty structural reworking of the bedroom farce (exposing the rules governing the construction of such generic products, parodying its protagonists, and deflating any potentially tender moments), *Tàlem* derives much of its dramatic strength from the structural liberties Belbel takes. The play's thirty-eight scenes both lead the action forward and take it back. Additionally, the second half of the play recontextualizes scenes featured in the early half. Meaning shifts according to where it is situated. As such the play comments on the complex processes of signification at work in every dissection of executed action(s).

Probably Belbel's most polemical work to date has been *Carícies* (1991), "a Catalan drama for the 1990s—violent, sexual, perverse and unequivocally modern."[3] Each of its ten scenes and epilogue consists of a dialogue between a pair of male characters, all of whom are given such generic names as Young Man. In the revised versions for the general public, the characters are the traditional couple, simply called Young Man and Young Woman. A pattern and sense of continuity are lent to its episodic structure by the inclusion of one of each pair of characters in the following scene. *Carícies* is essentially about a lack of communication between people, who perpetrate violence, both verbal and physical, on each other. The language of the play and the sexually explicit nature of some of the scenes led the play to receive a generally negative critical reaction.

In contrast to *Carícies, Després de la pluja* has proved a most popular work with the critics. The action takes place on the flat rooftop of a skyscraper in an unnamed city, but one more reminiscent of New York or Chicago than Barcelona. According to Belbel, this "great, modern city" [gran ciutat moderna] is the true protagonist of the play.[4] Staff from an office in the building escape to the rooftop in order to enjoy an illicit cigarette, as smoking is banned by their company.[5] To quote Belbel, "it's a play which speaks of the power relationships in the context of a modern, dehumanized and competitive company, which is to an extent a metaphor of the world in general" [és una obra que parla sobre les relacions de poder en l'àmbit d'una empresa moderna, deshumanitzada i competitiva, que em serviex una mica de metàfora del món en general].[6] Using a typically minimalist set, Belbel portrays the tensions and the underlying violence of a repressive postmodern society in which all the characters participate in restrictive surveillance.

The lack of communication between these characters is highlighted by the number of conversations that, although ostensibly dialogues, appear to be more like monologues or dialogues of the deaf. These scenes sometimes give rise to delightfully but disturbingly absurdist discussions, where motifs are juxtaposed and/or interwoven in unusual or conflicting ways. The tensions that punctuate the play occasionally surface in the form of verbal tirades, such as that of the Dark-Haired Secretary against her Red-Haired Colleague in Scene 6, or the extraordinarily violent and vulgar outburst by the Executive Manageress in Scene 11, which is directed against the Brown-Haired Secretary and is provoked by the latter's promotion to the Board of Directors.

As usual, Belbel explores in a disturbing but humorous way the relationships between individuals and groups. That between men and women is generally unhappy, although the final scene of the original Catalan version of the play does contain an element of hope. The Brown-Haired Secretary, having previously believed herself to be sterile, is expecting a child by the Computer Programmer, who had earlier been widowed. The optimism is reinforced by the arrival of the rain, providing relief after the drought. However, Belbel was not completely satisfied with this "happy" ending and, in his own Spanish translation, removed it. Another set of relationships in *Després de la pluja* are those between secretaries and their bosses, and these are given some humorous twists. For instance, executives as well as their secretaries resort to illicit smoking, including the seemingly proper and right-minded Executive Manageress, who is desperate to seek solace in a cigarette. We have already seen how she is further undermined by the promotion of the Brown-Haired Secretary. A similar kind of role-reversal occurs between the Blonde Secretary and her boss, the Administration Manager. The Blonde Secretary, brilliantly played by Laura Conejero in the original Catalan production, is on the surface a typical dumb blonde, although her long, inane speeches would suggest that the epithet "dumb" would be inappropriate. She has the measure of her boss, however, and is a good deal less stupid than she appears. In fact, in *Després de la pluja*, it is a case of secretaries on top!

The style and tone of the play are a typically Beckettian mixture of humor and seriousness, and of profundity and banality. The Red-Haired Secretary's almost philosophical angst, as she ponders the meaning of life, is calmed by a sexual adventure with the down-to-earth Runner, the size of whose sexual organ is first mentioned by the Blonde Secretary and then witnessed by the audience after the Red-Haired Secretary has ordered him to drop his pants. The juxtaposition between intellectual and carnal activity is highlighted in a large number of scenes, offering a humorous contrast in linguistic registers and deflating a number of the characters' grand ideas.

Belbel constantly frustrates our expectations. In Scene 10, what may be considered to be a typically secretarial discussion about the opposite sex is juxtaposed with the intellectual ramblings of the Red-Haired Secretary. Belbel's is not a thesis theater and, in its portrayal of thoroughly contemporary themes in a strikingly nonrealist form, is typical of much post-Francoist Catalan theater, which is far less blatantly preoccupied with political issues than that of the preceding generation.

Just as contrasting linguistic registers are set against each other, and intellectual and physical activities are intertwined, so are fantasy and reality often difficult to separate. For instance, the Brown-Haired Secretary recounts the sexual activities of an unhappily married wife with her lover in a neighboring building. The other secretaries believe she is making the whole thing up, but Belbel never resolves the question one way or the other. Scene 3 opens with the Runner observing a helicopter and then commenting "one day, one of those things is going to crash into a building." [algun dia, un trasto d'aquests xocarà contra un edifici] (p. 56). Immediately, the sound of a helicopter crashing is heard. In Scene 6, the Runner recounts the accident to the Dark-Haired Secretary with a sense of guilt that it was his psychic powers that caused the crash.

A particularly disconcerting instance of overlap between imagination and reality concerns the Computer Programmer's apparently throwing himself from the rooftop in Scene 4, observed by the Administration Manager, who counts the number of seconds it takes for the Programmer to fall to the ground. However, in Scene 4, the Administration Manager explains how he had had a nightmare the previous night, in which the Computer Programmer had thrown himself over the rail at the edge of the rooftop. This is also one instance of how, through the use of stage space, movement, and language, Belbel effectively communicates a sense of panic, tension, and even vertigo, which are associated with the play's elevated location. Also, Belbel's use of cross-referencing and repeated leitmotifs lend *Després de la pluja* a dramatic unity that defies its apparently episodic structure.

His latest work includes *Sóc lletja*, a hilarious black musical comedy cowritten with Jordi Sánchez in which a woman who is constantly taunted because of her ugliness turns into an obsessive man killer, and *La sang*, a powerful and thoughtful evocation of a terrorist kidnapping and the subsequent torture and murder of the victim. Finally, *El temps de Planck* is a musical, with words by Belbel and music by Oscar Roig. Since the late 1990s, much of Bebel's work has involved directing, including a Goldoni trilogy which was performed at the recently inaugurated National Theater of Catalonia in Barcelona in 1999, and Calderón's seventeenth-century Spanish masterpiece *El alcalde de Zalamea* in Barcelona and Madrid in 2000–2001. The move to collaborative writing in plays like *Sóc lletja* and *El temps de Planck* is reflected in the necessarily collaborative work involved in directing.

CRITICS' RESPONSE

Belbel has probably made a greater impact on the Catalan theatrical scene and at a younger age than any other post–Civil War Catalan playwright. The Catalan daily *Avui* summed up this impact (when Belbel was only twenty-five years old) with an article entitled "Catalan Theatre Is Called Sergi Belbel."[7]

Although the response of critics has been generally positive to Belbel as dramatist and as director, some older critics have been rather reluctant to accept him. Joan de Sagarra, for instance, was the only critic who thoroughly disapproved of Belbel's 1992 production of Àngel Guimerà's *La filla del mar* and compared it unfavorably with a 1971 production of the play by Ricard Salvat.[8]

Belbel has also been more widely criticized for what some have seen as a tendency to indulge in structural games and for a corresponding lack of social content, although, paradoxically, *Carícies* was condemned for an excess of social material. What has been termed a "tendency to treat the audience as ironic, intelligent onlookers or participants"[9] has led some to classify Belbel's plays as somewhat self-indulgent. In the words of Eduardo Galán: "His commitment is not to the audience, but to himself, to his project of theatrical creation, which, for the moment, refuses to make any concession to audiences" [su compromiso no es con el público, sino consigo mismo, con su proyecto de creación teatral, que por ahora se resiste a hacer concesiones al público].[10]

Those aspects of Belbel's theater that have most appealed to the critics are linguistic ones. He is praised for the agility of his dialogues and the rhythm of the language. Ironically, what is probably his least innovative and most conventional play, *Després de la pluja*, has proved to be his most popular with the critics. Joan-Anton Benach criticized the original ending, in his otherwise favorable review of the play: "It is possible that *Després de la pluja* is too long. And I could do without the happy ending, although I do understand that it might be a question of principle" [es posible que "Després de la pluja" se prolongue excesivamente. Y sobra, desde mi punto e vista, el "happy end," aunque comprendo que esta [*sic*] pueda constituir una cuestión de principio].[11]

Benach's dissatisfaction with the ending was one of only two slightly negative criticisms made in the press. The other came, also in an overall favorable review by Albert de la Torre in *El País* of October 30, 1993. De la Torre's view was that the limited number of rehearsals Belbel had conducted did show through in the first night. This does not detract from his overall satisfaction with the play's quality and does not prevent him from describing Belbel as "one of the most immaculate and skilful directors in Spain" [uno de los directores más pulcros y hábiles de nuestros escenarios], a point also made by David George in an article on Belbel's production of Guimerà's *La filla del mar*.[12] Although David George and John London concentrate exclusively on his dramaturgical work in *An Introduction to Contemporary Catalan Theatre*, they cite a commonly held view that Belbel is currently regarded "as the saviour of Catalan text-based drama"[13]—an extraordinary accolade for a dramatist still only in his thirties.

AWARDS AND DISTINCTIONS

Belbel has been the recipient of a number of prestigious awards since first coming to the critics' attention with his first play *Calidoscopios y faros de hoy*, awarded the Ministerio de Cultura's Premio Marqués de Bradomin in 1985. In 1987 alone he received three prizes: the Premio Ciutat de Granollers, Memorial Gregoir Resina for *Dins la seva memòria*; the Premi Nacional Ignasi Iglesias for *Elsa Schneider*; and the Barcelona Critics Prize for best direction for his staging of Josep Benet i Jornet's *Desig*. It is *Després de la pluja* that has been the most lauded of Belbel's plays, recipient of the Premio del a Crítica Serra d'Or for the best play staged or published in 1993, and the Premio Nacional de la Literatura Catalana for the best theater work staged or published between 1991 and 1993. *Morir* gained the Premio Born de Teatro in 1994, while Belbel's production of Georges Perec's *El aumento* received the Premio de la Asociación de Espectadores de Alicante in 1995. In 1993 Belbel's unique position as dramatist-director-translator was recognized by the award of the Premio Ojo Crítico de Teatro by Radio Nacional de España for his extensive body of plays. He has also received the Molière French Theatre prize for *After the Rain*, the French version of which was recently performed in Paris at the Theatre de Poche-Montparnasse Sergi. Belbel is an associate director of the Compañia Nacional de Teatro classico. He has directed Calderón's *El alcalde de Zalamea* in Madrid and Barcelona during 2000–2001.

NOTES

1. See Pep Blay, "Entrevista: Sergi Belbel," *Avui Diumenge*, 24 de febrero 1991: 6–7.
2. Sergi Belbel, *En companyia d'abisme i altres obres*, Els Llibres de l'Escorpí: Teatre/El Galliner, 116 (Barcelona: Edicions 62, 1990), 24.
3. David George and John London, "Avant-garde Drama," in *An Introduction to Contemporary Catalan Theatre*, ed. David George and John London (Sheffield: Anglo-Catalan Society, 1996), 95.
4. Interview with Sebastià Alzamora in *Diario de Mallorca*, 8 de abril 1994: 43.
5. Belbel was inspired to include the prohibition of smoking theme after spending seven desperate hours at the Romea Theatre in Barcelona reorganizing the set for *Car-*

ícies, where smoking was not allowed. See Santiago Fondevila, "Entrevista a Sergi Belbel," *La Vanguardia*, 12 de noviembre 1993: 48.

6. Interview with Sebastià Alzamora in *Diario de Mallorca*, 8 de abril 1994: 43.

7. Anon., "El teatre català es diu Sergi Belbel," *Avui*, 4 de enero 1989: 34.

8. *La Vanguardia*, 1 de noviembre 1992.

9. George and London, "Avant-garde Drama," 92.

10. Eduardo Galán, "Sergi Belbel: Artífice de la renovación escénica," *Primer Acto*, no. 233 (marzo–abril 1990): 82–88.

11. *La Vanguardia*, 30 de octubre 1993.

12. David George, "A Young Lad in the Arms of an Old Man—Sergi Belbel Directs Àngel Guimerà's *La filla del mar (The Daughter of the Sea)*," *Contemporary Theatre Review* 7.4 (1998): 45–64.

13. George and London, "Avant-garde Drama," 91.

BIBLIOGRAPHY

Plays: Collections

En companyia d'abisme i altres obres. Barcelona: (Els Llibres de l'Escorpí: Teatre/El Galliner, 116) Edicions 62, 1990. Includes: *En companyia d'abisme, L'ajudant and Tercet* (Catalan versions). The latter two plays have never been professionally performed, although they were performed by a semiprofessional Mallorcan group in 1993.

Plays: Original Stage Works (In Order of Performance)

Calidoscopios y faros de hoy (in Spanish; produced Madrid, 1986). Madrid: (Nuevo Teatro Español) Centro de Nuevas Tendencias Escénicas, 1986; *André Gide/Virginia Woolf: calidoscopis i fars d'avui.* Barcelona: Millà, 1994, Catalunya teatral, 2a època (Catalan version).

La nit del cigne (L'impossible silenci) (in Catalan; produced Terrassa, 1986). *Els Marges* 38 (September 1987): 61–79.

Tu, abans y després (written 1986–1987). Unpublished.

Dins la seva memòria (in Catalan; unperformed to date). Barcelona: (Els Llibres de l'Escorpí: Teatre/El Galliner, 104) Edicions 62, 1990 (Catalan version).

Minim.mal Show. Written in collaboration with Miquel Górriz (in Catalan; produced 1987, Barcelona). Valencia: Tres i Quatre, 1992.

Elsa Schneider (in Catalan; produced Barcelona, 1989). Barcelona: (Biblioteca Teatral 62) Institut del Teatre de la Diputació de Barcelona, 1988 (Catalan version); *El Público* 86 (septiembre–octubre 1991): 81–137 (Spanish version).

Òpera (in Catalan; produced Madrid, 1988) (in Catalan; produced Barcelona, 1989). Unpublished.

L'ajudant and Tercet (written in 1988).

En companyia d'abisme (in Catalan; produced Barcelona, 1989). In *En companyia d'abisme i altres obres; Primer Acto* 233 (1990): 89–109 (Spanish version).

Tàlem (in Catalan; produced Barcelona, 1990). Barcelona: Editorial Lumen, colecció

Teatre Català Contemporani—els Textos del Centre Dramàtic, 1992 (Catalan version); Madrid: Nuevo Teatro Español, no. 7, 1990 (Spanish version).
Carícies (in Catalan; produced Barcelona, 1992). Barcelona: (Els Llibres de l'Escorpí: Teatre/El Galliner, 127) Edicions 62, 1992 (Catalan version). *El Público* 86 (septiembre–octubre 1991): 16–78 (Spanish version).
Oh, San Francisco (written 1992). Unpublished.
Després de la pluja (in Catalan; produced Sant Cugat, 1993). Barcelona: Lumen colleción Teatre Català Contemporani, 1993 (Catalan version); Alicante: Gil Albert, 1994 (Spanish version).
Morir (Un moment abans de morir) (in Finnish; produced Helsinki, 1995); Valencia: Tres i Quatre, 1995 (Catalan version).
Ramon (in *Homes*) (in Catalan; produced Barcelona, 1994) (in Spanish; produced as *¡Hombres!* Madrid, 1995). Unpublished.
Al mateix lloc (written 1994). Unpublished.
La boca cerrada (in Spanish; performed by the Basque group Geroa as one of five short Spanish texts performed until the collective title *Por mis muertos* [1995]). Published in *Sibila* (Seville, February 1996).
Sóc lletja. Written in collaboration with Jordi Sànchez (in Catalan; produced Barcelona, 1997). Barcelona: (Els Llibres de l'Escorpí: Teatre/El Galliner, 158) Edicions 62, 1997.
La sang (in Catalan; produced in Barcelona, 1999).
El temps de Planck. Written in collaboration with Oscar Roig; produced in Barcelona, 2000.

Translations (by Belbel)

Fedra. Trans. into Catalan from the play by Jean Racine. Unpublished.
L'augment. Trans. into Catalan from the play by Georges Perec (produced Barcelona, 1988). Unpublished.
Passos. Trans. into Catalan from the play by Samuel Beckett (produced Barcelona, 1990). Unpublished.
Combat de negre y de gossos. Trans. into Catalan from the play by Bernard-Marie Koltès (produced Barcelona, 1998). Barcelona: Biblioteca Teatral del Institut del Teatre 61, 1988.
Combate de negro y de perros. Trans. into Spanish from the play by Bernard-Marie Koltès (produced Madrid, 1990). Madrid: Publicaciones del Centro Dramático Nacional, 1990.
En la soledad de los campos de algodón. Trans. into Spanish from the play by Bernard-Marie Koltès (produced Madrid, 1990). Unpublished.
La nit just abans dels boscos. Trans. into Catalan from the play by Bernard-Marie Koltès (produced Barcelona, 1993). Barcelona: Biblioteca Teatral del Institut del Teatre, 1993.
En la solitud dels camps de cotó. Trans. into Catalan from the play by Bernard-Marie Koltès (produced Barcelona, 1995). Valencia: Tres i Quatre, 1995.
L'hostalera. Trans. into Catalan from the play by Carlo Goldoni (produced Barcelona, 1995).
L'avar. Trans. into Catalan from the play by Molière (produced Barcelona, 1996).

Tabataba i altres textos. Trans. into Catalan from the play by Bernard-Marie Koltès and performed under the collective title *Perifèria Koltès* (produced Barcelona, 1998).

Rumors. Trans. into Catalan from the play by Neil Simon (performed Palma de Mallorca, 1999).

Translations (into English of Belbel's work)

After the Rain [Després de la pluja]. Trans. by Xavier Rodríguez Rosell, David George and John London. London: Methuen, 1996.

"Carresses" [Carícies]. First scene trans. Dominic Keown. Unpublished.

Carresses. Trans. John London. London: NickHern Books, 1999.

Fourplay (translation of *Tàlem*), by Sharon Feldman. Published with translations of three other contemporary Catalan plays by Methuen, 2000.

Deep Down (Eh companyia d'abisme). Trans. John London. *Modern International Drama* 26.2 (1993): 5–24.

Television

Adaptation of *Secrets de família*, by Ma Mercè Roca. Catalan television, 1995.

Ivern, series for Catalan television, 1996–1997.

Critical Studies

Blay, Pep. "Entrevista: Sergi Belbel." *Avui Diumenge* (24 de febrero 1991): 6–7.

Galán, Eduardo. "Sergi Belbel: Artífice de la renovación escénica." *Primer Acto*, no. 233 (marzo–abril 1990): 82–88.

George, David. "A Young Lad in the Arms of an Old Man—Sergi Belbel Directs Àngel Guimerà's *La filla del mar (The Daughter of the Sea).*" *Contemporary Theatre Review* 7.4 (1998): 45–64.

George, David, and John London, eds. *An Introduction to Contemporary Catalan Theatre.* Sheffield: Anglo-Catalan Society, 1996.

Orja, Joan. *Fahrenheit 212: Una aproximación a la literatura catalana recent.* Barcelona: Edicions de la Magrana, 1989, 103–106.

JACINTO BENAVENTE
(1866–1954)

John Dowling

BIOGRAPHY

Born in Madrid on August 12, 1866, into an upper-middle-class family, Jacinto Benavente y Martínez spent most of his life in his native city and died there on July 14, 1954. His father, Mariano Benavente, came from a family of modest circumstances. He studied medicine, becoming one of the first Spanish physicians to specialize in children and distinguishing himself as the author of scientific articles. The year that his third child, Jacinto, was born, his bust was placed in the Buen Retiro park, not far from the Niño Jesús Hospital where he served as director. Through his practice, the father cared for the children of rich bourgeois and aristocrat alike so that the family was familiar with the gamut of Madrid's upper classes. The Benaventes were also friendly with writers like Juan Valera and José Echegaray, politicians like Bravo Murillo and Francisco Silvela, and theatrical figures like Antonio Vico and Mario Calvo. Such were the people that Jacinto would later portray on the stage, where on occasion he would join the actors, satirizing a society that he knew intimately. Don Mariano died when his son Jacinto was nineteen years old. The youth dropped his legal studies and devoted himself to the life of a *señorito*, rich young man about town, tempered by serious reading of literature and travel in Europe.

In 1892, when Benavente was twenty-six years old, he published *Teatro fantàstico* [Fantastic Theater], a collection of four plays, one of which, *El encanto de una hora*, [The Magic of an Hour] (1905), was later produced.[1] The next year he published *Cartas de mujeres* [Letters from Women] (1893), imaginary letters that foretold the young man's understanding of the feminine psyche that he was to confirm when he undertook his career of writing for the theater.

Then, on October 6, 1894, when Benavente was twenty-eight, the actors Carmen Cobeña and Emilio Thuillier, under the direction of Emilio Mario, presented his first full-length play at the Teatro de la Comedia in Madrid. *El nido ajeno* [The Intruder)] depicts the return from the new world of Manuel, a rich, handsome bachelor, who lodges with his older brother, José Luis, recently married to María. The inevitable happens. Manuel is attracted to María, but the conflict is resolved when he moves out. The production was not an immediate hit, but it had the elements that were to lead Benavente to success: good actors, good direction, a good theater, a simple action, and sound psychology. These were the characteristics of Benavente's theater that were to appeal to the upper-middle-class audiences who frequented Madrid's best theaters in order to watch people like themselves on the stage. With such a formula and with outbursts of originality and creativity that carried him beyond his formula, Benavente held sway in the Spanish theater for sixty years.

His last play, *Por salvar su amor* [(To Save His Love)] was produced on November 3, 1954, a few months after his death in July at the age of eighty-eight. Pepe and Matilde, a poor but decent married couple, encounter Pepe's old school friend, Alberto, now rich and with a flashy American girlfriend, Letty. Alberto rescues them from Pepe's dead-end job, but he is drawn to Matilde. The two women avoid a conflict between their men by conniving to send them together on a business trip to the United States while they keep each other company in Spain. Such is the slender thread of action on which Benavente in many, many plays suspends his psychology of the sexes in order to keep his public interested.

First Period (1894–1912)

In earlier times, theatrical companies in Madrid were renewed during Lent to begin a new season on Sábado de Gloria—the evening before Easter Sunday. In more modern times, the season has run from September through August, with a high point during the Christmas season; a pause, sometimes prolonged, at Lent; renewal after Sábado de Gloria; and a waning during the dog days from early July to early September. After the performances of his first play in the 1894–1895 season, Benavente sat out the next. Then, with the 1896–1897 season, he premiered three plays, and the next season, two; after that, for ten years his production every season was from four to eight plays. They were the grandest years of a full life in the theater.

Gente conocida [Well-Known People] was first performed on October 21, 1896, at the beginning of the new season and, again, at the quintessentially bourgeois Teatro de la Comedia. Benavente's "scenes from modern life," as the subtitle reads, portray Spanish aristocrats and Madrid's upper-middle-class society. The Dowager Duchess of Garellano may disapprove, but she must accept the fact that her thirty-two-year-old son the Duke intends to maintain his liaison with his forty-eight-year-old mistress, a friend of his mother, while his marriage to an eighteen-year-old girl is being planned. The mistress, meanwhile, is about to marry a rich bourgeois while maintaining her liaison with the young Duke, whose fortune is not as great as that of the older man. The Duchess must also live with the knowledge that the husband of her pregnant daughter, the Marquis of Vivares, currently maintains a liaison with a certain Esperanza and borrows money from his mother-in-law to fend off his creditors.

But Benavente's satire was rarely mordant; he achieved his aim more by kidding than by biting. His aristocratic and bourgeois audiences saw themselves and their friends in his characters and situations, but they paid to come back for more.

His seventh play had more bitterness than others of the period, as its title suggests: *La comida de las fieras* [Food for Wild Beasts] was first performed on November 7, 1898. The date is significant, for Spain had just succumbed in its war with the United States. By the peace treaty signed in Paris on December 10, a month after the premiere of this play, it lost the final remnants of its colonial empire to an upstart republic in a hemisphere where it had once reigned supreme. Benavente belonged to the Generation of '98 that came to grips with the problem of Spain's place in the world and asked: Why had the nation sunk so low? As Ortega y Gasset, a younger man, was to do, Benavente laid blame at the door of the aristocracy and the upper bourgeoisie, who failed to provide leadership to the Spanish nation. In *La comida de las fieras* and other plays that were to follow, Benavente satirizes people more afflicted by foibles than by vices. Seldom will he create a tragic figure, but his comedy will serve as a catharsis for people who fail themselves and their country. They will pay good money to laugh at themselves and their friends and will keep coming to the theater to see themselves as Benavente saw them.

In the first decade of the twentieth century, Benavente added some sixty plays to his repertoire, including many that are good and several that are excellent. Among the good ones was *Lo cursi*, produced at the Teatro de la Comedia on January 19, 1901. Benavente dedicated it to the novelist and playwright Benito Pérez Galdós, who sometimes wrote about the same level of society that Benavente portrayed. "Lo cursi," that which is cheap, vulgar, or tawdry, was a word that flourished in the society of the Restoration (the last years of the nineteenth century and into the twentieth). It was thought to have been created by reversing the syllables in the surname Sicur of three Cadiz sisters who tried to be elegant but only appeared commonplace. The word and the condition were abhorrent to the bourgeois family that we see in the play: They are inherently "cursi," but they long to be distinguished and to exercise good taste.

In these years Benavente broadened the scope of his vision. Mostly, he scrutinized that Madrid society of bourgeois and aristocrats that he had known from childhood. But he selected other settings for many of his plays. In *La Gobernadora* [The Governor's Wife], premiered on October 8, 1901, at the Comedia in Madrid, Benavente invented his own provincial capital, which he ironically called Moraleda. It proves to be a town much like Madrid. *Los malhechores del bien* [The Evildoers of Good] was first performed on December 1, 1905, at Madrid's Teatro Lara, which also catered to an upper-middle class audience. The setting is a provincial port town where the ladies of distinction reveal their hypocrisy as they engage in acts of charity and do more evil than good.

Three outstanding plays belong to these years: *La noche del sábado* [The Witches' Sabbath] (1903), *Los intereses creados* [The Bonds of Interest] (1907), and *Señora ama* [The Lady of the House] (1908). The period of amazing creativity drew to a close with the performance in the 1909–1910 season of three plays for children. Two were given on December 20, 1909, at the Príncipe Alfonso Theater in Madrid to open the Christmas season: *El príncipe que todo lo aprendió en los libros* [The Prince Who Learned Everything from Books] and *Ganarse la vida* [Earning a Living]. The third, performed at the same theater on January 27, 1910, was *El nietecito* [The Grandson], inspired by a Grimm brothers tale. Then for three seasons, Benavente, the most prominent Spanish dramatist of his day, who had become a fixture of the Madrid theater, was barely represented: one play of his own, a translation of Shakespeare's *King Lear*, and a monologue.

He himself did not disappear from the literary scene, however. During these years he wrote for newspapers and lectured; and he was, as always, the man about town. Benavente was a small man, who wore lifts in his shoes to give himself height. He was dapper, he wore a toupee, and he cultivated a broad mustache and a goatee. He was known for big Havana cigars. He was devoted to his widowed mother. He never married, though there was a story of a love affair with a circus performer, a Britisher known as "the beautiful Geraldine." Gossip circulated for years of a long-term affair with a leading actress who introduced many of his plays, Rosario Pino, who was estranged from her husband, a minor actor. Benavente gave the name Villa Rosario to his retreat in the village of Aldeaencabo, province of Toledo; and a girl in the village whom he called his godchild was named Rosarito. He once traveled with a circus, and two of his plays deal with circus life: *La fuerza bruta* [Brute Force] (1908; and as a musical, 1919) and *Los cachorros* [The Cubs] (1918). His biography was his life in the theater.

Second Period (1913–1923)

In the 1913–1914 season Benavente returned to the Madrid stage with a masterpiece: *La malquerida* [The Ill-Beloved], known in its American production as *The Passion Flower* (1920). Its premiere was at the Princesa Theater (today's María Guerrero), Madrid, on December 13, 1913. Benavente dedicated the printed text to the great María Guerrero, who created the role of Raimunda.

Of more than twenty other plays produced in this period, a few have merited the esteem of retrospective criticism: *La propia estimación* [Self-Esteem] (1915), *El mal que nos hacen* [The Evil They Do Us] (1917), *La honra de los hombres* [Honor among Men] (1919), and the children's play *La Cenicienta* [Cinderella] (1919), a dramatic version of the fairy tale. A sequel to *Los intereses creados*, *La ciudad alegre y confiada* [The Happy, Confident City] (1916), successful in its day, has been seen as inferior by later critics. In *El audaz* [The Bold Man]

(1919), Benavente achieved the difficult task of adapting to the stage the 1871 novel by Pérez Galdós.

Third Period (1924–1939)

Although Benavente had been assailed by self-doubt during his absence from the Madrid theater, he returned with a very good play, not extraordinary, yet typical of his work: *Lecciones de buen amor* [Lessons on Good Love] (April 2, 1924), a simple psychological play about upper-middle-class people, ably performed at the Español by Pepita Díaz and her husband Santiago Artigas. *Afilarazos* [Pin Pricks] was produced in both Buenos Aires (1924) and Madrid (1925) so that after three seasons' absence, Benavente reestablished himself in the Madrid theater. Except for a couple of years with no or only one premiere, he was back into his rhythm of two to four new plays a season. Critics have rated several as good to excellent: *La otra honra* [Another Kind of Honor] (1924), *¿Si creerás tú que es por mi gusto?* [Do you Think I Like It?] (1925), *El demonia fue antes ángel* [The Devil Was Once an Angel] (1928), and *Cualquiera lo sabe* [Anyone Knows That] (1935). *Para el cielo y los altares* [For Heaven and Altar] (1928) challenged the Catholicism of the Primo de Rivera dictatorship and was closed. Successful was *Pepa Doncel* (1928)—named for the protagonist—which returned to themes of earlier years: aristocrats and social climbers in a provincial milieu.

During the Spanish Republic (1931–1936), Benavente traveled to Russia, and the result was a play, *Santa Rusia* [Holy Russia] (1932) that was intended to be the first of a trilogy that he did not complete. When Spain's first divorce law was being debated in the Republic's Cortes, Benavente joined the fray with a comedy, *La moral del divorcio, conferencia dialogada* [The Moral of Divorce, a Lecture in Dialogue Form] (1932).

In 1936 came the Spanish Civil War. Although he was suspect to the Left, Benavente remained in Spain, living mostly in Valencia, which was held by the Loyalists. But he was silent, for theater is a social art, and the society that Benavente knew and criticized was fighting for its existence.

Fourth Period (1940–1954)

The brutal Civil War ended on July 18, 1939, with the victory of the forces of General Francisco Franco. Amidst grief and mourning, the Madrid theaters reopened, and old plays from Benavente's repertory were produced. In the next season, 1940–1941, he offered two new plays to the public. The first, *Lo increíble* [The Unbelievable], was typical Benavente: upper-middle-class characters living in comfortable circumstances in a provincial town and gossiping about their neighbors. Benavente's "carpentry" was, as always, superb; and Spanish audiences clung to old patterns. In succeeding years—the period of World War II in Europe and of Spain's slow recovery from its own war—he produced several good to excellent plays: *La honradez de la cerradura* [Behind Closed Doors] (1942), *La culpa es tuya* [It's Your Fault] (1942), *Espejo de grandes* [An Image of Greatness] (1944), *Nieve en mayo* [Snow in May] (1945), and *La Infanzona* [The Noblewoman] (1945 in Buenos Aires; 1947 in Madrid). The last, similar to *La malquerida*, was a drama on the theme of incest in a rural setting.

Benavente's publisher, Aguilar, began a series of the best plays of the season with *Teatro español, 1949–1950* (ed. Federico Carlos Sainz de Robles, Madrid, 1951). In the next five seasons Benavente produced fourteen plays, including the esteemed *Mater Imperatrix* (1950), *El alfiler en la boca* [The Needle in the Mouth] (1953), and *Caperucita asusta al lobo* [Red Riding Hood Frightens the Wolf] (1953). Not one was selected to appear in these annual volumes. Among the five plays in that first volume was the young Antonio Buero Vallejo's *Historia de una escalera* [Story of a Staircase] (1949). Benavente was superannuated; the renovation of the Spanish theater in the second half of the century had begun. Today, with the end of that century, the assessment of Benavente's role in the history of the Spanish theater is under way.

DRAMATURGY: MAJOR WORKS AND THEMES

Benavente belongs to a Spanish tradition of prolific playwrights that begins with Golden Age authors Lope de Vega, Tirso de Molina, and Calderón de la Barca, and in the nineteenth century, Bretón de los Herreros. Benavente made his mark with 172 plays. Yet his nearest artistic model, who lived just a century before, was Leandro Fernández de Moratín. Moratín created only 5 original plays, but he engaged his audiences, as did Benavente, with a simple plot and convincing psychological penetration of character. Verisimilitude was the key to Moratín's theater, and Benavente, like his mentor, captured the truth of the society that he portrayed.

It is curious that of the four recognized masterpieces of Benavente's theater, not one is typical of the milieu that was distinctly his. Of 172 plays, 78 are set explicitly or likely in the Madrid of his day, mostly among people of the middle class and the aristocracy. Of 25 plays set in the provinces, most portray middle-class people or aristocrats. However, the characters in two of his best plays, *Señora ama* and *La malquerida*, recognized as masterpieces, are farm folk. They are well-to-do, to be sure, but they are far from the salons of Madrid or provincial capitals. The other two plays that have been called masterpieces are likewise distinct and very different from the others and from each other. The scene of *La noche del sábado* is laid in an international resort, and the characters form a bizarre gathering. *Los intereses creados* is a fantasy with characters from the Italian *commedia dell'arte* tradition, and the moral lesson is both serious and cynical. Three of the plays belong to Benavente's first period, that is, the first decade of the century when he was reaching toward maturity. The fourth, *La malquerida*, initiated his second period.

It is possible, even likely, that scholars will rediscover other plays by Benavente that truthfully and psychologically portray Spanish urban society in the first half of the twentieth century in such a way as to merit a renewal of esteem. Out of the array of his works, some may emerge that provide a valuable perspective nowhere else so well expressed. For the time being, the four works cited must be deemed his best. Two require brief description. Two merit more extended treatment.

The first of these was *La noche del sábado* [The Witches' Sabbath], performed March 17, 1903, at the Teatro Español, with María Guerrero in the role of Imperia, heading a cast of forty-four actors plus extras: princes, aristocrats, ladies, gentlemen, artists, circus performers, sailors, gypsies, servants, and police. The scene is an international "winter resort between Italy and France." It is a fantasy world that links Benavente, correctly associated with the Generation of '98, to the modernist movement of Rubén Darío in Spanish America and Spain. Critics have praised the spectacle, the dialogue, the expression of ideas. In English, it was produced in London, and Eva Le Gallienne played Imperia in New York in 1926. In Spanish, it held the stage for many years and was included in the repertory of the touring company that Benavente accompanied to America in 1922–1923 with Lola Membrives in the role of Imperia.

For some critics, *Señora ama*, premiered at the Princesa Theater, Madrid, on February 22, 1908, is Benavente's best work. In it he does for Spanish country life what he was doing at the same time for city life. The characters speak in the dialect of rural Castile, but their actions are not much different from those in *Gente conocida*. Dominica—the lady of the house—and her husband Feliciano live in comfortable circumstances, each having brought to the marriage a fair amount of property. Feliciano is a country Don Juan who has impregnated several of the young women around the countryside, but he and Dominica have no children of their own. They do arrange to get husbands for the women, and they provide for the children. Dominica defends her husband against gossip and even seems to take pride in his philandering. Feliciano for his part has been careful, as he confides in his best friend, Pilaro, not to get involved with María Juana. She is the illegitimate daughter of Dominica's father Tío Aniceto, and she is expected to marry Feliciano's brother José. There is even more scandal to gossip about so that one of the women who is taking part in the conversation is led to exclaim: "¡Yo me pasmo de oír estas cosas! Nunca creí que en lugares tan humildes fuera tanta la corrupción de costumbres" [I am taken aback to hear this stuff! I never believed that the corruption of manners was so great in such humble places].[2] In the third act, Dominica has become pregnant, and she asserts herself in a reversal that has earned the play the favor of critics who appreciate Benavente's treatment of feminine psychology. Its initial success owed much to Carmen Cobeña in the role of Dominica. She was the actress who, almost a dozen years before, had introduced Benavente to the Madrid public in *El nido ajeno*.

Los intereses creados (1907)

Leandro and Crispín come, as the latter puts it, to "two cities," explaining that one is "for people who arrive with money and the other for persons like us" (19).[3] Crispín is a roguish servant who belongs as much to the Spanish picaresque tradition as to the Italian *commedia dell'arte*. The two men are well dressed, and when Leandro wishes they had sold their clothes for the money they desperately need, Crispín declares, "I would sooner shed my skin than my good clothes" (21). When Leandro professes to feel faint-hearted—the role was created by an actress, Clotilde Domus, and is usually played by a woman—Crispín suggests that he should talk as little as possible but be very impressive. They must, he says, make the most of their talents and their effrontery, "for without effrontery talents are of no use" (21). Finding themselves before an inn on the main square, Crispín shouts boldly for attention. He persuades the Innkeeper that Leandro is a rich and powerful nobleman, traveling incognito with eight carts of baggage to follow, and is favoring him by choosing to lodge at his inn. When the Captain and the poet Arlequín stop by—Arlequín has written a sonnet praising the Innkeeper's stewed partridges and hare pie, although he has not tasted them—they too are convinced that Leandro is a great gentleman. The Captain laments that the "soldier's sword like the poet's lyre, is little valued in this city of merchants and traders" (35). Nevertheless, thanks to the credit that Crispín and Leandro are establishing at the inn and with Arlequín and the Captain, soon the whole city—a city much like Madrid—knows of Leandro's arrival.

Meanwhile, in another part of town, Doña Sirena, whose profession, like Celestina's, is to bring men and women together, laments to her maid Colombina that her credit is so poor that the caterers will not provision her evening party. Crispín changes that; with the help of Arlequín and the Captain, music, food, and drink are brought in for the guests who are eager to meet Leandro. Also expected is the rich Polichinela with his wife and his only daughter, Silvia, the richest heiress in the city. "My master," Crispín confides in Colombina, "has to fall in love with her, my master has to marry her; and my master will know how to reward in fitting fashion the good offices of Doña Sirena and yourself" (65).

The bonds of interest are encoiling the people of the city. Polichinela arrives late at the party with wife and daughter. Like husbands everywhere, he blames his wife, but with the self-satisfaction of the *nouveau riche*: "The delay was not my fault. It was my wife's, who, out of forty gowns to choose from, could never make up her mind which to put on" (79). While Doña Sirena takes Silvia to meet Leandro, Crispín accosts Polichinela as an old acquaintance. They once knew each other, it appears, as fellow galley slaves.

"Impudent scoundrel!" cries Polichinela. "Silence or . . ."

"Or you will do with me as you did with your first master in Naples," coolly responds Crispín, "and with your first wife in Bologna, and with that Jewish merchant in Venice . . ." (83).

When Crispín encounters Leandro later at the party, Leandro confesses his feelings after meeting Silvia: "You wanted me to pretend to be in love, but I have not been able to pretend it. . . . Because I really love her with all my heart. . . . I never believed it possible a man could love like this" (91). Even when Silvia comes with Doña Sirena to the house Leandro has rented and he confesses his lie to her, she returns his passion. She remains at his house while he goes in search of her mother.

The dénouement unfolds as the clever Crispín had planned it. The creditors demand their money. He makes them realize that they can get it only from the rich father. Polichinela resists until a curtain is drawn revealing Silvia and Leandro, Señora Polichinela and Doña Sirena, and Colombina. "Marry them! Get them married!" shout all. The Doctor—a lawyer—is ready with a document; by changing only a comma, he can apply it to the new circumstances.

Silvia has the last words of the play, which she directs to the audience. In this farce, she says, you have seen

how these puppets have been moved by plain and obvious strings . . . which were their interests, their passions, and all the illusions and petty miseries of their state. . . . But into the hearts of all there descends sometimes from heaven an invisible thread . . . of love, which makes these men and women, as it does these puppets, . . . almost divine and . . . lends wings to our drooping spirits, and whispers . . . that this farce is not all farce, that there is something noble, something divine in our lives which is true and eternal and shall not end when the farce of life shall end. (169)

Critics observe how rich the play is in literary allusion. They point to masters and servants in Latin comedy and to the multitude of pairs to be found on the stage in modern times: Mosca and Volpone in Ben Jonson's comedy (1605); Scapin and Léandre (like Benavente's Leandro) in Molière's *Les Fourberies de Scapin* (1671); Crispin (like Benavente's Crispín) and Éraste in Jean-François Regnard's *Le Légataire universel* (1708); Figaro and the Comte Almaviva in Beaumarchais's *Le Barbier de Séville* (1775). In our world, in which masters and servants hardly exist, it is curious to note Crispín's disquisition to Colombina on Leandro's character and his own. "We all have within ourselves a great and splendid gentleman of lofty hopes and towering ideals, capable of everything that is noble and everything that is good . . . and by his side, a humble and vile servant, who employs himself in the base actions to which we are enforced by life" (67). "The art of living," Crispín goes on to say, "is so to separate the two that when we fall into any ignominy we can always say: 'It was not my fault; it was not I. It was my servant.' "

Crispín's words—Benavente's words—have a special meaning when we know that the work that most likely gave impetus to *Los intereses creados* was Lope de Vega's *El caballero de Illescas* (ca. 1602), as the critic Dámaso Alonso has shown. The protagonist of the Lope play, Juan Tomás, encompasses both the noble and the vile in his persona. He led a depraved life before he arrived in Naples, where he passed for a gentleman of substance. He pretended to court Octavia, daughter of Count Antonio, who opposed the alliance. Together Juan Tomás and Octavia flee to Spain, and his feigned love becomes true, just as does Leandro's. He confesses his deception to her, she affirms her affection for him, and, after a series of incidents, the Count assents to the marriage.

"Believe me," says Crispín (a role that Benavente himself liked to play) as the farce ends, "the ties of love are as nothing compared to the bonds of interest" (169). Is Benavente a cynic, or is he being realistic? Leandro protests: "[W]ithout the love of Silvia, I should never have been saved" (169). Crispín, who had earlier exulted, "Who shall overcome us / when love beats the drum?" (103), counters with his own point of view: "I have always given due credit to the ideal, and I count upon it always" (169).

La malquerida (1913)

Some critics have called *La malquerida* a "rural tragedy" or a "domestic tragedy." Others have hesitated to denominate it a tragedy. Whether it is called a murder mystery, a melodramatic portrayal of a disaster, or otherwise, it is an impressively well-constructed drama.

The setting for the first act is a room in the house of a rich farm family located in the outskirts of a village in Castile. The second and third acts, which take place after the murder, are set in the entrance hall of the farmhouse where the family has sought isolation from the uproar in the village.

The exposition is simple. As the play opens, Raimunda, the mother, and Acacia, her daughter by a first marriage, are saying goodbye to friends—Gaspara and Bernabea among them—who have come to attend the engagement party of Acacia. Other friends—Doña Isabel and her daughter Milagros, together with neighbors, Engracia and Fidela—remain to chat a while longer.

The men—host and guests—have remained outdoors. Esteban, Raimunda's second husband, brings in Faustino with his father Tío Eusebio. They are from another village, Encinar, and the mother stayed home because poor eyesight makes it difficult for her to ride after dark. Young Faustino has forgotten until now to leave a second gift that he brought for Acacia, a scapular made by the nuns at Encinar especially for her. With that accomplished, all the guests but Milagros leave; she stays to keep Acacia company. Esteban sets out to go part way with Faustino and Tío Eusebio.

Acacia and Milagros sit by a chest to look at Acacia's things. Several are gifts from her stepfather Esteban, whom she refuses to call "father" as her mother wants. Norberto's last letter is there, too; and she tears it up and burns it in the lamp. She opens the window to throw away the ashes, and the two hear a distant shot. It is the point of departure for a plot that is built on disclosure and recognition. Shortly, the house is filled with people. Faustino is dead. Someone did not want him to marry Acacia. That someone must be Norberto. Act I ends on a note of high tension.

Days later, the family is now at the Grove, their country house. Tío Eusebio and Faustino's brothers threaten to kill Norberto, but he had a clear-cut alibi that the authorities accepted: On learning of the engagement party, he had set out alone with his rifle, intending to hunt; but he stopped at Los Berrocales to help his men with butchering and had spent the entire day with them. The town doctor saw him there and talked with him at the very hour the murder happened (227).[4]

Not knowing who the murderer is, people are fearful. Meanwhile, Esteban's farmhand, El Rubio, has been talking in town. When we hear the two of them speaking privately, we suspect that the hand that pulled the trigger was El Rubio's and that he did so believing that Esteban did not want Acadia to marry Faustino or anyone else.

Raimunda wants to talk to her nephew Norberto, and she gets him to come to her house. He is reluctant to speak, but from him she hears the song that leads her toward the truth:

> Whoever loves the girl at the Grove,
> is sorry to be alive.
> Because of who he is that loves her,
> they call her the Ill-beloved.

> El que quiere a la del Soto,
> tié pena de la vida.
> Por quererla quien la quiere
> le dicen la Malquerida.[5]

In Act III, tension rises as anagnorisis by one character after another leads to the terrible climax. Raimunda recognizes that her passion for Esteban was stronger than her love for her daughter. Esteban admits that he hungered for Acadia even while he lay in bed with his wife. We have been prepared for the final recognition by Juliana, who had foreshadowed Acacia's secret love for her stepfather, when she said that love had turned to hate. Raimunda cries for her daughter to throw her arms about Esteban's neck and call him father. Acadia embraces him, but she calls him Esteban and passionately kisses him. Raimunda cries: "Lip to lip, and you clutch her in your arms! . . . Now I see why you won't call him father" (266). Acacia confesses to herself and to all for the first time: "He is the only man I ever loved." With her world collapsing about her, Raimunda shouts Esteban's guilt for all to hear. He shoots her dead. The climax and the dénouement coincide, and the play ends, leaving the audience stunned.

The skillful use of light and sound in the play is notable, especially in the first act. As the women talk, a bell sounds for the evening Angelus, and they mumble the words of the prayer. Raimunda explains that neither Faustino nor Tío Eusebio will stay for supper. "There is no moon, so they should have been on the road long ago. It is getting late and the days are growing shorter. Before you know it, it is black night" (206). When Tío Eusebio enters, he excuses their prompt departure: "We must be off before dark" (206). When Doña Isabel leaves, she says, "Good night" (207), so that we suppose that the stage lights are gradually dimming. "Night is coming on," says Eusebio when he is urged to sit down (208). "It is getting dark," says Raimunda to her husband as he prepares to leave (209). A stage direction reads: "Meanwhile it continues to grow darker" (210). After Esteban leaves, Raimunda comments: "It is night before they start" (210). She tells Acacia: "Light the lamp dear. It makes me feel sad to sit in the dark" (210). When Acacia opens the window to throw out the ashes from Norberto's letter, she asks: "Did you ever see such a dark night?" Milagros exclaims: "It is black as pitch—no moon, no stars" (214). Out of the darkness is heard the shot. Who shot Faustino? "Nobody knows. It was too dark; they couldn't see" (216). Raimunda gives the order: "Light up the candles, Milagros, before the image of the Virgin" (217–218). We hear the women begin to tell the rosary as the curtain falls on Act I, which has been defined by dusk and darkness, dim light, religious chant by women, and a single, murderous shot. The drama ends with a second murderous shot.

Three characters require analysis: Acacia, Raimunda, and Esteban. Acacia is a desirable match: She is pretty and she is the heiress to the farmlands. "Your daughter," one guest tells Raimunda, "has had the pick of the entire village" (202). Doña Isabel observes, however, that "Acacia doesn't seem as happy as you might expect" on her engagement day (203). Her mother explains: "she is as innocent . . . as God made her. I never saw anyone like her; she is so silent. . . . For weeks together she has not one word to say. Then there are times when she begins to talk, and her tongue runs until it fairly takes your breath away" (203). After her father and Raimunda lost their sons, she was all they had and they spoiled her, so says one neighbor. Then, after her father's death and Raimunda's second marriage, which occurred too soon, Acacia confesses to feeling, she never got over the grudge according to another neighbor (203). Raimunda says that Acacia would never let her stepfather kiss her "even when she was a child, much less now" (204). Acacia tells Milagros, "I'd rather have been left alone with my mother" (213).

Everyone expected that Acacia would marry her cousin Norberto. Then he went chasing after another girl, and Acacia broke off their relationship. She does not grasp Norberto's rejection, but she understands the reason for the murder before her mother does. The scene in Act II between mother and daughter is superb (241). Of Esteban, Acacia says to her mother: "This man—this man is your husband; you love him; but all that he is to me is this man! . . . That is all he can ever be to me! . . . If he has sinned, he can pay for it. . . . Do you think I don't know how to guard my honor?" (241). She shows that she has understood her place in the house: "Would you have taken my word against this man, when you were mad for him? And you must have been mad not to see! He would eat me with his eyes while you sat there; he followed me around the house like a cat. What more do you want? I hated him" (241).

The old servant Juliana tells Acacia: "It was all your fault. . . . You were in love with him and you didn't know it. . . . A hate like that always grows out of a great love" (252). Juliana is preparing the way for Acacia's self-realization and the dénouement. Acacia asks: "Do you mean to tell me that I was in love with that man? Do you know what you are telling me?" (253).

Raimunda's character is less complex. She loved her first husband. Such is her passion for Esteban, whom she married soon after she was widowed, that her daughter feels left out. She disguises her passion as a practical need and out of gratefulness. Her brothers were victimizing her. "I didn't want to marry again. I should never have thought of it if my brothers hadn't turned out the way they did. If we had not had a man in the house to look after us, my daughter and I would have been in the street" (203). Raimunda is ever aware that she is mother to Acacia, and she is not jealous when Esteban brings his stepdaughter a gift and forgets his wife. She believes "it would be hard to say which of us loves or spoils her the most" (203), and she appears naive when she says that "it only makes me love him more to see how fond he is of her" (204). In the scenes with Norberto, with Esteban himself, as she comes closer and closer to the truth, she clings to the hope that the situation can be resolved, only to become herself the second murder victim.

Esteban wanted to be a good stepfather. The servant Juliana says that if Acacia "had been nice to him when she was little, he might have looked on her as his own daughter" (247). "If she had treated him like a father," Juliana laments. "I've seen him sit by himself and cry at the way the girl ran from him" (247). To his wife, Esteban confesses that the attraction he felt would not go away.

It became more fixed the more I struggled to shake it off. You can't say that I cast my eyes on other women. . . . But when I felt her by me my blood took fire. When we sat down to eat, I was afraid to look up. Wherever I turned she was there before me— always! At night, when we were in bed, and I was lying close by you in the midnight silence of the house, all I could feel was her. I could hear her breathe as if her lips had been at my ear. I wept for spite, for bitterness! I prayed to God, I scourged myself. I could have killed myself—and her! (260–261)

The play opened on a happy family occasion—outwardly. But each of the three main characters carried the seeds of destruction within. At the end, Raimunda is dead, Esteban will be charged in two murders, and Acacia will likely go to a convent. Benavente was known in the years preceding *La malquerida* for successive editions of his 1893 bestseller *Cartas de mujeres*, imaginary letters that revealed an uncommon penetration of feminine psychology. In the characters of Raimunda and Acacia, he confirmed that grasp. In Esteban and in the secondary and even in the protatic characters, he proved himself a master of human psychology.

María Guerrero, the most celebrated actress of the turn of the century, played the role of Raimunda, and her husband Fernando Díaz de Mendoza, that of Esteban. The part of Raimunda has long been a challenge as well as an opportunity for an actress when she reaches maturity. Acacia was played by María Fernanda Ladrón de Guevara during the second season after her debut, at a young age, on the Madrid stage. Her performance in *La malquerida* opened to her a long and successful career on both stage and screen.

CRITICS' RESPONSE

The critics of *El nido ajeno* and the plays that immediately followed dismissed the works of the new playwright. They were used to the dramas of José Echegaray, he of the tortured personalities, the contrived plots, and the gripping effects. Benavente gave the public low-key scenes from contemporary life. In time, by the strength of his own creativity, he won over the critics.

He did have problems with critics during World War I, a conflict in which Spain maintained neutrality. However, Spanish intellectuals tended to sympathize with France and the Allies. An independent Benavente did not conceal his Germanophilia and suffered a decline in popularity. A severe critic who emerged was Ramón Pérez de Ayala (1881–1962), a younger man, a novelist, poet, and essayist. His theatrical criticism he collected in two volumes entitled *Las máscaras* (1919). He included his acerbic critiques of seven of Benavente's new plays and two revivals performed between 1915 and 1919 (1: 105–213; 255–261). The dissension between the two persisted for years until it was dispelled at a meeting in the Argentine. Probably as a result of the posture of his critics, Benavente absented himself from the Spanish theater for a period of four years after *Una pobre mujer* [A Woman of the Poor] (1920), a play about poverty in Madrid and the indifference of the wealthy. He went to the Cono Sur with a theatrical company, and in Buenos Aires, he presented a single play and in Montevideo, a monologue.

AWARDS AND DISTINCTIONS

During his sixty years in the Spanish theater, Benavente garnered every significant award that was to be had. The achievements of his first period were recognized in 1912 by his election to the Royal Spanish Academy of the Language. However, he did not present the discourse required of an active member. In 1946, more than three decades later, he was named an honorary member.

In 1922, when he was still in his fifties, he was awarded the Nobel Prize in Literature. Word reached him where he was sleeping in a railway carriage on a siding in a remote Argentine town. He did not return to Europe to receive the award in person; the Spanish ambassador to Sweden accepted it for him.

NOTES

1. In most cases, the English version of titles of plays is that found in Peñuelas, *Jacinto Benavente*, pp. 163–174.
2. Act I, scene 4. The translation is by this author.
3. Page references of *The Bonds of Interest* are to the Underhill translation in the 1967 bilingual edition.
4. Page references of *La malquerida* are to the 1917 collection of *Plays* translated by Underhill.
5. The version is by this author. The Spanish is cited from the 1947 Manchester edition.

BIBLIOGRAPHY

Editions and Translations

Benavente's plays were normally printed shortly after they were performed, and many of them had several editions. None of these are given here; preference is given to the collected works. In the United States there have been several good school editions for the learning of Spanish. His authorized translator in the United States was John Garrett Underhill.

Obras completas. 11 vols. Madrid: Aguilar, 1940–1958. Most have appeared in more than one edition, sometimes with slight variants.
La malquerida. Ed. Paul T. Manchester. Authorized edition. 2d ed. New York: Crofts, 1947.
Comedias escogidas. Ed. Arturo Berenguer Carisomo. Nobel Prize Collection. 3d ed. Madrid: Aguilar, 1964.
Los intereses creados. Ed. Fernando Lázaro Carreter. Madrid: Cátedra, 1978.

Translations of Works by Jacinto Benavente

Plays. Trans. John Garrett Underhill. Authorized ed. New York: Charles Scribner's Sons, 1917. Contents: *His Widow's Husband. The Bonds of Interest. The Evil Doers of Good. La Malquerida.*
Plays. Second Series. Trans. John Garrett Underhill. Authorized ed. New York: Charles Scribner's Sons, 1919. Contents: *Beneventiana. No Smoking. Princess Bebé. The Governor's Wife. Autumnal Roses.*
Plays. Third Series. Trans. John Garrett Underhill. Authorized ed. New York: Charles Scribner's Sons, 1923. Contents: Theory and Criticism: Notes on the Plays. *The Prince Who Learned Everything Out of Books. Saturday Night. In the Clouds. The Truth.*
Plays. Fourth Series. Trans. John Garrett Underhill. Authorized ed. New York: Charles Scribner's Sons, 1924. Contents: On Theatre and Antitheatre. *The School of Princesses. A Lady. The Magic of an Hour. Field of Ermine.*
Saturday Night. Trans. John Garrett Underhill. Authorized ed. New York: Charles Scribner's Sons, 1926.

The Bonds of Interest (Los intereses creados). Trans. J. G. Underhill. Ed. Hymen Alpern. Bilingual ed. New York: Frederick Ungar, 1967.

Critical Studies

During Benavente's lifetime, a few books and many ephemeral articles appeared. At the time of his death, there was a spate of books and articles. Since then, scholarship on his life and works has been minimal.

Alonso, Dámaso. "De *El caballero de Illescas* a *Los intereses creados.*" *Revista de Filología Española* 50 (1967): 1–24.

Buceta, Erasmo. "En torno de *Los intereses creados.*" *Hispania* 5 (1921): 211–222.

Calvo Sotelo, Joaquín, and Gerardo Diego. *El tiempo y su mudanza en el teatro de Benavente.* Discurso leído el día 18 de diciembre de 1955, en su recepción pública, por el Excmo. Sr. D. . . . y contestación por el Excmo. Sr. D. . . . Madrid: Real Academia Española, 1955.

Cienfuegos, Casimiro. *Benavente y la crítica. Ensayos. Retrato y autógrafo de Benavente.* Covadonga: Editorial Covadonga, 1930.

Córdoba, Santiago. *Benavente desde que le conocí.* Madrid: Prensa Gráfica, 1954.

Guardiola, Antonio. *Benavente. Su vida y su teatro portentoso.* Madrid: Espejo, 1954.

Lázaro, Angel. *Biografía de Jacinto Benavente.* Madrid: Compañía Ibero-Americana de Publicaciones, 1930.

———. *Jacinto Benavente. De su vida y de su obra.* Paris: Agencia Mundial de Librería, 1924.

Mulvihill, E. R. "Benavente's Dramatic Technique." Ph.D. diss., University of Wisconsin, 1943.

Peñuelas, Marcelino A. *Jacinto Benavente.* Trans. Kay Engler. New York: Twayne, 1968.

Pérez de Ayala, Ramón. *Las máscaras.* 2 vols. Madrid: Saturnino Calleja, 1919.

Sainz de Robles, Federico. *Jacinto Benavente. Temas Madrileños,* XII. Madrid: Instituto de Estudios Madrileños, 1954.

Sánchez Estevan, Ismael. *Jacinto Benavente y su teatro. Estudio biográfico y crítico.* Barcelona: Ariel, 1934.

Starkie, Walter. *Jacinto Benavente.* London: Humphrey Milford/Oxford University Press, 1924.

Viqueira, José María. *Así piensan los personajes de Benavente.* Madrid: Aguilar, 1958.

Weiss, Rosemary Shevlin. "Benavente and Martínez Sierra on Broadway." *Estreno* 14.2 (1988): 30–33.

ANTONIO BUERO VALLEJO
(1916–2000)

Martha T. Halsey

BIOGRAPHY

The premiere of Buero Vallejo's *Historia de una escalera* [Story of a Staircase] in 1949 marked the resurgence of serious theater in Spain after the Civil War of 1936–1939. In contrast to the escapist fare then in vogue, Buero Vallejo's play about the hopes and illusions of working-class families in a dilapidated Madrid tenement reflected the painful reality of the postwar period. The play signaled the new direction to be taken by younger playwrights who felt an obligation to focus on the problems of their own time.

When *Story of a Staircase* opened, its author was virtually unknown. Born on September 29, 1916, Buero Vallejo studied at the San Fernando School of Fine Arts in Madrid before the Civil War and planned to become a painter. During the conflict he served in the medical corps on the Loyalist side, working under the direction of a Hungarian doctor of the International Brigades. At the end of the war he received the death sentence, which was later commuted to a long prison term. This was subsequently reduced to six years. Upon release in 1946, he found it difficult to resume painting after years of no practice and gradually came to realize that his deeper interest had always been the theater. *Story of a Staircase*, submitted anonymously, won Spain's coveted and most prestigious theater award, the Lope de Vega Prize. The premiere at Madrid's Español Theater, guaranteed by the award, was so successful that the traditional annual performance of José Zorrilla's *Don Juan Tenorio* was canceled, for the first time in theater history, so as not to interrupt its run. The play established Buero Vallejo's reputation as the first serious new playwright since the war.

During the Franco dictatorship Buero Vallejo had considerable problems in getting some plays approved by government censors, especially his antiwar *Aventura en lo gris* [Adventure in Grey], written in 1949 but not performed until 1963, and *La doble historia del doctor Valmy* [The Double Case History of Doctor Valmy], written in 1964, premiered in London in translation, but not performed in Spain until 1976, after Franco's death. After the Madrid opening of this play dealing with the torture and castration of a political dissident by a National Security policeman who later becomes one of the psychiatrist's patients, Buero Vallejo received death threats. However the work enjoyed a long and highly successful run. In the play, two of Dr. Valmy's former patients, acting as narrators, inform the spectators that the psychiatrist's story of torture is false or at least exaggerated. When the audience learns that these same patients—subjects of a prior case history—once interrupted to call the doctor a liar when he was telling the story of the policeman to a audience of other patients in his asylum, it is clear that these latter patients are the spectators, and the theater, the asylum. The implication was that if the spectators doubted the existence of torture in Spain, they were as insane as the doctor's patients.

Despite censorship, Buero Vallejo refused to make ideological concessions and continued to speak from a position of dissent. He endured the hardships imposed by a triumphalist and exclusionist Francoist culture that dominated the scene for some forty years and experienced the moral excision and marginality of those intellectuals who chose to remain in Spain. The reluctance of leftist writers to endorse any ideology that speaks from a position of power is well known; and after the end of the dictatorship Buero Vallejo continued to speak out just as sharply, or more so, than before, showing the grave contradictions and problems of Spain under the Socialists.

Buero Vallejo was Spain's foremost playwright of the second half of the twentieth century and perhaps the only genuine tragedian in the history of its theater. For more than two decades his plays have been performed regularly in Russia, Germany, Poland, Hungary, Rumania, Czechoslovakia, Sweden, Finland, Norway, and other countries. In Moscow he continues to be the only Spanish playwright to be staged in his own lifetime. Among internationally renowned directors who have staged his plays are Poland's Andrzej Wajda, Rumania's Liviu Ciulei, and Norway's Pål Løkkeberg. With the production of his *El sueño de la razón* [The Sleep of Reason] in 1984 at Centre Stage in Baltimore, in 1986 at the Wilma Theater in Philadelphia, and subsequently in Chicago, Buero Vallejo has begun to reach the professional stage in the United States.

In his lifetime, the playwright made several trips to the United States and lectured at major universities. His works are well known in academic circles for his articles and books of art and literary criticism such as his *Tres maestros ante el publico* [Three Masters on Stage] (1973), dealing with Valle-Inclán, Veláquez, and García Lorca.[1] His numerous essays on tragedy are also of considerable interest.

Buero Vallejo's first play, in which the unchanging staircase symbolized the fate of three successive generations who remained trapped in the same wretched situation, incorporated a tragic portrayal of human existence generally absent from twentieth-century Spanish stage. When Buero Vallejo began his career he expressed his view that the time had come for the theater to reflect the grave moment in history that Spaniards were experiencing and that what Spain needed was a return to the tragic sense or spirit that had characterized the most profound works of her art and literature: the paintings of Velázquez and José Gutiérrez Solana, the novel of Cervantes, the essays of Miguel de Unamuno, and the drama of García Lorca. All of Buero Vallejo's plays are tragedies that constitute critical inquiries into the problem of Spain and her destiny. At the same time, they are explorations of the human condition that are universal.

DRAMATURGY: MAJOR WORKS AND THEMES

Rejecting prescriptive considerations, Buero considers tragedy an expression of our struggle to free ourselves from the bonds—external and internal, social and individual—that enslave us.[2] Major obstacles to freedom are self-deception and unwillingness to face harsh realities. For Buero Vallejo tragedy does not imply any sort of radical pessimism but rather a desperate hope. He rejects the theories of Goethe, who maintains that the tragic vision has as its basis an antithesis that cannot be resolved and that any solution, or possibility of solution, negates tragedy; of Karl Jaspers, who affirms that to suggest any sort of rec-onciliation is to transcend tragedy; and of Lucien Goldmann, who calls tragedy ahistorical and contrary to the concept of the future, of progress, of realizable hope. Buero Vallejo's own tragedies reflect his understanding of the dialectical nature of history and are open in that they offer a degree of hope—however remote—at least for the audience, which must accept or reject the invitation the playwright extends to collaborate in creating a better future. His tragedies end with a question that only the audience can answer.

El tragaluz [The Basement Window] (1967), like *Story of a Staircase*, dram-atizes the continuing effects of the Civil War. The tragedy focuses on a family forced to take refuge at the end of the war in a dark basement apartment. The thoughts and actions of this obscure family are ostensibly represented through holograms projected by investigators from a future century. Spectators witness scenes that may be occurring only in the mind of a character seen lost in thought and thus are forced to identify with the character's point of view. Because of the presence of the investigators from the future, the spectators are also subjected to a sort of historical shock and, in judging the actions on stage, must also feel themselves judged for their own conduct and hence examine their own guilt. The structure of the drama underscores Buero's message: the solidarity of all persons with everyone who has ever lived, with past and future generations. Beginning as a portrayal of Spanish society of the Franco era, *The Basement Window* develops into an anguished inquiry into the human condition, into the mystery of the individual and of existence itself.

In his *El sueño de la razón* [The Sleep of Reason] (1970), which portrays the aging and deaf Goya in conflict with the tyrannical king Ferdinand VII, Buero Vallejo intensified his use of a subjective point of view on stage while exploring Spain's past. In *Las Meninas* (1960), he had pictured the moral and economic decadence, as well as the pretense and hypocrisy, of the Empire under Philip

IV—sad truths that Velázquez attempted to show in his famous painting. That drama ends with a tableau vivant of Velázquez's masterpiece as the audience is immersed in the moment, both fleeting and eternal, that the painting presents. The play is thus a mirror through which Buero invited the spectators to enter the world of the seventeenth century and, at the same time, the Franco period. *The Sleep of Reason* makes extensive use of the "immersion effect," a technique that has come to be associated with Buero Vallejo's name.[3] The phrase refers to an effect of psychic participation that allows the spectators to perceive reality through the perspective of a character or group of characters who suffer some type of physical defect or psychological abnormality. In *The Sleep of Reason* Buero Vallejo includes both possibilities. The audience shares Goya's deafness and his terrifying hallucinations. When the old man is on stage, the only sounds that are heard are the ones he imagines. His nightmares are fully externalized. Using a Brechtian multimedia technique, Buero Vallejo projects Goya's famous "Black Paintings," thus establishing the relationship between the aging painter's inner world and the artistic expression of his anguish. In all of his history plays, Buero Vallejo intends to stimulate an awareness of the tragic sense of Spanish history. Their originality lies in the fact that he makes historical distancing and emotive identification complementary functions of dramatic structure and establishes a dialectical synthesis between past and present. The end of the dramas is left open, for only the spectators can answer for the future.

La Fundación [The Foundation] (1974), one of Buero Vallejo's finest dramas, is the one play that he has said he had to write. Some twenty-seven years after his release, he used his observations as a political prisoner for the basis of a play. Other prisons had already appeared in his theater. *En la ardiente oscuridad* [In the Burning Darkness] (1950), set in an institution for the blind that is really a sort of prison, had pictured students who cheerfully ignored and even denied the existence of their affliction until a new arrival awakened them to a greater awareness. However, in no drama are spiritual blindness, self-deception, and alienation so clearly seen as in *The Foundation*. At the beginning, the action appears to take place in a room of an elegant center for research with a picture window opening on a magnificent landscape. At the end, the spectators find themselves in a prison cell and discover that the characters are not eminent writers and scientists with grants from a "Foundation" but political prisoners. The audience, although not realizing it until near the end of the drama, sees reality through the eyes of Tomás, a young prisoner who, unable to face reality, creates an illusory world. His gradual acceptance of the truth is represented visually by changes in stage decor as the pleasant furnishings of the "Foundation" vanish to be replaced with the sordid trappings of a cell. The set thus becomes a metaphor in movement. Since the spectators are forced to identify with Tomás, they, too, become victims of a delusion. However, when they participate, also, in his return to lucidity, their madness, like his, may result in a clearer understanding of their own situation.

The Foundation represented Buero's most extensive use up to that time of the "immersion effect." Since the audience sees reality through Tomás's eyes up until the final scene, he becomes, in effect, the narrator and the viewpoint, first person. When the set has been dismantled and Tomás's fictitious world has crumbled and reality has emerged, the spectators may see their own world for what it is and has been. At the end of the play, the cell is once again transformed into the elegant room seen at the beginning. Buero Vallejo thus invited his audience to reenter the "Foundation," together with its new inhabitants. The drama began all over. Buero's play constituted an attack upon political systems that deceive and enslave—upon the oppressive "Foundation" of the world. When Buero Vallejo himself was freed from prison, Franco's Spain was but another prison. The drama is also an expression of hope for a day in which a dark reality may be transformed into the luminous landscape seen by Tomás, who in his delusion saw a vision of what could become a future truth.

The marvelous Turner landscape the young prisoner Tomás sees, with its green mountains and meadows, clear sky, and sparkling silver lake, is the product of a delusion and, like the "Foundation" for scholars and scientists that he sees in place of the prison, is erased as he returns to reality. Nevertheless, the idyllic landscape seen through the window of the imaginary "Foundation" and accompanied by the serene Rossini pastoral functions as a symbol of freedom. Tomás's cellmate Asel—an author surrogate—tells the young prisoner that although he invented a rose-colored world, the landscape he saw is real. Buero thus expresses his hope for a better future that, even though glimpsed only through the eyes of delusion, may become reality. In the dialectical process depicted metaphorically by the drama, the reality of the prison vanquishes the imaginary "Foundation." Nevertheless, the ideal represented by the luminous Turner landscape remains.

The play is a commentary on Franco's Spain. At the same time, it is a parable of the human condition. The prisons of which Buero speaks in *The Foundation* are spiritual as well as physical. If the struggle for freedom implies a movement out toward an elsewhere, it also signifies a journey to an inner center where the individual must win a victory over the self. We see the movement toward an outside represented by the marvelous landscape. But just as important, we see the simultaneous movement inward: the quest for individual identity, memory, and authenticity as Tomás enters into himself. The journey toward liberation must be inward (in Tomás's case to his true past) and outward, through a series of concentric prisons from which tunnels must be opened toward an ever-brighter light. Of all Buero Vallejo's plays, *The Foundation* and *The Sleep of Reason* have brought him the most international acclaim.

In *Las Meninas* Buero Vallejo used Velázquez's masterpiece to make a powerful statement about an epoch of oppression and misery, of pretence and hypocrisy closely paralleling the Franco dictatorship. In *Diálogo secreto* [Secret Dialogue] (1984), he utilized another Velázquez painting, *The Spinner*, to express the tragedy of his protagonist, a famed art critic, and by extension, of Spanish society of the 1980s. Buero Vallejo's art critic, who is based on a case the playwright believes to be true, desperately conceals a terrible secret: He has always been color-blind. The audience shares the critic's affliction. As the latter gazes at the huge reproduction of *The Spinners* on his wall, its brilliant colors turn into lusterless ochre and sepia, somber browns and blues. This critic has made a victim, a young artist whom he condemned as a poor colorist; and when the youth commits suicide, the former must face the truth of the lie he has always lived. A series of secret or imaginary dialogues with his father, in which he accuses himself, are introduced by the brief "immersion" effects that communicate the critic's color blindness. Buero also communicates his guilt through his identification with Arachne in the painting. The critic imagines that her punishment was for weaving lies, that the defects she attributed to the gods were really her own. This is because the errors in color that he attributed to the youth were really the critic's own. Through his protagonist, who stands for anyone in a position of power, Buero renders a judgment on transition Spain, denouncing the hypocrisy, betrayal, and deception he saw present after two years of Socialist government.

In *Lázaro en el laberinto* [Lazarus in the Labyrinth] (1986), Buero used the image of the inextricable maze to suggest his protagonist's lack of freedom. The past that haunts Lázaro involves a student he loved twenty-two years earlier (about 1964) and who was beaten—fatally he will later learn—by fascist thugs after a protest demonstration. He remembers the past in two different ways. According to the first version, he intervened to try to save her; according to the second, he abandoned her to save himself. The labyrinth in which Lázaro is lost is thus the maze of memory where his doubts and fears hold him captive. When he hears that a friend thinks she is back in Madrid, he awaits her call to learn the truth. On several occasions Lázaro—and the spectators—hear nonexistent telephone rings as he awaits the voice that can "resurrect" him. The last possibility of a new life seems lost when Lázaro learns that the call will never come and when Amparo, a young woman he loves and sees as a new Ariadne who can lead him out of the labyrinth, reveals her belief that fear prevented him from saving the student and fear keeps him from accepting the truth of his cowardliness. The tragedy concludes with a startling "immersion effect"—one of Buero's best—as telephone rings that only Lázaro hears become louder and louder, awakening echoes all over the theater. The persistent rings at the end summon the spectators to examine their own conduct, to free themselves from their own labyrinths. Buero stated that the tragedy depicts a nation reluctant to recognize the errors of its collective past.

Música cercana (translated by Marion Holt with the title *The Music Window* (1986) features a ruthless executive, Alfredo, whose fortune—from sordid deals of which he feigns ignorance—permits him a life of luxury and privilege. However, middle-aged and lonely, he returns to his childhood home, with its window looking onto a courtyard where he hears melodies associated with a girl he once loved. Twice the audience shares his thoughts of Isolina, the girl he could possibly have made his wife, had he not let the opportunity slip by. As he becomes lost in memory, while listening to the music, the window to his back is suddenly opened by a charming young girl. These "immersion effects," in which the magical window opens silently in Alfredo's mind, are among Buero Vallejo's most original. Alfredo's other passion is his daughter, who will die after she is stabbed in the street. The tragedy consists of a series of revelations. Alfredo learns that his daughter was killed by an addict. Since he and his bank are involved in "laundering" drug money, he is indirectly responsible for her death. Alfredo receives a final revelation when, at the end, the real Isolina, now notably aged, appears at the window. When he whispers her name, she brusquely slams the window shut. To escape his meaningless life, Alfredo pins his hope on a route that leads, through a symbolic window, to an impossible past—a past that once could have been but was not and that now is impossible to recover. His situation suggests Spanish society in the late 1980s. Behind the bright facade of the economic boom, of a nation of frivolous big spenders and a cult of material success, is the reality evident in the references to alarms, locks, and the body-guards that Alfredo has follow his daughter. Spain has become another deceptive "foundation," that is, another prison.

Buero Vallejo's following play investigates the problem of coincidence in shaping human destiny. *Las trampas del azar* [The Traps of Fate] (1994) por-trays a young man who suffers nightmares involving shattered street lamps, whose full significance becomes clear only in the final scene. As a young boy, he threw a loose tile from his roof, shattering the lamp in front of his house, and although he heard a faint cry, he never investigated. He subsequently learns that, by a strange coincidence, his fiancée's back was horribly scarred by this same glass. Despite the repugnance he feels when he sees her back, he marries her. However, he never confesses that he threw the tile that disfigured her. A possible reason, it is suggested, is his desire to own the laboratory and factories that she will inherit. A major idea is the repetition of one generation's errors by the next. Although he attacks his father, a Francoist veteran of the Civil War who works in the laboratory producing war material, thirty years later we see that Gabriel, now middle-aged, profits from the same laboratory. Gabriel's judg-ment comes in the final scene. This scene, occurring in the protagonist's mind in the final moments of consciousness before his death, features another of Buero's startling "immersion effects." The audience sees Gabriel return to the street corner in front of his boyhood house. An old beggar, who has played his violin there for years, acts as Gabriel's alter ego, suggesting that the latter has dreamed of street lamps all his life to avoid dreaming of the victims of the arms from which he has profited. Matilde, it becomes clear, is only the first of those whom he has destroyed. As Gabriel approaches each of five lamps, its glass shatters; and the beggar makes it clear that the cries heard are of the countless people killed by the arms he helped produce. Gabriel lets himself be caught in the snares of fate that entrap him because he never has the courage to see himself as he really is until it is too late.

No image is so central to Buero's theater as is that of the prison, even though in only one play, *La Fundación*, is an actual cell seen on stage. The institution for the blind of *In the Burning Darkness*, the dark cellar apartment of *The Basement Window*, Goya's secluded villa in *The Sleep of Reason*, and the labyrinth where Lázaro is lost are all prisons of one sort or another. The elegant apartment with its bolts and guards in *The Music Window* is still another prison, and the title of Buero Vallejo's *The Snares of Fate* indicates the closing in of events that entrap the protagonist. If the playwright experiences an affinity for the idea of enclosure, immurement, or entrapment, it is because these states reflect his own condition and that of other Spaniards of his generation. These closed spaces are where the dialectical struggle between oppression and the dream of freedom that is at the core of Buero Vallejo's tragic vision occurs. The prison symbol carries its own contradiction within it. Like all symbols, it is potentially dynamic in that it implies reversibility. Prison walls imply an exit, and Buero Vallejo's purpose is to show the spectator this exit. For committed playwriters, to "unmask," to reveal the lies and hypocrisy behind the "Foundations" and institutions that oppress, is to issue an invitation to change.

CRITICS' RESPONSE

To date, there are over thirty scholarly monographs devoted to Buero Vallejo's theater. In his now classic *El teatro de Buero Vallejo*, Ricardo Doménech analyzes the thematics of the playwright's tragedies in their sociohistorical context. In this book he also coins the term "immersion effects" to describe the effects of interiorization that Buero Vallejo uses to bring the spectators to identify with his characters. This device—Buero Vallejo's answer to Bertold Brecht's "alienation effects"—has been studied by Victor Dixon in his excellent "The 'Immersion Effect' in the Plays of Antonio Buero Vallejo." In his pioneering book *La trayectoria dramática de Antonio Buero Vallejo*, Luis Iglesias Feijoo places what Doménech and Dixon call "immersion effects" in the broader perspective of structure, utilizing concepts from the study of the narrative. He shows that protagonists such as Goya of *The Sleep of Reason* and Tomás of *The Foundation* become first-person narrators since the action is for the most part the materialization of their thoughts. The critic shows that Buero Vallejo's theater constitutes a continuous experiment with dramatic structure. In *From Dictatorship to Democracy: The Recent Plays of Buero Vallejo (La Fundación to Músic certava)*. Halsey studies the recurrent symbol of the prison and the labyrinth in Buero Vallejo's plays but emphasizes the dialectic of freedom that reflects Buero Vallejo's dynamic view of history.

AWARDS AND DISTINCTIONS

Starting with *Story of a Staircase* in 1949, whose impact has been compared to that produced in the United States by Tennessee William's *The Glass Menagerie* (1944) or Arthur Miller's *Death of a Salesman* (1949), Buero Vallejo has authored some twenty-seven original plays. Virtually all have won awards. The esteem in which Buero Vallejo is held by writers and scholars of varying persuasions in Spain was evinced by his election, in 1971, to the Spanish Royal Academy. In 1978, he was elected an Honorary fellow of the Modern Language Association of America and invited to a special session in his honor at the organization's annual meeting. In recognition of his outstanding achievements, in 1987 he became the first playwright to be awarded the Cervantes Prize, an honor frequently referred to as the Nobel Prize of the Hispanic world.

If Buero waited more than thirty years to write *The Foundation*, based on his personal experiences in Franco's prisons at the end of the Civil War, almost sixty years passed before he dealt with another painful experience, that of the conflict itself, in which he fought on the Republican side. Buero Vallejo's final tragedy, *Misión al pueblo desierto* [Mission to the Deserted Village], (1999), constitutes a strong antiwar statement that returns to the pacifism of his very early *Adventure in Grey*. It deals with a Republican mission to rescue a painting of El Greco hidden in a village abandoned by both sides. The central action is the story of the rescue of El Greco's canvas being read to a cultural circle of our own time and reenacted on stage. This drama occurs within the outer drama of the debate by the circle over the story's relevancy to their own time. Since the lecture hall reassembles a theater, the spectators of Buero Vallejo's play are identified with the circle's members who listen to the tale; the action the spectators of the play see is thus what the members imagine.

Central to Buero's message is the opposition between Plácido—the village painter who wants to keep the canvas from harm even if that means leaving it for the other side, which, he also believes, will protect it—and the soldier who wants to fulfill his mission even at the risk of destroying the painting in getting it back to Madrid. Two debates show the contrast between the soldier's fanaticism and propensity for violence and Plácido's tolerance and pacifism. While the soldier, Damián, defends any atrocity—including murder and torture—for the sake of his cause, Plácido repudiates such crimes, stressing the need to reform the Revolution. Plácido, an author surrogate, rejects all violence and envisions a day when revolutionary goals will have been achieved through the legalization of new institutions—perhaps a reference to Spain's democratic transition of the 1970s. For half a century Buero Vallejo, who spoke out from the left, was the conscience of Spain, censuring both the injustices of the dictatorship and the insufficiencies of the new democracy. Now he stresses the need to reconcile the divisions remaining from the Civil War and to learn the lessons of peace.

NOTES

1. Antonio Buero Vallejo, *Tres maestros ante el publico* (Madrid: Alianza, 1973).
2. Antonio Buero Vallejo, "Sobre la tragedia," *Entretiens sur les Lettres et les Arts* (Rodez, France), no. 22 (1951): 83.

3. Ricardo Doménech, *El teatro de Buero Vallejo: Un meditación española*, 2nd ed. (Madrid: Gredos, 1993).

BIBLIOGRAPHY

Editions

Diálogo secreto. Madrid: Espasa Calpe, 1985.
La doble historia del Doctor Valmy. Mito. Madrid: Espasa Calpe, 1976.
En la ardiente oscuridad. Madrid: Espasa Calpe, 1993.
La Fundación. Madrid: Espasa Calpe, 1993.
Historia de una escalera. Las Meninas. Madrid: Espasa Calpe, 1993.
Lázaro en el laberinto. Madrid: Espasa Calpe, 1987.
Misión al pueblo desierto. Madrid: Espasa Calpe, 1999.
Música cercana. Madrid: Espasa Calpe, 1990.
El sueño de la razón. Madrid: Espasa Calpe, 1994.
El tragaluz. Madrid: Espasa Calpe, 1993.
Las trampas del azar. Madrid: Espasa Calpe, 1995.

Translations into English

The Basement Window. Trans. Patricia W. O'Connor. In *Plays of Protest from the Franco Era.* Madrid: Sociedad General de Libreria, 1981. 15–102.
The Double Case History of Dr. Valmy. Trans. Farris Anderson. *Artes Hispánicas/Hispanic Arts* (Indiana University) 1.2 (1967): 85–169.
Lazarus in the Labyrinth. Trans. Hazel Cazorla. In *Plays of the New Democratic Spain (1975–1990).* Ed. Patricia W. O'Connor. Lanham, MD: University Press of America, 1992. 381–479.
Las Meninas. Trans. Marion Peter Holt. San Antonio: Trinity University Press, 1987.
Three Plays (The Sleep of Reason, The Foundation, In the Burning Darkness). Trans. Marion Peter Holt. San Antonio: Trinity University Press, 1985.

Critical Studies

Cross Newman, Jean. *Conciencia, culpa y trauma en el teatro de Antonio Buero Vallejo.* Valencia: Albatros/Hispanófila, 1991.
Dixon, Victor. "The 'Immersion Effect' in the Plays of Antonio Buero Vallejo." In *Themes in Drama 2: Drama and Mimesis.* Ed. James Redmond. Cambridge: Cambridge University Press, 1980. 113–137.
Doménech, Ricardo. *El teatro de Buero Vallejo: Una meditacíon española.* 2d ed. Madrid: Gredos, 1993.
Halsey, Martha T. *Antonio Buero Vallejo.* New York: Twayne, 1973.
———. *From Dictatorship to Democracy: The Recent Plays of Antonio Buero Vallejo (From La Fundación to Música cercana).* Ottawa Hispanic Studies 17. Ottawa: Dovehouse Editions Canada, 1994.
Iglesias Feijoo, Luis. *La trayectoria dramática de Antonio Buero Vallejo.* Santiago de Compostela: Universidad de Santiago de Compostela, 1982.

Nicholas, Robert L. *The Tragic Stages of Antonio Buero Vallejo.* Valencia: Estudios de Hispanófila, 1972.

Paco, Mariano de. *De re bueriana.* Murcia: Universidad de Murcia, 1994.

————, ed. *Estudios sobre Buero Vallejo.* Murcia: Universidad de Murcia, 1984.

Ruiz Ramón, Francisco. "Buero Vallejo y la pasión por la verdad." In *Historia del teatro español. Siglo xx.* Madrid: Catédra, 1975. 337–384.

FERMÍN CABAL
(1948–   )

Candyce Leonard

BIOGRAPHY

Born in León on January 11, 1948, Fermín Cabal formed his identity as a playwright in the years he spent in the Independent Theater Movement which was at its height in the early 1970s. Initially, he was attracted by their efforts to defy conventional attitudes, to undermine the elitist social hierarchy, and to challenge the cultural imperatives of Francisco Franco's military dictatorship. Although his professional goal was to work in film, the acting experience of his school years and the friends he knew in theater circles influenced him to join Goliardos in 1972. One year later he became affiliated with Tábano where he spent the majority of his years with the independent theater. His initial contact with theater, however, was not as a writer. Rather, like other aspiring young thespians, Cabal did whatever was necessary—acting, accounting, or administrative duties—to keep the fledgling company afloat. While working with Goliardos, the Compañí monumental de las Ventas, or touring with Tábano, founding the Sala Cadarso and the Gayo Vallecano theaters, Cabal dreamed of a future Spain free from fascist rule. It was during these years of vital energy, enthusiasm, and creativity that he inadvertently launched his career as a dramatist. Unable to find dramatic works that conformed to Tábano's aesthetic and political imperatives, and already adept at writing dialogue and engineering scenic progression, Cabal joined his colleagues in writing collective texts. His own evolution as a writer caused him to end his alliance with the independent theater in 1978.

Among Cabal's first plays as an individual writer in the late 1970s were *Tú estás loco, Briones* [You're crazy, Briones]; *Fuiste a ver a la abuela???* [You Went to See Your Grandmother???]; and *Vade retro!* [Get Thee Behind Me!]. Some five years later in the published version of these three plays, Cabal observed that these texts typify his work after leaving Tábano. It was not until 1982 when *Vade retro!* was staged, however, that critics and audiences alike regarded his work apart from the independent theater. A definitive factor in Cabal's post–Tábano career was his association with two directors, Angel Ruggiero and Manuel Collado, who were instrumental in situating Cabal's theater within the post–Franco vanguard through their vision of his plays on stage. Ruggiero directed *Tú estás loco, Briones* and *Vade retro!*, and Cabal thought that he would never work with another director (Centeno, 1995, 8). In 1983, however, a collaboration with Manual Collado produced the stage triumph, *¡Esta noche, gran velada!: Kid Peña contra Alarcón por el título europeo* [Tonight, Main Event!: Kid Peña Fights Alarcón for the European Title], and affirmed his status as a dramatist. In 1985, Cabal and Ruggiero again collaborated to stage *Caballito del diablo* [Dragonfly], a play whose spatial and temporal structure as well as narrative flow reflect Cabal's continued interest in film, an interest that he was actively pursuing at that time.

Cabal lived in New York during 1987–1988. In addition to writing a dance script, "Jump Cat," for the Brooklyn Academy of Contemporary Arts, he accepted invitations to travel to numerous North American universities as a guest lecturer. Upon his return to Madrid, Angel Ruggiero prepared to stage *Ello dispara* [Shoot], Cabal's harsh denouncement of politics in contemporary Spain. Although *Ello dispara* referred to the Socialist government's death squads in response to Basque terrorism, a hotbed of political controversy that brought Socialist President Felipe González to trial in 1996, Madrid audiences showed little enthusiasm for the play's 1989 run. It was during this period that Cabal was dedicating most of his career time to film and television. This was due in part to his dissatisfaction, if not disillusionment, with the politics of theater scheduling and funding during the 1980s and in part to the monetary security that the newer media promised him. Despite this attraction to other art forms, Cabal continued to write theater and saw his next play, *Travesía* [The Voyage], win the coveted Tirso de Molina theater award in 1991. In 1993, the same year that he directed the premiere of *Travesía*, he completed his most recent play, *Castillos en el aire* [Lost Illusions]. Directed by José Luis Gómez, the drama opened in the spring of 1995 and reasserted Cabal's invective against Spain's political and moral values. *Castillos* was not only well received, but Cabal was named "Best Playwright" of 1994–1995 by Madrid's theater critics.

Some of the international stages where Fermín Cabal's plays have been performed are Greece, Colombia, Venezuela, Costa Rica, Germany, Portugal, Italy, Argentina, Russia, New York, and France. In spite of widespread international recognition and the translation of his plays into other languages, combined with the positive critical reception of his work, Cabal wrote primarily for television and film in the 1990s. Surprisingly, the fact that Cabal has chosen to limit the number of plays that he writes and to remove himself from the sometimes hostile atmosphere created by limited monies has had little effect on his powerful status as a playwright or the important effect he has had on burgeoning writers. Many younger writers credit him as their mentor, theater critics and contemporary Spanish writers in Spain acknowledge his valuable contributions to Spanish theater history, and scholars in the United States await his next play.

DRAMATURGY: MAJOR WORKS AND THEMES

Cabal's examination of the sometimes-delicate balance, but always definitive boundary, between good and evil resonates throughout his theater. His strengths lie in his vast capacity for storytelling, through both scenographic and linguistic modes, and his inexhaustible grievance against injustice. Although Fermín Cabal has a gift for making his audience laugh, entertainment is merely a byproduct of his sometimes-acerbic theater. His plays embrace both the hope and despair of his generation, a generation that once freed from Franco's dictatorship hoped to see their dreams for a more just society fulfilled, only to acknowledge that corruption infiltrates even a democracy. Thematically, Cabal's oeuvre preserves the critical posture of his independent theater days, whether tracing his own identity crisis during the transition to democracy in *Vade retro!* and *Travesía*, or denouncing moral corruption in *Esta noche, gran velada!*, *Ello dispara*, and *Castillos en el aire*. His plays examine both the powerful and the powerless through characters whose marginality or centrality to Spanish society defines their ambitions. Audiences readily identify with the contemporary language and problems that these characters embody.

Despite an eight-year interval between earlier and later works, his theater is united by recurring motifs. Written after the death of Franco, *Tú estás loco, Briones* and *Fuiste a ver a la Abuela???* illustrate Cabal's anger at the dictatorship. *Tú estás loco* lampoons Franco's regime through the protagonist's mental collapse during the transition from dictatorship to democracy. A Franco loyalist, Briones is unable to function apart from the fascist regime. At the play's abrupt close, he is accidentally killed in a psychiatric ward as attendants try to calm him. He therefore becomes a victim after all. In contrast, through use of a structure that manipulates time and space, *Abuela* chronicles a family's progression from the onset of the dictatorship to the early days of the democracy. It is a portrait of three generations affected by a society characterized by social, religious and sexual repression. These two early plays relentlessly inveigh against the despotic climate that Franco's regime produced.

Although written during the same period, *Vade retro!* surrenders the obvious anti-Franco rhetoric characteristic of Cabal's first two plays. The play premiered in Madrid in 1982, with a setting steeped in realism and humor. Two priests of different generations examine their lives within the context of their respective social and religious experiences. The younger priest, Father Lucas, renounces his call to the priesthood, choosing an entrepreneurial venture as a restaurant owner, while the older one, Father Abilio, affirms his choice to remain with the establishment. The conflict resides at the most fundamental levels of personality and chronological differences and is played out partly through language, not unlike Ionesco's absurdist play, *The Chairs*. When Lucas pulls out a cigarette and asks Abilio for a light, then a half hour later pulls out a cigarette lighter and innocently and sincerely denies that he ever said that he did not have one, Cabal emphasizes the inability of the two men to communicate. This linguistic game of cat and mouse is repeated several times in the play before the conflict between the two becomes physical. Imitating the famous sixteenth-century Protestant reformer, Martin Luther, who threw an inkpot at the devil in his study, Abilio hurls a sausage at the young Lucas when he finds out that Lucas has won the lottery. The moment is keen in its humor and poignant in its demonstration of post–Franco conflicts. In a metaphorical staging of the dark night of the soul, Abilio finds himself holding a knife to Lucas's throat in a sobering and dramatic moment that is broken by the ringing of the alarm clock. It is morning, and they amicably go their separate ways.

At an autobiographical level, Cabal sees the play as a crisis between conforming to a particular set of external rules and ideologies, and exploring other more personal options. Cabal perceived the independent theater of the post–Franco years to be yet another institution, with a set of criteria that no longer accommodated his professional or personal aspirations. He identifies himself as the young priest in the play, struggling to gain independence from an institution that was suffocating him (Leonard, 1987, 22). Divested of the author's personal interpretation, *Vade retro!* explores the transitional sociopolitical climate of Spain's early democratic history. His priests, invested with human frailties, mirror national crises. In a humorous but sobering self-examination, the younger priest's crisis of vocation represents the struggle of democratic Spain for a new independence from its oppressive past.

Written in 1981 and premiered in 1985 in the Círculo de Bellas Artes de Madrid, *Caballito del Diablo* [Dragonfly] is Cabal's most pessimistic play. Laying aside references to political repression, *Caballito* is firmly rooted in the drug culture of contemporary Madrid. Blanca, the protagonist whose names signifies both purity and heroine, seems to be the young adult who is most likely to fulfill the promises of a political and social democracy. She is immersed in the dark side of the democracy, however, and finds herself influenced, immersed, and contaminated by this dangerous element of her culture. Her death by drug overdose at the end of the play is Cabal's homage to his younger brother who also succumbed to the drug culture.

Caballito del Diablo is Fermín Cabal's most vanguard play and also the only one that appeals so directly to a younger audience. The spontaneous language of the young characters is truly colloquial and closely imitates the street language of the 1980s. The structure of the play is cinematic as the fluid scene transition associated with traditional theater gives way to breaks in scenes through the use of stage lighting. In his stage directions, Cabal writes: "The action of the characters should be superimposed, one scene upon another rather than by method of smooth transition," Such ruptured transition imitates the stage of being drugged, and it also reflects the internal chaos that runs through a society where freedom is dressed in the garb of drug addition.

With *¡Esta noche, gran velada!: Kid Peña contra Alarcón por el titulo europeo*, written one year after *Caballito* (1982) but premiered almost immediately (1983), Cabal experiments with a theater piece of greater commercial appeal.

Written according to traditional dramatic conventions, *Esta noche* elaborates the theme of social and moral bankruptcy. Kid Peña, approaching thirty and the end of his boxing prime, is within minutes of fighting a rigged match for the European title. It is a match that he must lose. While initially submitting to the scheme, after a "Dear John" from his girlfriend, Kid Peña loses all interest in the plot. When he finally agrees to fight, he is determined to win. Since his owners and other mob bosses have bet heavily against him, his moral victory seals his doom, and he is murdered shortly after he wins the title. Fermín Cabal's love of American cinema is reflected in the mob bosses and girlfriend who belong to 1940s Hollywood genre movies, and in Kid Peña, who like Marlon Brando's Terry Malloy in Elia Kazan's 1954 tour de force, *On the Waterfront*, wants to be a "contender" through his moral victory.

José Luis Alonso de Santos, Cabal's friend from the independent theater days, writes in the prologue to the play that the protagonist seeks to find his place in a filthy and meaningless world. The only rule of survival is to watch your back. In Cabal's view, democratic Spain had not been spared the pitfalls of human greed. Cabal's protagonists are innocent victims surrounded by fraud. When Kid Peña expresses surprise at the deceit that envelops him, his trainer admonishes his ingenuousness. Some fifteen years later, graft and cupidity resurface in *Castillos en el aire*, a play that achieves what Cabal's earliest plays had strained for. He suppresses his hyper-realistic style to build an energetic dialogue devoted to political commentary.

Martínez, the protagonist of *Castillos*, is older than Kid Peña and thinks he has a handle on the game of blackmail in a play that showcases how the game of corruption is played, and how some players more adept and successful at it than others. The characters have put aside the ideals of their youth and compete in a debauched battle over money, power, and turf. Martínez, the embodiment of both despair and hope, abandons the game, and through this act the moral triumph is his. The hope inspired by Martínez's character, however, is undermined in Cabal's metadramatic ending to the play when Martínez says: "A happy ending, just what the public is begging for." In other words, the play's happy resolution vis-à-vis Martínez's salvation is a sure box-office attraction. This reference could speak to the 1990 box-office failure of *Ello dispara*, Cabal's uncompromising reproof of Spain's failure to rise above corruption. Void of the author's characteristic humor, *Ello dispara*'s dark cynicism was more than either critic or audience could embrace in 1989. By 1995, however, *Castillos en el aire* seemed more palatable and its audience more receptive, perhaps because of the revelation and ensuing condemnation of the government death squads of the 1980s.

Castillos embodies the principal characteristics of Cabal's theater: humor, social criticism, and partisan dialogue. This play completes the trilogy begun in *Vade retro!* and continued in *Travesía*, a trilogy representative of Cabal's theater in general. These three plays follow the maturation of Cabal's generation from youthful cries for social justice to outrage at social fraud to resignation to the frailties of the human condition. Yearning for the ideals and optimism of youth, and acknowledging the greed that ambition and success breed, Cabal recognizes that even the smallest glimmer of hope redeems both his audience and his characters from complete depravity and despair.

CRITICS' RESPONSE

Since the late 1970s, Fermín Cabal has enjoyed the affirmation of theater scholars, audiences, and critics at both national and international levels. Numerous theater awards recognize the vigor that characterizes his theater, as well as his gifts for constructing dialogue and dramatic plots. Cabal's name invariably figures into discussions in Spain of the immediate post–Franco years for both his contributions to reshaping contemporary Spanish theater and his important influence on today's young writers. During the mid-1980s, he came to the attention of North American Hispanists whose studies of Cabal have appeared in a number of prestigious academic journals. Similarly, his theater has been a frequent focus of conference papers and other professional endeavors. Scholarly criticism is steady, yet no book-length analysis has appeared. While a key figure in contemporary Spanish theatre history, the lapse in his dramaturgic production between the years 1982 and 1989, and his yield of only two original plays in the 1990s has likely caused the temporary decline in research by North American scholars.

Cabal avoids alternative chic but refuses to acquiesce to commercial pressures. Critics applaud his sense of humor and dramatic strategies that break with conventional style (López Sancho; Tecglen), as well as his intrepid challenge to Spanish society (Alonso de Santos; Pascual; Siles). Enrique Centeno's introduction to Cabal's 1995 collection, which includes the play *Castillos*, provides not only an overview of Cabal's career, but also an insightful analysis of the author's thematic patterns. Sharon Feldman's theoretically based article on textual/theatrical space in *Ello dispara* confirms the substance of Cabal's theater, which readily lends itself to scholarly study, and Wilfried Floeck's analysis sorts Cabal's dramatic works according to dominant characteristics. Floeck concludes that the author's body of works rests on a tension between realistic and experimental theater.

AWARDS RECEIVED

1979: "Radio España," awarded for best play of the 1978–1979 Madrid theater season. *Tú estás loco, Briones.*

1980: "Long Play," awarded for best play of the 1979–1980 Madrid theater season. *Fuiste a ver a la abuela???*

1981: "Dos de Mayo," awarded in Madrid 1981. *Maladanza de Don Juan Martín.*

1983: "Premio Mayte," awarded for outstanding theater figure of the 1982–1983 Madrid theatre season.

1984: "Radio España," awarded for best play of the 1983–1984 Madrid theater season.
1991: "Tirso de Molina," 1991. *Travesía.*
1993: "Teatro de Rojas" awarded for best play of the 1992–1993 Madrid theater season. *Travesía.*
1993: Premio de la Crítica (Critics' Award) finalist for the 1992–1993 Madrid theater season.*Travesía.*
1995: Premio de la Crítica (Critics' Award) for the 1994–1995 Madrid theater season. *Castillos en el aire.*

BIBLIOGRAPHY

Dramatic Works

"Pérez. Un héroe de nuestros días." (1973). [Unpublished]
Cambio de tercio. (1976). Collective-writing text. Performed by Tábano in Spain in 1976. Madrid: Campus, 1978.
"El cisne." (1976). [Unpublished]
"¡Qué vivan las cadenas!" (1977). [Unpublished]
Tú estás loco, Briones. (1978). Performed in Spain in 1978. Directed by Fermín Cabal. Madrid: Fundamentos, 1982.
Vade retro! (1978). Performed in Spain in 1982. Directed by Angel Ruggiero. Madrid: Fundamentos, 1982 and 1987.
Fuiste a ver a la abuela??? (1979). Performed in Spain in 1979. Directed by Angel Ruggiero. Madrid: Fundamentos, 1982.
Malandanza de Don Juan Martín. (1981). Madrid: Fundación Banco Exterior, 1985.
Caballito del diablo. (1981). Performed in Spain in 1985. Directed by Angel Ruggiero. Madrid: Editorial Fundamentos, 1985, 1989, and 1995.
Esta noche, gran velada!: Kid Peña Contra Alarcón por el título europeo. (1982). Performed in Spain in 1983. Directed by Manuel Collado. Madrid: Fundamentos, 1985, 1989, and 1995.
"Chejoviana." (1987). Performed in Spain in 1987, adapted and directed by Angel Ruggiero. [Unpublished]
"Jump Cat." (1998). Performed at the Brooklyn Academy of Contemporary Arts in 1988. Directed by Fermín Cabal and Marga Guergué. [Unpublished]
Ello dispara. (1989). Performed in Spain in 1989. Directed by Angel Ruggiero. Madrid: Marsó-Velasco, 1991, and Madrid: Fundamentos, 1995.
Travesía. (1991). Performed in Spain in 1993. Directed by Fermín Cabal. Madrid: Instituto de Cooperacíon Iberoamericana, 1993, and Madrid: Fundamentos, 1995.
Castillos en el aire. (1993). Performed in Spain in 1995. Directed by José Luis Gómez. Madrid: Fundamentos, 1995.

Stage Adaptations

"La Cacatúa verde." (1973). Adaptation of Arthur Schnitzler's text. [Unpublished]
La ópera del bandido. (1980). Collective-writing version of John Gay's *La ópera del mendicante.* Performed by Tábano in Spain in 1975. Madrid: Ayuso, 1975.

"Sopa de mijo para cenar." (1978). Version of Darío Fo's *Aquí no paga nadie*. Performed in Spain in 1978. [Unpublished]

"El preceptor." (1980). Adaptation of Jacob Lenz's text, written in collaboration with Vicente Cuesta and Francisco Heras. Performed in Spain in 1980. [Unpublished]

Ahola no es de Leil. (1980). Partial revision in collaboration with Juan Margallo and Alfonso Sastre of Sastre's text. Performed in Madrid in 1980. *Primer Acto* (1980): n.p.

"La ópera de cuatro perras." (1980). Adaptation of Bertholt Brecht's text. [Unpublished]

"Veinticuatro horas del soldado Woyzeck." (1981). Adaptation of George Buchner's text. [Unpublished]

"Aurora de mi vida." (1983). Spanish version of Naum Alves de Sousa's text. [Unpublished]

"Y yo con estos nervios." (1989). Adaptation of Christopher Durang's *Beyond Therapy*. Performed in Madrid in 1989 and in Buenos Aires in 1992. Directed by Fermín Cabal. [Unpublished]

"El búfalo americano." (1990). Adaptation of David Mamet's text. Performed in Madrid in 1990. Directed by Fermín Cabal. [Unpublished]

"Estrellas en la madrugada." (1990). Adaptation of Alexander Galin's text. Performed in Spain in 1991. Directed by Angel Ruggiero. [Unpublished]

"Sabor a miel." (1991). Adaptation of Shelagh Delaney's text. Performed in Spain in 1991. Directed by María Ruiz. [Unpublished]

Entre tinieblas. (1992). Rewriting of Pedro Almodovar's filmscript. Performed in Spain in 1992. Directed by Fermín Cabal. Also performed in Lisboa in 1993 and Montevideo in 1994. Madrid: Sociedad General de Autores de España, 1994.

"La Estación." (1993). Free adaptation of Umberto Marino's text. Performed in Spain in 1993. Directed by Jaime Chávarri. [Unpublished]

"Mucho amor." (1993). Adaptation of Jean Paul Fargueau's text. [Unpublished]

Selected Works

"No hay que apretar." *Revista del Ateneo Puertorriqueño* 3.8 (1993): 46–55.

"Realidad en el teatro español." *El teatro se escribe hoy: Primer Congreso de la Asociación de Autores de Teatro*. Ed. Andrés Sorel. Madrid: Asociación Colegial de Escritores, 1992. 43–69.

La situación del teatro en España. Madrid: Asociación de Autores de Teatro, 1995.

Teatro español de los 80. Madrid: Fundamentos, 1985.

"El teatro español entre dos fuegos." *Estreno* 17.1 (1986): 21–30.

Translations

Get Thee Behind Me! Trans. Robert Sheehan. *Estreno* 14.1 (1988): 17–25.

Vade retro! Trans. André and Claude Demarigny. *L'Avant Scene de Paris*. 878 (1990). n.p.

Critical Studies

Alonso de Santos, José Luis. "Fermín Cabal: Un autor de nuestro tiempo." *Primer Acto* 196 (1982): 27–41.

———. "Fermín Cabal: Un autor de nuestro tiempo." *Primer Acto* 196 (1982): 27–41.

———. Prólogo. *¡Esta noche, gran velada!* By Fermín Cabal. Madrid: Fundamentos, 1983. 7–8.

Bigelow, Gary. "Fermín Cabal, cifra del teatro español actual: Fragmento de una entrevista," *Estreno* 11.2 (1995): 24–27.

———. "Interview with Fermín Cabal." *Estreno* 11.2 (1985): 24–27.

Centeno, Enrique. Prologue. *Travesía.* By Fermín Cabal. Madrid: Cultura Hispánica, 1993. 9–18.

———. "¿Una trilogía?." *Castillos en el aire.* By Fermín Cabal. Madrid: Editorial Fundamentos, 1995. 5–17.

Conesa, Maite. "Fermín Cabal: El teatro español tiene el pulso débil." *El Público* 68 (1989): 21–23.

Cuadros, Carlos. "Los viajes de Fermín Cabal." *Primer Acto* 251 (1993): 14–15.

Feldman, Sharon G. "Ello dispara de Fermín Cabal: Hacia una configuración posmoderna de espacio textual/teatral." In *De lo particuar a lo universal: El teatro español del siglo XX y su contexto.* Ed. John P. Gabriele. Madrid: Iberoamerica, 1994. 230–239.

Floeck, Wilfried. "Fermín Cabal y la poética de lo cotidiano." *Teatro Español contemporáneo: Autores y tendencias.* Eds. Alonso de Toro and Wilfried Floeck. Kassel, Germany: Edition Reichenberger, 1995. 339–365.

Giella, Miguel Ángel. "Fermín Cabal o el reencuentro del teatro español y el latinoamericano." *De dramaturgos: Teatro Latinoamericano actual.* Buenos Aires: Corregidor, 1994. 98–108.

Gómez, José Luis. Prólogo. *Caballito del diablo.* By Fermín Cabal. Madrid: Fundamentos, 1983. 81–84.

González Uribe, Guillermo. "*Caballito del diablo.* Contar en Bogotá la crónica de una juventud enganchada a la droga." *El Público* 77 (1990): 127.

Laborda, Angel. " 'Tú estás loco, Briones,' en la Sala Cadarso." *ABC,* 20 October 1978: 62.

Lamartina-Lens, Iride. "Sexo, drogas y rock y roll: Un estudio sobre la disidencia cultural en el teatro español contemporáneo." In *De lo particuar a lo universal: El teatro español del siglo XX y su contexto.* Ed. John P. Gabriele. Madrid: Iberoamerica, 1994. 211–218.

Leonard, Candyce. "Fermín Cabal y el teatro postfranquista: una entrevista." *Estreno* 18.2 (1987): 21–24.

———. "Interview with Playwright Fermín Cabal: From Dictatorship to Democracy to the Threshold of a New Century." *Western European Stages* 9.1 (1997): 47–50.

López Sancho, Lorenzo. " '¿Fuiste a ver a la abuela?', en la Sala Cadarso." *ABC,* 6 May 1979: 55.

Miralles, Alberto. Presentación. *La situación del teatro en España.* By Fermín Cabal. Madrid: Asociación de Autores de Teatro, 1994. 9–14.

Navarro, Ricardo. "Fermín Cabal." *Cinema 2001* (1983): 63–68.

Ortas Durand, Esther. "Metateatro y reteatralización en Fermín Cabal." *Cuadernos de Investigación Filológica* (1993–1994): 19–20, 39–60.

Pascual, Itziar. "El trozo de pan amargo." *Metropolí,* weekly supplement to *El mundo,* No. 257, 28 April 1995: 25.

Pérez Coterillo, Moisés. "Mesa Redonda con la Comisión de Teatro del PSOE." *Pipirijaina* 24 (1983): 22–28.

————. *"Vade retro!* de Fermín Cabal: Tentación venal." *Pipirijaina* 24 (1983): 44–46.

Perri, Dennis. "Fermín Cabal's *Tú estás loco, Briones*: Authoring the Self." *Estreno* 23.1 (1997): 29–32, 47.

Samaniego, Fernando. "Fermín Cabal plantea el conflicto de generaciones." *El País* 23 October 1982: 17.

Sheehan, Robert Louis. *"Get Thee Behind Me!* and *Mass Appeal*: A Case of Parallel Genesis." *Estreno* 14.2 (1988): 10–13.

————. "Tres generaciones miran la época postfranquista: Buero, Gala, Cabal." *Estreno* 13.1 (1987): 26–35.

Siles, Jaime. " 'Castillos en el aire.' " *Blanco y Negro*, Sunday supplement to *ABC*, 4 June 1995: 12.

Tecglen, Eduardo Haro. "Fermín Cabal, author de teatro." *Tú estás loco. Briones*. By Fermín Cabal. Madrid: Fundamentos, 1982. 7–13.

————. "Fermín Cabal y su 'Gran Velada.' " *El País*, 27 September 1983: 29.

————. "Vade retro! *El País*. 26 October 1982: 39.

Valiente, Pedro. *"Ello dispara*, de Fermín Cabal." *El Público* 79 (1990): 36.

————. "Fermín Cabal: Teatro para una vanguardia intelectual." *El Público* 78 (1990): 20.

Vicente Mosquete, José Luis. "Caballito: Fermin Cabal." *El Público* 21 (1985): 36–38.

Zalbidea, Victor and Carlos Cuadros. "Fermín Cabal." *Primer Acto* 251 (1993): 12–13.

ALEJANDRO CASONA
(1903–1965)

María M. Delgado with David Price-Uden

BIOGRAPHY

Under the pseudonym of Alejandro Casona (adopted in 1930), Alejandro Rodríguez Alvarez, the Spanish-born playwright who spent most of his creative life in self-imposed exile in Argentina, produced a prolific and varied body of work that achieved unprecedented commercial success on the stages of both Madrid and Buenos Aires. Born in an impoverished Asturian village to a family of schoolteachers, the landscape of his native region and his parents' profession were to have an influential and lasting impact on his dramaturgy. His nomadic youth, spent in the various Asturian towns where his father was posted as a teacher, familiarized him with the myths and legends of the land and was to inform the archetypal and transcendental nature of his work. Although Casona initially trained as a teacher, working in schools in the Pyrenees and León, he turned to writing and translating in the mid-1920s, completing his first full-length play, *Otra vez el Diablo* [The Devil Again], in 1928.

His first stage production was, however, a dramatic version of Oscar Wilde's *The Crime of Lord Arthur of Savile*, premiered as *El crímen de Lord Arturo* in Zaragoza during 1929. Although he worked as director of the Teatro del Pueblo for the government's Misiones Pedagógicas in the years between 1931 and 1936, staging a number of his own short plays and adaptations, national recognition as a playwright came in 1933 as his second full-length play *La sirena varada* [The Stranded Mermaid] received the prestigious Lope de Vega Prize. The reviews that greeted the play's production in 1934 heralded the presence of a vibrant new voice in contemporary Spanish dramaturgy. This view was verified by the success of his next play, *Nuestra Natacha* [Our Natacha], premiered in Barcelona in 1935, and later transferring to Madrid's Teatro Victoria in Feburary 1936, where it received a run of 500 performances—a feat until then unequaled in Spanish theater history. Although *Nuestra Natacha* received few negative reviews, fascist factions took exception to what they perceived as the play's criticism of conservative *señoritos*, singling Casona out as a Republican and targeting him as an antipatriotic figure. At the outbreak of the Civil War, the fate suffered by fellow dramatist García Lorca precipitated Casona's flight from Spain. He settled in Argentina, where he continued to work as a dramatist, collaborating with the touring Díaz-Collado company, which premiered many of his new works in the 1940s and early 1950s. Although he enjoyed veritable critical and commercial successes during these years, acclaim was tempered by a number of unfavorable comparisons with his earlier pre–Civil War plays.

After a brief period away from writing for the stage, Casona returned with what has come to be seen as one of his greatest plays, *La dama del alba* [The Lady of the Dawn], which opened in 1944 with the renowned actress Margarita Xirgu, also in self-imposed exile in Argentina, in the title role. Further collaborations with the Díaz-Collado company in these years included the production of *La barca sin pescador* [The Boat without a Fisherman], premiering at Buenos Aires' Teatro Liceo in 1945 and achieving a run of over 200 performances during that year alone, and the 1947 staging of *La molinera de Arcos* [The Miller's Wife], a reworking of Pedro de Alarcón's *El sombrero de tres picos*, which was greeted with a somewhat more muted response. Arguably his greatest success during this period was the 1949 production of *Los árboles mueren de pie* [Trees Die Standing] (1949), presented by the Luisa Vehil and Esteban Serrador company, which enjoyed a two-year run and extremely favorable reviews.

Although Casona's exile was punctuated by brief periods spent in his homeland, he only returned permanently to Madrid in the early 1960s, producing many of his own plays in the years between 1961 and his death in 1965. Undoubtedly the most important play of this period is *El caballero de las espuelas de oro* [The Knight with the Golden Spurs] (1964), a study of the satirist Francisco de Quevedo that received over 500 performances in Madrid's Teatro Bellas Artes. Casona's final completed work, a version of Fernando de Rojas's epic *La Celestina*, was presented after his death in October 1965 at the Teatro Bellas Artes. Casona died in Madrid on September 17, 1965, the result of complications following open-heart surgery. He was survived by his wife Rosalía Martín Bravo, whom he had married in 1928, and his daughter Marta Isabel, who had collaborated with him on adaptations of Shakespeare's *Richard III* and *A Midsummer Night's Dream*.

Although primarily known as a playwright, Casona was also a prolific essayist; wrote numerous screenplays (many of them adaptations of his own works); produced a libretto for Alberto Ginastera's opera *Don Rodrigo*, premiered in Buenos Aires in 1964 but later staged at the New York Metropolitan Opera House; and published numerous translations of foreign-language fiction works including plays by Lenormand and Strindberg. Although a small number of Casona's plays have been translated into English, it is in France, Italy, and Portugal that his work has most often been produced outside of Spain and Latin America.

DRAMATURGY: MAJOR WORKS AND THEMES

Although not as well known in English-speaking countries as he is in Spain and Latin America, it is impossible to deny the importance of Alejandro Casona to twentieth-century Spanish theater. Never achieving the critical success of his contemporaries García Lorca and Valle-Inclán, Casona should nevertheless be regarded as a prolific and innovative playwright who sought to challenge the dominance of the naturalistic play. His plays may not be as structurally sophisticated, ingeniously poetic, or dramatically inventive as those of his two illustrious contemporaries, but they are still adventurous explorations of the essentially subjective nature of what is habitually termed *reality*.

This is visible in his earliest dramatic works. *La sirena varada*, for example, written in 1929 but first staged in 1934, features an eccentric old man who returns to an old house to escape from the boredom of the world around him, which he views as bereft of imagination. Surrounding himself with like-minded individuals, he encourages them to find physical and emotional gratification through escapist fantasies. For the sexually abused María the assuming of a new identity as the frail Sirena (mermaid) is an attempt to reinvent her entire past. In many of Casona's works, conflicting realities come into play as characters from a recognizably human world are brought into conflict with those from beyond the grave. In *La casa de los siete balcones* [The House of the Seven Balconies] (1957), for example, the mute Uriel, one of the play's protagonists, finds solace in the visit of three long-dead relatives who appear to him dressed in white and comfort him at difficult moments. A number of his works, like *La molinera de Arcos* (1947) and *Corona de amor y muerte* [Love, Death, and a Crown] (1955), have their sources in well-known folktales and legends. Others, like *Siete gritos en el mar* [Seven Cries at Sea] (1952) and *La tercera palabra* [The Third Word] (1953), appear to work within an allegorical tradition that can be traced back to the Golden Age dramatist Pedro Calderón de la Barca's *autos sacramentales*. Often the plays are highly didactic, and the characters, rather than functioning as credible psychological constructs, operate as visible metaphors for certain states of mind. As such the wayward, unhappy protagonists of plays such as *La dama del alba* (1944) and *La barca sin pescador* (1945) often meet antagonists who are primarily alluring manifestations of eternal rest, lascivious temptation, or desire and clearly suggestive evocations of Death or Satan in disguise. Moralistic in tone, they recall the pastoral dramas of Lope de Vega, who also extolled the virtues of a simple rural life.

Idealizing the rural way of life of his native Asturias—to which he dedicated *La dama del alba*—and drawing on its pagan folkloric traditions, Casona crafted a series of plays that celebrated the "traditional" values that he felt were embodied in a rural way of life that was gradually being eroded by the increasing exodus to the cities. As such the city in *Romance en tres noches* [Ballad in Three Nights], first produced as *Romance de Dan y Elsa* [Ballad of Dan and Elsa] (1938), is a dangerous expressionistic abyss, where Elsa is lured into degenerate brothels. Far removed from Dan's rural home, it becomes a symbol for the corruption and vice of the new world order that Casona came to see as an intrinsic part of the post–World War I industrialized Spain. For those who sought solace and salvation in city life, like the grandson in *Los árboles mueren de pie* (1949) and Nina Pertus in *Siete gritos en el mar*, Casona found just punishments. His restless protagonists often meet with an untimely or gruesome death, thus offering a stark message for audiences about the dangers of bright city lights, get-rich-quick schemes, and foreign shores. Those who make desperate decisions for material gain find little lasting satisfaction in such strategies. Gothic figures punctuate a number of his plays. These are often characterizations of Satan and Death with an ability to metamorphosize into other more attractive shapes through which they endear themselves to the desperate protagonists. In *La dama del alba* Angélica, who abandoned her husband three days after their wedding, returns home, only to be lured to her grave by Death disguised as a lovely and vulnerable pilgrim. Placing her faith in this mysterious woman, Angélica is convinced that she no longer has a place in this community and drowns herself in the river. Death here is a gentle, alluring figure rather than an evidently malignant *femme fatale*. As with the Devil in *Otra vez el Diablo* (1935), she is characterized in an ambivalent manner, offering comfort as well as grief. In addition, her vulnerability renders her painfully human—an individual whom we pity rather than are in awe of. In *¡A Belén, pastores!* [To Bethlehem, Shepherds!], first produced in 1951, the Devil appears as a pathetic hen-pecked Scrooge-figure who stands in opposition to everything that Christianity teaches us Christmas is supposed to signify. In *Otra vez el Diablo* Satan manifests himself as an amusing misunderstood individual, aware of his unpopular status and capable of prayer, love, and affection. Both plays show Casona playfully reworking dauntingly severe conceptions of Satan, providing instead an ironic characterization that undermines popular preconceptions.

Archetypal characters and popular texts and myths form the basis of numerous Casona works. In his three historical dramas, *Corona de amor y muerte, Sinfonía inacabcda* [Unfinished Symphony] (1939), and *El caballero de las espuelas de oro*, Casona embellishes and remodels historical material in order to interrogate issues of political and artistic responsibility. Other plays are adaptations of key Spanish and foreign cultural works and include such pieces as *Carta de una desconocida* [Letter from an Unknown Woman] (1957), derived from Stefan Zweig's short story of the same name, as well as versions of Fernando de Rojas's *La Celestina* (1965), Tirso de Molina's *El burlador de Sevilla* [The Trickster of Seville] (1961), and Shakespeare's *A Midsummer Night's Dream* (produced as *Sueño de una noche de verano* in 1962). The reworking of such texts for modern audiences displays Casona's preoccupation with his cultural past. His educational work with the Misiones Pedagógicas in the early 1930s in promoting culture within the rural regions of Spain plays like *Nuestra Natacha* (1935), a call for widespread educational reform, and his dramaturgical work within children's theater points to a substantial interest in promoting theater's potential as an educational medium at a time where he felt society was moving in a number of dangerous amoral directions.

It is against the backdrop of an increasingly mechanized dehumanized society that Casona's work, from the early children's plays like *El lindo Don Gato* [Beautiful Mr. Cat] (1950) to the later comic and historical dramas like *Corona de amor y muerte*, is most clearly focused. The pressures that Casona perceived as generated by daily living in urban centers manifest themselves in a number of his plays. They are often recounted by emotionally disturbed characters who have retreated from society in differing ways.

Souls in crisis are a familiar motif in Casona's work, visible both in the "dream plays" (*La sirena varada, Prohibido suicidarse en primavera* [Suicide Prohibited in Springtime] [1937], and *Los árboles mueren de pie*), where the troubled protagonists locate temporary release from their miserable predicaments through illusionism, and in the historical dramas, like *Corona de amor y muerte* (a rewriting of the Ines de Castro legend) and *El caballero de las espuelas de oro*, where tormented figures come to terms with the conflicting responsibilities of their position. In *Prohibido suicidarse en primavera*, one of his most famous plays, the patients interned in the asylum for attempted suicides seek comfort from a world that has driven them to the brink of despair through illusionist theatrics. As in *Los árboles mueren de pie*, a recourse to illusion and role play offers a way for the characters to begin to confront their phobias, which, when articulated and faced are in Casona's view capable of cure. Unlike Pirandello, who displays a similar fascination with metatheater, Casona concludes that escapism through such illusionist games can only bring temporary satisfaction to the characters. Long-term angst is never confronted by such strategies. Casona's celebration of role play comes through an acknowledgment of its use in allowing the characters a possible way to begin to view the world anew. As such, in *Prohibido suicidarse en primavera*, "the patients" in the refuge for prospective suicides are encouraged to accept the wonders of that which immediately surrounds them. Only in *Los árboles mueren de pie* does a character, the grandmother, allow Mauricio (the Director of Dr. Ariel's institution for sick souls) and one of his patients Marta (also known as Isabel), who have pretended to be her long-departed grandson and his wife, to think that they have successfully deceived her in their performances. Here the theatrical performance is allowed to succeed because all the participants come to recognize its importance in securing lasting happiness for every party concerned.

A number of his latter plays written in exile also examine the role of the imagination in forging that which we commonly refer to as "reality." Their focus, however, is on the part played by dreams in this process, betraying Casona's increasing fascination in the 1950s with the theories of Freud, Jung, and Adler. *Siete gritos en el mar*, for example, is constructed around a dream in which the hyprocritical nature of the characters aboard a ship is revealed to a reporter. In *La llave en el desván* [The Key in the Attic] (1951), a play that Casona himself admitted owed much to Freud,[1] the disturbed protagonist Mario recounts three of his bewildering dreams to his friend and family doctor Gabriel Miranda and his sister-in-law Laura. The doctor, acquainted with Freudian ideas, locates Mario's angst in a childhood trauma that Mario does not remember when awake: dreams clearly functioning within the play as a manifestation of the unconscious.

An interplay between dreams and "reality," between the magical and the prosaic, and between paranormal characters and those more firmly grounded in this world, has often led to an assessment of Casona as a daring playwright concerned with pursuing a bold poetic theater. Nevertheless, his plays are in many ways deeply conservative. Transgression by wayward protagonists is generally punished. In addition, the plays are often overly reliant on incongruous plot devices. In *Prohibido suicidarse en primavera* and *Los árboles mueren de pie*, melodramatic conventions prevail as characters from the past appear at dramatically opportune moments. Equally, in both plays, coincidences abound. However, despite a clumsy recourse to laborious dramatic techniques and an excessive reliance on narrative closure neatly resolving all loose ends, there is no denying Casona's status as a prominent liberal humanist playwright. From his early works written in Spain in the 1930s, like *Nuestra Natacha*, to the varied body of plays produced abroad in the 1940s and 1950s, and his final completed dramatic venture, *El caballero de las espuelas de oro*, Casona demonstrated an astute ability to craft works that sought to restore to the Spanish stage the balance of *deleite* and *doctrina* that had proved such a cornerstone of the Golden Age writers he so admired.

Grounded within this pedagogical philosophy, *La barca sin pescador* incorporates the playwright's customary theatrical techniques to expose the moral degeneracy that Casona perceived to be an inherent part of the new urban societies. As with much of his work, plot construction remains contingent upon the characters' perceptions of events. By maintaining an element of suspense through a blurring of the boundaries of fantasy and reality, the play becomes a psychological drama tracing the shift in the moral perspective of its protagonist, Ricardo. Such a concern with the ideological development of his characters has infused much of Casona's work with a didacticism that has sometimes been judged in an unfavorable manner. First published in 1950, five years after its Buenos Aires premiere, *La barca sin pescador* features a protagonist who, embracing the ethics of a "new" commercial world, strikes a deal with the Devil. Ricardo escapes impending financial ruin by committing murder through intention, signing a document presented to him by this "caballero de negro."[2] The scream of the victim's wife Estela, however, is the catalyst that signals a reversal of Ricardo's ruthless unethical sensibility. Upon traveling to the Nordic village of the murdered man, a fisherman called Peter Anderson, he encounters in Estela the love that will provide him with redemption. Although certain critics deemed the subject matter of the play inappropriate and insensitive,[3] such a stance ignores Casona's preoccupation with the imagination and its power to enlighten humanity regarding the purifying effects of nature and the rural. Ricardo, symbolic of civilization's moral decline in Act One, learns from Estela to view his actions within the boundaries of a social conscience. As such Estela serves as the manifestation of Casona's ethical beliefs that "en la vida de un hombre está la vida de todos los hombres" [In the life of one man is the life of all men] (78), signaling explicitly that humanity has the moral obligation to fight against the dehumanized social structures so vividly documented in the first act of the play.

At the heart of Casona's imaginative vision is a relationship with his native land, nurtured during his youth, which is often manifest through the recognizably evocative Asturian settings of his plays. In *La barca sin pescador*, the rustic isolation of the Nordic village where men make an honest living from the land is reminiscent of Casona's recollections of his upbringing when much time was spent in the company of herdsmen recounting tales of the land.[4] Not that the play glibly extols the wonders of a rural way of life. Acknowledging that the commercial mentality is infecting even the farthest reaches of the world, Estela's family must find sustenance in the selling of souvenirs to foreign visitors. Nevertheless, for Casona it is largely through a harmonious relationship with the land that (wo)man may discover a mode of life in which personal actions have consequences and implications that reach beyond the limitations of human intention.

The idealization of this rural way of life often produces dramatic characters who are symbolic representations of traditional values. This is certainly the case in *La barca sin pescador*. The aquisition of imaginative insight gives Ricardo the ability to reject a way of life in which sentimentality distorts business acumen. Quoting the Devil's words of Act One, Ricardo acknowledges to Estela: " 'Para sufrir con el dolor ajeno, lo primero que hace falta es la imaginación' " [To suffer with someone else's pain the first thing you need is imagination] (78). The compassionate spirit manifest in the enigmatic Estela creates a character whose sharp insights into the complexity of human relationships far outweigh her humble education. As such she functions as a counterpoint to Ricardo; it is through her imaginative maturity and an ability to see beyond her constrained environment that we find a character equipped to provide Ricardo with the spirituality he lacks.

Of no less importance is the play's structural development from a dehumanized artificial world to one in which the characters, through the transforming power of love, repent their sins at the close. It is as a result of this strong mutual attraction, which transcends lust and physical desire, that both Ricardo and Estela are able to repent and forgive. Love, in its most spiritual manifestation, as opposed to desire, functions in much of his work as the antithesis to death—most notably manifest in *La barca sin pescador* by Lucifer. What prefigures the psychological makeup of Casona's characters in *La barca sin pescador* is the playwright's affinity with Christian theology and the issues of sin and redemption. As in much Golden Age drama, where the social order was disturbed only to be restored through forgiveness, in *La barca sin pescador* Ricardo, the complicitious sinner, is saved through repentence. Although some criticism has been leveled against Casona for displaying a lack of social responsibility in leaving Ricardo unpunished for his sin,[5] it is perhaps more constructive to see this aspect of the play as an affirmation of Casona's belief in the regenerative potential of selfless love. Rather than viewing Ricardo as a maladjusted human being whose moral decline was the result of a defective personality trait, we are invited by Casona to identify elements of ourselves in the troubled Ricardo. Thus, at the close of the play, forgiveness becomes the central theme: Estela forgives the repentant Christian for the murder of her husband; Frida relinquishes her fears that her husband, Christian, is in love with Estela; and Ricardo is willing to lay down his life in order to compensate for his sin of intent to murder.

This death drive, a facet demonstrated by many of Casona's characters, is an evident component of Ricardo's character. As Charles H. Leighton observes, the self-destruction that Freud read as the manifestation of a hypothetical death instinct, developed when the conflict between life and death remains internalized, never allowing the subject the opportunity to direct their aggression toward external objects, is here displaced through the reformation of Ricardo's personality:[6] an act achieved most notably through the life-affirming unconditional support offered by Estela, who looks to make good the "lack" within him.

The search for a fulfillment (usually satisfied, albeit temporarily, in heterosexual love) is what motivates the principal characters of *La barca sin pescador*. Conservative in his gender politics, Casona conceived of a world in which heterosexual union brought the benefits of stability and a sense of self-fulfillment. The central metaphor of the empty boat is indicative of a social order that in many ways is dependent on the male fulfilling a certain role. Without Peter Anderson, his family home becomes a soulless place, animated only by the arrival of another man, Ricardo. This is not to say that the gains from having a male present are purely financial, or that the men in Casona's plays exist independent of women. As Ricardo tells Estela as they pledge their commitment to one another: "No hay nada que un hombre no sea capaz de hacer cuando una mujer le mira" [There isn't anything a man isn't capable of doing when a woman looks at him] (89). Estela answers, "Esa es su gran fuerza" [That's his great strength] (89). Stability entails each recognizing and accepting particular "fixed" roles. Consistent within this union is the baptismal nature of Ricardo's relationship to Estela. The name Jordan, evocative of symbolic rebirth and the regenerative aspects of the Christian practice of baptism, is further strengthened through Estela's characterization as an angelic figure (as opposed to the "whorish" Devil) who leads him along the path to salvation.

Standing in opposition to the madonnalike figure of Estela is Satan, a metaphor for the protagonist's vulnerable and disturbed soul. Unlike Unamuno who was unable to reconcile the irrationality of death, Casona's drama allegorizes death through the Devil as a palpable aspect of everyday life. As articulated by Casona in a number of other plays as well as his own critical works on the subject—"El diablo en la literatura y el arte," presented as part of his studies at the Escuela Superior del Magisterio Madrid in 1926, and his 1955 article "Don

Juan y el Diablo"—Lucifer is a personification of the danger, both conscious and unconscious, present within us all. The Devil in *La barca sin pescador* is invested with the type of fallable qualities that locate him as a credible and tactile force. This is no harsh personification—rather, an articulate gentleman dressed in the attire of the bourgeoisie, attempting to go about his day-to-day business.

Humor, a tangible force in his works like *La molinera de Arcos* where habitual patterns of behavior are inversed, imbues *La barca sin pescador* with an optimism that some critics link to Casona's therapeutic intent.[7] Placing *La barca sin pescador* within the context of the morality plays of the Spanish Golden Age in which the happy ending often rests uneasily with a dark and disturbing narrative, humor serves to admonish those characters who frustrate the course of happiness with deceit. Thus the Devil, cheated from capturing Ricardo's soul, is earnestly seen crossing himself and praying. Humor, however, is not just the preserve of the principal characters. Secondary characters offering light relief become manifestations of a rustic wisdom that counters the excesses of urban life. Though Marco, the elderly and cantankerous fisherman, primarily adopts the position of foil to the forthright grandmother, his inability to understand the workings of the stock market, comparing the process to a magician's trick, is an example of Casona's confident use of satire. While offering a humorous reading of the commercial world, this episode is also an affirmation of prevailing common sense, an aspect of the rural way of life that permeates much of Casona's extensive body of work.

CRITICS' RESPONSE

The mere publication of an extensive bibliography of critical material on Casona's work in 1987 points to the substantial attention his plays have generated over the last fifty years.[8] Numerous prominent critics have been harsh on Casona's theater, chastising him for a failure to engage with the pressing political and social issues of the day and judging his theater as a largely escapist and at times ludicrously naive affair.[9] Nevertheless, despite these dissident views and the negative reviews a number of his plays received not only when first produced[10] but also when revived,[11] critics have tended to see in Casona's theater a bold use of the visual and aural possibilities of the stage to explore the fantastic and perplexing nature of "reality."[12] Illusionism and its possibilities as a form of therapy for Casona's characters have been the subject of numerous critical studies;[13] some have sought to look at the playwright's debt to Pirandello, attempting to locate Casona as part of a European rather than a specifically Spanish antinaturalistic movement.[14] Only Zatlin Boring, however, really draws attention to Evreinov's possible influence on Casona.[15] Thematic and stylistic parallels have also been drawn with the work of other playwrights including Federico García Lorca,[16] J. B. Priestley,[17] Maeterlinck,[18] and Calderón de la Barca.[19] Casona's fascination with the Devil, a subject of several studies,[20] has certainly been traced back to Calderón and the tradition of the *auto sacramental* by critics such as Harold K. Moon, Charles H. Leighton, and Federico Carlos Sainz de Robles;[21] as has his personification of death in *La dama del alba* been partly attributed to the influence of the renowned symbolist writers Maeterlinck and Baudelaire.[22]

The recurrent allure of the death wish visible in several of Casona's obsessive or suicidal characters has rendered numerous studies,[23] the best of which by the lucid and prolific Charles H. Leighton traces the playwright's debt to and divergence from Freudian theory.[24] The role of dreams in Casona's work has again been linked by Leighton and others to Freudian theories.[25] The location of key symbols in his work—the tree, the house, water, numbers, eyes—has offered scholars particular ways into his plays, facilitating a use of psychoanalytic theories for literary analysis.[26]

There is little doubt that Casona has polarized critics. The monographs of his work that followed the playwright's death have tended to be largely positive studies that have argued his status as a major playwright. Moon's study, published in 1985, cites the many international productions of Casona's plays in the 1950s to promote his reputation as a significant Spanish dramatist and firmly rebukes contemporary disdain of Casona's work.[27] There is no doubt that appreciation of Casona's ouevre in studies of twentieth-century Spanish theater has been somewhat more muted,[28] although César Oliva does acknowledge his widespread commercial appeal, pointing out that "Casona triunfó en la República, triunfó en el exilio, y triunfó en el franquismo" [Casona triumphed in the Republic, triumphed in exile, and triumphed during francoism].[29] It seems ironic that a political figure like Casona, who spent the 1940s and 1950s in exile, should have found his work so cautiously greeted by prominent critics on his return to Spain in 1963. Nevertheless, the Spanish premiere of *La dama del alba*, commonly acknowledged to be his finest play, like the Madrid productions of *La barca sin pescador, La sirena varada,* and *El caballero de las espuelas de oro* in the 1960s, received great public acclaim: a phenomenon referred to by the critic María Pilar Pérez-Stansfield as "fiebre Casona."[30] Since his death his plays have suffered a checkered production history; some like "María Curie" (1940) (cowritten with Francisco Madrid) and "El misterio del María Celeste" (1935) have faded into ignominy; whereas select others like *La dama del alba, La barca sin pescador,* and *El caballero de las espuelas de oro* have enjoyed high-profile productions. Perhaps G. Torrente Ballester offers the most perceptive judgment on Casona's work when he argues that the playwright's insistence on providing a "moral" (message) in his plays—rendering the changes of evasionism brought against his work as risible—actually limited their impact: "El pedagogo que cobija Casona en su alma impide a las más bellas de sus obras dramáticas alcanzar esa cima de la perfección poética en que el drama se justifica por sí mismo" [The pedagogue that resides in Casona's soul keeps his most beautiful dramatic works from reaching that peak of lofty poetic high where drama justifies itself].[31]

AWARDS AND DISTINCTIONS

National recognition for Casona was very much linked to his award of the Lope de Vega Prize in 1933 for *La sirena varada*. That same year his anthology of folktales *Flor de leyendas* received the National Prize for Literature. Awards received since then include: the Premio Nacional de Teatro "María Rolland" in 1963 for the Madrid production of *Los árboles mueren de pie*; the Premio de teatro de Valladolid, Medalla de oro for the staging of *La casa de los siete balcones* in 1964; the Premio de la Crítica de Barcelona in 1963; the 1977 premio de Teatro Valladolid "Leopoldo Cano" to the best play of the season for *El caballero de las espuelas de oro*.

NOTES

1. See Charles H. Leighton, "Alejandro Casona and the Significance of Dreams," *Hispania* 45.4 (December 1962): 697–703.

2. This is the name given to him in the play. See Alejandro Casona, *La barca sin pescador*, ed. José A. Balseiro and J. Riis Owre (New York: Oxford University Press, 1955), 4. All further references to this edition of the play are listed in the text.

3. See Harold K. Moon, *Alejandro Casona* (Boston: Twayne, 1985), 53, where he cites J. M. Velloso's comments on the insensitivity of composing such a piece in the immediate aftermath of the carnage of World War II.

4. For further details, see ibid., 2, 131.

5. For further details, see ibid., 58.

6. Charles H. Leighton, "Alejandro Casona and Suicide," *Hispania* 55.3 (September 1972): 436–445.

7. See, for example, John A. Moore, "Death as a Theme in Casona's Plays," *South Atlantic Bulletin* 39.2 (May 1974): 51–55.

8. Marsha Forys, "Alejandro Casona: A Bibliography of Criticism through 1987," *Hispania* 73 (September 1990): 577–592.

9. See, for example, Ricardo Doménech, "Para un arreglo de cuentas con el teatro de Casona," *Insula* 209 (April 1964): 15; Angel Fernández Santos, "Alejandro Casona," *Primer Acto* 68 (1965): 48–50; José Monleón, "Treinta años de teatro de la derecha," *Triunfo* (Madrid) 400.31 (January 1970): 7.

10. See, for example, "*Romance de Dan y Elsa.* Estrenó anoche la compañía M. Ortiz," *La Prensa* (Buenos Aires), 16 September 1939: 14; Moon, *Alejandro Casona*, 13–26.

11. See, for example, Ricardo Doménech, "*Los árboles mueren de pie*, de Alejandro Casona," *Primer Acto* 49 (January 1964): 52; José Monleón, "*Nuestra Natacha*, hoy," *Triunfo* (Madrid) 91.29 (January 1966): 7; Angel Fernández Santos, "*La casa de los siete balcones*, de Alejandro Casona," *Primer Acto* 52 (May 1964): 59–61; Moon, *Alejandro Casona*, 53–61.

12. See, for example, A. Wallace Woolsey, "Illusion versus Reality in Some of the Plays of Alejandro Casona," *Modern Language Journal* 38.2 (1954): 80–84; J. Frank Toms, "The Reality-Fantasy Technique of Alejandro Casona," *Hispania* 44.2 (May 1961): 218–221; Esperanza Gurza, *La realidad caleidoscópica de Alejandro Casona* (Oviedo: Instituto de Estudios Asturianos, 1968).

13. For example, José Caso González, "Fantasía y realidad en el teatro de Alejandro Casona," *Archivum* (Oviedo) 5.2–3 (1955): 304–318; Kessell Schwartz, "Reality in the Works of Alejandro Casona," *Hispania* 40.1 (March 1957): 57–61.

14. See Wilma Newberry, *The Pirandellian Mode in Spanish Literature from Cervantes to Sastre* (New York: New York University Press, 1973), 145–150; Phyllis Zatlin Boring, "Alejandro Casona and Nikolai Evreinov: Life as Theater," *Modern Drama* 22.1 (March 1979): 79–88; Charles H. Leighton, "Alejandro Casona's Pirandellism," *Symposium* 17.3 (Fall 1963): 202–214.

15. Zatlin Boring, "Alejandro Casona and Nikolai Evreinov: Life as Theater," 79–88.

16. Charles H. Leighton, "Casona and Lorca: A Brief Comparison," *Modern Drama* 7.1 (May 1964): 28–34; Luis E. Nieto Arteta, "Universalidad y Sexualismo en el teatro: Casona y García Lorca," *Revista de las Indias* (Bogotá) 36 (1941): 85–96: Bruce M. Goldfaden, *"Bodas de sangre* and *La dama del alba,"* *Hispania* 44.2 (May 1961): 234–36: Henryk Ziomek, "El simbolismo del blanco en *La casa de Bernarda Alba* y en *La dama del alba,"* *Symposium* 24.1 (Spring 1970): 81–85.

17. Leighton, "Alejandro Casona and the Significance of Dreams," 702.

18. Federico Carlos Sainz de Robles, "Alejandro Casona y su teatro," in Alejandro Casona, *Obras completas,* vol. 1, 6th ed. (Madrid: Aguilar, 1974), XI–CCXLIV.

19. Harold K. Moon, "Calderón and Casona," *Hispania* 48.1 (March 1965): 37–42; Charles H. Leighton, "Alejandro Casona and the Devil," *Hispania* 48.1 (March 1965): 29–36.

20. Robert Lima, "El demonio en la sangre: Génesis y superación del pacto diabólico en dos obras dramáticas de Alejandro Casona," *Romance Notes* 24.1 (Fall 1983): 10–16, Leighton, "Alejandro Casona and the Devil," 29–36; Rafael Vázquez Zamora, "Casona saca otra vez al diablo," *Insula* 200–201 (July–August 1963): 25.

21. See Moon, *Alejandro Casona,* 42, although Moon makes it clear that he believes Casona's Devil to be a more benign figure than Calderón's "awesome" Satan in *El mágico prodigioso*; Leighton, "Alejandro Casona and the Devil," 29–36; Federico Carlos Sainz de Robles, "Prologo," in Casona, *Obras completas,* vol. 1, LXXII.

22. Hilda Bernal Labrada, *Símbolo, mito y leyenda en el teatro de Casona* (Oviedo: Instituto de Estudios Asturianos, 1972), 137–149.

23. Harold K. Moon, "Death in the Theater of Alejandro Casona," *Brigham Young University Studies* 10.1 (Autumn 1969): 107–117; Moore, "Death as a Theme in Casona's Plays," 51–55; José Rodríguez Richart, "Death and Rebirth as a Double Mythic Dimension in *La dama del alba,"* *Kentucky Romance Quarterly* 31.3 (1984): 319–328.

24. Leighton, "Alejandro Casona and Suicide," 436–445.

25. Leighton, "Alejandro Casona and the Significance of Dreams," 697–703; Bernal Labrada, *Símbolo, mito y leyenda en el teatro de Casona,* 66–72.

26. Bernal Labrada, *Símbolo, mito y leyenda en el teatro de Casona,* 37–149; Thomas C. Turner, " 'Eyes' in the Drama of Alejandro Casona," *Hispaniófila* 61 (September 1977): 39–49.

27. Moon, *Alejandro Casona,* preface, 146–148.

28. See, for example, Cesár Oliva, *El teatro desde 1936* (Madrid: Alhambra, 1989), 50–53, 165–169; Francisco Ruiz Ramón, *Historia del teatro español, Siglo XX* (Madrid: Cátedra, 1984): 224–246; G. Torrente Ballester, *Teatro español contemporaneo* (Madrid: Ediciones Guadarrama, 1968), 352–354.

29. Oliva, *El teatro desde 1936,* 50.

30. María Pilar Pérez-Stansfield, *Direcciones de teatro español de posguerra: Ruptura*

con el teatro burgués y radicalismo contestario (Madrid: José Pornía Turanzas, 1983),
57.
   31. Torrente Ballester, *Teatro español contemporáneo*, 353.

BIBLIOGRAPHY

For a more comprehensive list of the many early editions of his plays, see either Harold
Moon, *Alejandro Casona* (Boston: Twayne, 1985), 141–146, or José Rodríguez Richart,
Vida y teatro de Alejandro Casona (Oviedo: Instituto de Estudios Asturianos, 1963),
185–190. Moon's study also provides a more comprehensive list of his prose work.

Plays: Collections

*Entremés del mancebo que casó con mujer brava, La sirena varada, Prohibido suicidarse
   en priavera.* Buenos Aires: Losada, 1941.
Retablo jovial. Buenos Aires: El Ateneo, 1949. (Includes *Entremés del mancebo que
   casó con mujer brava, Farsa del cornudo apaleado, Fablilla del secreto bien
   guardado, Farsa y justicia del corregidor,* and *Sancho Panza en la ínsula,* also
   known as *Sancho Panza en la isla Barataria.*)
Teatro. Buenos Aires: Losada, 1951. (Includes *La sirena varada, La barca sin pescador,
   Los árboles mueren de pie.*)
Nuestra Natacha, Otra vez el Diablo. Buenos Aires: Losada, 1965.
Teatro selecto. Madrid: Editorial Escelicer, 1966. (Includes *La sirena varada, Prohibido
   suicidarse en primavera, Los árboles mueren de pie, La casa de los siete bal-
   cones, El caballero de las espuelas de oro, Nuestra Natasha.*)
Obras completas 2 vols., 6th ed., ed. Federico C. Sainz de Robles. Madrid: Aguilar,
   1974.
Tres farsas infantiles. Gijón; Noega, Biblioteca de la Quintana, 1983. (Includes *El gato
   con botas, Pinocho y Blanca Flor, El hijo de Pinocho.*)
Farsas infantiles. Charlas radiofonicas. Articulos periodisticos. Oviedo: Hercules Astur
   de Ediciones, 1988.
Retablo jovial. Madrid: Bruño, 1995. (Includes *Entremés del mancebo que casó con
   mujer brava, Farsa del cornudo apaleado, Fablilla del secreto bien guardado,
   Farsa y justicia del corregidor,* and *Sancho Panza en la ínsula,* also known as
   Sancho Panza en la isla Barataria.)

Plays: Original Stage Works and Adaptations

Due to the exhaustive number of editions of many of Casona's works, not all editions
are listed here.

"El otro crímen," co-written with Salvador Ferrer c. 1925. Unpublished and unproduced.
El crímen de Lord Arturo, adapted from Oscar Wilde's *The Crime of Lord Arthur of
   Savile* (produced Zaragoza, 1929; revised version produced in Havana, 1938). In
   Obras completas, vol. 1, 1974.
La sirena verada (produced Madrid, 1934). In Buenos Aires: Losada, 1941.

Entremés del mancebo que se casó con mujer brava, based on *Enxemplo XXV* of *El conde Lucanor* by Infante don Juan Manuel (produced c. 1934, toured by the Teatro del Pueblo). In *Retablo Jovial*, 1949; in *Obras completas*, vol. 2, 1974; in *Retablo Jovial*, 1995.

"El médico a palos," adapted from Leandro Fernández de Moratin's play (produced c. 1934, toured by Teatro del Pueblo). Unpublished.

Sancho Panza en la ínsula (also referred to as *Sancho Panza en la isla Barataria*), adapted from Cervantes's *Don Quixote* (produced Madrid, c. 1934). In *Retablo Jovial*, 1949; in *Obras completas*, vol. 2, 1974; in *Retablo Jovial*, 1995.

"Balada de Atta Trol," adapted from a work by Heinrich Heine (produced c. 1935, toured by Teatro del Pueblo). Unpublished.

"El misterio del María Celeste," coadapted with A. Hernández Catá from his novel (produced Valencia, 1935). Unpublished.

Otra vez el Diablo (produced Madrid, 1935). In *La Farsa* (Madrid) 9.410 (27 julio 1935); Buenos Aires, Losada, 1943; Madrid: Escelicer, 1965; in *Obras completas*, vol. 1, 1974.

Nuestra Natacha (produced Barcelona, 1936). Madrid: Poveda, 1936; Buenos Aires: Losada, 1943; New York: Appleton Century Crofts, 1947; in *Obras completas*, vol. 1, 1974.

Prohibido suicidarse en primavera (produced Mexico City, 1937). Buenos Aires: Losada, 1943; Madrid: Escelicer, 1965; in *Obras completas*, vol. 1, 1974.

Romance en tres noches (produced Caracas as "Romance de Dan y Elsa," 1938). In *Obras completas*, vol. 1, 1974.

El hijo de Pinocho (written c. 1938). In *Tres farsas infantiles*, 1983.

Sinfonía inacabada (produced Mexico City, 1939). Buenos Aires: Losada, 1949; Madrid: Escelicer, 1965; in *Obras completas*, vol. 1, 1974.

"María Curie," cowritten with Francisco Madrid (produced Buenos Aires, 1940). Unpublished.

Las tres perfectas casadas, based on Arthur Schnitzler's *The Death of a Bachelor* (produced Buenos Aires, 1941). Buenos Aires: Losada, 1943; in *Obras completas*, vol. 1, 1974.

La dama del alba (produced Buenos Aires, 1944). Buenos Aires: Losada, 1944; New York: Charles Scribner's Sons, 1947; Madrid: Escelicer, 1965; in *Obras completas*, vol. 1, 1974; Madrid: Cátedra, 1984.

La barca sin pescador (produced Buenos Aires, 1945). Buenos Aires: Losada, 1950; New York: Oxford University Press, 1955; Madrid: Escelicer, 1964; Madrid: Ediciones Alcalá, 1966; in *Obras completas*, vol. 1, 1974; Madrid: Edas, 1983.

La molinera de Arcos (produced Buenos Aires, 1947). Buenos Aires: Losada, 1948; in *Obras completas*, vol. 1, 1974; Madrid: M. K. Ediciones, 1980.

Los árboles mueren de pie (produced Buenos Aires, 1949). Buenos Aires: Editorial Ateneo, 1949; Buenos Aires: Losada, 1951; New York: Henry Holt, 1953; Madrid: Escelicer, 1964; in *Obras completas*, vol. 1, 1974; Madrid: Edas, 1984.

El lindo don Gato (written c. 1950). In *Obras completas*, vol. 2, 1974.

¡A Belén, pastores! (produced Montevideo, 1951). In *Obras completas*, vol. 2, 1974.

La llave en el desván (produced Buenos Aires, 1951). In *Obras completas*, vol. 1, 1974.

Pinocho y Blancaflor (produced Buenos Aires, 1951 as *Pinocho y la infantina Blancaflor* infantiles, 1983.

Siete gritos en el mar (produced Buenos Aires, 1952). In *Obras completas*, vol. 2, 1974.

La tercera palabra (produced Buenos Aires, 1953). Buenos Aires: Losada, 1959; Madrid: Escelicer, 1965; in *Obras completas,* vol. 2, 1974; Madrid: Edas, 1993.

Corona de amor y muerte (Doña Inés de Portugal) (produced Buenos Aires, 1955, as *Inés de Castro).* New York: Oxford University Press, 1960; in *Obras completas,* vol. 2, 1974.

"Fuenteovejuna" (adapted from the play by Lope de Vega c. 1955). Unpublished. *El gato con botas.* In Tres farsas infantiles, 1983.

Carta de una desconocida, adapted from the story by Stefan Zweig, (produced Porto Alegre, Brazil, 1957). In *Obras completas,* vol. 2, 1974.

La casa de los siete balcones (produced Buenos Aires, 1957). Madrid: Escelicer, 1966; in *Obras completas,* vol. 2, 1974.

El anzuelo de Fenisa, adapted from the play by Lope de Vega (produced Buenos Aires, 1958). In *Obras completas,* vol. 2, 1974.

El burlador de Sevilla, adapted from the play by Tirso de Molina (produced Buenos Aires, 1961). In *Obras completas,* vol. 2, 1974.

Tres diamantes y una mujer (produced Buenos Aires, 1961). In *Obras completas,* vol. 2, 1974.

Peribañez y el Comendador de Ocaña, adapted from the play by Lope de Vega (produced Buenos Aires, 1962). In *Obras completas,* vol. 2, 1974.

"Cartas de amor de una monja portuguesa" (produced Buenos Aires, 1963). Unpublished.

El caballero de las espuelas de oro (produced Madrid, 1964). New York: Oxford University Press, 1968; in Federico C. Sainz de Robles, *Teatro español 1964–65.* Madrid: Aguilar, 1966, 125–91; in *Obras completas,* vol. 2, 1974; Madrid: Teatro Español, 1994.

La Celestina, adapted from the work by Fernando de Rojas (produced Madrid, 1965). In *Obras completas,* vol. 2, 1974.

Fablilla del secreto bien guardado (produced Melilla, 1967). In *Retablo Jovial,* 1949; in *Obras completas,* vol. 1, 1974; in *Retablo Jovial,* 1995.

Farsa del cornudo apaleado, adapted from Boccaccio's *The Decameron* (produced Melilla, 1967). In *Retablo Jovial,* 1949; in *Obras completas,* vol. 1, 1974; in *Retablo Jovial,* 1995.

Farsa y justicia del corregidor (produced Valencia, 1970). In *Retablo Jovial,* 1949; in *Obras completas,* vol. 1, 1974; in *Retablo Jovial,* 1995.

Opera Libretto

Don Rodrigo. Music by Alberto Ginastera (produced Buenos Aires, 1964).

Translations (Plays)

"Cuatro dramas en un acto de Strindberg." 1929.

"Los fracasados," "La loca del cielo," "La inocente," from three plays by Henri-René Lenormand. 1943 (all produced c. 1943).

"Sombra querida," a translation of Jacques Deval's *Ombre chère* (produced 1952). Unpublished.

Sueño de una noche de verano, undertaken with Marta Casona (produced Buenos Aires, 1962). In *Obras completas,* vol. 2, 1974.

Ricardo III, undertaken with Marta Casona. In *Obras completas*, vol. 2, 1974.
"El amor de los cuatro coroneles," from the play by Peter Ustinov (completed in 1958).

Adaptations and Translations (Prose)

"Los placeres y los tormentos del opio," a translation of Thomas De Quincey's *Confessions of an English Opium Eater*. 1926.
Novelas selectas de Voltaire. 1927.

Poetry

El peregrino de la barba florida: Leyenda milagrosa en poesía. Madrid: Editorial Caro Raggio, 1928; in *Obras completas*, vol. 1, 1974.
La flauta del sapo. Mexico: Instituto de Cultura Iberomericana, 1937; in *Obras completas*, vol. 1, 1974.

Screenplays

(Original screenplays unless otherwise listed.)

Nuestra Natacha (Spain, 1936).
Viente años y una noche (Argentina, 1940).
En el viejo Buenos Aires (Argentina, 1941).
La maestrita de los obreros (Argentina, 1941).
Concierto de almas (Argentina, 1942).
Ceniza al viento, one of the film's six episodes written by Casona (Argentina, 1942).
Cuando florezca el naranjo (Argentina, 1943).
Casa de muñecas, an adaptation of Ibsen's *A Doll's House* (Argentina, 1943).
Nuestra Natacha (Argentina, 1943).
Le María Celeste (Argentina, 1944).
Le fruit mordu, coadapted with Jules Superville from J. Jacques Bernard's *Martine* (Chile, 1945).
Margarita la tornera (Argentina, 1946).
El abuelo, adapted from the work by Benito Pérez Galdos (Argentina, 1946).
La dama del alba (Argentina, 1950).

Prose and Critical Works

Flor de leyendas. Madrid: Biblioteca Nueva, 1933; in *Obras completas*, vol. 1, 1974; Madrid: Espasa Calpe, 1978.
"El diablo: Su valor literario, principalmente en España." In *Obras completas*, vol. 2, 1974.
"Las mujeres de Lope de Vega." In *Obras completas*, vol. 2, 1974.
"Vida de Francisco Pizarro." In *Obras completas*, vol. 2, 1974.
Obra inedita de Casona: Charlas radiofónicas. Ed. Evaristo Arce. Oviedo: Instituto de Estudios Asturianos, 1982.

Translations (of Casona's Plays)

The Boat without a Fisherman. Trans. Richard Dumar. In *Modern Spanish Stage: Four Plays*, ed. Marion Peter Holt. New York: Hill and Wang, 1970.
"The Lady of the Dawn." Trans. Douglas Lylburn Heinsohn. M.A. thesis, University of Tennessee, 1959.
Lady of the Dawn; Love, Death and a Crown (Corona de amor y muerte). Trans. Graciela Miranda de Graves. Valencia: Albatros, 1972.
Suicide Prohibited in Springtime. Trans. Adam Horvath. In *Modern Spanish Theatre*, ed. Michael Benedikt and George E. Wellwarth. New York: E. P. Dutton, 1969.

Critical Studies

(Does not include works already listed in the notes.)

Anderson, Robert. "The Motifs of Death and Regeneration in *La dama del alma.*" *Hispanic Journal* 7.1 (Autumn 1985): 59–66.
Borrás, Angel A. "Musical Underscoring in the Dramas of Casona." *Hispania* 47.3 (September 1964): 507–509.
Burgess, Ronald. "Enigma, Paradox and Dramatic Movement in *La dama del alba.*" *Hispania* 68.1 (March 1985): 35–43.
Castellano, Juan R. "Casona y Asturias." *Hispania* 35.4 (November 1952): 392–394.
Díaz Castañon, Carmen. *Alejandro Casona.* Oviedo: Caja de Ahorros de Asturias, 1990.
Díez Taboada, Juan María. "El teatro de Alejandro Casona antes del exilio (1925–1937)." *Revista de literatura* 107 (1992): 269–282.
Edberg, George J. "Casona's Popularity." *Modern Language Journal* 44.4 (April 1960): 186–187.
Fernández Santos, Angel. "Alejandro Casona." *Primer Acto* 68 (1965): 48–50.
García Miñor, Antonio. "Alejandro Casona." *Boletín de Estudios Asturianos* 20.57 (April 1966): 89–106.
Goizueta Velasco, Teresa. "Efectos luminosos y musicales en el teatro de Alejandro Casona." *Boletín del Instituto de Estudios Asturianos* 132 (1989): 683–696.
Leighton, Charles H. "Alejandro Casona and the Revolt against 'Reason.' " *Modern Language Journal* 46.2 (February 1962): 56–61.
Llovet, Enrique. "Alejandro Casona o el evasionismo." *Mundo Hispánico* 21.242 (May 1968): 63–67.
Miras, Domingo. "Casona en perspectiva." *Primer Acto* 238 (1991): 10–13.
Moon, Harold K. "Alejandro Casona and the Christian Tradition." *Estreno* 122 (Autumn 1986): 9–11.
———. *Alejandro Casona.* Boston: Twayne, 1985.
———. *Alejandro Casona, Playwright.* Provo, UT: Brigham Young University Press, 1970.
Moore, John A. "Casona—Plays for Children." *Romance Notes* 16.3 (Spring 1975): 728–730.
Palacio, Adela. "Casona y la crítica actual." *Boletín del Instituto de Estudios Asturianos* 20.57 (April 1966): 115–146.

Plans, Juan José. *Alejandro Casona. Juego biográfico dividido en una raíz y tres árboles.* Oviedo: Grandío, 1965.
Sainz de Robles, Federico Carlos. "El humor en el teatro de Alejandro Casona." In *El teatro de humor en España.* Madrid: Nacional, 1966. 133–150.
Solís, Jesús-Andrés. *Alejandro Casona y su teatro.* Gijón: Solis, 1982.

RAMÓN DE LA CRUZ CANO Y OLMEDILLA
(1731–1794)

Rebecca Haidt

BIOGRAPHY

The fact that Ramón de la Cruz Cano y Olmedilla was a midlevel state bureau-crat during most of his career as a playwright is worth keeping in mind when studying the work of this eighteenth-century dramatist whose legacy of *sainetes* is fundamental in the history of modern Spanish theater. Able to write only at night, often until the early morning hours, Cruz was nevertheless prolific, pro-ducing on average twelve one-act and three two- to three-act plays per year during over thirty years of writing for the stage. Ramón de la Cruz was a functionary, but he was also a hardworking theatrical professional and creative genius who knew how to write what actors wanted to represent and audiences wanted to see.

Ramón de la Cruz was born March 28, 1731, in Madrid, the firstborn son of Raimundo de la Cruz, an Aragonese, and Mariá Rosa Cano y Olmedilla, from the Cuenca region of the Alcarria. Though Cruz had three brothers, one of whom, Juan (born 1734), was an engraver and cartographer who produced the famous *Collection of the Regional Costumes of Spain* [Colección de trajes de las provincias de España] in 1777, the other two are supposed deceased prior to 1762. Cruz is also known to have had a sister. Though Cruz's mother had descended from the lower nobility, the family was not monied. Cruz's father's profession is unknown; he probably brought the family to Ceuta in 1744, where they resided a few years and where Cruz wrote his first lines of poetry at the age of thirteen. Probably following the death of Cruz's father, the family re-turned to Madrid. While Cruz is not known to have been formally educated in the humanities, he may have had some studies with the aid of relatives and perhaps attended classes at Salamanca.

Six days before his twenty-eighth birthday, Cruz entered public service in 1759 as a third-ranking officer in the accounting division of the Department of Justice. Shortly after taking this employment Cruz married Margarita Beatriz de Magán, a native of Salamanca. Cruz's starting salary was meagre, 5,000 reales a year; he received only one promotion and one raise (in 1770) that doubled his salary but did not suffice for him to support a wife and several children adequately. Cruz began writing for the theater professionally in 1760 (though he had written theatrical works since 1757, the year of his first *zarzuela The Diety Loves a Sacrifice* [Quien complace a la deidad acierta a sacrificar]. He held his post in the accounting office for nearly thirty-five years, until lung troubles led in 1793 to a ten-month incapacitation and brought his death on March 5, 1794.

Cruz died surrounded by his family, in the house of his patron the Countess of Benavente; yet he died nearly destitute, his illness having blocked his earning power and used up the family's savings.[1] His widow had to petition Cruz's employer for 1,500 reales with which to bury the dramatist. Following his death Cruz's wife and daughter asked the Countess for financial assistance, which she granted them in the form of 6 reales daily until 1811, the probable date of the daughter's death. Born into less than comfortable circumstances, Cruz died in financial straits despite having worked unceasingly days (in the accounting office) and nights (writing for the theater) for thirty-five years.

Between 1765 and 1785 Ramón de la Cruz was one of the most powerful movers and shakers on the Madrid theater scene. His work may be divided into three periods suggested by the development of his career. In the first period, spanning roughly 1757 to 1764, Cruz gained a reputation for his *sainetes* and for his continuation of the successful *comedia de magia Marta la Romarantina*, titled *Martha Abandoned* [Marta abandonada] (1762).[2] Good examples of *sainetes* from this first period are *The Fashion Hospital* [El hospital de la moda] (1762) and *La civilización* (1763). The second period covers the nearly two decades between 1765 and 1784; during this time Cruz wrote across the spectrum of theatrical needs. He ceaselessly produced original *sainetes*, such as *The Craving for Seguidillas* [El deseo de seguidillas] (1769), the wildly popular and oft-imitated *Manolo* (1769), *The Boring Poet* [El poeta aburrido] (1773), *The Coif-Makers* [Las escofieteras] (1773), and *When Fools Regain Their Senses* [Los locos con juicio] (1778). He produced a steady output of original and adapted *zarzuelas*, with hits such as *The Farmgirls of Murcia* [Las labradoras de Murcia] (1769) and *The Girls from Fuencarral* [Las foncarraleras] (1772). Cruz was an innovator in the *zarzuela* form: He was the first to introduce local color (e.g., regional workers) into these operettas that traditionally had been drawn along mythological and pastoral lines and featured kings and gods.[3] In the composition of his *zarzuelas* and other theatrical works Cruz collaborated with some of the leading composers of the day, such as Rodríguez de Hita, Esteve, and Boccherini.[4] During this second period Cruz also won popularity for his *sainetes de costumbres teatrales*, skits dealing with the lives and escapades of the actors and acting companies themselves, representative examples of which are *The Theatre from Within* [El teatro por dentro] (1768), *The Guest Performer Consoled* [El huésped consolado] (1776), and *The Actors' Improvisation* [El repente de los cómicos] (1781). Cruz also translated or adapted a good number of comedies of various types, such as *La Eugenia* (1772, a translation from Beaumarchais) and *The Gleaner* [La Espigadera] Part I (1778, an adaptation of Favart's *Les moissoneurs*).[5] At the same time, Cruz was producing many *loas* and *introducciones* for his works and for the acting companies that would present them. In the final period, between 1785 and 1792, Cruz produced mostly *sainetes*, such as the 1787 *The Chestnut-Sellers Provoked* [Las castañeras picadas], and *loas*, along with two *zarzuelas*; as his health declines, so does his production, with illness severely limiting his ability to create between 1790 and 1792, the latter being the last year to which his work has been dated. Throughout these three periods Cruz also produced works for private patrons (e.g., the Countess of Benavente) and for public occasions, as, for example, in 1784 when Cruz was commissioned by the Ayuntamiento of Madrid to write *introducciones* and *fines de fiesta* for comedies to be performed in joint celebration of the birth of twins to Charles IV and the peace treaty with England.

The first few years of Cruz's second period coincided with the Arandan theater reforms (1767–1773), aimed at the improvement of the literary patrimony through the translation of foreign tragedies and the rehabilitation of theaters.[6] In an experiment to improve the national stage through an infusion of French models, *ilustrados* such as Gaspar Melchor Jovellanos and Pablo de Olavide translated works by Racine, Voltaire, and others for the newly established Sitios Reales Theatre, where actors recruited from Madrid's two companies performed plays believed by elite audiences to be the ultimate in enlightened taste. Between 1767 and 1773 Ramón de la Cruz produced many translations of Italian and French tragedies, too, but not for the Sitios Reales: *Aecio* (1767, a translation of Metastasio's *Ezio*), *Sesostris* (1767, a translation of Zeno and Pariati's *Sesostri re d'Egitto*), *Bayaceto*, (1769, from Racine's *Bajazet*), *Antigona* (1769), *Hamleto* (1772, a translation of Ducis's *Hamlet*), *Talestris* (1773, from Metastasio), and other Cruz tragedies were performed in the two Madrid coliseums during these six years, evidence of both the currency of the Arandan reforms and Cruz's versatility as a dramatist.

As a professional Cruz was eager to pick up on shifts in audience tastes, but he was not in league with the neoclassicists, and from the beginning of his career, he was embroiled in polemics instigated by jealous literati attacking his affectionate depictions of the customs of the lower classes and his influence in the acting companies; in response to their criticisms Cruz was fond of commenting "let them do it better" [háganlo otros mejor]. The polemics began when in 1762 Nicolás Fernández de Moratín (who was to work closely with Aranda), angry that actors didn't want to represent his comedy *The Primping Miss* [La petimetra] (1762), drew a distinction in his first *Lesson for the Spanish Theatre* [Desengaño al Theatro Español] between "high" and "low" contributions to the art of poetry and placed Cruz in the company of not the exalted Royal Spanish Academy and the Arcadia Romana but, rather, the lowly ranks of the hacks and hangers-on servicing dramatic troupes. In 1765 Francisco Mariano Nipho wrote *Satire Plagued by Modern Sainetes* [La sátira castigada por los sainetes de moda], a *sainete* lambasting Cruz for exceeding the bounds of respect for his contemporaries. In the same year Cruz responded with the *sainete The Public Complains* [El pueblo quejoso], mocking playwrights who disdain the tastes of the *pueblo* and write boring plays in the name of "rules." In a 1770s letter the neoclassicist Tomás de Iriarte expressed a litany of grievances encapsulating the attacks on Cruz's work. Iriarte wrote that Cruz did not respect the dramatic unities, that the language and characters in his plays were indecent and vulgar (and that he should be denounced to the authorities for the attendant corruption of public morals), that he poked fun at fellow writers in his plays and controlled the theatrical scene to the exclusion of opportunities for colleagues, and that though a veteran writer Cruz's "only excuse for not having advanced in this profession is his lack of training" [no tiene más disculpa para no haber adelantado en esta carrera que la falta de principios].[7]

Iriarte's characterization of Cruz as a writer who has not "advanced in this profession" perfectly reveals the profound difference between Cruz and the neoclassicist reformers who wanted to do away with the influence of popular theater. When Iriarte accuses Cruz of lacking professional training, he is speaking of the genteel exercise of the profession of "letters," not of the business of working in the theater. But Cruz *was* a professional writer, working rapidly and prolifically, with varied works covering all aspects of the theatre (*loas, introducciones, comedias*, etc.) and of acting (slapstick comedy, mimicry, song, etc.) and aimed at the pleasure of both performers and audiences. The theater reformers, conversely, idealized what had been theorized since Aristotle as the moralistic function of spectacle, and they labored to produce comedies and tragedies appropriate for the improvement of actors and the edification of audiences. The irony is that Cruz had advanced so far in his career by the early date of 1765 that he was made an honorary member of the Seville Royal Academy of Literature and inducted into the Arcadia Romana (the very one Moratín had claimed Cruz was not worthy of entering) with the name "Larisio Dianeo."[8] Iriarte and other writers bent on improving the state of the Spanish stage may have preferred elevated themes and material for their literary efforts, but because of his genius and hard work, Ramón de la Cruz entered their ranks anyway, enjoying at the same time a professional success in theater that they never were able to achieve. Ultimately Ramón de la Cruz became one of the most powerful dramatists of his time because he could do it all: tragedy, heroic comedy, burlesque parody, adaptations and translations, librettos—in any writing required for the theater of the day, Cruz outperformed his contemporaries.

DRAMATURGY: MAJOR WORKS AND THEMES

Cruz's work has many themes in various genres (e.g., *zarzuela, entremés*); as he is best known for his *sainetes*, this section will concentrate on the themes in those plays.[9] Cruz explored four central themes in his *sainetes*: (1) social types (e.g., *majos, payos*); (2) social panoramas; (3) class and gender differences; and

(4) the *sainetes* of theatrical life (*sainetes de costumbres teatrales*) and *sainetes* of parody or metatheater.

Several social types feature prominently in Cruz's *sainetes*.[10] *Petimetres* and *petimetras* are frequent subjects; representative treatment of these types is found in *The Fop* [El petimetre] (1764).[11] The *sainete* opens as Don Soplado the *petimetre* wakes around 10:00 A.M.; he proceeds to waste the rest of the morning at his *toilette* and in visits. First Don Zoilo, an abbé [abate], and Don Modesto, a gentleman [hombre de bien], arrive to chat with Don Soplado, giving Cruz ample time to contrast Modesto's integrity with Zoilo's and Soplado's superficiality. Then the three men pay a visit to the house of Don Simplicio, whose daughters are *petimetras* and whose house consequently is ill-maintained and in an uproar. Throughout the visit poor Don Simplicio pleads with his daughters to mend a hole in his stocking, but to no avail: As *petimetras* they are more interested in fashion and frivolity than in domestic pursuits. Don Zoilo is far from the only abbé featured in the *sainetes* of social types; his most famous kinsman is the scheming protagonist of *Guess Who's Coming to Lunch?* [El abate Diente-agudo] (1775), who spends an afternoon rushing from house to house, hoping to barter gossip for a repast. Though arriving inopportunely in each case (even stumbling into a deathbed scene in one house), the abbé insists on hinting at his being invited to lunch; in the end he winds up hungry and pitifully unaware of his rudeness and hypocrisy. Another frequently treated type is the country bumpkin [payo]; in the *sainetes* featuring *payos*, the contrast between city and country ways, between rustic simplicity and urban complexity is emphasized, as seen in *La civilización* (1763), where a landowner tries to "civilize" his laborers, introducing them to models of civilized behavior such as a *petimetre* and a lawyer. The *payos* know ridiculous behavior when they see it and end the play preferring their own ways to those of the simpering city folk.

During his time Ramón de la Cruz became known particularly for his portrayals of *majos* and their mannerisms, and in his *sainetes* one of the most frequently depicted social types is the *majo* and his feminine counterpart, the *maja*.[12] In the *sainetes* of *majos*, working-class neighborhoods (e.g., Lavapiés, Maravillas) come to life as residents celebrate native Spanish music and dance, confront *usías, petimetres*, and other upper-class intruders into their domain, and face the world with saltiness and inimitable vigor.[13] *The Majos in Fine Form* [Los majos de buen humor] (1770) is representative of Cruz's treatment of this social type. Two *majas* from Andalucía have caught the eye of a marquis and another *usía*, who snoop around their street, hoping for a glimpse of them. At the same time some young men try to capture the attention of the *majas*. The men play guitar and sing, demanding that they be let in to visit with the women; the women's boyfriends arrive, size up the situation, and let the admirers have a *fiesta* of dancing, singing, and jesting, during which the *majo* boyfriends force the callers to undress as proof of their admiration for the ladies, then throw the half-dressed men into the street—to the approval of the saucy *majas*.

The street is the site of the urban masquerade, where since *Lazarillo de Tormes* penniless nobility have donned their honor, pages passed for princes, and schemers of all kinds decked the dreams of the desperate. In the streets and open spaces of Cruz's *sainetes* persons of all regions, classes, and occupations mingle in the uncertainty and excitement of city life. This provides another major theme in the *sainetes*, that of the social panorama, where various types pass through a scene or event. In these plays *majos* and *petimetres*, water bearers and chestnut vendors, Galicians and Andalucians, mix in settings such as bullfights—as in *The Celebration of the New Bulls* [La fiesta de los novillos] of 1769, featuring *petimetres, payos*, constables, and others—and marketplaces—as in the 1770 *The Rastro in the Morning* [El Rastro por la mañana], showcasing sellers of various wares, a soldier, a page, foreigners, and locals. These *sainetes* depict in a sweeping manner the diversity of Spanish eighteenth-century urban society, something Cruz attempted to capture throughout his career.

Important aspects of the social diversity depicted in the *sainetes* are class and gender, a third major theme in Cruz's work. That *señores* differ from servants and men from women is to be expected, and Cruz satisfies the requirement of verisimilitude in his treatments of divergences—in everything ranging from sense of humor to integrity—between the sexes and among the classes. For the most part, even as diversity is depicted, deviant characters are put in their places: Social climbers are laughed at—as is the wife in *The Gathering Got Going Then Flopped* [La tertulia hecha y deshecha] (1774)—but so are social descenders (as in the case of the marquis and his friend in *Los majos de buen humor*); women who shirk their feminine duties are criticized—as in *Poor Men, Rich Wives* [Los pobres con mujer rica] (1767)—just as are men lacking the manly virtues (as in *El petimetre*). When a character betrays his class or gender "type," he is either put in situations that aright the deviation or contrasted with characters who show up his flaws. For example, dissolute and weak *petimetres* are corrected by more "manly" characters such as fierce *majos* and responsible *hombres de bien*. (A notable exception comes in the 1771 *Conquering the Majos* [Los majos vencidos], in which a *petimetre* beats up some *majos* who have tormented his *usía* friends; Cotarelo relates that the *sainete* is Cruz's response to comments that *majos* always got the better of *usías* in his plays.)[14] *The Republic of Women* [La república de las mujeres] (1771) provides a good example of the theme of class and gender differences.[15] The play takes place on an island and opens as a triumphant chorus of armed women escort a squadron of enslaved men onto the stage; the women proclaim their revenge upon the male sex, and the men lament their sufferings under the chains of "feminine arrogance" [femenil soberbia] (l. 10). Some shipwrecked men arrive and are captured by two women who inform them that fifty years previously ten women fed up with the yoke of patriarchy had fled society with followers and founded the republic of women. One of the shipwrecked arrivals tries to dress as a woman so as to avoid slavery; eventually the men are brought before the women's leader and attempt to appease her by promising that back in Spain "there are no more

spindles or barred windows,/no more escorts,/no bullying brothers,/neither husbands who lock doors,/nor watchful fathers" [ya no hay tornos, celosías,/no hay
escuderos, no hay dueñas,/hermanos espadachines,/maridos que cierren puertas,/
ni padres escrupulosos] (ll. 522–526). But these reassurances are unheeded, for
the women discover that an embarcation of men is approaching the island and
let loose the cry of war. One of the prisoners suggests to the leader that she
accept a tribute before going to battle; when a cache of glittering trinkets is
revealed, the men easily overcome the enraptured women and capture their arms.
The *sainete* ends with the women agreeing to return to society only upon three
conditions, notable among which is the demand that men be condemned for
adultery as severely as have been women. The play treats the clear differences
in social standards for men and women even as it reiterates popular conceptions
of gender difference (e.g., men keep their heads, women lose theirs over fripperies), and though the women agree once more to submit to male rule, one of
the men promises that "they'll see what's coming to them/in returning to our
power" [en volviendo a poder nuestro/verán lo que las espera] (ll. 646–647)—
suggesting that those breaking with society's gender norms will not be rewarded
after all for their experiment with liberty.

Some of Cruz's most innovative plays evidence the fourth major theme in his
work, that of *costumbres teatrales* and metatheater.[16] While *introducciones, loas,*
and *bailes* long had been used to present additions to theatrical companies or
introduce new repertory, Cruz began to craft *sainetes* around these same issues
and from there construct plays involving the talents and antics of the actors and
actresses playing themselves. The *sainetes de costumbres teatrales* serve the
purpose of highlighting and advertising acting companies' strengths and repertory (as did *loas*) but also treat the customs and relationships of those involved
in the theatrical world. Often in these *sainetes* the plot evolves from a group of
actors' rejecting material or improvising a new play, as in, for example, *When
Actors Are Writers* [Los cómicos poetas] (1776) and the 1778 *Improvised Sainete* [El sainete de repente]. In other *sainetes* individual actors are involved in
adventures and scrapes, as in *Chinica in the Countryside* [Chinica en la aldea]
(1767), in which the famous *gracioso* decides at the opening of the theater
season that he prefers country to city life but is persuaded to return to acting in
Madrid when nearly forced into marriage with a village maiden. Many *sainetes
de costumbres teatrales* depict performers interacting among themselves, as in
Ayala Gets Serious [Ayala por lo serio] (1764), in which the *gracioso* Ayala
complains to company director María Hidalgo that he never is allowed to have
"serious" parts and asserts that he will show everybody that he can do more
than be silly. Ayala auditions for his new role with a tragic scene, which of
course gives him ample opportunity to parody the components of tragic gravity
and highlight his own comic abilities.

Since Aristotle, tragedy has been the genre aligned with the nobility and the
high-born, comedy the genre representing the populace. It should not surprise
then that parodies of tragedy found particular favor with audiences. Between

1764 and 1792 Cruz produced at least ten *sainetes* that either are parodic tragedies (such as *Manolo* [1769]) or incorporate scenes parodying tragic declamation (as in *Ayala por lo serio*), along with numerous *loas* and *introducciones*
containing parodic elements. Some of these parodies spin off into metatheater,
being plays about the playing of parody; one such *sainete* is *The Comedy at
Valmojado* [La comedia de Valmojado] (1772), in which a group of *payos* re-
hearses a tragedy before members of one of the city troupes, imitating the gestures and inflections of beloved singers and actors while botching the tragedy
with inimitable crudity. Another metatheatrical *sainete* is *Zara* (written sometime in the 1770s).[17] The *sainete* opens played "straight," but rapidly the viewer
comes to understand that the characters are speaking as both characters (e.g.,
sultan, hero) and fellow actors. Thus the actor playing a sultan admonishes
another for not playing the sultan's confidant correctly; an actor hams it up
while listing the gory details of the battles he has waged for his beloved; and a
prompter appears several times before the actors to remind them that in tragedies
the deaths don't come until the *end* of the action—thereby so annoying the
character playing the sultan that he kills the prompter, proclaiming that the
victim had to die as punishment for having dabbled in a genre about which he
knew nothing.

CRITICS' RESPONSE

Cruz's work was polemical among peers in the academy, and eighteenth-
century critical histories of literature were not generally favorable to the dramatist: Pietro Napoli Signorelli dismissed Cruz's poetic ability in his *Critical
History of Ancient and Modern Theatre* [Storia critica dei teatri antichi e mod-
erni] (1777), an attack Cruz bitterly resented; and nearly half of Juan Sempere
y Guarinos's brief article on Cruz in the *Essay toward a Library of the Best
Writers of the Reign of Charles III* [Ensayo de una biblioteca española de los
mejores escritores del reynado de Carlos III] (1785) takes the form of citation
from Signorelli. Nevertheless, in an essay on eighteenth-century theater Leandro
Fernández de Moratín delivered favorable judgment of Cruz's *sainetes*: The
neoclassicist found fault with Cruz's celebration of popular vices but praised
his ability to imitate nature and create good comedy.[18] The younger Moratín's
approval of Cruz's verisimilitude informed nineteenth-century opinion of the
sainetes. Galdós praised Ramón de la Cruz for his realistic treatment of popular
themes. Menéndez y Pelayo lauded the dramatist in his *History of Aesthetic
Ideas in Spain* [Historia de las ideas estéticas en España] (1883–1901), describing Cruz as "the only original playwright of that century" [el único dramaturgo
original de aquel siglo] whose *sainetes* were "a faithful and poetic likeness of
the only national elements remaining in that confused and patchwork society"
[un trasunto fiel y poético de los únicos elementos nacionales que quedaban en
aquella sociedad confusa y abigarrada][19] By 1899, with the publication of Cotarelo y Mori's *Don Ramón de la Cruz and His Works* [Don Ramón de la Cruz

y sus obras], Cruz had become recognized as a major Spanish dramatist. Twentieth-century criticism has developed specific avenues for research into the *sainetes*.[20] One branch of Cruz studies has concentrated on the dramatist's sources in his many adaptations and translations; another has explored Cruz's treatments of popular culture; a third traces Cruz's place within the Enlightenment.

For its detailed information concerning Cruz's year-by-year output and the acting companies with which he worked, the most valuable study to date remains Cotarelo y Mori's *Don Ramón de la Cruz sus obras*. Don Emilio's text provides the plays with exquisitely detailed historical context but does not analyze them; his study is well supplemented by Mireille Coulon's recent *The Sainete in Madrid in the Era of Ramón de la Cruz* [Le sainete à Madrid à l'epoque de Don Ramón de la Cruz], an excellent analysis of the themes of *costumbres teatrales* and social types that provides a good discussion of the polemics surrounding the dramatist's work.

Cruz is best known for the *sainete Manolo: A Tragedy for Laughter or a Sainete for Tears* [Manolo: Tragedia para reír o sainete para llorar] (1769) and the accompanying *Introduction to the Ridiculous Tragedy of Manolo* [Introducción a la tragedia ridícula de Manolo]. The most valuable criticism of *Manolo* has been contributed by McClelland and Coulon.[21] McClelland places *Manolo* in the context of the eighteenth-century European vogue of burlesque tragedy. Coulon examines *Manolo* in light of Cruz's evolving treatment of *majismo* and further suggests that Cruz depicted *majos* with increasing frequency during periods in which he most was embroiled in polemic.[22] That *Manolo* was created within months of the failure of the elder Moratín's tragedy *Hormesinda* may be linked (according to Coulon) to Cruz's tendency to utilize *majismo* as a device for countering neoclassicist attempts at theater reform.[23]

Whether product of polemic or part of a larger trend toward burlesque tragedy, *Manolo* is a very funny play—but is it Cruz's most representative play? Indeed from Cruz's over 200 dramatic works in various genres, the selection of *one* representative play is nearly impossible. Yet *Manolo* and its *Introduction* do represent key elements of Cruz's writing for the theater: originality and adaptability; use of the important theme of *majismo*; clever burlesque; and in the *Introduction*, Cruz's innovative depiction of *costumbres teatrales*.

Manolo is a tragedy of ill-fated lovers that in its plot follows time-worn cues given glorious freshness through Cruz's having substituted *majos* and tavern owners for battling heroes and pensive kings, loudmouthed *majas* for distraught noblewomen, street corners and vegetable stands for palaces and battlefields, and plays on words for elevated poetic language. The protagonist, Manolo, returns from banishment (Cruz's twist on the tragic hero's return from battle). He had promised marriage years before to La Potajera, but back in Madrid he refuses to marry her; upon his return Manolo is promised in marriage to Remilgada, who loves another *majo*, Mediodiente. With the (questionable) honor of both La Potajera and Mediodiente at stake, Manolo and the other *majo* do battle, the valiant warriors' rowdy knife fight end in inevitable fatality.

Manolo operates in the interstices between the two genres of tragedy and comedy, as indicated in the subtitle of the play ("a tragedy for laughter or a *sainete* for tears"); this hybridity is hinted at in the *Introduction*, in which Chinica the *gracioso* (who claims authorship of the tragedy to follow) asserts that one may find all the tragic material one needs right in Madrid with no need to look back to Greece or Rome. Throughout *Manolo* Cruz plays with the distortion of genre in both the primary and secondary texts: for example, in Manolo's greeting of his mother: "Lady and mother mine!/Permit me to slather the sweet kiss of my dirty mouth/on your lovely paw" (¡Señora y madre mía!/Dejad que imprima en la manaza bella/el dulce beso de mi sucia boca] (ll. 189–191); or in the stage directions following Manolo's initial confrontation with Mediodiente, which describe the band of men to whom the protagonist points in his defense as "rascals" [pillos] (1. 302). But Cruz takes the parody still further: Manolo's mother drops dead at the sight of her son's body, and immediately afterward his stepfather dies "so as not to have to mourn or pay for a funeral procession" [por no hacer duelo ni pagar esequías] (1. 353); Remilgada determines to die next, followed by La Potajera, who instead of crashing to the floor, as did the others, decides to put herself in bed and call the doctor so she might "die with decency" [morir con convenencia] (1. 360). The remaining characters look at one another and ask, "Do we die too or what?" [Nosotros, ¿nos morimos o qué hacemos?] (1. 361), to which Mediodiente responds, "Friends, is this a tragedy or not?—we have to die" [Amigos, ¿es tragedia o no es tragedia?/Es preciso morir]—adding that only he who has the last word in a tragedy should be permitted by the poet to live (ll. 361–366). Cruz tests the limits of parody as the actors acknowledge the only rule that cannot be exorcised along with genre: that of the poet's power over his characters' fate.

McCelland suggests that parodies of tragedy—which layer vulgar language and characterization over elevated originals—were needed by audiences for relief from tensions imposed by theatrical reformers and neoclassicists (I: 274–275). But in *Manolo* careful cleverness far outweighs vulgarity. Cruz painstakingly tailors the conventions of one genre to those of another, not only for comic relief but also out of a desire for dramatic innovation: as Chinica says in the *Introducción*, "the key is in its pleasing/and in the viewer's realization/that the text is feeling its way/through new things for him to see" [todo está en que pete/ y se haga cargo el que vea/de que anda el discurso a tiento/buscándole cosas nuevas] (ll. 125–128). This sets the tension for the doubly-coded performance offered in *Manolo*: Every turn of plot, every gesture, every act of declamation that should carry the audience toward the gravity of tragic spectacle is designed to plunk the viewer squarely in the midst of a hilarious burlesque. *Manolo* is Cruz's ultimate adaptation in a career where adaptations of good plots and of interesting material were the writer's stock-in-trade. In many respects *Manolo* and its *Introduction* may be seen as representative of Ramón de la Cruz's prolific and varied dramaturgy: In these plays Cruz's passion for the portrayal of social types (in this case the *majo*) is patent, his devotion to the theme of *costumbres teatrales* displayed, his affection for audiences and good working relationship with the acting companies epitomized, and his flexibility and originality as a dramatist supreme.

NOTES

1. For more on Cruz's relationship with Faustina Téllez-Girón, the Condesa Duquesa de Benavente, see Emilio Cotarelo y Mori, *Don Ramón de la Cruz y sus obras: Ensayo biográfico y bibliográfico* (Madrid: José Perales y Martínez, 1899), 212–216.

2. For more on the popular theater of Cruz's day, see René Andioc, *Teatro y sociedad en el Madrid del siglo XVIII* (Madrid: Castalia, 1987); F. J. Blasco et al., eds., *La comedia de magia y de santos* (Madrid: 1992); and Emilio Cotarelo y Mori, *Colección de entremeses, loas, bailes, jácaras y mojigangas desde fines del siglo XVI a mediados del XVIII* (Madrid: 1911; NBEA XVII–XVIII).

3. For more on Cruz's *zarzuelas* and on eighteenth-century Spanish musical theater in general, see Emilio y Mori Cotarelo, *Orígenes y establecimiento de la ópera en España hasta 1800* (Madrid: Tipografía de la Revista de Archivos, Bibliotecas, y Muscos 1917); John Dowling, "Ramón de la Cruz: Libretista de zarzuelas." *Bulletin of Hispanic Studies* 68.1 (January 1991): 173–182; José Subira, "Repertorio teatral madrileño y resplandor transitorio de la zarzuela. (Años 1763 a 1771," *Boletín de la Real Academia Española* XXXIX. 158 (1959): 429–462; and Subirá's 3-vol. *La tonadilla escénica* (Madrid: 1928–1930).

4. It is worth keeping in mind that eighteenth-century theater involved music, singing, and dancing of many kinds and that Cruz's *zarzuelas* were not his only works calling for music: innumerable *sainetes, fines de fiesta,* and *loas* incorporate *seguidillas, bailes,* and so on. A good number of scores for such music await study and cataloguing in archives; many scores are lost or no longer available.

5. For more on Cruz's adaptations and translations from both Spanish and foreign sources, see Belorgey, Cirot, Coulon, Dowling, Gatti, Hamilton, Lafarga, Meregalli, and Nozick entries under "Critical Studies."

6. For more information on the reforms instituted by the Conde de Aranda and the establishment of the Sitios Reales theater, see Ivy McClelland, *Spanish Drama of Pathos 1750–1808,* 2 vols. (Liverpool: Liverpool University Press, 1970); and Cotarelo, *Orígenes y establecimiento de la ópera.*

7. Cited in Emilio Cotarelo y Mori, *Iriarte y su época* (Madrid: Sucesores de Rivadeneyra, 1897), 444. Did Cruz's *sainetes* disrespect the dramatic unities? Menéndez y Pelayo points out that the need for tightly reduced plots (given the time limit of *intermedios*) automatically confined the dramatist to "the greatest adherence to the unities of time and place" [la mayor rigidez en las unidades de lugar y de tiempo] and reminds readers that Cruz composed all types of works requiring knowledge of dramatic precepts and "rules." See his Historia de las ideas estéticas en España, vol. III (Madrid: CSIC, 1962), 315.

8. An honor of which Cruz was very proud, as is evident in the title of his ten-volume collection of works published between 1786 and 1791: *Theatrical works . . . of D. Ramón de la Cruz, Known among the Arcadians as Larisio* [teatro . . . de D. Ramón de la Cruz y Cano, entre los Arcades Larisio].

9. For more on Cruz's *zarzuelas*, see note 3.

10. One of Cruz's greatest strengths as a dramatist was his ability to depict the dozens of types populating the diverse social landscape of mideighteenth-century Madrid. For more on social types in the second half of the eighteenth century, see Cepeda reference under "Critical Studies."

11. Chapter VII of Coulon's *Le sainete à Madrid* . . . (Pau: Publications de l'Université de Pau, 1993), examines Cruz's treatment of *petimetres*.

12. The term *majo* is difficult to translate; generally *majos* are working-class people fiercely proud of their neighborhoods and their homegrown ways. In the *sainetes, majos* represent the celebration and preservation of Spanish popular culture in the midst of the capital's cosmopolitanism. For more on *majos* and *majismo* see Coulon, *Le sainete à Madrid*, chapter VI; Suppan, Varela, and Vilches entries in "Critical Studies" and Julio Caro Baroja, "Los majos," *Cuadernos hispanoamericanos* 299 (May 1975): 281–349.

13. *Usía*, a contraction of "vuestra señoría," was employed by servants or those of the popular classes when addressing superiors. In the *sainetes* of social types, an *usía* is one of privileged background who may or may not be in reduced circumstances and who is "slumming" in the domain of *majo* culture. In rare cases *usías* may befriend *majos* (as, for example, in the 1769 *sainete The Craving for Seguidillas* [El deseo de seguidillas]), but *majos* often employ the term disrespectfully, stressing their pride in the face of those who consider themselves socially superior.

14. Cotarelo y Mori, *Don Ramón de la Cruz*, 374.

15. For more on this play, see Coulon, "Ramón de la Cruz et le mythe des Amazones," *Bulletin Hispanique* 91 (1989): 5–19.

16. For more on this subject, see Coulon, *Le sainete à Madrid*, chapter IV; McClelland, *Spanish Drama of Pathos*; 91 (1989): 5–19. and Ermanno Caldera, "Il metateatro di Ramón de la Cruz," *Linguistica e Letteratura* II (1976): 81–113.

17. For more on *Zara* and Cruz's adaptation of its sources, see Lafarga, "Sobre la fuente desconocida . . ." *Anuario de Filología* 3 (1977): 361–371; and L. Teresa Valdivieso, "Regodeo burlesco de Don Ramón de la Cruz," *Dieciocho* 18.2 (Fall 1995): 253–259.

18. Leandro Fernández de Moratín, "Discurso preliminar," in *Obras de D. Nicolás y D. Leandro Fernández de Moratín*, BAE II (Madrid: Rivadeneyra, 1850), 317.

19. Menéndez y Pelayo, *Historia de las ideas estéticas en España*, 3: 315.

20. Studies referred to in this paragraph appear in the Bibliography.

21. For other articles on *Manolo*, see Carrasco, Courgey, Simón Díaz, and Suppan, entries in "Critical Studies."

22. See Coulon, *Le sainete à Madrid*, chapter VI, 338–342.

23. Ibid., 342.

BIBLIOGRAPHY

Editions

During his lifetime Cruz saw the publication of a ten-volume collection of his work, for which he wrote a prologue and commentary on the selections. The *Teatro o colección de los Saynetes y demás obras dramáticas de D. Ramón de la Cruz y Cano, entre los Arcades Larisio* (Madrid: Imprenta Real) appeared between 1786 and 1791.

The following bibliography of selected editions is in two sections. In the first I list useful editions and collections of Cruz's *sainetes* to date. In the second section I list several published or recorded *comedias* and *zarzuelas*. Much of Cruz's work remains without critical edition. There is also dire need for translations of his *sainetes*, as none is available in English.

Sainetes

Colección de los sainetes tanto impresos como inéditos, de D. Ramón de la Cruz, con un discurso preliminar de D. Agustín Durán, y los juicios críticos de los Señores Martínez de la Rosa, Signorelli, Moratín y Hartzenbusch. Ed. Agustín Durán. 2 vols. Madrid: Yenes, 1843.

Teatro selecto de D. Ramón de la Cruz. Colección completa de sus mejores sainetes, precedida de una biografía por Roque Barcía, ilustrada con láminas-acuarelas por Manuel Cubas. Madrid: José María Faquineto, 1882.

Sainetes inéditos de don Ramón de la Cruz existentes en la Biblioteca Municipal de Madrid y publicadas por acuerdo del Excmo. Ayuntamiento de esta villa. Ed. Carlos Cambronero. Madrid: Imprenta Municipal, 1900.

Sainetes de don Ramón de la Cruz, en su mayoría inéditos. Ed. Emilio Cotarelo y Mori. 2 vols. Madrid: Bailly-Vaillère, 1915–1928. Nueva Biblioteca de Autores Españoles, vols. 23 and 26.

Ocho sainetes inéditos de don Ramón de la Cruz, editados, con notas, segun autógrafos existentes en la Biblioteca Municipal de Madrid. Ed. Charles E. Kany. Berkeley: University of California Press, 1925. UC Publications in Modern Philology XXIII, 1.

Five Sainetes of Ramón de la Cruz. Ed. Charles E. Kany. Boston: Ginn and Co., 1926.

"Más sainetes inéditos de don Ramón de la Cruz." Ed. Charles E. Kany. *Revue Hispanique* LXXVI (1929): 360–572.

Diez sainetes inéditos de don Ramón de la Cruz. Ed. Luigi de Filippo. Madrid: Real Escuela Superior de Arte Dramático, 1955.

Doce Sainetes. Ed. José Francisco Gatti. Barcelona: Labor, 1972.

Tres Obras inéditas de don Ramón de la Cruz. Ed. Edward V. Coughlin. Barcelona: Puvill, 1979.

Sainetes. Ed. John Dowling. Madrid: Castalia, 1981.

Sainetes. Ed. Mireille Coulon. Madrid: Taurus, 1985.

Ten Unedited Works by Ramón de la Cruz. Ed. Edward Coughlin. Valencia: Albatros, 1987.

Sainetes. Ed. Francisco Lafarga. Madrid: Cátedra, 1990.

Comedias, Zarzuelas

Los dioses reunidos, o la fiesta de las musas, prólogo; y El tutor enamorado . . . puesto en idioma castellano por don Ramón de la Cruz, la música por don Luis Misón. Zarzuela. Madrid: A. Muñoz del Valle, 1764.

Marta abandonada y carnaval de Paris. Comedia. Ed. Felisa Martín Larrauri. Rome: Bulzoni, 1984.

Clementina. Recording with libretto. Zarzuela. Madrid: Consorcio para la Organización de Madrid Capital Europea de la Cultura, 1992.

Works

Cruz's dramatic works are too numerous to list here. The reader is referred to the following editions of the author's work in particular (complete bibliographical information for these and other editions of Cruz's work is found in the "Editions" section above)

Teatro o colección de los Saynetes y demás obras dramáticas. 10 vols. 1786–1791.
Sainetes de don Ramón de la Cruz, en su mayoría inéditos. Ed. Emilio Cotarelo y Mori.
  2 vols. 1915–1928.
Sainetes. Ed. John Dowling. 1981.
Sainetes. Ed. Mireille Coulon. 1985.
Sainetes. Ed. Francisco Lafarga. 1990.

Critical Studies

Alonso de Santos, José, and Fermín Luis Cabal. "Sobre Ramón de la Cruz." *Ínsula* 574 (October 1994): 21–23.
Barclay, T. B. "Reflections of Reality." In *The Theatre and Hispanic Life: Essays in Honour of Neale H. Tayler,* ed. Angelo Augusto Borrás. Waterloo: Wilfrid Laurier University Press, 1982. 33–53.
Belorgey, Jean. "Une exemple des infortunes de la censure en Espagne: Les traductions espagnoles de la *Zaire* de Voltaire." *Crisol* 7 (November 1987): 11–31.
Buck, Donald C. "Comic Structures and the *sainetes* of Ramón de la Cruz." In *Studies in Eighteenth-Century Spanish Literature and Romanticism in Honor of John C. Dowling,* ed. Douglas Barnette and Linda Barnette. Newark: Juan de la Cuesta, 1985. 65–76.
Caldera, Ermanno. "Il metateatro di Ramón de la Cruz." *Linguistica e Letteratura* II (1976): 81–113.
———. "Il riformismo illuminato nei *sainetes* di Ramón de la Cruz." *Letterature* I (1978): 31–50.
Cañas Murillo, Luis. "La poética del sainete en Ramón de la Cruz: De personajes, su tratamiento y su construcción." *Insula* 574 (October 1994): 17–19.
Carrasco, Hugo. "Manolo: Una tragedia paradójica." *Nueva Revista del Pacífico* 21 (1982): 31–45.
Cepeda Adán, José. "Tipos populares en el Madrid de Carlos III." In *El Madrid de Carlos III.* Madrid: Instituto de Estudios Madrileños del CSIC, 1988. 5–31.
Cirot, Georges. "Une des imitations de Molière par Ramón de la Cruz." *Revue de littérature comparée* III (1923): 422–426.
Cotarelo y Mori, Emilio. *Don Ramón de la Cruz y sus obras: Ensayo biográfico y bibliográfico.* Madrid: José Perales y Martínez, 1899.
———. *Orígenes y establecimiento de la ópera en España hasta 1800.* Madrid: Tipografía de la Revista de Archivos, Bibliotecas, y Museos, 1917.
Coughlin, Edward V. "Una obra inédita de D. Ramón de la Cruz: Su *Introducción para la tragedia Numancia destruída.*" *Boletín de la Biblioteca Menéndez Pelayo* LIII (1977): 307–316.
———. "*La Tertulia.* An unpublished 'sainete' by Ramón de la Cruz." *Dieciocho* I (1978): 46–62.

————. *"La tertulia de moda.* Sainete inédito de Ramón de la Cruz." *Dieciocho* 2 (1979): 166–188.

Coulon, Mireille. "Diecinueve sainetes desconocidos de Ramón de la Cruz." *Estudios escénicos* 21 (1976): 131–147.

————. "L'image du public dans les 'sainetes' de l'epoque de Ramón de la Cruz." In *IVe Table Ronde sur le Théâtre Espagnol (XVIIe-XVIIIe siècle).* Pau: Université de Pau et des Pays de l'Adour, 1983.

————. "Ramón de la Cruz." In *Siete siglos de autores españoles,* ed. Kurt Reichenberger and Theo Reichenberger. Kassel: Reichenberger, 1991.

————. "Ramón de la Cruz et le mythe des Amazones." *Bulletin Hispanique* 91 (1989): 5–19.

————. *Le Sainete à Madrid à l'epoque de Don Ramón de la Cruz.* Pau: Publications de l'Université de Pau, 1993.

————. "El sainete de costumbres teatrales en la época de don Ramón de la Cruz." In *Teatro menor en España a partir del siglo XVI.* Madrid: CSIC, 1983. 235–249.

Courgey, P. "A propos d'un air de famille: Réflexions sur le *Manolo* de Ramón de la Cruz et la *Farsa y licencia de la reina castiza* de Ramón del Valle Inclán." In *Mélanges à la mémoire de Jean Sarrailh.* 2 vols. Vol. I. Paris: Centre de Recherches de l'Institut d'Etudes Hispaniques, 1966. 281–289.

Dowling, John. "Los tres fines de siglo de Ramón de la Cruz." *Ínsula* 574 (October 1994): 7–9.

————. "Ramón de la Cruz: Libretista de zarzuelas." *Bulletin of Hispanic Studies* 68.1 (January 1991): 173–182.

Dufour, Gerard. "El público de Ramón de la Cruz." *Ínsula* 574 (October 1994): 19–20.

————. "Juan de Zabaleta et Ramón de la Cruz : Du 'galan' au 'petimetre.' " *Les Langues neo-latines* 212 (1974): 81–89.

Ebersole, Alva. *Los sainetes de Ramón de la Cruz: Nuevo examen.* Valencia: Albatros, 1983.

Filippo, Luigi de. "La satira del 'bel canto' en el sainete inédito de D. Ramón de la Cruz *El italiano fingido." Estudios escénicos* 10 (1964): 47–101.

Gatti, José Franisco. "La fuente de *Inesilla la de Pinto." Revista de Filología Hispánica* V (1943): 368–373.

————. "Las fuentes literarias de dos sainetes de Ramón de la Cruz." *Filología* I (1949): 59–67.

————. "Ramón de la Cruz y Dancourt." In *Homenaje al Instituto de Filología y Literaturas Hispánicas 'Dr. Amado Alonso' en su cincuentenario.* Buenos Aires: F. G. Cambero [distrib.], 1975. 117–121.

————. "Un sainete de R. de la Cruz y una comedia de Marivaux." *Revista de Filología Hispánica* III (1941): 374–378.

————. "Sobre las fuentes de los sainetes de Ramón de la Cruz." In *Studia Hispanica in honorem R. Lapesa.* 2 vols. Vol. I. Madrid: Gredos, 1972. 243–249.

————. *"Le triomphe de Plutus* de Marivaux y *El triunfo del interés* de Ramón de la Cruz." *Filología* XIV (1970): 171–180.

Hamilton, Arthur. "Ramón de la Cruz's Debt to Molière." *Hispania* IV (1921): 101–113.

————. "Ramón de la Cruz, Social Reformer." *Romanic Review* XII (1921): 168–180.

————. "A Study of Spanish Manners, 1750–1800, from the Plays of Ramón de la Cruz." *University of Illinois Studies in Language and Literature* XI (1926): 357–428.

———. "Two Spanish Imitations of *Maître Patelin.*" *Romanic Review* XXX (1939):
340–344.

Hidalgo, Ana María. "La mujer madrileña en don Ramón de la Cruz: Literatura y
realidad." *Anales del Instituto de Estudios Madrileños* XXIV (1987): 269–
287.

Huerta Calvo, Javier. "Ramón de la Cruz y la tradición del teatro cómico breve." *Ínsula*
574 (October 1994): 12–13.

Iacuzzi, Alfred. "The Naive Theme in *The Tempest* as a Link between Thomas Shadwell
and Ramón de la Cruz." *Modern Language Notes* LII (1937): 252–256.

Ingenschay, Dieter. "Ramón de la Cruz: Sainetes." In *Das spanische Theater: Vom Mittelalter bis zur Gegenwart*, ed. Volker Roloff and Harald Wentzlaff-Eggebert.
Dusseldorf: Schwann-Bagel, 1988.

Kish, Kathleen. "A School for Wives: Women in Eighteenth-Century Spanish Theater."
In, *Women in Hispanic Literature: Icons and Fallen Idols*, ed. Beth Miller. Berkeley: University of California Press, 1983. 184–200.

Lafarga, Francisco. "Ramón de la Cruz y el teatro europeo." *Ínsula* 574 (October 1994):
13–14.

———. "Ramón de la Cruz adaptador de Carmontelle." *Annali dell'Istituto Universitario
Orientale. Sezione romanza* XXIV (1982): 115–126.

———. "Ramón de la Cruz y Carmontelle." *1616* III (1980): 90–96.

———. "Sobre la fuente desconocida de *Zara*, sainete de Ramón de la Cruz." *Anuario
de Filología* 3 (1977): 361–371.

McClelland, Ivy. *Spanish Drama of Pathos, 1750–1808.* 2 vols. Liverpool: Liverpool
University Press, 1970.

Meregalli, Franco. "Goldoni e Ramón de la Cruz." In *Studi goldoniani.* Venice: Istituto
per la collaborazione culturale, 1960. 795–800.

Moore, John A. *Ramón de la Cruz.* New York: Twayne, 1972.

Nozick, Martin. "A source of Don Ramón de la Cruz." *Modern Language Notes* LXIII
(1948): 244–248.

Palacios Fernández, Emilio. "La descalificación moral del sainete dieciochesco." In *El
teatro menor en España a partir del siglo XVI.* Edn. Grupo de investigación sobre
teatro español. Madrid: CSIC, 1983. 215–233.

Palau, Francisca. *Ramón de la Cruz und der franzoesische Kultureinfluss im Spanien des
XVIII. Jahrhunderts.* Bonn: Rohrscheid, 1935.

Pérez Galdós, Benito. "Don Ramón de la Cruz y su época." *Revista de España* XVII
(1870): 27–52; XVIII (1871): 200–227.

———. "Ramón de la Cruz." In *Memoranda.* Madrid: Paez y Compañía, 1906. 145–
225.

Sala, José M. "Ramón de la Cruz entre dos fuegos: Literatura y público." *Cuadernos
Hispanoamericanos* 277–278 (1973): 350–360.

Sala Valldaura, Josep María. "Ramón de la Cruz, crítico de sí mismo: El prólogo de
1786." *Ínsula* 574 (October 1994): 5–7.

———. "Tradición y contexto: El sainete de finales del siglo XVIII." *Nueva Revista de
Filología Hispánica* 41.2 (1993): 459–470.

Simón Díaz, José. "Censura anónima del *Manolo.*" *Revista de Bibliografía Nacional* V
(1944): 470.

———. "Don Ramón de la Cruz y las ediciones fraudulentas." *Bibliografía Hispánica*
IV (1946): 712–722.

Subirá, José. "Lo que dicen sainetes y tonadillas: El Madrid musical en la época de Goya y Cruz." *Círculo de Bellas Artes* (1927): 65–72.

———. "Repertorio teatral madrileño y resplandor transitorio de la zarzuela. (Años 1763 a 1771)." *Boletín de la Real Academia Española* XXXIX. 158 (1959): 429–462.

Suppan, Steven. "Managing Culture. *Manolo* and the Majos' Good Taste." In *The Institutionalization of Literature in Spain*, ed. Wlad Godzich and Nicholas Spadaccini. Minneapolis: Prisma Institute, 1987. 125–168.

Valdivieso, L. Teresa. "Regodeo burlesco de Don Ramón de la Cruz." *Dieciocho* 18.2 (Fall 1995): 253–259.

Varela, Jose Luis. "Ramón de la Cruz y el majismo." In *La literatura española de la Ilustración: Homenaje a Carlos III*. Madrid: Universidad Complutense, 1989. 113–130.

Vega, José. *Don Ramón de la Cruz, el poeta de Madrid.* 1945. Madrid: Libros del ayer y del mañana, 1979.

Vilches Frutos, María Francisca. "El habla popular en los sainetes de D. Ramón de la Cruz." *Dieciocho* VI (1983): 116–137.

———. "Los sainetes de Ramón de la Cruz en la tradición literaria. Sus relaciones con la Illustración." *Segismundo* 39–40 (1984): 173–192.

ANA DIOSDADO
(1938–)

Iride Lamartina-Lens

BIOGRAPHY

In 1970 an unexpected phenomenon occurred in Madrid's Valle-Inclán Theater that rocked the theater establishment and altered the face and characteristics of the last genre of the twentieth century still monopolized by male authors. A young playwright by the name of Ana Diosdado staged her first original play, *Olvida los tambores* [Forget the Drums], and its extraordinary success not only launched the career of one of Spain's most renowned figures in contemporary theater but also paved the way for an entire generation of women dramatists in Spain. In that year, Ana Diosdado accomplished what no Spanish female predecessor in professional dramaturgy had achieved thus far: to capture the mainstream public's imagination, receive critical acclaim, win a prestigious theater prize, be the first woman dramatist to be included in F. C. Sainz de Robles's annual anthology of the best Spanish plays, and produce one of the season's major box office hits with 450 consecutive performances. Diosdado still holds the distinction of being Spain's foremost woman playwright of the postwar era and of prevailing throughout this period as one of the genre's most successful authors.

Ana Isabel Alvarez-Diosdado was born in Buenos Aires on May 21, 1938. Her early infancy was spent traveling throughout South America on a theater tour with her father, the distinguished actor and director Enrique Diosdado, who at the time was a member in Margarita Xirgu's theater company. While she was still a very young child, her parents divorced, her mother died shortly thereafter, and she was raised by her father and stepmother, the actress Amelia de la Torre. At the age of six, Diosdado made her stage debut in Xirgu's production of Federico García Lorca's *Mariana Pineda*. Under the tutelage of three of Spain's most celebrated actors, Xirgu, Diosdado, and de la Torre, the young girl received an exceptional formative education in the art of drama, and this exposure would greatly serve her in later years in her dual career as actress and playwright.

After her family's return to Spain in 1950, Diosdado dedicated herself to her studies, graduated from an elite French academy, and later entered the University Complutense of Madrid. The young woman soon dropped her studies and decided to return to her roots as a stage actress. With her father's encouragement, Diosdado also pursued her interest in writing, and in 1965, she published her first novel, *En cualquier lugar, no importa cuándo* [Anyplace, Any time]. In 1969 she wrote a second novel, "Campanas que aturden" [The Bewildering Bells], which was runner-up for the Planeta Prize but remains unpublished. The author's credits include a third novel published in 1986, *Los ochenta son nuestros* [The Eighties Are Ours], which is the narrative version of the play of the same title.

Notwithstanding Diosdado's relative success as a novelist, drama would provide the young writer with the best vehicle to fully develop her artistic talents. Throughout the first half of the 1970s Diosdado devoted herself entirely to writing, directing, and performing for the stage and/or television. During this intensive period of productivity, she wrote her first television series, *Juan y Manuela* (1974), in which Diosdado played the role of Manuela, and staged five original plays: *Olvida los tambores* [Forget, the Drums], 1970; *El okapi* [The Okapi] (1972); *Usted también podrá disfrutar de ella* [You, Too, Can Enjoy Her] (1973); *Los comuneros* [The Commoners] (1974); and *Y de Cachemira, chales* [And Shawls form Kashmir] (1976). The majority of these plays did not live up to the public's high expectations and received mixed reviews. However, *Usted también podrá disfrutar de ella* proved to be the notable exception, won two major literary prizes, and ran for more than 500 performances.

The political and cultural shifts resulting from Franco's death in 1975 greatly impacted Spanish society on the whole and the theater in particular. During this difficult transitional period from dictatorship to democracy, Diosdado temporarily retreated from authoring original plays and redirected her creative talents to translating/adapting foreign dramatic works and to writing television scripts. In 1983 her controversial adaptation of Henrik Ibsen's *A Doll's House* was staged in Madrid. Her version, imbued with feminist overtones, caused a stir among critics and theatergoers alike with her altered final scene of the play. In that same year, she wrote and starred in the enormously popular *Anillos de oro* [Wedding Rings], a series of thirteen hour-long television plays featuring a divorce lawyer who is faced with resolving a variety of matrimonial cases. In 1986 she wrote and starred in another widely viewed series, *Segunda enseñanza* [Secondary Education] in which she portrays the very real struggles of a teacher and a single mother. Both of these hit series reached millions of viewers in Spain and Latin America and have established Diosdado as an international celebrity.

In 1986 Diosdado returned to the stage after a ten-year absence with *Cuplé* [Ballad] (1988), which was staged by her own company and ran for four months in Madrid before touring the provinces. Its success initiated a second group of original plays that include: *Los ochenta son nuestros* [The Eighties Are Ours] (1988), the most commercially successful play of the 1987–1988 season; *Cam-*

ino de plata [The Silver Path] (1989), which ran for seven months in the 1988–1989 season before going on tour and featured Diosdado, her husband, Carlos Larrañaga, a well-known stage and film actor, and their daughter-in-law in the major roles; *Trescientos veintiuno, trescientos veintidós* [Three Twenty-one, Three Twenty-two] (1993), staged in the 1990–1991 season and directed by Larrañaga; *Cristal de Bohemia* [Bohemian Crystal] (1995), staged in 1994–1995; and most recently, "Decíamos ayer" ["As We Were Saying Yesterday"), 1997, and "La última a ventura" ("The Last Adventure"), 1999, both staged and directed by the author. Diosdado's credits also include the 1992 staging of her adaptation of Oscar Wilde's *Lady Windermere's Fan* and a fourth television series that same year, *Yo, la juez* [I, the Judge].

DRAMATURGY: MAJOR WORKS AND THEMES

One of the hallmarks that distinguishes Ana Diosdado's theater is an overall sense of balance that underlies and unites the structural, stylistic, and thematic aspects of her works. Her plays integrate high-quality craftsmanship with stimulating thematic content, incorporate innovative theatrical techniques to standard constructs of the well-made play, and provide a multiplicity of perspectives that invite reflection rather than reaction. In general, the dramatist recreates an identifiable reality that is inhabited by a repertoire of characters of diverse social backgrounds who express themselves in a colloquial and vibrant language.

Targeting significant issues of contemporary immediacy, her works embrace a wide range of themes including: the focus on interpersonal relationships based on freedom, equality, and mutual sensitivity; the search for sexual identity; the anguish of unfulfilled ambitions; the conflict between personal gratification and social responsibility; and the need to encounter purpose and meaning in a depersonalized society. These concerns are bonded by a critical underpinning that strongly condemns materialism and consumer society and its degrading effects on the human spirit.

Throughout her work, there is a concerted attempt to cultivate more social and political harmony among the class, gender, and ideological factions that currently polarize Spanish society on the whole and greatly influence interpersonal relationships in particular. While Diosdado's theater does not adhere to any one ideological stance; it unequivocally disputes and dismantles the political dichotomy (conservative/liberal) and deconstructs conventional paradigms of gender-assigned behaviors (strong/weak; positive/ negative; rational/emotional). But role reversal is only an initial step in the process of challenging sex-role stereotypes and in creating multidimensional characters of both sexes. For the dramatist also broadens her characters' range of emotional and behavioral experience and considers human complexity with all of its inherent contradictions. In so doing, her theater prompts new perspectives on past formulas and relationships.

One of Diosdado's most notable contributions is the creation of strong female characters for the stage. For the most part, the women she portrays are survivors, and they have the fortitude to triumph over societal obstacles and injustices much better than their male counterparts. It is important to note, however, that their victory does not necessarily conform to the prescribed male barometer of success, which is more materialistic than spiritual. These women's triumphs rise from an "emotional intelligence" fortified by the understanding of personal vulnerabilities and strengths, the compassion for others, the willingness to use intuition along with "cognitive intelligence", and the ability to adapt to outside changes.

Overall, Diosdado's plays fall into two major categories: The first group is more intimate in nature and probes issues of identity and personal relationships; the second examines broader issues of political and social concerns and foregrounds their impact on the individual and the society at large. Within this general framework, the dramatist often incorporates and interchanges characteristics between the two and uses a wide variety of approaches that range from realism to allegorical satire.

Characteristic of the first group, which includes *Olvida los tambores, Camino de plata*, and *Trescientos veintiuno, trescientos veintidós*, is the use of one setting and the precedence of dialogue and character development over exterior action. All three plays follow a realistic vein, develop within a chronological time frame, share a similar structure based upon the counterposition of two couples, spotlight sex roles and binary oppositions, and center on interpersonal relationships. Despite these similarities, close examination of these plays reveals several important differences that underscore Diosdado's evolution and maturation as a playwright.

Olvida los tambores mirrors the social and political revolutions of the late 1960s. The plot revolves around two young couples representing diametrically opposed lifestyles and ideological stances and their mutual disdain and intolerance for one another's differences. Alicia and Tony are the bohemian, idealistic couple who openly embrace the counterculture, have a liberal marriage, and reject materialism. On the other hand, Alicia's sister Pili and Lorenzo are the more traditional middle-class couple who thrive on social status and materialistic comfort and abide closely to their respective conventional roles. The main conflict arises when Lorenzo and Tony engage in an ideological spar that soon turns ugly and vindictive. Although Tony, a struggling musician, has consistently censured his rich brother-in-law's materialism, he now goes to him for a personal loan. Lorenzo sees this as an opportunity to get back at Tony for past offenses and refuses him the money. The incensed Tony decides to take revenge by taking away Lorenzo's most prized possession: his wife. Through sexual and intellectual manipulation, Tony recruits Pili against her husband and seduces her into having an affair with him. When Pili discovers that she has been nothing more than a sex object and/or status symbol for both men, she becomes embittered and decides to radically change her life. Lorenzo, on the other hand, cannot mentally cope with Pili's unfaithfulness, and he commits suicide. In order to balance the opposing ideological camps, Diosdado includes a fifth character, the buoyant and perceptive Pepe, who is Tony's lyricist and the true idealist in the play. This androgynous character, who promotes harmony and tolerance as a solution to conflict, will reappear in later plays and embodies the positive model needed for change.

With *Camino de plata* Diosdado resumes discussion of many of the themes and issues featured in *Olvida los tambores*. Her argument and characters reflect the changes in personal and social sensitivities that have evolved during these last two decades. This three-character play takes place over a period of several years and portrays the psychological and emotional maturation of a middle-aged couple, Paula and Fernando, and the evolution of their relationship within the scope of sexual politics. The second couple, in their early twenties, consists of Fernando's secretary, Mari-Carmen, and her unemployed, drug addict boyfriend who never appears on stage. This young couple is not concerned with ideological issues pertaining to freedom or sexual revolutions or even love. Rather, they reflect a desire to survive their dire reality, which is plagued by chronic unemployment, drugs, violence, and lack of hope for a better future.

In many ways, *Camino de plata* is a more mature, toned-down version of *Olvida los tambores* and resolves many of the unanswered questions posed by the earlier play. In *Camino de plata* the terms and the possibilities for female independence are more defined, and the solutions need not be as drastic as before. The play begins when Paula, a very traditional housewife and mother, is sent to a psychiatrist upon the insistence of her husband Andrés. Paula is fully aware of her husband's ploy to label her as unstable so that he can get a divorce and be free to date a younger woman. The play delineates Paula's progress from the initial stage of anger and confusion to the second stage of resignation and acceptance of her divorce to the final stage of emotional stability and economic self-reliance. Paula's evolution is not at the expense of her feminine qualities, however, nor does it exclude the human need for love and companionship. The ironic twist is that as Paula becomes more self-sufficient and confident, the two men in her life, Andrés and Fernando, grow less secure and more demanding of her time and affection. In the end, Paula maintains her hard-earned economic autonomy and redefines and balances her relationship with both men. In *Camino de plata*, the 1990s version of a "happy ending," is based on sexual equality, a sensitivity for personal differences, and a balance between love and independence.

Trescientos veintiuno, trescientos veintidós, which takes place in a hotel, contrasts young newlyweds, Jorge and Sara, with the middle-aged "couple" next door, Alberto, a politician, and Mercedes, an undercover journalist posing as a call girl. In this comedy of errors, Diosdado utilizes classic devices of role reversals, mistaken identities, and an imaginary friend (Buby the dog) to underscore the comic effect. The author focuses on male/female relationships and on the identity crisis faced by the two male characters. In the first couple, Sara is the stronger, more self-confident, and by far, the more sexually experienced and aggressive of the two. Jorge, on the other hand, is a timid virgin who relies on alcohol and Buby to give him courage. Upon Sara's persistent probing, Jorge reveals his sexual ambiguity; his resentment at having to choose between a stable career in business and his passion for music; his difficulty in living up to the traditional models of male behavior; and his uneasiness with relationships with women (his mother and Sara). Thinking that these are crises occurring only in youth, Sara and Jorge look wistfully at the seasoned couple next door, who seem to have all of the stability that they lack.

In the meantime, Alberto and Mercedes are having some difficulty in communication of their own as the unsuspecting Alberto divulges incriminating information about his intention to sell out to the opposition to the charming and witty Mercedes. Upon revealing her true identity, Mercedes gives him the choice to renege on his decision or she will expose him publicly, and she incites Alberto to come to terms with his lack of professional integrity and his personal failure as a father and husband. Inspired by Mercedes's commitment to principle and attracted by her openness and sensuality, Alberto hopes for a new life with her by his side. As the two, look nostalgically at the young, carefree couple next door, it becomes apparent that happiness is illusory at every stage of life.

In the second group of plays, Diosdado shifts her focus from the dynamics of the couple and addresses broader issues of contemporary social and political concerns. In many ways, *Usted también podrá disfrutar de ella* defines most of the characteristics prevalent in the remainder of her works. The play contains a complex structure that incorporates several innovative expressionist devices such as multiple staging used to accommodate rapid changes in time and space; the juxtaposition of time frames that highlight the dual perception of subjective and objective reality; and the doubling of one actor in various roles. In addition to these structural innovations, there is a critical underpinning that strongly attacks consumer society and focuses on manipulation by the media and its exploitation of women as sex objects. The action centers on a dual investigation of several unexplained deaths. The first is conducted in the present by a forensic specialist examining an apparent suicide. The second has occurred in the past and is evoked in an expressionistic fashion to tell us of a disillusioned journalist, Javier, who has been commissioned by a gossip magazine to interview a popular media icon, Fanny. The model has been associated with a product that seems to have caused the death of several children. During an intensive three-day interview, Javier and Fanny grapple with painful discoveries about themselves and the world in which they live that throw them into the grips of despair. Upon realizing that they have been made the scapegoats of a manipulative and exploitative society, they arrive at two major decisions: first, to expose the truth about a pharmaceutical company's cover-up of the children's deaths; second, to help one another commit suicide. Contrary to what was at first suspected, it is Javier who succumbs, while Fanny finds the defiant strength to survive and start anew.

The subsequent plays offer a multifaceted view of Spain within the context of its war-torn history, its troubled present, and its uncertain future. The first of these is the historical play *Los comuneros*, which is based on the sixteenth-century popular uprising against Spain's King Carlos I. Following expressionistic techniques, it uses two contradictory narrative voices of the king as a young boy and as an old man that discuss and analyze the events leading up to the defeat and execution of the rebellion's leaders. The dual characters' opposing political stances serve to contrast the intransigence and narcissism of the young monarch with the tolerance and wisdom of the older king. The play provides a hindsight view of the causes of civil war and its tragic aftermath, thus sustaining parallels with Franco's Spain.

El okapi depicts an authoritarian Spain of the early 1970s that denied personal freedom, stifled individualism, and resorted to fascist tactics of repression. The first act juxtaposes two separate plots that later converge in the second act. The first one centers on the carefree and indigent vagabond Marcelo, a survivor of the defeated Republicans, and his fight for survival. This action stands in marked contrast to the second plot, which takes place at the Happy Rest Home and features a group of senior citizens who live a regimented, nondescript life that is materially comfortable but spiritually devoid of meaning. After suffering an accident, Marcelo is sent to the Happy Rest Home to recover. His presence infuses hope into the dreary lives of the residents, inspires them to take control of their own destinies, and rekindles their forgotten aspirations for love and purposeful existence. When it becomes clear that Marcelo will never be permitted to leave the hospice, he, like the mythical *okapi* who cannot survive in captivity, dies. His influence on his companions, however, will continue to have long-lasting positive effects even after his death.

In the science fiction allegory *Y de Cachemira, chales*, Diosdado gives us a futuristic view of Spain after the end of the forty-year Francoist regime. The action centers on a group of survivors who have found a comfortable refuge in a department store in an attempt to isolate themselves from cataclysmic changes in the outside world. Juan, the elderly patriarch, insists on upholding the status quo and not risking the loss of material security for a precarious future based on too many unknown factors. His attitude conflicts with that of Dani, a newcomer, who speaks of creating new and better worlds based on the tragic lessons of the past. This struggle between the older authoritative forces and the younger promoters of freedom culminates in a violent encounter between Juan and Dani. Upon the patriarch's death, the remaining survivors abandon their illusory security and bravely go out to charter a new world.

The metaphor of a turbulent and paradoxical post-Francoist Spain first presented in *Y de Cachemira, chales* is reintroduced in *Cuplé* and *Cristal de Bohemia*. In these biting satires, Diosdado directs her criticism toward the morally and politically bankrupt consumer society that is at the root of the growing economic disparities between rich and poor, the spiraling unemployment rate and disenchantment among the young, the abandonment of the old, the exploitation of workers, the indifference of the middle class toward the needs of the disenfranchised, the diversion of Spanish capital to Swiss banks, and the rise in random terrorist acts. Both satirical farces feature an array of bawdy characters, which include prostitutes, pimps, progressive priests, fortune-tellers, murderers, and terrorists. In a quasi-esperpentic mode, Diosdado systematically reverses many expected roles, situations, and attitudes; by so doing, she underscores the tragic absurdity of a world gone awry, with displaced values and misdirected energies. Much of the comic effect of *Cuplé* is based on these inversions of roles, which feature a middle-aged mistress/ex-nightclub singer/conservative thinker Carmen, who has recently inherited her dead lover's wealth; Carmen's lover's second wife Leni, a young impoverished radical/terrorist involved in the Green movement; Balbina, Carmen's sixty-five-year-old maid who has embraced the liberation movement and needs to "find" herself; and the androgynous Grau, the new "maid" who turns out to be a disillusioned former history teacher. Although Grau's presence restores a sense of values and purpose in the other characters' lives, he cannot endure the pain of his own disenchantment, and after a series of humorous attempts at suicide, he finally succeeds at finding peace and happiness through death. Contemporary society's total disregard for the suffering of others and its dispassionate inclination to dispose of people or things that are no longer marketable are the overriding themes in the offbeat murder mystery *Cristal de Bohemia*. The play centers on the dismantling of a former house of prostitution and the ensuing inexplicable deaths among the bordello's retired prostitutes. Steeped in ironic overtones, the play contrasts the depravity and repression of the old authoritarian Spain with the indifference and depersonalization of the new Spain.

CRITICS' RESPONSE

In spite of Diosdado's exceptional commercial success, her theater has been largely ignored or often shrugged off as "well-made plays" for a bourgeois audience. In the most consulted history of twentieth-century Spanish theater (*Historia del teatro español: Siglo XX* [Madrid: Cátedra, 1975]), Francisco Ruiz Ramón documents hundreds of Spanish dramatists from important to minor to "underground" but refers to Diosdado only in the preface (10). In an important new history (*El teatro desde 1936* [Madrid: Alhambra, 1989]), César Oliva devotes a mere six lines of his 490-page study to Diosdado, labeling her work "bourgeois comedy" (458). Even though F. C. Sainz de Robles has praised Diosdado as one of the best dramatists in contemporary Spanish theater and has included *Olvida los tambores, El okapi*, and *Usted también podrá disfrutar de ella* in three volumes of *Teatro español*, his annual anthology of the best Spanish plays of the season (Madrid: Aguilar, 1970–1971; 1972–1973; 1973–1974), there has been a paucity of critical attention devoted to women dramatists in general and to Diosdado in particular (O'Connor 378–379). In Spain, critical reaction to her theater has ranged from Florencio Segura's identification of her work as a "comedy of manners" similar to the theater of Jacinto Benavente (348) to more favorable responses from Fernando Lázaro Carreter, theater critic for *Ga-*

ceta Ilustrada, and Lola Santa-Cruz, writer for *El Público*, who have singled out her work as intelligent, riveting, and in touch with contemporary reality.

It is to Hispanists in the United States, however, that one must turn in order to gain a more insightful and profound analysis of Diosdado's work. Joan Cain and Phyllis Zatlin, for example, have concentrated on Diosdado's mastery of theatrical techniques and her innovative approaches to structure and character development. Other critics, including Zatlin, Patricia O'Connor, Iride Lamartina-Lens, and Margaret Jones, have approached Diosdado's theater from a feminist perspective and have variously shown that the playwright's concern with sex roles, the deconstruction of binary oppositions of the patriarchy, the inclusion of a multiplicity of voices and viewpoints, her open-ended textuality, and her critical approach to historical and social issues does in fact coincide with contemporary feminist definitions of women's writing.

However, there has been some dissension among feminist critics as to the degree that Diosdado should be considered a feminist writer. Lamartina-Lens considers Diosdado a moderate feminist author whose work shepherds in the more radical women playwrights of the 1980s and 1990s. While O'Connor admires Diosdado for breaking away from the legacy of segregated and ideologically conservative feminine theater of the 1940s and 1950s, she believes that Diosdado, for the most part, sidesteps the feminist challenge and validates the masculine vision (381–382). Zatlin, on the other hand, commends Diosdado for her nonprescriptive male and female characters who tend to transcend both patriarchal and feminist canons of behavior and whose ambivalence toward the acceptance and/or rejection of traditional roles seems more authentic ("El teatro de Ana Diosdado" 136).

Close examination of Diosdado's most commercially successful play *Los ochenta son nuestros* might shed some light as to why there is a certain degree of ambivalence among feminist critics in regard to her work. The play is impeccably crafted, with a structure reminiscent of *Usted también podrá disfrutar de ella* and *Los comuneros* in its use of expressionistic techniques of multiple staging and dual time frames, but it is unique in its realistic portrayal of characters, situations, and dialogue. The play, whose cast is solely made up of teenagers, balances the author's concentration on interpersonal relationships of the young generation among themselves and with their parents with broader issues dealing with love, sex, sexuality, death, violence, prejudice, and rites of passage. The plot develops on two simultaneous temporal levels occurring at the same place but with a time difference of exactly one year. María Angeles, the narrator of the present, has returned in memory of the one year anniversary since her father's and Rafa's tragic deaths and also to fulfill a promise made to Miguel to wait one year before completing her rite of passage and offering him her virginity. As she waits for Miguel, she projects her memories into the past and evokes the tragic events of the previous New Year's Eve that so brutally brought her childhood innocence to an end and irrevocably shattered the security of her world. The main action takes place at a garage/clubhouse and revolves around a young group of friends and their preparation for that evening's festivities. Underneath the apparent innocence and normality of the characters and the circumstances, many unhealed wounds and prejudices fester that cause the death of two boys, El Barbas and Rafa, and the breakup of the closely knit band of friends. It is soon revealed that a gang of privileged young men, in retaliation for one of their girlfriend's rape, brutally beat up two suspicious-looking strangers. When the homeless drug addict, El Barbas, dies as a result of the beating, José, the most hostile and responsible of the gang, makes plans to escape to Italy. But Rafa, the group's most intelligent and perceptive member, feels equally responsible for El Barbas's death and initiates a gesture of reconciliation with the survivor, Miguel, by inviting him to the party. As soon as Miguel arrives, it becomes painfully clear to everyone present that he and Juan Gabriel, Rafa's older brother, have had a previous homosexual relationship and that he was the unnamed friend Juan Gabriel had been expecting. In the midst of these conflicts, there is one brilliant moment of peaceful coexistence and harmony between the opposing groups when they all put aside their differences and adapt a more tolerant attitude. The illusion soon vanishes when Rafa tries to defend Miguel from José's wrath and is accidentally killed.

Zatlin has recognized Diosdado for her open treatment of such sensitive issues as rape and its effect on the victim as well as on the victim's family and friends; prejudice based on class differences between the privileged and marginal groups; and the questioning of self-identity and sexuality. She also points out that Diosdado has deconstructed the liberal/conservative, good/bad, innocent/guilty dichotomies and has created psychologically integrated characters who go beyond stereotypes. O'Connor, on the other hand, interprets the author's treatment of these issues and characters as retrogressive, citing the fact that the majority of the characters do not steer substantially away from male prescripts of behavior, for even Cris, the young rape victim, seems to reduce the trauma to trivial proportions. Overall, Diosdado's theater does not provide a radical feminist response to the genre's dominant male canons. It does, however, raise the standard of theater written by both male and female playwrights as it furnishes a powerful and effective model of exquisite balance between exceptional form and compelling content and of memorable characters who ring of authenticity.

AWARDS AND DISTINCTIONS

Mayte Prize, for *Olvida los tambores*, 1970

Fastenrath Prize of the Real Academia Española, for *Usted también podrá disfrutar de ella*, 1973

Medalla de Oro de Valladolid, for *Usted también podrá disfrutar de ella*, 1973

BIBLIOGRAPHY

Plays

Olvida los tambores. Madrid: Escelicer, 1972. Teatro español, 1970–1971. Ed. F. C. Sainz de Robles. Madrid: Aguilar, 1972. Ed. Angel Rubio Maroto.

El okapi. Madrid: Escelicer, 1972. Teatro español, 1972–1973. Ed. F. C. Sainz de Robles. Madrid: Aguilar, 1974.

Los comuneros. Madrid: Ediciones MK, 1974. Madrid: Preyson, 1983.

Usted también podrá disfrutar de ella. Madrid: Ediciones MK, 1975. Teatro español, 1973–1974. Ed. F. C. Sainz de Robles. Madrid: Aguilar, 1975.

Y de Cachemira, chales. Madrid: Preyson, 1983.

Anillos de oro. 2 vols. Madrid: Espasa Calpe, 1985.

Cuplé. Madrid: Ediciones Antonio Machado, 1988.

Los ochenta son nuestros. Madrid: Ediciones MK, 1988.

Camino de plata. Madrid: Ediciones Antonio Machado, 1990.

Trescientos veintiuno, trescientos veintidós. Madrid: Sociedad General de Autores de España, 1993.

Cristal de Bohemia. Madrid: Sociedad General de Autores de España, 1996.

"Decíamos ayer." 1997.

"La última aventura." 1999.

Novels

En cualquier lugar, no importa cuándo. Barcelona: Planeta, 1965.

"Campanas que aturden." 1969. Unpublished.

Los ochenta son nuestros. Barcelona: Plaza y Janés, 1986.

Television Programs

Juan y Manuela. 1974.

Anillos de Oro. 1983.

Segunda enseñanza. 1986.

Yo, la juez. 1992.

Essays

El teatro por dentro: Ceremonia, representación, fenómeno colectivo. Barcelona: Aula Abierta Salvat, 1981.

Adaptations and Translations

Casa de muñecas. Madrid: Ediciones MK, 1983. [Adaptation of *A Doll's House* by Henrik Ibsen]

La gata sobre el tejado de zinc caliente. Madrid: Ediciones MK, 1984. [Trans. of *Cat on a Hot Tin Roof* by Tennessee Williams]

La Importancia de llamarse Wilde. Madrid: Ediciones MK, 1992. [Adaptation of *Lady Windermere's Fan* by Oscar Wilde]

Translation

"The Okapi." Trans. Marion Peter Holt. [Sponsored by the National Endowment for the Arts; unpublished]

Critical Studies

Anderson, Farris. "From Protest to Resignation." *Estreno* 2.2 (1976): 29–32.

Bremón, Anunchi. Interview with Diosdado. *El País Semanal* 1 (July 1984): 10–14.

Cain, Joan. "Ana Diosdado: Winner of the Fastenrath Prize." *Letras Femeninas* 5.1 (1979): 54–63.

Fagundo, Ana María. "El teatro de Ana Diosdado." *Alaluz* 18.2 (1986): 51–59.

Ferrero, Carmen. "La dialéctica del reconocimiento en *Usted también podrá disfrutar de ella* de Ana Diosdado." In *Entre Actos: Diálogos sobre teatro español entre siglos,* ed. Martha T. Halsey and Phyllis Zatlin. University Park, PA: *Estreno,* 1999. 49–54.

Floeck, Wilfried. "¿Arte sin sexo? Dramaturgas españolas contemporáneas." In *Teatro español contemporáneo: Autores y tendencies,* ed. Alfonso de Toro and Wilfried Floeck. Kassel, Germany: Reichenberger, 1995. 57–76.

Gopegui, Belén. "Camino de Plata, espectáculo de un solo público." *El Público* 62 (1988): 24–25.

Haro Tecglen, Eduardo. "Obras para que la burguesía se ría." *El País* 3 (October 1988): 22.

Jones, Margaret E. W. "La imagen, la mirada y la realidad en *Usted también podrá disfrutar de ella,* de Ana Diosdado." In *A Stage of Their Own/Un Escenario Propio,* ed. Kirsten Nigro and Phyllis Zatlin. 2 vols. Ottawa: Girol, 1998. 79–87.

Lamartina-Lens, Iride. "Contemporary Women Dramatists of the 80's and 90's." Paper presented to the Modern Language Association, Chicago, December 1990.

———. "Female Rage: Diosdado and Pedrero Deal with an Age-Long Problem in a New-Age Fashion." In *Entre Actos: Diálogos sobre teatro español entre siglos,* ed. Martha T. Halsey and Phyllis Zatlin. University Park, PA: *Estreno,* 1999. 63–68.

———. "Sex Roles in the Theater of Ana Diosdado." Paper presented at the Fifth Annual Wichita State University Conference on Foreign Languages, Wichita, Kansas, April 1988.

O'Connor, Patricia W. "Women Playwrights in Spain and the Male-Dominated Canon." *Signs* 15.2 (1990): 376–390.

Santa-Cruz, Lola. Interview with Diosdado. *El Público* 39 (December 1986): 28–30.

Segura, Florencio. "Olvida los tambores, ¿un teatro joven?" *Razón y Fe* 879 (1970): 347–350.

Zatlin, Phyllis. "Ana Diosdado." In *Spanish Women Writers: A Bio-Bibliographical Sourcebook,* ed. Linda Gould Levine et al. Westport, CT: Greenwood Press, 1993. 158–166.

————. "Ana Diosdado and the Contemporary Spanish Theater." *Estreno* 10.2 (1984): 37–40.

————. "El teatro de Ana Diosdado: ¿conformista?" In *Teatro español contemporáneo: Autores y tendencias*, ed. Alfonso de Toro and Wilfried Floeck. Kassel, Germany: Reichenberger, 1995. 125–145.

————. "The Theater of Ana Diosdado." *Estreno* 3.1 (1977): 13–17.

————. "Traditional Sex Roles in the Theatre of Ana Diosdado." *Mid-Hudson Language Studies* 10 (1987): 71–77.

JOSÉ ECHEGARAY
(1832–1916)

Wadda C. Ríos-Font

BIOGRAPHY

José Echegaray y Eizaguirre was born in Madrid in 1832, but he spent most of his childhood in Murcia. In 1847, at the age of fifteen, he returned to Madrid to begin his engineering studies in the Escuela de Caminos. He would join the faculty of the school shortly after the completion of his degree in 1854, teaching calculus and rational and applied mechanics, and decisively establish himself in the capital after his 1857 marriage to Ana Perfecta Estrada. The Escuela de Caminos was the center around which the young Echegaray would begin to build his reputation as a public man, since—as Javier Fornieles Alcaraz tells us—at this time in the nineteenth century the Spanish state was engaged in the massive construction of communications infrastructures, and consequently engineers were of enormous importance to a society, which in turn bestowed on them considerable prestige. In the context of his experience in the Escuela de Caminos Echegaray will begin to achieve renown as a mathematician and scientist, as well as to approach the public arena in regard to topics of economic and political importance.

Through 1868 Echegaray's intellectual life centers around the interests of his professional guild. Throughout the period he writes scientific pieces in publications such as the *Revista de obras públicas*, the *Revista para el progreso de las ciencias*, and the *Revista de España*, and in 1857 he debuts as an orator in the Ateneo with a talk on "Astronomía popular." Later on, in 1866, he would be inducted into the Real Academia de Ciencias Exactas in recognition of his long list of articles and books on calculus, geometry, physics, and thermodynamics. Engineers were also known for their espousal of the economic ideal of free trade and its political implications, and in this respect, Echegaray was one of their best-known representatives: In 1856 he founded, with his friend and colleague Gabriel Rodríguez, the free trade journal *El economista*.

The six-year democratic period following the Revolution of 1868 sees the active incorporation of Echegaray into Spanish political life. The first provisional administration names him, at the age of thirty-six, Director General de Obras Públicas—despite the fact that he did not at that time formally belong to any political party—and soon after, he joins the faction of monarchist democrats and is elected deputy to the Cortes Constituyentes for two different districts, Murcia and Avilés (he chooses the second). A speech on the issue of religious freedom pronounced at the Cortes earns him instant recognition as a brilliant politician. His success as a speaker, dependent "as much on the ability to connect with the feelings of the majority as on the eloquence of the speaker" [tanto en la habilidad para conectar con los sentimientos de la mayoría como en la elocuencia del orador] (Fornieles Alcaraz 226)—talents he would later make ample use of in his career as a dramatist—catapults his rise in the government, and he is soon reappointed as Ministro de Fomento, a position he will occupy uninterruptedly through 1871. In this character he will undertake economic reforms leading to the stimulation of private enterprise and educational reforms including the demand for university authorities to address the issue of women's low cultural standard.

As Minister he is chosen to be one of a committee of three in charge of welcoming Amadeo de Saboya on his arrival in Cartagena. Nevertheless, after the accession of the new king, the monarchist democrats' progressive distancing from his monarchy and Echegaray's integration into this new radical faction cause him to be overlooked for a ministerial position. From this point on, his political career will go through numerous changes, in accordance with the rapid succession of regimes in which he would participate as a member of the government. He serves for a period as parliamentary deputy, this time for Quintanar de la Orden, before being reappointed in 1872 as Minister of Works. In February 1873 Amadeo I abdicates, and the former minister of the parliamentary monarchy becomes the First Republic's Minister of Finance. He does not, however, hold the office for long. As a consequence of the ensuing confrontations between radicals and republicans, after a brief membership in the Asamblea Nacional he is forced into exile in April of the same year. He returns again in January 1874, after Pavía's new *pronunciamiento*, and retakes the Ministry of Finance in the cabinet presided over by Serrano. From this office he creates the Banco de España (a monopoly contradicting his early free trade ideals), introduces paper money, and works pragmatically to establish credit and financial credibility for the state.

It is during his brief period in French exile, in 1873, that Echegaray, dispirited by the uncertain course of political events, begins to write his first play. Upon his return to Spain in 1874, a friend was successful in getting this drama, *El libro talonario*, into the repertoire of the Teatro Apolo. Because of Echegaray's reputation as a statesman, it was decided to announce the author's name as Jorge Hayaseca, an anagram of José Echegaray, but Ramón de Campoamor took charge of spreading the rumor of his true identity. The play premiered to extraordinary success on February 18, 1874, and after this date Echegaray resigned his post as Minister of Finance. Although he would remain active in politics throughout his life and briefly reassume the same office in 1905, this moment marks a turning point in his activities, and until his death, he will remain first and foremost a playwright.

Echegaray's many successes—the greatest of which was *El gran Galeoto* in 1881 (others will be discussed in the following section)—earned him a literary renown as great as his reputation first as a scientist and then as a politician. In July 1882 he was chosen to occupy the place of the late Ramón de Mesonero Romanos in the Real Academia Española, and on November 13, 1904, he was awarded Spain's first Nobel Prize in Literature. The extraordinary command of Spanish theater he achieved and the extent to which he dictated the norms by which other playwrights were forced to abide generated, as we will see later on, both an enormous following and the enormous and eventually successful opposition of the group of intellectuals that would come to form the Generation of 1898. A new collection of artists with new aesthetic and political ideals would uncontestably leave him behind. Nevertheless, at the time of his death on September 14, 1916, Echegaray had lived one of the most influential lives of any of his contemporaries in all areas of Spanish culture and society.

DRAMATURGY: MAJOR WORKS AND THEMES

José Echegaray has long been considered to represent, in the words of Gonzalo Sobejano, "the typical melodrama of Restoration Spain" [el melodrama típico de la España de la Restauración], (93), and his works do indeed include most of the elements commonly associated with melodrama. His plays feature a conflict between good and evil expressed through high-pitched, emotional language and exaggerated acting. The best description of Echegaray's dramatic formula is perhaps the one made by the playwright himself in an often-quoted sonnet:

> I choose a passion, take an idea,
> a problem, a temperament, and infuse
> it, like solid dynamite, deep into
> a character my mind creates.
> The plot surrounds the character
> with several puppets, who in the world
> either flounder in filthy slime,
> or shine in Phoebean light.
> I light the fuse. The fire spreads,
> the cartridge inevitably bursts,
> and the principal star pay for it.
> Although, sometimes, too, in this siege
> I lay on art, which gratifies my instinct . . .
> the explosion cuts me right through the middle!

> [Escojo una pasión, tomo una idea,
> un problema, un carácter, y lo infundo,

cual densa dinamita, en lo profundo
de un personaje que mi mente crea.
La trama al personaje le rodea
de unos cuantos muñecos, que en el mundo
o se revuelcan por el cieno inmundo,
o resplandecen a la luz febea.
La mecha enciendo. El fuego se propaga,
el cartucho revienta sin remedio
y el astro principal es quien lo paga.
Aunque a veces también en este asedio
que al Arte pongo y que el instinto halaga . . .
¡me coge la explosión de medio a medio!] (Antón del Olmet 182)

It is an interesting fact, however, that not one of the more than sixty plays
written by Echegaray was explicitly designated as melodrama. Spain's first Nobel Prize winner did not consider his works melodramas, and neither his contemporary public nor the critics received them chiefly as such. José Echegaray's
work was melodramatic, but it was not, *in the context of its time*, melodrama,
and this distinction between adjective and noun is crucial to the assessment of
his dramatic career.

After the initial success of works generically known as melodrama in the first
half of the nineteenth century, in the second half of the century the label acquired
pejorative connotations because of its association with straining after effect and
extravagant displays of sentiment. As a result, although Echegaray's production
retains a strong melodramatic core, he distances it from melodrama through a
movement I have called *impersonation*: His melodramatic plays either incorporate features of other modes or overtly claim a kinship with prestigious theatrical forms—such as romantic and Golden Age theater, classical and modern
tragedy, realism and naturalism—often passing for those forms in the eyes of
the public. The donning of a mask is thus not limited to the actors playing
certain fictitious characters but extends to the work itself, which plays the part
of something else.

The process of impersonation emerges early on as a fundamental principle of
Echegaray's dramaturgy. Near the beginning of his career the playwright approximates two models that encourage his widespread perception as the reviver
of Spanish theater Calderonian and romantic drama. Early plays like *La esposa
del vengador* (1874) and *En el puño de la espada* (1875) resemble romantic
theater in features like their choice of distant times for their settings, their ample
use of verse, their stylization of Romantic staging conventions, and their exal-
tation of love as an overpowering passion. But most early (and many later) plays
also revolve around another concept, the powerful binomial of *honor* [honra],
which simultaneously evokes both the romantic and the Calderonian model.
Echegaray's works thus also hark back to the theater of Calderón, and superficial
though it may be, the connection between the two is soon established. It is

further strengthened through a process of *refundición*: Echegaray's own adaptation of *Semíramis o La hija del aire* premieres to wide acclaim in 1896.

If during Echegaray's early career the models were those of Romantic and Golden Age drama, in his mature period he tried to approximate other dramatic innovations finding their way into Spanish theater. Gonzalo Sobejano discusses how Echegaray attempts to conform to naturalism (*De mala raza, El hijo de Don Juan*) and to adapt Maeterlinck's symbolism (*La duda*) (98). Among the multiple currents and generic models he approaches throughout his career, one nevertheless stands out as a constant goal: He aspires especially to a "sublime horror *trágico*" (Echegaray, *Teatro escogido* 44), and tragedy appears everywhere as the generic paradigm he emulates. He sometimes invokes the paradigm directly, denominating his plays *drama trágico*, and also invokes it indirectly by repeatedly referring to his plays as "terriblemente trágicos" (Echegaray, *Recuerdos* 2:26).

There is plentiful indication that Echegaray's contemporaries did in fact perceive him as a writer of tragic drama, and the Secretary of the Swedish Academy echoes this perception in his speech at the award of the Nobel Prize to Echegaray: "After the splendor of hellenic theater, it is . . . among the English and the Spanish that a national dramatic art has developed. . . . Don José Echegaray . . . has a masterly command of the art of producing in the audience fear and pity, the well-known fundamental elements of tragedy" [Después del esplendor del teatro helénico, entre los ingleses y españoles es donde se ha desarrollado . . . un arte dramático nacional. . . . Don José Echegaray . . . domina magistralmente el arte de producir en el público el terror y la piedad, notorios elementos fundamentales de la tragedia] (qtd. in Lázaro Ros 12).

Throughout Echegaray's career critics echoed the Academy's judgments. In 1875 Manuel de la Revilla (usually censorious of Echegaray's work) wrote, referring to *En el puño de la espada*, that in its final acts "there is, not merely the dramatic sublime, but the tragic sublime with all its immense and magnificent horror" [está, no ya lo sublime dramático sino lo sublime trágico con todo su inmenso y grandioso horror] (qtd. in Baker 82). Almost twenty years later, a reviewer of *Mariana* quoted by José Yxart perceived the play as "terrible and terrifying . . . poignant and prodigious" [terrible y aterrador . . . conmovedor y prodigioso] (1:239). As these testimonies show, Echegaray's work effectively disguised its melodramatic core to become a plausible impersonation of tragedy. While my use of the word *disguise* may seem to imply a deliberate effort to deceive on the part of the writer, the network of reasons and explanations that account for the contemporary acceptance of his work as tragedy is more complex. At one level is the simple fact that, then as now, tragedy is a more prestigious model than melodrama. Tragic status is thus more likely to be granted to authors of great social reputation, and Echegaray, who already enjoyed professional and political fame before he wrote his first play, was a prime candidate for admission into this club. At another level, however, Echegaray's work reveals an honest impulse to create tragedy that follows personal theoretical reflection.

Echegaray's ideas of what is tragic generally conform, at least in principle, to classical definitions. One of the aspects he considers most central to tragedy is the Aristotelian concept of the character afflicted with a flaw. As Echegaray understands the flaw, it is an impulse that contradicts either the predominant direction of the character's nature or the imperative of social norms with grievous consequences. His idea resembles Robert Heilman's later interpretation of the flaw as "tragic dividedness":

In the concept of the good man with the flaw lies the germ of . . . a fundamental view of tragedy. . . . Goodness and flawedness imply different incentives, different needs and desires, indeed different directions. There is a pulling apart within the personality, a disturbance, though not a pathological one, of integration. The character is not "one," but divided. This is my basic assumption about the tragic experience. (7)

The notion of the person as inherently torn between contrary impulses is one of the most basic for Echegaray, who believes "that if one takes *the most virtuous man*, and at the same time *the most criminal man*, of all the evils of the latter there will be a trace, as microscopic as may be, but nevertheless a trace, in the former" [que si se toma *al hombre más virtuoso*, y a la par se toma *al hombre más criminal*, de todas las malas pasiones, de todos los vicios, de todas las negruras de este último, hay una representación . . . tan microscópica como se quiera, pero representación al fin, en el primero] (*Recuerdos* 1: 26). His characters are extraordinary examples of this ever-present conflict between opposing forces.

Echegaray's characters either fight parts of themselves that betray their ethical convictions or are unable to overcome pressures that threaten life as they know it. The tension between impulse and imperative is the tension between intimate feeling and public accountability portrayed in *O locura o santidad* (1877), where Don Lorenzo de Avendaño is driven insane by the conflict between his love for his daughter and his obligation to abandon riches not rightfully inherited and leave her devoid of the social position she needs to marry. It is also present in Echegaray's best-known play, *El gran Galeoto* (1881), in which the otherwise virtuous Ernesto tries to stave off the possibility of an adulterous act that he unconsciously desires and to which the pressure of others ultimately impels him. Insofar as it indicates unbearable irresolution between opposite drives, the concept of flawedness emerges as a structuring principle of Echegaray's dramaturgy. And it not only appears within the various plots but surfaces in the very titles of his plays and in the figures of speech that govern them. Antithesis (*El hijo de hierro y el hijo de carne* [1888], paradox (*Mancha que limpia* [1895], and oxymoron (*El loco dios*) occur repeatedly because they express the contest of contrary directions taking place in the characters' lives.

There are other ways in which Echegaray's dramas attempt to approach the tragic. One of the most significant is the profusion of disastrous endings, highly uncommon in melodramas of the period. Unlike the popular melodramatists, Echegaray insists that "I like dramas to end mournfully" [me gusta que los dramas acaben tristemente] (*Recuerdos* 1:35), and he equates misery with tragedy. Though the literary critic may sneer at this, his contemporary audience may have been more easily convinced: In making this equation Echegaray is adopting the popular use of the word *tragedy* to mean "disaster" or "calamity." But he goes further, emphasizing an Aristotelian dictum that stipulates the tragic plot as one in which characters go from happiness to unhappiness and "have done or suffered something terrible" (Aristotle 13.5).

The validity and success of Echegaray's attempt to write tragedy can of course be disputed. One may rightly argue that a terrible ending is not in itself definitory of tragedy. Heilman's own definition specifies that a monopathic character may be the victim of his or her own "darker side," and this false dividedness would belong not to tragedy but to a type of *melodrama* he calls drama of disaster. Two other critics, Oscar Mandel and George Steiner, isolate from Aristotle requirements that also serve to deny Echegaray's claim to tragedy. Mandel has stressed that tragic heroes "die and are not happy through their own efforts. And . . . *necessarily* as a condition contained in that effort" (24). Similarly, Steiner points out that "where the causes of disaster are temporal, where the conflict can be resolved through technical or social means, we may have serious drama, but not tragedy. . . . Tragedy is irreparable" (8). If the events of the play, horrifying as they may be, are caused by "chance encounter or affront . . . they provoke in us the momentary shock, the shiver in the spine . . . not the abiding terror of tragedy. And this distinction between horror and tragic terror is fundamental to any theory of drama. . . . *The difference is that between melodrama and tragedy*" (Steiner 164–165, my emphasis).

The precepts outlined by Mandel and Steiner are those of inevitability and irrevocability. Though in Echegaray's plays there is greater verisimilitude than in those overtly labeled melodrama, his characters do not obey the logic of their world; they have a different (higher, within the plays' scheme of values) moral code. And while their ethical beliefs are always ideal, they are not universal; the audience's acceptance of the characters' situation requires the temporary abandonment of everyday rationality. In addition, the events that lead the protagonists to succumb are often fortuitous, and their undoing seems preventable and sometimes even ludicrous. One gets the impression that Echegarayan characters could have avoided their fate if only they had made the choices that others in their situation would have made. According Mandel and Steiner, such a work is not tragedy but melodrama—which this critical view defines as a failed attempt at tragedy.

Applying these theories, the inevitable conclusion is that Echegaray's attempt to write tragedy is tainted by his misinterpretation of classical dicta and that this failure results in melodrama (a dramatic genre that exists by default of another). Such a conclusion is nevertheless problematic, since for one, as we have seen, it makes the twentieth-century critic ignore the horizon of expectations that governed Echegaray's original reception. The fact is that if one applies a different standard of tragedy—and views of tragedy, rather than remaining statically normative, have changed chronologically—it becomes easier to understand and accept the nineteenth-century reception of Echegaray's work as such. In his approach to the subject of tragedy, the playwright lives up to the epithet of *neorromántico*. As Michelle Gellrich explains, "[A] theory of tragedy centered on opposition and struggle seems first to emerge within the context of philosophically oriented Romantic treatments of sublimity." This view of tragedy, developed by Friedrich Schiller in *Das Pathethische* (1793), deemphasizes Aristotelian form and stresses the experience of conflict by the individual who encounters an overwhelming force: "tragic nobility [is] a direct consequence of a great soul's confrontation with oppressive or hostile forces inimical to his *grandeur d'âme* and moral freedom" (Gellrich 246). In reaction the heroes or heroines rely on personal will to resist all determinant pressures, often destroying themselves in the course of carrying out their purpose.

For Echegaray tragic conflict derives from collision with the sublime, that which has no limits and affords no comprehensive understanding. Tragedy and sublimity are both tightly linked to suffering: "The sublime in art lies in tears, pain, and death" [Lo sublime del arte está en el llanto, en el dolor y en la muerte] (*Recuerdos* 1:37). The response of Echegarayan characters to the insurmountable pressures they experience is one of protest, and here Echegaray, like Schiller, affirms the power of will "in accordance with a private, inner sense of commitment" (Gellrich 253). Their tragic nature is confirmed when they follow the dictates of their will even at the risk of their own ruin. In *O locura o santidad* Lorenzo de Avendaño destroys himself and his daughter in assuming his perceived duty. In *Mariana* the title character defeats her own weakness in the face of adulterous temptation by calling on her husband (known as a *médico de su honra* once) to act out his revenge.

As with other definitions of tragedy, Echegaray's plays do not meet all, or perhaps most, of the criteria of the Schiller model. But despite deviations from the model, they benefit once again from a system of association. They incorporate signs from a tragic system with which Spanish audiences—who had experienced the throes of Romanticism much later than other Europeans—were familiar and so become identified with that system. In this manner, Echegaray makes use of the public's ideas of tragedy to credibly implant tragic "genes" into his melodramatic works. With regard to tragedy or to nineteenth-century dramatic currents, the result is a fusion of theatrical sign systems. The particular relationship created is one in which each individual play assumes the identity of the more prestigious form while remaining melodramatic in essence. Under the variable rubrics of Spanish classical theater, naturalism, realism, or tragedy, it is melodrama that acts as the centripetal force of Echegaray's works.

So far I have referred to Echegaray's "impersonation" as a process of literary codification. Nevertheless, it goes beyond the realm of style and genre and extends to the ideological space of melodrama. As Peter Brooks has documented, melodrama originated in France after the Revolution as a way of legitimizing and perpetuating moral and social value systems:

> [Melodrama] comes into being in a world where the traditional imperatives of truth and ethics have been violently thrown into question, yet where the promulgation of truth and ethics, their instauration as a way of life, is of immediate, daily political concern. . . . The word is called upon to make present and to impose a new society, to legislate the regime of virtue. (15)

Melodrama was ethical drama showcasing the strength of the institutions that structured society: family, law, government, prescribed class, and gender roles. Victim-protagonists, always virtuous, are identified with this "regime of virtue," and villains personify the threat of social disorder.

The conservative values characteristic of melodrama are inherent in Echegaray's dramaturgy, but this is not always immediately apparent to a spectator or reader. Many of Echegaray's plays promote liberal ideas he himself has espoused in politics: freedom of religious belief, a degree of independence for women. Nevertheless, the characters that incarnate these ideas are not reaffirmed in the conciliatory endings distinctive of works generically known as melodrama but vanquished by a society that cannot understand or accept them. In this way the works that seem to propose radical ideological changes always end—as in the generic tradition of French and Spanish melodrama—with a return to the initial order.

While the years 1874–1888 saw massive successes of Echegaray works like *En el puño de la espada, El hijo de hierro y el hijo de carne* (1888), and *Lo sublime en lo vulgar* (1888), during the 1889–1890 season only three of his dramas are staged—the new *Los rígidos* and repeats of *Lo sublime en lo vulgar* and *El gran Galeota*—and they run for only five, four, and three nights, respectively (*Lo sublime* originally ran for twenty-four consecutive nights). This decline in popularity has been linked to the death in 1888 of the actor Rafael Calvo, who together with Antonio Vico constituted the tormented protagonist duo of Echegaray's neo-Romantic plays. The bad spell would begin to subside around 1890, when Echegaray finds a new protagonist in María Guerrero. Her performance of *Siempre en ridículo* that year ran for sixteen nights; the newly found success would continue and culminate with *Mariana* (1892) and last well into the decade.

Another circumstance combined with the forced change in protagonists and the need to regain lost popularity to make Echegaray alter his dramatic formula: the personal contact with Benito Pérez Galdós and the expectations that the latter's influential drama *Realidad* (premiering in 1892 and starring Guerrero) generated in theatrical audiences. The public's new expectations of realism and actuality in the theater induce Echegaray to modernize his theatrical production, and to do this he resorts once again to a process of impersonation—this time of ideas and controversies as well as of dramatic modes. Probably the best example of this operation is his apparent turn from the portrayal of weak and subordinate female characters to that of strong and self-sustaining heroines, through which he once again distances his work from melodrama (which traditionally stressed the role of women insofar as they supported men's actions or the integrity of the family) and brings it closer to the realist novel.

In this regard Echegaray's early neo-Romantic plays had remained close to melodrama. Toward the 1890s, however, Echegaray writes for María Guerrero parts in which she would be able to unleash all her acting power. A typical character of this period is the Fuensanta of *El loco dios* (1900), a rich widow who thrives without a man until she falls in love with her lawyer Gabriel. Even as she acknowledges the depth of her love, however, she firmly states her independence and ultimately chooses marriage as the lesser of two evils: Gabriel's authority as a husband is preferable to her than the influence of relatives who have previously dominated her. Through her urge to be independent, Fuensanta trespasses, both socially and sexually, the boundaries of the feminine. Echegaray does not, however, showcase her boldness but instead punishes her for this transgression. After their marriage Gabriel goes mad, believing he is God, and kills her in a fire as he screams that "you refused to respect your God, wretched creature!" [¡no quisiste respetar a tu Dios, mísera criatura!] (*Loco dios* 106). With characters like Fuensanta, Echegaray seemingly constructs plays that appear to advocate a greater freedom for women—a contemporary controversy in which Echegaray himself had participated. Nonetheless, these characters are vanquished in their attempts to subvert prescribed roles.

The protagonists of plays like *El loco dios* and *Mariana* all perish because of their inability to cope with patriarchal customs and beliefs. Echegaray never really questions traditional configurations of power, and his heroines only emerge triumphant through the public's compassion for their suffering (and, most frequently, their death). The "feminine" disguise is, however, effective, and at a time when audiences were increasingly reading about nascent feminism, Echegaray could not but find his popularity renewed. *Mariana*, for example, had forty-six performances during the 1892–1893 season—more than any other drama (Galdós's *La loca de la casa* was second with twenty-two, and *Don Juan Tenorio* was fourth, with fourteen).

The appropriation of modern and progressive currents of thought occurs also with regard to other issues, giving Echegaray's theater a reputation as a platform for liberal ideas: religious tolerance in *Dos fanatismos* (1887); the dangers of the doctrine of hereditary determinism in *De mala raza* (1886) and *El hijo de don Juan* (1892); the evils of *caciquismo* in *Comedia sin desenlace* (1891). Echegaray, who as a statesman often fought against reactionary positions—as Ministro de Fomento, for example, he undertook legal reform that would allow religious freedom in education—undoubtedly favors many of the ideas he attempts to propagate. This favor is, however, marked by an underlying ambivalence. In both life and work, there is a singular combination of conservative and liberal ideology. In life, it shows in Echegaray's negotiation with and participation in opposite ideological regimes. In work, it shows in characters who ostensibly stand for progressive ideals yet always fall outside society through insanity, criminality, or death and thus have no influence over a state of things that both precedes and survives them. Ultimately Echegaray's theater is a theater of hegemony: It appeals to (and thus obtains the consent of) liberal-minded audiences by showcasing an ideology it does not decisively embrace and covertly supports the exact opposite of that ideology.

The balance between melodramatic effect and dramatic as well as ideological novelty catapults Echegaray to the foreground of nineteenth-century Spanish theater. At the economic level, he could boast late in his career that since he began writing plays "I have lived on almost nothing else" [casi no he vivido de otra cosa] (Antón del Olmet 187)—and he made almost 5,000 duros a year, an extremely comfortable living at the time. At a second level, through this movement of impersonation, Echegaray created a hybrid genre that "rescued" melodrama: Because of his tremendous success, melodrama ceased to belong in the second-class theaters and entered—through covertly—the theatrical mainstream. Echegaray's melodramatic recipe would often be equated with the essence of the Dramatic and became the very standard of expectation for audiences of the time. The first consequence of this phenomenon was the creation of a school of followers—Eugenio Sellés, Leopoldo Cano, José Feliú y Codina, Joaquín Dicenta—that consolidated this theater's command over the Spanish stage. The second was the sparking of a polemic about the need for theatrical reform that alone grants the playwright an important position as a catalytic force in the modernization of Spanish theater.

CRITICS' RESPONSE

Echegaray's integration of "cultured" and "popular" theater and the success it achieved became a matter of much controversy. Dramatists like Benito Pérez Galdós and Enrique Gaspar rejected his theater's affectation and advocated a more realist type of theater. Echegaray's most successful dramatic scion, Jacinto Benavente (Spain's second Nobel Prize winner), followed their line in the pursuit of naturalness. The members of the Generation of 98 reacted much more violently against Echegaray, and near the turn of the century their public protests against his drama were a common occurrence in theaters. After the award of the Nobel Prize in 1904, the journal *Gente vieja* organized an homage to Echegaray in the name of "toda la intelectualidad española" [all of Spain's intellectuals]. The act, endorsed by authors like Emilia Pardo Bazán, Joaquín Dicenta, Serafín and Joaquín Álvarez Quintero, was boycotted by a group of fifty young intellectuals, among them Miguel de Unamuno, Rubén Darío, Ramiro de Maeztu, Manuel Bueno, Manuel and Antonio Machado, Enrique Díez Canedo, José Martínez Ruiz (Azorín), Ramón del Valle-Inclán, and Pío Baroja.

The protesters signed a document stating that

part of the Press initiates the idea of an homage to Don José Echegaray, and it claims to represent all Spanish intellectuals. Having the right to be included among them, and without discussing now the literary personality of Don José Echegaray, we certify that our ideals are others and our admirations very different.

[parte de la prensa inicia la idea de un homenaje a don José Echegaray, y se abroga la representación de toda la intelectualidad española. Nosotros, con derecho a ser comprendidos en ella, sin discutir ahora la personalidad literaria de don José Echegaray, hacemos constar que nuestros ideales son otros y nuestras admiraciones muy distintas] (qtd. in Castilla, "Echegaray en su tiempo" 243)

Appropriately conflating the artistic and the political, this group of intellectuals rejected Echegaray's dramaturgy and the values it represented. Their rising influence and the authority subsequently acquired by their individual voices triggered a process that culminated in the twentieth-century dismissal of Echegaray's importance in the literary context of his time.

What began with the Generation of 98 was one of the most successful instances of redefinition of the literary canon. Dramatists like Valle-Inclán strongly attacked Echegaray's style, and others would subsequently forget about him. Echegarayan melodrama was once at the center and zenith of Spanish theater, and in a sense this very fact generated its demise. In its comprehensive success Echegaray's theater became what Hans Robert Jauss has termed "culinary art" (25)—it lost its artistic value and provoked numerous (and ultimately victorious) attempts at negating the aesthetic experiences it afforded. His name and those of his followers were largely erased from "the chronology of great authors" (4). Thus it has remained in literary limbo—theater historians such as Francisco Ruiz Ramón have referred to it as "teatro ripio"—where it awaits, if not a change in our tastes, an interest in revising the trajectories of the noncanonical.

AWARDS AND DISTINCTIONS

Real Academia Española, 1882
Nobel Prize in Literature, 1904

BIBLIOGRAPHY

The following is a selection from the more than sixty works written by the playwright, in the editions I have used.

El bandido Lisandro. Madrid: Imprenta de José Rodríguez, 1886.
Bodas trágicas. 2d ed. Madrid: Hijos de A. Gullón, 1881.
Un crítico incipiente. Madrid: Imprenta de José Rodríguez, 1895.
La desequilibrada. Madrid: E. Velasco, 1904.
Dos fanatismos. Madrid: Imprenta de José Rodríguez, 1887.
Haroldo el normando. 4th ed. Madrid: Sociedad de Autores Españoles, 1902.

El hijo de Don Juan. Madrid: Florencio Fiscowich, 1892.
El hijo de hierro y el hijo de carne. 2d ed. Madrid: Florencio Fiscowich, 1901.
El hombre negro. Madrid: Florencio Fiscowich, 1898.
El loco dios. 8th ed. Madrid: Sociedad de Autores Españoles, 1907.
Mancha que limpia. 2d ed. Madrid: Florencio Fiscowich, 1895.
Mariana. Madrid: Imprenta de José Rodríguez, 1892.
La rencorosa. Madrid: Florencio Fiscowich, 1894.
Lo sublime en lo vulgar. Madrid: Florencio Fiscowich, 1888.

Collections and Current Editions

El gran Galeoto. Ed. James H. Hoddie. Madrid: Cátedra, 1989.
Teatro escogido. Ed. Armando Lázaro Ros. Madrid: Aguilar, 1957.

Translations

The Great Galeoto. Trans. Eleanor Bontecou. In *Continental Plays*, ed. Thomas H. Dickinson. New York: Houghton Mifflin, 1935.
The Great Galeoto. Trans. Barrett H. Clark. In *Masterpieces of Modern Drama*. New York: Duffield and Co., 1917.
The Great Galeoto. Trans. Jacob S. Fassett, Jr. Boston: R. G. Badger, 1914.
The Great Galeoto. Trans. Hannah Lynch. Garden City, NY: Doubleday, 1916.
The Great Galeoto. Folly or Saintliness. Two plays done from the verse by José Echegaray into English Prose. Trans. Hannah Lynch. London: J. Lane, 1895. New York: H. Fertig, 1989.
Madman or Saint. Trans. Ruth Lansing. Boston: R. G. Badger, 1912.
Mariana. Trans. James Graham. Boston: Roberts Brothers, 1895. London: T. F. Unwin, 1895.
Mariana. Trans. Federico Sarda and Carlos D. S. Wupperman. New York: Moods, 1909.
The Son of Don Juan. Trans. James Graham. Boston: Roberts Brothers, 1895. London: T. F. Unwin, 1895.

Critical Studies

Antón del Olmet, Luis, and Arturo García Carraffa. *Echegaray*. Madrid: Imprenta de "Alrededor del Mundo," 1912.
Aristotle. *Poetics*. In *Aristotle's Theory of Poetry and Fine Art with a Critical Text and Translation of the Poetics*, ed. S. H. Butcher. 4th ed. London: Macmillan, 1927. 6–111.
Baker, Clayton. "Echegaray and His Critics." Ph.D. diss., Indiana University, 1969. Ann Arbor: UMI, 1969. 6914695.
Bosch, Rafael. "La influencia de Echegaray sobre *Torquemada en el purgatorio*, de Galdós." *Revista de estudios hispánicos* 1 (1967): 243–253.
Bueno, Manuel. *Teatro español contemporáneo*. Madrid: Biblioteca Renacimiento, 1909.
Bustillo, Eduardo. *Campañas teatrales (crítica dramática)*. Madrid: Rivadeneyra, 1901.
Cabrales Arteaga, José Manuel. "El teatro neorromántico de Echegaray." *Revista de literatura* 55.101 (1989): 77–94.

Cabrera, Vicente. "Valle-Inclán y la escuela de Echegaray: Un caso de parodia literaria." *Revista de estudios hispánicos* 7 (1973): 193–213.

Canals, Salvador. *El año teatral 1895–96.* Madrid: Establecimiento tipográfico de *El nacional,* 1896.

Castillo, Rafael Alberto. "Echegaray en su tiempo." Ph.D. diss., Harvard University, 1974.

———. "Una parodia de *El gran Galeoto." Hispanófila* 26. 3 (1983): 33–40.

Echegaray, José de. *Recuerdos.* 3 vols. Madrid: Ruiz Hermanos, 1917.

Fornieles Alcaraz, Javier. *Trayectoria de un intelectual de la Restauración: José Echegaray.* Almería: Caja de Ahorros, 1989.

Gellrich, Michelle. *Tragedy and Theory: The Problem of Conflict since Aristotle.* Princeton, NJ: Princeton University Press, 1988.

Gregersen, Halfdan. *Ibsen and Spain.* Cambridge: Cambridge University Press, 1936.

Heilman, Robert. *Tragedy and Melodrama.* Seattle: University Washington Press, 1968.

Hernández, Librada. "El teatro de Echegaray: Un enigma crítico." Ph.D. diss., UCLA, 1987. Ann Arbor: UMI, 1982. AAC 8719921.

Herrán, Fermín. *Echegaray, su tiempo y su teatro.* Madrid: Imprenta de Fortanet, 1880.

Jauss, Hans Robert. *Toward an Aesthetics of Reception.* Trans. Timothy Bahti. Minneapolis: University of Minnesota Press, 1982.

Lázaro Ros, Armando. Prologue to his edition of *Teatro escogido,* by José de Echegaray. 11–47.

Loss, Archie K. "Everyman Blooms as Everybody." *A Wake Newslitter: Studies in James Joyce's Finnegan's Wake* 13 (1976): 96–98. [Claims an influence of JE on James Joyce]

Mandel, Oscar. *A Definition of Tragedy.* New York: New York University Press, 1961.

Mansour, George P. "Time in the Prose of José Echegaray." *Kentucky Romance Quarterly* (Supp.) 13 (1967): 17–24.

Mathias, Julio. *Echegaray.* Madrid: EPESA, 1970.

Menéndez Onrubia, Carmen, and Julián Avila Arellano. *El neorromanticismo español y su época: Epistolario de José Echegaray a María Guerrero.* Madrid: CSIC, 1987.

Montero Padilla, José. "Echegaray visto por Benavente." *Revista de literatura* 13 (1958): 245–248.

Palau, Melchor de. "Acontecinnentos literarios: Mariana, drama original, en tres actos y un epílogo, estrenado en el Teatro de la Comedia, la noche del 5 de diciembre." *Revista contemporánea* 88 (1892): 638–647.

Paolini, Gilbert. "Noctis imago en *El hijo de don Juan* de Echegaray y *Los espectros* de Ibsen." *Letras peninsulares* 5 (1992–1993): 337–345.

Pí y Arsuaga, Francisco. *Echegaray, Sellés y Cano: Ligero exámen crítico de su teatro.* Madrid: Imprenta de Alfredo Alonso, 1884.

Revilla, Manuel de. *Obras.* Madrid: Víctor Saiz, 1883.

Ríos-Font, Wadda C. "The Impersonation of the Feminine: Gender and Melodramatic Discourse in the Theater of José Echegaray." *Hispanófila* 106.1 (1992): 21–30.

———. "The Melodramatic Paradigm: José Echegaray and the Modern Spanish Theater." Ph.D. diss., Harvard University, 1991. Ann Arbor: UMI, 1991. AAC 9132026.

———. *Rewriting Melodrama: The Hidden Paradigm in Modern Spanish Theater.* Lewisburg, PA: Bucknell University Press, 1997.

Rubio, Isaac. "Galdós y el melodrama." *Anales galdosianos* 16 (1981): 57–67.

Ruiz Ramón, Francisco. *Historia del teatro español (desde sus orígenes hasta 1900)*. Madrid: Cátedra, 1986.

Sánchez, Roberto G. "Mancha que no se limpia o el dilema-Echegaray." *Cuadernos hispanoamericanos* 297 (1975): 601–612.

Sobejano, Gonzalo. "Echegaray, Galdós y el melodrama." *Anales Galdosianos* (Supplement) 13 (1978): 91–115.

Sparks, Amy. "La refundición por Echegaray de *La hija del aire* (segunda parte) de Calderón." In *Calderón: Actas del Congreso Internacional sobre Calderón y el teatro español del siglo de Oro*, ed. Luciano García Lorenzo. Madrid: CSIC, 1983.

Steiner, George. *The Death of Tragedy*. New York: Oxford University Press, 1980.

Weisler, Shawney Anderson. "Melodrama and the Beginnings of Spanish Social Drama." Ph.D. diss., University of North Carolina at Chapel Hill, 1984. Ann Arbor: UMI, 1984. AAC 8425525.

Yxart, José. *El arte escénico en España*. 2 vols. Barcelona: La Vanguardia, 1894–1896.

ANTONIO GALA
(1936–   )

Hazel Cazorla

BIOGRAPHY

Over the centuries Andalusia has been the cradle of some of Spain's greatest writers, painters, and musicians, among them Lorca, Juan Ramón Jiménez, Velázquez, Picasso, and Manuel de Falla. Being an "andaluz" has always carried with it a strong sense of historical identity and a characteristic philosophy of life, modifying a refined aestheticism with a resilient stoicism. Though born not in Andalusia, but in the Castilian province of Ciudad Real, Antonio Gala nevertheless considers himself to be a true andaluz. His family moved, soon after his birth in 1936, to Cordoba, that most Andalusian of cities, capital in medieval times of the Islamic Caliphate of Spain. He speaks, thinks, and conducts himself with the innate elegance and wit of Andalusia, while responding profoundly to its underlying tragic sense of life.

One of five children born to a comfortably well-off physician and his wife, Gala spent his childhood in the tense and confining conditions of the Spanish Civil War (1936–1939) and its aftermath, the emotional and psychogical scars of which are to be seen in his literary work. As an adolescent he proved to be a precociously brilliant student, entering first the University of Seville at the age of sixteen and later the University of Madrid, graduating within six years with three degrees, one in law, another in history, and the third in political science and economics. During his university years in Seville the future playwright made his debut as a poet, and his literary career seemed about to take wing. However, in 1958, in compliance with his father's wishes, he prepared for the competitive national examinations, known as the *oposiciones*, for one of the few coveted positions of "Abogado del Estado," the gaining of which would mean an assured and distinguished future within the Spanish legal system. Under the strain of the examinations, the young writer suffered a severe emotional crisis, withdrew from competition, and entered the Carthusian monastery at Jerez de la Frontera for some months of spiritual retreat. The year 1959 found him once more in Madrid, where he resumed his literary activity, winning an *accesit* (second place) in the national Adonais Prize for Poetry. During the next two years he continued to write poetry and short fiction, supporting himself by working at various jobs before eventually becoming manager of a commercial art gallery, then leaving for Florence to manage a similar enterprise there.

In 1963, when Gala had been in Italy for scarcely a year, news of his father's grave illness brought him hurriedly back to Spain. In the midst of his distress over the subsequent death of his father, Gala learned of his first big literary success. He had been awarded the national Calderón de la Barca prize for his first play: *Los verdes campos del Edén* [The Green Fields of Eden]. This award, together with the accompanying staging of the play at the Maria Guerrero theater in Madrid, brought him instant celebrity, a status that has not dimmed over the succeeding three decades, during which Gala has not only staged some twenty plays but has also gone on to achieve equal fame as an essayist and journalist, a film-script writer, novelist, and poet, while becoming himself a well-known television personality and popular literary figure, widely sought after for personal appearances and lectures. He has continued to write poetry over the years, while publishing relatively little of it, since, he has said, poetry is the most intimate of literary confessions, not always to be made public.[1] Yet in 1997 he came out with *Poemas de amor*, an astonishingly popular collection of poems that sold a record number of copies in the prestigious national Book Fair in Madrid that year. Turning to narrative, Gala published his first novel, *El manuscrito carmes*, in 1990, following it in 1993 with the phenomenally successful bestseller *La pasión turca*. In rapid succession thereafter came three more novels: *Más allá del jardín* (1995), *La regla des tres* (1996), and *Las afueras de Dios* (1999), leaving no doubt about the extraordinary range of Gala's literary genius.

Antonio Gala occupies a very special place within the history of the post–Civil War Spanish theater, for while he has been endlessly innovative, he has not allowed himself to be sidetracked by the merely experimental and has deftly avoided the dead end of the fashionable avant-garde. Gala's theater is marked, above all, by two components: first, its brilliantly colorful, lyrical, and witty language, equally expressive in both the comic and tragicomic mode, and secondly, an essentially ethical preoccupation with the pursuit of happiness, hope, and justice for all.

DRAMATURGY: MAJOR WORKS AND THEMES

Gala's first play, which catapulted him to national prominence, called into question the aesthetics of the serious theater of the 1960s, the time of the so-called Realist generation, and created something of a scandal, even as it evoked the same ethical concerns that motivated the best contemporary Realist writers such as Antonio Buero Vallejo, Lauro Olmo, and Carlos Muñiz. *Los verdes campos del Edén* signaled a radical departure from the current neo-Realist theater not only in its disturbingly unfamiliar setting but also in its strongly allegorical overtones paralleling figures and episodes from the New Testament. Nothing on the contemporary stage could have prepared the audience for the strangeness of the setting: a stage split between the interior of a family tomb on the lower level and the upper scenic space that was illuminated, as needed, to serve as deserted cemetery, country roadside, town market, or boardinghouse, enabling the action to pass fluidly from one area to another but focusing the main action on the inside of the tomb. Nor was there any precedent for the cast of characters: a heterogeneous group of cheerful outcasts from society, beggars and young delinquents, kind-hearted prostitutes, a homeless couple, a mentally disturbed, middle-aged widow, all of whose lives are changed by the arrival of a mysterious, charismatic stranger who befriends them and takes them into the only "home" he has, a family tomb inherited from his grandfather. According to its author, the play was about human redemption, a daring theme at a time when a drab and pragmatic social realism set the tone in the arts. In bringing a poetic glimpse of a transcendent reality to the stage, Gala was vulnerable to the attacks of certain uncomprehending critics who accused him of offering a saccharine-sweet evasion of society's "real" problems. Since the play was an enormous popular success, a heated controversy ensued, during which Alejandro Casona, the grand old man of the pre–Civil War theater, published his now-famous letter to the author, praising the play for bringing to the stage its "humor, poetry and tenderness precisely at the moment when poetry, fantasy and laughter are in danger of being derided by those who dictate fashion in our theater" [la carga fresca de humor, de poesía y de ternura precisamente en un momento en que la poesía, la fantasía y la sonrisa empiezan a estar muy mal vistas entre los que dictan la moda en nuestro teatro].[2]

   In spite of his success in the theater, Gala has always insisted that he is not a playwright but a writer who happens to write sometimes for the stage, for whom theater is a literary text entrusted, upon completion, to a director, scenic designer, actors, and technicians for its realization upon a stage. But let there be no misunderstanding: This emphasis upon the supreme importance of the written word in no way diminishes the essential theatricality of his work. For Antonio Gala, the dialogue is inseparable from all the other elements of theater, such as lighting and sound, together with gesture and movement, all of which he often specifies in his stage directions. Moreover, he conceives his characters not only as living embodiments of human behavior but also as pieces in a complicated scenic game invented by him, in which each piece moves in response to an inner dynamic.

   The organizing principle of most of Gala's theater is the allegorical form. Starting with *Los verdes campos del Edén* (1963) and continuing through *Los bellos durmientes* [Sleeping Beauties] (1994), *Café cantante* (1997), and *Las marganas del viernes* (1999), with only one exception, *Samarkanda* [Samarkand] (1985), Gala has constructed his plays on the principle of a sustained metaphor, a central image providing the focus for the plot, which functions simultaneously on two levels: that of the literal reality it presents and another, often transcendent one, which constitutes the ultimate meaning of the play.

After the popular but controversial triumph of his first play, Gala returned to the stage three years later, undeterred by the polemic, with another fundamentally allegorical piece: *El sol en el hormiguero* [The Sun on the Ant Heap] (1966), the action and characters of which are based on a universally known myth, that of Swift's *Gulliver's Travels*. This time, the play failed to convince either critics or public, and it was quickly closed. Yet within a year, most of the critics were hailing the playwright as what they termed "the new Gala," on the occasion of the premiere of *Noviembre y un poco de yerba* [November and a Bit of Grass], (1967). This play tells the story of an ex-soldier from the defeated Republican army of the Spanish Civil War, a man who has survived by living in hiding with his female companion and her mother since the Franco victory some twenty years before. It is a tale of entrapment and imprisonment, both physical and psychological, which is brought to a climax when he makes the decision to give himself up to the authorities after the proclamation of a general amnesty. In an ironical final twist of fate, Diego finds not freedom and happiness but a meaningless death as he trips and falls on the very gun that he had kept for so long and was now about to surrender.

Although this play differs in many ways from the preceding ones, it shares certain characteristics with them, and with the rest of Gala's subsequent theater. There is an obvious parallel between the hiding place, an abandoned cellar beneath the disused canteen of a remote, rural whistlestop, and the underground tomb of Gala's first play. Each of them is a form of the enclosed space in which Gala most often places his characters. Both are suggestive of an inner reality, signaling a lack of freedom, both physical and psychological, on several levels of human existence. The characters in both plays are all losers, defeated in the struggle of life, since the freedom they seek can be achieved only in the act of dying. The action of both plays is allegorical, even though Gala does draw on contemporary events in *Noviembre y un poco de yerba*. A general amnesty for ex-Republicans had in fact been proclaimed in Spain shortly before the staging of the play, and the national newspapers had carried the startling news of the emergence of a Republic soldier after years in hiding. In any case, Gala had apparently redeemed himself in the judgment of those who demanded greater "realism" in the theater and for whom the oft-cited "humor, poetry and tenderness" were simply escapist platitudes. The audience, however, did not agree. The play was one of Gala's very few box-office failures and was soon withdrawn.

During the decade of the 1970s, a number of "New Authors" with experimental tendencies sought to incorporate into the Spanish scene some of the theories of Brecht, Artaud, and Grotowski, which had been a strong influence in the rest of Europe for some time but had encountered the opposition of strict and puritanical censorship in Spain. Some authors evaded the censors but drew only marginal audiences by writing in a deliberately enigmatic, antinaturalistic mode, and Gala himself wrote at least two avant-garde plays of this nature, *El caracol en el espejo* [The Snail on the Mirror] (1970) and *El veredicto* [The Verdict] (written in the 1970s but not published until 1983). Neither one has ever been staged, and it is clear that Gala quickly abandoned this direction. It seems obvious that the radical dehumanization that characterizes such plays does not reflect the temperament of Antonio Gala, and he himself apparently recognized such experimentation as a virtual dead end.

After the failure of *Noviembre* in 1967, Gala withdrew from the stage for some five years, except for the production of a short, cabaret-style, musical piece with an English title: *Spain's striptease* (1970). When, at the end of those five years, Gala returned to the theater, he was to produce four of his best-known plays in rapid succession: *Los buenos días perdidos* [The Bells of Orleans] (1972); *Anillos para una dama* [Rings for a Lady] (1973); *Las cítaras colgadas de los árboles* [The Harps Hanging from the Trees] (1974); and *¿Por qué corres, Ulises?* [What Makes You Run, Ulysses?] (1975). In these years of intense dramatic creativity Gala also wrote a satirical, contemporary musical, *¿Suerte, campeón!* [Good Luck, Champ!]), which was prohibited by the censors on the eve of its premiere in September 1973 and has never been produced since.

Of these four plays, according to Gala's most recent biographer, José Infante, *Anillos para una dama* is the one that has received the most awards and has been most frequently staged (Infante, *Antonio Gala*, 329). A detailed study of it will be found at the end of this section.

Its predecessor by one year, *Los buenos días perdidos* is a contemporary allegory that has been called a "rich, lusty fable" telling the story of "a quartet of characters caught in a changing and uncaring world."[3] It is set in a highly symbolic place: an unused side-chapel of a sixteenth-century parish church, crudely remodeled and vulgarly furnished to meet the housing needs of an oddly matched young couple, (the church sacristan who moonlights as a barber and his wife), who share the space with his mother, a former madam with aspirations to middle-class gentility. The simple-minded wife is a dreamer, seduced by the hope of a new life in a promised land, offered to her by a handsome visitor who stays with the family as the new church bell-ringer while doubling as the local gigolo. In contrast with the gentle protagonist of Gala's first play, this savior from nowhere is a false one, who eventually deceives and betrays them all. The suicide of the young Consuelo, echoing the seeming hopelessness of the ending of *Los verdes campos del Edén*, does nevertheless leave the audience with an overwhelming sense of the transforming power of hope: the vision of a promised Paradise lives on, though Gala's characters may not reach it here on earth.

In the other three plays of this group, produced in the waning years of the Franco regime, Gala begins to explore a type of theater for which he has subsequently shown a special predilection: plays based on an historical and/or mythological theme, which he systematically proceeds, in the course of the work, to demythify and subvert, thus exposing, beneath the mask of allegory, the age-old fanaticisms and worn-out prejudices of today. Historical drama, favored by several postwar Spanish writers, beginning with Antonio Buero Vallejo's *Un soñador para un pueblo* (1958), proved a convenient vehicle for the expression of sociopolitical criticism since it enabled them to evade the censorship of the Franco regime, and Gala certainly has been attracted to the genre, not only as an anticensorship device but also because he believes it is important to tell the Spanish people the story of their past: "I am certain," he has said in his Autocrítica to *Las cítaras colgadas de los árboles*, "that Spaniards must be sincerely reconciled with their own past if they are to be reconciled with others" [Tengo la seguridad de que el español debe convivir sinceramente con su propio pasado para poder después convivir con su prójimo].

Las cítaras colgadas de los árboles (1974) and *¿Por qué corres, Ulises?* (1975) are both examples, like *Anillos para una dama*, of plays demythifying the past in order to create a better understanding of it. In *Las cítaras*, Gala turns a harsh spotlight upon another historical period, which, like that of El Cid, forms part of the legendary past of the nation: the Golden Age of Spanish conquests in the Americas, coming hard upon the taking of Granada from the Moslems and the expulsion of the Spanish Jews. In this, Gala's most eloquent and violent tragedy of racial hatred, he makes what Enrique Llovet has called a "frontal attack upon an entire period of history, upon its habitual practices in the exercise of Power, upon its social structure and its expressions" [un ataque frontal a toda una época histórica, a sus hábitos de ejercio del Poder, a su organización social, a sus expresiones] (24) It deals with the eternal theme of oppressor and oppressed, of the recurrent civil war between "the two Spains," between the powerful, "official" Spain and that inhabited by the marginalized and powerless minorities, in this case represented, on the one hand, by the rich landowner and, on the other, principally, by a young woman of Jewish ancestry, a *conversa*, and the man who had wished to marry her against the prejudices of the time. In seeking to make his fortune in the Americas, he was not only rendered impotent by a terrible wound but underwent a revulsion against all forms of violence and oppression. Upon his return to Spain, he finds that she has been subjected to all sorts of degradation and that the powerful and their sycophants are united in their rejection of his vision of peace and reconciliation. The two are the objects of a bloody manhunt, at the end of which, the young *conversa* takes it upon herself to slay her beloved in his sleep, to save him from the unspeakable death promised him by their pursuers, after which she calmly awaits her own destruction at their hands.

The last play in this group, *¿Por qué corres, Ulises?* is an esentially comic reworking of the Ulises and Penelope myth, in a way that strips the two figures of their Homeric grandeur and places them in an atemporal context, in which the senseless horror of war, even if it was the war against Troy, can easily be seen to apply to more contemporary situations, including the Spanish Civil War, the long shadow of which still projected itself upon the social and political landscape of the country.

Upon the death of Franco in 1975, Spain threw herself euphorically into an orgy of freedom for the next few years, known as the period of transition to democracy. Between 1975 and 1980 Gala again withdrew from the theater, an absence due, as he has since explained, to his awareness that "the audience was living its own drama, out in the streets" [El público vivía su propio drama en las calles].[4] He was referring to the countless street protests, placards, political gatherings, and graffiti that appeared everywhere, the product of a political energy hitherto suppressed. When, for the second time in his career, Gala returned to the stage, it was to produce once more a quick succession of theatrical triumphs, the three dramas that he later published together as *Trilogía de la libertad* [The Freedom Trilogy] (1983). In 1980 came both *Petra Regalada* and *La vieja señorita del Paraíso* [The Old Lady of the Paradise Café], followed by *El cementerio de los pájaros* [The Bird Cemetery] (1982). As their collective title indicates, these three plays offer, again in allegorical form, three different perspectives upon the possible future of Spanish society, or any society, finding itself suddenly and disconcertingly free, after the collapse of an authoritarian regime. Each of the three plays is a demonstration of the difficulty, the almost impossibility of accepting the responsibilities imposed by human freedom.

The inauguration of a democratic, socialist government in the 1980s brought state patronage of certain sectors of the theater, favoring the performance of proven classics considered to be part of the national heritage. Lavish, state-subsidized productions of well-known works in a few national theaters made survival for commercial theaters and private productions difficult, and many of them were forced to close. But in spite of these conditions, Gala was able to stage two new works in 1985: *Samarkanda* [Samarkand] and *El hotelito* [The Family Mansion].

In the second of these plays, *El hotelito*, Gala uses the allegorical mode without any ambiguity or subtlety to pursue the theme of human dissensions and hatred that are constantly proving to be obstacles on the road of the human search for a Paradise regained. The play functions, simultaneously, on the level of a sociopolitical satire upon the effects of the newfound freedoms and regional autonomies of the democratic Spain. The entirely female cast of characters consists of five argumentative and highly amusing stereotypes, each one from a different area of Spain (Castile, Andalusia, Galicia, Catalonia, and the Basque Country, the five historic regions of the nation), each speaking her own regional dialect and thus adding to the comic confusion. These five ladies are the last surviving members of a once-powerful, aristocratic, but now impoverished family who have gathered at the family mansion, their only remaining asset, in order to try to agree on how, and to whom, to sell it, shabby and in need of repair though it is. They bicker and fight among themselves while waiting to hear from a mysterious lady from abroad, who never materializes. Their noisy squabbling is suddenly brought to an end by the persistent ringing of the doorbell and a warning from the police to evacuate the house because of a possible terrorist bomb that may have been left on their doorstep. They agree to disregard the warning and to overcome their differences, joining merrily together in a spontaneous folk dance as the curtain slowly begins to fall. It seems that the five of them have finally found a way of living together, but just as the curtain comes to rest, the audience hears a tremendous explosion, and then—silence. There is no explanation, no comforting end to what had seemed to be a critical and wryly amusing commentary on Spain's unending problem of regional separatism. The dilapidated family mansion is an obvious metaphor for Spain, divided since medieval times by internal, regional differences, but as scattered references in the dialogue make clear, there is now a wider threat from outside, the worldwide menace of nuclear weapons. This last explosion on stage is unexpected and disquieting, leaving the audience uneasy that the joke should turn out to have such an apocalyptic punchline.

Samarkanda, staged a few months before *El hotelito*, stands apart from the rest of Gala's dramatic works. As the author explained in his prologue to the play: "For the first time, when I wrote *Samarkanda*, it was not my intention to write a play, but a truth. . . . I have asked the actors not to act, but to be" (31). That is to say, Gala abandoned his customary allegorical approach to his theme and communicated here in direct terms. In this play there is no poetic transformation of the reality lived by the three characters: Their actions and words convey the only level of meaning in a tragic, heartrending situation that unfolds simply and inevitably before the audience. These people do not imply any collective or national message: They represent nothing and no one except themselves: two men and a woman seeking refuge in a remote mountain location, from the injustice and hatred of the outside world, only to find themselves cornered and hunted down by the violence that stalks them. In this play, Gala deals more explicitly than in any other with the theme of homosexuality, although such a relationship forms part of the plot also of *La vieja señorita del Paraíso* and is the theme of one of the four erotic episodes of *Carmen Carmen* (1975, staged 1988). In all three dramatic works, Gala denounces the hypocrisy of a society that condemns such men to a life of pretense and shame.

The last play staged by Gala before launching a series of musical dramas was *Séneca o El beneficio de la duda* [Seneca or The Benefit of the Doubt] (1986), a psychological drama with a philosophical and historical setting, in which the author recreates a legend, much as he did in *Anillos para una dama* and *¿Por qué corres, Ulises?* by destroying and reinterpreting the original myth. In this play, Gala returns to the mode of the sociopolitical allegory, in which the dilemma of a historical figure, in this case, the Roman Seneca, serves a a metaphor for that of today's individual. It is a text of powerful sociopolitical criticism in the form of an almost classical dialogue about ethics in politics. It lends itself, however, to lengthy speeches that slow down the dramatic movement of the action. Such lack of theatricality is unusual in Gala and may be the reason for the play's lack of success on stage.

Between 1986 and 1992 Gala staged three musical dramas: *Carmen Carmen* (1988), *Cristóbal Colón* [Christopher Columbus] (presented as the libretto for an opera, 1989), and *La Truhana* [Truhana] (1992). All of them were mounted with an orchestral score, using lavish sets and costumes, a large cast of actors and singers, along with elaborate lighting and sound effects. The first, *Carmen Carmen*, written in 1975 and somewhat revised for the staging in 1988, was an enormous box-office success. It shares with the other two musicals an imaginative recreation of a myth, giving new life on stage to a literary legend, the nineteenth-century creation of Prosper Mérimée, the gypsy Carmen. Gala's protagonist, who has "Carmen" as both her Christian name and surname, is the latest in a long line of reincarnations, all of them rooted in the equally mythical Andalusia of the popular imagination. What Gala has done with her is subvert the meaning of the legendary Romantic heroine and turn her into a picaresque antiheroine who, in the end, takes on a certain tragic dignity. Carmen, as recreated by Gala, is a triple metaphor for human love, for the pursuit of happiness and for life itself, all willingly surrendered in an act of self-sacrifice. This demythification and subsequent remythification of the traditional Carmen is similar to the process used by Gala with the figure of Jimena, widow of El Cid, with Homer's Ulysses and with Christopher Columbus, obliging the audience to reflect critically upon some well-worn myths and offering, at the same time, the possibility of reformulating the ideal, creating another form of the myth more expressive of the times we live in. Gala's Carmen is one of the kind-hearted, generous prostitutes who abound in his dramatic world. She is courted, loved, and murdered, four times, in four successive episodes, by four men who are comical parodies of their respective Spanish stereotypes: the military man, the politician, the man of religion, and the bullfighter. The cast is rounded off by a ridiculously funny group of "Carmen Carmen's enemies" who change uniform in accordance with each change of lover, becoming, successively, soldiers accompanying the military man, bodyguards with the politician, transvestites who taunt the man of religion, and lastly, the matador's team of professional assistants. At the same time, a changing chorus of neighborhood women, factory girls, or bullfight spectators comment in turn, as in a Greek tragedy, upon the unfolding action as it leads inevitably to the grotesquely repeated, ritual murder of Carmen Carmen.

Cristóbal Colón, written as the libretto for an opera with the music composed by Leonardo Balada, deals imaginatively with the story of Columbus's first voyage to the Americas and the circumstances leading up to it. Interested in more than the mere outward events, Gala reveals the inner doubts, fears, and loves of his protagonist, turning history into a dramatization of an inner spiritual journey, a discovery of self. It is a voyage leading not only to a geographical New World but also to a vision of a newfound Paradise on earth, a new Jerusalem.

The protagonist of the third, and up to now, the latest of the musical plays, *La Truhana* (1992), is a quasihistorical, seventeenth-century figure, a famous actress, who is sought out by the King of Spain to be his mistress but who flees from the nobleman sent to pursue her. The action consists of her adventures during her flight across the breadth of Spain, in a series of nine separate episodes. Thus the work offers us yet another journey, both physical and spiritual, that ends, in this case, with the triumph of love, the love discovered by Truhana and the nobleman she spends most of the action trying to elude. In the final scene, as the new couple set sail for the Americas, together with all the friends and followers collected by Truhana on the way, Gala again presents us with the optimistic image of a new beginning in the New World, symbol of human hope for a return to an earthly Paradise lost.

Two years after *La Truhana* in which the characters leave behind an Old World, confident of the existence of that earthly Paradise at the end of their journey, Gala brings to the stage a vision of the false Paradise that has in fact materialized as the twentieth century draws to its close. *Los bellos durmientes* [Sleeping Beauties] (1994) is set precisely in what the stage directions call "a frigid Paradise" [un gélido paraíso], an immaculate, designer-decorated apartment, complete with high-tech appliances and futuristic labor-saving devices. It would seem to be a "dream home," but it is in fact only a luxurious living space, sterile and meaningless, lacking the warmth of real human love. The residents, Diana, a successful young lawyer and her equally successful live-in lover, are concerned only about success in a competitive world. In moments taken from their busy schedules they engage in sex, but routinely, like sleepwalkers. But Chance (or is it something else?) brings a stranger to live with them, in the person of Marcos, a musician. As in so many of Gala's plays, the unknown outsider is often the herald of Paradise, a savior who sometimes turns out to be a deceiver. In this case, Marcos has a mission: to reveal to the young couple the truth about the false Paradise they inhabit and to awaken them to life in all its fullness. Through Marcos, Diana awakens to the reality of the life she is leading and discovers a love that is not limited to sex and the pursuit of money. In the gradual process of revelation, she achieves freedom from the pseudo-Paradise inhabited by the "Beautiful People" of a materialistic society. In this, the latest of his dramatic allegories, Gala's heroine is awakened, like the Sleeping Beauty of the fairy tale, by a kiss from a stranger and is restored to the world of reality by the power of love.

The ultimately optimistic tone of *Los bellos durmientes* reappears in yet another allegorical comedy, *Café cantante* [Café singer] (1997), in which Gala's theatrical metaphor for Spain is a rundown, dilapidated house, the ground floor of which had once been a thriving and popular nightclub. Its sole inhabitant is an aged female, María, formerly the toast of the town, famed for her seductive talents as a dancer and singer, now left to face old age and death alone. A very brash and "hip" young woman, Yeni, presents herself on María's doorstep and settles in as a somewhat unwanted guest. The play offers us a visual image of the conflict between the old Spain, left over from the Franco years (incarnated in María), and the new generation (Yeni), born of the transition to a democratic society. In *Café cantante* Gala happily combines allegorical elements from earlier plays like *La vieja señorita del Paraíso* and *Los buenos días perdidos* with the musical component that gives a lighthearted, lyrical tone to *La Truhana*, for example.

In his latest play to date, *Las manzanas del viernes* (1999), Gala again takes up a theme that runs throughout his theater with more or less insistence: the tragicomedy of human love, with all its highs of passion and its lows of deception and abandonment. In his later years, Gala has stressed the inevitability of aging and its effects on the human need for love. Such is the theme of this somewhat bitter piece about the passionate love of an older, successful businesswoman for a much younger man, whose only passion is money and the good life it can bring. It provides us with another portrait of a female protagonist, this time painted in somewhat more sombre tones than before but still a fitting addition to the extensive Gala gallery of women who belong to two worlds: that of mundane reality and that of myth.

At first sight, and on one level, *Anillos para una dama* (1973) is a psychological study of a famous woman in Spanish history who long ago became a legendary figure: Jimena, wife of the greatest Spanish hero of all time, El Cid. The action on stage begins soon after El Cid's death and will soon reveal, to our astonishment, that Jimena had, for years, only been playing the part of the loving, faithful wife and mother. Contrary to popular belief, she and El Cid had never really loved each other, and consequently, her life with him had been empty and frustrated. Now, as his widow, she proclaims her desperate need to be herself, instead of the Jimena that everyone expects her to be. She declares her need to discover what it is to love and to be loved.

There is an additional reason, however, for the playwright's interest in this figure, since she becomes also a way of looking at the past while reflecting on the contemporary reality of Spain in the early 1970s, years of change and transition that offered some interesting parallels with the politics of Castile under Alfonso VI. The implications of the play still hold true in the 1990s, and not only in Spain but also in many other countries of the world today where unexpected and swift-moving changes are transforming human lives. Gala chooses Jimena, not only as a fascinating subject for the study of female frustration but also as a metaphor for Spain herself in the process of transformation. The play may be understood as an allegory for Spain as the nation made the transition to democracy after almost four decades of dictatorship, seeking to free itself from some of the myths, half-truths, and lies that had kept the country immobilized and bound to the past. Jimena personifies Spain as they both seek freedom of action in order to look for the truth about themselves and thus define themselves for the future instead of being defined by their past, however glorious that past might be.

In *Anillos para una dama*, the drama is enacted on two battlegrounds, one personal and intimate, the other national and public. The story of a love that might have been, between the widowed Jimena and Minaya, the dead Cid's friend and second in command, reflects a frustrated search for truth on the emotional plane: It is a battle between love and the power of public opinion that demands that the widow of the hero remain firmly isolated upon the pedestal where they had placed her, frozen forever in a kind of Spanish Camelot. On the public plane, two opposing political attitudes confront each other: Alfonso the King demands that the patriotic myth remain intact, that nothing change, while Jimena yearns for freedom from the past in order to enjoy the right to choose her destiny. The human drama consists of Jimena's struggle to escape from her isolation and to realize herself as a woman; the political drama reflects a parallel longing to escape from virtual imprisonment into freedom: In both we witness the search for identity, as the woman and, implicitly, Spain, attempt the difficult task of choosing between dreams and reality.

Jimena's story plays like an elegy with three themes, corresponding to the three men who shape her destiny, and in three movements, corresponding to the past, the present, and the future. El Cid is an overpowering shadow from the past; Alfonso the King is the imperative voice of the present; Minaya, the desire for a future different from the past but as yet still undefined. These three figures not only give form to a story of impossible love but also define the larger conflict between dreams and reality. Gala asks the eternal questions about this conflict: What are dreams? What if freedom is also a dream? Can we afford the luxury of dreaming any more? Where can we find the truth? In the official history books or in the prosaic doings of ordinary beings? Among legendary heroes or within the "silent majority" represented by Minaya? Must we stop dreaming in order to survive, or do we need to dream in order to make sense of our existence?[5]

Challenging the pragmatic present of Alfonso and the legendary past of El Cid, Minaya, the third man in Jimena's life, represents the dream of a free future. When the proud, independent Jimena finally dismisses Minaya from her life, accepting her role as widow to a legend, we know that she acts not out of fear or lack of spirit. Why, then, does she give in? How does her submission to the King become an act of defiance and self-affirmation? Why does she voluntarily and irreversibly identify herself with the myth of El Cid's life, relinquishing the dream of her own freedom? The answer is to be found in the cynicism of the King who, in the face of renewed Arab attacks, planned to set fire to Valencia, the dream city whose capture had been the jewel in the crown of El Cid's achievements, comparing it to a "nest of scorpions." Jimena then realized that she herself had been part of El Cid's life's work and as such could never consent to its total obliteration. By denying the myth of El Cid, she would be denying her own life, making nonsense of everything, of her dreams as well as his. If El Cid's life could be made, in the jargon of the official spin-masters, "non-operative," what then would remain of her sacrifices, of her entire life spent at his side? What would happen to the confidence that so many had placed in him and his cause? It was then that she became capable of the definitive sacrifice of herself so that others might not lose their faith in the legend of the past, so that they might not falter on the march into the future. In the name of an ideal, she voluntarily condemns herself to live as the prisoner of a myth, a myth that gave comfort and strength to others, helping them to continue striving for their own ideal. Thus has Gala most skillfully interwoven the intimate story of a woman's impossible love with a symbolic, national meaning, converting her into a tragic and heroic figure who struggled to free herself from the myth that had informed her life but who finally had to give in to the powerful reality of that very myth, enabling it to live on as an inspiration to her compatriots.

AWARDS AND DISTINCTIONS

These are national awards for plays and publications in the field of theater:

Calderón de la Barca Theater Award, 1963, for *Los verdes campos del Edén*

Foro Teatral Award, 1970, for *Spain's striptease*

Premio Nacional de Teatro, 1972, for *Los buenos días perdidos*

Premio Mayte, 1972, for *Los buenos días perdidos*

El Quijote de Oro, 1973

Premio Nacional de Guiones, 1973, for the TV series *Si las piedras hablaran*

Libro de Oro de los Libreros Españoles, 1983

Honored as "Andaluz universal," 1983, by the government of Andalusia

First Prize in the Letras Andaluzas Award, 1989

NOTES

1. Antonio Gala, "Gala contra Gala: Lectura de su poesía," Symposium Gala sobre Gala, El Escorial, 1 julio 1992.
2. Alejandro Casona, "Carta a Antonio Gala en las cien representaciones de *Los verdes campos del Edén*," *Primer acto* 51 (1964): 29–30.
3. Jeff Storer, Introduction. *The Bells of Orleans*. Trans. Edward Borsoi (University Park, PA: Estreno, 1994), viii.
4. Antonio Gala, personal interview, Madrid, May 1981.
5. Hazel Cazorla, "Antonio Gala y la desmitificación de España: Los valores alegóricos de *Anillos para una dama*," *Estreno* 4.2 (1978): 13–15.

BIBLIOGRAPHY

Editions of Plays by Antonio Gala

Anthologies

Obras escogidas. Ed. Fausto Díaz Padilla. Madrid: Aguilar, 1981. (*Los verdes campos del Edén; El caracol en el espejo; El sol en el hormiguero; Noviembre y un poco de yerba; Spain's striptease; Los buenos días perdidos; Anillos para una dama; Las cítaras colgadas de los árboles; ¿Por qué corres, Ulises? Petra Regalada; La vieja señorita del paraíso.*)

In Three Annual Anthologies Edited by Federico Carlos Sainz de Robles

Teatro español, 1963–64. (*Los verdes campos del Edén*) Madrid: Aguilar, 1964.
Teatro español, 1972–73. (*Los buenos días perdidos*) Madrid: Aguilar, 1973.
Teatro español, 1973–74. (*Anillos para una dama*) Madrid: Aguilar, 1974.

Plays Published in Madrid by Espasa-Clape in the Colección Austral

Los verdes campos del Edén. Los buenos días perdidos. 1975.
Las cítaras colgadas de los árboles. ¿Por qué corres, Ulises? 1977.
Trilogía de la libertad. Petra Regalada. La vieja señorita del paraíso. El cementerio de los pájaros. 1983.
Samarkanda. El hotelito. 1985.

Other Editions Containing Two or Three Plays

Antonio Gala: El caracol en el espejo. El sol en el hormiguero. Noviembre y un poco de yerba. Madrid: Taurus Ediciones, 1970.
Noviembre y un poco de yerba. Petra Regalada. Madrid: Ediciones Cátedra, 1981.
Los verdes campos del Edén. El cementerio de los pájaros. Barcelona: Plaza & Janés, 1986.
Los buenos días perdidos. Anillos para una dama. Madrid: Castalia, 1987.
Los verdes campos del Edén. Los buenos días perdidos. Madrid: Espasa-Calpe, 1994.

Editions of Single Individual Plays (in order of their original stage productions)

Los verdes campos del Edén. Primer acto 51 (1964): 31–53.
Los verdes campos del Edén. Madrid: Escelicer, 1964.
Los verdes campos del Edén. Salamanca: Almar, 1983.
El sol en el hormiguero. Madrid: Ediciones MK, 1984.
Noviembre y un poco de yerba. Primer Acto 94 (1968): 19–45.
Noviembre y un poco de yerba. Madrid: Preyson, 1983.
Cantar de Santiago para todos. Madrid: Ediciones MK, 1974.
Los buenos días perdidos. Primer Acto 150 (1972): 31–57.
Los buenos días perdidos. Madrid: Escelicer, 1973.
Los buenos días perdidos (with *Las cartas boca abajo* by A. Buero Vallejo). Tarragona: Ediciones Tarraco, 1976.
Los buenos días perdidos en Años difíciles: Tres testimonios del teatro español contemporáneo. Barcelona: Bruguera, 1977.
Anillos para una dama. Madrid: Júcar, 1974.
Anillos para una dama. Madrid: Ediciones MK, 1982.
Anillos para una dama. Madrid: Bruño, 1991.
Las cítaras colgadas de los árboles. Madrid: Preyson, 1983.
¿Por qué corres, Ulises? Tiempo de Historia II. 15 (1976): 70–101.
¿Por qué corres, Ulises? Madrid: Preyson, 1984.
Petra Regalada. Madrid: Ediciones MK, 1980.
Petra Regalada. Madrid: Editorial Vox, 1980.

La vieja señorita del paraíso. Madrid: Ediciones MK, 1981.
El veredicto. Cuadernos Hispanoamericanos 407 (1984): 35–46.
El veredicto. Estreno II. 1 (1985): 6–12. (*El veredicto* remains unstaged.)
Samarkanda. Madrid: Ediciones MK, 1985.
Samarkanda. Madrid: Ediciones Antonio Machado, 1986.
El hotelito. Madrid: Ediciones Antonio Machado, 1986.
Séneca o El beneficio de la duda. Madrid: Espasa-Calpe, 1987.
Carmen Carmen. Madrid: Espasa-Calpe, 1988.
Cristóbal Colón (libreto de ópera). Gestos 3.6 (1988): 177–213.
Cristóbal Colón. Madrid: Espasa-Calpe, 1992.
La Truhana. Madrid: Espasa-Calpe, 1992.
Los bellos durmientes. Madrid: Espasa-Calpe, 1994.
Café cantante. Madrid: Espasa-Calpe, 1997.
Las manzanas del viernes. Madrid: Espasa-Calpe, 1999.

Translations

Into German

Schuch, Wolfgang. *Petra Regalada*. Berlin, n.d.
Arca, Conrado. *Los verdes campos del Edén*. n.p., n.d.

Into Arabic

Sobh, Mahmud. *Samples of Contemporary Spanish Theater*.
Bagdad: Iraq Ministry of Information, 1980. (An anthology of several Spanish authors.)
Abd al-Latif Abd al-Halim. *Anillos para una dama*. Kuwait: Kuwait Ministry of Information, 1984.

Into English

O'Connor, Patricia W. *The Green Fields of Eden*. In *Contemporary Spanish Theatre: The Social Comedies of the Sixties*. Madrid: Sociedad General Española de Librería, 1983.
Borsoi, Edward. *The Bells of Orleans (Los buenos días perdidos)*. University Park, PA: Estreno, 1994.

Into Italian

Montanari, Ugo. *Perche corri, Ulisse?* Cento, 1986.

Into Portuguese

Los verdes campos del Edén. Brazil, 1965.

Into Russian

Los verdes campos del Edén. Los buenos días perdidos. Petra Regalada. La vieja señorita del Paraíso. Moscow, 1984.

Critical Studies

Alcolea, Ana. Introducción. *Anillos para una dama*. Madrid: Editorial Bruño, 1991. 9–66.

Amorós, Andrés. Introducción. *Los buenos días perdidos. Anillos para una dama*. Madrid: Castalia, 1987. 9–116.

Anderson, Farris. "From Protest to Resignation." *Estreno* 2.2 (1976): 29–32.

Cazorla, Hazel. "Antonio Gala, ¿vanguardista arrepentido?" *Estreno* 12.2 (1986): 25–28.

———. "Antonio Gala y la desmitificación de España: Los valores alegóricos de *Anillos para una dama*." *Estreno* 4.2 (1978): 13–15.

———. Introducción. *Los verdes campos del Edén*. Salamanca: Ediciones Almar, 1983. 13–35.

———. "El libreto *Cristóbal Colón* de Antonio Gala: Dramatización histórico-alegórica de un viaje humano." *Estreno* 13.2 (1992): 27–30.

———. "El retorno de Ulises: Dos enfoques contemporáneos del mito en el teatro de Buero Vallejo y Antonio Gala." *Hispanófila* 97 (1986): 43–51.

———. "*El veredicto* de Antonio Gala: Un 'anti-auto' de nuestro tiempo." *Estreno* 11.1 (1985): 4–5.

Cibreiro, Estrella. "Tensión antitética: Estilo y contenido en el teatro de Antonio Gala." *Hispania* 78 (March 1995): 1–12.

Díaz Castañon, Carmen. Estudio preliminar. *Trilogía de la libertad*. Madrid: Espasa Calpe, 1983. 11–73.

———. Introducción. *Antonio Gala. Andaluz*. Madrid: Espasa-Calpe, 1994.

———. Introducción. *El águila bicéfala/ Textos de amor*. Madrid: Espasa-Calpe, 1993.

———. Prólogo. *Samarkanda. El hotelito*. Madrid: Espasa-Calpe, 1985. 9–28.

———. "El teatro de Antonio Gala: Veinte aõs después." *Cuadernos hispanoamericanos* 407 (1984): 48–72.

Díaz Padilla, Fausto. *El habla coloquial en el teatro de Antonio Gala*. Oviedo: Universidad de Oviedo, 1985.

———. Prólogo. *Obras escogidas*. Madrid: Aguilar, 1981. ix–clv.

Garijo Galean, Carmen. "Visión sociológica." *Cuadernos del Sur, Suplemento de Cultura de Diario Córdoba*, 11 (December 1986): 24.

Harris, Carolyn. *El teatro de Antonio Gala*. Toledo: Zocodover, 1986.

Infante, José. "Antonio Gala." In *Gran Enciclopedia de Andalucía*. Anel, 1983.

———. *Antonio Gala. Un hombre aparte*. Madrid: Espasa Calpe, 1994.

———. "La poesía de Antonio Gala." *Cuadernos del Sur. Suplemento de Cultura de Diario Córdoba* 11 (December 1986): 22–23.

Kirsner, David M. "The Function of Children in Three Representative Plays by Antonio Gala." In *Proceedings of the Symposium on "El niño en las literaturas hispánicas,"* Indiana University of Pennsylvania, October 20–21, 1978, 241–250.

———. "The Image of Spain in the Theater of Antonio Gala." Ph.D. diss., University of Illinois, 1988.

———. "The Theater and Politics of Antonio Gala." *Proceedings of the Symposium on Hispanic Literature and Politics*, Indiana University of Pennsylvania, October 8–9, 1976, 241–250.

Lamartina-Lens, Iride. "*Petra Regalada*: Madonna or Whore? *Estreno* 11.1 (1985): 13–15.

Llovet, Enrique. Prólogo. *Las cítaras colgadas de los árboles. ¿Por qué corres, Ulises?* Colección Austral. Madrid: Espasa-Calpe, 1977.

López Estrada, Francisco. "El drama de Antonio Gala sobre la Jimena del Cid." In *Pliegos de Cordel.* Roma: Instituto Español de Cultura, 1983. 31–49.

Martínez Moreno, Isabel. "Orleans, espacio de libertad en *Los buenos dias perdidos.*" *Anuario de Estudios Filológicos* 15 (1992): 217–225.

———. Prólogo. *Los bellos durmientes.* Madrid: Espasa Calpe, 1994.

———. "El universo simbólico en la obra de Antonio Gala." *Revista de Literatura* 50.100 (1988): 485–506.

Newberry, Wilma. "Antonio Gala's *El cementerio de los pájaros* and the Problem of Freedom." *Hispania* 70.3 (1987): 431–436.

Padilla Mangas, Ana María. *Tipología en la obra dramática de Antonio Gala.* Córdoba: Universidad de Córdoba, 1985.

Pérez Coterillo, Moisés. Prólogo. *La Truhana.* Madrid: Espasa-Calpe, 1992. 9–20.

Robertson, Victoria. *El teatro de Antonio Gala: Un retrato de España.* Madrid: Editorial Pliegos, 1990.

Romera Castillo, José. Introducción. *Los verdes campos del Edén. El cementerio de los pájaros.* Barcelona: Plaza 7 Jánes, 1986. 13–115.

———. Prólogo. *Carmen Carmen.* Madrid: Espasa-Calpe, 1988. 9–44.

———. Prólogo. *Cristóbal Colón.* Madrid: Espasa-Calpe, 1990. 9–65.

Sádaba, Javier. Introducción. La fuerza de la moral. *Séneca o El beneficio de la duda.* Madrid: Espasa Calpe, 1987. 19–46.

Salvat, Ricard. Prólogo. *Años dificiles: Tres testimonios del teatro español contemporáneo.* Barcelona: Bruguera, 1977: 5–48.

Sheehan, Robert Louis. "Antonio Gala and the New Catholicism." In *The Contemporary Spanish Theater: A Collection of Critical Essays*, ed. Martha T. Halsey and Phyllis Zatlin. Lanham, MD: University Press of America, 1988. 113–129.

———. "Antonio Gala's *Cristóbal Colón*: A Preliminary Note." *Estreno* 18.2 (1992): 19–20.

Zatlin-Boring, Phyllis. "De *Petra* a *Pájaros*: Gala y el tema de la libertad." *Explicación de Textos Literarios* 16.2 (1987–1988): 1–10.

———. Introducción. *Noviembre y un poco de yerba. Petra Regalada.* Madrid: Cátedra, 1981. 9–109.

———. "Martínez Mediero, Gala, and the Demythification of Spanish History." *Modern Language Studies* 16.4 (1986): 3–8.

———. "La mujer en su teatro." *Cuadernos del Sur. Suplemento de Cultura de Diario Córdoba* 11 (December 1986): 17.

———. Prólogo. *Los verdes campos del Edén. Los buenos días perdidos.* Madrid: Espasa-Calpe, 1994. 1–37.

———. "The Theater of Antonio Gala: In Search of Paradise." *Kentucky Romance Quarterly* 24 (1977): 175–183.

ANTONIO GARCÍA GUTIÉRREZ
(1813–1884)

George P. Mansour

BIOGRAPHY

Antonio García Gutiérrez was born on July 5, 1813, and raised in Chiclana, a village near Cádiz.[1] His experiences in school there offered him little of interest. Contrary to his own wishes, but at the insistence of his father, he enrolled in the School of Medicine of the University of Cádiz. Uninterested in medicine, he would spend his study time composing poetry, an activity to which his father strongly objected. Such was the opposition to writing verses that García Gutiérrez developed the subterfuge of utilizing minute cursive characters for his poems so they would go unnoticed by the father. Although Antonio eluded the objections of his father, this practice seriously affected his eyesight, resulting in a condition that persisted throughout his life.

In 1833 García Gutiérrez, in the company of a friend, left his parents for Madrid to try to make it on his own as a writer. The road to success was not an easy one. The trip, which had to be made on foot, lasted at least seventeen days. Work was not easy to secure. He eventually was given odd jobs in different publishing houses, and through the intervention of Juan Grimaldi, leading theater impresario of the day, García Gutiérrez was hired on the editorial staff of the *Revista Española*, a position by which he financially eked out a living but which, more important for him, represented an opportunity to put some of his own work into print.

His success as a dramatist was not immediate. He undertook the translation of plays that had good box-office appeal in France. In 1834 and 1835 he translated three plays of Eugène Scribe: *Le vampire* [The Vampire], *Batilde*, and *Le quaker e la Danseuse* [The Quaker and the Dancer].

The initial plays of Spanish romanticism during these same years influenced García Gutiérrez's view of drama. In 1835 he penned his most important play, *El trovador*, which he offered to Grimaldi for production in the Teatro de la Cruz. Adams has described how an inferior theatrical troupe became convinced by an unsympathetic stage prompter that the play was impossible to present

(12). Discouraged, García Gutiérrez enlisted in the army to help quell the Carlist uprisings. He was sent to Leganés. He was there for only a short while when he received word that Espronceda had responded enthusiastically to reading *El trovador*, and with the help of Grimaldi once again, this play was to be produced. The play premiered on March 1, 1836. Without seeking permission from his commanding officer, García Gutiérrez abandoned his military duties in Leganés to attend the performance in Madrid. The performance was an overwhelming success, and as reported repeatedly by his biographers, the audience insisted that the unknown author come onto the stage for recognition. The impact of the play was such that it had one of the longest stage runs of any work in years, the first edition of the drama was exhausted within days, and the author was granted a full discharge from military service. His career as dramatist was under way.

The next year he produced three plays, *El paje* [The Page], *El sitio de Bilbao* [The Siege of Bilbao], *Magdalena*, and the translation *La Pandilla* [The Gang] by Scribe, a pace that he maintained for several years. Between 1838 and 1842 he published and produced fifteen plays, seven of which were translations from the French. In 1839 he translated *La chute d'un ange* of Alexandre Dumas as *Don Juan de Marana o La caída de un ángel* [Don Juan de Maraña or The Fall of an Angel], a translation that was perhaps the most important for the development of Spanish drama, for some believe this work to be one of the sources of José Zorrilla's *Don Juan Tenorio* in 1844. During this period, the dramatist also collaborated with such other writers as Zorrilla, with whom he wrote *Juan Dandolo*; Isidoro Gil y Baus, *Juan de Suavia*; and Luis Valladares y Garriga and Carlos Garía Doncel, *De un apuro, otro mayor* [From the Frying Pan into the Fire]. The rate of productivity during this period, however, exceeded that of success.

In 1843, however, he regained renown with the premiere of *Simón Bocanegra*, at which the audience repeated its demand of seven years earlier that the author come onto the stage. It is reported that in addition to his required appearance before the audience, he was crowned for his mellifluous verse and dramatic achievement. Since the coronation was a spontaneous gesture of laud, some of his acquaintances rummaged about the stage properties and borrowed the paper crown that had been used in a performance of another play. Although the production of his plays continued virtually annually, he was not to achieve similar acclaim as dramatist until the performance of *Venganza catalana* in 1864, which ran for fifty-six nights.

During the interim between successes, García Gutiérrez's talent did not go unnoticed, at least by maestro Giuseppe Verdi, who was fascinated by some of the characters and complex intrigues the dramatist created. He selected two plays: He and his librettist adapted *El trovador* and composed *Il Trovatore* between 1850 and 1852; he also adapted *Simón Bocanegra*, presenting it as an opera in 1857 and subsequently revising it in 1881. García Gutiérrez went to Cuba during this interim, where he worked for a newspaper, and then subsequently to the Yucatán, where he lived for a few years during which he continued to compose plays.

In 1855 he was named to a government post in London as "Head of the Spanish Financial Commission in London," a position he held for two years. While there he learned that his brother's house in Seville was damaged by fire and that the manuscript of his play *Roger de Flor* had been destroyed. Sometime after his return to Spain he recast the lost piece into the new play *Venganza catalana* [Catalan Vengeance], first performed on February 4, 1864, a work that symbolically stands as one of his last but largest successes and a work on the occasion of whose performance he was lauded with a laurel crown before the audience. The following year he released *Juan Lorenzo*, a work that further secured his position as a major dramatist in Spain.

In addition to works of little significance for the development of Spanish theater, during the period 1853–1865 he worked with such composers as Emilio Arrieta and Francisco Asenjo Barbieri to produce a number of *zarzuelas*, short dramatic pieces that intermingle spoken and sung parts. In 1868 and 1869 he held consular posts at Bayonne and Genoa. During the last twelve years of his life, 1872 to 1884, he served as Director of the Archaeological Museum of Madrid. He died on August 26, 1884.

DRAMATURGY: MAJOR WORKS AND THEMES

At least seventy-five dramatic works are attributed to Antonio García Gutiérrez as dramatist, translator, collaborator, or librettist. His original works include principally comedies and dramas, the latter genre of which is the source of his greatest fame. Many of these include topics from Spanish or peninsular medieval or renaissance history poeticized through complex dramatic structures of intrigue and multiple actions. The following are representative of this author's successful plays.

El trovador [The Troubadour], which premiered on March 1, 1836, in the Teatro del Príncipe, is a drama in five acts that juxtaposes the themes of love and vengeance. The action occurs in Aragón during the fifteenth century. The two themes are introduced in the initial scenes by secondary characters from whom we learn that the brother of the Count of Luna as a child fell victim to a spell cast upon him by a gypsy. After the gypsy was burned at the stake, the health of the child improved, but he soon mysteriously disappeared. The charred remains of a child, believed to be his, were found near the site of the gypsy's execution. We also learn that the Count of Luna is involved in a love triangle in which he loves Leonor, who prefers Manrique, the Troubadour, who wounded the Count in a duel.

Leonor, believing that the Troubadour has been killed during his travels, refuses to marry the Count and chooses to enter the convent. Following the ceremony at which she makes her vows as a nun, however, she sees Manrique, who has returned. Manrique hears from Azucena, a gypsy whom he believes to be his mother, that years earlier she witnessed the execution of her own mother and that, seeking revenge, she tried to incinerate the Count's son, only to discover that she mistakenly threw her own child into the flames. In a powerful scene, Leonor confronts the dilemma of having made insincere vows to God when she still loves Manrique; removing her nun's veil, she abandons her spiritual husband for the Troubadour. Both Manrique and Azucena are taken prisoner. Leonor offers herself to the Count of Luna in exchange for Manrique's freedom. She goes to the Troubadour's cell, informs him that he is to be freed, reveals that she poisoned herself, and dies in his arms. The Count orders Manrique's execution, which he requires be witnessed by the gypsy Azucena, who subsequently informs the Count that he executed his own brother Manrique and dies shouting that her mother is now avenged.

In *El page* [The Page], first performed on May 22, 1837, the action occurs in Cordoba and Seville in the midfourteenth century. Ferrando, the fifteen-year-old page of Don Martín, the Count of Niebla, is in love with the Countess Blanca. Blanca, currently married to Don Martín, was formerly the lover of Rodrigo with whom she had a child. He is still in love with her and wants her to run away with him. Rodrigo tells her that years before he entrusted their child to an older man and has since lost track of him. Rodrigo, wanting to have Blanca for himself, plots to kill his rival Martín. Ferrando learns that he was an abandoned child, news that saddens him. Blanca tries to console him, only to have him reveal his own love for her. She tells the page that he could prove his love for her by killing her husband Don Martín, who is already seriously wounded. She encourages him with her own words of love. The page carries out the request, only to see Blanca leave with Rodrigo.

Ferrando learns that Rodrigo is his father, and saddened, he pledges to die avenged of the woman whom he loves but who deceived him. The day of the marriage of Rodrigo and Blanca, Ferrando gains entry into Blanca's bedroom, accuses her, and drinks poison from a vial. He informs her that Rodrigo is his father. Rodrigo enters as Ferrando takes his last breath, and he curses Blanca, the mother of their now-dead child.

Simón Bocanegra, first performed on January 17, 1843, consists of a prologue and four acts. The prologue occurs in Genoa in 1338 and depicts the plot to have the pirate Simón Bocanegra named Dux. Years before, Bocanegra had seduced Mariana and had a daughter with her. Still in love with her, he tells her father he wishes to marry her, but he becomes aware that she has just died. In Act One, which takes place in Genoa in 1362, one learns that Gabriel is in love with Susana in whom Bocanegra, now Dux for twenty-four years, has also expressed an interest. Gabriel and others conspire to overthrow Bocanegra. Susana is abducted by Paolo, who is also in love with her, and is entrusted to another conspirator. Bocanegra and Susana recognize that she is his daughter, a fact they intend to keep secret. Gabriel, about to assassinate Bocanegra, is stopped by Susana. Bocanegra reveals the identity of Susana and gains the loyalty of Gabriel. Mariana's father, incited to rage by Paolo, by his insistence on the shame that she brought to his family, attempts to poison Bocanegra, who drinks from the drugged cup, asks Mariana's father for forgiveness, and toasts Gabriel and Susana, naming Gabriel the new Dux of Genoa.

Venganza catalana [Catalan Vengeance], a four-act drama that premiered on February 4, 1864, dramatizes a historical incident made melodramatic through the complications of love intrigues. The action takes place in Andrinopolis and Apros in 1304. It is the story of Roger de Flor whose Catalonian and Aragonese armies assist the Emperor of Byzantium in his battles against the infidels. Roger is married to Maria, the cousin of the Emperor. Gircon, head of the Emperor's allies, the Alans, had a daughter Margarita who had been seduced by someone whose identity she took with her to the grave. Gircon and his son Alejo have repeatedly tried to discover who dishonored Margarita. The intrigue is further complicated by the fact that Alejo and Maria, Roger's wife, had been lovers and had pledged to maintain their love for each other. Roger de Flor informs them of his previous secret marriage to Margarita and that while he was at war she committed suicide, thinking herself abandoned. Gircon learns of the relationship and calls for vengeance. At a dinner, he assassinates Roger. The joint armies of Roger and Miguel, now headed up by Berenguer, triumphantly avenge the murder of Roger de Flor in bloody battles.

CRITICS' RESPONSE

El trovador is unquestionably the play for which García Gutiérrez is best remembered both nationally and internationally. The initial critical reception in 1836 mirrored the enthusiastic response of the initial viewing audience. Within a few days of the first performance, Mariano José de Larra reviewed the work, extolling its dramatic artistry and the poetic and emotional heights the author evokes. Although the reviewer considered the complexity of action a possible flaw, he recognized that it clearly sustained the audience's interest. In criticizing the play, Larra mentions such defects as the limited development of some characters and a certain, unbelievable suddenness in their change of heart. He did not insist on the need for drama to adhere faithfully to such neoclassical tenets as the unities; however, he invoked verisimilitude as a criterion in formulating a critical judgment, a principle that did not constitute part of the dramaturgy of Romantic plays.

Juan Eugenio Hartzenbusch speaks in his prologue to the *Obras escogidas*, published in 1866, of the influence Rivas's play *Don Alvaro o la fuerza del sino* [Don Alvaro or the Power of Fate], staged one year earlier, exercised on *El trovador*. He further observes that through García Gutiérrez's play the Spanish *comedia* of old finally triumphs over the presence of the rigid, French critical perspectives of drama (xvi). Although the recovery of Spain's medieval past and Golden Age theater is typically Romantic, Hartzenbusch's association of *El trovador* with Golden Age theater does not change the fact that in its external structure and conflict, high-pitched language, and acting *El trovador* reflected the dramatic taste and principles of its own day.

Nicholson B. Adams's book *The Romantic Plays of García Gutiérrez* was long considered the authoritative reference for studies on the dramatist. In his commentary on the play (59–101), Adams principally demonstrates his interest in literary and historical sources and influences: using titles for each act (Hugo's *Hernani*), having five acts instead of three (French drama), mixing prose and verse (Rivas's *Don Alvaro*), introducing the theme of vengeance (Dumas), and making political references in the play that are documentable (e.g., "Chronicle of John II"). Adams offers an elaborate comparison of the play and Larra's *Macías* of 1834, showing similarity in structure, themes, and character configuration. He considers most interesting the sinister figure of Azucena, the gypsy, and her compelling passion for vengeance.[2]

Carmen Iranzo's book on García Gutiérrez provides the broadest published review of the scholarship on the play from the first performance to the time of its writing for Twayne Publishers; however, she presents a severely critical view toward foreigner's (i.e., non-Spanish) commentary on the play.

María Luisa Guardiola-Ellis has published the most recent book (1993) on García Gutiérrez, an insightful and useful compendium of the themes and the roles of women in the plays. Her commentary on *El trovador*, for example, reflects the paradigm she establishes for the study: female protagonists, women within the family context, women in society, religion and women—a critical structure within which she relates the dramatist's portrayal of women and their presence in nineteenth-century Spain. Thus, her observations on the play, although important, are filtered through the critical construct and per force appear sporadically throughout the study.

El trovador occupies a significant place in Spanish Romantic drama, a genre known for its emotive, symbolic, subversive elements, multiple dramatic actions that elucidate usually one central theme, and its subordination of characterization to action. It is a spectacle that addresses the spectator principally through the senses. In this play García Gutiérrez bombards the audience's senses and emotions through vivid imagery evoked in poeticizing the Troubadour's passion for Leonor, the gypsy's profound desire for revenge, the incineration of the gypsy's own child, the terrifying discovery that brother has executed brother. In addition to provoking powerful sense impressions, as was done in other Romantic plays, this author also attends to character development, masterfully and boldy depicting through Leonor an extraordinarily strong woman who defies the values and institutions of her patriarchal society. She opposes the will of her brother—a substitute *pater familias*, unjust class distinctions, the church, and God. The convent scenes (III, 4–5) are the centerpiece of the play; where she articulates the dilemma of her passion—having taken the vows of a nun while still clinging to her love for the Troubadour—which culminates in her abandoning the spiritual marriage with God in favor of the flesh and blood of the Troubadour. She says to him:

Tus brazos son mi altar, seré tu esposa,
Y tu esclava seré; pronto, un momento,
Un momento pudiera descubrirnos,
Y te perdiera entonces. (III, 5)

[Your arms are my altar; I shall be your wife;
I shall be your slave. Hurry, a moment,
In a moment we could be discovered,
and I would then lose you.]

This scene occupies the geometric center of the play, a point in Romantic drama regularly reserved for a significant act, gesture, or metaphor of the entire work. In *El trovador* it is a symbolic point not only in the drama of Leonor and Manrique but for what it represents as well outside of the play for Spain of the mid-1830s. Previous dramatists—for example, Mariano José de Larra (*Macías*, 1834), Martínez de la Rosa (*La conjuración de Venecia*, 1834), Duque de Rivas (*Don Alvaro o la fuerza del sino*, 1835)—had depicted in their plays defiance of and resistance to such established values and institutions as inherited nobility, legitimate and illegitimate absolutist governments, repressive social classes and hierarchies, and the church. Through the words and action of a woman, García Gutiérrez boldly extends the resistance to a metaphysical level, a symbolic step that further subverts the established order. In spite of the resounding reception of *El trovador* in 1836 and in subsequent years, Leonor's love of Manrique is doomed from the beginning of the play, a trajectory that parallels somewhat the fate of the efforts to modify or to liberate the order of things in nineteenth-century Spain.

AWARDS AND DISTINCTIONS

In 1862, García Gutiérrez was named member of the Real Academia Española de la Lengua (Spanish Royal Academy of Language), an honor bestowed upon a limited number of writers and intellectuals. He was recipient of several badges of public recognition, among which are the Great Cross of the Order of Charles III in 1856, of that of María Victoria, of Isabel la Católica, and of the Concepción de Villaviciosa of Portugal in 1864.

In 1864, following the premiere of *Venganza catalana*, ten supporters formed a commission to offer the dramatist testimony of esteem for his significant contributions to Spanish theater. With the help of three publishers who released the rights they owned to some of the plays, a major collection of his plays was published in 1866 as *Obras escogidas de Don Antonio García Gutiérrez, edición hecha en obsequio del autor* [Select Works of Don Antonio García Gutiérrez, an Edition Issued in Honor of the Author]. This volume brings together nineteen of his dramatic works, fourteen plays, and five *zarzuelas*, a collection that continues to be the highest number of his dramatic pieces collected in one volume.

The book emulated the format, size, and binding of the *Biblioteca de Autores Españoles*, published also by Rivadeneyra, a feature that unofficially placed García Gutiérrez among the distinguished authors whose works were included in this major series of Spanish authors.

NOTES

1. Biographical sources for Antonio García Gutiérrez are rare, as Iranzo regularly notes in her book. The information provided above is based on data presented by Adams, Rosell, and Iranzo. See "Critical Studies."
2. Jerry Johnson's brief study examines more closely this character and her conflicting needs to avenge her mother's death and for the Troubadour's affection. See also Siciliano's article in "Critical Studies."

BIBLIOGRAPHY

Editions

Obras escogidas de Antonio García Gutiérrez, edición hecha en obsequio del autor. Prologue by Juan Eugenio Hartzenbusch. Madrid: Imprenta y Estereotipia de M. Rivadeneyra, 1866.
Venganza Catalana; Juan Lorenzo. Ed. José Lomba y Pedraja. Madrid: Espasa-Calpe, 1958.
The Troubadour. In *Spanish Plays of the Nineteenth Century.* Trans. Rachael Benson. Ed. Roberto O'Brien. New York: Las Américas, 1964.
El trovador, drama caballeresco en cinco jornadas, en prosa y verso. Ed. José Hesse. Madrid: Aguilar, 1964.
El trovador. Ed. Alberto Blecua. Barcelona: Labor, 1972.
El trovador, drama; Los hijos del tío Tronera, sainete. Ed. Jean-Louis Picoche. Madrid: Alhambra, 1979.
El trovador. Ed. Antonio Rey Hazas. Barcelona: Plaza y Janés, 1984.
El trovador. Sound Recording. Compañía de Actores de Radio Nacional de España. Coproducción de Radio Nacional y el Ministerio de Cultura, Secretaría General Técnica. Madrid: Diapason, 1984.
The Troubadour. In *Three Spanish Romantic Plays.* Trans. Luis Soto-Ruiz and Georgia Papanastos. Ed. Anne Pasero. Mérida, Mexico: Producción Editorial Dante, 1989.
El trovador; Simón Bocanegra. Ed. Luis F. Díaz Larios. Barcelona: Planeta, 1989.
El grumete, zarzuela en un acto: En el centenario de la muerte de Emilio Arrieta Corera. Música de Emilio Arrieta. Madrid: Instituto Complutense de Ciencias Musicales, 1994.

Critical Studies

Adams, Nicholson Barney. *The Romantic Plays of García Gutiérrez.* New York: Instituto de las Españas en Estados Unidos, 1922.

Alicna Franch, Juan. "El trovador." In *Teatro romántico*. Barcelona: Bruguera, 1968. 11–50.

Cattaneo, María Teresa. "Inventare il vero: A proposito di *El teatro del rey* di Antonio García Gutiérrez." In *La scena e la storia: Studi sul teatro spagnolo*, ed. María Teresa Cattaneo, Bologna, Italy: Cisalpino, 1997. 215–232.

Eckard, Robert Emmett. "A Critical Study of the Later Plays (1849–80) of Antonio García Gutiérrez." Ph.D. diss., University of Kentucky, 1979.

Ferrer del Río, Antonio. *Galería de la literatura*. Madrid: Mellado, 1846.

Guardiola-Ellis, María Luisa. *La temática de García Gutiérrez: Indice y estudio: La mujer*. Barcelona: Promociones y Publicaciones Universitarias, 1993.

Guaza y Gómez Talavera, Carlos. *Músicos, poetas y actores*. Madrid: Maroto e hijos, 1884.

Iranzo, Carmen. *Antonio García Gutiérrez*. Boston: Twayne Publishers, 1980.

Johnson, Jerry. "El antagonista romántico: Una reconsideración." *Romance Notes* 27 (1987): 239–243.

———. "Azucena, Sinister or Pathetic?" *Romance Notes* 12 (1970): 114–118.

Larra, Mariano José de. "El trovador." In *Artículos de crítica literaria y artística*, ed. José Lomba y Pedraja. 1836. Madrid: Espasa-Calpe, 1960.

Lemartinel, Jean. "*El trovador* de García Gutiérrez: Objet d'une recherche collective." In *Aspects de XIXe siècle iberique et ibero-americain: Actes du XIIe congrès de la société des hispanistes français de l'enseignement superieur, Lille, 1976*. Lille: Université de Lille, 1977. 9–16.

López Funes, Enrique. *Don Antonio García Gutiérrez, estudio crítico de sus obras dramáticas*. Madrid: Suárez, 1900.

Menarini, Piero. "García Gutiérrez e l'autoparodia del *Trovador*." *Spicelegio Moderno: Saggi e Ricerche di Letterature e Lingue Straniere* 8 (1977): 115–123.

Ribao, Montserrat. "La teatralidad externa de *El trovador*." *Siglo Diecinueve* 3 (1997): 53–68.

Rosell, Cayetano. "D. Antonio García Gutiérrez." In *Autores dramáticos contemporáneos y joyas del teatro español del siglo XIX*," ed. Pedro de Novo y Colson. 2 vols. Madrid: Fortanet, 1881. 1: 81–96.

Ruiz Díaz, Adolfo. "Motivos románticos europeos en *El trovador* de García Gutiérrez." *Revista di Letterature Moderne* 13 (1973): 151–190.

Ruiz Silva, Carlos. "García Gutiérrez: Política y guerras civiles." *Cuadernos Hispanoamericanos* 415 (1985): 91–100.

———. "*El trovador*, de García Gutiérrez, drama y melodrama." *Cuadernos Hispanoamericanos* 335 (1978): 251–272.

Siciliano, Ernest A. "La verdadera Azucena de *El trovador*." *Nueva Revista de Filología Hispánica* 20 (1971): 107–114.

Varela, José Luis. "Verdi ante el *Simón Bocanegra* de García Gutiérrez." In *Estudios románticos*. Valladolid: Patronato Quadrado, del CSIC, 1975. 327–343.

Vilarnovo, Antonio. "Poética del sonido en *El trovador*." *Revista de Literatura* 48 (1986): 101–113.

FEDERICO GARCÍA LORCA
(1898–1936)

Ada Ortúzar-Young

BIOGRAPHY

Poet. Playwright. Creator of myths. Primitive yet very modern. Federico García Lorca, or just Lorca, as most critics call him, is considered today, over sixty years after his untimely death, one of the most major figures in Spanish literature of all times. His works, along with those of Cervantes, are among the most often translated and recognized outside Spain. The year of his birth (1898) and that of his death (1936) coincided with two major historical events in his nation. In 1898 the Spanish-American War closed Spain's imperial expansion and marked its retreat to the Iberian peninsula. For three years, between 1936 and 1939, Spaniards, deeply divided, fought among themselves. The Civil War has been considered by many Spain's single most far-reaching event in the twentieth century. It altered the destinies of many of its citizens as it shaped their economic, intellectual, and political future.

Lorca was born on June 5, 1898, in Fuente Vaqueros, a small town near Granada. His father, Don Federico García Rodríguez, was a well-to-do landowner. He married Doña Vicenta Lorca Romero, a schoolteacher who has been credited with nurturing her son's artistic interests. In 1909 his family moved to Granada and established their residence near Sacro Monte, the area where many gypsies lived. This seems to have made a lasting impression on young Lorca, since years later two of his most important works—*Romancero gitano* [Gypsy Ballads] (1928) and *Bodas de sangre* [Blood Wedding] (1933) would incorporate the caves of Sacro Monte, and the gypsies as protagonists. He briefly attended the Colegio del Sagrado Corazón de Jesús and later enrolled at the University of Granada to study law. However, his interests were elsewhere, and he was beginning to pursue writing, literature, and the arts in general. He was becoming an accomplished guitar and piano player. This period of his life is marked by two prominent men of letters. Fernando de los Ríos, president of the Centro Artístico de Granada [Granada's Artistic Center], took an interest in him, and his friendship would leave a lasting imprint on his career. Lorca's music professor Martín Domínguez Berrueta would also recognize his talents. A tour of Spain for his Theory of Literature and Art class would lead to the publication of his first book before age twenty, a travelogue entitled *Impresiones y paisajes* [Impressions and Landscapes] (1918).

Lorca's decision in 1919 to move from provincial Granada to Madrid and his stay at the famous Residencia de Estudiantes ("la Resi") would be one of the most decisive steps in his career. By the end of his stay at "la Resi" some eight years later, Lorca had already achieved an international reputation. There he had been in close contact with numerous European intellectuals and with such emerging Spanish poets as Rafael Alberti, Dámaso Alonso, Gerardo Diego, Jorge Guillén, and Pedro Salinas. He also established a close and eventually painful friendship with Salvador Dalí and Luis Buñuel, who within a short time would revolutionize Spanish plastic arts and film directing, respectively. His stay in the Spanish capital coincides with a period of intense artistic activity dominated by Surrealism other avant-garde movements imported from various European countries. The 1920s also witnessed the expansion of the movie industry and the first steps toward the interaction between the cinema and literature. The cinema will be particularly attractive to the young poets of the time who were trying to experiment, creating unusual poetic images with words. They saw in the incipient art form a wealth of possibilities for combining images, sounds, and rhythms in a multiplicity of unexpected ways. In 1925, inspired by the new medium, Lorca wrote "El paseo de Buster Keaton" [Buster Keaton's Stroll], which would be followed by the cinematic skits "La doncella, el marinero y el estudiante" [The Maiden, the Sailor and the Student] and "Quimera" [Chimera], published under the title of *Teatro breve* [Short Plays] (1928). His filmscript "Viaje a la luna" [Trip to the Moon] (1929) was written as a response to Buñuel's audacious "Un chien andalou" [An Andalusian Dog].

The culmination of these newly found avant-garde interests came for Lorca and his group with the celebration of the tercentenary of the death of the seventeeth-century Spanish baroque poet Luis de Góngora. This led to the labeling of the group as the "Generation of 1927," also called the Lorca generation. Lorca paid hommage to the baroque poet with his essay "La imagen poética de don Luis de Góngora" [Luis de Góngora's Poetic Image] (1926). The adoption of Góngora as a hero was a significant one for the young poets. The baroque poet had been a polemical figure in his time. His ingenious play with words and images, his metaphorical ornamentation, and his highly elaborate poetry were very much akin to what his countrymen were doing some 300 years later. Furthermore, by associating with Góngora the young poets of 1927 were showing their contempt for the conventional art of the time and for the Spanish Academy, which had decided to overlook the commemoration of Góngora's death.

Equally contemptuous and a reflection of the profound division between old and new aesthetic conceptions was a book planned by Dalí and Lorca around 1926, tentatively entitled "Los putrefactos" [The Putrid Ones]. The term "putrefacto," with its allusions to the odor produced by a corpse in the process of decomposition, denoted, in particular, those intellectuals who professed conservative aesthetic values and for this reason did not partake of the latest avant-garde currents. The book would not come to fruition due to the break of Dalí and Lorca's friendship resulting from aesthetic and personal differences. In 1928, as new avant-garde literary magazines flourished in Spain, Lorca would make his own contribution with the publication in Granada of the journal *Gallo* [Rooster].

In the summer of 1929 Lorca departs for New York, via Paris and London, with his friend and former teacher Fernando de los Ríos. He studies English at Columbia University, but without much success. His interests are elsewhere, in nearby Harlem, home of the African descendants who, like the gypsy of Granada, would become the subject of many of his poems. He feels passion for jazz. There he starts working on two of his most surrealist works: *Poeta en Nueva York* [Poet in New York] and *Así que pasen cinco años* [Once Five Years Pass], which will be completed upon his return to Spain. Lorca is then invited to Cuba for a series of lectures, and with Lydia Cabrera, the renouned African folklorist, he further explores the lives and the music of the African population in the island. In their primitive dances and corporal expressions he believes to find traces of his native Andalusian "cante jondo" [deep song]. In Havana he is hard at work on a highly experimental play, *El público* [The Public] that would never be represented during the author's life, perhaps due to its highly experimental character and to the subject matter, where the author tries to vindicate the rights of those sexually different, particularly homosexuals. According to biographer Ian Gibson, while in Cuba Lorca manifested more openly his own homosexuality.

Lorca returns to Spain in the summer of 1930. There are signs of the social and political turmoil that would lead to the Second Republic and the Spanish Civil War. He participates in an important cultural project of the Republic with the creation of "La Barraca" [The Hut], a troupe of traveling theater of the University of Madrid, which he codirects with Eduardo Ugarte. Between 1932 and 1936 the group will draw from Spain's well-established classical tradition to stage in numerous Spanish cities works by such masters as Cervantes, Tirso de Molina, Lope de Vega, and Calderón de la Barca. In the last three years of his life he will experience an unparalleled success. His *Romancero gitano* has established his reputation as a poet, which is further enhanced by the publication of *Llanto por Ignacio Sánchez Mejías* [Lament for Ignacio Sánchez Mejías] (1935). *Bodas de sangre* has been warmly acclaimed by the Spanish public, and he is invited to Buenos Aires where his works will be produced in 1933. *Yerma* [Barren] (1934) and *Doña Rosita la soltera* [Rosie the Spinster] (1935), bring him to the peak of his fame.

The year 1936 marks the beginning of the Spanish Civil War. Fearing the turmoil in Madrid, on July 16 Lorca returns to his parents' home at the "Huerta de San Vicente" in Granada seeking safety. The situation in Granada is critical, and his family, sensing the danger, sends him to the home of a friend, the poet Luis Rosales, who has Falangist connections. All efforts are in vain. In the midst of the turmoil, Lorca is taken away by the Francoists, and on August 19, the order for execution is given. Many details about the last days of his life and the actual execution remain unclear. His remains were placed in an unmarked grave in the hills of nearby Viznar.

DRAMATURGY: MAJOR WORKS AND THEMES

The dramatic work of Federico García Lorca has traditionally been divided, both thematically and qualitatively, into two broad categories, mostly along chronological lines. This neat division, however, is somewhat deceiving. While it is true that his dramatic career evolves and matures over a period of a decade and a half, some of his works have been produced a decade after they have been conceived. It is even more difficult to establish clear boundaries between genres. In Lorca's case it is impossible to separate the poet from the dramatist since similar lyric and dramatic techniques are reelaborated in most works. A small number of themes recur over a fifteen-year period: the marginal situation of certain members of society (gypsies, women, homosexuals); the individual's natural instincts as they clash with the intolerance of established norms; the forces of death, destruction, and violence in general. The treatment of cosmos, images, light, and sound conveys a particularly dramatic texture regardless of the genre, and similar symbols and motifs (such as the horse and the moon) predominate over this universe where colors acquire a force of their own. It is only an accident of fate that *La casa de Bernarda Alba* [The House of Bernarda Alba] (1936) is the last point of reference of a literary career that ends abruptly and unexpectedly.

Lorca's interest in the theater started as a child, according to his brother Francisco. He has commented on young Federico's fascination from a very early age about playing with puppets and marionettes and building toy theaters. His first play *El maleficio de la mariposa* [The Butterfly's Evil Spell] (1920) is a poetic fantasy. On a bright summer day a brilliantly colored wounded butterfly falls into an Andalusian field among a colony of cockroaches. Having never seen such a creature, the insects feel frightened by the intruder, except for one who becomes hypnotized by the beauty and mystery of the invader. The enchantress tells him about the world of sunlight and flowers, thus tempting the lowly cockroach to agitate his wings and attempt to fly away, just to realize that he cannot rise himself above the grass. The day comes when the butterfly regains the use of her wings and flies away, leaving behind the anguished cockroach, victim of her spell and condemned forever to dream about the open-air paradise he will never enjoy. *El maleficio de la mariposa* was negatively received by the Madrid audience and had only one perfomance.

Lorca's childhood interest in marionettes led him in 1923 to present in collaboration with composer Manuel de Falla a series of puppet plays for their friends to celebrate the Twelfth-Night holiday. In addition to a Cervantes *entremés* (short farce interlude) and a medieval mystery play, *Los reyes magos* [The Three Kings], Lorca presented one of his own plays, now lost, *La niña que riega la albahaca y el príncipe preguntón* [The Girl Who Waters the Basil and the Inquisitive Prince]. Later, in 1928, he wrote another puppet farce, *Los títeres de cachiporra: Tragicomedia de don Cristóbal y la señá Rosita* [The Billy Club Puppets: Tragicomedy of Christopher and Rosie]. While frivolous on the surface, the puppet theater allowed Lorca, and some of his contemporaries (Jacinto Grau and Ramón del Valle-Inclán), to make human comparisons with the wooden figures. Critics have often regarded these early puppet pieces as improvisations for the more elaborate social farces such as *La zapatera prodigiosa: Farsa violenta* [The Shoemaker's Prodigious Wife: Violent Farce], (1930), *Retablillo de don Cristóbal* [Don Cristobal's Little Stage], (1934), and *Amor de don Perlimplín con Belisa en su jardín* [The Love of Don Perlimplín with Belisa in His Garden] (1933).

La zapatera prodigiosa, similar in theme and spirit to Alarcón's *El sombrero de tres picos* [The Three-Cornered Hat] also shares some similarities with Valle-Inclán's *Los cuernos de don Friolera* [Don Friolera's Horns]. It was successfully produced in Madrid in 1930. The first of Lorca's plays with a woman as a central character, it draws from folklore to make a farcical representation of a young and lively woman married to an older man who remains faithful despite her unhappiness. The "zapatera" is full of zest for life. She spurns young suitors that besiege her attracted by her provocative appearance, with her bare arms in her flame-red dress. Lorca's treatment of the theme follows closely the tradition of the *entremés*. He makes extensive use of pantomimes and ballet choreography. In terms of language and spirit Lorca remains very close to the common people. The *zapatera* sings the refrains of popular songs, and at the end, the playwright introduces a Puppet Show in which the Puppeteer-Shoemaker recites the ballad of the Saddler and the Saddler's Wife, which is used to reinforce the burlesque tone of the play.

In 1931 Lorca returns to the theme of the mismatched marriage with another puppet play, *Retablillo de don Cristóbal*. The grotesque Cristóbal buys in marriage the exhuberant and erotic Rosita, just to be deceived by her later. Critics have often considered these puppet pieces improvisations to the more elaborate farce *Amor de don Perlimplín con Belisa en su jardín*, which carries the subtitle of "Aleluya erótica" [Erotic Hallelujah]. Don Perlimplín is a respectable elderly man. At the suggestion of his maid, he proposes marriage to her neighbor, the young and voluptuous Belisa. On the wedding night, a marriage bed appears on the stage, with the anguished Don Perlimplín fearful of not being able to consummate the marriage. The room opens to five balconies, with ladders leading outside, and five hats beneath, serving as evidence that five men have visited his wife during the night. Don Perlimplín appears fully clothed, sitting in his bed with two horns grown on his forehead. Lorca further elaborates on the situation of the cuckold and his loss of honor. As Belisa prepares to be serenaded by a sixth lover in the garden's moonglight, Don Perlimplín puts a dagger into his heart and falls dead in Belisa's arms, thus making a transition from farce to tragic farce.

Mariana Pineda, a historical play subtitled "Romance popular en tres estampas" [Popular Ballad in Three Scenes] was first produced in 1927 with limited success. Lorca's adaptation is based on a real-life figure, a widowed mother of two children who sewed the flag of the Republican conspirators who were trying to overthrow the monarchy of Ferdinand VII in the early part of the nineteenth century. The historical Mariana was an active conspirator who gave her life for freedom. Lorca's melodramatic interpretation makes her romantic and idealistic. She is a symbol of liberty and is fully committed to the man she loves. When caught by the king's police, she refuses to divulge the names of the conspirators who have succeeded in escaping Spain and is put to death. She becomes a symbol of the search for human liberty.

El público and *Así que pasen cinco años* are Lorca's most experimental plays. It seems that Lorca started to write *El público* at a moment of personal crisis during his trip to New York and Cuba. It is very influenced by surrealism and deals somewhat in disguise with the subject of homosexuality. This is something he could not express openly at a personal level or in the theater in the society in which he lived. It also poses the larger question of representing truth in the theater. The playwright continues his exploration of avant-garde techniques in *Así que pasen cinco años*, a disconcerting play due to its treatment of characters, space, and time. Critics have felt disturbed and confused by the lack of plan and the automatic like behavior of the characters. The dialogue is enigmatic. Time seems to take place in the mind of a young child, identified with the author.

Lorca's four best-known plays were written within a few years during the 1930s—*Bodas de sangre* [Blood wedding], *Yerma*, and *La casa de Bernarda Alba* [The House of Bernarda Alba] are known as the rural trilogy. The highly successful *Doña Rosita la soltera o El lenguaje de las flores* [Rosie the Spinster or The Language of Flowers] (1935), shares numerous similarities with the trilogy. The spectacular public reception of *Bodas de Sangre* established Lorca's reputation as a playwright. His inspiration for this play came from an event that occurred in the town of Níjar, in the Andalusian province of Almería, where a bride runs away with a former sweetheart after taking her wedding vows. Lorca transforms this real-life situation into a play of mythic proportions where two of life's major rituals, marriage and death, are brought together with tragic consequences. The inevitable forces of fate loom from the offset of the play. In a way reminiscent of *Romeo and Juliet*, the Mother of the groom fears about her only surviving son who is about to be united in matrimony with the daughter of a feuding family. They had caused the violent death of her husband and elderly son. Only one character, Leonardo Félix, has a proper name. The rest are known for the family relations they perform. The Bride, feeling passionately attracted to Leonardo, elopes with him. The groom's need to avenge his honor gives way to a persecution of cosmic proportions. Critics (most notably Higginbotham, among others) have pointed out that the real characters of the play are allegorial in nature. Death appears as a Beggarwoman, and the Moon is personified as a young woodsman. Together they create a chilling effect, and after a frantic persecussion, the inevitable death of Leonardo and the groom is carried out. *Yerma*, which Lorca subtitled "Poema trágico en tres actos y seis cuadros" [Tragic Poem in Three Acts and Six Scenes] has no plot, according to comments made by the playwright himself. It does have a theme that is carefully elaborated throughout the play. *Yerma* is about a barren woman. She gladly married the man that was chosen for her by her father because it meant the possibility of having a child. Allusions about Juan's possible impotency abound, as he spends the evenings away from home irrigating his crops. Yerma, close to the earth and aware of her fertile surroundings, and very much a part of a culture that destines women to be mothers, feels dry and unfulfilled as a woman because she has not experienced maternity. Her character hardens and becomes bitter. She has the opportunity to commit adultery and become impregnated by another man, but in the best Calderonian tradition, Yerma insists she has "honra" [social honor, reputation]. If she is going to have a child, it can only be by her husband. At the end of the play, in a ritualistic scene where the boundaries between Christianity and paganism blur, Juan confesses to Yerma that he will not give her a child. Yerma strangles him, losing the last hope of ever becoming a mother.

Part comedy and, in a sense, part tragedy, *Doña Rosita la soltera* is Lorca's second Granada play. It was an astounding success when it was first produced in Barcelona in 1935. Created as a "pieza de época" [period piece], it is divided into periods (or "gardens" in Lorca's language of the flowers): 1885, 1900, 1911, each one representing a moment in the life of the protagonist. Rosita is engaged to a man who later abandons her to go to America. Despite his promise of a marriage by proxy, the necessary papers never arrive, and Rosita finds out years later that her fiancé had been married to someone else all that time. The faithful bride-to-be loses her youth and with it every possibility of marrying. Lorca presents this fact poetically with the symbol of the beautiful but short-lived "rosa-mutabile" [mutable rose], which Rosita's uncle cuts from the greenhouse. In this play Lorca intends to dramatize the "cursilería española" [Spanish bad taste] and the plight of the old maid. For the former, Lorca resorts to comic characters who border on the grotesque, such as the spinster sisters, reminiscent of his early theater. But as an old maid, Rosita is above all a tragic figure. She has lost her youth behaving precisely in the way society expected her to do, and as a consequence she suffered a spiritual death. She is therefore closer to the tragic young women in Lorca's trilogy.

The manuscript of *La casa de Bernarda Alba* indicates that it was finished on Friday, June 19, 1936, just two months before the playwright's death. Like his other plays, this one is deeply rooted in Andalusian tradition. Near Lorca's hometown, in a village called Arquerosa, now Valderrubio, lived a strange family, Frasquita o Francisca Alba, with her daughters, and also a man that served as inspiration for Pepe el Romano. The plot is simple and straightforward. The curtain rises as three generations of women, María Josefa (Bernarda's mother), Bernarda, and her five unmarried daughters, ages twenty to thirty-nine, return from the burial of the man of the house. Bernarda insists on adhering to tradition, as she understands it, and the daughters must prepare themselves to spend eight years in mourning. Lorca subtitled this play "Drama de mujeres en los pueblos de España" [Drama of Women in Spanish Towns]. When Pepe el Romano, attracted by the eldest daughter's dowry, asks her in marriage, rivalry and discord prevail among the other four sisters. They all desire the only man available. Adela, the youngest, violating her mother's tight vigilance and society's mandate that a woman must remain pure until marriage, or lose her honor, establishes an illicit relationship with Pepe, which will lead to her suicide, when sister Martirio betrays her by informing their mother. More than the loss of a daughter, Bernarda is concerned with the damage her daughter's transgression of the honor code might have on her reputation. The neighbors must believe that her daughter has died a virgin.

Critics have often emphasized the visual nature of the *casa* [house] neatly framed in the stage with its thick jaillike walls and a few windows and doors leading to the outside world. However, this powerful visual image transcends the limits of the concrete. This *casa* is, above all, a sociocultural institution. Within the confines of its walls, in ritualistic fashion, Bernarda and her family repeat centuries-old traditions, like many generations of women that preceded them. This repetitive and collective act obliterates the uniqueness of the individual for the sake of preserving patriarchal hegemony. *La casa de Bernarda Alba* is not so much about what we see as about what we hear. Unlike most of Lorca's plays—and this is particularly the case with *Bodas de sangre* and *Yerma*—where there is extensive use of ballet, choreography, music, and poetry, *La casa de Bernarda Alba* relies almost exclusively on dialogue. Limited in terms of movement and space, its force is auditory, not visual. The playwright tells us that the three acts are intended to be a photographic document. In his time, photographs were in black and white, and these two colors are emphasized throughout the play: the black dresses of the women in mourning, in contrast to the very white walls of the house. Bernarda's authoritarian voice stands out as she commands, "!Silencio!" [silence!] at the opening and end of the play, closely related in each case to the death of one member of the family and the spiritual death of those living. Despite Bernarda's call for silence, other sounds succeed in penetrating the thick walls and contribute to define the nature of their society and the dichotomy between being a man and being a woman, between life inside and outside the house. The distant tolling of the bells reminds of the presence of the church, the mob that wants to lynch the unwed mother represents public morality, the songs of the harvesters point to the freedom men enjoy in the open fields, and the most persistent of them all, the horse—a symbol of virility—betrays the unseen presence of Pepe el Romano.

Bernarda's *casa* is a household without men. This is by fate as well as by design. Upon the death of her husband, she must assume the patriarchal role of guarding her daughters' honor and forbids the presence of men within the confines of the house, thus limiting the world her daughters are allowed to know. Her *casa* is clearly governed by patriarchal forces. Pepe el Romano, the male character we do not see but hear about, is the strongest motivating force in the play. Bernarda's authoritarian discourse adamantly reenacts what she learned from her father and her grandfather. In doing so, she adheres to an old Spanish obsession with their "casta" [the purity of her lineage, the quality of her race] that links Lorca to the literature of the Spanish Golden Age. This concept also associates property with social class, as Bernarda is well aware. When one of her daughters has the opportunity of marrying, she does not allow it because the groom's father was a "gañán" [a wage earner]. The situation within the walls of her house would have been quite different had Bernarda found enough men of her social condition to marry her daughters.

Lorca indicts society, and the spectator might be inclined to condemn Bernarda as well. Although she is not aware of it, Bernarda is a victim turned victimizer. In the same way that her daughter Adela is symbolically asphyxiated by her mother's oppression (as she commits suicide by hanging), Bernarda's maternal feelings have been suffocated by society. As a widow, she uses her newly found powers to perpetuate those values that benefit men. She becomes their accomplice. Her husband was a womanizer, and she claims that men should enjoy the freedom of the streets. Women should be confined in the house, against their natural instincts. Bernarda is, at best, an imperfect man, as exemplified in her failed attempt to use the gun—a phallic symbol. Within this play another mother figure, María Josefa, vehemently distances herself from Bernarda and approaches Adela. Her name is a combination of that of Jesus's parents (Mary and Joseph), and as such she leads the spectator to consider another way of parenting closer to early Christian values. She sings a lullaby while holding a "baby" (a lamb) in her arms, an act that Bernarda—devoid of maternal instincts—seems incapable of performing. Her association with Adela makes Bernarda's youngest daughter a lamb scarified to atone the sins of a society that oppresses the individual against their natural feelings. Bernarda as a mother figure becomes dehumanized and therefore closer to the puppet figures that we encountered in Lorca's early theater, almost to the point of having the dimensions of a grotesque caricature. At the beginning of the play the maid La Poncia, a modern Pontius Pilate, threatens Bernarda's public image with her gossip. At the end of the play, and despite Bernarda's call for silence, we know that the neighbors have awakened. The thicks walls have been rendered useless.

CRITICS' RESPONSE

By 1936 Federico García Lorca had become the best-known poet and dramatist of his generation, justly recognized both in Spain and abroad. He was only thirty-eight years old. One can only wonder what was yet to come and how he would have helped shape Spanish literature in the twentieth century. Perhaps it would have been comparable to what Luis Buñuel did for cinema, and Salvador Dalí and his fellow Andalusian Pablo Picasso did for the visual arts. The circumstances surrounding Lorca's execution at the hands of the Falangists and the fact that the Francoists would rule Spain until 1975 imposed, at least in the beginning, a rigid censorship on Lorca's works, his personal circumstances, and the staging of his plays. They also created obstacles for the scholars investigating his life and works. Despite these official efforts Lorca's appeal has increased steadly in the past sixty years, both in the academic community and with the public at large. His major plays have become classics on the stages in Spain and the Americas. A bibliographical search shows several thousands of items produced since his death. However, the quality of these studies is uneven, and there are still certain areas that merit further analysis by critics. Given the fact that in Lorca's theater most main characters—and a considerable number of secondary ones—are women and that female characters also abound in his poetry, the paucity of critical studies that deal with this subject stand out; and even more noticeable is the absence of studies that incorporate the latest theories on gender and class. These approaches would be invaluable and would shed new light on the work of this writer who has repeatedly been praised for unabashedly exalting the traditional elements of his rural Andalusia. Another area that is beginning to be addressed by biographers and critics is the question of Lorca's homosexuality.

Despite the voluminous nature of Lorca studies, an introduction to his works is made easy by some landmark works, by recent full-length annotated bibliographies, and by bibliographical resources included at the end of most studies listed in this bibliography. In addition, the most outstanding scholars within the last one or two decades have carefully incorporated previous seminal investigations, by continually gathering and synthesizing hard-to-find materials while at the same time opening new grounds. Francesca Colecchia's bibliographical editions *García Lorca: A Selectively Annotated Bibliography of Criticism* and *García Lorca: An Annotated Primary Bibliography* and the "Selectively Updated Bibliography" in *Lorca's Legacy* by Manuel Durán and Colecchia are an excellent starting point for the Lorca neophyte. Familiarity with an author's life, immediate surroundings, and particular historical circumstances is essential for an understanding of his or her works, and Lorca is no exception. Ian Gibson has spent several decades investigating Lorca's life. His works provide a wealth of details about the dramatist, his family, and formative years. Of particular interest is *The Death of Lorca*, originally published in 1971 in Spanish as *La represión nacionalista de Granada en 1936 y la muerte de Federico García Lorca* [The Nationalist Repression in Granada in 1936 and the Death of Federico García Lorca]. Gibson, quite appropriately, details the circumstances of Lorca's life in Granada and his death resulting from a national conflict between the Republic and the Falangists and the repression that followed. This study discusses and substantiates the sources of different rumors as to the motivations for Lorca's death, as it tries to establish the facts about his arrest and execution. Gibson includes numerous photographs that help bring to life the facts he discusses.

Lorca's homosexuality has been discussed openly by some critics. Some two decades earlier his distinguished biographer Marie Laffranque lamented the situation of the scholar interested in exploring the more unorthodox aspects of his life. The existence of moral and material obstacles led to the publication of selected aspects of Lorca's life and works, while others remained inaccessible to the public. Angel Sahuquillo's *Federico García Lorca y la cultura de la homosexualidad masculina. Lorca, Dalí, Cernuda, Gil-Albert, Prados y la voz silenciada del amor homosexual* [Federico García Lorca and the Culture of Masculine Homosexuality. Lorca, Dalí, Cernuda, Gil-Albert, Prados and the Silenced Voice of Homosexual Love] has tried to fill this gap. This is a thorough and well-researched book but difficult to read. It discusses in detail cultural issues and the subject of homosexuality in Lorca's criticism by tracing the subject throughout the poet's works and giving concrete examples. By placing homosexual repression within a patriarchal and classist context, the Lorca reader can easily relate the dramatist's personal situation to that of many of his characters, such as the gypsies, women, and blacks, in their marginalized and powerless condition, searching for freedom of expression. In addition, this book also sheds light on similar circumstances faced by other members of Lorca's group of intellectuals.

Many of Lorca's contemporaries (Dámaso Alonso, Vicente Aleixandre, Jorge Guillén, Pedro Salinas, among others), along with some of his relatives, have written about his life and work. Their testimonies have contributed to a more personal knowledge of the author, although in some cases it is tinted by the admiration they felt for the playwright or by the desire to preserve a good family image. *In the Green Morning*, a translation of *Federico y su mundo* [Federico and His World] by Francisco García Lorca, the dramatist's younger brother, provides an insider's view of his brother's life and times, as he was growing up in the Granada area. Using his privileged position, he provides family details and personal anecdotes that shed light on the popular sources of his brother's inspiration as well as his creative process. The continuous efforts to recover the variety of Lorca's production led to the publication of *"Los putrefactos" de Dalí and Lorca. Historia y antología de un libro que no pudo ser* ["The Putrid Ones" by Dali and Lorca. History and Anthology of a Book That Could Not Be], by Rafael Santos Torroella. By discussing the "theme of putrefaction" as it relates to the intellectual movement of the 1927 group and the avant-garde visual artists, particularly Dalí, Santos Torroella contributes to the understanding of the Lorca-Dalí relationship at a time of changing aesthetic orientation in Europe. Over time, Lorca's copious production has been gathered by Aguilar in the *Obras completas*, a two-volume edition prepared by Arturo del Hoyo, including some of Lorca's drawings, as well as an extensive bibliography and chronological information—perhaps not the definitive Lorca collection, but the best available at the moment. The best studies to understand Lorca's works are those of a panoramic nature, given the fact that a small number of themes and motifs recur throughout his poetic and dramatic work to culminate in the 1930s in his mature theater. A number of full-length studies accomplish the quite well. *Sobre García Lorca*, by his fellow Andalusian Antonio Gallego Morell, presents an overview of Lorca's life and his growth as a poet and playwright. His letters and drawings provide a fuller understanding. Equally useful in Gil's *Federico García Lorca. El escritor y la crítica*. The editor gathers a number of landmark articles about Lorca's poetry and the theater that are quite representative of the best about the playwright. The selections from reviews in the local press included in the appendix give the reader an invaluable insight that would otherwise be hard to obtain. One of the most complete and current studies on the dramatist is *García Lorca en el Teatro: La Norma y la Diferencia*. Fernández Cifuentes carefully considers the aesthetic currents that influenced Lorca and provides a detailed study of his major dramas. This work, along with the specific studies by Doménech and Klein, should be essential readings.

Lorca's legacy is very much alive. The cinematic representation of *Bodas de sangre* and two versions of *La casa de Bernarda Alba*, one Spanish and one British, have made his works more accessible to the public. The interest in his life and works continues to grow. The film biography *A Murder in Granada* focuses on his works and on interviews of family members and friends. *El balcón abierto* [The Open Balcony] explores Lorca's influence in today's Spain. In 1995 the "Huerta de San Vincente," the family home in Granada, was designated as a museum—a last hommage to the poet in his native Andalusia.

BIBLIOGRAPHY

Work

Obras completas. Madrid: Aguilar, 1991 (Volumes I, II, III).

Major Dramas

El maleficio de la mariposa [The Butterfly's Evil Spell], 1920.
La niña que riega albahaca y el principe preguntón [The Girl Who Waters the Basil and the Inquisitive Prince], 1923.
Los títeres de cachiporra: Tragicomedia de don Cristóbal y la señá Rosita [The Billy Club Puppets: Tragicomedy of Christopher and Rosie], 1928.
Teatro breve [Short Plays], 1928.
Así que pasen cinco años [Once Five Years Pass], 1930.
El público [The Public], 1930.

Amor de don Perlimplín con Belisa en su jardín [The Love of Don Perlimplín with Belisa in his Garden], 1933.
Bodas de sangre [Blood Wedding], 1933.
Mariana Pineda [Mariana Pineda], 1933.
La zapatera prodigiosa: Farsa violenta [The Shoemaker's Prodigious Wife: Violent Farce], 1933.
Yerma [Yerma], 1934.
Doña Rosita la soltera o El lenguage de las flores [Rosie the Spinster or The Language of Flowers], 1935.
La casa de Bernarda Alba [The House of Bernarda Alba], 1936.

Translations

Bauer, Carlos, trans. *The Public and Play without a Title: Two Posthumous Plays.* New York: New Directions, 1983.
Dewell, Michael, and Carmen Zapata. *The Rural Trilogy: Blood Wedding, Yerma, The House of Bernarda Alba.* New York: Bantam, 1987.
Edwards, Gwynne, and Peter Luke. *Three Plays.* Metuchen, NJ: Scarecrow Press, 1987.
Logan, William B., and Angel G. Orrios. *Once Five Years Pass, and Other Dramatic Works.* Barrytown, NY: Station Hill Press, 1989.
Macpherson, Ian, and Jacqueline Minett. *Yerma: A Tragic Poem* (bilingual edition). Warminster, UK: Aris & Phillips, 1987.
O'Connell, Richard L., and James Graham-Luján. *Five Plays: Comedies and Tragicomedies.* New York: Penguin, 1987.

Critical Studies

Anderson, Reed. *Federico García Lorca.* London: Macmillan, 1984.
Colecchia, Francesca, ed. *García Lorca: An Annotated Primary Bibliography.* New York: Garland, 1982.
———. *García Lorca: A Selectively Annotated Bibliography of Criticism.* New York: Garland, 1979.
Doménech, Ricardo, ed. *"La Casa de Bernarda Alba" y el teatro de García Lorca.* Madrid: Ediciones Cátedra, 1985.
Durán, Manuel, and Francesca Colecchia, eds. *Lorca's Legacy. Essays on Lorca's Life, Poetry, and Theatre.* New York: Peter Lang, 1991.
Edwards, Gwynne. *Lorca. The Theatre Beneath the Sands.* Boston: Boyars, 1980.
Feal, Carlos. *Lorca: Tragedia y mito.* Ottawa: Dovehouse Editions, 1989.
Fernández Cifuentes, Luis. *García Lorca en el teatro: La norma y la diferencia.* Zaragoza: Universidad de Zaragoza, 1986.
Frazier, Brenda. *La mujer en el teatro de Federico García Lorca.* Madrid: Playor, 1973.
Gallego Morell, Antonio. *Sobre García Lorca.* Granada: Universidad de Granada, Spain. 1993.
García Lorca, Francisco. *In the Green Morning: Memories of Federico.* Trans. Christopher Maurer. New York: New Directions Publishing Corporation, 1986.
Gibson, Ian. *The Death of Lorca.* Chicago: J. Philip O'Hara, 1973.
———. *Federico García Lorca: 1. De Fuente Vaqueros a Nueva York (1898–1929).* Barcelona: Grijalbo, 1985.

————. *Federico García Lorca: 2. De Nueva York a Fuente Grande*. Barcelona: Ediciones Grijalbo, 1987.

————. *García Lorca*. Barcelona: Editorial Atlántida, 1992.

Gil, Ildefonso-Manuel, ed. *Federico García Lorca. El escritor y la crítica*. Madrid: Taurus, 1989.

Higginbotham, Virginia. *The Comic Spirit of Federico García Lorca*. Austin: University of Texas Press, 1976.

Klein, Dennis A. *Blood Wedding, Yerma, and The House of Bernarda Alba. García Lorca's Tragic Trilogy*. Boston: Twayne Publishers, 1991.

Martín, Eutimio. *Federico García Lorca, heterodoxo y mártir. Análisis y proyección de la obra juvenil inédita*. Madrid: Siglo XIX, 1986.

Martín Recuerda, José. *Análisis de doña Rosita la soltera, o el lenguaje de las flores. [de Federico García Lorca] tragedia sin sangre*. Salamanca: University of Salamanca, 1979.

Martínez Nadal, Rafael. *Cuatro lecciones sobre Federico García Lorca*. Madrid: Cátedra, 1980.

Morris, C. Brian, ed. *"Cuando yo me muera . . ." Essays in Memory of Federico García Lorca*. Lanham, MD: University Press of America, 1988.

Rodrigo, Antonina. *Lorca-Dalí: Una amistad traicionada*. Barcelona: Planeta, 1981.

Sahuquillo, Angel. *Federico García Lorca y la cultura de la homosexualidad masculina. Lorca, Dalí, Cernuda, Gil-Albert, Prados y la voz silenciada del amor homosexual*. Alicante: Instituto de Cultural "Juan Gil-Albert," 1991.

Sánchez Vidal, Agustín. *Buñuel, Lorca, Dalí: El enigma sin fin*. Barcelona: Planeta, 1988.

Soria Olmedo, Andrés, ed. *Lecciones sobre F.G.L.* Granada: Comisión Nacional del Cincuentenario, 1986.

Vitale, Rosanna. *El metateatro en la obra de Federico García Lorca*. Madrid: Editorial Pliegos, 1991.

AGUSTÍN GÓMEZ-ARCOS
(1933–1998)

Sharon G. Feldman

BIOGRAPHY

Agustín Gómez-Arcos, a bilingual dramatist and novelist, was born in 1933 in the village of Enix (Almería). The origins of his theater can be traced to his childhood experiences, in which he witnessed firsthand the horrors of the Spanish Civil War and the dark clouds of oppression of the Franciost regime, images that left indelible imprints on his literature and his life.[1] Although in the future he would leave behind both native country and language, his memories of the Civil War and postwar period would continue to surface in his plays.

The evolution of Gómez-Arcos's career as a writer entails four stages that are delineated by several shifts in residence, literary genre, and language. His artistic trajectory began during the 1950s when, as a law student in Barcelona, his fascination with drama grew with his involvement in various university theater productions. Eventually, he completely abandoned his legal studies in order to pursue a life in the theater in Madrid. His public debut as a dramatist took place in 1960 with the premier of *Elecciones generales*, a "farsa político-disparatada" based on Nikolai Gogol's *Dead Souls*, which won a prize at the Primer Festival Nacional de Teatro Joven. During the 1960s he wrote a total of fifteen plays (listed here in order of composition): *Doña Frivolidad; Unos muertos perdidos; Verano; Historia privada de un pequeño pueblo; Elecciones generales; Fedra en el Sur; El tribunal; El rapto de las siamesas* (in collaboration with Enrique Ortenbach and Adolfo Waitzman); *Balada matrimonial; El salón; Prometeo Jiménez, revolucionario; Diálogos de la herejía* (staged 1964); *Los gatos* (staged 1965, 1992–1993); *Mil y un mesías;* and *Queridos míos, es preciso contaros ciertas cosas* (staged 1994–1995). He also adapted and translated into Spanish Jean Giraudoux's *La loca de Chaillot* (staged 1962, 1989) and *Intermezzo* (staged 1963), René-Jean Clot's *La revelación* (staged 1962), and Thorbjorn Egner's *La villa de los ladrones* (staged 1963).

In 1962, he won the Premio Nacional Lope de Vega for his historical drama *Diálogos de la herejía*, but the prize was swept from his hands in a wave of controversy, annulled in a blatant gesture of censorship that signified the Franco regime's official response to his unorthodox choice of thematic material. It was not until 1964 that Gómez-Arcos finally saw a censored version of his play premier to conflicting reviews at Madrid's Teatro Reina Victoria. Also that year, the censored text appeared in *Primer Acto* with a series of articles addressing the play's audacious subject matter and its polemical production/reception (see bibliography). The controversy surrounding *Diálogos de la herejía* would serve as a prelude to a series of combative encounters with Francoist censorship that eventually prompted Gómez-Arcos's voluntary exile from Spain in 1966. That year, upon receiving his second Lope de Vega for *Queridos míos, es preciso contaros ciertas cosas*, he used the prize money to buy a ticket to London, and two years later, he moved to France.

The second stage of his career began amid the Parisian *café-théâtres*, where he was employed as a playwright, director, actor, and sometimes even a waiter. His Parisian debut took place in February 1969 at the Latin Quarter's Café-Théâtre de l'Odéon where French spectators witnessed the dual premiere of *Et si on aboyait? (Adorado Alberto)* and *Pré-papa (Pre-papá)*. Together, these one-act absurdist pieces share an inseparable history and exemplify his creative output during this period. Both were originally conceived in Spanish and subsequently translated into French by his friend and fellow actress Rachel Salik (who also played the role of Mademoiselle Adèle in *Pré-papa*). They were then staged in French under Gómez-Arcos's direction at the Odéon, where their extremely successful run of seventy-one performances led to the subsequent publication of Pré-papa in the bimonthly *L'Avant Scène Théâtre*. The events surrounding this Parisian debut constitute a significant moment in Gómez-Arcos's artistic evolution, for it was on this occasion that he began to comprehend fully the creative implications of his exile and his freedom from censorship. During this period, he also wrote *Sentencia dictada contra P y J, Dîner avec Mr & Mrs Q* (staged at the Café-Théâtre Campagne in 1972), and *Interview de Mrs. Muerta Smith por sus fantasmas*. In November 1972, he accepted an invitation to present *Et si on aboyait?* and *Pré-papa* at the Université de Paris-Sorbonne on the occasion of the Jornadas Internacionales Universitarias sobre el Teatro Español Contemporáneo (chronicled by Moisés Pérez Coterillo, Vicente Romero, and Ricard Salvat in the January 1973 issue of *Primer Acto*). There, he participated in a round-table discussion of the "new Spanish theater" along with playwrights Fernando Arrabal, Josep Maria Benet i Jornet, and Francisco Nieva. Both *Et si on aboyait?* and *Pré-papa* were met with enthusiastic applause, and following the *mise en scène* at the Sorbonne, the plays enjoyed still another successful run at the Café-Théâtre de l'Odéon in 1973.

The third stage in Gómez-Arcos's literary trajectory began one evening at the Odéon in 1973. An editor from Éditions Stock, captivated by what he had witnessed on stage, asked his unsuspecting waiter if the playwright was in the house. The waiter responded, "C'est moi!" And the result of this fortuitous encounter was Gómez-Arcos's first novel in French *L'agneau carnivore*, which won Prix Hermès in 1975 (ironically, the same year as Franco's death). Since that time, Gómez-Arcos's publication of fifteen novels, written in French and translated into several languages, has earned him international acclaim. His narrative voice in French, his language of exile, expresses a cry of defiance, freedom, and openness.

The fourth and current stage of Gómez-Arcos's career can be described as a "tale of two cities," in which he divided his time between Paris and Madrid. During the 1990s, his theater underwent a renaissance on the stages of his native Spain, where seemingly overnight he has succeeded in reestablishing his prestige as a dramatist. In February 1991, the premier of *Interview de Mrs. Muerta Smith por sus fantasmas* at Madrid's Sala Olimpia (Centro Nacional de Nuevas Tendencias Escenicas) marked his triumphant return to the Spanish stage after an absence that had endured nearly twenty-six years. *Los gatos* opened at the Teatro María Guerrero (Centro Dramático Nacional) in November 1992 and was promptly selected for a national tour of Spain. Then, in December 1994, the long-overdue premier of *Queridos míos, es preciso contaros ciertas cosas* took place at the María Guerrero, twenty-eight years after it originally received the Lope de Vega prize. All three productions were directed by Carme Portaceli, and all received subventions from Spain's Ministry of Culture. It appears that Gómez-Arcos's life finally came full circle in that the Spanish government that once denigrated his work, with the advent of democracy, began to promote it. He died in 1998 in his beloved Paris.

DRAMATURGY: MAJOR WORKS AND THEMES

For Gómez-Arcos, the stage is a battleground where allegorical wars are waged, always in the name of freedom. His theater is "committed" in the sense that it is never oblivious to history and sociohistorical circumstance; yet at the same time, it resists identification with any particular political or ideological designation. Echoing the "realist" perspective of theatrical predecessors such as Alfonso Sastre and Antonio Buero Vallejo, Gómez-Arcos affirms that "el artista debe estar al servicio de la sociedad, y además, en la manera más difícil del mundo, es decir, como Casandra, haciéndole ver las cosas que no quiere ver" [the artist should be at the service of society, and moreover, in the most difficult way in the world, that is, like Cassandra, making people see what they don't want do see] (Interview with Montero 7–8). His plays employ an allegorical language of the stage as a tropological weapon in the irreverent violation of taboos and systems of oppression. The allegorical nature of his theater is a crucial thread that links his work to that of other censored playwrights of his postwar generation. However, throughout his career as both dramatist and novelist—and during the past three decades of living (and writing) in exile, far from Spain and what was Spanish fascism—he has, curiously, continued to develop and refine his allegorical strategies. The metaphoric inversions, hyperbolic depictions, and dark humor of his allegorical domains are tendencies that situate his theater within the European and Spanish traditions of the absurd, the car-nivalesque, the *esperpento*, the grotesque, the surreal, and even the postmod-ern—epitomized in twentieth-century Spain by the work of artists, such as Ramón del Valle-Inclán, Salvador Dalí, Luis Buñuel, Fernando Arrabal, and Pedro Almodóvar.

In *Diálogos de la herejía*, history is allegorized as an endless quest for free-dom of expression. Set amid the sacrificial flames of the Spanish Inquisition, this historical drama portrays the turmoil and hysteria that rock a sixteenth-century Extremaduran village when its inhabitants are entranced by a bizarre outbreak of *alumbrismo*, embodied in the characterizations of a lustful religious pilgrim and two sensuous nuns. In a grotesque parody of the Immaculate Con-ception, the pilgrim (*el Peregrino*) seduces a wealthy noblewoman (Doña Tris-teza de Arcos) and convinces her that she is pregnant with the son of God. At the end of the play, the *alumbrados* are burned at the stake for engaging in "heretical dialogues," a gesture that establishes a clear correspondence between censorship and the sacrificial flames of the Inquisition.

With *Los gatos*, Gómez-Arcos continues the exploration of sacrifice, oppres-sion, eroticism, and religious fanaticism that he initiated in *Diálogos de la herejía*; however, this time, he casts these themes within a modern, bourgeois setting. *Los gatos* depicts the story of two virgin sisters in their fifties, aptly and ironically known as Pura and Angela, whose beliefs have become so twisted and misconstrued that they have lost all sense of differentiation between right and wrong. When they learn of the pregnancy of their young unmarried niece (Inés), their obsession with her sexual promiscuity compels them to commit a perverse act of murder. They bludgeon Inés to death and throw her body to their hungry cats. Hence their blind adherence to sociocultural taboos converts them into transgressors in a grotesque portrait of religious and sexual repression.

Pré-papa, a short absurdist piece containing interesting reversals of gender, is situated in the doctor's office of a science-fictive world in which the young couple John and Mary (the biblical reference is obvious) await a diagnosis for John's mysterious malady. As the audience listens to the dialogue between John and Mary, they are simultaneously subjected to the sanctimonious judgments of Mademoiselle Adèle, a devout Catholic who prays to God over the telephone, as well as the scientific-philosophical discourse of an iconoclastic female Pro-fessor. The Professor (with the help of a male nurse) informs John that he is pregnant, and his wife consequently abandons him. The Professor then proposes that John exile himself to the realm of outer space in order to express himself freely and perpetuate a new race. His baby will be born in a completely unstruc-tured universe, free of censorship, intolerance, and restrictions.

The setting for *Interview de Mrs. Muerta Smith* is an even more elaborate—though less optimistic—futuristic universe of surreal invention, *guignolesque* caricature, and dark humor. In this dream world of phantoms and nonsensical language, Mrs. Muerta Smith, a resuscitated cadaver (and ex-American diplo-mat), disillusioned with how things have turned out on earth, traverses the barriers of space and time as part of her quest for an interview with God. Her ultimate desire is to colonize the heavens and impose her authoritative (North American) system upon the celestial world. She is accompanied by two faithful companions: Boby, her talking dog, and "Doble Nick, blanco y negro," her gigolo. On her voyage, she discovers that both the celestial world and the underworld have been sold as material commodities to left-wing governments, and in the end, she has no other choice but to return to earth empty-handed.

Queridos míos, es preciso contaros ciertas cosas enjoyed an eleven-week run at Madrid's Teatro María Guerrero during the 1994–1995 theater season. It is, perhaps, the play that best exemplifies Gómez-Arcos's continued interest in the themes of censorship and exile. In this work, the scenic space functions as a metaphoric representation of the notion of eternal return, whereby certain universal characteristics appear forever engraved in the souls of all human beings and in the framework of their societies. In his stage directions, Gómez-Arcos calls for the construction of an allegorical theatrical realm whose concrete spatiotemporal dimensions seem infinitely and instantaneously alterable: "El escenario, es un ámbito especial que puede ser o convertirse en todo: palacio, cárcel, plaza pública, calle, campo, o cualquiera de las cinco partes del mundo, o cualquier nación, o cualquier ciudad, o cualquier casa" (17). As the play progresses, the scenic space seamlessly transforms itself into several historical contexts, transgressing the limits of linear and rational chronology: that is, a seventeenth-century Spanish colony, the nineteenth century, the Middle Ages, 1966, Nazi Germany, and so on. The characters appear indifferent to these successive transfigurations. They emerge and reemerge, scene after scene, within the different periods and places as reincarnations (and *pre*incarnations) of their former selves. The transformative setting, as a result, signifies an ambiguous "everywhere": the combination of past, present, and future. It evokes a sensation of timelessness, of a never-ending "process" and a "closed cycle" (to translate the playwright's words) in which history seems forever condemned to repeat itself (18).

The first scene is situated on the public plaza of a seventeenth-century Spanish colony where the supreme figures of sociocultural authority emerge as a collection of absurd incarnations. They include an Ubuësque Governor, the Governor's Wife, a Captain, and a pompous Duchess. The play commences with the arrival of a sideshow tumbrel that immediately infuses the stage with an air of the carnivalesque. The tumbrel is accompanied by a raucous barker (*el Feriante*) and Cassandra, his main attraction. They are clad in a slovenly sort of garb that clashes with the more aristocratic, ostentatious attire of the Governor and his counterparts.

In his opening speech, the Barker, addressing the audience as well as the characters on stage, urges passersby to witness the forecasts and divinations of Casandra, a psychic visionary who knows all and who always speaks the truth: "(*A gritos*) ¡Señoras y señores, piadosos, pecadores, hijos de España y de las Indias de España, en una palabra, cristianos, ha llegado el carro de Casandra, la adivina, lectora de manos y de naipes, lectora del corazón, visionaria de la fortuna y del destino, de la tempestad y la plaga, del oro y la calderilla" [(Shouting) Ladies and gentlemen, saints and sinners, sons of Spain and the Spanish Indies, Christians, in a word, here you have Cassandra's cart. Cassandra, the sibyl, reader of hands and cards, reader of the heart, teller of fortunes and foreteller of fate, of tempest and plague, of gold and coppers]. (19). Imbedded in the Barker's discourse is a warning to the spectator to proceed with caution when venturing into this mythical realm: "Lo difícil es reconocer a la injusticia, saber cuáles son sus diversos camuflajes, bajo qué disfraces de orden o desorden, de paz o revolución se esconde. Por eso, queridos míos, es preciso contaros ciertas cosas" [The difficult thing is to recognize injustice, to know what its various camouflages are, under what masks of order and disorder, peace or revolution, it disguises itself. That is why, my dear friends, it's time we get certain things straight] (420). Within this theatrical space, several versions of the truth will be placed on display for all to behold. Injustice, for example, may assume several disguises. The task put forth for the spectator, therefore, is that of a quest for the truth that lurks behind an infinite assortment of masks and veils.

Through the art of divination, as the Barker infers, Casandra will play a revelatory role in this scheme, disclosing "certain things" that lie beneath the exterior facade of the Governor's realm. However, it is unclear whether the sacred words of this unkempt-looking sorceress will serve as remedies or poisons. Her name, derived from classical mythology, is an allegorical allusion to prophesy and revelation, but here the allusion is also an ominous and ambiguous one: the Cassandra of ancient myth, having resisted Apollo's love, witnessed as punishment a systematic rejection of her truths when he extinguished her prophetic abilities.

Casandra and the Barker are bearers of new, foreign ideas and "poisons" (communism, for instance), and their arrival threatens to open windows of change into the minds and souls of the people of the Governor's realm. The Duchess describes Casandra as "Una especie de quiromante, o bruja, or estudiante, or judía, o negra prosélita de la palabra 'no' vestida de greñas, peinada de harapos . . . que anda por los caminos del reino, por las calles de la ciudad, por las cafeterías, por los nightclubs, por los hipódromos y los campos de fútbol llamándolo al pan vino y al vino pan" [A sort of palmist, or witch, or student, or Jewess, or Negress, or devotee of contradiction . . . who travels the paths of the kingdom, roams the city streets, wanders through cafes, night clubs, racetracks, football fields, calling black white and white black] (47–48). Despite her nonsensical tone, her commentary subtly reverberates with the familiar sounds of fascism, the Inquisition, Nazism, and other oppressive orders. In effect, Casandra is the simultaneous embodiment of all marginalized, exiled, and disenfranchised "Others" whose voices have questioned and challenged the dominant hierarchy at one time or another. Like a censored writer, condemned for her artistic creations, her words are regarded as her most volatile weapon.

Casandra looks into the Duchess's eyes and foresees a future of sin, death, and misery, but this is not the sort of truth that the Duchess was hoping to hear. The Governor decides that Casandra must be silenced in order to suppress the power of her contaminated words. He calls for her arrest, and she is promptly quarantined within the silent walls of his prison. Eventually, the Governor offers to grant her freedom in exchange for her silence. But when Casandra rejects his proposal of censorship, exile is offered as a final solution.

If Casandra is the truth, then the hatred and censorship that challenge her words and thoughts represent a rejection of the truth. The Governor's presumptuous decision to silence the voice of a prophetess implies a denial of her premonitory visions and therefore a complete rejection of the future as well as the historical past. In order to perpetuate his system, he recognizes the need to remove the past and future from her hands, so that he may fabricate his own "false" truths. He and his cohorts are hypocrites, more concerned with appearances and falsely contrived realities than with the veritable, underlying truth.

The Captain is granted permission to escort Casandra to the border region of the Governor's realm, to a narrow strip of land known as the "tierra de nadie." In this empty zone of nothingness, they are at last able to speak freely and openly, without fear of censorship. Casandra's truth-seeing eyes and truth-bearing words have penetrated ("contaminated," in the Governor's opinion) the Captain's mind and soul. He realizes that Casandra not only *speaks* the truth; she is the embodiment of truth. "Casandra," the Captain declares "es otra cosa. Es una verdad" [is something else. She is the truth] (144). Before bidding farewell to his prisoner, he candidly reveals the (com)passion and hope that she has inspired in him: "¡No mueras nunca! ¡Necesito que vivas! Todos los días que termine mi guerra, antes de acostarme, pensaré en ti. Pensaré: 'Ella vive. Yo también.' Déjame tener esa esperanza" [Don't ever die! I need for you to live! Every day, when my war ends, before I go to bed, I'll think about you. I shall think: "She is alive. I am, too." Permit me that hope.] (63–64). But for Casandra, the distinctions between life and death do not apply. She is an immortal being: timeless, ageless, and eternal.

In the final scene, the Governor, his Wife, and the Duchess—glasses of scotch in hand—lament the unexpected return of Casandra who, according to the Duchess, is now twice as mattedly dressed and raggedly combed (161). They can no longer tolerate Casandra's ceaseless cries. This time, in order to silence her, the Governor decides to have her tongue surgically extracted. The censorship of Casandra is performed as a surgical rite of purification. The Barker plays the role of surgeon, dressed in a white robe. The ruthless stoicism maintained by the Governor and his loyal subjects clashes with the piercing scream that Casandra unleashes as her final expression of truth. The Barker/Surgeon summarizes the results of his medical exploits: "(*Con tono profesional.*) Ha sido muy sencillo. Una incisión limpia. Los nervios perfectamente degollados. El foco de infección, en vulgo, la lengua duerme en la basura el sueño de los justos. Quiero decir el sueño de Luzbel. ¡Agua de rosas para lavarme la sangre de las manos!"

[(*Professional tone.*) It was very simple. A clean incision. The nerves perfectly severed. The center of infection; in vulgar terms, the tongue sleeps the sleep of the just in the garbage pail. The dream of Beelzebub, that is. Rose water to wash the blood off my hands!"] (168).

The spectator is left with the revelation that the truth has been tossed into the trash can. As the play concludes, the Barker assumes his original stance, as in the opening scene, shouting, "¡Señores y señoras, piadosos y pecadores, ciudadanos del mundo" ["Ladies and gentlemen, saints and sinners, citizens of the world"] (170). This time, he offers to sell Casandra's story in leaflet form. The story of Casandra thus seems forever governed by the singular presence of History, forever enslaved by the authority of the Governor's system, and condemned to repeat itself ad infinitum.

CRITICS' RESPONSE

On the occasion of the premier of *Diálogos de la herejía*, Elías Gómez Picazo wrote: "La crítica, sea de individuos o de sistema, no se ve por ninguna parte. . . . No basta con encadenar blasfemias para conseguir, por el desagradable impacto que produce en los oídos, que se considere valiente al autor e importante la obra. . . . Hubo, afortunadamente, bastantes protestas, lo que salva al buen gusto de nuestro público." [It's not enough to link together a series of blasphemies so that, through the disagreeable impact produced in one's ears, the author may be considered daring or the play may be considered important. . . . Fortunately, there was a substantial amount of protest, which salvaged the good taste of our audience.]

In his 1965 review of *Los gatos*, Enrique Llovet wrote: "La aventura de Gómez-Arcos merece repeto. *Los gatos* es obra de un escritor. Nadie ha sostenido que la misión de la literatura sea, en nuestro tiempo, una misión azucarante." [The adventure that Gómez-Arcos has offered us deserves respect. *Los Gatos* is the work of a real writer. Nobody has ever claimed that the mission of literature, in our time, should be a sugar-coated one.] Following the 1992 premier of the same play, Javier Villán wrote: "Gómez Arcos aprovecha como elemento dramático el brutal contraste de un marco intolerante y atroz y el júbilo de la juventud y la vida que lo invade. La dirección de Portaceli lo subraya con tacto." [Gomez-Arcos takes full advantage of the dramatic possibilities derived from the brutal contrast between an intolerant, horrific context and the joyful youth that invades it. Portaceli's taging tactfully underlines this situation.]

Referring to the 1991 production of *Interview de Mrs. Muerta Smith por sus fantasmas*, Enrique Centeno wrote: "*Interview* es un texto todavía sorprendente. . . . Exceptional equipo para un montaje ha dirigido magníficamente Carme Portaceli en una escenografía espléndida—decrepitud, holocausto, ironía—donde Julieta Serrano muestra su inacabable talento junto a un espléndido Manuel de Blas. A todos ellos, y a lo que el estreno significaba, dedicó el púbico muchos aplausos la noche del estreno." [*Interview* is still a surprising text . . . An exceptional team for a production that Carme Portaceli has magnificently directed with a splendid set design—decrepitude, holocaust, irony—where Julieta Serrano displays her endless talent along with a splendid Manuel de Blas. To all of them, and to what the premier signified, the audience devoted much applause the night of the premiere.]

Following the premier of *Queridos míos, es preciso contaros ciertas cosas* in 1994, Javier Villán wrote: "*Queridos míos* . . . mantiene su desafío agitador y ni siquiera para un público anestesiado por una historia fatal resulta cómoda." [*Queridos mios* . . . maintains its rousing defiance and not even for an audience anesthetized by its own dreadful history does it result comfortably.]

AWARDS AND DISTINCTIONS

During the 1960s, Gómez-Arcos won the following Spanish prizes: Premio Primer Festival Nacional de Teatro Nuevo (1960) for *Elecciones generales*, Premio Nacional Lope de Vega (1962) for *Diálogos de la herejía* (subsequently annulled), and Premio Nacional Lope de Vega (1966) for *Queridos míos, es preciso contaros ciertas cosas.*

In addition, he has been consistently recognized by French literary circles with awards for his writing (Prix Hermès, Prix de Livre Inter, Prix Roland Dorgelès, Prix Thyde-Monnier de la Société de Gens de Lettres, Prix Européen de l'Association des Écrivains de Langue Française, Prix du Levant, and Prix Littéraire du *Quotidien du Médecin*). Gómez-Arcos has been twice a finalist for the Prix Goncourt—for *Scène de chasse (furtive)* (1978) and *Un oiseau brûlé vif* (1984)—and in 1985, he became, at the time, one of only four Spaniards (along with Picasso, Bergamín, and Alberti) ever to be decorated by the French Legion of Honor as "Chévalier de l'Ordre des Arts ès Lettres."

NOTE

1. I wish to express my appreciation to Mr. Agustín Gómez-Arcos for sharing with me the biographical data included in this entry. Most publications by and about Gómez-Arcos erroneously list his birthdate as 1939.

BIBLIOGRAPHY

Editions and Translations

Plays

Diálogos de la herejía. Written: 1962. Published (censored) version: *Primer Acto* 54 (June 1964): 26–53. Unpublished new restructured version: Paris, 1980.
Los gatos. Written: 1963. Published: Madrid: Sociedad General de Autores de España, 1994.
Queridos míos, es preciso contaros ciertas cosas. Written: 1966. Published: Madrid: Centro Dramático Nacional, 1994.

Pre-papá. Written: 1968. Published in French as *Pré-papa.* Trans. Rachel Salik. *L'Avant-Scène Théâtre* 434 (1969): 37–44. Staged: 1969, 1972, and 1973 (Paris) as *Pré-papa.* (Later converted into the novel *Pré-papa ou Roman de fées.*)

Interview de Mrs. Muerta Smith por sus fantasmas. Written: 1972. Bilingual French/Spanish edition: *Interview de Mrs Morte Smith par ses fantômes/Interview de Mrs. Muerta Smith por sus fantasmas.* Trans. Rachel Salik. Arles: Actes-Sud, 1985. Spanish edition: Intro.

Moisés Pérez Coterillo and Lola Santa-Cruz. Teatro 15. Madrid: *El Público/*Centro de Documentación Teatral, 1991.

Novels

L'agneau carnivore. Paris: Stock, 1975. Seuil "Points Roman," 1985.

Maria Republica. Written: 1975. Paris: Seuil, 1983.

Ana non. Paris: Stock, 1977. Stock "Livre de poche," 1980.

Scène de chasse (furtive). Paris: Stock, 1978.

Pré-papa ou Roman de fées. Paris: Stock, 1979.

L'enfant miraculée. Paris: Fayard, 1981.

L'enfant pain. Paris: Seuil, 1983. Seuil "Points Roman," 1987.

Un oiseau brûlé vif. Paris: Seuil, 1984.

Bestiaire. Paris: Le Pré aux Clercs, 1986.

Un pájaro quemado vivo. Madrid: Debate, 1986. (Gómez-Arcos's Spanish translation/adaptation of *Un oiseau brûlé vif.*)

L'homme à genoux. Paris: Julliard, 1989.

L'aveuglon. Paris: Stock, 1990.

Marruecos. Madrid: Mondadori, 1991. (Gómez-Arcos's Spanish translation/adaptation of *L'aveuglon.*)

Mère Justice. Paris: Stock, 1992.

La femme d'emprunt. Paris: Stock, 1993.

L'ange de chair. Paris: Stock, 1995.

Essay

"Censorship, Exile, Bilingualism." In *Critical Fictions: The Politics of Imaginative Writing,* ed. Philomena Mariani. Seattle: Bay Press, 1991. 220–222.

English Translations of Novels

Ana No. Trans. John Becker. London: Secker and Warburg, 1986.

The Carnivorous Lamb. Trans William Rodarmor. Boston: Godine, 1984. New York: Plume, 1986.

A Bird Burned Alive. Trans. Anthony Cheal and Marie-Luce Papon. London: Chatto and Windus, 1988.

Critical Studies

Adorado Alberto (Et si un aboyait?)

Pérez-Coterillo, Moisés. "Teatro actual español en la Sorbona. Los espectáculos." *Primer Acto* 152 (enero 1973): 60–67.

Diálogos de la herejía

Doménech, Ricardo. "*Diálogos de la herejía* de Agustín Gómez-Arcos." *Primer Acto* 54 (junio 1964): 51–52.

Feldman, Sharon. "Agustín Gómez-Arcos's *Diálogos de la herejía* and the Deconstruction of History." *Gestos* 18 (noviembre 1994): 61–80.

Llovet, Enrique, Elías Gomez Pícazo, and Alfredo Marquerie. "Tres críticas de la prensa diaria a *Diálogos de la herejía.*" *Primer Acto* 54 (junio 1964): 24–25.

Monleón, José. "Los mitos embalsamados." *Primer Acto* 54 (junio 1964): 17–18.

Morera, José María. "Reflexiones de un director después de un estreno polémico: *Diálogos de la herejía.*" *Primer Acto* 54 (junio 1964): 23.

Los gatos

Feldman, Sharon. "*Los gatos*: Gómez-Arcos's Spectacle of Sacrifice." *Estreno: Cuadernos del teatro español contemporáneo* 23.1 (primavera 1995): 38–44.

Haro Tecglen, Eduardo. "Injusticia mal reparada." *El País*, 12 noviembre 1992: 34.

Llovet, Enrique. "Estreno de *Los gatos* en el Teatro Marquina." *ABC*, 27 septiembre 1965: 91.

Monleón, José. "*Los gatos* de Agustín Gómez-Arcos." *Primer Acto* 68 (octubre 1965): 53–54.

Villán, Javier. "Sombría historia." *El Mundo*, 12 noviembre 1992: 43.

Interview de Mrs. Muerta Smith por sus fantasmas

Centeno, Enrique. "Una justa recuperación." *Diario 16*, 25 febrero 1991.

Feldman, Sharon. "Sanctifying the Scatological and Debasing the Divine: Postmodernist Allegory and Gómez-Arcos's *Interview de Mrs. Muerta Smith por sus fantasmas.*" *España Contemporánea* 8.1 (1995): n.p.

Haro Tecglen, Eduardo. "La señora se pudre." *El País*, 25 febrero 1991: 31.

Pérez Coterillo, Moisés. "Breve interrupción de una ausencia." Introduction. *Interview de Mrs. Muerta Smith por sus fantasmas*. By Agustín Gómez-Arcos. Teatro 15. Madrid: El Público/Centro de Documentation Teatral, 1991. 9–12.

Santa-Cruz, Lola. "Agustín Gómez-Arcos." Introduction. *Interview de Mrs. Muerta Smith por sus fantasmas*. By Augustín Gómez-Arcos. Teatro 15. Madrid: El Público/Centro de Documentation Teatral, 1991. 13–15.

———. "La mortaja del Tío Sam." *El Público* 84 (mayo–junio 1991): 26–29.

Vizcaíno, Juan Antonio. "Gómez Arcos vuelve a la escena española tras más de 20 años de ausencia." *El País*, 25 febroro 1991: 31.

Pré-papa

Gérome, Raymond. *Pré-papa. L'Avant Scène Théâtre* 434 (1969): 37.

Pérez-Coterillo, Moisés. "Teatro actual español en la Sorbona. Los espectáculos." *Primer Acto* 152 (enero 1973): 64–66.

Queridos míos, es preciso contaros ciertas cosas

Centeno, Enrique. "Las cosas que nos prohibían." *Diario 16*, 9 diciembre 1994: 44.

Torres, Rosana. "Gómez Arcos recibe grandes honores de dramaturgo con 30 años de retraso." *El País*, 7 diciembre 1994: 36.

Villán, Javier. "Entre Franco, Sófocles y Felipe. *El Mundo*, 9 diciembre 1994: 80.

General

Aragonés, Juan Emilio. *Teatro español de posguerra.* Temas españoles 520. Madrid: Publicaciones españolas, 1971.

Feldman, Sharon. *Allegories of Dissent: The Theater of Agustín Gómez-Arcos.* Lewisburg, PA: Bucknell University Press, 1998.

Monleón, José. "Gómez-Arcos: La honesta herejía." *Primer Acto* 238 (marzo–abril 1991): 132–144.

Oliva, César. *El teatro desde 1936.* Historia de la Literatura Española Actual 3. Madrid: Alhambra, 1989.

Zatlin, Phyllis: *Cross-Cultural Approaches to Theatre: The Spanish-French Connection.* Metuchen, NJ: Scarecrow Press, 1994.

Interviews

with José Benito Fernández. "Voy a contaros ciertas cosas . . . : Entrevista con Agustín Gómez Arcos." *Quimera* 117 (1993): 49–55.

with Karl Kohut. *Escribir en París.* Barcelona: Hogar del Libro, 1983. 128–55.

with Rosa Montero. "Agustín Gómez Arcos: El creyente de la palabra." *El País* (Suplemento dominical): 4–10.

with Vicente Romero. "Entrevista con un autor casi olvidado: Agustín Gómez Arcos." *Primer Acto* 148 (septiembre 1972): III–IV.

with Lola Santa-Cruz. "Agustín Gómez-Arcos: El teatro es subversión." *El Público* 84 (mayo–junio 1991): 30–32.

JUAN EUGENIO HARTZENBUSCH
(1806–1880)

Linda S. Materna

BIOGRAPHY

The first son of Santiago Hartzenbusch, his German-born father, and María Josefa Martínez Calleja, Juan Eugenio Hartzenbusch y Martínez was born in Madrid on September 6, 1806. His principal contemporary biographers—Aureliano Fernández-Guerra y Orbe, Antonio Ferrer del Rio, and Eugenio de Ochoa y Ronna—trace his introverted, taciturn, humble, and industrious temperament to an impecunious and melancholy childhood. It was punctuated by the death of his mother in 1808 two weeks after giving birth to his brother, Santiago, and by the poverty to which political liberalism and ill health condemned his father, in whose furniture shop Juan Eugenio and his brother worked and grew up in relative isolation. Enrolled by his father in the Colegio de San Isidro el Real (1818–1822) to prepare for the priesthood, Juan Eugenio instead studied Latin and philosophy. Continuing as an apprentice in his father's shop, he studied French and Italian on his own, reading some plays, learning poetic meter from the treatise of Father Losada, and using his scant savings to buy books. The beginning of the "Ominosa Década" (Ominous Decade) and the return of absolutism brought financial disaster to the family with the confiscation of Santiago's assets. Despite his literary aspirations, Hartzenbusch increasingly was compelled to hire out as a furniture maker to support the family.

A passion for the theater undoubtedly was sparked in December 1824 when Hartzenbusch attended his first theatrical performance, a one-act opera; that same year he also saw Manuel Bretón de los Herreros's *A la vejez viruelas* [A Pox on Old Age]. Despite the hardships of poverty and the demands of manual labor, by 1823 Juan Eugenio had begun to read plays, translating several from French. The first work Hartzenbusch staged in a public theater was a *refundición* [recasting or "rewrite"] of Francisco de Rojas Zorrilla's *El amo criado* [The Master Servant], performed in the Príncipe theater in 1829 to a positive reception. Later that year his translations of two French plays were staged at the Cruz theater with moderate success: *El regreso inesperado* [The Unexpected Return] of Jean-

François Regnard and *El tutor* [The Tutor] of Florent Carton Dancourt. Given his immersion in classical Spanish and French theater, Hartzenbusch channeled his passion for Golden Age theater by writing two additional *refundiciones* in 1829: Pedro Calderón de la Barca's *Los empeños de un acaso* [Chance Undertakings] and Agustín Moreto's *La confusión de un jardin* [Confusion in the Garden]. The year 1830 was one of both personal happiness and tragedy: In April, he married María Morgue, an actress; in June, his father died after a long period of financial hardship and declining health.

The opportunity to stage these two latest *refundiciones* came when Hartzenbusch was invited to adapt the ridiculous but potentially lucrative eighteenth-century comedy *La restauración de Madrid* [The Restoration of Madrid], of Manuel Fermín de Laviano. Having accepted the proposition with the stipulation that the theater impresario would stage his own play, *El infante Don Fernando de Castilla*, Hartzenbusch took from the original only its plot, eliminating the Virgin of Atocha's resuscitation of the beheaded daughters of Gracián Ramírez and retitled it *Las hijas de Gracián Ramírez o la restauración de Madrid*. Unfortunately, the premiere (1831) was jeered, and the impresario who hired him blamed the failure on his unauthorized radical revision of the original text and refused to stage *El infante*. Present at the humiliating premier, Hartzenbusch made and subsequently kept a vow never to attend the openings of his plays. Wary of criticism, he continued to write in isolation, rarely benefiting from the opinions of critics and writers.

Wounded but undaunted, Hartzenbusch returned to translation. His first verse translation was written in 1833, rewritten in 1834, and published with the title of *Floresinda* in 1844. Loosely based on Voltaire's *Adélaide du Guesclin*, he adapted the original to Romantic tastes, disguising its origins to pass the censorship that banned Voltaire's works in Spain. Nevertheless, theater producers turned down even the rewritten version. Neither his translations of Vittorio Alfieri's *Mérope* (1833), his *refundición* of Voltaire's *Edipo* [Oedipus, lost], nor his original play *Medea* (lost) were staged. The Spanish stage, alive with the new Romantic aesthetic, had no place for the neoclassical inspiration of these plays, written by Hartzenbusch in the relative isolation of his workshop.

To improve his economic fortunes, Hartzenbusch enrolled in 1834 in the Madrid School of Stenography. In 1835, he became a temporary stenographer for the *Gaceta de Madrid* and later for *El Diario de las Cortes*, positions that afforded him more money and more time for writing. Since 1831, he had been composing a drama in prose on the legend of the lovers of Teruel and had been encouraged by Ramón de Mesonero Romanos. When Mariano José de Larra staged his *Macías* in 1834, however, Hartzenbusch was so shocked by its similarity to his script that he abandoned his efforts until 1836. Although he suffered the death of his wife that year, Hartzenbusch renewed his attempt to create a new dramatization of the legend. He improved upon the plays that Tirso de Molina and Juan Pérez de Montalbán had dedicated to the subject, adding verse and changing the plot and characterization.

His industry and persistence finally paid off. Like Antonio García Gutiérrez after the 1836 premiere of his play, *El trovador* [The Troubadour], Juan Eugenio Hartzenbusch stepped into the limelight of instant success when *Los amantes de Teruel* [The Lovers of Teruel] premiered in the Príncipe Theater on January 19, 1837. Larra himself helped consecrate the play's canonical status and Hartzenbusch's fame with his review in *El español*. Perhaps hoping to compensate for his merciless review of *Las hijas de Gracián Ramirez* several years before, Mesonero Romanos initiated that night the process to admit Hartzenbusch into the Ateneo Literario y Científico of Madrid [Literary and Scientitic Atheneum]. In 1838 the young writer repeated the success of *Los amantes de Teruel* with *Doña Mencía o la boda en la Inquisición* [Doña Mencía or The Wedding in the Inquisition]. That same year he married a widow, Salvadora Vercruysse, born Hiriarte, who brought five children to her marriage. He and Salvadora had one child, Eugenio Máximo, born in May of 1840. Now a celebrity, Hartzenbusch was sought for lectures and commissions. In 1844, he was named Chief Clerk of the Biblioteca Nacional [National Library], and in 1847, he was admitted to the Real Academia Española [Spanish Royal Academy]. In 1854 he was appointed Director of the Escuela Normal Central de Maestros [Central Normal School for Teachers], returning to the Biblioteca Nacional in 1857 as Chief Librarian. At the death of Agustín Durán in 1862, the Biblioteca Nacional named him its Director.

Hartzenbusch was one of the most prolific dramatists of his time. Until declining health ended his dramatic career in the early 1860s, he wrote twenty-nine original plays in many theatrical genres and was apparently working on a comic opera (Conliffe 559). Showing a constant preoccupation for the resuscitation of the Spanish stage and for the development of a vital national theater, Hartzenbusch composed at least twelve *refundiciones* of Golden Age theater. He wrote at least twenty-nine translations and imitations of foreign plays, most from the French. In the year immediately following *Los amantes de Teruel* and *Doña Mencía, La redoma encantada* [The Enchanted Flask] (1839), a *comedia de magia* [comedy of magic], was an extraordinary success. In 1841 another *comedia de magia, Los polvos de la Madre Celestina* [Mother Celestina's Powders], (pub. 1840), and his superb but underrated historical play *Alfonso el Casto* [Alfonso the Chaste] were box-office hits.

Besides his activity as a dramatist, Hartzenbusch worked simultaneously throughout his career in numerous literary and scholarly endeavors. In his indispensable *Bibliografía*, Eugenio enumerates the following works of his father: fifteen collections (which include various editions of his works), ninety-four plays, 236 poems, 231 verse fables, nineteen speeches, eight biographical articles, fifteen short stories, fourteen costumbristic articles, nine articles of literary criticism, three articles of theatrical criticism, thirty-three prologues, twenty-two articles on annotations of *Don quijote*, twenty-two diverse articles, and nine collected or annotated works of diverse articles. Among his fables, first published in 1848, there are both original pieces and translations and adaptations from German (especially works of G. E. Lessing), French, and several Golden Age Spanish writers. *Ensayos poéticos y artículos en prosa, literarios y de costumbre* [Poetic Essays and Prose, Literary and Costumbristic Articles] (1843) incorporates many of his articles and includes a "dramatic story," "Querer de miedo" [Love Out of Fear]. While his lyric poetry is unremarkable, a translation of Friedrich Schiller's "Das Lied von der Glocke" [The Song of the Bell], entitled "La campana" [The Bell] is of interest. His critical expertise is evident in his prologues to the works of José Zorrilla and Carolina Coronado and his editions of works of the Duque de Rivas and García Gutiérrez. In the prologue to the works of Bretón de los Herreros, Hartzenbusch credits him with the resurrection of Spanish theater to which he dedicated his own career. With daily access to the documents of the Biblioteca Nacional, he prepared important editions of the works of Calderón, Tirso, Felix Lope, deVega Carpio, and Juan Ruiz de Alarcón and the posthumous works of Leandro Fernández de Moratín. His love for the *Quijote* led to his publication of *Las 1.633 notas puestas por el Excmo. e Ilmo Señor D. Juan Eugenio Hartzenbusch a la primera edición de "El ingenioso hidalgo"* [The 1,633 Notes of the Most Excellent and Illustrious Gentleman, Don Juan Eugenio Hartzenbusch to the First Edition of "The Ingenius Hidalgo"] (1874). Much of his literary criticism and philological writings is still lost in magazines, newspapers, and other publications of difficult access. While Hartzenbusch was not always accurate nor meticulous in these endeavors, his critical editions are still of value, and he is considered a precursor of the modern literary researcher. As a member of a commission for the *Diccionario de la Real Academia Española* [Dictionary of the Royal Spanish Academy], he wrote many of the dictionary's definitions and the prologue to the *Gramática de la lengua castellana por la Real Academia Española* [Grammar of the Spanish Language by the Royal Spanish Academy]. Among Hartzenbusch's contributions to many newspapers and magazines are his drama reviews for the newspaper *El español* in 1846, 1847, and 1857.

A member of various professional associations, Hartzenbusch played a central role in the support and protection of his fellow playwrights and actors. He was a close friend of García Gutiérrez, Zorrilla, Cecilia Böhl de Faber, and other writers of the day. In 1839, he helped create the Liceo Artístico y Literario de Madrid [Literary and Artistic Liceum of Madrid], and in 1841 he founded the Academia Hispano-Alemana [Hispanic-German Academy] to foster better relations between Spain and Germany. An active supporter of the rights of authors and actors, he became a member of the Sociedad de Socorros Mutuos de Actores de España [The Association for the Mutual Assistance of Spanish Actors], the Junta Consultiva de Teatros [The Theater Advisory Board], and in 1874, the Consejo de Instrucción Pública [The Public School Board]. He received numerous distinctions, including the Cross of Isabel the Catholic, the supernumerary cross of Charles III, and a medal from the Emperor of Brazil (Conliffe 10–11).

Hartzenbusch began to complain of health problems in 1862. His creative writing declined, but despite failing eyesight, he continued his bibliographic and critical investigations. Salvadora's death in 1867 further debilitated him. He retired as Director of the Biblioteca Nacional in 1875, and illness subsequently prevented him from attending meetings of the Spanish Royal Academy. His extraordinary personal and professional status, however, led the other Academy members to declare him present at all meetings until his death on August 2, 1880. Considered one of nineteenth-century Spain's greatest men of letters by his contemporaries, and the most erudite writer among the Romantics, Hartzenbusch was a central figure in the literary and scholarly world of his times. Despite his status and success, he died in the poverty in which he had been raised. Throughout his life, he showed the humility, methodical industriousness, penchant for detail, gravity, and dedication to duty evident in his youth. Among Romantics, Hartzenbusch has been called a classic or an eclectic. While sharing the Romantic enthusiasm for Medieval and Golden Age Spain, he imbues them with a moral and philosophical focus and a concision and a discretion that separate him from the unbridled passions and rhetorical excesses of his contemporaries.[1] Literarily, Hartzenbusch's reputation today derives primarily from his first resounding success, *Los amantes de Teruel*, the definitive masterpiece in a long line of works dedicated to the legend.

DRAMATURGY: MAJOR WORKS AND THEMES

The dramaturgy of Juan Eugenio Hartzenbusch, incorporating original plays, *refundiciones*, and translations, received little comprehensive monographic attention in the twentieth century, reflecting his relegation into the ranks of Romantic writers of secondary status. Such is the opinion of influential critics such as Ángel Valbuena Prat who declares that *Los amantes de Teruel* was the best effort possible from a man "saturated" with libraries.[2] Francisco Ruiz Ramón notes that after 1850 Hartzenbusch's historical drama ceased to interest the public. For this critic, he occupies a position in the vast museum of Spanish theater, an evaluation reiterated by Donald L. Shaw, who extends his "just" oblivion to "most of his critical and editorial labours."[3] Carmen Iranzo criticizes negatively most of his plays except *Los amantes de Teruel*, focusing primarily on their inner contradictions. Ermanno Caldera and Antonietta Calderone classify Hartzenbusch with playwrights who, primarily dedicated to other cultural activities, are not therefore true professionals of the stage.[4] Only Ricardo Navas Ruiz and Grafton J. Conliffe have been generally positive in their judgments of his theater. His primary nineteenth-century critics—Fernández-Guerra, Ferrer del Río, Ochoa, Leopoldo Augusto de Cueto, Manuel Cañete and others—had praised it highly, but they were friends, and their commentary often is biased.

This lukewarm critical assessment of Hartzenbusch's creative talents has relegated almost all of his works to library shelves. Other than *Los amantes de Teruel*, his only drama published in the twentieth century are *La jura en Santa Gadea* [The Oath in Saint Gadea], edited with *Los amantes de Teruel* in 1964, and alone in 1971, and *La cojay elencogido* (The Lame Girl and the Bashful Man), published in a bilingual edition in 1902. His fables were edited by Navas Ruiz in 1973.

Original Dramaturgy

Hartzenbusch's original dramaturgy traditionally has been divided by critics into two periods. They are differentiated by greater stylistic simplicity and restraint after 1843, with more care in plot construction, the avoidance of extraneous incidents, less varied metrical forms, and an increasing use of verse over prose. Nevertheless, the works of both periods show the same general ideological focus, compositional strategies and preoccupations, themes, and motifs. Unlike the drama of his Spanish Romantic contemporaries, Hartzenbusch's theater is philosophical and moral, his goal being both to entertain and, especially, to instruct the public. His emphasis on the subordination of individual rights and self-interest to duty, as well as his respect for the monarchy reveal a conservatism contrary to the individualism and rebelliousness of liberal Romanticism. Nevertheless, Hartzenbusch did profess liberal ideas, condemning religious fanaticism and the Inquisition, royal absolutism, censorship, economic injustice, the corruption of the privileged, and the limitation of individual freedom, especially that of women. The compositional strategies of his theater also remain constant. Hartzenbusch reedited and recast many of his original plays, often to make additional income but also to perfect their narrative logic and language. Critics agree that this obsessive rewriting complicates the editing and chronological ordering of his works, frequently fails to improve them, and often wrests spontaneity from his verse.

The primary theme of his plays is a moral lesson: the necessary subordination of egotistical desires and self-interest to duty and virtue. The Romantic pursuits of psychological unification of the subject and social legitimacy through love function as the narrative through which this lesson is taught. The dramatic action results in tragedy or happiness for the protagonists, depending upon their ability to assert virtue and love over vice and egocentrism. Their tragedy is self-inflicted when vice derives from personal moral flaws such as pride, lust, anger, avarice, and jealousy. In several dramas, innocent protagonists fall prey to the immorality of others. Thus, in his most Romantic play, *Los amantes de Teruel*, Margarita's adultery and the lust, pride, and anger of Zulima and Azagra combine to set in motion the fatal mechanism of time and cause the lovers' deaths. Mirroring Catholic doctrine, Hartzenbusch's plays trace the Christian narrative of salvation through love or, in his tragedies, either the failure of love to conquer vice and fatality, or the necessity to sacrifice love for duty. This latter message is summed up in the famous lines from *La jura en Santa Gadea* [The Oath in Saint Gadea] (1845), "[B]etween duty and love, duty comes first."[5]

Many secondary themes and motifs expressive of this primary theme incorporate the forms of Romanticism, if not its more rebellious ideology. The Romantic preoccupation with subjectivity and the forging of an autonomous individual from the ruins of an *ancien régime* of noble and collective privilege, for example, find expression in the question of the protagonist's legitimacy. Thus, Hartzenbusch frequently creates protagonists who are orphaned and/or of unknown and mistaken identity, locating their "nobility" not in heredity but in moral virtue. The confusion created by uncertain identities provides much of the dramatic intrigue, especially in his philosophical-symbolic plays and comedies of character and manners. This strategy derives not only from Romanticism, but also from the motif of *engaño* [deception] through appearances that permeates the Golden Age drama that so influenced Hartzenbusch and other Spanish Romantics.

The motif of misreadings, as yet unexamined by critics, is the most intriguing strategy through which the relationship between identity and virtue or vice is communicated, although Navas Ruiz does mention the abundance of plots based on changes of personality, the hiding of origin, or errors of opinion (*Romanticismo* 211). This misreading of identity is located in spoken and particularly written texts: untranslatable texts (the riddle in *La redoma encantada*, and the letters identifying the legitimate heirs in *Doña Mencía, El bachiller Mendarias, o los tres huérfanos* [Learned Mendarias or the Three Orphans] and *Honoraria*), falsified texts (the report of Don Apolinar's death in *Derechos póstumos ad hoc* [Posthumous Rights after the Fact] and the message that Rufino transforms into a love letter in *La coja y el encogido*), and sabotaged texts (Margarita's love letters, which Azagra uses for blackmail in *Los amantes de Teruel*). The presence of letters also reflects both Hartzenbusch's fascination with language and his "deciphering" work as a translator and critic.

Other themes include a critique of economic injustice, royal absolutism, the Inquisition and religious fanaticism, and a support of the right of women to choose their spouse. Typically Romantic is Hartzenbusch's dramatization of Spain's medieval and Golden Age past, accomplished with an erudition absent in most other Romantic playwrights. The theme of love is dominant, and love often conflicts with duty and honor. Hartzenbusch frequently extols the very unromantic theme of conjugal love (*La archiduquesita* [The Little Archduchess], *Doña Juana Coello, El bachiller Mendarias, La redoma encantada*, and *Los polvos de la Madre Celestina*). His representation of the feminine merits attention since he often reveals sympathy for the plight of women, a sex exploited by men, unfairly vulnerable to moral condemnation for sexual transgressions, and limited in marital choice. Although the Romantic heroine is central to the hero's quest narrative in Romantic theater, Hartzenbusch is exceptional in Spanish Romantic and classical drama in his creation of many protagonist mothers (e.g., Margarita in *Los amantes de Teruel*, Pelayo's mother Doña Juana Coello and Doña Críspula in *La visionaria* [The Visionary]). In two plays—*Los amantes de Teruel* and *El bachiller Mendarias*—he depicts an adulterous woman whose sin serves the blackmail of an egotistical rival of the hero. The theme of incest, unusual in Spanish literature and present in *Alfonso el Casto, Doña Men-*

cía, and *Honoraria* (Navas Ruiz, *Amantes* 10), the asexual cohabitation of Honoraria and Jimén in the last-mentioned play, and the suicides in *Doña Mencía* and *Primero yo y siempre yo* [I Always Come First] (1842) undoubtedly are inspired in French Romantic theater and Rivas's *Don Alvaro o la fuerza del sino* [Don Alvaro or the Force of Destiny].

Hartzenbusch's twenty-nine original plays are best analyzed chronologically by genre: historical drama, philosophical-symbolic drama, biblical drama (one play), comedy of character and manners, *comedia de magia, zarzuela, loa*, and children's drama (one play). The dates given here and in the bibliography and notes refer to the stage premiere unless otherwise indicated.[6]

Hartzenbusch's historical drama is considered his best genre and includes the majority of the plays most applauded in his time: *Los amantes de Teruel, Alfonso el Casto, La jura en Santa Gadea, La madre de Pelayo* [Pelayo's Mother], *La ley de raza* [The Race Law], and *Vida por honra* [Life for One's Honor]. All deal with Spanish medieval and Golden Age legends and history. The historical periods used are always rigorously researched, and the protagonists are generally drawn from history.

Hartzenbusch's first staged historical play, *Las hijas de Gracián Ramírez*, had been full of melodrama and Romantic excess and was booed from the stage. By contrast, *Alfonso el Casto* (1841) was highly acclaimed and is worthy of critical attention. Inspired in history and Alvaro Cubillo de Aragón's *El conde de Saldaña* [The Count of Saldaña], the action is set in 792 in Oviedo during the Reconquest. It is based on the love of Sancho Saldaña and Jimena, King Alfonso's sister, from whom Bernardo del Carpio will be born. The play depicts the conflict between their love and King Alfonso's jealousy because of his incestuous desire for Jimena, whom he has coerced to become a nun both to atone for their father's patricide and to keep her from other men. The illegitimacy of this love is duplicated politically in the rebellious uprising against Alfonso that the treacherous Ordoño leads. Alfonso, who has repressed his passion for Jimena, is forced by the mother-figure Bernarda to face his desire and to temper vengeance with compassion. Ordoño is justly killed, and contrary to historical accounts documenting Alfonso's cruel punishment of Sancho, the King allows him to escape with Jimena into exile. The use of complicated plots, love triangles, jealousy, a sabotaged letter that impedes revelation of the real traitor, a strong mother-figure, and the bourgeois solution of marriage and self-sacrifice over the exercise of vengeance are typical of Hartzenbusch. The incest motif, the notion of ill-fated love, and the protagonism of time as a tragic force operating through the mechanisms of the *plazo* (time limit), memory, and fear of the future recall *Los amantes de Teruel* and *Doña Mencía* (Caldera and Calderone 509).

La jura en Santa Gadea (1845) is the only Hartzenbusch play edited in the twentieth century, besides *Los amantes de Teruel*. The action occurs in 1073 and centers around the tradition of the Cid, dramatizing events just before those of the epic poem. The Cid's adherence to the principle of honor compels him to demand King Alfonso's oath of innocence in the murder of the King's brother, Sancho of Castile, even though the Cid risks losing Jimena's hand in marriage as a result. Having killed Vellido Dolfos to prevent his revelation that Elvira herself ordered the assassination, the evil Gonzalo falsifies Vellido Dolfos's testimony and accuses the Cid. Maligned, the hero slays Gonzalo in a duel, and Alfonso capitulates to the Cid's arrogant command, swearing his innocence three times. He then gives the hero Jimena's hand in marriage, but punishes him with a three-year exile, which the Cid boldly extends to four. Hartzenbusch emphasizes the Cid's Spanish virtues of patriotism, religiosity, courage and respect for the law, Jimena's constancy in love, and the victory of virtue over vice.

Hartzenbusch wrote two historical dramas in a Gothic setting: *La madre de Pelayo* (1846) and *La ley de raza* (1852). Set in 653, *La ley de raza* dramatizes the events leading up to the abolition of the race law, which prohibited the marriage of Goths with Hispano-Romans. Taking place in 702, after the law's abolition, *La madre de Pelayo* focuses on the heroic figure of Luz, a symbol of the new Spain and mother of its first hero, Pelayo. *Vida por honra* (1858), *La archiduquesita* [The Little Archduchess] (1854), and Hartzenbusch's last original drama *Doña Juana Coello* (written in 1861; unpublished and never staged) are set in Golden Age Spain. Full of falsified and secret information, *Vida por honra* depicts the deceit and consequently just murder of the libertine Count of Villamediana in 1622. *La archiduquesita* (1854), written for the child actress Rafaela Tirado, is a sentimental story about efforts to convince the fourteen-year-old Mariana of Austria to marry her forty-one-year-old uncle and King of Spain, Philip IV. *Doña Juana Coello*, set during the reign of Philip II, portrays the life of the heroic and virtuous wife of Philip's treasonous Minister of State, Antonio Pérez.

Hartzenbusch's four philosophical-symbolic dramas—*Doña Mencía, Primero yo y siempre yo, El bachiller Mendarias o los tres huérfanos*, and *Honoraria*—reveal his efforts to imbue Spanish drama with the philosophical and symbolic depth of German literature. All teach a moral lesson through the personification in a character of a vice or a virtue (Conliffe 219–220). While this moral and philosophical focus remits back to Calderonian drama, the historical settings, melodrama and rhetorical outbursts, suicides, and torturous plots reflect their Romantic patrimony. All but the popular *Doña Mencía* were a box-office failure, and Hartzenbusch soon abandoned this genre.

Riding the wave of popularity of *Los amantes de Teruel*, *Doña Mencía* (1838) was a smashing Romantic success, although like many modern critics, Caldera and Calderone claim that its characters are lost in a "*mare magnum* of daggers, of discoveries and fatal equivocations of identity" (494). It was staged in 1838 for seven consecutive days, and every year between 1842 and 1849, except 1846. Set during the reign of Philip II, it contains an outspoken criticism of the Spanish Inquisition and of religious fanaticism. The examination of incestuous love and its tragic consequences suggests to a modern reader versed in Freud an implicit relationship between repressed incestuous desires and religious intolerance. As in *Primero yo*, the outcome is the suicide of the protagonist, in this instance, Doña Mencía. Attempting to prevent illegitimacy and incest, she ironically has fallen in love with and married her own father, Gonzalo. Implacable destiny has pursued the lovers; Mencía's fanaticism, malice, and deceit have recoiled upon her, just as Gonzalo's secret sin of adultery has condemned him. Of admirable psychological penetration and daring themes, it justly deserves critical attention.

Primero yo is a detectivesque drama in which the egotistical, arrogant, and wealthy Luciano betrays his virtuous friend Isidoro and accuses his own wife Rosalía of poisoning him, all in order to pursue his secret passion for Mariana. In it, Hartzenbusch condemns capitalistic utilitarianism and the reduction of relationships to the principle of self-interest. Set in Soria in 1388, *El bachiller Mendarias* (1842) reveals the Romantic themes of the mysterious and mistaken identities of three orphaned protagonists, the defense of the freedom of the medieval *fueros* [local or regional law codes] against royal absolutism, and the primacy of love over all desires, including freedom. In *Honoraria*, Hartzenbusch's use of the psychological conflicts and/or moral failures of female characters propel the action and to determine the tragic fate of love finds expression in Honoraria and Desideria, exaggerated portrayals of charity and envy. The play appears to defend the right of a woman—and man—to satisfy forbidden love in chaste friendship and to condemn a society whose gossip and envy make this relationship impossible.

Hartzenbusch's only biblical drama, *El mal apóstol y el buen ladrón* [The Bad Apostle and the Good Thief] (1860), is a psychological portrayal of Judas and Dimas, the criminal who was crucified with Christ. The play recalls Tirso's *El condenado por desconfiado* [Condemned for Lack of Faith] and the *auto sacramental*. It emphasizes the redemptive power of Christian faith.

Hartzenbusch wrote seven comedies of character and manners over a period of fourteen years. Most were commissioned or written to highlight the performance of a specific actor. Showing psychological penetration and the study of customs, they also criticize a personal or social defect and end with the punishment of the character who incarnates it. Hartzenbusch situates the action in various epochs, and the customs studied are historicized accordingly. Most were well received by the public and by critics.

La visionaria (1840) takes place in Palma de Mallorca in 1805 during Admiral Nelson's blockade of Gibraltar. Written to educate the public against judging by first impressions and caprice, its comedic and didactic center is the scatterbrained Doña Críspula. Although a self-proclaimed "visionary," Críspula's self-interest, foolishness, and wild imagination lead her to misread the hearts and minds of those around her. *Es un bandido! o juzgar por las apariencias* [He's a Bandit!, or Judging by Appearances] (1843), *Una onza a terno seco, o la fortuna rodando* [A Gold Coin for a Lottery Ticket, or Changing Fortunes] (1845), and *Jugar por tabla* [To Play by the Board] (1850) are light pieces written in collaboration with Manuel Juan Diana, Tomás Rodríguez Rubí, and

Luis Valladares y Garriga and Cayetano Rosell, respectively. *¡Es un bandido!* teaches that judging by appearances can lead to negative consequences. *Una onza a terno seco* criticizes economic injustice, and *Jugar por tabla*, loosely drawn from *Gabrielle*, by Émile Augier, deals with a troubled marriage.

La coja y el encogido (1843) is a study of a timid young man Fabián and his transformation into a self-assertive pretender of the heroine Adela. Through Fabián's conquest of love and analogous economic turn of fortune, and by means of the punishment of the licentious, greedy, and self-interested Rufino, Hartzenbusch criticizes utilitarianism. In the highly popular farce *Juan de las Viñas* [Juan of the Vineyards] (1844), Hartzenbusch ridicules individuals who complain that their good intentions always produce bad results while failing to locate this misfortune in their own ignorance and imprudence. Staged in 1852, *Un sí y un no* [A Yes and a No] is considered his best comedy of manners. In the play he criticizes and punishes those who contract marriage for personal gain, that is, when the favorable balance of "yeses" outweighs the "noes." Thus, just like Rufino in *La coja y el encogido*, the immoral lawyer and charmer Florencio is left without a girlfriend or a fortune, while the prudent García wins Pilar's hand. The plot relies on letter documents to verify wealth and identity. Falsified identity unmasks vice when García's strategic lie about Pilar's disinheritance convinces the status seeker Florencio to abandon plans to marry her. Ultimately Pilar and García's virtue triumphs over greed and egotism.

Hartzenbusch's *comedias de magia*—*La redoma encantada* (1839), *Los polvos de la madre Celestina* (1841; revised in 1862), and *Las Batuecas del duque de Alba* [The Duke of Alba's Rural Lands] (1843)—were his most popular plays. *La redoma encantada*, for example, was staged initially for thirty-four consecutive nights, by 1875, it had seen 292 performances.[7] Immensely popular in the eighteenth century, and reborn in Juan de Grimaldi's *La pata de cabra* [The Goat's Hoof] (1829), the economic promise of the *comedia de magia* attracted many writers. Next to Grimaldi, Hartzenbusch became its most important practitioner, infusing the genre with literary quality (Gies 79).

In *La redoma encantada* he uses elements from *La pata de cabra*, Molière's *El anfitrión* [The Host], *La piel de asno* [The Ass's Skin], and Madame Beaumont's story *Les trois souhaits* [The Three Wishes] to develop his story: the resurrection or disenchantment of Enrique de Aragón, Marqués de Villena, considered a sorcerer in the first half of the fifteenth century. The Marqués is resuscitated in 1710, during the reign of Philip V and the War of Succession, and the drama recounts the victory of the true nobility of character over a corrupt and powerful nobility of blood, by means of the contrast between virtuous Enrique and the nefarious Count, whose allies are the German aggressors. Two parallel love triangles—one between the noble Enrique, the Count and Dorotea, and the other between the lower-class *gracioso* [fool] Garabito, don Laín, and Pascuala—propel the plot in which sorcery aids both sides. Fantastic settings, disappearances and transformations, and misreadings through the doubling of identities populate the play. Garabito's fears, slapstick actions, and the inclusion of misunderstood German phrases add humor. Always moralistic, Hartzenbusch teaches that love is the greatest good—especially conjugal love—and that it ultimately prevails. He also condemns religious fanaticism and the exploitation of women. The medieval Spanish, created for Enrique's speech, and the use of German phrases and Andalusian dialect reflect the author's passion for language and translation.

Los polvos de la Madre Celestina was of equal popularity, with nearly 300 performances before the author's death (Gies 79). An imitation or free translation of *Les pilules du diable* [The Devil's Pills] (1839) of Ferdinand Laloue, its action occurs during the reign of Charles II, and his dementia has a fictional parallel in that of the comic Junípero Matranzos, a ridiculous but rich gentleman whom the pharmacist Maese Nicodemus Chirinela wants as a husband for his pupil and sister-in-law Teresa. Teresa also is loved by the virtuous but impoverished poet Don García. At the same time and by means of a gentleman's embrace and promise of marriage, Celestina quests to exchange her immortality and miserable old age for mortality and youth. The path to the final happy solution—the union of García with Teresa and of Celestina with Junípero—is obstructed and finally cleared by fantastic and humorous occurrences, caused by the conflicting magic of Locura (Madness), protectress of lovers, and of the egotistical Celestina. The play's fundamental and final magical transformation, the replacement of Celestina's medieval magical powders with the gold wealth of Junípero, can be read as a symbolic analogy for the historical replacement of power based in the "magic-like" divine rights of nobility with the material power of gold and capital of the new bourgeois order. Hartzenbusch's last *comedia de magia, Las Batuecas del duque de Alba*, was a stage failure. Cast in allegorical and intellectual terms, it traces the victory of wisdom and virtue over wealth.

Less important in Hartzenbusch's original dramaturgy are his two *zarzuelas*, two *loas* and children's play. His first *zarzuela, La alcaldesa de Zamarramala* [The Woman Mayor of Zamarramala] (1846), contributes to the newly popular Andalusian *zarzuela*.[8] The action takes place in the town of the title and alludes to the custom of some towns to set aside a day in which women are in control. *Heliodora o el amor enamorado* [Heliodora or Love in Love] (never staged; pub. 1864) portrays the love story of Cupid and Psyche, the latter given the name of Heliodora. Hartzenbusch wrote two *loas*, short pieces used to initiate a performance and to render homage to writers, actors, or political figures. *Derechos póstumos ad hoc* (1856) was written for the production celebrating the birth of Calderón. Its action traces the acquisition by Don Apolinar of the rights to his works and of Rosita's hand in marriage. *La hija de Cervantes* [Cervantes' Daughter] (1861), written to commemorate the death of Miguel de Cervantes, depicts the life of his bastard daughter Isabel. It includes some of his fictional characters and commentary on his works. Around 1837, Hartzenbusch wrote a children's play, *El niño desobediente* [The Disobedient Boy], which for years was staged without his knowledge (Conliffe 484). In it two boys are frightened and punished for disobeying an order not to enter a forest.

Los amantes de Teruel

The legend of the lovers of Teruel has taken literary form in the texts of many Spanish writers—including the plays of Andrés Rey de Artieda, Tirso de Molina, and Pérez de Montalbán published, respectively, in 1581, 1614, and 1638. Nevertheless, it is Hartzenbusch who gives the legend definitive dramatic and literary form with *Los amantes de Teruel*, premiered on January 17, 1837, at the Principe Theater. A great success, it was staged for ten consecutive days and five more times that year. Published frequently, it has inspired subsequent literary works as well.[9] The alleged historicity of the legend itself has divided critics. Arguments of its veracity derive from the 1619 document of the Teruel notary and town clerk Juan Salas de Yagüe. His document is a copy of yet another copy an archival document entitled *Historia anónima de los amantes de Teruel* [Anonymous History of the Lovers of Teruel]. Hartzenbusch himself asserts the truth of the tradition. The most recent summaries of this polemic by Picoche (1970; 1980 in Spanish) and Conrado Guardiola Alcover (1988) still leave open the question of its veracity.

Imbued with the spirit of Romanticism, Hartzenbusch adds to the plots of his dramatic predecessors greater psychological realism, the narrative catalyst of Isabel's adulterous mother, Margarita, and the oriental motif of seditious Moors, headed by the lustful and vengeful Queen Zulima. He also locates the action in 1217 to make it coincide with the legend. The plot of his 1836 play is as follows: Juan Diego (Martínez Garcés) de Marsilla, a young man without familial prestige or money, has fallen in love with the rich and beautiful Isabel de Segura. Her father, Don Pedro, refuses to accept him as a husband for Isabel because of his poverty, but Diego secures from him a six-year time period [*plazo*] to gain fame and fortune. Marsilla sets off to win riches in war, and Isabel promises fidelity. The action begins when Marsilla, triumphant, returns to Valencia with only six days left in the agreement. Misfortune pursues him, and he is captured by the Moors, whose Queen Zulima falls in love with him. Rejected by him, she takes revenge by impeding his timely return to Teruel and by delivering to Isabel the false message of his death.

Meanwhile, Isabel's father has pressured her to marry the noble and wealthy Rodrigo de Azagra to whom he has promised her. Azagra first tries to break Isabel's resistance. He blackmails her and her mother Margarita, threatening to expose the latter's youthful love affair unless Isabel marries him. Isabel ultimately puts duty before love, a decision reinforced by the report of Marsilla's death and his affair with the Moorish queen. Azagra now promises to let Isabel retain her chastity if only she will marry him. A stoic Isabel finally surrenders to fate and weds him.

Marsilla, however, is still alive, impeded from arriving in time to stop the wedding by bandits hired by Zulima. The Moor Adel murders Zulima in the name of the Emir, her husband, whom Zulima had rebelled against because he took another wife. Marsilla, furious at Isabel's inconstancy and rebelling against fate and social law, swears to kill Azagra. When Isabel and Marsilla finally meet, she declares that although she loves him, she is duty bound to her husband. However, when he informs her that Azagra, wounded in duel with him, has vowed to expose her mother's love letter in revenge, she frantically turns against and cries out the famous repudiation of her love, "I detest you." Marsilla falls dead immediately. Loveless and therefore lifeless without him, Isabel throws herself on his body and dies, uttering the final words of the play: "I loved you, I always loved you . . . You wept when I belonged to another, I die belonging to you."

The Romantic extravagance, exoticism, and fatality of the 1836 plot were modified by Hartzenbusch for his now-definitive 1849 play. Picoche has thoroughly studied the manuscripts of each version and the nineteen editions of minor changes published in the author's own lifetime. He concludes that the changes in the 1849 version are so numerous and substantial that the latter is essentially a new drama. In summary, these changes reflect an attenuation of Romanticism and an effort to enhance narrative verisimilitude. The 1836 mixture of prose and verse gives way to a dominance of verse in the 1849 text, and the acts are reduced from five to four, with the rectification of some historical data. Margarita is not called an adulteress and is less egotistical, a change influenced by negative criticism of the play. Isabel expires near rather than on top of Marsilla's body, Zulima and Marsilla die off stage, and the costumbristic element of the bandits, criticized as silly by Larra, is gone. Isabel sentimentally pardons Zulima, whose vengeance she forgives because it was an act of love. The Moor Zeangir's name is changed to Osmin, and that of Mari-Gómez to Teresa, with an elimination of the maid's earthy humor. Isabel's final words are more sentimental than passionate: "My dear, pardon my fatal spite. I adored you. I was yours, I am yours: in pursuit of your spirit my enamored spirit sets forth."

Refundiciones of Spanish Golden Age Theater

Except for the unpublished work of Conliffe and several articles by other critics, no studies have been dedicated to Hartzenbusch's *refundiciones* of Spanish Golden Age theater. The total number reaches twelve. Seven were successfully staged and have been preserved in print; in his *Papeles* [Papers], willed to the Biblioteca Nacional, Hartzenbusch has left notice of five more.[10]. The writing of *refundiciones* was a common activity during the period, and no one was better able nor more authorized to compose them than Hartzenbusch, given his archival and library work and his experience in writing original theater. These works were part of his effort to educate the public in classical drama and to resuscitate Spanish theater. Hartzenbusch's modifications of the original texts, like those of other "recasters," focus on external structure and language and seek to maintain the philosophical content and the same general plot. His goals were always faithful restoration tempered with verisimilitude for audience understanding.

Conliffe comments that this generally meant a reduction to three or four acts, the elimination and reordering of scenes, and the addition of episodes that enhance narrative logic. Hartzenbusch also reduced the number of characters, eliminated unrealistic asides, and shortened soliloquies. He omitted plot complications, justified entrances and exits, reduced lengthy time periods, and ennobled characters by eliminating offensive words and actions. He retained the language of the era but modernized the vocabulary when necessary to make it accessible to nineteenth-century audiences.

Translations

In his authoritative book, Corbière enumerates twenty-two translations of plays that Hartzenbusch made from French originals; he also translated Alfieri's *Mérope* from Italian (written 1854; published 1870) and Lessing's *Emilia Galotti* from German (probably dating from 1840). Most of the translated plays date from the eighteenth century, and his revisions often involve the elimination of potentially suggestive "indecency or a lack of respect for social conventions" (Corbière 77). Given the revolutionary ideology of French Romanticism and Hartzenbusch's moral conservatism, it is not surprising that *Ernesto*, his 1837 translation of Alexandre Dumas *père*'s *Angèle* of 1833, differs greatly from the original. Hartzenbusch's hero Ernesto is an aggressive man of action and lacks the Romantic melancholy, introspection, and fatalism of Dumas's Alfred. The unbridled passions of the original Romantic play, which protests against conventional morality and criticizes the institution of marriage, are mitigated in his adaptation. Thus Carolina is the sister-in-law rather than the mistress of the Minister of Foreign Affairs, and Enrique's chastisement of Ernesto for his moral conduct has no counterpart in the French play (Corbière 35). In *El barbero de Sevilla o la inútil precaución* [The Barber of Seville or the Useless Precaution] from Pierre Beaumarchais's 1775 play, Hartzenbusch reduces the role of Figaro, eliminating "those deft allusions to politics and society that foretold the approaching end of the old order" (Corbière 37).

Critics' Response

Critical studies of Hartzenbusch's works are also limited in scope and number. With the exception of the book by Iranzo, the unpublished dissertation of Conliffe and Dolores E. Farkas, and Anthony Sylvain Corbière's published dissertation on Hartzenbusch and the French theater, his life and works receive only brief treatment in the histories of Spanish theater. Only Navas Ruiz dedicates a comprehensive chapter to Hartzenbusch. The vitality of *Los amantes de Teruel*, on the other hand, has led to numerous critical editions of the play, including the definitive one of Jean Louis Picoche, the thesis of M. E. Butterfield, Farkas's comparative study, and a number of articles. Nicholson Barney Adams, J. Sarrailh, and James C. Nicholls have written articles on *Sancho Ortiz de las Roelas,*

Alfonso el Casto, and *La coja y el encogido*, respectively. Rich, varied and influential in its time, however, Hartzenbusch's dramaturgy merits a comprehensive critical reexamination. Criticism of the play has been laudatory, beginning with Lara's January 27, 1837, review in *El español*. Fernández Guerra and Ferrer del Río are effusive. Navas Ruiz and Salvádor García Castañeda prefers the spontaneity and passion of the first version to the external perfection of the second. García Castañeda calls the *plazo* the real protagonist (20–21). Navas Ruiz emphasizes the opposition between a system of collective coexistence to which the individual is tied by duty and an individual desire that rebels against this system in search of happiness (*Romanticismo* 214). Ruiz Ramón cites with praise the twin themes of time and fatality but criticizes Romantic "tricks" that make fatality "a gross 'deus ex machine' " (386). Caldera and Calderone say that the play takes the theme of time modeled by its Romantic predecessors—*Macías, Don Alvaro*, and *El trovador*—and makes time a cosmic threat in the form of the *plazo* (467). David T. Gies notes that "*Los amantes de Teruel* is not a drama of rebellion or cosmic angst, but it is nevertheless a profoundly Romantic drama because of its deep pessimism" (122).

Picoche's text is authoritative and indispensable (1970 French edition; 1980 in Spanish). He studies the Madrid theater of the period, the legend, and Hartzenbusch's sources. He analyzes the themes, structure, and staging of the 1836 play and the reasons for and nature of the 1849 *refundición*. His diagrammatic analyses of the narrative and the pattern of dramatic intensity prove the play's equilibrium and careful emotional rhythm. He notes Hartzenbusch's aim to write the great Spanish work on love. Given the complexities of the variations and chronology of the manuscripts and editions, Picoche presents the two principal versions successively, incorporating the variants found in different editions. The study ends with an exhaustive bibliography of editions, translations, and creative and critical works on the theme.

Conliffe calls the separation of the two lovers until the end a defect that may derive from a timidity to present intense love, a lack of talent, or an overdependence on the legend (36). Francis B. Rang emphasizes the scholarly sources of Hartzenbusch's Romanticism. Farkas compares the play with Pedro Antonio de Alarcón's 1880 novel *El niño de la bola*. Iranzo's greatest contribution to studies of the legend is her 1971 edition of Rey de Artieda and Tirso's plays. Richard A. Curry shows how Hartzenbusch maintains the play's dramatic tensions, despite the audience's prior knowledge of the story, by means of interior and exterior structures (37). Kay Engler finds narrative unity in Marsilla's struggle against the obstacles that thwart his desire.

I propose a feminist interpretation that centers on the feminine agents who act as the obstacles to love's realization.[11] As obstacles that impede the satisfaction of the principle of pleasure (Eros), these agents are what Freud has called the "law of the Other" (Thanatos), the projected half of the subject that serves in its otherness as a rejected or repressed difference, through which and against which the subject defines himself. Imposing death as the inevitable solution for the reintegration of the self, this resistant and dangerous Other of *Los amantes de Teruel* is embodied in the autonomous feminine Other of Margarita and Zulima. Interestingly, they are the two principal characters whom Hartzenbusch added to the legend, revealing also in his creation of Zulima the influence of Romantic Orientalism. While the heroine, Isabel, is a positive feminine figure through whom the alienated Romantic hero tries to reunite his divided self and gain access to patriarchal society, the acts of rebellious autonomy of Margarita and Zulima—adultery, sedition, and vengeance—make them a destructive force. The dangers these women represent are controlled—through Isabel's self-sacrifice and Zulima's death—but not before their autonomy destroys the two lovers. The remorse and penance of Margarita, and the silencing of her narrative through a denial of positive power to the love expressed in her letters, evince the same authorial rejection of rebellion present in other plays. This rejection and silencing are also revealed in Zulima's inability to translate Marsilla's written warning to the Emir in Act I, a translation that Osmín, her male subordinate, can realize. This inaccessible document ultimately provides evidence of her conspiracy with Merván against her husband and thus causes her death. In both instances, the resistant feminine Other is deprived of the power to tell and control her story, which is assimilated instead into the predominant masculine narrative of the hero and canonical Romanticism.

NOTES

1. Ricardo Navas Ruiz, *El romanticismo español*, 4th ed. (Madrid: Cátedra, 1990), 208.

2. Angel Valbuena Prat, *Teatro moderno español* (Zaragoza: Partenón, 1944), 48.

3. Francisco Ruiz Ramón, *Historia del teatro español, I (Desde sus orígenes hasta 1900)* (Madrid: Alianza, 1967), 387; and Donald L. Shaw, *A Literary History of Spain. The Nineteenth Century* (London: Ernest Benn, 1972), 26.

4. Ermanno Caldera and Antoinetta Calderone, "El teatro en el siglo XIX (I) (1808–1844)" in *Historia del teatro en España. Tomo II. Siglo XVIII. Siglo XIX*, dir. José Manā Diez Borque (Madrid: Taurus, 1988), 508.

5. All translations of Hartzenbusch's works and those of the critics belong to this author.

6. Fernández-Guerra, Conliffe, and Navas Ruiz divide Hartzenbusch's dramaturgy by genre. I have followed the divisions used by Conliffe, except his commissioned works (the *loas, zarzuelas*, and children's play), which Conliffe combines into one category. The absence of a definitive published study of Hartzenbusch's theater has led to a confusion in numerical totals for his original plays; Fernández-Guerra counts twenty-five, Navas Ruiz twenty-seven, and Gies twenty-nine. Given the unpublished fragments of plays and lost texts documented in Eugenio Hartzenbusch's bibliography, this issue is even more problematic.

7. Corbière, 78, quoted in David Thatcher Gies, *The Theatre in Nineteenth-Century Spain* (Cambridge: Cambridge University Press, 1994), 79.

8. The new attention to the Andalusian *zarzuelas* probably follows in the wake of Rodríguez Rubí's popularization of Andalusian themes and theater in the early 1840s.

9. Subsequent works on the legend include Enrique Gil's 1844 novel *El señor de Bembibre* [The Gentleman from Bembibre], Gertrudis Gómez de Avellaneda's *La flor del ángel* [The Flower of the Angel] (1871), Alarcón's 1878 *El niño de la bola*, and numerous nineteenth-century dramatic parodies (Gies 285, 333–334).

10. The seven staged and published *refundiciones* are Rojas Zorrilla's *El amo criado* (1829), *El médico de su honra* (1844) of Calderón, *La esclava de su galán* [Her Suitor's Slave] (1847) of Lope de Vega, Tirso de Molina's *Desde Toledo a Madrid* [From Toledo to Madrid] (1847), *Sancho Ortiz de las Roelas* (1852) (an adaptation of Cándido María Trigueros's 1800 play of the same name, which had been a *refundición* of Lope's alleged play *La Estrella de Sevilla* [The Star of Sevilla]), Tirso's *La prudencia en la mujer* [A Woman's Prudence] (1858), and Lope's *El perro del hortelano* [The Gardener's Dog] (1862). Ferrer del Río adds the two *refundiciones* done in 1929, Calderón's *Los empeños de un acaso* [Chance Undertakings] and Moreto's *La confusión de un jardín* [Confusion in a Garden]. The five plays mentioned in his *Papeles* are Calderón's *Guárdate del agua mansa* [Beware of Still Waters], Antonio Coello's *Dar la vida por su dama* [To Give Your Life for Your Lady], and Francisco de Bances Candamo's *Por su rey y por su dama* [For His King and His Lady]. Hartzenbusch also attempted to recast Rojas Zorrilla's *Progne y Filomena* and *La Estrella de Sevilla* but abandoned them after several scenes; he returned to the latter play indirectly in his recasting of Trigueros's *Sancho Ortiz*.

These *refundiciones* and Hartzenbusch's professional and scholarly activities merit critical attention. Given the abundance of documentation on this work and all his theatrical activity, Jesús Rubio Jiménez calls for a detailed investigation of his theatrical ideas and of the activities leading to his virtual omnipresence over many decades in the institutions that controlled and shaped the direction of Spanish theater (Caldera and Calderone 634 [note 4]). He remarks that Leonardo Romero Tobar evaluates Hartzenbusch's work on the theater of his era in *La teoría dramática española (1800–70)* [Spanish Dramatic Theory (1800–70)] (Madrid: Facultad de Filosofia y Letras, 1970).

11. Linda S. Materna, "Lo femenino peligroso y el orientalismo en *Los amantes de Teruel* de Juan Eugenio Hartzenbusch," in *Actas del XII Congreso de la Asociación Internacional de Hispanistas* (Birmingham, UK, 1995). Vol. IV, *Del Romanticismo a la Guerra Civil*, ed. Derek W. Flitter (Birmingham, UK: University of Birmingham, 1998), 192–201.

BIBLIOGRAPHY

Available Editions and Translations of *Los amantes de Teruel*

There are no translations in print. The primary Spanish editions in print are listed below, including the version of the play chosen by the editor. A virtually exhaustive list of all of the editions published can be found in Picoche.

Alcina Franch, Juan, ed. *Teatro romántico*. 3d ed. Barcelona: Bruguera, 1984. (Follows 1850 Baudry edition, that is, the 1849 version).
García Castañeda, Salvador, ed. *Juan Eugenio Hartzenbusch. "Los amantes de Teruel."* Madrid: Castalia, 1971. (1836 version).
Gil Albacete, Alvaro, ed. *Juan Eugenio Hartzenbusch. "Los amantes de Teruel." "La*

jura en Santa Gadea." 1st ed. 1935 Madrid: Espasa-Calpe, 1964. (Follows 1850
  Baudry edition).
Iranzo, Carmen, ed. *Juan Eugenio Hartzenbusch. "Los amantes de Teruel."* Madrid:
  Cátedra, 1989. (1858 version, improved version of 1849 text).
Navas Ruiz, Ricardo, ed. *Juan Eugenio Hartzenbusch. "Los amantes de Teruel."* Madrid:
  Espasa-Calpe, 1992. (1836 version with some simultaneous transcription of the
  1849 version).
Picoche, Jean-Louis, ed. *Juan Eugenio Hartzenbusch y Martinez. "Los amantes de Te-
  ruel."* Paris: Centre de Recherches Hispaniques, 1970. (All versions).
————. *Juan Eugenio Hartzenbusch. "Los Amantes de Teruel."* Spanish translation of
  1970 Paris edition. Madrid: Alhambra, 1980.

Principal Editions

Except for Navas Ruiz's 1973 edition of Hartzenbusch's *Fábulas* and the numerous
editions of *Los amantes de Teruel*, editions of his works are partial and date from the
nineteenth century. His plays can be found in the three *Obras* listed below. The location
in these *Obras* of individual original plays is shown next to each play by means of a
number code (1, 2, or 3) and volume code. (1:4), for example, means volume four of
the Tello edition. There are many unpublished works and materials in the *Papeles de
Hartzenbusch* of the Biblioteca Nacional in Madrid and some in the Archivo Municipal
de Madrid.

(1) *Obras de Don Juan E. Hartzenbusch.* Pro. Aureliano Fernández-Guerra. 5 vols. Ma-
    drid: Tello, 1887–1892. Volume 1 includes the Fernández-Guerra prologue and
    poetry, and volume 2, the fables. Volumes 3–5, entitled *Teatro 1, 2,* and *3,*
    respectively, include theater.
(2) *Obras de encargo.* Madrid: Sucesores de Rivadeneyra, 1864.
(3) *Obras escogidas de Don J. E. Hartzenbusch.* Prologue. Eugenio de Ochoa. Paris:
    Baudry, 1850.
(4) *Obras escogidas de Juan Eugenio Hartzenbusch.* Bio. Antonio Ferrer del Rio. 2 vols.
    Leipzig: Brockhaus, 1863.

Original Dramaturgy

Dates in parentheses correspond to the stage premiere. Plays that premiered in the
same year are ordered chronologically by premiere. The bibliographical status (publication, etc.) of works never staged is indicated. For published works not included in the
Obras editions, the monograph publication information is given.

Las hijas de Gracián Ramírez, o la restauración de Madrid (1831). Never published.
  Act I and First and Last Scenes of Acts II–IV in E. Hartzenbusch's *Bibliografía*
  Ms. in Archivo Municipal de Madrid.
Los amantes de Teruel (1837) (1:3; 3; 4:1; as well as aforementioned editions available).
El niño desobediente (written circa 1837; staged without author's knowledge or author-
  ization). Published *Semanario Pintoresco Español,* 25 Marzo, 1849.
Doña Mencia o la boda en la Inquisición (1838) (1:3; 3).

La redoma encantada (1839) (1:3).
La visionaria (1840) (1:4; 3).
Alfonso el Casto (1841) (1:4 and 3).
Los polvos de la Madre Celestina (1841) (1:4).
Primero yo, y siempre yo (1842) (1:4; 3).
El bachiller Mendarias o los tres huérfanos (1842) (1:5; 3).
La coja y el encogido (1843) (3; see also "Translations").
Honoraria (1843) (1:5; 3).
¡Es un bandido! o juzgar por las apariencias (1843). In collaboration with Manuel Juan Diana. Madrid: Yenes, 1843.
Las Batuecas del duque de Alba (1843). Madrid: Repullés, 1843.
Juan de las Viñas (1844) (3; 4:1).
La jura en Santa Gadea (1845) (3; see also available editions of *Los amantes de Teruel*).
Una onza a terno seco o la fortuna rodando (1845). In collaboration with Tomás Rodríguez Rubi. Madrid: Repullés, 1845.
La madre de Pelayo (1846) (3).
La alcaldesa de Zamarramala (1846). Manuscript in *Papeles*.
Jugar por tabla (1850). In collaboration with Luis Valladares y Garriga and Cayetano Rosell. Madrid: Omaña, 1850.
La ley de raza (1852) (4:2).
Un si y un no (1854) (4:2).
La archiduquesita (1854) (4:2).
Derechos póstumos ad hoc (1856) (1:5; 2).
Heliodora o el amor enamorado (written 1857–1858; staged posthumously in 1880). Published as *El amor enamorado* (1864) (2); and a *refundición* for staged version published Madrid: J. Rodríguez, 1880.
La vida por la honra (1858) (4:2).
El mal apóstol y el buen ladrón (1860) (4:2).
La hija de Cervantes (1861) (2).
Doña Juana Coello (begun in 1861; never staged; manuscript in *Papeles*; Act I and First and Last Scenes II–III in Eugenio Hartzenbusch *Bibliografía*).

Refundiciones of Golden Age Spanish Theater

Dates in parentheses correspond to the stage premiere. Plays that premiered in the same year are ordered chronologically by premiere. The bibliographical status (publication, etc.) of works is indicated. The name of the original play and author are given in parentheses before the date of the premiere, if staged. Grafton Conliffe is the best source of information about the *refundiciones*.

El amo criado (Donde hay agravios no hay celos, y amo criado of Francisco de Rojas Zorrilla; 1829). Madrid: Yenes, 1841.
Los empeños de un acaso (Los empeños de un acaso of Pedro Calderón de la Barca; circa 1829 as documented by Antonio Ferrer del Río). Never staged; no extant text.
La confusión de un jardin (La confusión de un jardin of Agustin Moreto; of approximate date of *Empeños*). Never staged; manuscript in *Papeles*.

El médico de su honra (El médico de su honra of Pedro Calderón de la Barca; 1844).
Madrid: D. Marcos Bueno, 1844.
Desde Toledo a Madrid (Desde Toledo a Madrid of Tirso de Molina; 1847). In collaboration with Manuel Bretón de los Herreros. In Biblioteca Municipal of Madrid
(*Comedias de Tirso de Molina* [Madrid: 1907]).
La esclava de su galán of Lope Félix de Vega Carpio; 1847). Madrid: J. González y A.
Vicente, 1848.
Sancho Ortiz de las Roelas (adaptation of 1800 play of the same title by Cándido María
Trigueros, which had been a *refundición* of *La Estrella de Sevilla* attributed to
Lope Félix de Vega Carpio; 1852). Madrid, 1852.
La prudencia en la mujer (La prudencia en la mujer of Tirso de Molina; 1858). Madrid:
Est. Tip. "Sucesores de Rivandeneyra," 1902.
El perro del hortelano (El perro del hortelano of Lope Félix de Vega Carpio; 1862).
Published March 21, 1903. Manuscript in *Paples.*
Dar la vida por su dama (Antonio Coello), *Por su rey y por su dama* (Francisco de
Bances Candamo), and *Guárdate del agua mansa* (Pedro Calderón de la Barca)
are listed by Aureliano Fernández-Guerra. Never staged; no extant text.

Translations

Dates in parentheses correspond to the premiere. The bibliographical status (publication, etc.) of works is indicated. The name of the original play and author are given
before the date of the premiere, if staged. Anthony Sylvain Corbière and Eugenio Hartzenbusch are the best sources of information about the translations.

La escuela de los padres (L'Ecole des Pères of D'Alexis Piron, 1827). Manuscript in
Papeles.
El regreso inesperado (Le Retour Imprévu of Jean-François Regnard; 1829). Manuscript
in *Papeles.*
El tutor (Le Tuteur of Florent Carton Dancourt; 1829). Manuscript in Archivo Municipal
de Madrid.
La pupila y la péndola (1830). Madrid: V. de Lalama, 1848.
Mérope (Mérope of Alfieri). Translated 1833; never staged. Published in *Teatro selecto
antiguo y moderno nacional y extranjero.* Ed. Francisco Orellana. Barcelona,
1870.
La independencia filial (L'Independence Filiale of Emile Augier; 1837). *Semanario Pintoresco Español,* June 10, June 24, and July 1, 1949.
Ernesto (Angèle of Alexander Dumas *père*; 1838). Madrid: Hijos de Doña Catalina Piñuela, 1837.
El barbero de Sevilla o la inútil precaución (Le Barbier de Seville of Pierre Beaumarchais; circa 1838 and 1860). Madrid: Repullés, 1840.
Función de boda sin boda (La Noce sans Mariage of Louis Benoît Picard; 1839). Madrid:
Repullés, 1839.
Emilia Galotti (Emilia Galotti of G. E. Lessing). Probable translation circa 1840. Manuscript in *Papeles.*
Los polvos de la Madre Celestina (a free adaptation of *Les Pilules du Diable* by Ferdinand Laloue; 1841). Listed and discussed here under "Original Dramaturgy"
because of the degree of adaptation.

El abuelito (*Le Bon Papa, ou la Proposition de Mariage* of Eugène Scribe and M. Mélesville; 1842). Madrid: Yenes, 1842.

El novio de Buitragio (*Le Vogage Interrompu* of Louis Benoît Picard; 1843). In collaboration with Eugenio González D'Apousa. Originally translated only by Hartzenbusch and staged in the Teatro de Buenavista with the title *El viaje interrumpido*. *El novio de Buitragio* was published: Madrid: V. de Lalama, 1846.

La Abadia de Penmarch (*L'abbaye de Penmarch* of Pierre Tournemine and Thomas James Thackeray, 1844). Correction by Hartzenbusch of translation of Nemesio Fernández Cuesta entitled *La Abadia de Penmarck*. Hartzenbusch play published: Madrid: M. Bueno, 1844.

Floresinda (free translation of *Adélaide du Guesclin* of Voltaire). Never staged. Originally written in 1827 with the title *Doña Leonor de Cabrera*. Retouched in 1830. Published as *Floresinda*: Madrid: J. Repullés, 1844.

El doctor Capirote o los curanderos de antaño (*Les Empiriques D'Autrefois* of Eugène Scribe, 1846). Madrid: V. de Lalama, 1850.

Los dos maridos (*Les Deux Maris* of Eugène Scribe and M. Varner, 1847). Madrid: V. de Lalama, 1850.

Jugar por tabla (*Gabriela* of Émile Augier; 1850). Listed and discussed under "Original Dramaturgy." Madrid: S. Omaña, 1850.

El padre pródigo (*Un Père Prodigue* of Alexandre Dumas, *fils*; staged in Zaragoza). In collaboration with Cayetano Rosell. Madrid: C. González, 1861.

Corbière also lists the following five adaptations from French, preserved only in manuscript form without dates, and perhaps never presented: *Olindo y Sofronia*, imitation of a play by Louis-Sébastien Mercier in collaboration with Juan Manuel González Acevedo; *Don Junípero Bausán, o ¡cómo se pasa el tiempo!* (*Marion Delorme* of Louis Benoît Picard); *El espíritu de contradicción* (*L'Esprit de Contradiction* of Charles Rivière Dufresny; *Aviso a las casadas*, from Alexandre Guillavme Mouslier de Moissy; and *María Delorme* (*Marion Delorme* of Victor Hugo). Eugenio Hartzenbusch lists, using his own information and other sources, *Nanina* (*Nanine* of Voltaire), *La escocesa* (*L'Ecossaise* of Voltaire), *El hijo pródigo* (*L'Enfant prodigue* of Voltaire), and *Edipo* (*Edipo* of Voltaire).

Poetry, Fables, and Short Narrative

Volumes I and II of the Tello edition of his *Obras* contain his poetry and fables, respectively. The Brockhaus edition of his *Obras escogidas* contains stories, poetry, and fables. The Baudry *Obras escogidas* contains stories, several speeches, poetry, and fables. Ricardo Navas Ruiz (*Romanticismo* 206) lists several other works.

Cuentos. Madrid: Espasa-Calpe, 1924.

Cuentos y fábulas. Madrid: Rivadeneyra, 1861. Second corrected edition in 1862.

Ensayos poéticos y artículos en prosa, literarios y de costumbres. Madrid: Yenes, 1843. (21 poems).

Fábulas. 1888. Definitive version according to Ricardo Navas Ruiz.

Fábulas. Ed. Ricardo Navas Ruiz. Madrid: Espasa-Calpe, 1973.

Fábulas en verso castellano. Madrid: Sociedad de Operarios, 1848. Two expanded editions in same year.

Obras. Poesías. Colección de Escritores Castellanos Líricos. Vol. 1. Madrid: Tello, 1887. (65 poems).

Criticism and History

Ricardo Navas Ruiz reports that between 1839 and 1857 Hartzenbusch published in various newspapers theater chronicles entitled *Crónica dramática, Crítica dramática,* and *Revista dramática,* none edited for publication. The reader is referred to Navas Ruiz for a bibliographical list of some important articles, speeches, and prologues (*Romanticismo* 206–207). Other articles and prologues can be found in different publications including *El Español, La Iberia, La Constitución, Revista de Europa, El Heraldo, La Gaceta de Madrid, Revista de Teatros, Las Novedades, Semanario Pintoresco Español, Los Niños, El Corresponsal, El Laberinto, El Entreacto,* and *Revista de España y del Extranjero.*

Critical Editions of Spanish Classics

Comedias de don Juan Ruiz de Alarcón y Mendoza. Vol. XX. Biblioteca de Autores Españoles. Madrid: Rivadeneyra, 1852.
Comedias de don Pedro Calderón de la Barca. Vols. VII, IX, XII, XVI. Biblioteca de Autores Españoles. Madrid: Rivadeneyra, 1848–1850.
Comedias escogidas de Fray Gabriel Téllez (El Maestro Tirso de Molina), juntas en colección e ilustradas por D. Juan Eugenio Hartzenbusch. Vol. V. Biblioteca de Autores Españoles. Madrid: Rivadeneyra, 1848.
Comedias escogidas de Fray Lope Félix de Vega Carpio. Vols. I–IV, XXIV, XXXIV, XLI, and XLII. Biblioteca de Autores Españoles. Madrid: Rivadeneyra, 1853–1857.
"El Ingenioso Hidalgo Don Quijote de la Mancha," compuesto por Miguel de Cervantes Saavedra. Vols. I–IV. Argamasilla de Alba: Rivadeneyra, 1863.
Las 1,633 notas puestas por el Excmo. e Ilmo. señor don Juan Eugenio Hartzenbusch a la primera edición de "El ingenioso hidalgo." Barcelona: Ramírez y Cía., 1874.
Obras póstumas de don Leandro Fernández de Moratín. 3 vols. Madrid: Rivadeneyra, 1867–1868.
Romancero pintoresco o colección de nuestros mejores romances antiguos. Madrid: J. R. Benedicto, 1848.
Teatro escogido de Fray Gabriel Téllez, conocido con el nombre de El Maestro Tirso de Molina. 12 vols. Madrid: Yenes, 1839–1842.

Translations of Works by Hartzenbusch

The Lovers of Teruel. Trans. Henry Thomas. Rev. ed. London: Oxford, 1950. (1st ed., Montgomeryshire: Gregynog, 1938).
La coja y el encogido (The Lame Girl and the Bashful Man). Bilingual. Ed. Floyd B. Wilson. New York: R. F. Fenno, 1902.
Die Liebenden von Teruel. Trans. Adolf Seubert. Stuttgart: Druck von G. A. Landenberger, 1853. Leipzig: Druck und Verlag von Philipp Reclam, 1875?
Die Liebenden von Teruel. Trans. Wilhelm Altenburg. 1857–1860?

Critical Studies

Adams, Nicholson Barney. *Hartzenbusch's "Sancho Ortiz de las Roelas."* Rpt. from *Studies in Philology* 28.4 (1931): n.p.

Brett, Lewis E. *Nineteenth Century Spanish Plays.* New York: Appleton-Century Crofts, 1935.

Butterfield, M. E. "Two Dramatic Versions of *Los amantes de Teruel*." Master's thesis, University of Oklahoma, 1931.

Caballero, Fernán. *Cecilia Bohl de Faber (Fernán Caballero) y Juan Eugenio Hartzenbusch, una correspondencia inédita.* Ed. Theodor Heinermann. Madrid: Espasa-Calpe, 1944.

Chevalier, Maxime. "Pour les sources des fables d'Hartzenbusch." *Bulletin Hispanique* 81 (1979): 303–310.

Colecchia, Francesca. "Funeral en Teruel: Evocaciones modernas de una leyenda antigua." *Crítica Hispánica* 16:2 (1994): 241–247.

Conliffe, Grafton J. "El teatro de Juan Eugenio Hartzenbusch." Ph.D. Diss., Northwestern University, *DAI* 35 (1975): 4508A.

Corbière, Anthony Sylvain. "Juan Eugenio Hartzenbusch and the French Theater." Ph.D. Diss., University of Pennsylvania, 1927.

Curry, Richard A. "Dramatic Tension and Emotional Control in *Los amantes de Teruel*." *West Virginia University Philological Papers* 21 (1974): 36–47.

Engler, Kay. "Amor, muerte y destino: La Psicología de Eros en '*Los amantes de Teruel*.' " *Hispanófila* 70 (1980): 1–15.

Farkas, Dolores E. "*Los amantes de Teruel* de Hartzenbusch y *El niño de la bola* de Alarcón: un estudio comparativo." *DAI* 36 (1976): 1487A.

Fernández-Guerra, Aureliano. *Hartzenbusch.* Madrid: Imprenta de la Cía de Impresores y Libreros, n.d.

———. "Hartzenbusch, estudio biográfico y crítico." *La España* (Madrid), 8 abril 1855.

Ferrer del Río, Antonio. *Galería de la literatura.* Madrid: Mellado, 1846.

Flitter, Derek. "The Romantic Theology of *Los amantes de Teruel*." *Crítica Hispánica* 18.1 (1996): 25–34.

Fournier, Anne. "Les Ressorts dramatiques dans le théâtre de J. E. Hartzenbusch. Étude du drame *Alfonso el Casto*." In *Romantisme, realisme, naturalisme en Espagne et en Amérique Latine.* Lille: PU de Lille 3, 1978.

Gonzalo Morón, Fermín. "Juicio crítico de las tragedias y comedias de don Juan Eugenio Hartzenbusch." *Revista de España y el extranjero* III (1842): 130–139.

Guardiola Alcóver, Conrado. *La verdad actual sobre los Amantes de Teruel: Orientación crítica de los estudios amantísticos.* Teruel: Instituto de Estudios Turolenses, 1988.

Hartzenbusch, Juan Eugenio. "Los amantes de Teruel." *El laberinto* (Madrid), 16 diciembre 1843.

Hartzenbusch e Hiriart, Eugenio Maximino. *Bibliografía de Hartzenbusch. (Excmo. Sr. D. Juan Eugenio) formado por su hijo D. Eugenio Hartzenbusch.* Madrid: Sucesores de Rivadeneyra, 1900.

Heinermann, Theodor. *Cecilia Böhl de Faber (Fernán Caballero) y Juan Eugenio Hartzenbusch.* Madrid: Espasa-Calpe, 1944.

Hobbs, Gloria L. "Odyssey of *Los amantes de Teruel*." *South Central Bulletin* 26.4 (1966): 4–9.

Iranzo, Carmen. *Juan Eugenio Hartzenbusch.* Boston: Twayne, 1978.
Juretschke, Hans. "La recepción de la cultura y ciencia alemanas en España durante la época romántica." In *Estudios románticos.* Valladolid: Patronato Quadrado del CSIC, 1975.
Larra, Mariano José de. *"Los amantes de Teruel." El español* (Madrid), 27 enero 1837. In *Articulos de crítica literaria y artística* Clásicos Castellanos. Ed. José Lomba y Pedraja. Madrid: Espasa-Calpe, 1960.
Materna, Linda S. "Lo femenino peligroso y el orientalismo en *Los amantes de Teruel* de Juan Eugenio Hartzebusch." In *Actas del XII Congreso de la Asociación International de Hispanistas* [Proceedings of the XII International Congress of Hispanists] (Birmingham, UK, 1995). Vol. IV, *Del Romanticismo a la Guerra Civil,* ed. Derek W. Flitter (Birmingham, UK: University of Birmingham, 1998).
Mesonero Romanos, Ramón. "Hartzenbusch." In *Memorias de un setentón.* Madrid: La Ilustración Española y Americana, 1880.
Nicholls, James C. "Variations on the Motif of the One-Eyed Lover from Marmontel to Hartzenbusch." *Revue de Litterature Comparée* 43 (1969): 15–22.
Picoche, Jean Louis. *"Los amantes de Teruel* avant et aprés." *Recherches sur le monde hispanique au dix-neuvième siécle.* Paris: Eds. Universitaires, 1973.
————. "Les Manuscrits d'Hartzenbusch a la Bibliotheque Nationale de Madrid." *Bulletin Hispanique* 70 (1968): 525–529.
————. *"Mil y una noches españolas* (Madrid 1845): Una colección poco conocida de cuentos históricos: Intención y realización." *Romanticismo 3–4: Atti del IV Congresso sul romanticismo spagnolo e ispanoamericano (Bordighera, 9–11 aprile, 1987).* In *La narrativa romantica.* Intro. Ermanno Caldera. Genoa: Biblioteca di Lett, 1988.
Rang, Francis B., II. "The Erudite Romanticism of Juan Eugenio Hartzenbusch in *Los amantes de Teruel." DAI* 32 (1972): 7000A–7001A.
Rodriguez López Vázquez, Alfredo. "Claramonte, El rey Don Pedro y la mixtificación de Hartzenbusch." In *Varia hispánica: Homenaje a Alberto Porqueras Mayo,* ed. Joseph L. Laurenti and Vern G. Williamsen. Kassel: Reichenberger, 1989.
Sarrailh, J. "L'Histoire et le Drame Romantique. A Propos d' *Alfonso el Casto." Bulletin Hispanique* 38 (1936): 1920.
Sparks, Amy. "Honor in Hartzenbusch's 'Refundición' of Calderón's *El médico de su honra." Hispania* 49 (1966): 410–413.

ENRIQUE JARDIEL PONCELA
(1901–1952)

Douglas McKay

BIOGRAPHY

At his 1983 induction into the Spanish Royal Academy, the playwright José López Rubio spoke of a special generation of innovators of contemporary humor who, like himself, shared a fondness for the dissemination of nonsense on the Spanish stage.[1] Among "the artisans of the new humor" were Antonio de Lara (Tono), Edgar Neville. Miguel Mihura, López Rubio, and especially the one playwright and novelist whom Francisco García Pavón had singled out as both the inaugurator and leading voice of the vanguard of humor, Enrique Jardiel Poncela (1901–1952).[2]

Jardiel's contributions to a resplendent new direction in theater humor, registered between 1927 and 1949, is the justifiable basis for assigning him the seminal role as spokesman for that generation of important playwrights. His demonstrated commitment to the cultivation of strange, illogical, and unusual stage action and dialogue garnered for Jardiel his recognition of leadership among the purveyors of the Spanish theater of the absurd.[3]

Jardiel Poncela was born October 15, 1901, in Madrid. His apprenticeship at theater writing began at the age of fifteen. He had already completed over thirty full-length plays in collaboration with Serafín Adame Martínez before staging, in 1927, his first comedy as an independent playwright. Throughout the last twenty years of his life he experienced severe negative criticism from enemies of the press. His own overreaction to that criticism only intensified the vituperation, which left him exhausted and cynical from many vain efforts to vindicate his unconventional career. He died in despair and bitterness on February 18, 1952, in Madrid.

His legacy to the modern stage includes a surface comicity that still maintains its unique appeal in surprise of action and complication of plot. An unusually large number of characters comprises the cast of his major plays; their farcical development is based on witty, unexpected dialogue and a startling, often outrageous plot line. Jardiel is most revolutionary in his use of verbal nonsense and irrational happenings to point out the insufficiency of commonplace stage humor. His technical skills lifted the absurd from the plane of wild caricature to a level of solid construction, melding the improbable with an occasional serious tone and a timely poetic vein. Today his name is generally recognized as a pioneer of bold endeavors and new departures, one who established an eccentric albeit creative struggle against the conservative blandness of such earlier playwrights as José de Echegaray and Jacinto Benavente. His best comedies had a profound influence on a large number of writers of Spanish theater humor.[4]

DRAMATURGY: MAJOR WORKS AND THEMES

The following eight productions, spanning eighteen years of Jardiel Poncela's most creative period as an independent playwright, illustrate his innovative contributions to the theater of his day. They speak eloquently to Jardiel's firm resolve to counter the conservative blandness of Spanish drama with daring experiments in the field of comedy, with original and surprising stagecraft.

A Sleepless Spring Night [Una noche de primavera sin sueño]

Having repudiated everything he had written before 1927, Jardiel insisted that A Sleepless Spring Night (premiere 1927) was his legitimate debut as a dramatist.[5] A work of incipient audacity, its effectiveness depends on the use of unanticipated revelations, comic reversals, and a burlesque tone applied to both situation and dialogue. Its action begins during the final moments of an all-night dispute between Mariano and Alejandra, a young married couple. The husband bolts from the apartment in anger, only to be replaced by Valentín, a handsome stranger who spends the rest of the morning hours chatting with Alejandra. When Mariano returns with his lawyer, intending to initiate divorce proceedings, and sees Valentín, he accuses his wife of adultery and threatens to kill her alleged lover. The young wife, convinced now that Mariano's display of jealous rage is a token of his love for her, turns her wrath on the intruder for having contributed a possible motive for divorce action. In the end the two men reveal that they are really old friends and had prearranged the entire charade of accusation and threatened homicide as a stratagem to enable Mariano to solidify Alejandra's affection for him. This revelation comes as a complete surprise both to Alejandra and the audience.

Jardiel's accumulation of farcical tricks, combined with a comic perversion of logic and congruity in an unstructured sequence of events, sufficed to bestow a revolutionary tag on this work: It was judged shocking, unorthodox, bold, and provocative by his many outraged critics, but it has remained a popular work among Spanish playgoers and American students of Spanish.

Angelina, or A Brigadier's Honor [Angelina, o El honor de un brigadier]

Angelina (premiere 1934) is a verse parody of nineteenth-century melodrama. Its humor results from a heavy use of caricature to exaggerate the frills, costumes, customs, and stereotypes of the post-Romantic theater of José Echegaray and his disciples. Set in the year 1880, it deals with a man's overwrought concern for his honor. The story line is quite simple but predictably implausible: Angelina, the daughter of Don Marcial, the brigadier of the play's subtitle, elopes with Germán on the very day of her engagement to Rodolfo, a young poet who travels about on a bicycle. Don Marcial's honor has been compromised by this impertinent act, so he and the jilted cyclist chase after the wayward lovers. Discovering his daughter's seducer at long last, Don Marcial challenges Germán to a duel. In the heat of combat, Don Marcial learns that his own wife, Marcela, has also betrayed him, and with none other than the same rogue who ran away with his daughter and who stands in mortal peril before him. All of the characters plead with Don Marcial to spare Germán and to forgive the dishonored Marcela, just as Rodolfo has consented to do with Angelina. Confused, enraged, but doubting his own powers of judgment, Don Marcial invokes the spirit of his departed father for some wise supernatural guidance. The ghost appears and persuades Don Marcial to pardon his spouse. Don Marcial agrees to leave the country, intent upon fighting to his death for a remote cause in a distant war. And thus ends this outlandish burlesque that mocks the ideal of honor, satirizes the notion of sacrifice for a noble cause, and spoofs without acrimony many bygone theatrical mannerisms.

The importance of *Angelina* stems from the elegance of its poetic form and the good-humored tone of its content. It is a finished piece of writing, providing the reader with one of those rare moments in Jardiel Poncela's repertory: a play of solid literary quality, with no loss of evenness or spontaneity despite its zany intrusions into caricature.

Four Hearts in Check and Backward March [Cuatro corazones con freno y marcha atrás]

Jardiel believed that this comedy (premiere 1936) was one of the best plays he had written. He rejoiced in its improbability and esteemed the imaginative fantasy and extravagance of its plot far above the best qualities of his previous and later writings.[6]

The plot concerns the discovery in 1860 of a secret saline solution extracted from algae that stops the aging process and thus assures perpetual youth. The discoverer invites a group of friends to join him to prolong their mortal existence indefinitely. Their exhilaration and optimism while seeking immortality are the focus of the first act. Act Two takes place in the year 1920, sixty years later. The privileged immortals are now in a state of forlorn misery and ennui, self-exiled to a remote desert island. They have withdrawn from the rest of the human race, owing to the terrible tedium of changelessness. The jarring contact with unceasing mortality is too much for them to bear; life has lost its meaning and pleasures with no end in sight. The bliss with which they had contemplated perpetual youth has now turned sour, and their days are filled with contention, recrimination, and grief. Act Three initially resolves their plight: They have moved ahead in time another sixteen years. Another discovery from a similar saline distillation will enable them to become progressively younger until they return to the moment of birth and then . . . disappear! Each person accepts this option with glee, recognizing that by reversing the chronology of one's life, he can once again infuse his existence with meaning. This inversion of the natural order, however, effects an equal distortion upon the social and moral orders. The subjects' children and grandchildren are now obliged to care for their irresponsible parents who have passed 100 years of age and yet act more and more like adolescents. Bickering breaks out anew and contentions flourish. The play ends without a clear resolution after all: Each individual awaits the certain oblivion that will follow his infancy.

A pervasive levity obviates our taking seriously the work's occasional forays into philosophical musing. Jardiel's theater of superficial amusement reduces important problems to a level of nonsense and triviality, stripping thought of its intellectual challenge to supplant it with easy laughter.

A Round-Trip Husband [Un marido de ida y vuelta]

A Round-Trip Husband (premiere 1939) enjoyed an unusually clamorous and widespread success. Jardiel himself judged it "the most perfect work of art that our imperfect human state is capable of creating."[7] It is developed along highly improbable lines, not unlike other major productions of "Jardielismo." We meet the three main characters at a costume party hosted by a married couple named Leticia and Pepe. During the course of the evening Pepe extracts a promise from his best friend, Paco, that Paco will never marry Leticia in the event of Pepe's death. Suddenly, Pepe succumbs to a heart attack. In spite of his promise, Paco does marry Leticia, and this action so enrages the spirit of the departed Pepe that he returns as a ghost to reproach them both. He is still dressed in the bullfighter's costume that he had worn at the party when he died. Pepe's ghost convinces Leticia that she should leave Paco and that she should live alone until such time that she too departs mortality to join her late husband. Leticia intends to comply with Pepe's request and does so unexpectedly: In a sudden encounter with a truck, she too is whisked away to the great beyond.

Playgoers will recognize at once a striking thematic parallel between Jardiel's comedy of 1939 and Noel Coward's Blithe Spirit of 1941. Jardiel, in fact, accused Coward of plagiarism.[8] A Round-Trip Husband has more to commend it than a mere historical importance as forerunner to Coward's well-known play. The two ingredients that give the comedy its own dynamism are, first, the high level of sophisticated humor by which the comic conflict is upheld and, second, Jardiel's tender and compassionate treatment of his characters.

Heloise Lies Under an Almond Tree [Eloísa está debajo de un almendro]

Heloise (premiere 1940) is a play of bewildering, sophisticated madness. It consists of a long delightful prologue that has nothing whatever to do with the two acts that follow; a plot of great complexity that has relatively nothing to do with the play's popularity; no less than thirty characters, few of whom have any affiliation with rational behavior; and a staggering conglomeration of hilarious scenes that have no connection with the norms of conventional humor. *Heloise*, to be savored, must be viewed or read to be appreciated; for one who lacks a personal acquaintance with the play, only the broad surface mechanics of its construction can be apprehended.

The highly esteemed prologue to *Heloise* is a veritable *entremés*, an independent vignette of Madrilenean *costumbrismo*. Its action takes place in the last row of a *barrio* movie house where some nineteen moviegoers plus an usher face the audience in anticipation of the beginning of a film. Their antics, quips, repartee, and rejoinders serve to prepare our minds for the dazzling absurdities to follow. Subsequently, many strange people say and do many strange things throughout the two long acts of this strange comedy. Perhaps the strangest creature of them all is Edgardo Briones, who has spent over twenty years in bed listening to the radio, shooting his gun to test the nervous disposition of new maids, and pretending to travel every evening on a locomotive. His behavior conveys the greatest dramatic impact with a strong tinge of pathos, since it is the result of his having witnessed, several years before, the murder of his wife Heloise at the hands of his demented sister Micaela, whom he now protects by his own feigned madness in order to avoid sending her to an institution. He himself had buried Heloise in the garden under an almond tree.

Another unusual type is Ezequiel, who throughout the play is taken for a pathologic murderer. In truth he slays only cats for an experiment, but in recording the details of each assassination, he makes it appear as if his victims were women. Ezequiel is loved by a psychotic woman named Clotilde, whose affection for him is based on her suspicion that he dispatches his victims for purely sadistic pleasure. Yet another memorable abnormal character is the garrulous maid, Praxedes, an individual who talks to herself incessantly by asking and answering her own questions. This gallery of deranged or eccentric characters, thrown together in an excessive number of seemingly inexplicable actions and situations, is obliged to move about on a stage teeming with an outrageous number of furnishings. The play calls for the use of more physical props for a single stage setting than any other production of our time, with the possible exception of Ionesco's short farce *The New Tenant*.

Heloise contains all of the characteristics of Jardiel's passion for originality as well as all of the ingredients of that passion's intemperance. The superabundance of his audacity earned him a unique status in the annals of theatercraft, yet by his singular love for the unusual and his disdain for conventionality, he incurred the wrath of a reactionary press and a tradition-bound public. He then became overly sensitive and defensive in the face of adverse criticism and allowed his detractors to canker his soul. *Heloise* not only marks the high point of Jardiel's long-coveted triumph in the theater, but it heralds as well the coming tempest, a climate of rancor that will ultimately lead to his despair and will hasten his death.

We Thieves Are Honorable People [Los ladrones somos gente honrada]

We Thieves Are Honorable People (premiere 1941) builds on a progressive swell of complications, reversals, and improbable situations, which tend to mislead and taunt the audience with a constant intermeshing of false identities, assumed names, and unsuspected surprises. It opens with the intrusion of Daniel and his band of thieves at a wealthy manor where a party to celebrate Herminia's social debut is under way. The thieves' intended assault is suddenly thwarted when Daniel, the head thief, falls in love with the young heroine. Although she pretends to be an older, experienced, sophisticated woman, and he tries to pass as a refined, worldly gentleman, their respective masquerades do not impede a mutual affection. Within a few months' time, Daniel marries Herminia and brings one of his criminal companions to the mansion to serve as his butler. Two other thieves, miffed over their earlier failure to pull off the robbery, also enter the home, but they are obliged to pass as Daniel's poor relatives. This multiplication of simulation and disguise mushrooms into a hilarious game of cops and robbers. A police inspector, learning of an earlier crime involving Herminia's family, pretends to be a bungling hack detective in order to win the household's confidence. The inspector is fooled into thinking that one of the thieves, who is also attempting to clear up the mystery, is a famous sleuth. In the end, the original thieves collaborate with the police to solve the crime. They receive an acquittal for their efforts. Herminia's family, on the other hand, having appeared to be honest, upright, good-natured people, are guilty of a dastardly crime. The result is a delightful farce in which the clash between appearance and reality is sustained by the exaggeration of comic situations and by an interplay of deception and subterfuge on the part of all the characters.

The playwright's clever manipulation of false clues, misleading data, and shifting suspicions enlarges the mystery to such an extent that his spectators remain as baffled as the characters appear to be.

Blanca on the Outside and Rose Within
[Blanca por fuera y Rosa por dentro]

Conceived initially as a psychological comedy, *Blanca* (premiere 1943) proved to be an outrageous farce that sacrifices sound observation of character and solid construction for an amusing carnivalesque production employing more than the usual exaggeration of comic situations. Carried away by his fondness for shocking his audience with an incremental succession of complications derived from a single episode, Jardiel brings the action of this play to a state of pandemonium. From the opening scene, whose chaos is advanced by a fierce domestic squabble between the main characters, Blanca and Ramiro, to a closing scene of cosmic disorder, with the reenactment of a train derailment in the protagonists' living room, the play can best be described as a work of sustained hilarity and madness.

Jardiel's inventiveness is nowhere more apparent than in this play. At one point he brings together twelve characters and engages them in simultaneous action and dialogue. Perhaps his most noteworthy accomplishment is achieved by the use of several distancing techniques in the Brechtian manner. Even the characters seem free to identify with or to comment upon the zany proceedings. Both the real and the simulated train crashes required by the action, complete with special lighting and sound effects, signs, physical movement on and off stage, and overt parody, contribute in no small degree to establish the practical application of the so-called theory of alienation, wherein the audience observes but does not identify with the stage experience.

You and I Make Three [Tú y yo somos tres]

In You and I Make Three (premiere 1945), once again a Jardielesque characteristic prevails: Chaos evolves from a single happening. That single happening concerns the marriage-by-proxy of Manolina to Rodolfo, who appears before his bride arm in arm with his Siamese twin Adolfo. Manolina resolves to have the brothers separated, and thus she commissions Dr. Loriga to perform the delicate operation. Once the two men are detached, Adolfo, who exhibits certain tendencies toward being a scoundrel, departs into the world of riotous living. However, Adolfo's unrestrained dissipation effects serious consequences in Rodolfo, who suffers both physically and psychologically the results of his twin brother's extravagant behavior. Since Rodolfo cannot face the prospect of married life while still dependent in a psychic way on Adolfo, Manolina prompts an all-out effort to locate the profligate half of Rodolfo's personality. Once the prodigal is found, Dr. Loriga subjects the twins to a special therapy in order to restore to each his normal sense of individuality.

Technically, this is a good play, but it is no more revolutionary and renovating than any single play of Jardiel's earlier successful productions. Its humor borders at times on low comedy, and the situations often imply an attitude of mockery at the medical profession, reminiscent of Latin farces. The physician in this case, Dr. Loriga, is in fact a quack of a quite conventional character, just another undistinguished doctor who prescribes needless treatments and who receives many satirical buffetings in the name of stage amusement. With this play Jardiel has begun a long, painful, frustrating, and humiliating descent, not in terms of any loss of creativity or technical skill but in his overinsistence on launching absurdity for its own sake and his dogged persistence in defending himself against the verbal lampoons of his many detractors.

CRITICS' RESPONSE

In the same way that the preceeding eight plays accurately reflect Jardiel's significant achievements in the Spanish theater of humor, so too does the general critical response to those representative productions summarize the nature of the support for and the disdain toward his dramatic expressions.

A Sleepless Spring Night (1927), for example, was hailed "an outline of new intention" by Jardiel's chief advocate Alfredo Marqueríe. He declared that it set "the keynote for much of Jardiel's subsequent theater."[9] Elsewhere, Marqueríe lauded the rapid burlesque tone of its dialogue and the explosion of paradoxical situations, affirming that the work initiated the distinctive nature of Jardielesque humor, which would "be confirmed, ratified, and amplified in all the rest of the playwright's stage productions."[10]

While Jardiel basked in the luxury of much positive acclaim for his first "official" play, thanks principally to Alfredo Marqueríe's unqualified praise, he was also hounded by the first annoying outburst of gibes from several detractors. Unfortunately for his state of unease, Jardiel lacked resilience in the face of negative criticism. He singled out Enrique Díez-Canedo, for instance, for having "poisoned his happiness" with destructive comments.[11]

The hostility was augmented with *Angelina* (1934). Díez-Canedo condemned it "as perishable as the timeworn dramas it parodies."[12] In contrast to Díez-Canedo's rage, the famous Catalonian essayist and critic Eugenio d'Ors invited his readers of the Madrid newspaper *El Debate* to examine the original, thought-provoking notions and the unusual humor underlying Jardiel's lively parody.[13] Yet even d'Ors modified his favorable opinion some twelve years later, calling Jardiel "an eccentric of theater literature . . . who passed each day as if he were hallucinating."[14]

With the production of *Four Hearts* (1936), Jardiel's critics were more set on countering the playwright's self-laudatory expectations about the play's status as "an exceptional work in its genre"[15] than they were in judging its worth as dramatic comedy. This adversarial attitude diminished over the Civil War years, and by late 1939 there was even a tone of restraint and amelioration between Jardiel and his critics. *A Round-Trip Husband* (1939) fared so well in the Spanish capital that it was accorded an unprecedented spate of flattering reviews. In fact, the play was so well received that some of Jardiel's most relentless adversaries tended to yield their only recorded compliments to the playwright.

Heloise (1940), despite its tight construction and lavish embroidery, but also because of its surface incoherence, signaled a return to critical condemnation. Francisco Ruíz Ramón summarized its defects as "an operation of purely cerebral" exercise, overly concerned with plot development and a complicated intrigue at the sacrifice of character development and deeper meanings."[16]

Throughout the 1940s Alfredo Marqueríe continued to defend Jardiel against the unrestrained carping and sniping of his impassioned critics. He lauded Jardiel's technical mastery of the mystery genre in *We Thieves Are Honorable People* (1941), a play whose plot, he says, "is filled with constant and unsuspected surprises."[17] And with respect to the playwright's Brecht-like achievement of alienation in *Blanca* (1943), Marqueríe remarked how expertly Jardiel had managed to dehypnotize the spectators, "making them depart and then recover from the suggestion that the dialogue and the sweeping course of the action exercised upon them, obliging them to reflect and to reconsider the course of the comic or dramatic grotesque events to which they had been a witness."[18]

Marqueríe reserved his most energetic endorsement for *You and I Make Three* (1945), overcompensating perhaps for the intense barrage of critical derision that descended on this and other Jardielesque plays from most Spanish reviewers. He devoted the last section of a forty-seven-page monograph written about Jardiel's theater to this play.[19] Among his several epithets of praise, he called it "a revolutionary and renovating work . . . of exceptional comic value."[20] Marqueríe often allows his enthusiasm for the play to color his critical judgment; technically, it is a praiseworthy comedy, but it is no more "revolutionary and renovating" than any single play of Jardiel's earlier repertory. Acutely aware of the singular damage hostile criticism was doing to Jardiel's sense of well-being, Marqueríe became his unwavering protector in the press and seemingly his only advocate in critical circles.

AWARDS AND DISTINCTIONS

Jardiel Poncela's career as playwright, script writer, and novelist preceded the era of lavish literary awards. Nevertheless, he waggishly conferred a myriad of self-generated distinctions on his own stage productions and works of fiction. Owing to the negative judgments of his many detractors, the literary world did not accord him a recognition equal in splendor to his own positive assessments.

NOTES

1. See José López Rubio, Discourse: "La otra generación del '27," Madrid, Real Academia Española, 1983.

2. Francisco García Pavón, "Inventiva en el teatro de Jardiel Poncela: *Cuatro corazones con freno y marcha atrás*," in *El teatro de humor en España* (Madrid: Editora Nacional, 1966), 90.

3. See the summary of Jardiel's place in the contemporary theater of humor by María José Conde Guerri in *Insula* 50. 579 (1995): 11–13.

4. Alfredo Marqueríe mentions the following nine playwrights as having profited markedly by Jardiel's example: Edgar Neville, José López Rubio, Joaquín Calvo Sotelo, Miguel Mihura, Antonio de Lara (Tono), Alvaro de Laiglesia, Alfonso Paso, Carlos Llopis, and Juan José Alonso Millán. Based on remarks conveyed in personal correspondence with Alfredo Marqueríe, April 5, 1972.

5. *A Sleepless Spring Night* was the sixty-fourth play that Jardiel had written and the twelfth he had staged. He disavowed fifty-three titles in manuscript form, twenty-eight of which were written in collaboration with Serafín Adame Martínez. He also refused to release eleven plays for publication that had been performed between 1919 and 1926.

6. In the more than forty years since Jardiel's death, critical opinion has tended to vindicate the playwright's personal judgment. Francisco Ruíz Ramón, for example, agrees that together with *A Round-Trip Husband*, *Four Hearts* represents for its time the culmination of Jardiel's artistic passion for the absurd: *Four Hearts* was his prewar masterpiece, and *A Round-Trip Husband* was his most significant play of the post–Civil War period. See Francisco Ruíz Ramón, *Historia del teatro español* (Madrid: Alianza Editorial, 1971), 2:306.

7. Jardiel Poncela, *Obras completas*, I: 1106.

8. Quoted by Alfredo Marqueríe, "Novedad en el teatro de Jardiel," in *El teatro de humor en España* (Madrid: Editora Nacional, 1966), 77.

9. Quoted in Phyllis Zatlin-Boring, "The Bases of Humor in the Contemporary Spanish Theatre" (Ph.D. diss., University of Florida, 1966), 39.

10. Marqueríe, "Novedad en el teatro de Jardiel," 72.

11. See Alfredo Marqueríe, *Veinte anos de teatro en España* (Madrid: Editora Nacional, 1959), 66.

12. Enrique Díez-Canedo, *Artículos de crítica teatral: El teatro español de 1914 a 1936* (México: Joaquín Mortiz, 1968), 4:260–261.

13. Eugenio d'Ors's commentaries about Jardiel are reproduced in chapter 24 of Rafael Florez's gossipy compilation *Mío Jardiel* (Madrid: Biblioteca Nueva, 1966), 213–220.

14. Ibid., 222.

15. Francisco García Pavón, *Textos y escenarios* (Barcelona: Plaza y Janes, Editora, 1971), 104.

16. Ruíz Ramón, *Historia del teatro español*, 2:306.

17. Alfredo Marqueríe, *El teatro de Jardiel Poncela* (Bilbao: Ediciones de Conferencias y Ensayos, 1945), 15.

18. Marqueríe, "Novedad en el teatro de Jardiel," 77.

19. Marqueríe, *El teatro de Jardiel Poncela*, 15.

20. Ibid., 40, 46.

BIBLIOGRAPHY

Works

Obras teatrales escogidas. Madrid: Aguilar, 1964.
Obras completas. 5 vols. Barcelona: Editorial AHR, 1965.
Obra inédita. Barcelona: Editorial AHR, 1967.

Plays: Editions and Translations

Una noche de primavera sin sueño. Ed. Francisco C. Lacosta. New York: Appleton Century Crofts, 1967.
Eloísa está debajo de un almendro. Madrid: Centro Dramático Nacional, 1984.
Eloise Is under an Almond Tree. Trans. Steven Capsuto. In *Plays of the New Democratic Spain (1975–1990),* ed. Patricia W. O'Connor. Lanham, MD: University Press of America, 1992. 1–102.

Critical Studies

Books

Areza Viguera, Manuel. *Enrique Jardiel Poncela en la literatura humorística española.* Madrid: Editorial Frague, 1974.
Conde Guerri, María José. *El teatro de Enrique Jardiel Poncela (Una aproximación a los humoristas de la vanguardia española).* Zaragoza: Caja de Ahorros, 1984.
Cuevas García, Cristóbal. *Jardiel Poncela. Teatro, vanguardia y humor.* Málaga: Editorial Anthropus, 1993.
Díez Canedo, Enrique. *Artículos de crítica teatral. El teatro español de 1914 a 1936.* 4 vols. Méjico: Joaquín Mortiz, 1968.
Dougherty, Dru, and María Francisca Vilches de Frutos, eds. *El teatro en España. Entre la tradición y la vanguardia (1918–1939).* Madrid: Fundamentos, 1992.
Marqueríe, Alfredo. *El teatro de Jardiel Poncela.* Bilbao: Ediciones de Conferencias y Ensayos, 1945.
———. *Veinte años de teatro en España.* Madrid: Editorial Nacional, 1959. 61–73.
McKay, Douglas R. *Enrique Jardiel Poncela.* New York: Twayne, 1974.
Ruíz Ramón, Francisco. *Historia del teatro español. Siglo XX.* Madrid: Cátedra, 1975. 269–278.
El teatro de humor en España. Madrid: Editora Nacional, 1966.

Unpublished Dissertations

Hammarstrand, Robert Edward. "The Comic Spirit in the Plays of Enrique Jardiel Poncela." University of California, Berkeley, 1966.
Page, Richard J. "Humor in the Plays of Enrique Jardiel Poncela." University of Illinois, 1974.
Pérez Rasilla Bayo, Eduardo. "El teatro policiaco de Jardiel Poncela y otros autores del teatro español de posguerra (1940–1969)." Navarra, 1988.

Seaver, Paul William, Jr. "La primera época humorística de Enrique Jardiel Poncela, 1927–1936." University of Maryland, 1980.

Articles

See also articles by diverse authors compiled by Cuevas García and in *El teatro de humor en España*, cited above.

Anderson, Farris. "Hacia el teatro de Jardiel Poncela: Una noche de primavera sin sueño." *Papeles de Son Armadans* (Mallorca) 68 (1973): 313–340.

Antlitz, Horst Kassel. "Enrique Jardiel Poncela und das Moderne Spanische Theater." *Maske und Kothurn* I (1965): 55–77.

García Ruíz, Víctor. "Teatro español de preguerra y de posguerra: Ruptura y continuidad." *Journal of Hispanic Research* 1 (1992–1993): 371–382.

Kaatz, Gerda R. "Three Escapes from Reality: Pirandello's 'Henry IV,' Durrenmatt's 'Die Physiker' and Jardiel Poncela's 'Eloísa está debajo de un almendro.' " *Language Quarterly* 17. 1.2 (1978): 33–38, 47.

Seaver, Paul William, Jr. "La desmitificación del donjuanismo en las obras de Enrique Jardiel Poncela." *Hispanic Journal* 8.2 (1987): 51–66.

Studies Not Recommended

The following published writings are generally included in bibliographies pertaining to Jardiel Poncela, but they lack either reliability, critical substance, or scholarly value.

Bonet Gelabert, Juan. *El discutido indiscutible. Jardiel Poncela*. Madrid: Biblioteca Nueva, 1946.

Canay, Alberto. *Recuerdo y presencia de Enrique Jardiel Poncela*. Buenos Aires: Edición del autor, 1958.

Escudero, Carmen. *Nueva aproximación a la dramaturgia de Jardiel Poncela*. Murcia: Universidad de Murcia, 1981.

Florez, Rafael. *Jardiel Poncela*. Madrid: EPESA, 1975.

———. *Mío Jardiel: (Jardiel Poncela está debajo de un almendro en flor)*. 1966. Madrid: Gráficas Pedraza, 1993.

JOSÉ LÓPEZ RUBIO
(1903–1996)

Marion Peter Holt

BIOGRAPHY

As a playwright, film scenarist, and author of innovative teleplays, José López Rubio enjoyed a successful career that spanned almost six decades. He also translated some twenty foreign plays for the Madrid stage, directed six films between 1940 and 1947, and published a novel and a collection of short stories. Born in the Mediterranean city of Motril on December 13, 1903, he spent his childhood in Granada, where from an early age he saw numerous productions of touring theater companies. An influential part of his secondary education was at the Colegio de los Agustinos in Madrid, and he would maintain close ties with teaching members of the Augustinian order in later years. After a period of study at Madrid's Universidad Central, he gave up formal education to pursue a literary career. By 1926, he was an editor of the magazine *Buen Humor*, attempting to write for the theater with his friend Enrique Jardiel Poncela and attending the influential literary gatherings presided over by the unconventional Ramón Gómez de la Serna. He also participated in the avant-garde theater group El mirlo blanco [The White Blackbird].

In 1928, the Madrid daily *ABC* sponsored a playwriting contest for new authors, guaranteeing a professional production for the winning entry. The first prize, chosen from 884 plays submitted, went to *De la noche a la mañana* [Overnight], an intellectual comedy that López Rubio had written in collaboration with Eduardo Ugarte. Performed in 1929 at the Teatro Reina Victoria, with Josefina Díaz and her husband Santiago Artigas in leading roles, it was a critical and popular success. The following year, *La casa de naipes* [The House of Cards], a second play by López Rubio and Ugarte, was staged at the Teatro Español by the capable director Cipriano Rivas Cherif.

López Rubio had also collaborated with another friend, Edgar Neville, on several plays that never reached the stage, and it was Neville, now the Spanish consul in Los Angeles, who was instrumental in obtaining for López Rubio and Ugarte a contract with MGM to adapt several of the studio's early talking pictures for Spanish versions. On his first day in Hollywood, the young playwright met Charles Chaplin and soon became a regular guest at Chaplin's social gatherings for international celebrities and leading figures of the film world. When MGM closed its Spanish department in 1932, López Rubio moved to Fox Films (later 20th Century Fox), where he acquired experience in all aspects of filmmaking and participated in the production of some fifteen Spanish-language films.

Although busily engaged in screenwriting, López Rubio had not lost interest in the theater. In 1935 he began a new play, *Celos del aire*, which would establish him as a major dramatist some fifteen years later. He completed more than half of the first act before returning to Spain under contract to direct several films in his homeland. The filming of the first production, a version of Benavente's *La malquerida* (known as *The Passion Flower* in the United States, was scheduled to begin on July 20, 1936, but was halted by the outbreak of the Spanish Civil War. He soon left for France, where he completed the first act of his new play before returning to the United States to work for Fox again. In 1939 he went to Mexico to prepare a script for the filming of Jorge Isaac's novel *Maria*; however, the war in Spain ended, and he returned to Madrid. In 1940 the filming of the postponed *La Malquerida* was finally realized, and until 1947, López Rubio devoted himself principally to scriptwriting and directing. Still, he found time to write for the stage again, completing two new plays, *Alberto* and *Una madeja de lana azul celeste* [A Skein of Sky Blue Wool]. His translation of Benn W. Levy's *Mrs. Moonlight* [El tiempo dormido] was staged in 1947 and, the following year, his new Spanish version of Molière's *Le bourgeois gentilhomme*.

The premiere of the seriocomic *Alberto* on April 29, 1949, marked the beginning of López Rubio's second career as a playwright and the start of his most important and intense period of creative activity for the theater. *Celos del aire*, which had been completed at the urging of director Cayetano Luca de Tena, opened less that a year later at the Teatro Español. It elicited admiring praise from both critics and audiences and confirmed the playwright's position in the contemporary Spanish theater. In 1951 three new plays by López Rubio reached the stage: *Veinte y cuarenta* [Twenty and Forty], another serious comedy with touches of engaging whimsy; *Cena de Navidad* [Christmas Dinner], an atypical serious drama; and *Una madeja de lana azul celeste*, a minor sophisticated marital comedy. For the season of 1952, he wrote *El remedio en la memoria* [Remedy in Memory], a serious Pirandellian tour de force dedicated to the actress Tina Gascó. That season he also adapted Miller's *Death of a Salesman* and Wilde's *The Importance of Being Earnest*.

With the production of *La venda en los ojos* [The Blindfold] in March 1954, López Rubio added substantially to his reputation. The play dealt with a young wife's creation of a feigned delusion to cope with her husband's callous desertion. With its blend of near-absurdist humor, genuine human conflicts, and a dramatic situation that suggested the influence of Evreinov's concepts of "theatre in life," it was the author's most important play since *Celos del aire*. Yet his next play, *Cuenta nueva* [A New Account], turned out to be one of his least successful and was dismissed by critics at its Barcelona premiere as dated and discursive. A few weeks after the Barcelona failure, López Rubio had occasion to forget, for the first performance of *La otra orilla* [The Other Shore], on November 4, 1954, was met with the kind of enthusiastic approval accorded *La venda en los ojos*. The plot of this seriocomic "ghost" play harked back to the playwright's effective use of the fantastic in *De la noche a la mañana*. Contributing to the play's success were the skillful direction of Edgar Neville and the acting of the talented comedienne Conchita Montes.

López Rubio's next venture was a musical comedy entitled *El caballero de Barajas* [The Gentleman from Barajas], for which he wrote the book and lyrics. Manuel Parada composed the score, and the playwright himself directed the production in September 1955. The same year his adaptation of Rodgers and Hammerstein's *South Pacific* [Al sur del Pacífico] opened to favorable critical reception; however, the musical did not create the kind of public enthusiasm it had enjoyed in the United States. In February 1956, the playwright presented another new work in Barcelona, only to meet with the most unequivocal failure of his career. With it extraterrestrial theme, *La novia del espacio* [The Love from Space] might have been expected to have considerable appeal, but the critical comments were uniformly negative. *Un trono para Cristy* [A Throne for Cristy], which also opened in 1956, was a more typical comedy dealing with the efforts of an American woman living in Mallorca to achieve royal status for her daughter.

The following year, at the beginning of the theatrical season, López Rubio offered a totally atypical work, different in its stark treatment of guilt from either his seriocomic plays or the essentially serious dramas *Cena de Navidad* and *El remedio en la memoria*. Modern in tone but a tightly constructed play of classical lineage, *Las manos son inocentes* [Our Hands Are Innocent] dealt with the power of economic deprivation to break down moral constraints and to bring a middle-aged couple to the point of attempting a bloodless murder. In spite of the play's excellence, the public reception was lukewarm, and López Rubio never thwarted his audiences' expectations again with a work of such tragic implications. His next two plays were comedies, replete with humorous situations, sparkling dialogue, and deft touches of satire. Both *Diana está comunicando* [Diana's Mind Is Busy] (1960) and *Esta noche, tampoco* [Not Tonight, Either] (1961) were designed for the talents of the popular Conchita Montes, whom López Rubio habitually referred to as his favorite actress.

Now, after more than fifteen years of almost continual involvement in the theater—writing, translating, and participating in various aspects of production— López Rubio slowed his pace. He had found a retreat in a turn-of-the-century hotel in San Lorenzo de El Escorial, where the air was clear and yet the lights of Madrid were visible in the distance at night. He also began to travel widely, taking trips to South America and Scandanavia. Although several of his translations were staged, it was not until 1964 that his next original play, *Nunca es tarde* [It's Never Too Late] had its premiere. In some respects the play was in the style of his best seriocomic works and had an optimistic ending; at the same time it was decidedly a pièce noire in which a principal character is killed at the end of the second act.

In the winter of 1966–1967, López Rubio accepted an invitation from Hiram College in Ohio to be playwright-in-residence, and he returned to the United States for the first time in twenty-eight years. After his stay at Hiram, he conducted seminars at the State University of New York in Albany and at the University of Missouri at St. Louis before traveling on to California to revisit the film capital. On his return to Spain he wrote *La puerta del ángel* [The Way of the Angel], a serious drama with frank sexual motivations. Since no producer was willing to deal with the potential objections of the censors, he put the play aside and found a new and productive outlet for his creative talents in television drama. His series of short plays called *Al filo de lo imposible* [At the Edge of the Impossible] was telecast in 1970. One of the best of the series, *Veneno activo* [Active Poison] was adapted for the stage and opened at the Café Teatro Stefanis in 1971. The following year, López Rubio returned to the stage with an original full-length play, *El corazón en la mano* [With Heart in Hand]. Although it lacked the sheer theatricality of the playwright's most memorable works, it was a compelling and topical play deemed worthy of the National Prize for Drama for 1972. Returning to television drama, López Rubio wrote his second series of teleplays, entitled *Mujeres insólitas* [Exceptional Women], after extensive research into the lives of some thirteen famous women of history and the literary treatments or legends they had inspired.

On June 3, 1983, López Rubio occupied a seat of the Spanish Royal Academy to join the small number of contemporary dramatists to receive this highest recognition for literary achievement. His induction presentation, in which he recalled and defined the aesthetics of his contemporaries (Tono, Jardiel Poncela, Neville, and Mihura) was titled "La otra generación del 27" [The Other Generation of 27]; it remains an essential document on the group of seriocomic writers who had experienced the intellectual ferment of the 1920s. With censorship no longer an issue, *La puerta del ángel* reached the stage at last in 1986 under the direction of Cayetano Luca de Tena, who had prompted López Rubio to complete *Celos del aire* more than three decades earlier. In 1990 a successful revival of *Celos del aire* in Madrid's Centro Cultural de la Villa provided a decisive reconfirmation of López Rubio's distinctive talents, and Spain's senior playwright stepped onstage to receive the warm applause of a new generation of theatergoers. The continued appeal of his serious comedies was demonstrated again by a revival of *La otra orilla* at the Teatro Maravillas in 1995, with the king and queen of Spain in attendance on opening night to honor the playwright.

DRAMATURGY: MAJOR WORKS AND THEMES

Although José López Rubio's nineteen full-length plays vary considerably in concept, theme, and importance, none is without scenes that illustrate his skillfully measured and often ironic dialogue as well as his talent for delineating character subtly. His best works are skillfully structured, with a masterly melding of dialogue and visual effect. Too often the early plays he wrote with Ugarte are treated as historical footnotes, and neither has been revived since its original staging. Nevertheless, both are accomplished theatrical pieces, and both reflect themes and scenic devices that figure in several of the plays of López Rubio's second career.

As the title suggests, the action of *De la noche a la mañana* [Overnight] takes place literally overnight. Early in the play the protagonist, Mateo, is joined onstage by the physical representation of his *conciencia*, called Don Mateo. Their late-night discussion is interrupted by the unexpected arrival of an impetuous young woman (Silvia) and her blasé husband (Jacobo), who are seeking shelter from the rain after their car has broken down. In the course of events, both Mateo and his better self, Don Mateo, become hopelessly infatuated with the provocative and illogical Silvia. At the end of the play, Silvia and Jacobo depart as quickly as they had arrived. Don Mateo rushes off in hopeless pursuit of his love, leaving Mateo without his *conciencia* and in mental confusion. With its convincing treatment of the unreal as real, its skillful blending of dialogue and visual symbolism, and its experiment with Pirandellian role-playing, *De la noche a la mañana* could never be confused with a drawing-room comedy by Benavente.

In *La casa de naipes*, López Rubio and Ugarte turned from the highly fanciful to the treatment of ordinary people in realistic dramatic conflicts. The setting is the Madrid pension of Doña Rita, whose daughter Elena is being educated as a "señorita." Two of the boarders, the professional magician Alejandro and a law student named Andrés, are attracted to Elena. Finding Andrés too indecisive, Elena goes off with Alejandro. In the final act she returns, sadly disillusioned, to try to recapture Andrés's interest; but it is too late. The play is rich in nonverbal effects, such as the sound of a music student playing a simple practice exercise throughout the opening scenes. The most startling and imaginative scene ends with a performance of magical tricks by Alejandro. As a pigeon flies from a hat, a secondary character tosses a plate to Doña Rita, who is caught off guard. The plate shatters, providing an unconventional curtain for the first act as well as a prefiguration of the failures to come.

When López Rubio returned definitively to the theater in 1949, it was with a play that had some obvious similarities to *La casa de naipes* as well as aesthetic differences. *Alberto* is also set in a pension, and the theme of the play is the creation and destruction of illusions. However, the new element is the use of theater-within-theater as a plot device. In this case, the boarders invent an imaginary personality to take charge when the owner of the pension leaves to join a man she has loved in memory for some thirty years. The instigator for the creation of "Alberto" is a young stenographer named Leticia, who has a hyperactive imagination. Ultimately, her fiancé resorts to inventing a "play" in which Alberto is portrayed as weak and capable of deceit to cure Leticia of her growing obsession with a man who is only a fiction. The "cure" has a stunning effect on Leticia, and the play ends with her note of uncertainty about reality and illusion.

In virtually all of López Rubio's plays, self-theatricalization occurs to some degree, and illusion may fail or triumph; yet only a few of his plays are authentic "metaplays" in the strictest application of Abel's original definition of metatheatre. *Alberto*, the first of these, not only contains role-playing-within-the-role and plays-within-the-play, but the dramatic action centers on the concept of life as theater and the characters exist essentially as self-dramatizers to serve the playwright's exploration of the illusion-reality conundrum.

While *Alberto* provided a clear reconfirmation of López Rubio's talent, *Celos del aire* established him as Spain's finest creator of serious comedy at that point in time. The setting for this impeccably constructed metaplay is a remote country house in the Pyrenees, in "a year without war." The elderly owners, Don Pedro and Doña Aurelia, have rented their house for the summer because their resources have dwindled; however, they have insisted on a pretense that divides the house into two worlds and admit no direct communication with their younger tenants, Bernardo and Cristina. An old servant named Gervasio comically recognizes either couple when it is expedient. Cristina is uncontrollably jealous, even when she has her husband completely isolated from potential rivals. When Enrique, a playwright, arrives with his wife Isabel for the weekend, he recommends that Bernardo pretend to deceive Cristina with Isabel to cure her. In reality that pretense is unnecessary, since Bernardo and Isabel have been having an affair. The subsequent action is viewed in part by Don Pedro and Doña Aurelia who sit at one side in their armchairs as an onstage audience. Cristina changes the course of events by taking over as "director" and ordering Enrique to feign a love scene with her for the benefit of Bernardo and Isabel. When the playwright can think of nothing to say, Cristina tells him to recite the names of the provinces of Spain in a romantic way. In the final act, Isabel senses that Bernardo is falling in love with his wife again and decides that it is time to bow out. But she has a moment of vengeance before her exit. Earlier, Cristina had discovered the adulterous pair in the garden in a "love scene." She is not certain whether it was staged for her benefit or played in sincerity; Isabel coldly tells her it was for real. The final dialogue falls to the elderly pair. They have also faced the problem of deception, and their union has survived. By listening to a retelling of a marital crisis that had occurred years before, Cristina and Bernardo are able to apply the narrated reconciliation to their own lives. References to theater abound in the dialogue as the characters almost gleefully resort to self-dramatization as a means to self-realization.

In writing *La venda en los ojos*, some three years after the staging of *Celos del aire*, the playwright allowed his imagination free rein, creating his most affecting play and, arguably, his best. This seriocomic metaplay opens with a highly amusing comic twist that is a send-up of a clichéd exposition scene. A maid relates to a younger servant newly arrived from the provinces the scandalous things she has observed. Then she abruptly discloses that she had been talking about her former employers, and the audience realizes that nothing that has been said in the opening scene has anything to do with what is to follow. At that point, Carolina, the elderly aunt of the protagonist, Beatriz, enters and casually asks the maid if she has informed the new girl that everyone in the house is utterly mad. It is an overstatement, but there is much subsequent behavior to make it seem plausible. Ten years earlier, Beatriz's husband Eugenio had failed to return from a business trip to Barcelona, but she has continued to go to the airport every morning as if no time had elapsed. She also has lengthy telephone conversations with a supposedly imaginary friend. At the end of the first act she brings home a substitute Eugenio who is actually an architect named Germán. To the dismay of her aunt and uncle, Germán elects to play the role of Eugenio. The uncle is in the habit of luring potential buyers to the apartment by advertising false objets d'art, and the aunt dresses in different costumes according to her mood. The buyer of the day is fascinated by the bizarre behavior and remains through much of the play as an audience for these energetic self-dramatizers. When the real Eugenio returns in the final act, Beatriz rejects him in a powerful confrontation scene and proceeds to manipulate time once again, now reversing it to a year before she had even met her real husband. In a final telephone monologue she implies that she will recreate her life with a young architect named Germán. A telephone is frequently used for plot purposes in López Rubio's plays, but in no other play except the teleplay *El último hilo* is it so fundamental to the dramatic situation.

In *La venda en los ojos* all the significant influences on López Rubio's dramaturgy are in evidence. A strong affinity with Evreinov's "theatre in life" can be seen in the dramatic action; the amusing and unexpected shifts from logic in the dialogue reflect an aesthetic akin to that of Jardiel Poncela as well as the influence of Ramón Gómez de la Serna. In the dialogue there are several direct references to Hollywood and cinema, and there is a hint of the Hollywood madcap comedies that the playwright came to know in the 1930s. The moments of poetic eloquence, as in Beatriz's re-creation of her honeymoon for the substitute Eugenio, are as measured as they are dramatically effective. Since Beatriz's rewriting of life's script to improve it represents a striving toward an ideal, *La venda en los ojos* may best be described as a Quixotian metaplay.

La otra orilla, the third of López Rubio's most important seriocomic plays, differs from its predecessors in the use of the supernatural and a shift from the more overt metatheatricality of *La venda en los ojos* and *Celos del aire*. The four principal characters are killed in the opening moments of the play and then appear as ghosts who can discuss their predicament among themselves but cannot communicate with the survivors. An adulterous couple, Leonardo and Ana, are shot by Ana's "wronged" husband, Jaime, who is in turn killed by the police. The fourth victim, Martín, had been walking his dog and happened to get in the way of Jaime's first shot. As their survivors begin to arrive, all of the betrayals and mistakes of their former existences are laid bare with telling comic irony. The second act ends with the startling news that one of the four "dead" characters is only in a coma. Through gradual elimination it becomes apparent which of the characters are really dead, for they begin to disappear through the French windows of the living room: first Jaime, and then Leonardo. When Martín and Ana are alone, Martín declares his love for a woman he has met in a postmortem situation. Now Ana begins to disappear, and Martín calls after her in desperation. The telephone rings and a policeman (as well as Martín and the audience) receives the news that the surviving victim has now died. Thus the plays ends as Martín vanishes through the windows calling Ana's name. Unlike Coward's *Blithe Spirit* and Jardiel's *Un marido de ida y vuelta* [A Round-Trip Husband], plays in which ghosts figure prominently, *La otra orilla* develops from the perspective of the ghosts rather than that of the living characters, and the audience's interest is focused on them.

López Rubio's other major play of the 1950s, *Las manos son inocentes*, represents a total departure from his most familiar style and is his only work of tragic implications. While *Cena de Navidad, El remedio en la memoria*, and the later *La puerta del ángel* are indeed serious dramas, they still reflect the playwright's metatheatrical bent either in scenes or in concept. The playwright called the work a *comedia dramática* rather than a tragedy—though the title is derived from a passage in Racine's *Phèdre*. A critical event that is fundamental to the action takes place just before the opening scene of the play. It is the death of a boarder who had been living in the shabby apartment of Germán and Paula, a middle-aged couple beset by failure and in dire financial need. Tempted by the money the boarder had in his possession, they had plotted to poison him. The inner action of the two acts develops from a series of revelations concerning the actual cause of death. Ultimately, an autopsy proves that the supposed victim had died of natural causes; however, Germán and Paula must carry with them the guilt of a crime they intended to commit. *Las manos son inocentes* is a modern work in a classical mode; the unities are carefully observed; a woman concierge functions as a chorus, and a modern device, the telephone, serves as the "messenger." The dramatic tension is achieved through the reversal of the situation and revelations progressing through three stages. This play must be included among López Rubio's most important works for the stage, and it is essential to any consideration of the scope of his dramatic talent and the literary merits of his plays.

Unquestionably, López Rubio's most inventive and memorable writing of his later career is in his two series of teleplays. The episodes of *Al filo de lo imposible* vary considerably in theme, style, and mood—from black ironic comedies such as *La casi viuda* [Almost a Widow] to a two-part Jardielesque romp about bungling kidnappers entitled *El secuestro* [The Kidnapping] and *El rescate*

[(The Ransoming)]. In a totally different vein there is the outstanding *El último hilo* [The Last Connection], a riveting depiction of old age and lost illusions. In yet another mode, *Veneno activo* [Active Poison] is an exercise in ironic, macabre theater in which the dialogue is intentionally deformed to resemble an overly literal translation from the French. The second series, *Mujeres insólitas*, deals with thirteen famous women of history who have been subjects of literary treatments and legend and the descrepancies between historical fact and imaginative literary recreations. Some of the subjects, such as Cleopatra, Alfonsine Plessis (Camille), and Lola Montés are known internationally; others such as Juana la Loca and Inés de Castro are less familiar outside the Iberian peninsula. Each teleplay opens on a bare set, with a stage manager (Pepe) and the protagonist present on stage. Distancing effects are used liberally, and the scenes from dramatic treatments of the women's lives by Shakespeare, Tamayo y Baus, and others are interpolated with originality and dramatic impact.

CRITICS' RESPONSE

The productions of López Rubio's first collaborative plays in 1929 and 1930 elicited favorable critical response with minor reservations. Both stagings profited from the participation of leading figures of the Madrid stage whose talents no doubt contributed to the attention given the two plays. By the time the dramatist returned to the theater in 1949, Spain had passed through the Civil War and a decade of dictatorship. The critics of Madrid's dailies, most notably the respected Alfredo Marqueríe of *ABC*, were generally favorable to his best works and mildly critical of the perceived flaws of lesser efforts. Invariably there was praise for the scintillating and often eloquent dialogue as well as for the careful construction of most of his plays. In Barcelona the reception was often more tempered—though Angel Zúñiga of *La Vanguardia* did not hesitate to lavish warm praise on *Celos del aire*. Enrique Sordo, critic for the weekly *Revista*, reviewed many of the stagings of López Rubio's plays and translations in Barcelona, at times with rather grudging respect and at other times with sharp disapproval. Most critics focused on the text of the plays itself and the participation of leading actors; however, there is scant record of overall production values or ways in which stagings may have affected the public and critical reception of the plays. Intentionally or otherwise, few noted the delightfully subversive lines that evaded the censors of the dictatorship. In the 1950s anti-establishment critics such as Juan Emilio Aragonés and José Monleón often referred to the plays of López Rubio and his contemporaries as "teatro de evasión." For these critics the term identified plays that in any sense were perceived to evade reality through illusion or theatricalism or that seemed to uphold the conservative values of Spanish society. In practice it was applied to works of the most divergent themes and dramatic styles without regard for aesthetic values. With the successful revivals of *Celos del aire* (1990) and *La otra orilla* (1995), a younger generation of critics in democratic Spain have seen the plays as enduring comic pieces within the larger context of Spanish humoristic theater. The most detailed critical studies of individual plays are by Holt (*Alberto* and *Las manos son inocentes*) and Zatlin (*Celos del aire*), published in scholarly journals in the United States. Articles by José María Torrijos and Eduardo Pérez-Rasilla have provided new insights into the influences on and the artistic aims of the playwright and his generation.

Of all of López Rubio's works, *Celos del aire* is the play most widely admired and deemed illustrative of his finest writing for the stage. The ironic humor, polished dialogue, and a dramatic development that has both intellectual and emotional appeal have given this play enduring viability. *Celos del aire* lacks the humorous sublots of López Rubio's other major seriocomic plays and focuses principally on the intrigues of two couples, observed and commented on by the elderly pair who enter directly into the action in the final moments of the play. While the play has always been admired for its verbal grace, the dialogue is frequently punctuated with stage directions for silences, a suggestion from the playwright that this is not a brisk farce but rather an intellectual comedy. One of the most memorable scenes, involving an uncertain Cristina and the watchful older couple, is totally silent, and the thought is conveyed by the actors through movement and facial expression. This self-reflective comedy, in which the actors declare their own theatricality and become directors of their own playacting, is an unequivocal metaplay in which life is theatricalized on many levels with engaging abandon.

AWARDS AND DISTINCTIONS

1928: *ABC* Prize for New Playwrights for *De la noche a la mañana* (shared with Eduardo Ugarte).

1950: Fastenrath Prize of the Royal Spanish Academy for *Celos del aire*. Rosario de Santa Fe Prize for best foreign production (Argentina) for *Celos del aire*.

1954: National Theatre Prize for *La venda en los ojos*.

1955: María Rolland Prize for *El caballero de Barajas* (shared with composer Manuel Parada).

1970: National Prize for Television and the "Ondas" Television Prize for *Al filo de lo imposible*.

1983: Elected to seat "ñ" of the Real Academia Española.

1990: *ABC* Gold Medal and the Mayte Prize for Theatre.

BIBLIOGRAPHY

Editions and Translations

The following plays by López Rubio were published by Escelicer in the series "Colección Teatro" (CT) between 1951 and 1974: *Celos del aire* (CT2), *Cena de Navidad*

(CT7), *Una madeja de lana azul celeste* (CT14), *Alberto* and *Veinte y cuarenta* (CT30), *El remedio en la memoria* (CT48), *Estoy pensandao en ti* (one act)(included in CT100), *La venda en los ojos* (CT101), *La otra orilla* (CT119), *El caballero de Barajas* (CT151), *Un trono para Cristy* (CT174), *De la noche a la mañana* and *La casa de naipes* (CT190), *Las manos son inocentes* (CT272), *Diana está comunicando* (CT331), *Esta noche, tampoco* (CT461), *Nunca es tarde* (CT464), *El corazón en la mano* (CT759). Ten of López Rubio's translations also appeared in the same series.

The following plays were included in the yearly anthology *Teatro español*, published by Aguilar and edited by F. Sainz de Robles, with selected reviews and the playwright's *autocríticas*: *Celos del aire* (1949–1950), *Veinte y cuarenta* (1950–1951), *Una madeja de lana azul celeste* (1951–1952), *La venda en los ojos* (1953–1954), *La otra orilla* (1954–1955), *Las manos son inocentes* (1958–1959), *Diana está comunicando* (1959–1960), *Esta noche, tampoco* (1961–1962), *Nunca es tarde* (1964–1965).

Homenaje a José López Rubio: Celos del aire. Ed. José María Torrijos. Madrid: Centro Cultural de la Villa, 1990. (The definitive text of the play, with tributes by editor Torrijos, Conchita Montes, Juan José Alonso Millán, Fernando Lázaro Carreter, and Francisco Nieva).

Translations

The Blindfold. Trans. Marion [Peter] Holt. In *The Modern Spanish Stage: Four Plays*, ed. Marion [Peter] Holt. New York: Hill & Wang, 1970.
In August We Play the Pyrenees (*Celos del aire*). Trans. Marion Peter Holt. University Park, PA: Estreno, 1992.

Works

Alberto. Madrid: Editora Nacional, 1949.
Al filo de lo impossible. Ed. José Luis Herrera. Madrid: Ediciones Guadarrama, 1971. (16 teleplays from the series).
Celos del aire. Madrid: Publicaciones Españolas, 1950.
Cuentos inverosímiles. Madrid: Rafael Caro Raggio, 1924.
Entrevista con la madre Teresa de Jesús. Madrid: Biblioteca de Autores Cristianas, 1982.
La otra generación del 27: Discurso leído el día 5 de junio de 1983, en su recepción pública, por el Excmo. Sr. Don José López Rubio y contestación del Excmo. Sr. Don Fernando Lázaro Carreter. Madrid: Real Academia Española, 1983.
La otra orilla. Introduction by José María Torrijos. Madrid: Sociedad General de Autores, 1995.
La otra orilla/Las manos son inocentes. Colección Austral 1678. Madrid: Espasa-Calpe, 1988.
La puerta del ángel. Madrid: Ediciones Antonio Machado, 1987.
Roque Six. Madrid: Rafael Caro Raggio, 1927.
Son triste. Granada: Ediciones Antonio Ubaga, 1996.
Teatro select de José López Rubio. Madrid: Escelicer, 1969. (Contains *Celos del aire, La venda en los ojos, La otra orilla, Las manos son inocentes, Nunca es tarde*).

Critical Studies

Holt, Marion Peter. *José López Rubio*. Boston: Twayne/G. K. Hall, 1980.

———. "López Rubio's *Alberto*: Character Revelation and Form." *Modern Drama* 10.2 (1967): 144–150.

———. "López Rubio's Venture into Serious Drama." *Hispania* 49.4 (1966): 764–768.

———. "The Metatheatrical Impulse in Post–Civil War Spanish Comedy." In *The Contemporary Spanish Theater: A Collection of Critical Essays*, ed. Martha T. Halsey and Phyllis Zatlin. Lanham, MD: University Press of America, 1988. 79–91.

López Rubio, José. Interview with Eladio Cortés. *Estreno* 4 (1978): 6–7.

Pérez-Rasilla, Eduardo. "José López Rubio y la otra generación del 27." *Reseña* 28.221 (1991): 2–7.

Pinto, Alfonso. "Hollywood's Spanish Language Films: A Neglected Chapter of the American Cinema, 1930–1935." *Films in Review* 24.8 (1973): 474–483.

Torres, Augusto M., ed. *Cine español: 1896–1983*. Madrid: Editora Nacional, 1984. 110–112, 342.

Torrijos, José María. "Chaplin y los humoristas españoles: A la sombra de Hollywood." *Reseña* 199 (1989): 2–6.

———. "El más antiguo alumno: José López Rubio cumple 90 años." *L.E.A.: La Escuela Agustiana* 47 (1994): 34–44.

———. "El otro grupo del 27: Del humor al teatro." *Religión y Cultura* 35 (1989): 397–418.

Zatlin, Phyllis. "López Rubio and the Well-Made Metaplay." *Modern Drama* 32.4 (1989): 512–520.

FRANCISCO MARTÍNEZ DE LA ROSA
(1787–1862)

Robert Mayberry and Nancy Mayberry

BIOGRAPHY

In his history *The Spirit of the Age* [El espíritu del siglo], Francisco Martínez de la Rosa described his birth as follows: "I was born at the outbreak of the French Revolution, as if fate, I know not if fortunately or unfortunately, had destined me to be a witness to the grave events that in a short time have turned the world upside down" [Cabalmente nací al estallar la revolución francesa; como si la suerte, no sé si por fortuna o por desgracia, me hubiese destinado a ser testigo de los graves acontecimientos que en poco tiempo han trastornado el mundo].[1] In fact, the author's works reflect this lifelong interest in political, historical, and moral theory, particularly the problem of how to balance freedom from tyranny with justice and order. The play for which he is best known, *The Venice Conspiracy* [La conjuración de Venecia], is based on this same preoccupation and has the honor of being the drama generally accorded the distinction of having introduced the Romantic movement to Spain.

Born on March 10, 1787, in Granada into a wealthy family, the youth received an excellent education, excelling in classical studies, philosophy, and logic.[2] At the age of fifteen he entered the University of Granada and two years later, in 1805, received the Doctor of Civil Law. The following year, at the astonishingly young age of eighteen, he was granted the chair of moral philosophy at the University of Granada. Martínez's literary education was based on the strictly neoclassical principles of the eighteenth century as they had been outlined in Luzán's *Poética* (1737). These included the imitation of Greek and Latin models where certain rules of form were considered inviolable. In drama this included a strict observance of the unities of time, place, and action, in five acts of hendecasyllabic verse. The didactic function of literature was valued over entertainment, with reason, restraint, balance, measure, and harmony being the stylistic ideals. Under this influence, the author's first literary endeavors involved neoclassic poetry—satiric epigrams, patriotic and religious odes—in the style and form of the classical poets.

In political theory, Martínez was a follower of the English theorist Jeremy Bentham, who believed that political institutions and laws should serve moral and social ethics. Moral philosophy was the other shaping influence in both Martínez's literary production and his politics. He was incensed, for example, at Napoleon's treacherous invasion of Spain in 1808, and he wrote newspaper articles denouncing the emperor. Other political activities included patriotic odes and a military venture to Gibraltar in 1808, where he acquired ammunition and rifles for the Spanish resistance. He also took a trip to England in 1810, the motive for which is shrouded in secrecy but which may have involved a secret mission for the Spanish Central Junta. On his return from England, his family having moved to Cadiz, Martínez settled in that city where his career as a dramatist began.

Martínez's political writings, poems, and plays brought him sufficient renown to have him elected in 1813 to the Cortes as a deputy from his native Granada. One political action was to have disastrous effects. He introduced a bill in the Cortes forbidding the alteration of the 1812 constitution for eight years. The king, Fernando VII, on his return to Spain from a French prison in 1814, annulled the constitution, restored absolute monarchy, and had Martínez de la Rosa arrested and eventually sentenced to eight years' imprisonment at the Peñón de la Gomera in North Africa. Oddly enough, the author's literary production, essays, translations, a play, and literary criticism continued during his imprisonment. These writings demonstrate the author's interest in political theories of rebellion and patriotic love of native land in confrontation with ethical and moral dilemmas—particularly those related to family matters—all of which became characteristic of his dramaturgy.

In 1820 the king's tyranny was curbed by another rebellion that forced him to swear to uphold the 1812 constitution, and a new representative government freed Martínez de la Rosa from prison. Martínez, however, was no longer a passionate young liberal but a moderate ready to accept constitutional monarchy. This led Fernando VII to name Martínez de la Rosa to head the government as Prime Minister. The office lasted only a few months, for Martínez suffered the fate of most moderates, being thoroughly despised by both the Absolutists, who supported a monarchy, and the Liberals, who supported the 1812 constitution. Martínez lost even the king's support when he advocated a change in the constitution based on the British system of two chambers. Named Prime Minister in March 1822, Martínez resigned in July. With the return to absolute monarchy in 1823 the former Prime Minister went into exile in France.

The seven years spent in exile were definitive. The influence of the French Revolution was felt in all avenues of society, and new tendencies in literature were evident among the poets, novelists, and dramatists who frequented the literary salons of Paris. Here began Martínez's lifelong study of the history of the French Revolution, its sources, its excesses, and its results. Here, too, he was introduced to the poetry of Lamartime and Byron, the historical novels of Walter Scott and Stendahl, the dramas of Mérimée and Victor Hugo. Although a French translation of one of his neoclassic comedies was successfully performed in Paris in 1826, the literary climate in France was quite different from that in Spain. In 1827, Hugo's preface to *Cromwell*, a veritable romantic manifesto was published. There the neoclassic rules were claimed unnecessary and freedom in art proclaimed. That same year, Martínez published his *Poetics and Annotations* [Poética y anotaciones]. The *Poetics*, written in verse, demonstrate a rigid adherence to neoclassical principles, while the prose *Annotations* indicate an increasing moderation. In a series of *Appendices* to the *Poetics*, Martínez evidenced a growing acceptance of what he called "historical" drama, a form almost unknown to the classicists.

While in France, Martínez de la Rosa began publication of his complete *Obras literarias* (1827–1830). These included a history of Spanish literature, a translation of Horace's *Letter to the Pisos*, and other literary criticisms. Volume 5 contained the two new plays on which Martínez's fame as a dramatist mostly rests: *Aben-Humeya or the Rebellion of the Moors* (Aben-Humeya o la rebelión de los moriscos) and *The Venice Conspiracy* [La conjuración de Venecia]. The year of their publication, 1830, was an important one in the history of both French and Spanish drama. In France it saw the triumph of the new style of drama advocated in Hugo's preface in *Cromwell* but not assured until the first performance of that dramatist's *Hernani* in February 1830. Martínez de la Rosa attended the famous stormy premiere of that historical event when fights broke out at the beginning line and whistles drowned out the dialogue in which the rules of verse meter were being broken. Only a few months later, Martínez's French version of *Aben-Humeya ou La Révolte des Maures sous Philippe II* was successfully performed in Paris. An essay entitled "Notes on Historical Drama" [Apuntes sobre el drama histórico], which accompanied the published version, explains Martínez's theories concerning the innovations in his two "historical" plays. There he admits, "In the midst of the hard-fought war being waged today by two opposing literary camps, I believe that in this point [the unity of place], as in many others, the truth lies in the golden mean" [En medio de la guerra encarnizada que mantienen en el día los dos campos literarios opuestos, creo que sobre este punto, así como sobre muchos otros, la verdad está en un justo medio] (*O* 1: 291). It was this moderation, both in politics and in literature, that have been considered by most critics the hallmarks of Martínez de la Rosa's career.

Martínez returned to Spain in 1831, taking up residence again in Granada and having performed both a comedy and tragedy. His play *Edipo* was so successfully staged in Madrid that one reviewer reported that it was necessary to erect barriers at the ticket booths in order to avoid disorder.[3] Meanwhile, Martínez's star was also rising politically. When Fernando VII died in 1833, leaving his wife Maria Cristina as regent of the infant Isabel, the harried regent asked Martínez to form a new government as Prime Minister once again. April of 1834 marks the height of Martínez de la Rosa's literary and political career. On the tenth of that month a Royal Statute, almost exclusively composed by the Prime

Minister, was adopted by the Cortes; on the twenty-second a quadruple alliance
was signed by France, Portugal, England, and Spain; and on the twenty-third,
The Venice Conspiracy had its wildly successful premiere in Madrid. It was the
first representation of the new Romantic school in Spanish drama, and its success
is proven by its record number of performances. In fact, its fame was of such
magnitude that for months afterward the ladies of Madrid were reported to have
worn their hair and dress in the Venetian style.[4]

But as quickly as his star had risen, so did it decline. The royal statute was
not completely embraced by the Liberals, who split into two groups, the Moderates headed by Martínez and the Progressives, some of whom were radicals,
while the Conservatives supported Fernando's brother Carlos in his attempt to
win the throne. From 1833 to 1840 the first of the Carlist civil wars raged
throughout the country. On June 7, 1835, Martínez de la Rosa, unable to control
the rising anarchy, was forced to resign as Prime Minister, although he continued
as head of the Moderate party. His literary career also declined. The Spanish
performance of *Aben-Humeya* in Madrid in 1836 had a much cooler reception
than when it was so well received in its original French in Paris. Increasingly
the author turned to history, political essays, and a long historical novel *Doña
Isabel de Solís, Queen of Granada*, the first part of which was published in
1837. Oddly, the author never attempted another drama in the Romantic style,
even though the Romantic plays of the Duque de Rivas, Gutiérrez, and Hartzenbusch were triumphing on the boards. In fact, in his literary essays appearing
in the *Revista de Madrid* after the author and politician became director of the
Royal Spanish Academy in 1839, he roundly denounced the doctrines of fatalism
and the portrayal of blind fate as opposed to a benevolent God.[5] Trying to take
advantage of the vogue for reworkings of Golden Age drama, he wrote a comedy, *A Spaniard in Venice* [El español en Venecia] in imitation of Tirso de
Molina's cape and sword drama. It was performed in Madrid, but the lack of a
foreword and faint praise from the reviewers indicates its lack of success.

Martínez's political career also continued to wane when both he and the queen
regent were forced into exile in October of 1840 after a Spanish soldier, Espartero, took over the government. In France, Martínez became a member of
the historical society and concentrated on the writing of his monumental history
The Spirit of the Age. With the fall of Espartero in 1843, he was able to return
to Spain, where he was subsequently named minister of external affairs. The
writer's declining years were dedicated to both political ambassadorships in Italy
and in France and to publishing his complete works. His two tragedies published
in 1848 and 1856 were unsuccessful, although their author continued to hold
important political posts. The aging statesman then wrote only occasional political and historical essays until his death in 1862.

DRAMATURGY: MAJOR WORKS AND THEMES

Martínez wrote six tragedies and five comedies. With the exception of *Edipo*,
an adaptation of Sophocles's famous play, all of the tragedies deal with the

subject of historical and unsuccessful rebellions against tyranny. The first, *Padilla's Widow* [La viuda de Padilla] (1812), dramatizes the moral dilemma of Padilla's widow concerning the wisdom of continuing to defend the besieged city of Toledo against the superior forces of the Castilian nobles. The circumstances in Toledo during the Castilian war of the *comunidades* were similar to the city of Cadiz in 1812, and the play represents Martínez's custom of adapting his drama to the political, social, and moral situation of the time. The form of the play is strictly neoclassical, five acts of hendecasyllabic verse, following the unities of time, place, and action. There is little movement or action, for it is mostly a political debate between the widow and her advisers.

Morayma, written in prison in 1818, deals with the rebellion of the Abencerrajes in Martínez's native Granada. This play again has as its main character a widow, Morayma, who prefers death to tyranny. While in the traditional neoclassic verse form of five acts, there is a slight variation in the unity of place, for the setting changes from room to room in the royal Moorish palace. The staging is more luxurious and exotic, the widow's laments much more pathetic and sentimental. A love interest in the form of a nonhistorical character and an unsuccessful suspenseful conspiracy to save Morayma's son give much more interest and movement to this play. Morayma unwittingly causes her son's death, and the final scene shows her dying of grief over her son's body. The drama is a curious mixture of neoclassic form with Romantic tone and content. It amply demonstrates that even before his experience in France, the author was predisposed to certain Romantic characteristics, particularly love of political freedom, exotic settings, and sentimental scenes of foreboding in historical plots freely adapted to the prevailing political climate.

Although not a historical play, Martínez's *Edipo* also demonstrates the author's fascination with sentimental scenes of moral family dilemmas in lugubrious and foreboding settings. This adaptation of Sophocles's play was first published in France in 1828 but not performed until 1830 in Seville, and 1832 in Madrid. The form is still the neoclassic five acts of mostly hendecasyllabic verse but is again a mixture of neoclassic form and Romantic content. The hero is much more sentimental than Sophocles's original archtypal figure of the man who tragically kills his father and marries his mother, all the while attempting to escape that very prophecy. Martínez suppresses the character flaws evident in Oedipus's character in other renditions of the plot and makes of his hero a tragic plaything of his fate. Sections of his *Poetics* explain that in dealing with tragedy one should keep the audience vacillating between hope and terror in order to evoke the emotions of pity and fear. The use of a blind, undeserved fate was a useful instrument in evoking these emotions, Martínez claimed, even though it was opposed to Christian belief. Again Martínez was capitalizing on the prevailing atmosphere in France where eighteenth-century rationalism was being replaced by greater emphasis on the individual, the emotions, imagination, and tender sentiments, rather than the public good.

Martínez's first truly successful tragedy *Aben-Humeya or the Revolt of the Moors* was originally written in French and performed in Paris. The author modestly attributed its success to "the richness of the sets and costuming, the propriety with which the actors zealously presented the work on stage, the enchantment of the music and choruses composed by my compatriot señor Gomis" [La riqueza de las decoraciones y de los trajes, la propriedad con que se la ha presentado en la escena, el celo de los actores, el encanto de la música, los coros, compuestos por mi compatriota el señor Gomis].[6] The subject is again an unsuccessful rebellion against tyranny, this time the Moorish uprising against Philip II's repressive laws. The situation was similar to the contemporary politics in France where Charles X was instituting repressive laws against the freedoms won in the revolution.[7] Again, moral dilemmas conflict with political ideals. The plot deals with the family of Aben-Humeya, the leader of the rebellion, his wife Zulima, and her father Muley. The latter pleads for moderation, rescues a Christian woman, and sends a letter to the Christian enemy pleading for the safety of his family. This leads to a final confrontation in which Zulima discovers her father's suicide is at her husband's instigation. She is killed by another conspirator, her husband is shot, and the play ends with the dying Aben-Humeya warning his assassin that the same fate will befall the new Moorish leader. The form reflects the changing climate of literary rules, for it is three acts of prose rather than five acts of verse, and the unity of place is again somewhat freer. The preface to the 1861 edition maintains that while the author was aware of the quarrels between the classics and the Romantics, he had friends in both camps and preferred to follow the unique rule of good taste. His *Poetics* had outlined this rule of good taste as the ideal of verisimilitude, with the theatrical illusion presented in as realistic a manner as possible.

The play for which Martínez de la Rosa is best known, and which guarantees his inclusion in the history of Spanish literature, is his *The Venice Conspiracy* [La conjuración de Venecia]. Published in 1830 in France, it was not performed until 1834 in Madrid. Its premiere heralded the triumph of the new style of drama in Spain. It dramatizes the story of a young hero, Rugiero, who plots to overthrow the cruel tribunal governing Venice. The conspiracy plans are overheard by spies as the hero shares them with his beloved Laura in a scene in a pantheon. He had married her in secret out of fear of Laura's uncle, the hated Pedro Morisini, head of the tribunal. The rebellion fails, and Rugiero is arrested. An almost demented Laura begs her father to intercede with his brother Pedro to save Rugiero. Pedro refuses to let family devotion interfere with political duty, even though he himself lost a child. During a dramatic trial scene where three doors are labeled Truth, Justice, and Eternity, Rugiero describes his being stolen as a child off a Greek ship near Candia. Pedro suddenly recognizes that Rugiero is his long-lost son and faints. The trial continues, Rugiero is condemned to death, and his plea to be allowed to embrace his father is rejected. Laura is torn from his arms as the curtains part to reveal the gallows, and Laura falls lifeless in her maid's arms.

The success of the play was immediate and no doubt surprised its author who considered it a "historical" drama. The only innovation from his earlier tragedies was the use of ordinary people speaking in a less-elevated style in prose. The play is not entirely Romantic, for it lacks the intense lyricism of later more truly Romantic drama, maintains the five-act neoclassic form, with the unity of place stretched to include the whole city of Venice, and the unity of time to cover a few days. The content, however, demonstrates again the author's love of tender scenes of heartrending emotions, gloomy forebodings in settings of ruins, tombs, and pantheons, and most important, political liberty thwarted and families torn apart. The hero of unknown origins pursued by an unjust fate seems to have derived from Sophocles's Oedipus. The theme of a son killing his father is reversed, and its effect was so powerful that the killing of one family member by another became a standard feature of later Romantic drama. The play lacks a truly metaphysical depth or malaise such as became apparent with the more extreme forms of Romanticism that followed.

In fact, Martínez was alarmed by this feature of later Romantic drama, for he never again wrote a tragedy in the Romantic vein. Instead, he took part in his literary essays in what Donald Shaw has labeled "The Anti-Romantic Reaction."[8] His last two tragedies were unsuccessful. The first, a melodramatic historical play set during the French Revolution, is entitled *A Father's Love* [Amor de padre]. In it a noble family flees the excesses of the rebelling mob, takes refuge at an inn, then a monastery where there is a familiar scene among tombstones. The family is captured, and the father substitutes for his son's execution. The author seems to have tried to capitalize on those scenes that were so successful in *The Venice Conspiracy*, a ruined monastery, the trial scene, the lugubrious sound of the wind, the tender, fainting heroine's forebodings, and a son becoming the inadvertent cause of his father's death. The play is not well structured, being overly episodic with melodramatic language. Its five acts of prose, with an attempt at unity of time, represents that author's dogged resistance to a complete abandonment of neoclassic rules of form.

The tragedy *The Parricide* [El parricida] (1856) is a sentimental melodrama that was not published in the author's own collection of his complete works. Ojeda Escudero suggests that the play may have been written much earlier than its publication date, or that it may be mistakenly attributed to Martínez, or that it might be a translation of another play. Its themes, however, are remarkably similar to those so characteristic of this author's work. Set in England the plot is the familiar one of separated families reunited in tragic circumstances. The hero had killed his father because of the parent's opposition to his son's marriage with a commoner. The son then married and inexplicably abandoned his beloved Matilde. In an inn in England he finds his lost wife, learns he has a daughter whom he is able to legitimize, thus making her eligible to marry the nobleman who has planned to marry her against his family's wishes. The many lachrymose scenes include the hero's hallucinations over his guilty conscience, an attempted suicide, and final death in the tender arms of his long-lost family. The title page identifies it as a sentimental drama in two acts in prose and may represent the author's attempt at imitating the sentimental and lachrymose vein of drama popular in the middle of the century.

Four of Martínez's five comedies are neoclassical imitations of the style of drama initiated by Moratín the son. There are no innovations, and the comedies are moralizing attempts to correct through ridicule the vices and errors common in middle-class society. The first, *The Power of a Position* [Lo que puede un empleo], was performed in 1812 in Cadiz during a bombardment. It deals with a parasitical clergyman, Melitón, who opposes liberal reforms and thwarts the marriage of a young couple. He is revealed as a hypocrite when he accepts with alacrity a well-paid position in the liberal government. The second, *The Daughter at Home and the Mother at the Masquerade* [La niña en casa y la madre en la máscara] was first performed in Madrid in 1821. Its obvious aim is to criticize both the bad examples of heedless mothers as well as the shallow education afforded the females of the age. A young woman is intrigued by the promises of a seducer while her mother is off at a mascarade. Her ruin is averted by the stalwart hero, and the mother promises closer supervision. The play is written in octosyllabic verse and was successfully translated and performed in French in Paris in 1826. *Unfounded Jealousy or The Husband in the Fireplace* [Los celos infundados o el marido en la chimenea] was given as a benefit in Granada and later in 1833 in Madrid. A lighthearted farce in two acts, the play pokes fun at excessive jealousy in a typical drawingroom style. *The Wedding and the Wake* [La boda y el duelo], performed in Madrid in 1839, counterposes a young countess supposedly mourning her old husband's death while secretly helping her brother win the girl being sacrificed to a rich old suitor by a greedy mother. The obvious moral aim is the criticism of forced marriages for monetary gain. His final comedy, *The Spaniard in Venice or the Enchanted Head* [El español en Venecia o la cabeza encantada], published in 1843 and performed in 1840 and 1843, is the only comedy not written in imitation of Moratín. Rather than a comedy of manners, this is a typical cape and sword play in imitation of Tirso de Molina. In it a habitual liar is forced to reform through the dubious use of an enchanted head. The heroines are modeled on Tirso's females who cleverly manipulate their faithless lovers. The drama marks again the author's proclivity for imitation of models and for adapting his style to the prevailing literary or political climate.

CRITICS' RESPONSE

Contemporary critics are reevaluating Martínez's place in literary history, noting his important contributions to a patriotic defense of Spanish literature as well as being the first to introduce Romantic drama to Spain.[9] Of particular importance is the monumental study of Ojeda Escudero, published in 1997, which examines in great detail the form, structure, themes, historical setting, prior influences, language, characters, literary method, and critical response to each of Martínez's plays. His conclusions are that, while there is a progression in the themes of rebellion, from liberal support for uprisings against tyranny in his first plays to a conservative denunciation of revolution in *A Father's Love*, Martínez's overriding ideology was the golden mean, mixing both neoclassic and romantic characteristics in his drama.

The drama *The Venice Conspiracy* rightfully holds an important place as the first play in a Romantic style to triumph in Madrid. The young critic Larra (537–543) wrote a glowing review of the premiere, praising the play's superior construction, the natural exposition, the scenes in the pantheon, Laura's confession to her father, and the overwhelming nature of the last act. Today the play narrowly escapes melodrama, lacking the lyricism of the best Romantic drama but succeeding with its scenes of dark conspiracies alternating with light scenes of gaiety, the happy songs of Carnival contrasting with the lugubrious sound of the wind in the dark pantheon. Love scenes of moderate, urbane dialogue contrast with the weighty, legalistic language of the tribunal, which ignores a frantic father's pleas for mercy. The Romantic nature of the hero Rugiero has also received critical attention. While Allison Peers (1: 157) called him the first Romantic hero in Spanish drama, Michael McGaha has convincingly demonstrated that he is modeled on the hero of unknown origins in Jovellanos's *El delincuente honrado* (242). Donald Shaw suggested that the hero "lacks both the insight and symbolic role of the genuine Romantic hero,"[10] although he later noted that he did represent the hero whose experience could not "conciliate earthly experience with belief in a divinely ordained and hence benevolent pattern of existence."[11]

While the themes introduced in *The Venice Conspiracy* certainly had considerable influence on the more truly Romantic drama to follow, Martínez de la Rosa was obviously not a hot-headed romantic rebel against God or bourgeois values, or an overthrower of accepted patterns of eighteenth-century rationalism. This aspect of Romanticism plainly bothered the dramatist whose preface to *The Wedding and the Wake* demonstrates his dislike for this direction in Romantic drama. It is evident that what offended the author was not so much the breaking of neoclassical rules of form as his fear of the underlying metaphysics of the movement. In the preface, he claims this tendency was threatening "to infect our theater not only in its literary aspect but in another of greater importance and transcendence" [inficionar nuestro teatro no sólo en la parte literaria, sino en otra de más importancia y transcendencia] (*O* II: 9). His literary speeches and essays reveal a moderate stance as he defended classical paganism against the ultraconservative Catholic defenders of morality such as Donoso Cortés, while at the same time warning against the dangerous destruction of morality inherent in doctrines of fatalism. He remained a firm believer in neoclassic rules of form that contributed to making the theatrical illusion as real as possible. His literary essays demonstrate his strictly Catholic orthodoxy in matters of faith, and he rejected the depiction of an uncaring or hostile God, favoring instead a God of benevolence and providence. He likewise rejected the idea of blind fate and supported instead the concept of free will.

AWARDS AND DISTINCTIONS

The career of Martínez de la Rosa was filled with honors and distinctions in both political and literary fields. He was the holder of the chair of Moral Philosophy at the University of Granada at the age of 18. After abandoning the role of professor, he became an important political figure, holding such important posts as prime minister of Spain, ambassador to France, ambassador to Italy, minister of state, and president of the Cortes. On the literary front, his first two historical plays were heralded in both France and Spain. He became a member of the Royal Academy of Spain and was elected director in 1839. He was president of the Ateneo of Madrid, and he read and published many important political, philosophical, historical, and literary essays, both in French and and in Spanish.

In spite of these distinctions, he continues to be remembered primarily as the author who heralded Romantic drama into Spain with the successful performance in Madrid of *The Venice Conspiracy*. It is a great irony that the author had no intention of introducing French, German, or English. Romanticism, for as a champion of moderation and the golden mean, he greatly feared the excesses inherent in that movement. As Menéndez Pelayo stated so accurately:

This after all was the constant fate of Martínez de la Rosa, both in politics and in literature, to be the herald of revolutions and then to be frightened by them, and in the same way in art, without ever having been romantic, to open the door to romanticism and to be the first to triumph on the boards in the name of the new school. [Este al fin y al cabo, fué destino constante de Martínez de la Rosa, así en política como en literatura; ser heraldo de revoluciones y asustarse luego de ellas, y de la misma manera, en el arte, sin haber sido nunca romántico, abrir la puerta al romanticismo y triunfar el primero en las tablas, en nombre de la nueva escuela.] (4:175)

NOTES

This chapter is based on (excerpted and adapted from) Francisco Martínez de la Rosa by Robert Mayberry and Nancy Mayberry. Copyright © 1988 by G. K. Hall & Co. Used with permission of Twayne Publishers, an imprint of Simon & Schuster MacMillan.

1. *Obras de Don Francisco Martínez de la Rosa*, ed. Carlos Seco Serrano, *BAE* vols. 148–156 (Madrid: Ediciones Atlas, 1962), V: 7. Henceforth, all quotations from this work will be indicated by the abbreviation *O*, followed by the volume number and the page number of that edition. All translations from the Spanish are our own.

2. We follow the biographies of Jean Sarrailh and Luis de Sosa (See "Critical Studies").

3. The review appeared in *Cartas Españolas* February 9, 1832, and is reported by John Cook, p. 446 (see "Critical Studies").

4. The incident is reported in George Northup, *An Introduction to Spanish Literature*, 3d ed., rev. Nicholson B. Adams (Chicago: University of Chicago Press, 1960), 351.

5. See Nancy Mayberry's "The Adverse-Fate Theme" in "Critical Studies."

6. See Sarrailh's edition of *Obras dramáticas*, 137, in "Editions."
7. See Dowling's. "The Paris Premiere" in "Critical Studies."
8. Donald Shaw, "The Anti-Romantic Reaction in Spain," *Modern Language Review* 58 (1963): 606–611.
9. See Alborg's "Martínez de la Rosa," 426–428 in "Critical Studies."
10. Donald Shaw, and Ojedo Escudero, *A Literary History of Spain, The Nineteenth Century* (New York: Barnes and Noble, 1972), 8.
11. Ibid., 357.

BIBLIOGRAPHY

We cite the first editions only.

Plays

Lo que puede un empleo. Cadiz, 1812.
La viuda de Padilla. Madrid: Imprenta que fue de García, 1814.
Edipo. Paris: Baudry, 1829.
Aben-Humeya ou la révolte des maures sous Phillipe II. Paris: Didot, 1830. (Text in both French and Spanish.)
La conjuración de Venecia. Paris: Didot, 1830.
Los celos infundados o el marido en la chimenea. Madrid: Repullés, 1833.
La niña en casa y la madre en la máscara. Paris: Baudry, 1838.
La boda y el duelo. Madrid: Impr. Del Colegio de Sordo-Mudos, 1839.
El espannol en Venecia, o La cabeza encantada. Madrid: Vicente de Lalama, 1843.
El parricida. Matanzas: La Aurora, 1856.
El parricida. Madrid, 1856.

Poetry

Odas a los atributos de Dios que brillan en la Sacrosanta Eucaristía. Granada: Gómez, 1805.
Zaragoza. London: Bensley, 1811
Poesías. Madrid: Jordan, 1833.
Poesías; poética española, apéndices sobre la poesía didáctica, la tragedia y la comedia. Paris: Baudry, 1845.

Narrative Prose

Hernán Pérez del Pulgar el de las hazañas. Madrid: Jordan, 1834.
El espíritu del siglo. Vols. 1–4, Madrid: Jordan, 1835–1838. Vol. 5, Madrid: Alegría & Charlain, 1842. Vol. 6, Madrid: Vicente de Lalama, 1843. Vol. 7, Madrid: Viuda Jordán & Hijos, 1846. Vols. 8–10, Madrid: Agustín Espinosa, 1847–1851.
Libro de los niños. Madrid: Compañía Tipográfica. 1839.
Bosquejo histórico de la politica de España, desde los tiempos de los reyes Católicos hasta nuestros días. 2 vols. Madrid: Rivaddeneyra, 1857.

Novel

Doña Isabel de Solis, Reina de Granada. Vols. 1–2, Madrid: Jordán, 1837–1839. Vol. 3, Madrid: Caballero de la Gracia, 1846.

Essays

These are only those essays of importance to the author's literary theories and that we were able to locate. Martínez published large numbers of newspaper articles, essays, and so on.

"¿Cuál es el método o sistema preferible para escribir la historia?" *Revista de Madrid*, 2d ser., 2 (1839): 531–540.

"Del influjo de la religión cristiana en la literatura." *Revista de Madrid*, 2d ser., 3 (1839): 139–146.

"El sentimiento religioso." *Revista de Madrid*, 3d ser., 2 (1841): 313–322.

"¿Cuál es la influencia del espíritu del siglo sobre la literatura?" *Revista de Madrid*, 3d ser., 3 (1842): 148–158.

Scholarly Editions

La conjuración de Venecia. Edited by E. Arthur Owen and John Lister. Chicago: Sanborn & Co., 1925.

Obras dramáticas. Edited by Jean Sarrailh. Clásicos castellanos, vol. 107. Madrid: Espasa-Calpe, 1933. (Includes *La Vivda de Padilla, La conjuración de Venecia* and *Aben-Humeya.*)

La conjuración de Venecia. Edited by José Paulino Ayuso. Madrid: Taurus, 1988.

La conjuración de Venecia. Edited by María José Alonso Seoane. Madrid: Catedra, 1993.

Collected Works

Obras literarias. 5 vols. Paris: Didot, 1827–1830.

Obras literarias. 4 vols. Barcelona: Oliva, 1838. Reissued in London: Imprenta de Samuel Bagster, 1838 in 6 vols.

Obras dramáticas. Paris: Beaudry, 1843.

Obras completas. Colección de los mejores autores españoles antiguos y modernos. Vols. 28–32. Paris: Beaudry, 1844–1845.

Obras dramáticas. 3 vols. Madrid: Rivadeneyra, 1861.

Obras de Don Francisco Martínez de la Rosa. Ed. Carlos Seco Serrano. *BAE* vols. 148–156. Madrid: Ediciones Atlas, 1962.

Critical Studies

Books

Cook, John. "Neo-Classic Comedy after Moratín: Martínez de la Rosa." In *Neo-Classic Drama in Spain: Theory and Practice.* Dallas, TX: Southern Methodist Press, 1959.

Larra, Mariano José de. *Artículos Completos*. Ed. Melchor de Almagro San Martín. Madrid: Aguilar, 1961.

Mayberry, Robert, and Nancy Mayberry. *Francisco Martínez de la Rosa*. Twayne World Authors series 618. Boston: G. K. Hall, 1988.

Ojeda Escudero, Pedro *El justo medio: neoclasicismo y romanticismo en la obra dramática de Martínez de la Rosa*. Burgos: Universidad de Burgos, 1997.

Peers, Edgar Allison. *A History of the Romantic Movement in Spain*. 2 vols. Cambridge: University Press, 1940.

Sarrailh, Jean. *Un homme d'état espagnol. Martínez de la Rosa, 1787–1862*. Bardeaux: Feret et Fils, 1930.

Shearer, James. *The Poética y Apéndices of Martínez de la Rosa: Their Genesis, Sources and Significance for Spanish Literary History and Criticism*. Princeton, NJ: Princeton University Press, 1941.

Sosa, Luis de. *Don Francisco Martínez de la Rosa: Político y poeta. Vidas españolas del siglo XIX*. No. 2. Madrid: Espasa Calpe, 1930.

Unpublished Works

Alfaro, Arsenio. "Francisco Martínez de la Rosa (1787–1862): A Study in the Transition from Neo-Classicism to Romanticism and Eclecticism in Romantic Literature." Ph.D. diss., Columbia University, 1965.

Articles and Chapters

Alborg, Juan Luis. "Martínez de la Rosa." In *Historia de la literatura española: El romanticismo*. Madrid: Editorial Gredos, 1980. Vol. 4, 417–453.

Avrett, Robert. "A Brief Examination into the Historical Background of Martínez de la Rosa's *La Conjuración de Venecia*." *Romantic Review* 21 (1930): 132–137.

———. "A Glimpse into the Historical, Basis of Martínez de la Rosa's *Aben-Humeya*." *Romantic Review* 23 (1932): 30–33.

Caldera, Ermanno. "Presenza del teatro sentimentale nella 'Conjuracion de Venecia." In *Studi di letteri iberiche e ibero-americane offerti a Giuseppe Bellini*, ed. Giovanni Battista De Cesare and Silvana Serafin. Rome: Bulzoni, 1993. 109–15.

Cebrián, José. "Significación y alcance de la *Poética* de Martínez de la Rosa." *Revista de Literatura* 52.103 (1990): 129–150.

Dendle, Brian. "A Note on the Valencia Edition of Martínez de la Rosa's *La viuda de Padilla*." *Bulletin of Hispanic Studies* 50 (1973): 18–22.

Dowling, John. "The Paris Première of Francisco Martínez de la Rosa's *Aben-Humeya*, (July, 1830)." In *Homenaje a Rodriguez-Moniño*. Madrid: Castalia, 1966. 1:147–154.

Geraldi, Robert. "Francisco Martínez de la Rosa: Literary Atrophy or Creative Sagacity?" *Hispanófila* 79 (1983): 11–19.

González de Garay y Fernández, Teresa. "De la tragedia al drama histórico: Dos textos de Martínez de la Rosa." *Cuadernos de Investigación Filológica* 9 (1983): 199–234.

Lloréns, Vicente. "Martínez de la Rosa: Literatura y política." In *El romanticismo español*. Madrid: Fundación Juan March y Editorial Castalia, 1983. 86–111.

Mansour, George. "An *Aben-Humeya* Problem." *Romance Notes* 8 (1967): 213–216.

———. "The *Edipo* of Martínez de la Rosa and Romantic Dramaturgy." *Revista de Estudios Hispánicos* 18 (1983): 239–252.

Mayberry, Nancy. "Martínez de la Rosa and the Adverse-Fate Theme." In *La Chispa '85: Selected Proceedings of the Sixth Louisiana Conference on Hispanic Languages and Literatures*, ed. Gilbert Paolini. New Orleans: Tulane University Press, 1986. 251–258.

————. "More on Martínez de la Rosa's Literary Atrophy or Creative Sagacity." *Hispanófila* 93 (1988): 29–36.

————. "El parricida. An unknown sentimental drama by Martínez de la Rosa." *Romance Languages Annual* 2 (1990): 474–476.

McGaha, Michael. "The 'Romanticism' of Martínez de la Rosa's *La conjuración de Venecia*." *Kentucky Romance Quarterly* 20 (1973): 235–242.

Menéndez Pelayo, Marcelino. "Don Francisco Martinez de la Rosa." 1882. Rpt. in *Estudios y discursos de crítica histórica y literaria*. Vol. 4 of *Edición nacional de las obras completas de Menéndez Pelayo*. Santander: Aldus, 1942. 263–288.

Miguel y Canuto, Juan Carlos. "Casi un siglo de crítica sobre el teatro de Lope: de la *Poética* de Luzán (1737) a la de Martínez de la Rosa (1827)." *Criticón* 62 (1994): 33–56.

Navas Ruiz, Ricardo. "Francisco Martínez de la Rosa." In *El romanticismo español*. Madrid: Cátedra, 1982. 150–163.

Romera Tobar, Leonardo. "Notas sobre Martínez de la Rosa en el centenario de su muerte." *Revista de Literatura* 22 (1963): 78–82.

Rubio, Enrique. "Martínez de la Rosa: *La conjuración de Venecia*, realidad y ficción." In *Teatro politico spagnolo del primo ottocento*, ed. Ermanno Caldera. *Biblioteca de Cultura* 438. Rome: Bulzoni Editore, 1991. 153–166.

MANUEL MARTÍNEZ MEDIERO
(1937–   )

John P. Gabriele

BIOGRAPHY

The third of four children of a prominent physician and his wife, Manuel Martínez Mediero was born in Badajoz, Spain, on March 12, 1937, during the Spanish Civil War. Little did anyone know at the time how profoundly the tumultuous and disquieting social and political situation of postwar Spain would impact on the playwright's artistic vision. After receiving his primary and secondary education at the Colegio de los Hermanos Maristas in his native Badajoz, Mediero earned a bachelor's degree in economics from the University of Bilbao. While economics is never a concrete theme in Mediero's theater, his knowledge of economic systems and structures has undoubtedly sensitized this perception and heightened his awareness of the inequities that exist in our social and political institutions as well as our understanding of gender issues. Currently, Mediero serves as the Director of the Territorial Council on the Cultural Heritage of Extremadura. Badajoz remains his permanent place of residence, where he lives with his wife Francisca, an interior decorator who manages her own small business, and his two children, Manuel and Eva. Despite the fact that Mediero lives in Badajoz, he visits Madrid frequently, stays exceptionally well informed about current theatrical events, and is himself no stranger to the Spanish capital's inner circle of theater professionals.

Manuel Martínez Mediero's career as a playwright spans thirty-five years. He has written an astonishing quantity of plays, fifty-three to date. All have been published except two.[1] Mediero belongs to a group of playwrights of the 1960s and 1970s whose work was a direct response to the authoritarian tactics of the Franco regime. Appropriately dubbed underground or silenced dramatists, their work was the target of official censorship and performed only by experimental theater groups and most often in university settings or at theater festivals outside Madrid. Mediero's theater posits a critical view of a reality that championed totalitarian ideals and suppressed free ideological and artistic expression. Tenacious in his belief of an individual's right to free expression and undaunted by the threat of official censorship, Mediero was determined to confront Spain's social and political situation. His theater is identified by a resolute objective to provoke an awareness of the oppressive social and political underpinnings of hierarchically conceived societies that promote a disparaging sense of community. Deeply committed to human values, Mediero admits that he began writing theater because he felt a moral responsibility to the human condition (Isasi, "Entrevista" 47). For Mediero, theater is merely a "means of communicating with the people" (Gabriele, "Breve encuentro" 47).

The evolution of Mediero's theater is inextricably linked to the social and political tenor of postwar Spain. Yet his message is universal in scope. The plays written between 1965 and 1974 are works of protest and disillusionment with Francoist Spain. In spite of government censorship, Mediero managed to publish an impressive number of plays during this period: *Jacinta se marchó a la guerra* [Jacinta Goes to War] (1965), *Espectáculo siglo XX* [Spectacle of the Twentieth Century] (1967), *Mientras la gallina duerme* [While the Chicken Sleeps] (1968), *El convidado* [The Guest] (1968), *El último gallinero* [The Last Chicken Coop] (1968), *Perico, Rey* [Pete, the King] (1969), *El regreso de los escorpiones* [The Return of the Scorpions] (1969), *Las planchadoras* [The Ironing Women] (1970), *Perdido Paraíso* [Paradise Lost] (1971), *Los herederos* [The Heirs] (1971), *El hombre que se fue a todas las guerras* [The Man Who Went to All the Wars] (1971), *El Fernando* [Ferdinand] (1972), *Las hermanas de Búfalo Bill* [Buffalo Bill's Sisters], (1972), *El automóvil* [The Automobile] (1972), *Denuncia, juicio e inquisición de Pedro Lagarto* [The Denunciation, Judgment and Inquisition of Pedro Lagarto] (1973), *Un hongo para Nagasaki* [A Mushroom Cloud for Nagasaki] (1973), and *El bebé furioso* [The Angry Infant] (1974).[2] The conflict between what reality appears to be and what it actually is constitutes a common narrative thread in these early works and provides the basis for dramatic tension. Freedom and repression, both social and psychological, is a major theme. Violence and cruelty are constant motifs.

Of these early works, *Las hermanas de Búfalo Bill* deserves special mention. As Franco lay dying in his private residence on the outskirts of the Spanish capital, the play opened in Madrid's Valle-Inclán Theatre on October 8, 1975. Little could anyone attending the play have known to what extent its content would prove prophetic of what was soon to transpire in their own reality. In the simplest of terms, the play depicts the difficulties that confront individuals during a period of transition. A play about the abuse of power, *Las hermanas de Búfalo Bill* portrays a grotesque dying old man who oppresses his sisters both during his lifetime and as a ghost after his death. Considered a parody of the Franco regime, it was not until recently that Mediero confirmed this speculation: "[W]hen I wrote *Las hermanas de Búfalo Bill* I wanted to write a work about the Dictator and anticipate his death" (Gabriele, "Martínez Mediero habla" 221). When Franco died on November 20, 1975, Mediero was catapulted into notoriety. For all intents and purposes, *Las hermanas de Búfalo Bill* was the last play of the Franco Era and the first of New Democratic Spain. Several months later, on March 5, 1976, while the play was still enjoying a successful run, a right-wing group staged a protest. Claiming that the play was an affront to national honor, they hurled bombs into the theater, thereby ending its run.

Not unlike many other Spanish authors, Mediero withdrew from writing during the difficult period of Spain's transition from dictatorship to democracy that followed Franco's death. By 1979 Mediero had resumed his writing. The few works he wrote between 1975 and 1979 and those he wrote after 1979 present the eternal conflict of historical past and present. They represent a reality in flux, comparable in all regards to Spain's own social and political situation. The difficulty of abandoning the sense of security that comes with imposed control and order in an effort to shape one's own destiny is a prevalent theme, as in *El día que se descubrió el pastel* [The Day They Discovered the Scheme] (1975) and *Los clandestinos* [Clandestine People] (1978). Freedom and the theme of national identity also continue to be of major concern to the playwright, as evidenced in *La patria está en peligro* [The Country Is in Danger] (1979), *Las bragas perdidas en el tendedero* [Stray Panties] (1980), *Heroica del domingo* [Sunday Afternoon Heroics] (1984), and *Las hermanas de Búfalo Bill cabalgan de nuevo* [Buffalo Bill's Sisters Ride Again] (1986).

What truly distinguishes Mediero's recent work is a focus on gender issues and a predominant use of a historical revisionist perspective. Lisístrata [Lysistrata] (1980), *Fedra* [Phaedre] (1981), *Madrecita del alma querida* [Beloved Mother] (1983), *Juana del amor hermoso* [A Love Too Beautiful] (1983), *Lola, la divina* [Lola, the Divine] (1988), and *La Edad de Oro de mamá* [Mother's Prime] (1996) are representative of plays that showcase the reality of women and their plight at the hands of patriarchal social structure. As regards a critical historical perspective, Mediero makes use of the conflict of past and present in order to dispel certain social and political myths in *Aria por un papa español* [Aria for a Spanish Pope] (1985), *Carlo Famoso* [Charles the Famous] (1987), *¡¡¡Tierraaa . . . a . . . laaa . . . vistaaa . . . !!!* [Land Ho!] (1987), *Las largas vacaciones de Oliveira Salazar* [The Long Holiday of Oliveira Salazar] (1990), *El Niño de Belén* [The Child from Bethlehem] (1992), *El gato Félix* [Felix the Cat] (1996), and *¡Adiós, muchachos!* [So Long Fellows!] (1999), among others. The protagonists of these plays are historical figures: The Spanish born Pope Alexander VI, the Spanish explorers Vasco Nuñez de Balboa and Francisco Pizarro, the Portuguese dictator Antonio Oliveira de Salazar, the Emperor Charles I of Spain, a Christ, and General Antonio Tejero Molina. Underscoring the basic human nature of these characters, the playwright steers us away from the traditional interpretation of their lives to posit a critical view of history, both past and present.

If box-office success and long-running engagements are any indication of a playwright's public appeal, then Mediero has enjoyed such recognition for nearly three decades. Beginning in 1968 with the premiere of *El último gallinero*, his plays have been performed regularly in some of Madrid's most prestigious theaters as well as playhouses throughout Europe, the United States, and

South America. Most recently, *"La vida sexual"* . . . *de Egas Moniz* ["Sex Life" by Egas Moniz] was staged in Lisbon in 1999. In addition to *Las hermanas de Búfalo Bill*, mentioned earlier, other performances include *El convidado* in 1971, *El Fernando* in 1972, *El bebé furioso* in 1974, *El día que se descubrió el pastel* and *Mientras la gallina duerme* in 1976, *Las planchadoras* in 1978, *La novia* [The Girlfriend] and *Lisístrata* in 1980, *Fedra, Tito Andrónico* [Titus Andronicus], *Juana del amor hermoso* and *La loca carrera del árbitro* [The Referee's Wild Career] in 1983, *Aria por un papa español* in 1985, *Carlo Famoso* in 1987, *¡¡¡Tierraaa . . . a . . . laaa . . . vistaaa . . . !!!* in 1989, *Badajoz, puerto de mar* [Badajoz, Seaport] in 1992, *El Niño de Belén* in 1994, *El marco incomparable* [The Incomparable Place] in 1995, and *Las largas vacaciones de Oliveira* in 1997.

Inasmuch as Manuel Martínez Mediero shows no signs of slowing down, it is probably safe to say that he will not relent in his quest to spark our awareness of the human condition in future works. Given his general approach to social and political issues, Mediero's dramaturgy provides the necessary link between the socially objective work of the Realist Generation of the 1960s and the more thematically ambitious theater of present-day Spain.

DRAMATURGY: MAJOR WORKS AND THEMES

Thematically speaking, the focus of Mediero's theater is life itself. Drama, as the playwright himself admits, "is an art form that most closely approximates life in every sense of the word" (Gabriele, "Martínez Mediero habla," 217). Yet it is not objective reality with which Mediero is concerned but that which lies underneath. His work delves below the surface to explore the very essence of reality and the dynamics of human interaction. Introspective in nature, Mediero's dramatic universe abounds in motifs, metaphors, symbols, and situations that spring from the drama of our everyday existence.

Mediero concerns himself with the inconspicuous inequities of modern-day society, the infringement of free expression and choice, and the fraudulence of traditional social, political, and gender-related myths that, perpetuated throughout time and seldom challenged, have led us to accept as real what is illusory and paradoxical at best. In order to transcribe visually on the stage his particular worldview, Mediero makes use of a series of opposing concepts such as the use and abuse of power, human exploitation and repression, dominance and servility, oppression and passivity, cruelty and compassion, and the primitivelike, yet intriguing, inherent need in human beings to exercise control, as if instinctually, over the destiny of others while all along masking their own deep-seated insecurities and fears. Often farcical and absurd in content, his work is both social and existential in scope.

Mediero's first play, *Jacinta se marchó a la guerra*, introduces themes that characterize his theater. *Jacinta se marchó a la guerra* paints a realistic and deeply moving portrait of a onetime well-to-do countess, now an impoverished and lonely woman who has been abandoned by her family and friends. Despite the abject and the adverse condition of her social circumstances, Jacinta strives to maintain her human dignity in a society that is deeply rooted in the opportunistic exploitation of unfortunate individuals. Jacinta's actions transcend the immediacy of her situation to put us in contact with a world that has overextended itself in its dehumanizing dimension. Through Jacinta's characterization, Mediero is able to convey that the unkind and demoralizing treatment to which individuals are often subjected is not cause enough to compromise human dignity. As Jacinta herself explains, "If voluntary death is humanity's greatest weakness, then a life of sufferance is the worst humiliation possible" (160).

The social and personal deprivation so vividly portrayed in *Jacinta se marchó a la guerra* takes on very definite political connotations in *El último gallinero*. The play uses animal symbolism to parody authoritarian social structure. The play is set in a run-down chicken coop where its inhabitants, cut off from the outside world, consider banding together against their oppressors on the outside. Castelar, evicted from another chicken coop because of his libertine ideals, is placed in the "last chicken coop" where he quickly makes his thoughts known: "[T]rue freedom is in our souls. Doors and walls cannot prevent us from exercising our freedom of speech" (364). Eventually, Castelar's ideas incite suspicion within the chicken coop as expressed by Hermógenes, the head rooster and dictatorial figure: "[W]e cannot trust anyone. He [Castelar] could be a spy. What other reason could there be for removing him from his chicken coop" (357). In time, petty insecurities and doubts undermine the sense of community that once existed. A chaotic struggle for power ensues. Castelar's alternative way of thinking leads to his tragic end. Absorbed by their determination to eliminate Castelar, the chickens lose sight of their original communal objective, and machines from the outside destroy the chicken coop. Clouded by an insatiable thirst for power, no less reprehensible than the tactics of their oppressors, the inhabitants of the chicken coop have fallen prey to their own self-centered ideals. Ironically enough, their actions sustain rather than arrest the oppressive outside forces.

Las planchadoras relies on two of Mediero's major thematic concerns: freedom and control. What is more, it points to the pivotal role of women in Mediero's dramatic stage rhetoric. *Las planchadoras* portrays a world of exile where violence and cruelty have become a prerequisite for survival. Cruelty is elevated to a level of spectacle along Artaudian lines, taking on definite cathartic dimensions. Human interaction is reduced to a ludicrous but conscious game of control in which everyone participates. The play centers on the lives of three sisters: Libertad, Clavellina, and Dionisíaca. Boasting of her virginity and condemning Clavellina for her erotic thoughts, Dionisíaca appears to exert control over her sister. At the level of subtext Clavellina also exerts control. Questioning the importance of sexual abstinence and chiding Dionisíaca for her moral reprobation, Clavellina teases her sister with stories of erotic sexual encounters that, albeit fabricated, succeed in inciting her sister's anger. Erotic dreams and sexual frustration serve as metaphors for repression. With the return of Libertad ("Liberty"), who years ago was evicted from the house for prostitution, Mediero draws attention to the theme of freedom, as her name implies. Although free of Dionisíaca's tyrannical control, Libertad's life has not been easy. In her struggle to survive, she has learned that freedom is as much a social responsibility as a personal one: "We must learn to be less egotistical and self-centered and put the interests of others before our own wants and desires" (59).

The debut of *Las hermanas de Búfalo Bill*, as indicated earlier, represents a momentous occasion for the contemporary Spanish stage. It is undoubtedly the play for which Mediero is best known. A disturbing portrayal of a society faced with the unknown, *Las hermanas de Búfalo Bill* depicts a world that is essentially disconnected and dysfunctional where human relationships are characterized by an inability to communicate. It portrays a society whose past weighs heavily on its present, a society incapable of finding effective means to effectuate change and bring about solidarity. The play is at once reminiscent of the highly critical vision of Mediero's early plays and indicative of the more liberating nature of his later works.

Dressed as a gun-wielding cowboy of the American Old West, Amadeo tyrannizes his sisters, Cleo and Semíramis, chaining them in order to prevent them from being seduced by the world that exists outside the four walls of their home. They live in an imaginary past, out of touch with reality. Amadeo spends his time defending his territory from imaginary Indians while forcing his sisters to confess their illicit sexual thoughts. The moral taboos associated with a dictatorship are the target of Mediero's criticism. Curiosity with the forbidden pleasures of sex is the play's central metaphor. Suddenly and unexpectedly, illusion becomes reality when Amadeo is pierced by an arrow. Following his death, the scenery is the first indication we have of the change that has taken place. The small rooms of the house have suddenly taken on a modernistic air. The guns have disappeared, and Cleo and Semíramis don contemporary clothes and makeup. Yet their grotesque nature persists. They remain obsessed with sex. Not surprisingly, Amadeo is still present, appearing from time to time as a ghost who reminds them of their aberrant behavior and immoral thoughts. Amadeo's presence in the second act suggests that the sudden death of a figurehead who embodied authoritarian ideals does not erase years of indoctrination and submission to a prescriptive lifestyle. Nowhere is this more evident than in Cleo's and Semíramis's first attempt to exercise their newfound freedom. They decide to kidnap the neighborhood baker, lock him up in the basement, and take advantage of him sexually at will. Yet they fail in their objective. The inability to realize their personal desire is indicative of the extent to which past taboos infiltrate the present, as Semíramis herself proclaims, "I sense that Amadeo is still with us. He's here and he hears us" (238), and Cleo concurs: "It's evident that we are not free of him even after death" (244). When we learn that Amadeo's ghost is the product of the sisters' imagination, it is clear that their difficulty in adjusting to a society in which they are now essentially free to think and act for themselves is the result of a lifetime of physical and psychological oppression. Their task involves developing faculties heretofore repressed. Ultimately, *Las hermanas de Búfalo Bill* illustrates Mediero's intent to demythify Spain's recent past and work against the perpetuation of old myths in the future. The plays written after 1979 pick up the metaphor of Spain after Franco's death. Essentially, these works explore identity on a national and personal level. Mediero's use of gender roles in *Lisístrata* and *Juana del amor hermoso* proves an effective means of exploring identity. Both plays convey Mediero's concern for feminist issues. The first play is based on the classical Greek play of the same title by Aristophanes. The second is a revisionist look at the life of Queen Joanna of Castile. Both protagonists are rebellious women determined to affirm their individual identities in both social and political terms. In both plays, Mediero draws on feminist theory in presenting his image of the Spanish female in order to destroy universal myths about gender in an effort to move toward cultural change. Typical of Mediero's strong-willed and indomitable characters, both Lisístrata and Juana challenge authoritarian ideals. Their struggle represents that of any individual who wishes to become integrated into society and overcome his or her historical marginality. In both plays, Mediero attacks the hypocrisy of social and political institutions as it regards the status of women. Both Lisístrata ("We want to create a progressive society, where there is no violence, no oppressors, no oppressed" [72] and Juana ("I refuse to be used" [371] espouse egalitarian principles and promote liberal ideals with regard to the social condition of women. In dramatizing a feminist consciousness, Mediero continues his crusade against society's paradoxical nature, showing how intransigent traditions persist in a democratic society when individuals, women in particular, seek to legitimize themselves.

    Carlo Famoso: Sueño histórico and *El Niño de Belén* are revisionist in perspective. *Carlo Famoso: Sueño histórico* is set in the Yuste Monastery where Charles I of Spain spent his last days. Mediero's portrait of Charles is that of a frail, compassionate human being who recalls tender moments of his past and displays genuine concern for the political direction of his country. What Mediero portrays stands in direct contrast to the cold and austere image of the Spanish monarch popularized in paintings, legends, and historical accounts. What Mediero dramatizes in the play gives new meaning to the interplay of illusion and reality, the fundamental concepts at the very base of the social paradox that informs Mediero's dramaturgy as a whole. Less concerned with the magnificence of his historical image, Charles defines greatness and power in terms of personal human aspirations. When the king's sister tells her dying brother that he is "the most powerful person of his time," Charles responds, "[T]hat is what the history books will say, the truth is quite different. . . . You are not powerful or great because you possess nations and lands you don't even know. . . . You are great when your personal dreams and aspirations come true" (424).

    Mediero's last work, *El Niño de Belén*, is by far his most ambitious work to date. The protagonist, as the title of the play suggests, is Christ. Mediero's Christ is as critical of how society has evolved as any of the author's previous protagonists. Moreover, he reveals a propensity toward rebellion. Espousing liberal ideals, he abandons his privileged place in the Holy Trinity to realize his personal aspirations to become a bullfighter and perform in Spain's famous Maestranza bullring in Sevilla. Highly disillusioned and critical of a world that has falsified his image and erroneously interpreted his message, Mediero's protagonist declares that "what I want is to undo my historical past. My life and death have been the subject of many precious paintings that fill palaces, churches and libraries all over the world. . . . Yet my example has not served to solve human suffering, envy, political tyrannies, nothing" (251).

Christ's expresses disenchantment with a reality that has distanced itself progressively from the humanitarian principles his life exemplified. As Christ performs in the Maestranza bullring, under the assumed name of "The Child from Bethlehem," he is struck by a bullet that kills him instantly. This leads the Virgin Mary to exclaim that "do what you will, history repeats itself" (321). The Virgin Mary's final words are indicative of the way in which Mediero views the heroic stature of his characters. When asked to expound briefly on what constitutes victory for his protagonists, who characteristically face a hopeless situation and meet a tragic end, Mediero is quick to explain their cause in transcendental terms. Victory, he says, "consists in the struggle itself, the desire to confront the situation. My protagonists, each in his or her own way, combats injustice. Not to face and combat injustice implies acceptance and approval. Their victory is measured in spiritual terms, not material" (Gabriele, "Martínez Mediero habla" 217).

CRITICS' RESPONSE

Although the author of a considerable number of plays, Mediero's individual accomplishments as a playwright have not been widely discussed. A number of scholarly studies focus on Mediero's theater in relationship to that of other underground playwrights but offer little in the way of analysis of specific aspects of the playwright's dramaturgy. The studies of Francisco Ruiz Ramón, George Wellwarth, María Pilar Pérez-Stansfield, Miguel A. Medina, Alberto Miralles, and Hazel Cazorla are typical of this general approach to Mediero's theater. The importance of this approach notwithstanding, these studies are less a critical assessment of the ideology and aesthetics of Mediero's work than a general overview of his theater as a cultural phenomenon of a specific political and social national reality. More important still is the degree to which critical opinion regarding the overall importance of Mediero's dramaturgy varies. Francisco Ruiz Ramón, for example, openly expresses doubt about the artistic value of Mediero's work and questions its limited thematic scope (538), whereas Hazel Cazorla finds his work rich in content and theme and universal in scope (199). Of these general considerations, Miralles's is the only study that makes an effort to elaborate a critical evaluation based on dramatic form and theory as well as content.

Studies of a general nature that focus specifically on the individual merit of Mediero's contributions to the Spanish stage are virtually nonexistent. As regards criticism of Mediero's work of the Franco Years, the short studies of Fábregas, Isasi, and Petit do much to provide a global view of the playwright's early works, contextualize the theme of freedom, and offer a theoretical assessment of his use of cruelty. Gabriele's study of *El convidado* ("El tema bíblico") and *El último gallinero* ("Sacrificio ritual y convención dramática") are the only detailed analyses of Mediero's plays that date from the Franco Period. In these studies, Gabriele illustrates, respectively, how the playwright's use of a biblical source and ritual sacrifice serve to posit a social critique that is at once national and universal in scope. Gabriele's "Teatro español de urgencia. El caso de Manuel Martínez Mediero" represents the first attempt to view the evolution of Mediero's theater within the context of national and international trends in twentieth-century drama, drawing parallels between Mediero and Valle-Inclán, Nieva, Spain's Realist Generation, Brecht, Artaud, and Piscator.

It is Mediero's theater written after 1979 that has generated the most sustained treatment. The focus of this work has centered almost exclusively on the author's prevalent use of a historical revisionist perspective and his concern with feminist issues. Phyllis Zatlin ("Martínez Mediero, Gala, and the Demythification") and Denise DiPuccio ("*Juana del amor hermoso*: A Struggle"), for example, illustrate how Mediero presents thematic parallels between Imperial Spain and Democratic Spain to realize "his serious commentary on contemporary society" (Zatlin 7). As regards a feminist reading, a series of recent articles by John Gabriele ("*Lisístrata*, de Manuel Martínez Mediero": "Performing Feminisms"; "Gender and Patriarchy"; "Politics and the Discourse of Violence") illustrates to what degree Mediero's drama subscribes to a feminist ideology and feminist dramatic theory in order to promote alternative ways of thinking. As suggested by these more recent studies, Mediero's use of historical revisionism and feminist concerns may indeed provide the most logical critical approach to the essential elements of the playwright's artistic vision: social commitment, demythification, and liberal ideals.

Only recently has the first comprehensive study of the playwright appeared: John Gabriele's *Manuel Martínez Mediero: Deslindes de un teatro de urgencia social* (2000), which traces the evolution of Mediero's thirty-five year career. The first chapter focuses on the principal thematic and formal elements of Mediero's theater and divides his work into several phases and cycles. The four remaining chapters constitute a phase-by-phase analysis of the author's fifty-one published plays to date based on a variety of twentieth-century dramatic theories.

AWARDS AND DISTINCTIONS

Premio Nacional Teatro Universitario (1967 and 1970)
Premio del Festival de Sitges (1969 and 1972)
Premio Ciudad de Alcoy (1971)

Premio Radio España de Teatro (1974)
Premio el Espectador y la Crítica (1975)
Premio Long Play (1975)
La Medalla de Extremadura (1999)

NOTES

1. The following plays by Mediero remain unpublished, cited here with their date of composition: *La reina fofa* [The Shallow Queen] (2000) and *La verdadera historia imposible* [The Impossibly True Story] (2000).
2. The titles of plays are given with their dates of definitive composition. Regarding the publication of Mediero's plays, Editorial Fundamentos has recently published all but four of the playwright's works in their definitive version in eight volumes (see the bibliography).

BIBLIOGRAPHY

Editions and Translations

¡Adiós, muchachos!. In *Manuel Martínez Mediero. Obras completas*. Vol. 8. Madrid: Editorial Fundamentos, 2000.
Aria por un Papa español. In *Manuel Martínez Mediero. Obras completas*. Vol. 5. Madrid: Editorial Fundamentos, 1999.
El automóvil. In *Manuel Martínez Mediero, Obras completas*. Vol. 2. Madrid: Editorial Fundamentos, 1999.
Badajoz, puerto de mar. In *Manuel Martínez Mediero. Obras completas*. Vol. 6. Madrid: Editorial Fundamentos, 1999.
El bebé furioso. In *Manuel Martínez Mediero. Obras completas*. Vol. 2. Madrid: Editorial Fundamentos, 1999.
Las bragas perdidas en el tendedero. In *Manuel Martínez Mediero. Obras completas*. Vol. 3. Madrid: Editorial Fundamentos, 1999.
Carlo Famoso. In *Manuel Martínez Mediero. Obras completas*. Vol. 5. Madrid: Editorial Fundamentos, 1999.
César y Cleopatra. In *Manuel Martínez Mediero. Obras completas*. Vol. 6. Madrid: Editorial Fundamentos, 1999.
Los clandestinos. In *Manuel Martínez Mediero. Obras completas*. Vol. 3. Madrid: Editorial Fundamentos, 1999.
El convidado. In *Manuel Martínez Mediero. Obras completas*. Vol. 1. Madrid: Editorial Fundamentos, 1999.
Denuncia, juicio e inquisición de Pedro Lagarto. *Primer Acto* 153 (1973): 51–55.
El día que se descubrió el pastel. In *Manuel Martínez Mediero. Obras completas*. Vol. 3. Madrid: Editorial Fundamentos, 1999.
La Edad de Oro de mamá. In *Manuel Martínez Mediero. Obras completas*. Vol. 7. Madrid: Editorial Fundamentos, 1999.
Espectáculo siglo XX. In *Manuel Martínez Mediero. Obras completas*. Vol. 1. Madrid: Editorial Fundamentos, 1999.

Manuel Martínez Mediero: Deslindes de un teatro de urgencia social. Madrid: Fundamentos, 2000.

―――. "Gender and Patriarchy in *Juana del amor hermoso.*" In *Selected Proceedings of the Pennsylvania Foreign Language Conference 1991*, ed. Gregorio C. Martín. Pittsburgh: Duquesne University, 1995. 84–90.

―――. "*Lisístrata*, de Manuel Martínez Mediero: En busca de una identidad femenina en la España de transición." *Anales de la Literatura Española Contemporánea* 17.1–3 (1992): 229–241.

―――. "Martínez Mediero habla de su teatro." *Anales de la Literatura Española Contemporánea* 20.1–2 (1995): 223–231.

―――. "Performing Feminisms in Manuel Martínez Mediero's *Lisístrata* and *Juana del amor hermoso*: A View from the Masculine." *Revista de Estudios Hispánicos* 27 (1993): 257–274.

―――. "Politics and the Discourse of Violence in Manuel Martínez Mediero's *Lisístrata*." In *La Chispa '97: Selected Proceedings*, ed. Claire J. Paolini. New Orleans: Tulane University, 1997. 153–161.

―――. "Teatro español de urgencia. El caso de Manuel Martínez Mediero." *El teatro español contemporáneo. Autores y tendencias*, ed. Alfonso de Toro and Wilfried Floeck. Kassel: Edition Reichenberger, 1995. 217–242.

―――. "El tema bíblico y la crítica sociopolítica en *El convidado.*" *Hispanófila* 90 (1987): 1–7.

Isasi, A. Carlos. "Entrevista desde Alemania." *Primer Acto* 153 (1973): 47–50.

―――. "El teatro de Mediero." *Primer Acto* 153 (1973): 37–46

López Mozo, Jerónimo. "Y unas palabras de un amigo . . ." *Estreno* 6.2 (1980): 12–13.

Martínez Mediero, Manuel. "Algo de mí y de mi teatro." *Primer Acto* 197 (1983): 64–71.

―――. "Largo camino hasta el cachondeo." *Primer Acto* 175 (1974): 45–47.

Martínez Mediero, Manuel, and Jerónimo López Mozo. "*Las hermanas de Búfalo Bill* . . . cinco años después." *Estreno* 2.1 (1980): 11–13.

"Martínez Mediero en la hora presente." *Yorick* 38 (1970): 10–11.

Medina, Miguel A. "Manuel Martínez Mediero." In *Teatro español en el banquillo.* Valencia: Fernando Torres Editor, 1976. 41–48.

Miralles, Alberto. *Nuevo teatro español: Una alternativa social.* Madrid: Editorial Villalar, 1977.

Monleón, José. "Teatro antropofágico de Martínez Mediero." *Triunfo*, 17 junio 1978: 65–66.

Pérez-Stansfield, María Pilar. *Direcciones de teatro español de posguerra: Ruptura con el teatro burgués y radicalismo contestatario.* Madrid: Porrúa, 1983. 296–298.

Petit, Hèrve. "El teatro de la crueldad." *Primer Acto* 175 (1974): 26–29.

Ruiz Ramón, Francisco. *Historia del teatro español. Siglo XX.* 9th ed. Madrid: Cátedra, 1992. 535–538.

Salvat, Ricardo. "Entevista con M.M.M." *Tele-expres*, 28 marzo 1972: 26.

Torres Nebrera, Gregorio. "Mediero en media docena de estrenos." *Anuario de Estudios Filológicos* 20 (1997): 409–423.

Valdivieso, L. Teresa. *España: Bibliografía de un teatro "silenciado."* Lincoln, NE: Society of Spanish and Spanish-American Studies, 1979. 43–48.

Wellwarth, George. *Spanish Underground Drama.* University Park: Pennsylvania State University Press, 1972. 91–96.

Zatlin, Phyllis. "Martínez Mediero, Gala, and the Demythification of Spanish History." *Modern Language Studies* 16.4 (1986): 3–8.

JOSÉ MARTÍN RECUERDA
(1925–   )

Denise G. Mills

BIOGRAPHY

The works of José Martín Recuerda are a rich tapestry illustrating the turbulent passions and politics of Spain. This prize-winning playwright's literary career spans nearly fifty years of crisis, repression, hope, disillusion, and struggle.

José Martín Recuerda was born in 1925 into a working-class home in Granada, whose colors, sounds, smells, and music are evident in his later plays. Recuerda obtained a degree in Arts and Letters from the University of Granada in 1947 and pursued his literary calling while engaged in a variety of teaching positions. The economic necessity of teaching was not without its benefits: During eight years at the Teatro Universitario Español at the University of Granada, he had the invaluable opportunity to experience drama from the director's interpretive and technical point of view.

Deprived of employment as a result of denunciations against his work, Recuerda spent much of the late 1960s as a visiting professor in several North American universities. His appointment as chair of the "Juan del Encina" Theater of the University of Salamanca in 1971 gave Martín Recuerda a venue from which he could continue to develop his dramatic talent.

Martín Recuerda is included in what critic José Monleón calls the "Realist Generation" (*Cuatro autores* 11). The common themes of this Realist Generation concern issues of social justice, the exploitation of the working and middle classes, and the moral and social hypocrisy of established society.

The critical stance of Realist Generation authors toward Spanish society did not endear them to the government censors who could, and did, reject controversial or critical portrayals of Spanish life, especially those with negative reference to the government, the armed forces, the Catholic Church, or the devastating Spanish Civil War.

Spain is the soul of José Martín Recuerda's work. This fixation is a painful one at times. "In the body of my work there has been a logical evolution, but my fundamental emphasis or concern is rooted in analyzing what Spain is. This, perhaps, is my greatest flaw as an author" [En mi obra ha habido una lógica evolución, pero mi tendencia o preocupación fundamental radica en analizar lo que España es. Este quizá sea mi gran pecado como autor] (Ruiz Molinero 5). It is a concern that guided him through periods of exile, periods of unemployment, periods of despair and anger.

DRAMATURGY: MAJOR WORKS AND THEMES

With even a superficial reading of Recuerda's published plays, the central point is obvious: to expose the side of Spain—often more specifically of Andalusia—that is a far cry from the sunny, colorful tourist facade portrayed in the Quinteros' dramas. The Spain of Martín Recuerda's dramas stifles variance and dissension and crushes the hearts and souls of misfits and rebels.

The Plain [La llanura] (1947) deals with a woman's refusal to resign herself to the loss of her husband who was summarily shot by the Nationalists at the height of the Spanish Civil War.[1] This woman is haunted by the idea that her husband's body was left unburied outside the town. Her daily pilgrimage to the plain and to the municipal offices seeking information humiliates and eventually destroys her family.

The Illusions of the Travelling Sisters [Las ilusiones de las hermanas viajeras], written in 1955 but not published until 1981, is a gentle play focusing on the stagnant lives and wistful dreams of three sisters and their aged tenant.

Don Ramón's Little Theater [El teatrito de don Ramón] (1957), the Lope de Vega prizewinner for 1958, is a drama about an amateur theatrical company whose love of the theater and need for companionship go hand in hand. The negative critical response was a blow to Martín Recuerda, and he reacted by vowing that Don Ramón would be the last of his characters to accept defeat gracefully.

Julita Torres, the schoolteacher protagonist of *Like the Dry Stalks along the Way* [Como las secas cañas del camino] (1960), loses both her position and her reputation when her kindness to a young male student is maliciously misinterpreted by the hypocritical social leaders of the town of Salobreña.

Savages in Puente San Gil [Las salvajes en Puente San Gil],[2] written in 1961, indicates Martín Recuerda's developing social conscience and increasing power as a dramatist. The play deals with a travelling show of dancing girls whose arrival in Puente San Gil provokes furious denunciation on the part of the priest and the wives of the hierarchy, smirking lust on the part of the men, and violence and rape on the part of some frustrated youths. While protagonists of the earlier plays were unwilling and/or unable to defy the social order that suppressed them, the dancing troupe responds with fierce rebellion. *Las salvajes* marks the inception of collective defiance as an important dramatic technique in Martín Recuerda's work.

Francisco Ruiz Ramón captures the essence of *The Christ* [El cristo] (1964), calling it "a violent criticism of popular Spanish Catholicism" [una violenta crítica del catolicismo popular español] (*Historia del teatro español. Siglo XX* 506). The play centers on a young, idealistic priest's failed attempts to instill real religious faith in his superstitious parishioners.

Who Wants a Verse from the Archpriest of Hita [¿Quién quiere una copla del Archipreste de Hita?] (1965) is Martín Recuerda's first drama to explore the connections between historical and contemporary Spain and features Juan Ruiz, the Archpriest of Hita and author of the Book of Good Love [El libro de buen amor]. The fourteenth-century setting of a desperate Spain bereft of young men, money, and ideals lost to the interminable war against the Muslims portends Martín Recuerda's time.

The Man from Caracas [El caraqueño] (1968), a product of Recuerda's exile in the United States, treats the crisis provoked by the return to Spain of Emilio, who has made his fortune in Caracas. The struggle between Emilio and his father embodies the confrontation between a traditional generation and a changing one.

Martín Recuerda maximizes the dramatic and technical possibilities of the theater in *The Inmates of the Convent of Saint Mary Egyptian* [Las arrecogías del Beaterio de Santa María Egipciaca] (1970), his compelling portrayal of the popular nineteenth-century Granadine heroine Mariana Pineda.

The Man Who Is Deceived [El engañao] (1972) is the story of San Juan de Dios, who Martha Halsey calls "a saint who embodies perfectly José Martín Recuerda's idea of the Christian religion" [un santo que encarna perfectamente la idea de la religión cristiana que tiene José Martín Recuerda] ("*El engañao* o el nuevo drama" 40). This historical drama follows the holy man's struggle to minister to Granada's poor against a backdrop of Imperial corruption and indifference.

Unbridled Horses [Caballos desbocaos] (1978) is a reworking of the plot of *Like the Dry Stalks along the Way*. But where the title *Dry Stalks* evokes the withered fragility and hollowness of Julita Torres's life, *Unbridled Horses* presents the Andalusian town twenty years later amid the reckless and unrestrained chaos of the early post-Franco period.

Conversions [Las conversiones] was conceived in 1973 and not finished until 1980. The play treats the classical Spanish literary character of the Celestina. Martín Recuerda recounts a series of betrayals that twisted an innocent Jewish convert girl into Fernando de Rojas's malevolent character.

La Trotski (1984) is a harsh view of post-Franco Spain. The protagonist indicts the government for its failure to improve the life of the working class. The disillusion and despair of the defeated Republicans of the late 1930s are repeated in the anguish of the late 1980s.

The Scar [La cicatriz] (1985) extends the common Martín Recuerda theme of searching for acceptances and love in a rigid and callous society to explore homosexual love. The play takes place in a monastery where men struggle with the question of authority, faith and identity.

Trotski goes to the Indies [La Trotski se va a las Indias] (1986) revisits the character of the 1984 play. Where the earlier Trotski play denounced post-Franco Spain, this play projects the protagonist's fury on the exposition proposed for Seville. Trotski sneers at national and local governments' failure to stimulate economic and/or moral prosperity and rages at the waste of creative and financial resources on Expo-92.

Martín Recuerda's play *Amadis of Gaul* [Amadis de Gaula] (1991) reiterates the author's affinity for Spain's literary and historical past. Rather than the accustomed series of heroic adventures, Martín Recuerda's Amadis and the magician Arcalaus embody the struggle to find love. The bitter and cruel magician denies its existence, and Amadis, anguished, defeated, and disillusioned, strives to find it.

Carteles rotos/Torn Posters (1982) is a despairing look at the moral, physical, and economic disintegration of a once powerful and prosperous family which mirrors the unsettled and aimless late transition period in Spain.

Las Reinas del Paralelo/ The Queens of Paralelo (1991) displays several Martín Recuerda hallmarks: the choral character, the *teatro-fiesta*, the play within the play, and an elaborate, grotesque stage setting. This play, set in late 1940s Barcelona, is another critical but loving look at the marginal, desperate, and suffering side of Spain embodied in the artists, customers, dissidents, and authorities who work in and around a squalid nightclub.

La Trotski descubre las Américas/Trotski Discovers America is the final piece in the Trotski trilogy which finds the dispirited, yet defiant, heroine striking out for new territory. Other later plays include *El carmen en Atlántida*, *El payaso y los pueblos del sur*, and *Los últimos días del escultor de su alma*.

CRITICS' RESPONSE

Martha T. Halsey must be mentioned first among a growing list of Hispanists investigating Recuerda's role in modern Spanish Literature. Angel Cobo Rivas, Marion Holt, Antonio Morales, José Monleón, Francisco Ruiz Ramón, Sixto Torres, and Barry Weingarten have also contributed to the body of work on this playwright.

Most analyses of Martín Recuerda's work have concentrated on the central issue of social criticism. Monleón divides Recuerda's work into two phases: the early plays that are critical, but whose protagonists are victims who suffer in silence, and the later plays, distinguished by the rebellion of the characters and their invitation to the public to do likewise.

Francisco Ruiz Ramón agrees with the two-phase division, noting that Recuerda himself has said that he made a conscious decision after the premiere of *El teatrito de Don Ramón*. "I promised myself that my characters would always rebel, that they would raise consciousness, that they would scream, that they would never let themselves be destroyed" [Me prometí que mis personajes se rebelarían siempre, que exaltarían sempre las conciencias, que gritarían, que no se dejarían hundir en ningún momento] ("Pequeñas memorias" 55).

Martha Halsey affirms that the plays following *El teatrito de Don Ramón* (which she calls "violent dramas") are Recuerda's most important, because they force the spectator to identify with either the victim or the oppressor. In an introductory essay to *El engañao* and *Caballos desbocaos*, Angel Cobo prefers to divide the plays into three parts: the lyrical-dramatic poems, violent choral theater, and theater-celebration. [poema lírico-dramático, teatro de expresión coral y violenta, y teatro-fiesta] (24).

Whether Recuerda's plays are divided into two or three phases, in most studies the emphasis has been on the element of social criticism and the characters' reaction to their oppression.

An element that is usually missing, or mentioned in passing, is one of tantamount importance in the study of Martín Recuerda's work—the author's dramatic technique or stagecraft. In his classic essay on the theater, Antonin Artaud utterly rejects "a theater which subordinates the mise en scène and production, i.e., everything in itself that is specifically theatrical, to the text" (41). To genuinely appreciate Martín Recuerda's craft, one must focus on the entirety of his work, a creative process involving not only plots, themes, personalities, and social commentary but also the craft of the playwright: staging, plotting, the introduction and development of collective characters, the use of playmaking as a technique, gestures, signs, lighting, and music.

Recuerda's inspired skill in staging is of fundamental importance to the exciting quality of his plays. The pathetic little theater of Don Ramón within Recuerda's stage, depicting a shabby, sorry garret, is a distant antecedent to the fascinating set of *Las conversiones*, which includes a multi-level stage divided by draped bolts of slashed brocade and velvet, a terrible hanging of animal carcasses, skins, and hides, platforms, a trapdoor, and an elevated nest of twigs.

Another significant technique is the playwright's use of the fiesta motif. *Las arrecogías* is subtitled "Spanish Celebration in Two Parts" [Fiesta española en dos partes], and the subtitle of *Caballos desbocaos* is "Theater-Carnaval in Two Parts" [Teatro carnaval en dos partes]. Martín Recuerda's use of festivity as a backdrop for the grim realities of his plays begins in *La llanura* with flashbacks to the wedding day of the protagonist and develops in later works to merge fiesta and drama. The festival atmosphere lends itself naturally to the inclusion of music and dance, which may add a note of gaiety or serve as a grotesque or pathetic parody of fiesta.

Martín Recuerda also uses drama as a technical device. His play-within-the-play is not a Pirandellian awareness of the author as character and the character as actor. Instead, he uses playmaking and performance, especially unsuccessful attempts, to emphasize the futility and fragility of his characters.

Another component of Recuerda's maturation as a dramatist is the development of the chorus and the collective character. In *La llanura* there is merely as an offstage presence a singer of Gypsy ballads who echoes the author's beliefs. In *Las conversiones* it is imposing and ever present, narrating, assuming, reacting, assuming the parts of ruffians, workers, and prostitutes. The role of this collective character often reflects that of the audience and has evolved in Recuerda's dramas from that of a passive onlooker to aroused participant.

If success for a dramatist need not depend on the amount of profit made or the length of a play's run, but can be defined by appreciation and interest, then Martín Recuerda was a success before *Las arrecogías del Beaterio de Santa María Egipciaca* took the 1977 season by storm. It was this play, however, that brought him critical, financial, and public success with its premiere under the direction of Adolfo Marsillach just after the death of the dictator.

Las arrecogías is the most well-known, the most acclaimed, and the most analyzed of Martín Recuerda's plays. In this play the dramatist demonstrates his mastery of what Artaud calls the "poetry in space" of the theater—"music, dance, plastic art, pantomime, mimicry, gesticulation, intonation, architecture, lighting, and scenery" (39)—which carry meaning just as valid, if not more so, than the spoken word.

Las arrecogías, preoccupied with the theme of rebellion, sacrifice, and solidarity, is Martín Recuerda's first overtly political play. The play deals with the historical figure Mariana Pineda, a Liberal sympathizer who facilitated the escape of political prisoners during the repressive years of the reign of Fernando VII in the first third of the eighteenth century. Mariana is arrested and jailed in the Convent of Saint Mary Egyptian, which serves as a sort of woman's reformatory. Mariana's story is echoed in the stories of the other women, and the audience comes to see that they are all condemned by the repressive regime.

The impact of the staging of *Las arrecogías* is as powerful as the absorbing political message. In this play, arguably his finest, Martín Recuerda succeeds in bringing together the elements of scenery, costume, sound, and light as an integral part of this dynamic piece.

Martín Recuerda's staging in this play is superb: The stage represents the streets of Granada and the convent of St. Mary Egyptian, which is behind walls that can be raised to the ceiling for scenes within the convent. The set is designed to make the aisles in the seating area merge with Granada's hills in the scenery. On either side of the stage are the windows and balconies of nearby houses. In order to engage the audience, Martín Recuerda makes extraordinary use of the entire theater. Ruiz Ramón notes that as soon as the playgoer enters, he becomes a part of he action of the play. The musicians and some of the actors are milling about, greeting the public and handing out flowers. In his introduction to the play, Ruiz Ramón observes: "When this celebration is moved to the stage the spectators will already have begun to participate in it, or, at least will have been caught up in its atmosphere" [Cuando la fiesta se traslade al escenario, los espectadores habrán empezado ya a participar en ella, o, al menos, a ser envueltos por su atmósfera] (*Las salvajes*, 21).

The convent is a closed space within the city that Ruiz Ramón calls another closed space because of the repressive political atmosphere. Recuerda makes the audience a part of the closed space by having characters move in and out of the stage area from the seating area. At the end of the first part, the prisoners join

Mariana Pineda in expressing their furious rebellion by singing, clapping, and stamping. At this point actors who are seated in the theater seats rise to join the defiance. The women leave the stage area and join them in the aisles, clapping and chanting. As they leave the stage, replicas of prison bars descend from around the ceiling, effectively making prisoners of the entire audience. The women return to the stage, their fury spent, as the bars rise to permit the heavy convent walls to seal them up in the convent again. This movement of the convent walls is especially convincing; they can focus attention where needed, and when they are raised, the audience is conscious of being confined in the convent prison.

More than in previous plays Martín Recuerda supplies visual richness. Upon entering the theater the spectator sees various handwritten signs on the convent walls insulting the authorities of the King and encouraging rebellion. Pieces of cloth in the form the banners, bandages, or clothing are prominent in this play. Lolilla, the liberal seamstress, brandishes a red banner on which is written "You are not alone, Inmates" [No estaís solas, arrecogías]. One of the manacled prisoners, repeating the plea of Christ, begs for a scrap of cloth dipped in vinegar to soothe her swollen wrists. A tortured Gypsy girl is bandaged with scraps of cloth torn from the clothing of the inmates. Sor Encarnación, a peasant novice with liberal sympathies, pulls the veil from her head and tears her religious habit.

There is great contrast between the exaggerated French styles worn by Lolilla and her seamstresses and their nationalistic, revolutionary sentiments. There is also great visual contrast between the jagged edges of the tatters worn by the inmates and the solemn orderliness of the nun's habits and the soldiers' uniforms.

Sound plays a major role in this drama. Bells signify prayer, alarm, and death. When Mariana has been taken away the sound of tolling bells inundates the theater, and the echo of the bells lingers as the inmates announce her execution. The grating clash of metal against metal is heard as the women bang their manacles and chains against the bars that imprison them.

Lighting is another element employed with the purpose of turning the spectators into accomplices. When the inmates invade the seating space of the theater at the end of Part One, the house lights are turned up. The lights, the physical positions of the actors, the descending bars, the ascending walls all serve to eliminate the barrier between character and spectator.

In *Las arrecogías* the elements of playacting and fiesta are vehicles for social commentary and political statement interwoven in the action of the play. All elements of society are involved in deception: As the nuns sing, they also permit torture and abuse in the King's name; as the town readies itself for the bullfight, furtive rebellion is glimpsed behind windows and doors; as acrobats perform, they threaten violence to reactionary forces; as Lolilla dances, she tosses a message of solidarity to the imprisoned women.

Martín Recuerda often creates characters who function as a chorus. In *Las arrecogías* there are three main choruses: Lolilla and her seamstresses, the nuns, and the inmates. Lolilla and her *costureras* embody all of the choric possibilities: They comment on and participate in the action; they provide information; and they set the mood for much of the play. The seamstresses deliberately propagate the notion that they are silly, shallow girls concerned only with fashion and parties in order to disguise their rebellion against the Crown. The altruistic seamstresses are consistent with the heroine who sacrifices her body, her lover, and her life to the cause of liberty.

The nuns of *Las arrecogías* are a chilling chorus. The nuns are made ominous and anonymous by their sanctioned use of force hidden behind massive walls. Under the guise of reforming "fallen women," the nuns conspire, and perhaps participate, in the detention, abuse, torture, and death of the prisoners. The security offered by membership in this group is absolute: Their vow of obedience releases the nuns, and the commands of the King release the Mother Superior, from responsibility for their actions.

The inmates are a diverse group: Among them are prostitutes, criminals, political activists, liberal sympathizers, conspirators.[3] In "Martín Recuerda: El estado de sitio," Ruiz Ramón characterizes the inmates as "divided and mutinous" [divididas y enfrentadas] (207) and notes that their eventual identification with Mariana Pineda is their means of achieving solidarity. Slowly the inmates recognize that Mariana is as alone, abandoned, and terrified as they are. Instrumental in the unification process are Mariana's fury at the sight of the tortured Gypsy girl and her scornful refusal of an offer to secure her own release by betraying the noblemen who helped her. *Las arrecogías* is ostensibly the story of Mariana Pineda, but neither she nor any one inmate is the protagonist of this drama. Collectively, as a group whose consolidation has meant sacrifice on the part of all its members, the inmates become the focal point of the play. Indeed, the process of unification of the protagonist is the point of the play and the point Recuerda is making about oppression: that in unity there is moral, emotional, and political strength.

AWARDS AND DISTINCTIONS

José Martín Recuerda is the only author who has twice been awarded the prestigious Lope de Vega National Theater Prize [Premio Nacional de Teatro Lope de Vega]—in 1959 for *El teatrito de don Ramón* and again in 1976 for *El engañao.*

Las arrecogías del Beaterio de Santa María Egipciaca, Recuerda's most renowned play, has received the Provincial Prizes "Radio Popular de Madrid" and "Vivarambla." In 1980 this play was performed in English at Pennsylvania State University's Resident Theater Company. In that same year the play was performed at the Sorbonne in Paris.

There has been considerable interest in Recuerda's work. An English translation of *La llanura* was aired by the BBC in 1954, and in 1965 Antonio Ribas directed a film version of *Las salvajes en Puente San Gil* that was screened at the Cannes Film Festival. *Como las secas cañas del camino* was televised in 1968 and *El teatrito de don Ramón* in 1969 by TVE Estudio 1. *El Cristo*, not produced in Spain until 1983, received one of Coventry Cathedral's International Prizes in 1969 and was broadcast in an Italian translation by RAI (Italy's national TV network) in 1972 and 1975.

NOTES

1. Martha T. Halsey notes, "To Martín Recuerda belongs the distinction of having had staged, however mutilated by the censors, the earliest play to deal explicitly with the continuing effects of the Civil War" (Halsey and Zatlin 12).

Recuerda himself says that *La llanura* was mutilated by the censors (Monleón, *Cuatro autores* 46). After months of waiting, the play was approved. The approval was predicated, however, upon removal of mention of the Civil War or shooting. An executed man was to be the victim not of political reprisals but of some vague neighborhood quarrel.

2. The dramatist received such a storm of protest because *Secas cañas* named the towns of Salobreña and Motril that he later created the name Puente San Gil, and although the episode of *El Cristo* is based on a true story, the author carefully does not name the village.

3. Emilio Orozco Díaz, the Director of the Department of Spanish Literature of the University of Granada, investigated the Convent of Saint Mary Egyptian's documents for the year 1831, *after* reading Recuerda's manuscript of *Las arrecogías*, and found historical references that coincide with the stories created by Martín Recuerda (from the playbill of the Madrid premiere).

BIBLIOGRAPHY

Editions/Translations

La llanura (1947)

Estreno 3.1 (Spring 1977): T1–T16.
>   Granada: Don Quijote, 1982. Ed. Antonio Morales.
>   Motril: Ayuntamiento, 1996. Intro. Angel Cobo Rivas.

Las ilusiones de las hermanas viajeras (1955)
>   Murcia: Godoy, 1981. Ed. Antonio Morales.

El teatrito de don Ramón (1957)
>   Madrid: Taurus, 1969. Ed. José Monelón.
>   Madrid: Escelicer, 1969.
>   Barcelona: Plaza y Janés, 1984. Ed. Gerardo Velázque Cueto.

Como las secas cañas del camino (1960)
>   Madrid: Escelicer, 1967.
>   Barcelona: Plaza y Janés, 1984.

Las salvajes en Puente San Gil (1961)

> *Primer Acto* 48 (1963): 29–71.
> Madrid: Aguilar, 1964. Ed. F. C. Sáinz de Robles.
> Madrid: Escelicer, 1965.
> Madrid: Taurus, 1969. Ed. José Monleón
> Madrid: Cátedra, 1977. Ed. Francisco Ruiz Ramón.

El Cristo (1964)

> Madrid: Taurus, 1969. Ed. José Monleón.
> Granada: Don Quijote, 1982. Ed. Antonio Morales.

¿Quién quiere una copla del Archipreste de Hita? (1965)

> Madrid: Nacional, 1965.
> Madrid: Escelicer, 1966

El caraqueño (1968)

> *Primer Acto* 107 (1969): 35–78.
> Madrid: Escelicer, 1971.

Las arrecogías del Beaterio de Santa María Egipciaca (1970)

> *Primer Acto* 169 (1974): 16–61.
> Madrid: Cátedra, 1977. Ed. Francisco Ruiz Ramón.

The Inmates of the Convent of Saint Mary Egyptian (1980)

> Trans. Robert Lima in Drama Contemporary: Spain.
> New York: Performing Arts, 1985.

El engañao (1972)

> Madrid: Cátedra, 1981. Ed. Martha T. Halsey and Angel Cobo Rivas.

Caballos desbocaos (1978)

> Madrid: Cátedra, 1981. Ed. Martha T. Halsey and Angel Cobo Rivas.

Las conversiones (1980)

> Murcia: Godoy, 1981. Ed. Antonio Morales.

La Trotski (1984)

> *Primer Acto* 207 (1985): 57–96.
> Sevilla: Andaluzas Unidas, 1990. Intro. Angel Cobo Rivas.
> Motril: Asociación Cultural Guadalfeo, 1998. Ed. Angel Cobo Rivas.

La cicatriz (1985)

> Canente 7 (1990): 79–110.
> Salobreña: Alhulia, 1998. Intro. Angel Cobo Rivas.

La Trotski se va a las Indias (1986)

> Sevilla: Andaluzas Unidas, 1990. Intro. Angel Cobo Rivas.
> Motril: Asociación Cultural Guadalfeo, 1998. Ed. Angel Cobo Rivas.

Amadis de Gaula (1986)

> Murcia: Universidad de Murcia, 1991. Intro. Jacobo Fernández Aguilar.
> Miami: Universal, 1995. Ed. Sixto Torres.

Las reinas del Paralelo

    Primer Acto 261 (1995): 48–93.

Carteles rotos

    Miami: Universal, 1995. Ed. Sixto Torres.

El carmen en Atlántida

    Salobreña: Alhulia, 1998. Intro. Angel Cobo Rivas.

El payaso y los pueblos del sur

    Murcia: Escuela Superior de Arte Dramático, 1998.

La Trotski descubre las Américas

    Motril: Asociación Cultural Guadalfeo, 1998. Ed. Angel Cobo Rivas.

Los últimos días del escultor de su alma.

    Peligros, Granada: Comares, 1998.

Other Works

"A los que pueden escucharnos y entendernos." *Primer Acto* 158 (1973): 73–74.
De mis recuerdos más queridos en Motril. "La Caramba" en la iglesia de San Jerónimo el Real. Motril: Ingenio, 1996.
"Desahogo sobre algo de mí y de las salvajes." *Primer Acto* 48 (1963): 26–28.
Génesis de El engañao: Versión dramática de la otra cara del Imperio. Salamanca: Universidad de Salamanca, 1979.
"Manifiesto de *El caraqueño.*" *Primer Acto* 107 (1969): 32–34.
"Notas para un nuevo teatro español." In *El teatro y su crítica.* Servicio de Publicaciones. Málaga: Instituto de la Diputación Provincial, 1974. 313–329.
"Pequeñas memorias." In *Teatro: El teatrito de Don Ramón, Las salvajes en Puente San Gil, El Cristo.* Madrid: Taurus, 1969. 54–59.

Critical Studies

Acerete, Julio C. "*Como las secas cañas del camino* de José Martín Recuerda." *Primer Acto* 73 (1966): 62.
Artaud, Antonin. *The Theater and Its Double.* New York: Grove Press, 1958.
Cazorla, Hazel. "Literatura y realidad histórica en *Las conversiones* de Martín Recuerda." *Romance Quarterly* 35 (February 1988): 75–79.
Cobo Rivas, Angel. "Apunte biográfico-creador de José Martín Recuerda." *Cuadernos de Dramaturgía Contemporánea* 3 (1998): 31–40.
———. *José Martín Recuerda: Génesis y evolución de un autor dramático.* Granada: Diputación Provincial, 1993.
———. "Martín Recuerda, reciente." *Primer Acto* 257 (1995): 33–38.
Fernández Santos, Angel. "Un estreno agitado." *Primer Acto* 48 (1963): 24–25.
Halsey, Martha T. "Dramatic Patterns in Three History Plays of Contemporary Spain." *Hispania* 71 (March 1988): 20–30.
———. "*El engañao* and the Primitive Christianity of Juan de Dios." *American Hispanist* 4.32–33 (1979): 3–7.

————. *"El engañao* o el nuevo drama histórico de la posguerra." In *El engañao,* ed. Martha T. Halsey and Angel Cobo. Madrid: Cátedra, 1981. 27–50.

————. "Introduction to the Historical Drama of Post–Civil-War Spain." *Estreno* 14.1 (1988): 11–17.

————. "Juana la Loca in Three Dramas of Tamayo y Baus, Galdós and Martín Recuerda." *Modern Language Studies* 9.1 (Winter 1978–9): 47–59.

————. "Martín Recuerda's *Las arrecogías del Beaterio de Santa María Egipciaca:* A Contemporary Celebration of Mariana de Pineda and Her Sisters." *Kentucky Romance Quarterly* 20.30 (1979): 305–318.

————. "The Violent Dramas of Martín Recuerda." *Hispanófila* (September 1980): 71–93.

Halsey, Martha T., and Angel Cobo, eds. *El engañao, Caballos desbocaos.* By José Martín Recuerda. Madrid: Cátedra, 1981.

Halsey, Martha T., and Phyllis Zatlin, eds. *The Contemporary Spanish Theater: A Collection of Critical Essays.* Lanham, MD: University Press of America, 1988.

Heras, Santiago de las. "Un autor recuperado: Una entrevista con José Martín Recuerda." *Primer Acto* 107 (1969): 29.

Holt, Marion. *"The Inmates of the Convent of Saint Mary Egyptian." Theatre Journal* 32.3 (1980): 390–91.

Laín Entralgo, Pedro. "En el redaño de Iberia." *Primer Acto* 48 (1963): 21–23.

Méndez Moya, Adelardo. *"La cicatriz* de José Martín Recuerda: Una visión de amor total." *Canente* 7 (1990): 71–77.

Miras, Domingo. *"El paralelo* de Martín Recuerda." *Primer Acto* 261 (1995): 42–45.

Molero Manglano, Luis. *"El teatrito de don Ramón* y su mejor crítica." *La Estafeta Literaria* 172 (1959): 16.

————. "Teatro Español. *El teatrito de don Ramón,* Premio Lope de Vega, 1959." *La Estafeta Literaria* 169 (1959): 16.

Monleón, José. *Cuatro autores críticos.* Granada: Gabinete de Teatro, Secretaria de Extensión Universitaria, 1976.

————. "Entrevista con José Martín Recuerda." *Primer Acto* 169 (1974): 8–11.

————. "Martín Recuerda en Salamanca." *Primer Acto* 143 (1972): 67–70.

————. "Martín Recuerda o la otra Andalucia." In *Teatro: El teatrito de don Ramón, Las salvajes en Puente San Gil, El Cristo,* ed. José Monleón. Madrid: Taurus, 1969, 9–21.

————, ed. *Teatro: El teatrito de don Ramón, Las salvajes en Puente San Gil, El Cristo.* Madrid: Taurus, 1969.

Morales, Antonio. *"La llanura* o la conciencia temprana." In *La llanura. El Cristo.* Granada: Don Quijote, 1982.

————. "Martín Recuerda en la periferia." *Primer Acto* 210 (1985): 186–187.

————. "La obra ignorada de José Martín Recuerda: *El Cristo."* In *La llanura. El Cristo.* Granada: Don Quijote, 1982.

Oliva, César. "El personajé perdedor en la generación teatral realista: El caso límite de José Martín Recuerda." *Cuadernos de Dramaturgia Contemporanea* 3 (1998): 41–49.

Ruiz Molinaro, Juan J. "José Martín Recuerda o el teatro subterráneo." *Ideal* [Granada], 14 abril 1974: 5–6.

Ruiz Ramón, Francisco. *Historia del teatro español. Siglo XX.* 3d ed. Madrid: Cátedra, 1977.

————. "Martín Recuerda: El estado de sitio." In *Studies in Honor of Gustavo Correa*, ed. Charles D. Faulhaber, et al. Potomac, MD: Scripta Humanística, 1986.

————. "Notas para una lectura de *Las arrecogías*." *Primer Acto* 169 (1974): 14–15.

————, ed. *Las salvajes en Puente San Gil, Las arrecogías del Beaterio de Santa María Egipciaca*. By José Martín Recuerda. Madrid: Cátedra, 1977.

Torres, Sixto L. "*Carteles rotus*: A Postista Vision of Recent Spain." *Círculo Cultural Panamericano* 18 (1989): 223–229.

————. "José Martín Recuerda's New Play: *La Trotski*." *Estreno* 14.1 (1988): 3–4.

————. "Martín Recuerda's *Caballos desbocaos* and the Quality of Life in Post-Franco Spain." *Hispanic Journal* 8.1 (1986): 61–68.

Vallejo, Javier. "Las dos Españas en un café cantante. *La Trotski* de José Martín Recuerda." *El Público* 93 (1992): 42–43.

Vaquero Cid, Benigno. "Sobre *La llanura*." *Estreno* 3.1 (1977): 18–19.

Velázquez Cueto, Gerardo. "De Lorca a Martín Recuerda: Crónica de una violencia siempre anunciada." *Insula* 440–441 (julio–augusto 1983): 23.

Weingarten, Barry E. "Form and Meaning of José Martín Recuerda's Social Dramas: *Las salvajes en Puente San Gil*." *Estreno* 6.1 (1980): 4–6.

————. "José Martín Recuerda's *Como las secas cañas del camino* and the Rural Drama." *Hispanic Review* 51 (1983): 435–448.

————. "José Martín Recuerda's *La Trotski*: Post-Franco Spain as Esperpento." *Estreno* 19.2 (1993): 44–47.

ALFONSO PASO GIL
(1926–1978)

Núria Triana Toribio

BIOGRAPHY

Born in Madrid on September 12, 1926, Alfonso Paso Gil seemed predestined to become a playwright. Although he obtained a degree in American History in 1951 and had one or two scholarly articles published, he decided not to pursue his studies further. From childhood he had been immersed in the world of theater. His father was Antonio Paso, the Andalusian author of comedies, and his mother was the actress, Juana Gil. His father showed Paso the mechanics of theater, a fact that biographers see as having a deep influence on his young mind. He even married into the theater; his first wife was Evangelina, daughter of the acclaimed author of the 1940s, E. Jardiel Poncela. Soon after his marriage, he aroused the hostility of his family by deciding to become totally independent. In these first years he lived the familiar story of the unsuccessful young writer concealing his struggle against poverty from his ostentatious theater colleagues. Nonetheless, it was generally believed that Paso, with strong family connections in the world of theater, would easily succeed.

During these early years as a playwright, Paso was a founding member of the avant-garde group *Arte Nuevo*, a university theater organization that sought to revitalize the Spanish theater (see Dramaturgy). Later, when the movement broke apart, Paso still cultivated the friendship of some of its members. For a while his theater remained socially responsible and engaged, as that of the group had been. His friend and biographer, Alfonso Marqueríe, recalls that, for the first ten years, it was very difficult for the playwright even to get his work staged; in his study *Alfonso Paso y su teatro*, Marqueríe relates several anecdotes about the setbacks Paso suffered in his early career.[1]

Marion P. Holt points out the important effect of these early years of privation on the young writer's decision to compromise his beliefs.[2] Some years later, in a long interview, Paso himself adduced this need for financial security as one of the reasons he embraced less controversial stances.[3] Economic necessity, combined with the conviction that the Spanish theater could be renewed "from within," led to the "second start" of his career. In 1956, he abandoned all the *Arte Nuevo* postulates and subsequently became the most prolific playwright in Spain, specializing in comedies and farces. He was awarded several prizes, although he was not much respected by the more erudite public and critics. His sympathies with conformist ideas, and the fact that he was seen as having given in to the demands of petit-bourgeois audiences earned him the hatred of many critics and fellow-writers.

Paso's output was well over 100 titles, some of which have had over 100 or even 200 productions. Parallel to his career as a playwright, he also became interested in writing and directing cinema. In the mid-1950s, he started to write film scripts in collaboration with the successful producer José Luis Dibildos. From this collaboration came, among other works, *Felices Pascuas* [Happy Christmas] (1954), directed by J. A. Bardem, and Antonio del Amo's *Sierra Maldita* [Cursed Sierra] (1954). Paso soon became one of the most prolific scriptwriters of the period. He collaborated in *La noche y el alba* [The Night and the Dawn] (1958), directed by José María Forqué; *Los que tocan el piano* [Those Who Play Piano] (1968), and *Lola, espejo oscuro* [Lola, Dark Mirror] (1965). He became further involved in cinema through the many adaptations of his comedies. Beginning in 1969, Paso himself became an actor and directed some of his films. Among them were *Los extremeños se tocan* [The Men from Extremadura Touch Each Other] (1969) and *La otra residencia* [The Other Dwelling] (1970).

Paso died in Madrid in 1978. Although some of his plays have been revived for production, his name is rarely mentioned today. For one reason, his work was closely identified with the Franco dictatorship. More than that, his name connotes selling out to audience-ratings, total escapism, and the denial of social responsibility.

DRAMATURGY: MAJOR WORKS AND THEMES

Paso's creative career falls into two distinct periods. In order to characterize them properly, it is necessary to describe the prevailing socioeconomic climate in Spain in the 1940s and early 1950s. In those years, the situation in the Spanish theater was similar to that which prevailed following the crisis of 1898. Theaters were mainly showcasing comedies for the bourgeoisie, plays that encouraged an irresponsible escapism rather than recognition of the country's deep social divisions in the aftermath of the Civil War.

In 1945, against this background of denial and escapist art, a group of young students and theater enthusiasts adopted attitudes that challenged the status quo. Alfonso Paso was a member of this group, together with other young playwrights such as Medardo Fraile and Alfonso Sastre, and the budding critics Alfredo Marquerie, Haro Tecglen, and Martín Zaro. The group was named *Arte Nuevo*, and, as Alfonso Sastre explains, "[it] was born as a perhaps confused and excited way of saying 'no' to the existing state of affairs; and the state of affairs for those of us who felt a theatrical vocation was precisely the sort of play that was produced on our stages" [*Arte Nuevo* nació como una forma—quizás tumultuosa y confusa de decir que no a lo que nos rodeaba; y lo que nos rodeaba a nosotros que sentíamos la vocación del teatro, era precisamente el teatro que se producía en nuestros escenarios].[4]

The group's fight for an engaged and socially responsible theater was not eased by the fact that the contemporary Spanish cultural scene was then under the close scrutiny of the *Movimiento*. Despite opposition, the group struggled for two years to reform the Spanish theater. It is difficult to pinpoint their ideological stance, for, as their later careers would reveal, the group comprised members with sometimes opposite points of view. Moreover, some members were not interested in taking an openly political line.

In order to assess the group's overall intention, it is important to consider César Oliva's study *El teatro desde 1936* in which he analyzes the common purpose of *Arte Nuevo*:

"It would be difficult to say here what were the motives that drove the 1945 generation to experimentation. However, solely on the basis of the subsequent careers of the protagonists of the movement we are led to believe that, with some exceptions, the attempt was centered on renewing the theatre from within. Politics had not yet reached the theatre, for obvious reasons. This did not prevent the fact that, through those very experiments, those young "fighters" started to acquire a political conscience which they would further develop in later years."

[Sería difícil asegurar aquí cuáles fueron los motivos que impulsaron hacia la experimentación de la España del 45. Pero la simple trayectoria de los protagonistas invita a pensar que, salvo excepciones, el intento se centraba en renovar la escena desde la escena misma. La política no llegaba aún a los teatros por razones obvias. Lo que no impidió que, de esa experimentación misma, algunos de aquellos jóvenes luchadores fueran cobrando una conciencia política que desarrollarían años después.][5]

During his *Arte Nuevo* period, Alfonso Paso wrote mainly short works and other works in collaboration with like-minded young dramatists. This collaboration ended after just two years, after the group fell into debt and suffered from lack of support. Paso's subsequent career is somewhat surprising considering this avant-garde beginning.

During the 1950s, Paso's career went into a new direction: he increasingly accepted the impositions of the established theater, abandoning attempts to change or renew Spanish theater. His defense of his changed attitude in the theatrical journal *Primer Acto* sparked a polemical debate in the 1960s (*Posibilistas* versus *No posibilistas*), which turned into a sour dialogue among Buero Vallejo, Sastre, and Paso. As Oliva sums it up, the playwrights envisioned three possible strategies: Paso believed it was negative to ignore the restrictions imposed on artistic creation by the regime and better to fight from within; Sastre was totally opposed to this attitude; and Buero Vallejo attempted to adopt a position between the two.[6]

By the end of the 1950s, as the Cold War brought about a shift in the priorities of the victors of World War II, the Franco regime slowly gained recognition from the Western powers. Spain could now be considered an ally in the fight against communism rather than being dismissed as a fascist dictatorship. The United States began to establish links with Franco with a view to exploiting the strategic importance of the Iberian peninsula. With foreign investment and a series of *planes de desarrollo* (Economic Development Plans), Spain slowly recovered from bankruptcy, and its population began to enjoy a certain degree of prosperity.

Against this background of increasing stability and growth, the opposition was almost silenced. By playing the card of the economic boom, Franco managed to convince the bulk of the population that only under his dictatorship could a lasting peace and economic development be achieved. As the historian Edouard de Blaye suggests:

There can be no doubt that if completely free elections had ever been held, between 60 and 70 per cent of Spaniards would have voted unhesitatingly for Franco. Many would have done so out of habit, or from fear of chaos—others from profound conviction. Besides the Army and the Church, authority's objective allies, the Caudillo could always be sure of the backing of at least three categories of citizens: women, businessmen and the middle classes.[7]

Art in general was affected by this acceptance of the status quo, but the theater was especially vulnerable in as much as its audience was predominantly middle class. To this picture we must add the existence of a regressive censorship which ensured that the people would not be confronted by a view of alternative worlds. Oliva summarizes the result as follows:

The theatre, definitively wedded to a paternalistic censorship which prevented audiences from seeing anything unfavorable, could do no more than to vegetate in its own mediocrity, the same mediocrity that motivated Spanish petit bourgeois aspirations in the 1960s.

[El teatro, pues, casado definitivamente con una paternalista censura que impedirá ver el lado malo de las cosas, no tiene más remedio que vegetar en medio de su mediocridad. La misma mediocridad que mueve las aspiraciones del pequeño burgués español de los sesenta].[8]

Paso's plays reflect this complacency, which characterizes the second period of his career.

Although the whole body of work of such a prolific author is not easily classified, a few recurrent themes can be detected. A significant part of Paso's work is inspired by social concerns, and although he often denied any interest in the class struggle, he certainly makes an overt attempt to address middle-class problems in these plays. Among them we find *Los pobrecitos* [Poor

Things] (1957) and *La boda de la chica* [The Daughter's Wedding] (1960) in which a respectable middle class is contrasted with an upper class that possesses wealth but lacks morals and responsibility. There are also some elements of social criticism in *Enseñar a un sinvergüenza* [Teaching a Crook] (1968), and even though the action takes place in England, it is consistent in situating corruption among the upper classes. In *La Corbata* [The Tie] (1963), the middle-class hero is oppressed by both the upper class and the working class, which seem to be the ones profiting from the current state of affairs. However, despite the grim neorealist portrayal of the central family, absurd or even grotesque elements in the plot preclude easy identification with the hero's problems. Later in his career, his social commentary petered out, becoming even anecdotal or topical (e.g., see *Juan jubilado* [Retired Juan], 1961).

Another distinctive group of Paso's plays may be classified as thriller plots formulated along the lines of Agatha Christie; these works were clearly influenced by his father-in-law Jardiel Poncela's crime plays. Some of Paso's most accomplished work belongs to this group of plays. In these works, plot unfolds through witty dialogue, and Paso demonstrates expert cutting from scene to scene. *Usted puede ser el asesino* [You Could Be the Assassin] (1957) is perhaps the finest example; other plays in this group are *Veneno para mi marido* [Poison for My Husband] (1953) and *Receta para un crimen* [Recipe for a Crime] (1959).

Among Paso's most popular plays are the light comedies, which follow a predictable pattern. They present disillusioned characters who suddenly find in romanticism a reason to go on living. *Cosas de Papa y mama* [Mum and Dad's Affairs] (1960) and *Cuarenta y ocho horas de felicidad* [Forty-eight Hours of Happiness] (1952) transport the audience to a utopian fantasy, with a happy ending that comes about in the most unexpected manner—not unlike the melodramatic closures prevalent in Spanish popular cinema at that time as in the benign family romances *Un rayo de Luz* (Lucia, 1960) or *La gran familia* (Palacios, 1962), or the romantic platonic comedies *Las chicas de la cruz roja* (Salvia, 1958).

Paso was also attracted by a less popular genre: historical drama. Oliva remarks that his interest in this type of theater was not successful with his middle-class audiences. Moreover, these plays are full of anachronisms and deploy the same technique as that used in his *comedias de salón*. Perhaps the most notorious example is *Nerón-Paso* (1969).

CRITICS' RESPONSE

The main characteristics of Paso's theater are, of course, his prolific output and his success. Both characteristics are of crucial importance in any analysis of his work; he worked fast to a formulaic pattern, and he allowed his public to dictate his themes and style. His target audience in the 1960s, the petit bourgeoisie of Madrid and the provinces, was a society that, for the first time, after considerable pain and struggle, was enjoying a measure of prosperity. As Olivia reminds us, it was a society with no other aim than its own stability, a society that consumed, applied for credit to pay for its homes and electric appliances [[U]na sociedad sin más alicientes que su establidad; una sociedad que pide créditos para, por fin, comprar a plazos vivienda y electrodomésticos.][9]

Some contemporary theater critics were in sympathy with the regime and therefore believed that the blind acceptance of social and economic gain outweighed the lack of political freedom. These critics saw the need for an entertainment without other pretensions, and Paso, with his trite plots and simple play structures, seemed to fill such a role. On the other hand, many critics and writers, generally hostile to the Franco regime, viewed the theater as an arena for political and social comment and accordingly disparaged Paso's work. In their opinion, he ensured that audiences would not confront their own failings; with the middle classes thus reassured, the status quo of 1960s Spain was therefore condoned.

Alfredo Marquerie is one of the few critics who defended Paso's theater. A contemporary Marquerie wrote one of the very few books favorable to the author, supporting the *posibilista* ideal and approving of Paso's pact with the petit bourgeoisie. Understandably, Marquerie gives little time to Paso's early career and his brief period as a would-be reformer of the Spanish stage. His admiration for the author starts only when Paso "turned a new leaf" in 1956 and decided to pander to the middle classes and their idiosyncrasies. In all fairness, Marquerie's work cannot be considered as properly evaluative of Paso's worth or lack of it, for he allows the author himself to express his views and attack his opponents. The critic does not sufficiently distance himself from the author to allow even a pretense of objectivity. L. Rodríguez Alcalde, another Paso contemporary, takes a more neutral and cautious attitude toward Paso's success in *El teatro español contemporáneo*:

Comedy writers like Alfonso Paso have always existed, and their existence is not a sin. However, the success of these interval entertainments is a bit worrying especially since there is not anything before or after them.

Comediógrafos como Alfonso Paso existen siempre, y su existencia no es pecado. Ahora bien, el éxito de ese amable intermedio puede ser intranquilizador cuando no hallamos otra cosa antes y después de su intervención.)[10]

Later on, the writer praises Paso's early plays and regrets that their charm and wit gave way to the cliched expression of the later works.

More frequently, Paso's work has attracted harsh criticism from theater academics and writers. In 1970, Medardo Fraile remarked on the author's unfortunate characterization of the working class as lazy and easily corruptible, which we find in *La Corbata*.[11] Fraile rightly points out that this is an easy way out for the author. Since no one of that class would be in the audience, he could directly pander to the prejudiced middle-class view of the poor as scroungers who had brought their plight on themselves, something that was likely to earn him complicit applause.

Contemporary writers on Spain's postwar theater stress their disapproval of such practices and often refuse to give Paso more than the dutiful mention which his productivity and commercial success merit. César Oliva, for example, in his chapter "Un teatro para un régimen" [A Theatre for a Regime], though admitting the skillful structure of some of Paso's plays, dismisses his entire output as conventional. He does not deny that a reference to Paso is unavoidable in a comprehensive study of theater under Franco, but he maintains that Paso's work was interesting only in its early stages. The fact that he moved to less demanding forms of theater has meant that Paso, despite his undoubted potential, will not be remembered as another Buero Vallejo or Sastre.[12]

Clearly, then, critics have tended to condemn Paso's comedies for their blatant ideological conformism; these are certainly not texts that encourage audiences to demand political freedom. However, the themes of the plays cannot be attributed solely to his acceptance of the political regime. Popular authors of the past (including Benavente, Arniches, Alvarez Quintero) had constructed comedies in much the same way, with a similar repetition of trite themes, appealing to similar theatre audiences.

Even if Paso's contribution as a playwright is not impressive, he is an interesting author to study from a sociopolitical point of view; indeed, his plays provide a barometer of popular taste in the 1960s. Paso's plays had a particular function: to meet the laws of consumer demand and to encourage Spaniards to count their economic and social blessings. Without this cosy self-assurance as a safety net, the next generation would probably have been less insistent in its demands for more political freedom. Furthermore, through the omissions in Paso's plays, through their failure to address the extremes of the class system (the very poor or the very rich, as *La Corbata* exemplifies, often take the blame for society's evils), a whole reading of Spanish society in the 1960s can be made.

AWARDS AND DISTINCTIONS

Barcelona Prize for *Sueño de amor en la solapa*, also known as *Cuarenta y ocho horas de felicidad* [Forty-eight Hours of Happiness] (1952).

Carlos Arniches Prize (given by Alicante Town Hall) for *Los Pobrecitos* [Poor Things] (1956).

Premio Nacional de Teatro for *El cielo dentro de casa* [Heaven at Home] (1958).

Alvarez Quintero Prize instituted by the *Real Academia Española*, for *El cielo dentro de casa* [Heaven at Home] (1958) given to the author in 1959.

María Rolland Theatre Prize for *Las que tienen que servir* [Those Who Have to Serve] (1962).

Barcelona Critics' prize for *La corbata* [The Tie, 1963].

NOTES

1. Alfredo Marqueríe, *Alfonso Paso y su teatro* (Madrid: Escélicer, 1960), p. 18.
2. Marion P. Holt, *The Contemporary Spanish Theater (1949–1972)* (Boston: Twayne Publishers, 1975), p. 18.
3. The alluded interview is included in Amando Isasi Angulo, *Diálogos del Teatro de la posguerra* (Madrid: Editorial Ayuso, 1974), pp. 155–181.
4. César Oliva, *El teatro desde 1936* (Madrid: Alhambra, 1989), p. 188.
5. Ibid., p. 189.
6. Ibid., p. 191.
7. Edouard de Blaye, *Franco and the Politics of Spain* (Hammondsworth: Penguin, 1974), p. 378.
8. Oliva, *El teatro desde 1936*, p. 193.
9. Ibid., p. 207.
10. L. Rodríguez Alcalde, *Teatro español contemporáneo* (Madrid: Epesa, 1973), p. 189.
11. Medardo Fraile, "Teatro y vida en España *La Camisa, La Corbata* y *Tres sombreros de copa*," *Prohemio* 1.2 (1974): 254–269.
12. Oliva, *El teatro desde 1936*, p. 197.

BIBLIOGRAPHY

Editions

The following editions of Paso's plays are still available in various reprints. Data are from the Ministerio de Cultura (Dirección General del Libro y Bibliotecas). Unfortunately, in many cases, no information was available on the date of the particular edition.

Los pobrecitos. Madrid: Escélicer, 1957.
Catalina no es formal. Madrid: Escélicer, 1958.
Papá se enfada por todo. Madrid: Escélicer, 1958.
El canto de la cigarra. Madrid: Escélicer, 1958.
Hay alguien detrás de la puerta. Madrid: Escélicer, 1958.
Juicio contra un sinvergüenza. Madrid: Escélicer, 1958.
Cena de matrimonios. Madrid: Escélicer, 1959.
Usted puede ser el asesino. Madrid: Escélicer, 1959.
Receta para un crimen and *Preguntan por Julio César*. Escélicer, 1960.
La boda de la chica. Madrid: Escélicer, 1960.
Cosas de papá y mamá. Madrid: Escélicer, 1960.
Cosas de papá y mamá. In Federico Carlos Saínz de Robles, ed., *Teatro español 1959–60*. Madrid: Aguilar, 1961.
Aurelia y sus hombres. Madrid: Escélicer, 1961.
Las buenas personas. Madrid: Escélicer, 1961.
Cuándo tú me necesites. Madrid: Escélicer, 1961.
Juegos de marido y mujer. Madrid: Escélicer, 1961.
Una tal Dulcinea. Madrid: Escélicer, 1961.
Vamos a contar mentiras. Madrid: Escélicer, 1961.

Cómo casarse en siete días. Madrid: Escélicer, 1962.
¿Conoce usted a su mujer? Madrid: Escélicer, 1962.
Las que tienen que servir. Madrid: Escélicer, 1962.
El mejor mozo de España. Madrid: Escélicer, 1962.
Sosteniendo el tipo. Madrid: Escélicer, 1962.
La Corbata. Madrid: Escélicer, 1963.
Los derechos del hombre. Madrid: Escélicer, 1963.
Sí, quiero. Madrid: Escélicer, 1963.
Un treinta de febrero. Madrid: Escélicer, 1963.
De pronto, una noche . . . Madrid: Escélicer, 1964.
Mamá con niña. Madrid: Escélicer, 1964.
Prefiero España. Madrid: Escélicer, 1964.
Casi Lolita. Madrid: Escélicer, 1967.
¡Cómo está el servicio! Madrid: Escélicer, 1967.
Desde Isabel con amor. Madrid: Escélicer, 1967.
¡Estos chicos de ahora! Madrid: Escélicer, 1967.
Atrapar a un asesino. Madrid: Escélicer, 1968.
En el Escorial cariño mío. Madrid: Escélicer, 1968.
Enseñar a un sinvergüenza. Madrid: Escélicer, 1968.
Esta monja. Madrid: Escélicer, 1968.
España es diferente. Madrid: Escélicer, 1968.
Las que tienen que alternar. Madrid: Escélicer, 1968.
Un matrimonio muy . . . muy . . . muy feliz. Madrid: Escélicer, 1968.
El armario. Madrid: Escélicer, 1969.
Nerón-Paso. Madrid: Escélicer, 1969.
Juan jubilado. Madrid: Escélicer, 1961.

Critical Studies

García Lorenzo, Luciano, ed. *Documentos sobre el teatro español contemporáneo.* Madrid: SGELSA, 1980.
García Pavón, Francisco. *Teatro social en España* Madrid: Taurus, 1962.
Holt, Marion P. *The Contemporary Spanish Theater (1949–1972).* Boston: Twayne Publishers, 1975.
Marqueríe, Alfredo. *Alfonso Paso y su teatro.* Madrid: Escélicer, 1960.
———. *Veinte años de teatro en España.* Madrid: Editora Nacional, 1959.
Monleón, J. *Treinta años de teatro a la derecha.* Barcelona: Tusquets, 1971.
Oliva, César. *El teatro desde 1936.* Madrid: Alhambra, 1989.
Pérez-Stanfield, María Pilar. *Direcciones de Teatro español de postguerra.* Madrid: José Porrúa Turranzas S.A., 1983.
Rodríguez Alcalde, Luis. *Teatro español contemporáneo.* Madrid: Epesa, 1973.
Ruiz Ramón, Francisco. *Historia del teatro español: Siglo XX.* Madrid: Cátedra, 1989.
Saínz de Robles, Federico Carlos, ed. *Teatro español 1959–60.* Madrid: Aguilar, 1961.
Torrente Ballester, Gonzalo. *Teatro español contemporáneo.* Madrid: Ediciones Guadarrama, 1957.

PALOMA PEDRERO
(1957–   )

Candyce Leonard

BIOGRAPHY

In his 1989 article about young Spanish playwrights, Sabas Martín cites only one female, Paloma Pedrero. This inclusion of one prominent figure and the omission of others calls attention to the slow pace at which women writers gained recognition toward the closing decade of the century in Spain's already full-blown democracy. Indeed, by the 1990s, Pedrero had matured into an international figure, and she remains the most celebrated female playwright to appear during the democratic period. Born in Madrid on July 3, 1957, Pedrero found herself working in an urban hospital by the age of seventeen due to economic hardships at home. Her ten years at the hospital, along with an awareness of her mother's struggles as a single parent to raise four children alone, shaped the future author's sensitivity and responsiveness to the social conditions for women, which would later form the core of her theater.

Paloma Pedrero's affinity for theater began in her teen years when she was cast in the annual plays at a private school for boys only (Galán, "Paloma Pedrero, una joven dramaturga," 11; Lamartina-Lens, "Paloma Pedrero," 389). From 1978 to 1984 while attending college, Pedrero pursued her love of the theater by performing with the independent theater company, Cachivache, and then dedicated herself full time to a career in theater as she turned to writing. During these early years of study and preparation, Pedrero found mentors in such notable figures as John Strasberg, Zulma Katz, Jesús Campos, Dominic de Fazio, Fermín Cabal, and Alberto Wainer. She credits Wainer, whom she knew as both drama teacher and acting coach, with guiding her beyond the traditional space for women in theater as an actress and into the traditionally masculine space of stage directing and playwriting (Galán, "Paloma Pedrero, una joven dramaturga," 11; Lamartina-Lens, "Paloma Pedrero," 389). Pedrero recalls that Fermín Cabal, a principal figure in the Independent Theater Movement in the 1970s, also influenced her transformation from actor to writer when he challenged her to write a play. After a marathon writing session resulted in her first play, Cabal christened Pedrero "playwright." At that moment she knew that her years of study and experience in the theater had determined her future (Johnson, 17; Galán, "Paloma Pedrero, una joven dramaturga," 11; Serrano, "Introducción," 11–12).

Shortly thereafter, *La llamada de Lauren* ("The Call of Lauren"), a protest against gender-role stereotyping that won her an award in the Valladolid Teatro Breve competition in 1984, inspired her creative passions, and by 1985, Pedrero had authored three more plays:*Resguardo personal* ("The Voucher"), *Besos de lobo* ("Wolf Kisses"), and *Invierno de luna alegre* ("Winter's Happy Moon"). This succession of plays, including her powerful work *El color de agosto*, published in 1989, brought increasing attention by scholars and peers. Nonetheless, at the beginning of the 1990s, Pedrero entered a period of crisis that proved critical to her maturation as a writer. This three-year period that affected Pedrero both personally and creatively was nurturing in the best of all possible ways. Pedrero, the budding writer of the early 1980s, had been transformed into an author of considerable creative vigor and social insight well able to negotiate the competitive atmosphere of theater life in Madrid.

Perhaps the most distinctive characteristic of the young playwrights with whom Pedrero is chronologically associated (their theater dates after 1975) is their formal training and experience as actors and directors. With plays that range from the neorealist to the experimental, and from artistic exploration to social comment, these authors are united by the diversity and dynamics of their dramas that resist conventional categories. The sociopolitical and cultural events that reshaped Spain's national identity after 1975 produced an atmosphere of artistic freedom so that Pedrero found a friendly environment for a burgeoning writer. She found herself liberated, from a psychological point of view, and free from the government or self-censorship experienced by those writing under the fascist dictatorship of Francisco Franco (Leonard, personal interview, June 4, 1994). The introduction of government subsidies in the early 1980s, however, and the climate of rivalry and self-censorship that they fostered in the midst of Spain's shifting political climate, prompted Pedrero's 1995 challenge of government sponsorship that might favor commercial theater and compromise the vitality of Spain's young authors (Villán, 61). The irony of the curious transition from Spain's fascist government whose censorship determined which plays would be staged to Spain's democratic government whose grant monies determined which plays would be staged was not lost on Pedrero. In spite of her considerable exposure and corpus of published and unpublished plays, Pedrero, along with her contemporaries, often finds herself struggling for stage space and funding in a consumer-driven and technologically seductive climate.

By the late 1980s, Pedrero had established her individuality and scope as a playwright, and by the early 1990s she marked a new era in Spanish theater history by becoming mentor and teacher to a new generation of young writers launching their respective careers. Her audacious writing about social and sexual repression in latter-day Spain has secured her reputation among scholars and students of contemporary Spanish theater as well as among theater cognoscenti. Three of her plays from the mid-1990s, *Una estrella* ("A Star"), *De la noche al alba* ("From Darkness to Dawn"), and *El pasamanos* ("The Handrail"), were given a special reading at Madrid's Centro Cultural de la Villa in May 1995. Lourdes Ortiz and José María Rodríguez Méndez, both noted Spanish writers, hosted the ceremonial evening and praised Pedrero for her unique contribution to contemporary theater through the style, timeliness, and thematic originality of her theater in democratic Spain. During the final years of the century and into the twenty-first century, Pedrero continued her playwriting, teaching, and traveling as international recognition of her theater flourished. She has altered the course of Spanish theater history.

DRAMATURGY: MAJOR WORKS AND THEMES

Stylistically, Pedrero's method tends toward verbal economy, metadramatic devices, and linguistic vogue. The terseness with which she argues her theses leaves her audiences at once confronted and exhilarated by the impact of her dramatic voice. While her theater avoids commercial platitudes such as the predictable denouement or reinforcement of bourgeois ideologies, the structural components of her plays remain within the scope of traditional dramatic conventions, as they are not inclined toward techniques associated with experimental theater. Her work does, however, incontrovertibly reflect her perception of theater as the locus of freedom, agitation, and the exploration of the human condition and its historical circumstances (Villán, 60). Her style ranges from very short works such as *Esta noche en el parque*, a play that requires minimal set design and number of props, to the full-length drama *Locas de amar*, which has a distinct character of realism. The author's principal concerns are contemporary society vis-à-vis gender identity specifically associated with female sexuality, and renegotiating the male/female paradigm within our existing social systems. These concerns are unconditionally interrelated and focused in her characters who are, invariably, the socially disinherited.

Pedrero's penchant for subverting established gender/sexual roles dates from her earliest plays and finds expression in both her male and female characters. She calls for a reckoning of female sexuality that has long been typecast, distorted, or simply ignored, and she incites rebellion against the socially acceptable generic paradigms that govern traditional Spanish society. Female characters of wide-ranging personal circumstances and individuality inhabit her plays to express female sexuality and autonomy, two personal conditions that in Pedrero's plays are mutually dependent. Two of the characters of *Besos de lobo*, for example, Luciano, a seventeen-year-old homosexual, and Ana, an eighteen-year-old with a long-distance fiancé, befriend each other in a rural town inhospitable to the nonconformity of their sexual behavior. Sent away after her mother's death so that her aunt could more freely become involved with her father, Ana defiantly returns home. She talks with her young homosexual friend about their respective sexual frustrations, telling him that she satisfies her own sexual desires. In spite of the explosion against repression that accompanied the democratic period, evident in the reinstitution of divorce in Spain in 1981, the social climate in Spain remained restrained. Thus, Ana's explicit reference to female sexuality became more than a mere challenge to cultural double standards. Through her character Ana, Pedrero dared to demystify female sexuality and proclaim the legitimacy of sexual desires with a boldness that provoked anxiety, curiosity, and anticipation in Spanish audiences. Rather than marry the fiancé whom she has long awaited, Ana subverts the conventional model of the Spanish female by her guilt-free sexual attitude and by her choice to fashion her own future by leaving the small town and her fiancé behind.

La llamada de Lauren and *Invierno de luna alegre*, also written in the mid-1980s, approach female gender roles and sexuality through their two dissimilar protagonists, Rosa y Reyes. *La llamada de Lauren*, one of the most performed of Pedrero's early plays, reiterates the theme of gender-role expectations in a young married couple. The action occurs one evening during Carnival, a setting that underscores the masks, games, and instabilities associated with the socially prescribed gender paradigm. Rosa's husband has selected costumes that allow him to inhabit a gender personality that he embraces: Pedro assumes a Lauren Bacall identity while Rosa somewhat unwillingly performs the Humphrey Bogart character. As Pedro becomes aroused through their respective alternative gender identity, Rosa learns that her husband prefers the so-called feminine role, that his brief marriage to her has been a masquerade, and that she must redefine her life. The closing moments find Rosa at home alone, void of the marriage and family she had chosen according to established social norms while Pedro joins the Carnival festivities dressed as Lauren Bacall. Although the focus of *La llamada de Lauren* appears to be Pedro's gender-role liberation, the fact that his sexual orientation impacts Rosa's own sexual satisfaction as well as her role in a society comprised of traditional couples urges audience members to interrogate the imperatives of cultural approbation and the circumstances of individuality happiness.

Far removed from the small-town metaphor that Ana escapes, or the traditional marriage and family that Rosa needs, Reyes, the seemingly self-assured Generation X-er of *Invierno de luna alegre*, enjoys the urban life of sex and drugs in Madrid. Her vibrant sexuality and *joie de vivre* stir the three men whose lives she briefly intersects. Joining Olegario's street show, a bullfight suggestive of the sexual tension she inspires, Reyes' economic contributions bring monetary security to the older vagabond who offers her shelter and who ultimately and hopelessly falls in love with her. Driven by her restlessness and sense of adventure, Reyes secures a temporary job as a topless hostess and takes off with Olegario's lusty twenty-four-year-old neighbor. Like Ana of *Besos de lobo* who rejects a socially prescribed marriage, Reyes spurns conventional behavior and thinks about her immediate future based on her own needs and desires rather than on the compliance or noncompliance of the prevailing social attitudes governing Madrid. Reyes does not, however, discover independence in the way that Ana and Pedro do. Rather, she assumes that she always had it, and this is the radical point that Pedrero asserts: the socially unacceptable are emancipated by their individuality and endurance in the face of oppressive tradition.

Within a relatively short period of time, Pedrero's female protagonists move from merely alluding to their sexual desires to openly demanding sexual satisfaction. Yolanda, the young protagonist of *Esta noche en el parque* ("Tonight in the Park"), calls Fernando to meet with her again in the park after a one-night stand a few days earlier. She demands her turn at the sexual gratification that Fernando's masculine privilege disregarded during their first encounter. Fernando kills her, the absolute deed of silencing. It is the price that Yolanda pays for her attempt to exact sexual pleasure and, ostensibly, to reverse gender roles in terms of who initiates and consummates the relationship. In contrast, sexuality in *El color de agosto* is framed within the art world where market demands, that is cultural values—always relative and capricious—determine success. Laura and María, both artists in their thirties, meet together after an eight-year estrangement so that we first see them as they discuss their respective personal, professional, and sexual disillusionments. The play is steeped in artistic imagery that depicts emotional rupture, both between the man whom they have mutually desired, and between each other. Perhaps the most iconic scene of the plays is the sexually charged moment when the two women paint each other's nude body, a scene that provoked comments by critics and scholars about lesbian overtones in the play. While such an analysis is not without merit, it is also true that in "writing the body" the author exposes the arbitrary nature of conventional body praxis and gender representation. Pedrero tests conventions through the relationship between the two women and through the ability of one of them to reconstitute herself in a realization of personal autonomy. *El color de agosto* revels in examining and undermining standards of appraisal, not only in terms of the social and commercial values that construct and instruct gender and sexual behavior, but also in terms of the art world where conformity to market demands dominates creativity. Such overt reference to the commercialization of art surely reflects the difficulties that playwrights encounter when issues of money influence which play audiences will see performed on which stage.

Two plays published in 1995, *El pasamanos* and *De la noche al alba*, illustrate a slight departure from Pedrero's thematic trajectory. A third play, *La isla Amarilla*, signals a more major thematic detour. It is about materialism and the magnetism of gold. Pedrero dramatizes what she perceives as a historic irony. Her play considers and equates the repeated criticism of Spain's excessive materialism and drive for gold which in the fifteenth and sixteenth centuries brought conquistadors in an island in the Caribbean and today's main ambition, the pursuit of money, in another island of the Americas. Both plays continue to focus on the male-female relationship, but now with a decided turn toward the tenderness, companionship, and respect that suggest an emotional relationship. The mid-thirties night-club hostess of *De la noche al alba* characterizes the fatigue of sexual adventures that emotional poverty produces. Vanesa's life is tedious, and her relationship with her callous live-in pimp is vacuous. While trying to catch a taxi late one night after work, Vanesa has a conversation with Mauro, a young man who has known and admired her from afar. His pledge of love and protection is met by the arrival of Vanesa's pimp/boyfriend, Ramón, whose brusque and unloving behavior sets in relief Mauro's affection and sincerity. As Vanessa pauses longingly and then runs to catch up with Ramón, Pedrero's audience turns from issues of female sexuality and desire to emotional salvation in a culture of personal greed. Such is the satisfaction that the golden-aged couple of *El pasamanos* enjoys in the warmth of a relationship nurtured through years of mutual support, compromise, and understanding. The couple fights the sociopolitical battles of aging, media exploitation, and individual rights as the elderly husband insists that a handrail be installed to assist him down the stairs of his apartment building. Perhaps, as José Monleón suggests, the couple of *El pasamanos* finds emotional fulfillment because their younger years of sexual appetite and games of domination and aggression have passed. The metaphor of the handrail, however, suggests the companionship of a loving partner whose moral and unconditional support eases the journey down life's path.

Pedrero's most recently published play, *Locas de amar*, premiered in 1997 in the Centro Cultural de la Villa of Madrid. It represents one of the most carefully crafted of Pedrero's theater pieces for its use of the traditional structure of the *comedia* designed to accommodate traditional thematic content. Pedrero locates the key to the play within the text itself, "with a dash of delirium and a touch of catharsis, organically performed, but always with feet on the ground even when the head is in the air" (Personal interview. May 16, 1997). Purposefully ironic, Pedrero appropriates this dramatic structure, almost exclusively associated with male writers, not only to subvert the notion of masculine space but also to create tension between the structure and content of the play by introducing a contemporary theme. In a middle-aged clichéd attraction to a younger woman, Paco abandons Eulalia, his wife of over twenty years. After locking herself in her bedroom, weeping and refusing to eat in an effort to avenge herself by starvation, forty-something Eulalia emerges with a slimmer figure like that of her twenty-year-old daughter. Accustomed to the comfortable life-style that her husband's salary has afforded and indentured to the bourgeois image of a middle-aged housewife, Eulalia is devastated by her new social status. In fact, Eulalia proclaims to her daughter that she has nothing left in life. Her brief tryst with a young man posing as a psychologist is a gesture of spiritual renewal at the same time that it is a rupture with Eulalia's implicit social instincts, but Pedrero's message is not wrapped around sexual escapades as any sort of short- or long-term solution. Rather, *Locas de amar* proposes that strict adherence to social codes of conformity cannot guarantee a happy marriage. Furthermore, Eulalia's physical restitution is duplicitous regarding her attractiveness toward men, and it must be read on a figurative level as an exteriorization of the internal fat of social convention that has been trimmed away.

Finally, Eulalia refuses Paco's repentance after his romantic interlude when she recognizes that there is a difference between desiring and needing a man. The twenty-first-century content of Pedrero's theater has dramatically altered the confines of the traditional structure that she has employed. While swathed in a humor that exploits the often comical patterns of obsessive-compulsive sexual/romantic behavior that audience members easily recognize in themselves, and rather than merely grope about philosophically with the elusive nature of love or attempt any romanticized attempts to understand it, Pedrero allows this personal crisis in Eulalia's life to be a turning point when the character casts off middle-class conventions in favor of personal authority.

Paloma Pedrero is acknowledged as the single playwright who consistently challenges social perception and response to female sexuality. Her theater, however, eschews the gratuitous or impulsive use of sex or anything relating to sex. Rather, the author's careful choices regarding how and when to shape her dramas around female sexuality—whether as metaphor or as practice—are always grounded by her passion for social and political equality.

CRITICS' RESPONSE

Paloma Pedrero's theater invariably attracts critical attention, as much for her challenge to the establishment as for scholars' concerted efforts to create a space for the female voice, or for the fact that she is the only contemporary Spanish playwright who insistently focuses on women. Translations of her plays into English, German, and French have guaranteed a wider market of distribution for her theater and situate her among the vanguard of post-Franco dramatists. Since the late 1980s, Pedrero has received the national and international acclaim of audiences and critics alike, along with numerous awards presented to her during the initial phases of her career. Her theater is the frequent focus of conference papers, articles, and doctoral dissertations in the United States.

Criticism surrounding her theater is sharply divided between scholars and theater critics as they react to the male-female paradigm that resonates throughout Pedrero's theater. She refuses easy conventional prototypes to generate a new model infused with the female identity (Berardini; Podol; Zatlin, "Paloma Pedrero"). Some approaches to her work involve analyses of the technical strategies that identify her plays (Gabriele; Harris, "Juego y metateatro" Zatlin, "Intertextualidad y metateatro"; Leonard, "Body, Sex, Woman"; Makris). Other interpretations focus on her plays' overtures to feminism. Hers is a bold voice raised in the democratic period to summon female identity, self-awareness, and experience so long repressed in Spain (Gabriele; Harris, "La experiencia femenina"; Lamartina-Lens, "*Noches de amor efímero* de Paloma Pedrero" Leonard, "Body, Sex, Woman"; Weimer).

Although Pedrero's theater has stimulated research among academic scholars in the United States and has inspired a new generation of writers in Spain, not all commercial criticism has been felicitous. Some reviewers are wary of her forthright dialogue, or feel that the topics of marriage, women, or women's shifting roles within today's society are not substantial enough for serious theater. It must be acknowledged, however, that virtually all of Madrid's theater critics are male so that the possibilities for women as either writer or critic remain small. Outspoken Madrid theater critic Eduardo Haro Tecglen, for example, writers that Pedrero's *Noches de amor efímero* ("Parting Gestures: Three Plays") is trivial, unimportant, and lacking in real substance, being witty more than anything else. Tecglen's masculinist response to Pedrero's theater in general and to this trilogy in particular overlooks the metaphorical nature of the repressed female sexuality and gender identity that Pedrero's theater elaborates. Further more, such masculine and dismissive interpretation imitates precisely the male-inscribed gender values against which Pedrero's female protagonists continually struggle. The derisive title of Tecglen's review, "Orgasmos perdidos y hallados" ("Orgasms Lost and Found") ironically captures the female condition today. Pedrero's theater asserts that what has been "lost" in contemporary Spain is woman's voice, a metaphorical orgasm that her dramatic works satisfy and that fill a void in contemporary Spanish theatre.

AWARDS RECEIVED

During the brief time that Pedrero has been writing, her theater has garnered numerous awards. Since the late 1980s, she has received both national and international acclamation of audiences and critics. Among her awards are the "Valladolid del teatro breve," Second Place Award, 1984, for *La llamada de Lauren*; Finalist in the First Premio Nacional de Teatro Breve de San Javier, 1987, for *El color de agosto*; the prestigious "Tirso de Molina" national theater award, 1987, for *Invierno de luna alegre*; and Best Writer of the VI Muestra Alternative de Teatro del Festival de Otoño de Madrid in 1994.

BIBLIOGRAPHY

Plays: Editions

"Imagen doble." 1984. [Unpublished]
La llamada de Lauren. Teatro breve 1984. Valladolid, Spain: Caja de Ahorros Provincial, 1985; Madrid: Ediciones Antonio Machado, 1987.
Besos de lobo and *Invierno de luna alegre.* Madrid: Espiral/Fundamentos, 1987. "Las fresas mágicas." 1988. [Unpublished]
Resguardo personal. Dramaturgas españolas de hoy, ed. Patricia O'Connor. Madrid: Espiral/Fundamentos, 1988. 97–105.
El color de agosto. Madrid: Ediciones Antonio Machado, 1989.
La noche dividida. Madrid: Ediciones Antonio Machado, 1989.
Esta noche en el parque. Estreno 16.1 (1990): 15–17.
Noches de amor efímero. Murcia, Spain: Secretariado de Publicaciones. Universidad de Murcia, 1991; Madrid: Sociedad General de Autores de España, 1994.

Solos esta noche. Murcia, Spain: Secretariado de Publicaciones. Universidad de Murcia, 1991.

Una estrella. Madrid: La Avispa, 1995.

Besos de lobo. Madrid: La Avispa, 1995.

La isla amarilla. Ciudad Real: AGESPA, 1995.

El pasamanos. *Primer Acto* 258 (1995): 67–90.

De la noche al alba. Madrid: Sociedad General de Autores de España, 1995.

Cachorros de negro mirar. Madrid: Teatro del Alma, 1998. "En el túnel un pájaro" [unpublished]

Locos de amar. Madrid: Sociedad General de Autores de España, 1996; Ottawa, Ontario: Girol, 2001.

"En el túnel un pájaro." [Unpublished]

Translations

L'apelle de Lauren. Trans. André Camp. Paris: L'Avant Scène, 1989. n.p.

The Color of August. Trans. Phyllis Zatlin. *Parting Gestures: Three Plays*. Estreno: University Park, 1994.

A Night Divided. Trans. Phyllis Zatlin. *Parting Gestures: Three Plays*. Estreno: University Park, 1994.

Tonight in the Park. Trans. Phyllis Zatlin. *Collages & Bricolates* 6 (1992): 104–111.

Tonight We're Alone. Trans. Phyllis Zatlin. *Collages & Bricolates* 7 (1993): 80–89.

The Voucher. Trans. Phyllis Zatlin. *Parting Gestures: Three Plays*. Estreno: University Park, 1994; and *The Literature of Democratic Spain* (1976–1992). Ed. Cecilia C. Lee. *The Literary Review* 36.3 (1993): 389–97.

Critical Studies

Asenjo, Enrigue. "*Locas de amor*, una interesante Comedia que va de la sensualidad a la carcajada." *ABC*, 3 May 1996: 111.

Berardini, Susan. "El toreo como vía de la identidad en *Invierno de luna alegre*." In *De lo particular a lo universal. El teatro español del siglo XX y su contexto*. Ed. by John P. Gabriele. Frankfurt am Main, Vervuert-Madrid: Iberoamericana, 1994. 181–187.

Canovas, Elena. "Con Elena Canovas." *Primer Acto* 265 (1996): 135–138.

De la Fuente, Manuel. "Paloma Pedrero, loca de amar." *ABC*, November 11, 1996: 103.

Fagundo, Ana María. "La mujer en el teatro de Paloma Pedrero." In *Literatura femenina de España y las Américas*. Madrid: Fundamentos, 1995. 155–165.

Flores, Sofía. "*Noches de amor efímero* de Paloma Pedrero: Los amores fáciles." *El Público* 82 (1991): 108.

Gabriele, John P. "Metateatro y feminismo en *El color de agosto de Paloma Pedrero*." In *Lecturas y relecturas de textos españoles, latinoamericanos y US latinos*. Ed. by Juan Villegas. Irvine: Universidad de Califronia, 1994. 158–164.

Galán, Eduardo. "Paloma Pedrero, una joven dramaturga que necesita expresar sus vivencias." *Estreno* 16.1 (1990): 11–13.

Haro Tecglen, Eduardo. "En busca del feminismo perdido." *El País*, April 14, 1996. n.p.

———. "Orgasmos perdidos y hallados." *El País*, November 15, 1990: 46.

Harris, Carolyn. "Concha Romero y Paloma Pedrero hablan de sus obras." *Estreno* 19.1 (1993): 29–35.

———. "Juego y metateatro en la obra de Paloma Pedrero." In *De lo particular a lo universal. El teatro español del siglo XX y su contexto.* Edición de John P. Gabriele. Frankfurt am Main, Vervuert-Madrid: Iberoamericana, 1994. 170–180.

———. "La experiencia femenina en escena: *Besos de lobo y El color de agosto de Paloma Pedrero.*" *Confluencia* 10.1 (1994): 118–24.

Hodge, Polly J. "Photography of Theater: Reading between the Spanish Scenes." *Gestos* 22 (1996): 35–58.

———. "Poetic Drama, Images, and Windows: Aliento de equilibrista by Paloma Pedrero and Isabel Ordaz." *Estreno* 23.2 (1997): 30–37.

Johnson, Anita. "Dramaturgas españolas: Presencia y condición en la escena española contemporánea." *Estreno* 19.1 (1993): 17–20.

Lamartina-Lens, Iride. "Paloma Pedrero." In *Spanish Women Writers. A Bio-Bibliographical Source Book.* Ed. by Linda Gould Levine, Ellen Engelson Marson, and Gloria Feiman Waldman. Westport, CT: Greenwood Press, 1993. 389–396.

———. "*Noches de amor efímero* de Paloma Pedrero: Tres variaciones de un tema." In *Discurso femenino actual.* Ed. by Adelaida López de Martínez. Puerto Rico: Universidad de Puerto Rico, 1995. 295–305.

———. "Female Rage: Diosdado and Pedrero Deal with an Age-Long Problem in a New-Age Fashion." In *Entre Actos: Diálogos sobre teatro español entre siglos.* Ed. by Martha Halsey and Phyllis Zatlin. University Park, IL: Estreno, 1999. 63–68.

———. "Paloma Pedrero: A Profile." *Western European Stages* 9.1 (1997): 53–54.

Leonard, Candyce. "Body, Sex, Woman: The Struggle for Autonomy in Paloma Pedrero's Theater." In *La Chispa '97. Selected Proceedings.* Ed. by Claire Paolini. New Orleans: Tulane University, 1997. 245–254.

———. "Women Writers and Their Characters in Spanish Drama in the 1980s." *Anales de la Literatura Española Contemporánea* 17.1–2 (1992): 243–256.

———. Personal interview. June 4, 1994.

———. Personal interview. May 16, 1997.

Lopez Mozo, Jerónimo. "*El color de agosto.*" *Primer Acto* 267 (1997): 44–45.

López Sancho, Lorenzo. "*Locas de amar,* de Paloma Pedrero, en el Centro Cultural de la Villa." *ABC,* April 13, 1996: 85.

Makris, Mary. "Metadrama, Creation, Reception and Interpretation: The Role of Art in Paloma Pedrero's *El color de agosto.*" *Estreno* 21.1 (1995): 19–23.

Martín, Sabas. "Joven teatro español." *Cuadernos Hispanoamericanos* 466 (1989): 171–179.

Miranda, José Luis. "Con José Luis Miranda." *Primer Acto* 262 (1997): 58–61.

Monleón, José. "Paloma Pedrero." *Primer Acto* 258 (1995): 3.

O'Connor, Patricia. "Postmodern Tendencies in the Theatre of Marisa Ares and Paloma Pedrero." *Letras Peninsulares* 4.2–3 (1991): 307–318.

Oliva, María Victoria. "Paloma Pedrero. El espaldarazo del Tirso." *El Público* 52 (1988): 41.

Podol, Peter. "The Father-Daughter Relationship in Recent Spanish Plays: A Manifestation of Feminism." *Hispanic Journal* 17 (1996): 7–15.

———. "The Socio-Political Dimension of Sexuality and Eroticism in Contemporary

Spanish Theater." *Anales de la Literatura Española Contemporánea*, 17.1–3 (1992): 257–270.

Rodríguez, Alfredo. "La mujer en el teatro español del siglo XX: De María Martínez Sierra a Paloma Pedrero." *Estudios sobre mujer, lengua y literatura*. Santiago de Compostela, Spain: USCompostela, 1996. 121–136.

Rossetti, Ana. "A modo de epílogo," *Locas de amar*. Madrid: Fundación Autor, 1997. 97–98.

S.G. "*Locas de amar*, viaje al corazón de una mujer." *ABC*, April 17, 1996: 121.

Serrano, Virtudes. "La personal dramaturgia de Paloma Pedrero." *Primer Acto* 258 (1995): 62–66.

———. Introducción a *Paloma Pedrero. Juego de noches. Nueve obras en un acto*. Ed. by Virtudes Serrano. Madrid: Ediciones Cátedra, S.A., 1999.

Sullivan, Mary Lee. "The Theatrics of Transference in Federico García Lorca's *La casa de Bernarda Alba* and Paloma Pedrero's *La llamada de Lauren*." *Hispanic Journal* 16.1 (1995): 169–176.

Torres, Rafael. "Noches de amor." *El mundo*, November 15, 1990: 62.

Torres-Pou, Joan. "El elemento paródico en *La llamada de Lauren* de Paloma Pedrero." *Estreno* 19.1 (1993): 26–28.

———. "Síntesis e inversión: Dos rasgos del teatro del Paloma Pedrero." *Alaluz* 25.1–2 (1992): 89–92.

Villán, Javier. "Con Paloma Pedrero." *Primer Acto* 258 (1995): 58–61.

Weimar, Christopher. "Gendered Discourse in Paloma Pedrero's *Noches de amor efímero*." *Gestos* 16 (1993): 89–102.

Zatlin, Phyllis. "Intertextualidad y metateatro en la obra de Paloma Pedrero." *Letras Femeninas* 19.1–2 (1993): 14–20.

———. "Paloma Pedrero and the Search for Identity." *Estreno* 16 (1990): 6–10.

BENITO PÉREZ GALDÓS
(1843–1920)

Lisa Pauline Condé

Benito Pérez Galdós has been widely acclaimed as Spain's greatest writer since Cervantes, although until fairly recently, this acclaim has been based largely upon his achievements as a novelist. However, the last couple of decades have seen a considerable resurgence of interest among Galdós scholars in the turn of the great writer to the stage in 1892, and in his subsequent, somewhat traumatic career as a dramatist.[1] The "experimental daring" [atrevimiento experimental][2] of Galdós's first staged play, *Realidad*, was acknowledged as bringing "a breath of fresh air" [un soplo de esperanza][3] to the late nineteenth-century Spanish stage, notwithstanding the mixed and at times confused reaction of the contemporary public and critics to the new dramatist's work.[4] The audience's confusion, particularly over Galdós's first, most ambitious play, was compounded by the effects of the considerable compromise to which he was subjected during the creative process, as a study of the manuscripts reveals.

BIOGRAPHY

Recent biographical studies of Galdós have tended to reflect the renewal of interest in his theatrical venture. The standard biography remained to the point of preparing this essay in 1995, that of H. Chonon Berkowitz entitled, not inappropriately, *Pérez Galdós: Spanish Liberal Crusader* (1948). In addition to Galdós's very considerable artistic talent, it was this "crusading" element of his work that prompted my own biographical sketch *Stages in the Development of a Feminist Consciousness in Pérez Galdós* (1990), which traces the evolution of the writer's portrayal of women's roles in society, culminating in his projection of "the new woman" [la mujer nueva] on stage—hence the progression of my own interest in Galdós as novelist to his career as dramatist. Other relatively recent biographical studies have focused on this later phase in Galdós's life and work, including Benito Madariaga's *Biografía Santanderina* (1979) and Carmen Menéndez Onrubia's study *El dramaturgo y los actores: Epistolario de Benito Pérez Galdós, María Guerrero y Fernando Díaz de Mendoza* (1984). The second volume of Armas Ayala's biography, *Galdós, Lectura de una vida* (1995), also focuses on this later phase of Galdós's life and career, especially on his theatrical venture.

Another area of increasing interest to most biographers of Galdós is his particular experience and understanding of women from many different walks of life, which clearly inspired his portrayal of the female roles so often predominant in both his novels and his plays. It is only quite recently that much of this personal biographical information and related correspondence has come to light, leading to such major studies as Carmen Bravo-Villasante's *Vida y obra de Emilia Pardo Bazán: Correspondencia amorosa con Pérez Galdós* (1973) and Sebastian de la Nuez Caballero's study of the last love in Galdós's life, *El último gran amor de Galdós: Cartas a Teodosia Gandarias desde Santander (1907–1915)* (1993), in addition to a number of articles.[5]

Galdós, the great writer and philosopher, perceived by his contemporaries as a meek and mild man who lived quietly, seems in fact to have enjoyed a very colorful love life—hence the convincing nature of his portrayal of women on both the page and the stage. The year of his turn to the stage, 1892, is of particular interest in this regard as the young actress with whom he was currently involved, Concha-Ruth Morell, was clearly the inspiration both for the protagonist of his novel of that year, *Tristana*, and for the development of the role she herself was to play on stage as Clotilde, the precursor of "the new woman" in his dramatic début *Realidad*.[6] The leading lady of this play, María Guerrero, whose influence was subsequently to lead to the further development of the role of the new woman, played the part of Augusta, whose infidelity had in turn been inspired by Galdós's former lover, the writer Emilia Pardo Bazán.[7]

Galdós never married, although in 1891 he had a daughter Maria, by Lorenza Cobián, a woman of the *pueblo*. His early years in Las Palmas, where he was born in 1843, are described in some detail by Berkowitz, as is the strength and influence of his mother, "Mama Dolores." It was she who engineered the breakup of his relationship with his cousin, Sisita, due to the girl's illegitimacy, by arranging for him to go to Madrid to study and for Sisita to return to Cuba. A strict Catholic, his mother's inflexible conservatism seems to have contributed to the anticlerical nature of Galdos's early novels and to his own increasingly "liberal" outlook, reinforced on his arrival in Madrid by the influential Krausist philosophy imported from Germany by Sanz del Río.

Galdós was nineteen when, in 1862, his mother persuaded him to go to Madrid to study law. He understood her motives for sending him away, and although he would presumably have liked to assert himself against her so far as Sisita was concerned, according to Berkowitz he was not only somewhat fearful of going so directly against his mother's wishes but aware that his own plans for a literary career would be best realized in the capital.[8] Unhappily, it seems Galdós's mother gained little satisfaction from her son's literary achievements. When he finally abandoned his law studies, the tie was effectively broken, and apparently Galdós did not see her again after 1869 when his abortive university career ended. Donald Brown's study of their relationship concludes of Mama Dolores: "She may have had good motives but certainly her domineering conservatism produced many unhappy results."[9] Galdós's mother has been seen as having directly inspired such works as *Doña Perfecta* (1876) and the character of Dona María in the *Episodio Nacional, Cádiz* (1874) and may well also have influenced the creation of Doña Sales in his later novel *Angel Guerra* (1890).[10]

By the time time of his arrival in Madrid, Galdós had already tried his hand at penning a number of plays, for, as he was later to recount in his *Memorias*, it was in the theater that his dreams always lay [siempre tenía puesta mi ilusión].[11] He was, however, to become disillusioned by these early attempts and turn his hand to the novel, soon earning considerable recognition (and not inconsiderable hostility) for his novels and *Episodios Nacionales*. Galdós was a prolific writer, the author of a number of political and literary articles and reviews, forty-six *Episodios*, thirty-one novels, and twenty-two published plays (a number of which were adapted from novels). By the time of his final turn to the stage in 1892 at the age of forty-nine, he had already fully exploited the potential of the realist novel and was seeking an alternative mode of artistic expression as well as a more direct means of confronting the public with his ideas.

Clearly, the liberal approach of the Krausist philosophy was attractive to the young Galdós. Juan López Morillas defines Krausism as more than a philosophy, rather a "way of life" [estilo de vida] that, founded on a secular and liberal basis, placed primary emphasis on moral integrity and the formation of the whole person, regardless of their sex.[12] The Krausists' contribution to educational reform was considerable, and these ideas, together with the fundamental Krausist tenets of tolerance, reason, and conciliation, are reflected throughout Galdós's work in varying degrees and not least in his drama.

Galdós's particular concern over the lack of education and opportunities available for women is apparent in his writing from the early "thesis" novels. The influence of the real women in his life upon the fictional women of his work is equally apparent, regardless of whether or not one currently approves of any kind of "biographical" approach to a text. Sociological, political, historical, and religious issues are also invariably woven into the tale Galdós is telling or, in the case of the theater, "showing." We see such influences quite clearly from the thesis novels of "the first period" [la primera época]: concern over religious intolerance from *Doña Perfecta* (arguably inspired by Mama Dolores), lack of intellectual freedom for women stressed in *Gloria* (evidently inspired by the second woman in Galdós's life whom he nearly married, Juanita Lund)[13] and so on. The parallels continue, with recurring, arguably "feminist" images of restriction and confinement, on the one hand, and knowledge and awareness, on the other, highlighting the issues confronted, particularly with regard to women's roles in society (e.g., "the doll," "the corset," "light," "wings," etc.).[14] These same images return in Galdós's drama, to be reworked as the victimized heroine of his novels turns triumphant on stage, again arguably reflecting the lives of the successful women with whom the writer later became involved.[15]

Various threads of Galdós's life and work can be seen to converge at his point of transition in 1892, as we find letters from the women currently in his life reproduced on the page in his novel *Tristana*, while the women themselves are found on the stage in his first play, *Realidad*. There is no doubt that Concha-Ruth Morell's letters to Galdós are "literally copied" [literalmente copiadas][16] onto the pages of *Tristana*, and the heroine's dilemma was clearly prompted by her ideas and those of Emilia Pardo Bazan.[17] Both these women find themselves physically on the stage of *Realidad*, Concha Ruth playing the part of Clotilde and Doña Emilia attending a number of rehearsals, much to Clarín's disapproval and Concha Ruth's discomfort.[18] However, it is the leading lady, María Guerrero, who was subsequently to be the greatest source of inspiration to the new dramatist.

It is clear that "Sisita," Juanita Lund, Concha-Ruth Morell, and Emilia Pardo Bazán all heightened Galdós's awareness of the extent of woman's repression in the society of his time, culminating in the ultimate demands of the eponymous heroine of *Tristana*, directly inspired by Concha-Ruth as Gilbert Smith and others have illustrated. The young actress failed to realize her hopes and ambitions, as did Tristana, whose reasons for failure have led to considerable debate among critics. So far as Concha-Ruth was concerned, it seems that a combination of illness, emotional and financial dependence, and a lack of real acting talent led to her sad demise. Nevertheless, she had caused Galdós to focus his attention on both woman's plight and potential, and the relevance of this issue to societal reform, further reinforced by Emilia Pardo Bazán, was to prove crucial in his dramatic career.

Galdós's "new woman," evolving from Concha-Ruth's inspiration and depiction of Clotilde in *Realidad*, was to become incarnate in his leading lady, María Guerrero. It was she who was invariably to be the carrier of the new dramatist's message and instrumental in effecting the changes leading toward his vision of "a new society" [una sociedad nueva].

María Guerrero was virtually unknown to Galdós prior to the staging of *Realidad*, although he recalls the first time he saw her in a production of *Felipe Derblay*, when "I was enchanted by the actress's voice, manner and elegance" [la voz, el gesto y la prestancia de la actriz me encantaron].[19] When he was subsequently introduced to her by the director, Emilio Mario, the new dramatist was further impressed by her exceptional memory. María had already read the novel version of *Realidad* and was quick to grasp the essence of the role of Augusta, which, as observed, had been inspired by the infidelity of Emilia Pardo Bazán. Although it seems that María was not ideally suited to this role, being at the time insufficiently mature, she was well placed to interpret Galdós's evolving concept of an alternative heroine, the new woman, whose precursor Clotilde was originally inspired and interpreted by Concha-Ruth Morell. Where Concha-Ruth failed, María was to succeed, for as Menéndez Onrubia observes: "María

Guerrero had Concha's strengths but not her weaknesses, because she was certainly qualified, and very well qualified, to fulfil her ambitions as an actress" [María Guerrero tiene las virtudes de Concha y no tiene sus defectos, porque sí está capacitada, y muy bien capacitada, para realizarse como actriz].[20] From this point on, Concha Ruth effectively faded into the background, while María went on rapidly to assume and incarnate this new role.

From the correspondence available in the Casa Museo Pérez Galdós in Las Palmas, much of which has now been published by Carmen Menéndez Onrubia, we know that Galdós created a considerable number of the female protagonists of his plays directly for his leading lady and through her inspiration. María herself was to remind Galdós of this in no uncertain terms on one occasion when he was slow to comply with her wishes, writing to him in large letters and underlining twice: "¡¡I am the inspiration!!" [¡¡Yo soy la inspiración!!].[21] Indeed, María Guerrero was to prove an extremely strong and influential character in Galdós's dramatic career, as Emilia Pardo Bazán and Concha-Ruth Morell both withdrew to the wings, leaving the leading lady center stage. The letters available show that the relationship between dramatist and leading lady became increasingly familiar and dependent, although María's marriage to the actor Fernando Díaz de Mendoza in 1896 probably ensured that it did not become intimate. At the same time, Galdós was to adopt an increasingly idealized view of women that was to persist to his last works and his last love, Teodosia Gandarias.

DRAMATURGY: MAJOR WORKS AND THEMES

Galdós wrote twenty-two plays between 1892 and 1918, of which the most ambitious and complex was his first and, arguably, his finest, *Realidad* (1892). Unfortunately, however, this work proved to be too much, too soon, in almost every sense, for the majority of the contemporary audience. In terms of form, it came too close to the "baggy monster" of the novel to be acceptable, and in terms of content, Marina Mayoral's summation of Galdós's novel of the same year, *Tristana*, applies equally insofar as the work was ahead of its time with its ideas—and was not understood.[22]

As a result of the fundamental lack of understanding of this first play on the part of the contemporary audience, subsequent plays were to become increasingly schematic, and much of the new dramatist's innovation and potential was lost in the attempt to conform to current theatrical exigencies and expectations.

Galdós's original intention was to reform the Spanish stage in the same way as he had the novel. In his "Observaciones sobre la novela contemporánea en España" of 1870, he set out his ideas for realism in the novel. In 1885 he declared: "In order that realism should be established in the theatre, it is essential that a determined and resourceful writer should break the present mould and set this crucial reform in motion" [Para que el teatro entre con pie derecho en la escuela de la naturalidad, es preciso que un autor de grandes alientos rompa la marcha y acometa con recursos de primer orden esta gran reforma].[23] In each case, Galdós was to rise to his own challenge, but while there is little dispute over his success as "the creator of the modern novel in Spain,"[24] his "bold experimentation" in the theater was frequently frustrated.

While the new dramatist was increasingly prepared to compromise on form, he was less willing to compromise on the essential content of his plays, remaining convinced that "literature should enlighten, illustrate" [la literatura debe ser enseñanza, ejemplo].[25] Through the modernization of the Spanish theater, Galdós sought to relate his ideas for a more enlightened society directly to his audience, sharing Azorín's view that "art is the key to revolution" [el arte es el principal factor de la revolución].[26]

Thus rather than seeking temporary dramatic *effect*, Galdós was anxious to *affect* more permanently the minds and consciousness of the public. Unfortunately, his public was more accustomed to and expectant of the melodrama of Echegaray, and Galdós was often bitterly disappointed by their apparent inability to grasp the essence and point of much of his work. He was still more bitterly frustrated by the failure of many of his critics to collaborate in this new direction, and by the superficial nature of their often dismissive reviews.

Despite the fact that Galdós's ambitions were curtailed by contemporary theatrical exigencies and that his intentions were frequently not fully understood, many of his plays did enjoy considerable success, and one, whose message was particularly timely, *Electra*, enjoyed almost delirious acclaim. Berenguer's major study *Los estrenos teatrales de Galdós en la crítica de su tiempo* (1988) analyzes both the public's response, as reported by the critics, and the critics' own evaluations of the plays. He concludes that the public responded favorably 80 percent of the time and that critics wrote 77 percent positive or rave reviews. Only two plays were badly received, *Gerona* (1894) and *La fiera* (1896), while *Los condenados* (1894) was a total failure.[27] This compares with Sackett's slightly earlier study that concluded thirteen plays to be successes, five partial successes, and four to be failures.[28]

Galdós's first play, *Realidad*, appears at the crossroads of the writer's trajectory as he turns from the frequently ambiguous presentation of the complex social and moral issues found in the *novelas contemporáneas* to the more schematic and symbolic work that was to follow. *Realidad* was adapted from the dialogue novel of the same name; yet despite the novelty of the form of the original version, the work belongs more to the former than to the latter phase of his work, having much of the characteristic complexity and ambiguity of the novels of the 1880s. Such complexity was to entail prolixity, both of which were to cause problems and confusion for the audience presented with this work on the stage. For as Ocatvio Picón concluded in his review of the opening night: "*Realidad* makes one think" [*Realidad* hace pensar].[29]

In terms of structure, Galdós nurtured for some time the notion of a symbiotic form of "dialogue novel" [novela dialogada], "read theater" [teatro leído], or "spoken novel" [novela hablada], although ultimately he was forced to conform to the "narrow limits" [límites estrechos] of the contemporary stage. Somewhat late in the day, a number of eminent critics, including Leopoldo Alas ("Clarín") were to lament this conformity. There were those, though, who recognized the value of Galdós's dramatic début as "a breath of hope in the stagnant darkness of our theatre" ["un soplo de esperanza en la noche y estancamiento de neustra literaturay teatral].[30]

The contemporary plays of Galdós's "first period" (most notably *Realidad* and *Voluntad*), through which he explored his ideas for a possible future based on a more egalitarian and enlightened society, are not only the most complex but arguably the most modern of his dramatic career. Alongside the moral, psychological, and philosophical concerns of these works runs a quest for liberation from sexual as well as from class prejudice and injustice. Increasingly, these ideas were presented from a moral rather than a socio-economic perspective (although such reform was implied), and this better suited the dramatic form nevertheless, by the time of *Voluntad* (1895), Galdós's new heroine had entered the male world of commerce and seized control.

A number of later contemporary plays, notably *Mariucha* (1903), fit into this early group in the increasingly utopian quest for "a new society" [una sociedad nueva], whose catalyst is invariably the new woman. This whole notion of reform, working through "the new couple" [la pareja nueva], "a new society," and "a new Spain" to "a new world" [un mundo nuevo] persists to Galdós's last "theatrical fable" [fábula teatral], *La razón de la sin razón*, which has a 1700s precedent in a satiric essay with the same title. It was probably written by Jovellanos, whose Enlightened liberal philosophy, ideas on science, aesthetics, religion, work, happiness, and prosperity, Galdós inherits. Here a form of Utopia or "new world" is realized, generated from the new "superior" woman [la mujer superior]. The message was reinforced directly by the writer himself in 1917, when he declared that "the day women succeed in emancipating themselves, the world will be different" [el día en que la mujer consiga emanciparse, el mundo será distinto].[31]

In the quest for a more egalitarian society, Galdós attempts to break down barriers of both class and gender. Arguably, however, the most progressive aspect of his contemporary drama lies in his treatment of sexual politics, as his rather romanticized notion of socialism has been seen to become increasingly outdated. Nevertheless, such plays as *La de San Quintín*, which dealt in simple and symbolic terms with the ideal of class equality, were very well received at the time, despite their obvious limitations to the modern reader/would-be spectator. (It is worth noting that an adaptation of *La de San Quintín* performed at the María Guerrero in 1983 was not so successful.)

Such immediate emotive response as that received by *La de San Quintín* in 1894 reached the point of delirium in the case of Galdós's wildly successful play *Electra* (1901), which fits into another category of his drama concerned directly with religious prejudice and intolerance. Within this smaller group of plays, the writer returns to the theme of his early "novels of the first period" [novelas de la primera época]. Indeed, a trilogy can be identified as paralleling the three novels described by L. B. Walton as "The Unholy Trinity" [*Doña Perfecta* (1876), *Gloria* (1877), and *La familia de Leon Róch* (1878)] in the drama version of *Doña Perfecta* (1896), the hugely successful play *Electra* (1901), and the drama version of *Casandra* (1910). This trilogy earned the new dramatist more immediate recognition and acclaim than some of his earlier, arguably more modern plays. Of course, the religious question was very pertinent to the contemporary Spanish society and the timing of *Electra* notably propitious, following the controversial case of Adelaida de Ubao.[32] The play, widely interpreted as a highly political statement, enjoyed an almost ecstatic reception that reverberated over the continent and South America.

As in the case of Galdós's earlier highly successful play *La de San Quintín*, however, *Electra* now appears rather facile and dated, although it continues to provoke critical interest among Galdós scholars. *Doña Perfecta*, on the other hand, well received at the time of its début, remains a work of considerable substance, inherent drama, and artistry, albeit of primarily historical interest. *Casandra* was less enthusiastically received at its first showing in 1910, although this was the work chosen by Francisco Nieva for a modern adaptation performed at the Teatro Pérez Galdós in Las Palmas in 1983. Drawing on the symbolic elements of the original novel version, the adaptation aroused considerable interest, if not great enthusiasm, indicating, perhaps, that such a work could only really succeed within its historical context.

Other plays for which Galdós enjoyed contemporary recognition due to their dramatic artistry and moral grandeur were *El abuelo* (1904) and *Santa Juana de Castilla* (1918). Clara Hernández Cabrera has recently concluded *El abuelo*, seen by some as a Galdosian *King Lear*, to be Galdós's finest play.[33] *Santa Juana de Castilla*, his last play, was also widely praised for the artistry of its composition. It is clear that Galdós took much time and trouble over the creation of this work, in consultation with his last great love, Teodosia Gandarias, and that despite his advancing years, his efforts were not in vain. Contemporary critical reaction was summed up by Gutiérrez, who confirmed that "almost all began by praising Galdós in his glorious old age and stressing the sober intensity of his dramatic composition" [comienzan casi todos elogiando a Galdós en su gloriosa ancianidad y coinciden en poner de relieve la sobriedad e intensidad de la composición dramática].[34] Indeed, the poet Manuel Machado wrote following the opening night: "I was aware during this sober and powerful drama of moments of great artistic truth, and there were times when my spirit was moved by the reverberation of such supreme beauty" [yo he creído notar en este drama sobrio y fuerte que la mano del genio entreabría a veces las puertas de la gran verdad artística, y el estrecimiento de la suprema belleza ha conmovido mi espíritu en ciertos momentos].[35]

It is noteworthy that, having created a "new woman" in his contemporary drama, Galdós should return to the past in his final work to glorify the now-sanctified female victim of history, effectively rewriting "her-story."[36] It is perhaps also fitting that Galdós should return to the issue of religious intolerance, which was so prominent in his early "thesis" novels. As in earlier plays, however, not only are tolerance and conciliation promoted in *Santa Juana* but also the concept of progress through work. In this play and in *La razón de la sinrazón*, his last "novel," (or rather, "fábula teatral") the stress is on work "on the land and in the arts" [en la labor de la tierra y en las artes], although the benefits of scientific progress are also promoted in such plays as *Celia en los infiernos* (1913).

It can be seen that Galdós did not shrink from confronting a wide and often controversial range of issues on stage in spite of the various pressures to compromise, some of which he felt obliged to heed. Such compromise was most evident in the structure and form of his plays rather than in their essential content, although this was frequently modified to the point that the message became less clear. It could certainly be argued that Galdós's concession to contemporary theatrical exigencies was prejudicial to his artistic development as a dramatist. While some of his plays did show considerable artistic merit as well as moral grandeur and social significance, I would not totally agree with Finkenthal's recent conclusion that "Galdós was a great dramatist" [Galdós fue un gran dramaturgo].[37] Nevertheless, his drama certainly contained elements of greatness, displayed considerable innovation, and advanced the ideas he inherited from eighteenth-century thinkers.

CRITICS' RESPONSE

As a result of the innovative and controversial nature of Galdós's drama, critical response was correspondingly varied. As noted above, his main biographer, Berkowitz, defines Galdós as a "Spanish Liberal Crusader," and indeed by the time of the writer's contemporary drama, the term *liberal* might almost be extended to *socialist* and, arguably, to *feminist*.

Perhaps the most striking feature of contemporary critical response to Galdós's drama is not so much the anticipated hostility from neo-Catholic, conservative elements but rather the initial reservations from such major critics and writers as Clarín, which undoubtedly contributed to the pressure on the new dramatist to modify his artistic ambitions for the theater. This is most evident in the case of Galdós's dramatic début, his adaptation of the dialogue novel *Realidad* for the stage.

This first play of Galdós's was highly polemical in terms of both form and content, leaving some spectators horrified, some confused, and others aware of having witnessed a superior and extraordinary work without having fully understood it. Of particular interest on the opening night of *Realidad* was the reaction of the great academic Menéndez Pelayo who, notwithstanding his own conservative ideology, exclaimed, "How wonderful! . . . This is our Ibsen, this is how we like him!" [¡Qué hermoso es esto! . . . ¡Esto es nuestro Ibsen, así le queremos!].[38]

Galdós's own "liberal" ideology was very apparent in his dramatic debut, which attempted to present "reality" itself on stage and took a highly unconventional approach to the theme of adultery, traditionally revenged on the Spanish stage. In Galdós's complex play of social conventions, politics, morals, marriage, friendships, love, and lust, the adulterer, while not condoned, is not automatically condemned nor is revenge sought. Furthermore, the sympathetic portrayal of a common prostitute was compounded by the subtle suggestion that she might actually be of greater moral worth than the upper-class, socially respected heroine, although such suggestion was toned down considerably in the final *adaptación*, presumably at the hand of director Emilio Mario.[39]

As indicated, much is suggested rather than spelled out in *Realidad*, which was censured by many for lacking the constant melodramatic effects of the drama of Echegaray, who had been popular for so long in Spain. There was also a major problem in the fact that the particular complexity of this play led to prolixity, and the contemporary theatergoing public was totally unaccustomed to such lengthy, thought-provoking work. So radical a departure from the relatively simple, romantic melodrama of Echegaray inevitably led to disappointment in some and confusion in others.

Nevertheless, such praise as that expressed by so distinguished a critic as Menéndez Pelayo goes some way to refute the claim that the enthusiastic ovation enjoyed by Galdós on the opening night was purely attributable to his popularity as a novelist. As indicated, a number of serious critics were of the view that the enthusiasm was largely due to an acknowledgment of having witnessed a superior work without necessarily having reached full understanding of it. Galdós himself was subsequently to lament: "Among the various critics, there was not one who penetrated the issues or the characters of the drama being judged" [Entre las diversas críticas, no hubo ninguna que profundizase en el asunto y caracteres juzgados].[40] At the same time, however, he was clearly relieved and pleased by the reception he received on the opening night, aware that, as Octavio Picón pointed out, "he hadn't presented the audience with just another play, but a play which differed greatly from those they were used to seeing" [no se ha hecho un drama más, sino un drama que se diferencia mucho de cuantos hemos visto hasta ahora].[41]

Realidad, therefore, marks not only a crucial turning point in Galdós's own career but also a significant landmark in the history of the Spanish stage, which was apparently not quite ready for such a work. Notwithstanding the length of the play, the unconventional treatment and resolution of adultery, along with the progressive social and moral implications, were largely misunderstood or unrecognized by the contemporary audience. Yet despite the increased confusion resulting from the compromise to which Galdós had been subjected in the creative process, it was recognized that "*Realidad* makes one think" [*Realidad* hace pensar].[42] This, of course, was highly problematic in itself, as the contemporary Spanish public was more accustomed to feeling than thinking in the theater—hence the general failure to grasp the full implications of the characters' behavior in this play.

As in his novels, we find that the female characters in Galdós's plays tend to predominate, and this is reflected in the works' titles. In the majority of the plays, these female characters tend to be the strongest as well as the most developed and the most subject to reworking through the creative process. In *Realidad* the character of Augusta (as noted above, inspired by the infidelity of Galdós's former mistress, the writer Emilia Pardo Bazán) is probably the most complex and arguably the most disturbing. *Four* sets of manuscripts involving the repeated reworking of Augusta's presentation in Act One reveal the importance Galdós attributed to her role and the subsequent difficulty he experienced in compromising over the psychology of her situation.[43]

Despite the fact that he had earlier called for such realism in the theater, Leopoldo Alas (Clarín) was among the many contemporary critics who initially criticized Galdós for writing a "psychological" drama that was "novelistic" in conception. Ironically, when the new dramatist subsequently attempted to reduce the level of psychological penetration in his plays, Clarín bemoaned the loss, declaring *Realidad* to be Galdós's finest play, despite its weaknesses.[44]

Although later plays of Galdós may be more tightly and effectively structured and their plots and/or themes less complex, I, too, am of the view that this first play, *Realidad*, shows the greatest innovation and potential. Close study of all the manuscripts and *adaptaciones*, together with relevant correspondence and reviews available in the Casa Museo Pérez Galdós in Las Palmas and the Biblioteca Nacional in Madrid, has convinced me of the scope and modernity of this progressive play, as well as revealing the extent of the compromise to which the new dramatist was subjected in the creative process.

As indicated, the major theme of *Realidad* was inspired by the infidelity of Galdós's mistress, Emilia Pardo Bazán, although the female protagonist, Augusta, was some way from being a carbon copy of Doña Emilia. Nevertheless, she herself did acknowledge: "I recognised myself in that lady so loved despite her infidelity and cheating. God help me! I can assure you that I myself don't know how I came to *that*" [Me he reconocido en aquella señora más amada por infiel y por trapacera. ¡Valgame Dios, alma mía! Puedo asegurarte que yo misma no me doy cuenta de cómo he llegado a *esto*].[45]

Menédez Onrubia has recently concluded of *Realidad*: "Augusta Cisneros is the Spain which is dying, while Clotilde Viera is that which is reborn" [Augusta Cisneros es la España que muere, mientras Clotilde Viera es la que renace].[46] However, a closer analysis of the behavior, psyche, and situation of these female characters, further complicated by the role of Leonor, the prostitute referred to as "la Peri," shows the issues confronted in this play to be considerably more complex than those reflective of so straightforward a thesis.

Among those issues that compromise obscured but that the manuscripts reveal Galdós originally wished to explore and to stress are the following: first, the causes and implications of the breakdown of the marriage between Augusta and Orozco, resulting both in the adultery between Augusta and Federico (brother of Clotilde and close friend of the married couple) and in the impossibility of reconciliation, despite Orozco's willingness to forgive and Augusta's wish to confess. Given the couple's apparent incompatability and their lack of communication, Galdós wished to explore the social and psychological factors that contributed to Augusta's decision to break her marriage vows. These factors were more sharply depicted and closely analyzed in his final *adaptación* prior to the last-minute modifications.

Crucial among social factors were the limited horizons of the heroine in terms of both vision and opportunity. To illustrate and stress this situation, Galdós used some of the contrasting images of awareness and constriction found in the *novelas contemporáneas*, highlighting these in the original manuscripts. In the final *adaptación*, for example, we see Galdós originally intended Orozco to tell his wife: "Your intelligence is great, but you have accustomed yourself to seeing only limited horizons. You need to see more, more" [Tu inteligencia es grande, pero la has acostumbrado a no ver más que horizontes limitados. Conviene ver más, más].[47] This developed version offers a deeper insight into the situation as well as a more sympathetic portrayal of Orozco as a human being and of Augusta as a victim of societal restriction. Augusta herself is not unaware of this restriction, which the image of the corset is used to reinforce, as she recoils against "these social demands, this puritanical and restrictive upbringing that disfigures our souls just as the cursed corset disfigures our bodies" [este compás social, de esta educación puritana y meticulosa que nos desfigura el alma como el maldito corsé nos desfigura el cuerpo].[48]

On the psychological level, Galdós, in true Cervantine fashion, stressed the conflict between reality and illusion, emphasizing the delusion behind Augusta's desperate escape from the mold prepared for her by society into the fantasy of "romance." As the reality of her situation is unsatisfying to her, Augusta becomes increasingly dependent upon and susceptible to the unreal. Both her early inclination to fuse the two concepts and her later involuntary confusion between reality and illusion were stressed by Galdós but then modified in the final *adaptación*, where such statements as "I want to fuse illusion with reason" [Es que aspiro a fundir la ilusión con la razón][49] were deleted.

The second major issue was the whole nature of the adulterous relationship between Augusta and Federico. This was more closely analyzed in Galdós's original manuscript, and the danger of the couple's unbridled passion contrasted with the danger of Orozco's emotional denial, further underlining the inherent complexity of these issues. A number of references to the "madness" ["locura"] of Augusta and Federico's passion were deleted, including Augusta's declaration "I love you madly" [Te quiero locamente].[50]

Third, Galdós clearly wished to stress the sincerity and value of the relationship between Federico and the prostitute Leonor, "la Peri," and contrast this with the insincerity of the relationship between Federico and Augusta. Again, he had to "backtrack" at the eleventh hour in his exploration of the social and moral implications to the point where, somewhere between the final *adaptación* and the version performed and published, an incident involving Federico's mother's prayerbook was introduced that effectively contradicted some of the earlier, progressive suggestions made.[51] Certainly the notion of true, disinterested friendship between members of the opposite sex (as well as from very different backgrounds) was a novel one and, indeed, is still a polemical subject.[52] In *Realidad*, Federico shares a very special friendship with Leonor and an understanding and honesty that is lacking in his relationship with Augusta. She herself envies the closeness of spirit her lover enjoys with Leonor, while he sadly acknowledges the incompleteness of his relationship with Augusta: "I am her lover, not her friend" [Soy su amante; su amigo, no].[53]

Finally, we find the expansion and development of the role of Clotilde as the precursor of "the new woman," on which Galdós was little prepared to compromise, despite the director's protestations. For as Casalduero was later to conclude: "Clotilde represents the vital solution" [Clotilde representa la solución vital].[54]

Notwithstanding the difficulties and compromise involved, *Realidad* ran successfully at the Teatro de la Comedia in Madrid for twenty-two consecutive nights (a lengthy run for the period) and was equally successful in Barcelona, despite the somewhat vitriolic criticism received from certain quarters.[55]

Although he was subsequently to modify his approach, Galdós the dramatist battled on in his quest to open the eyes and the minds of his spectators not only to the possibility of a new, enlightened society but also to a greater understanding of that present and past.

AWARDS AND DISTINCTIONS

On February 6, 1897 Galdós was elected to the Spanish Royal Academy. He joined the Republican party and became a parliamentary deputy for Madrid in 1906. In 1910 he was elected a member of the Spanish parliament for the Republican-Socialist Union in Madrid, and in 1912 he was nominated for the Nobel Prize. In 1919 the sculpture of Galdós by Victorio Macho was inaugurated in El Retiro Park in Madrid, and the day of his death, January 4, 1920, became one of national mourning.

NOTES

1. In addition to a marked increase in the number of articles published and conference papers given on Galdós's theater, two full-length introductions have been published: Stanley Finkenthal, *El teatro de Galdós* (Madrid: Editorial Fundamentos, 1980); Carmen Menéndez Onrubia, *Introducción al teatro de Benito Pérez Galdós* (Madrid: CSIC, 1983).

2. Gonzalo Sobejano, "Efectos de *Realidad*," *Estudios Escénicos*, no. 18 (septiembre 1974): 41.

3. Rafael Altamira y Crevea, "El teatro de Pérez Galdós," in *De historia y arte* (Madrid: Suárez, 1898), 275.

4. See Lisa P. Condé, *Women in the Theatre of Galdós* (New York: Mellen Press, 1990), chapter V, for details.

5. Including Gilbert Smith, "Galdós, *Tristana*, and Letters from Concha-Ruth Morell," *Anales Galdosianos* X (1975): 91–120.

6. See Lisa P. Condé, *Stages in the Development of a Feminist Consciousness in Pérez Galdós (1843–1920)* (New York: Mellen Press, 1990), chapter V, for details and additional bibliography.

7. See Carmen Bravo-Villasante, *Vida y obra de Emilia Pardo Bazán: Correspondencia amorosa con Pérez Galdós* (Madrid: Editorial Magisterio Español, 1973), for details.

8. H. Chonon Berkowitz, *Pérez Galdós: Spanish Liberal Crusader* (Madison: University of Wisconsin Press, 1948), p. 40.

9. Donald F. Brown, "More Light on the Mother of Galdós,"*Hispania* XXXIX (1956): 403–404.

10. Condé, *Stages*, 24–26.

11. B. Pérez Galdós, *Memorias*, ed. Alberto Ghiraldo (Madrid: Renacimiento, 1930), 158.

12. Juan López Morillas, *El Krausismo Español* (Mexico: Fondo de Cultura Económica, 1980).

13. Condé, *Stages*, chapter II.

14. See Lisa P. Condé, "Feminist Imagery in Galdós," in *Galdós' House of Fiction* (Oxford: Dolphin Book Co., 1991), 99–125.

15. Condé, *Stages*, chapters VIII and IX.

16. Quoted by A. F. Lambert, "Galdós and Concha Ruth Morell," *Anales Galdosianos* VIII (1973): 34.

17. See Benito Madariaga, *Pérez Galdós: Biografía Santanderina* (Santander: CSIC, 1979), 84.

18. See Condé, *Stages*, 158, 197.

19. Pérez Galdós, *Memorias*, 17.

20. Carmen Menéndez Onrubia, "Presencia de María Guerrero en la obra dramática de Galdós," in *Actas del Tercer Congreso Internacional de Estudios Galdosianos* (Las Palmas: Cabildo Insular de Gran Canaria, 1990), 433.

21. Letter conserved in the *Casa-Museo Pérez Galdós*, Caja 6, Carp. 24, Leg. 66.

22. Marina Mayoral, "*Tristana*: ¿una feminista galdosiana?" *Insula*, nos. 320–321 (1973): 28.

23. B. Pérez Galdós, *Nuestro teatro*, ed. Alberto Ghiraldo (Madrid: Renacimiento, 1923), 141.

24. L. B. Walton, *Pérez Galdós and the Spanish Novel of the Nineteenth Century* (New York: Dutton, 1927).

25. Quoted by Antón del Olmet and García Carraffa, *Los grandes españoles*.

26. Quoted by R. Cardwell, "Juan Ramón, Ortega y los intelectuales," *Hispanic Review* 53 (1985): 333.

27. Angel Berenguer, *Los estrenos teatrales de Galdós en la crítica de su tiempo* (Madrid: Consejería de Cultura, 1988).

28. Theodore Sackett, *Galdós y las máscaras* (Verona: Instituto di Lingue e Letterature straniere di Verona, 1982).

29. J. Octavio Picón, "Estreno de *Realidad*," *El Correo*, 16 marzo 1892.

30. Altamira y Crevea, "El teatro," 275.

31. Reported by Angel Martín (Galdós's coachman in 1917) in *Excelsior* (Mexico City), November 11, 1917. Quoted by W. Pattison in *Benito Pérez Galdós* (New York: Twayne, 1975), 19.

32. See E. Inman Fox, "Galdós' *Electra*," *Anales Galdosianos* I (1966), who explains

the events coinciding with the presentation of *Electra*; and Juan López Nieto, "*Electra o la victoria liberal* (Una nueva interpretación a la luz de la situación española de hacia 1900)," in *Actas del Cuarto Congreso Internacional de Estudios Galdosianos* (1990) (Las Palmas: Cabildo Insular de Gran Canaria, 1993), 711–730. L. B. Walton coined the phrase "The Unholy Trinity" in *Pérez Galdós and the Spanish Novel of the Nineteenth Century* (London: Dent, 1927).

33. Clara Hernández Cabrera, "*El abuelo* y la prensa de su epoca," in *Actas del Tercer Congreso Internacional de Estudios Galdosianos* (Las Palmas: Cabildo Insular de Gran Canaria, 1989), 395–403.

34. Jesús Gutiérrez, "La "Pasión" de Santa Juana de Castilla," *Estudios Escénicos* 18 (septiembre 1974): 203.

35. Manuel Machado, *El Liberal* (Madrid, 9-V-1918).

36. As stressed by John Gabriele in a paper given on August 21, 1995, at the *XII Congreso* of the *Asociación International de Hispanistas* at Birmingham University, entitled "Historia y feminismo en *Santa Juana de Castilla* de Galdós."

37. Finkenthal, *El teatro de Galdós*, 205.

38. Quoted by Altamira y Crevea, *De historia y arte*, 281.

39. See Condé, *Women in the Theatre of Galdós*, chapter III.

40. Pérez Galdós, *Memorias*, 176.

41. In Octavio Picón, "Estreno de *Realidad*."

42. Ibid.

43. *Casa-Museo Pérez Galdós*, Caja 14, Núm. 1–2.

44. See Condé, *Women in the Theatre of Galdós*, chapter V.

45. Quoted by Bravo-Villasante, *Vida y obra*, 143.

46. Menéndez Onrubia, "Presencia de María Guerrero," 429.

47. Final *adaptación, Casa-Museo*, Caja 14, Núm. 2.

48. B. Pérez Galdós, *Realidad*, ed. Lisa Condé (New York: Mellen Press, 1993), 28.

49. Final *adaptación, Casa-Museo*, Caja 14, Núm. 2.

50. Ibid.

51. See Condé, *Women in the Theatre of Galdós*, chapter III.

52. Witness the debate sparked off by the relatively recent American film *When Harry Met Sally!*

53. From the original novel version, B. Pérez Galdós, *Obras Completas*, ed. F. Sainz de Robles (Madrid: Aguilas, 1973), *Novelas II*, 1252.

54. Joaquín Casalduero, "*Ana Karenina* y *Realidad*," *Bulletin Hispanique* XXXIX (1937): 395.

55. Pedro Bofill, for example, warned: '¡Madres que tenéis hijas, no las llevéis al teatro!' [Mothers who have daughters—don't take them to the theater!], *La Época*, 16 marzo 1892.

BIBLIOGRAPHY

Published Works

Obras inéditas. Ed. Alberto Ghiraldo. Vol. V, *Nuestro teatro*. Madrid: Renacimiento, 1923.

Obras inéditas. Ed. Alberto Ghiraldo. Vol. X, *Memorias*. Madrid: Renacimiento, 1930.

"Observaciones sobre la novela contemporánea en España." 1870. Reproduced in *Ensayos de crítica literaria*. Ed. Laureano Bonet. Barcelona: Ediciones Peninsula, 1971.

Obras Completas. Ed. Federico Saínz de Robles: *Novelas I; Novelas II; Novelas III; Cuentos, Teatro y Censo*. Madrid: Aguilar, 1973.

Teatro Selecto. Realidad, Abuelo, Doña Perfecta. Ed. Rodolfo Cardona and Gonzalo Sobejano. Madrid: Escélicer, 1973.

Plays: Modern Editions

Electra. Madrid: Editorial Hernando, 1981.
Casandra. Versión de Francisco Nieva. Madrid: Ediciones MK, 1983.
La de San Quintin y *Alma y vida*. Ed. Isaac Rubio. Salamanca: Ediciones Almar, 1987.
The Theatre of Galdós: Realidad (1892). Ed. Lisa P. Condé. New York: Edwin Mellen Press, 1993.
The Theatre of Galdós: La loca de la casa (1893). Ed. Lisa P. Condé. New York: Edwin Mellen Press, 1995.
The Theatre of Galdós: Voluntad (1895) Ed. Lisa P. Condé. New York: Edwin Mellen Press, 2000.

Critical Studies

Altamira y Crevea, Rafael. *De historia y arte*. Madrid: Suárez, 1898.
Antón del Olmet and Arturo García, Carraffa. *Los grandes españoles: Galdós*. Madrid: 1912.
Armas Ayala, Alfonso. *Saldós, Lectura de una vida*. Santa Cruz de Tenesife: Servicio de Publicaciones de la caja general de Ahorros de Cenarias, 1989–1995.
Bastons Carles, and Nonteys, Míriam. "Ecos en Cataluña del estreno de *Electra* en Madrid." *Homenaje a Alfonso Armas Ayala*. Las Palmas: Ediciones del Cabildo de Gran Canaria, 2000. 139–158.
Berenguer, Angel. *Los estrenos teatrales de Galdós en la crítica de su tiempo*. Madrid: Consejería de Cultura, 1988.
Berkowitz, H. Chonon. *Pérez Galdós: Spanish Liberal Crusader*. Madison: University of Wisconsin Press, 1948.
Boo, Maltilde L. "El manuscrito de *La de San Quintín* (Estudio preliminar)." *Anales Galdosianos* 18 (1983): 125–130.
Bravo-Villasante, Carmen. *Galdós*. Madrid: Mondadori, 1988.
———. *Vida y obra de Emilia Pardo Bazán: Correspondencia amorosa con Pérez Galdós*. Madrid: Editorial Magisterio Español, 1973.
Brown, Donald F. "More Light on the Mother of Galdós." *Hispania* XXXIX (1956): 403.
Casalduero, Joaquín. *Vida y obra de Galdós*. Madrid: Editorial Gredos, 1974.
Condé, Lisa P. "The Adaptation of Galdós' *Realidad* for the Stage: A Preliminary Manuscript Study." *Anales Galdosianos* XXV (1990): 95–111.
———. "Adultery in Galdós's *Realidad*." *Romance Studies*, No. 31 (Spring 1998): 19–32.

————. "The Complexity of Women's Roles in Galdós' *Realidad.*" *Forum for Modern Language Studies* 28.2 (1992): 173–188.

————. "Feminist Imagery in Galdós." In *Galdós' House of Fiction.* Oxford: Dolphin Book Co., 1991. 99–125.

————. "Galdós and His Leading Ladies." *Bulletin of Hispanic Studies*, 75 (1998): 79–91.

————. "From *El sacrificio* (n.d.) to *La loca de la casa* (1893)." In *A Sesquicentennial Tribute to Galdós 1843/1993*, ed. Linda Willem. Newark, DE: Juan de la Cuesta Press, 1993. 283–297.

————. "The Spread Wings of Galdós' 'Mujer Nueva.' " In *Feminist Readings on Spanish and Latin American Literature*, ed. Lisa P. Condé and Stephen M. Hart. New York: Mellen Press, 1991. 13–35.

————. *Stages in the Development of a Feminist Consciousness in Pérez Galdós (1843–1920).* New York: Mellen Press, 1990.

————. "*Voluntad*: ¿Una obra feminista?' *VI Congreso Internacional Gladosiano (1997).* Las Palmas: Ediciones del Cabildo de Gran Canaria, 2000. 254–266.

————. "Womanpower in Galdós *Voluntad* (1895)." In *New Frontiers in Hispanic and Luso-Brazilian Scholarship*, ed. Oakley Dadson and Odber de Baubeta. New York: Mellen Press, 1994. 209–223.

————. *Women in the Theatre of Galdós.* New York: Mellen Press, 1990.

Finkenthal, Stanley. *El teatro de Galdós.* Madrid: Editorial Fundamentos, 1980.

González Santana, Rosa Delia. "Electra. Un personaje femenino entre mundos divergentes." *VI Congreso Internacional Galdosiano (1997).* Las Palmas: Ediciones del Cabildo de Gran Canaria, 2000. 772–781.

Hernández Cabrera, Clara. "El abuelo y la prensa de su epoca." In *Actas del Tercer Congreso Internacional de Estudios Galdosianos.* Las Palmas: Cabildo Insular de Gran Canaria, 1989. 395–403.

Inman Fox, E. "Galdós' *Electra.*" *Anales Galdosianos* I (1966): 131–141.

Lambert, A. F. "Galdós and Concha Ruth Morell." *Anales Galdosianos* VIII (1973): 34. 33–49.

López Morillas, Juan. *El Krausismo español.* Mexico: Fondo de Cultura Económica 1980.

López Nieto, Juan. "*Electra* o la victoria liberal." In *Actas del Cuarto Congreso Internacional de Estudios Galdosianos* (1990). Las Palmas: Cabildo Insular de Gran Canaria, 1993. 711–730.

Madariaga, Benito. *Pérez Galdós: Biografía Santanderina.* Santander: CSIC, 1979.

Mayoral, Marina. "*Tristana*: ¿una feminista galdosiana?" *Insula*, núms. 320–321 (1973): 28.

Menéndez Onrubia, Carmen. *El dramaturgo y los actores: Epistolario de Benito Pérez Galdós, María Guerrero y Fernando Díaz de Mendoza.* Madrid: CSIC, 1984.

————. *Introducción al teatro de Benito Pérez Galdós.* Madrid: CSIC, 1983.

————. "Presencia de María Guerrero en la obra dramática de Galdós." In *Actas del Tercer Congreso Internacional de Estudios Galdosianos.* Las Palmas: Cabildo Insular de Gran Canaria, 1990.

de la Nuez Caballero, Sebastiën. *El último gran amor de Galdós: Cartas a Teodosia Gandarias des de Santander (1907–1915).* Santander: Concejalia de Cultura del Gxcmo Ayuntamiento de Santander, 1993.

O'Byrne Curtis, Margarita. "El retorno de Casandra: La inversión del mito en el drama galdosiano." *Anales Galdosianos* 31/32 (1996/1997): 75–82.

———. "*Santa Juana de Castilla*: Una reconstrucción heterológica del pasado nacional." *VI Congreso Internacional Galdosiano (1997)*. Las Palmas: Ediciones del Cabildo de Gran Canaria, 2000. 536–546.

Ortiz-Armengol, Pedro. *Vida de Galdós*. Barcelona: Crítica. 1996.

Palomo, Maria del Pilar. "*El Abuelo* galdosiano: de la novela al cine pasando por la escena." *Homenaje a Alfonso Armas Ayala*. Las Palmas: Ediciones del Cabildo de Gran Canaria, 2000. 513–536.

Paolini, Gilberto. "*Voluntad* y el ideario galdosiano." *Estudios Escénicos*, no. 18 (1974): 63–78.

Pattison, W. *Benito Pérez Galdós*. New York: Twayne, 1975.

Rios Font, Wadda. "Galdós, Renovación teatral y economía cultural." *VI Congreso Internacional Galdosiano (1997)*. Las Palmas: Ediciones del Cabildo de Gran Canaria, 2000. 810–821.

Sackett, Theodore. *Galdós y las máscaras*. Verona: Instituto di Lingue e Letterature straniere di Verona, 1982.

Smith, Gilbert. "Galdós, *Tristana*, and Letters from Concha-Ruth Morell." *Anales Galdosianos* X (1975): 91–120.

Sobejano, Gonzalo. "Efectos de *Realidad.*" *Estudios Escénicos*, no. 18 (septiembre 1974): 41–61.

DUQUE DE RIVAS (ANGEL DE SAAVEDRA)
(1791–1865)

Alvin F. Sherman, Jr.

BIOGRAPHY

Angel de Saavedra Ramírez de Baquedano, Duque de Rivas, was born in Cordova on March 10, 1791. He was the second son of Juan Martín de Saavedra y Martínez and María Dominga Ramírez de Baquedano y Quiñones, both of whom came from prominent Spanish families. Because of the family's unique social standing, young Angel enjoyed many privileges and honors. At the age of six Angel was given the title of Captain of the Princes Regiment, with its corresponding salary. By the time he was eight years old Rivas had received both the Order of Santiago and that of San Juan of Jerusalem. In 1802 his father died, and the title of the Duke of Rivas passed on to Angel's older brother, Juan Remigio. The next year Angel entered the Real Seminario de Nobles in Madrid. However, after only three years he left the Seminario and accepted a commission as a captain in the Royal Guards. In his youth, Rivas began to demonstrate a penchant for literature, especially poetry. It is during his early years that Angel began to compose and compile his own works.

With the outbreak of the War of Independence young Rivas participated in several significant battles, including Sepúlveda, Tudela, Uclés and Talavera. During the early skirmishes of the battle of Ocaña he was gravely wounded. The injuries he received were often referred to as the "eleven mortal wounds." Reports of these wounds developed over time into an elaborate myth surrounding the young nobleman. However, historical records verify that he only received three, one of which pierced his chest, punctured his lung, and left him physically disabled for the rest of is life. After a long convalescence, Angel returned to military service. In 1810 he was assigned to work for the general staff of the Spanish Army in Cádiz. Soon thereafter he was promoted to the rank of captain. After the War of Independence, Rivas moved back to Cordova and dedicated his time and effort to honing his painting and writing skills.

Angel's fondness for the arts brought him into intimate association with several notable literary and political leaders of the time, including Martínez de la

Rosa, Arriaza, Quintana, Juan Nicasio Gallego, and the Count of Haro, later the Duke of Frías. In 1814 Rivas published his first collection of poetry consisting of thirty short compositions and *El paso honroso*, a more extensive poetic work. That same year he completed his first historic drama, *Ataúlfo*. This piece was harshly censured and never appeared on stage. Undaunted, Rivas moved forward in his creative endeavors. In the years before his exile Rivas wrote several historic tragedies, including *Aliatar* (1816), *Doña Blanca de Castilla* (1817, now lost), *El duque de Aquitania* [The Duke of Aquitaine] (1818), *Malek-Adhel* (1819), and *Lanuza* (1822).

In 1821 he represented Cordova in the new liberal Córtes in Madrid. Unfortunately, after the triumph of Fernando VII in 1823, Rivas was exiled. Like many of his cohorts, Rivas migrated to London. However, after only six months, he left England en route to Italy. The trip was interrupted by a short layover in Gibraltar where he married María de la Encarnación de Cueto. Finally, when he arrived in Liorna, Italy, the papal authorities denied residency to him. Again, he was forced by circumstances to find another safe haven for himself and his wife. They finally settled in Malta. While in Malta he befriended John Hookham Frere, who introduced Rivas to the works of William Shakespeare and Sir Walter Scott, as well as the writings of several Spanish Medieval and Golden Age writers. This new literary perspective enriched Rivas's appreciation for the *belles arts* and supplied him with a rich and endless source of material from which he developed his own writing style. More important, these works tutored the young writer in the fundamentals of traditional Romanticism that would prove a vital resource in the development of the author's artistic ideology. However, Rivas' study of literature was not limited to this orthodox point of view. Frere also introduced Rivas to the writings of Lord Byron, whose brandish style and sensuality later surfaced in Rivas's characterization of Don Alvaro.

While Rivas resided in Malta, King Ferdinand VII issued an edict condemning him to death. This action further delayed Rivas's hopes of returning to Spain. It was during these latter years of his exile that Rivas composed three more works: a tragic history, *Arias Gonzalo* (1827?); a comedy, *Tanto vales cuanto tienes* [What You Have Is What You're Worth] (1828); and a poem "El faro de Malta" [The Lighthouse of Malta] (1828). In 1829 he began work on one of his most significant contributions to Spanish Romanticism, *El moro expósito* [The Abandoned Moor].

In spring 1830 Rivas and his family, comprising his wife and three children, departed from Malta on a yacht, which was headed for France. First the Rivas family was detained in Marseille in accordance with an edict issued by the French government regarding Spanish immigrants. From there the family was relocated to Orleans, where Rivas set up shop as a painter and instructor. In Orleans the family lived poorly, surviving on the meager income that Rivas earned from his painting and tutoring. Within a few months of their arrival in Orleans, Rivas moved his family to Paris, where he again painted and taught Spanish. During this phase of his life Rivas made it a point to avoid involvement with those who promoted revolution and the overthrow of the Spanish monarchy. Shortly after the birth of his fourth child, the family was forced to move to Tours due to an outbreak of cholera in the French capital. Here he wrote the most applauded of his theatrical works, *Don Alvaro o la fuerza del sino* [Don Alvaro or the Force of Destiny] (1832). His original intention was to stage a French version of the work in the Port de San Martin in Paris. However, with the promise of amnesty and a long-awaited return to Spain, the staging of this romantic drama was delayed. The following year he completed work on *El moro expósito* (1833).

With the death of Fernando VII (1833) the Spanish government issued a decree of general amnesty. Unfortunately, Rivas was not among those who was allowed to return to the country. However, later that same year the Queen Regent issued another amnesty edict that opened the door for Rivas. Rivas returned to Spain on January 9, 1834, after more than ten years of exile. Soon after his arrival to Spain, all his rights, honors, and possessions were restored to him. In May of the same year his older brother Juan Remigio died, and Angel inherited the title Duke of Rivas. The honors continued to mount when in October he became a member of the Royal Spanish Academy. Despite all these significant events in his life, none was to have the profound impact and long-lasting effect as the staging of *Don Alvaro o la fuerza del sino* on March 22, 1835, at the Príncipe theater in Madrid. This important work launched Rivas into the forefront of the Romantic movement in Spain and established him as one of its chief contributors.

In his political career, Rivas joined the ranks of the moderates, a move that would end in another brief exile to Gibraltar in 1836. In August 1837 he returned to Madrid, at which time he was elected to be the first president of the Ateneo Literario. By 1840 Rivas had moved his family to Seville. This period was the beginning of a very productive phase in Rivas's literary career. From 1840 to 1842 he published the *Romances históricos* [Historical Romances] (1841) and four comedies, including *Solaces de un prisionero* [A Prisoner's Consolation] (1840), *La morisca de Alajuar* [The Morisco of Alajuar] (1841), *El crisol de la lealtad* [The Crucible of Loyalty] (1842), and *El parador de Bailén* [The Inn at Bailén] (1842), and a fantasy drama, *El desengaño en un sueño* [Disillusionment in a Dream] (1842). This period of frenetic and continuous literary production was followed by an appointment from his longtime friend González Brabo to be Spain's Minister Plenipotentiary and Ambassador to the court of Fernando II, King of the Two Sicilies. Rivas served in this position for six years.

After returning to Spain from his assignment in Italy, Rivas began editing his works, and in 1854 and 1855 he published them in five volumes. Interestingly he omitted from this collection his eight historical dramas, including *Ataúlfo, Aliatar, Doña Blanca, El duque de Aquitania, Malek-Adhel, Lanuza, Arias Gonzalo*, and the comedy *El parador del Bailén*. The complete reasoning for this omission is unclear. However, in the introduction to his complete works, Rivas suggests that the pieces were of little literary value.

In 1857 General Ramón María de Narváez named Rivas to the post of Ambassador in Paris, which he occupied until the next year. After many years serving in political appointments, Rivas returned to Spain and settled into a quieter life out of the public eye. However, the poet's talents could not so easily go unnoticed. In 1862 he was appointed Director of the Royal Spanish Academy, a position he held until his death on June 22, 1865. During the years immediately preceding his death, both his peers and the state recognized Rivas's valuable contributions to the politics and literature of the nation. From 1863 to 1864 he presided over the Council of State. Soon thereafter Queen Isabel II decorated him with the Collar of the Golden Fleece.

DRAMATURGY: MAJOR WORKS AND THEMES

Rivas's work, both dramatic and poetic, is a reflection of the political and social upheavals of a country coming to grips with its identity and individuality. Instead of the strictly patriotic works of his youth, Rivas's latter tragedies and comedies reflect the poet's quest to understand humanity's role in the cosmos as well as its place in the more finite spaces of day-to-day human interaction. Paramount to the poet's pursuit is his belief in the innate goodness of his country and its people manifested in the frequent use of themes such as love, loyalty, faithfulness, and patriotism. These elements appear as essential themes in Rivas's early tragedies.

From the appearance, and eventual censoring, of *Ataúlfo* (1814) to the publication of *Lanuza* (1822) there operates one central theme: the unpredictable nature of life and the role fate and destiny play in its outcome. Rivas's preoccupation with these two enemies surfaces in amorous encounters, in political intrigues, and in interpersonal relationships. The influence of these two forces assails his characters and leaves them vulnerable to other more sinister constraints. These *dramatis personae* can neither control nor change the events that lead to their destruction. However, in some instances, Rivas counteracts the negative effects of fate and destiny by imbuing his heroes and heroines with moral and spiritual virtue. Thus, their victimization or death produces a political or social icon to be venerated. More important, these tragedies afford a nascent concept of the Romantic self that will find its full expression in Rivas's most famous drama, *Don Alvaro o la fuerza del sino*, and in Rivas's favorite piece, *El desengaño en un sueño*.

Stylistically, Rivas's tragedies closely follow the French model. In every case the hero or the heroine meets an untimely death or some other tragedy that leaves them powerless. Within the framework of these plays the heros become essential symbols of virtue, loyalty, purity, and valor. These essential traits become the basis of Rivas's concept of national identity. More important, Rivas's faithful Catholic personae are not the only ones who possess these essential qualities but also many of his Moorish characters. This hybridization of two cultures to reflect a single identity casts a unique light on Rivas's perspective of Spanish nationalism. Rivas augments this motif by locating his characters within historic or geographic locales that are simultaneously familiar to his audience (e.g., Zamora, Aragón) and imbued with patriotic significance. He further expands his referential territory by including personalities from Spanish history (e.g., Urraca, Philip II) whose contribution to the building of the nation is understood. Around these symbols of national identity he engenders characters whose purpose it is to demonstrate the elevated ideals of Spanish patriotism and honor.

Already noted is the fact that the possession of these virtues is not reserved for the Christian majority. Rivas often imbues some Moorish characters with these essential traits. It is equally important to note that many of his Christian characters personify greed, ambition, and corruption. This interesting twist compels the audience to reconsider the long-held premise that virtue and honor are exclusive rights held by certain races or religions. This movement away from a Eurocentric/Catholic concept of self toward a more pluralistic concept of national virtue places Rivas at the forefront of independent, liberal thought.

Ataúlfo (1814) is one of two plays believed to be lost. However, in 1984, Juan Manuel Cacho Blecua tracked down a manuscript version of the work that had been donated by Enrique Ramírez de Saavedra, the son of the Duke of Rivas, to Víctor Balaguer and preserved in the Biblioteca-Museo Balaguer in Villanueva y Geltrú (Barcelona). This discovery was a fortunate turn of events inasmuch as the work was never staged nor included in any collection after it was censored in 1814. This work is an important indicator of Rivas's dramaturgic attitudes and ideological underpinnings.

The work focuses on the love of Ataúlfo, King of the Goths, for Placidia, a Roman princess. Contrary to the wishes of his advisers, Ataúlfo chooses to marry the princess and thereby establish a pact with Emperor Honorio and the Roman state. When all persuasion fails to convince the King that the marriage is not in the best interest of the kingdom, Vinámaro, an Arria priest, plots to usurp power from the king. After Vinámaro's plot is discovered, the king orders his imprisonment. However, Vinámaro manages to convince Sigerico, captain of the King's Guards, that if he were released he could stay any rebellion among the masses. Believing the priest, Sigerico removes the priest's chains and lets him go. Immediately, Vinámaro begins to incite the people against Ataúlfo. With a group of followers, Vinámaro enters the palace, sets a trap for the king, and then kills him.

Ataúlfo was censored by the Fernandine government because it suggested too strongly the idea of revolution. Donald Shaw notes that *Ataúlfo* "serves to illustrate the giant stride forward in technical ability, but especially in outlook, which Rivas accomplished between 1814, the date of its composition, and 1834, when he prepared the final version of *Don Alvaro*, which marks a watershed in the history of the modern Spanish theatre" (*Hispanic Review* 231).

Rivas's second tragedy, *Aliatar* (1816), was the first of his early works to be staged and to receive high acclaim from both the critics and the public. This piece examines the traditional conflict between Christian and Moor. Similar in tone to other works of this type, Rivas vilifies the Moorish protagonist and exalts his Christian rival. As the work opens, Aliatar has captured Doña Elvira and holds her captive in his fortress. Soon Don García, a rich nobleman and Elvira's lover, presents himself to Aliatar as Elvira's brother and asks permission to see her. When the two of them meet, they embrace and begin to speak of their love and devotion one for another. The two do not realize that Caleb, one of Aliatar's Jewish slaves, has hidden himself in the chamber and has overheard their conversation. Caleb soon reports his findings to Ismán, another slave. Jealousy and anger motivate Ismán to lash out at Elvira because he, too, loves the young Christian. When Aliatar hears the news of Don García's deception, he declares war against the nobleman and his army. Unfortunately, Aliatar cannot withstand the army's onslaught and retreats to his fortress. Enraged by Elvira's deception and the resulting conflict, Aliatar takes Elvira, stabs her, then, in the presence of Don García, kills himself. Rivas completes the tragic love triangle (Aliatar, Ismán, Elvira) by informing the audience that Ismán was killed during a battle with the Christians. Interestingly, this tragic demise falls upon two contrasting figures. Like Rivas's tragic pair from *Don Alvaro*, Aliatar and Elvira embody all the positive and negative aspects of society. Both Don Alvaro and Aliatar are marginalized because of their ethnicity and their social standing. In a similar fashion, Doña Leonor and Elvira are victims of their virtue.

The other tragedies from this early period have remained virtually unnoticed by critics. This fact is unfortunate since each of these works proffers an interesting vision of Rivas's ever-evolving literary style. In brief, *El duque de Aquitania* (1818) traces the intimate struggle among family members as they vie for political power. Integrity plays an essential role in Rivas's *Malek-Adhel* (1819) as Ricardo, Matilde's brother, forces her to marry Lusiñán, not because he is good or that he loves her but rather to create a political alliance. The tension of the work surfaces when Malek-Adhel, a noble and virtuous Moor, aspires only to show Matilde the respect he feels that she deserves as a woman. *Lanuza* (1822), written on the eve of the return of Fernando VII and the beginning of the "ominous decade" [década ominosa], examines the importance of sovereignty and autonomy. Throughout this final work Rivas criticizes the wanton power of despots, especially those whose aims do little to serve the needs of the country and its people.

During his ten-year exile in Malta, Rivas writes only two works. First, *Arias Gonzalo* (1827?) examines the importance of individual honor and virtue. The second of these two works is a comedy, *Tanto vales cuanto tienes* (1828). In this play Rivas formulates a complex web involving pride and deceit. The audience is informed that Don Blas has written his brother Alberto, his sister Rufina, and his nephew Miguel from Lima to tell them that he is returning to Spain. In the letter he announces that he brings a huge fortune with him that he is willing to share with all. The siblings and nephew are selfish spendthrifts and have squandered their money and all that Blas has sent them in the past. Because they fear that Don Blas will reject them and disinherit them because of their lifestyle, they begin a complete renovation of their home. Unfortunately, they must rely on credit and the "kindness" of others in order to accomplish their task. When Blas's family can no longer borrow the much-needed money from legitimate sources, they are obligated to borrow 3,000 ducats from Don Simeon, a usurer. When Don Blas arrives in Seville, the family learns that all the money was lost to Moorish thieves, thereby leaving their once wealthy brother and uncle destitute. Immediately Rufina chastises her brother and asks that he leave the house. When he asks how he is to live, she responds that he must beg, because their social station could not allow them to deal with people of his type. However, Don Blas has the last laugh. The siblings and nephew are informed by Don Juan, Don Blas's co-conspirator, that their brother had insured the fortune and that he was still solvent. Just as quickly as she kicked him out, Rufina tries to make amends, suggesting that all that she had said was in jest. Don Blas does not believe her. The audience learns that upon his arrival in Cádiz from the Americas, Don Blas had been apprised of his siblings' wanton and deceitful attitude. Though he refused to believe such rumors, he soon realized that the theft of his money provided him with the perfect opportunity to test their filial love. Of course they failed miserably and, as a result, Don Blas disinherits them. However, to Paquita, the only family member to show him any compassion, he gives 50,000 ducats as a dowry so that she can marry Don Juan. In the end, Rufina remains steadfast in her pride and arrogance.

While exiled in Tours, Rivas composes his most famous drama, *Don Alvaro o la fuerza del sino* (1832). Originally Rivas had thought to stage a French version of the play in Paris, but with the assurance of his amnesty, Rivas returned to Spain in January of 1834. On March 22, 1835, as noted, *Don Alvaro* debuted at the Príncipe Theater in Madrid. The play soon gained widespread popularity and returned numerous times to the stage. In this important work Rivas resorted once again to the theme of destiny, which had played an important role in several of his early works.

The work opens in a tavern near Seville as residents and travelers discuss the events of the day. Soon the subject turns to young Don Alvaro and his nightly excursions to the estate of the Marquis of Calatrava. All those present find the young gentleman to be worthy of Leonor's attention, though they are dubious regarding his origins and lineage. The only person who appears concerned with Don Alvaro's frequent outings is the local priest, who is the Marquis's confidant and friend. Because of his sense of obligation, the priest reports his findings regarding Don Alvaro to the Marquis. Meanwhile, Don Alvaro secretly infiltrates the Marquis's estate and enters Doña Leonor's bedroom through the balcony. As the two lovers speak, the Marquis enters the room with a sword in hand. He reviles his daughter and Don Alvaro for their clandestine affair and laments the shame it has brought to him and to his household. In an attempt at submission, Don Alvaro kneels before the Marquis, removes his pistol from his belt, and throws it to the floor. As the revolver hits the floor, it discharges, mortally wounding the Marquis.

Act II opens again in a tavern, this time in the village of Hornachuelos. Travelers and locals are drinking, singing, and talking. Soon they begin to question Uncle Trabuco regarding the mysterious traveler who has accompanied him to the tavern. Unwilling to reveal the person's identity, or simply ignorant of the fact, Uncle Trabuco remains silent as each of the guests attempts to ascertain the traveler's identity. Meanwhile, one of the guests, a student from Salamanca, explains that he has come to Hornachuelos to find the murderer of his friend's father. When all decide to retire to their rooms, the student is overcome by curiosity and tries to enter the room of the unknown traveler. However, he is thwarted in his attempts by the innkeeper, who directs him to the habitation he is to occupy for the night.

Early the next day we see Doña Leonor, disguised as a man, approaching the convent of Los Angeles. During her ascent to the convent she laments the tragic circumstances that have brought her to this spot and speaks of the forgiveness she hopes to achieve. At the door of the monastery she meets Father Melitón. She pleads with him to call Father Guardián so that she might ask permission to occupy a hermitage that once belonged to a saint who lived in the nearby mountains. The scene ends with Doña Leonor entering the cloister supported by Father Guardián.

Acts III and IV take place in Italy. We first meet Don Carlos de Vargas, an officer in the King's army and brother to Doña Leonor. He is playing cards with other officers from the regiment. When the game goes awry, Don Carlos is forced to defend himself. At that moment Don Alvaro hears the commotion and comes to Don Carlos's aid. Not wanting to reveal their true identity, each man introduces himself using an alias. Don Carlos tells Don Alvaro that he is Don Felix de Avendaña. In turn, Don Alvaro presents himself as Don Fadrique de Herreros. Immediately Don Carlos recognizes Don Alvaro's pseudonym as the name of a valiant and courageous soldier in the king's army. Soon the two become inseparable friends and both enter the campaign to defend Naples.

During a battle for the city, Don Alvaro is seriously wounded. He is carried by the army surgeon and Don Carlos to the chief officer's lodging. Fearing that he might die, Don Alvaro entrusts the key to a small box that is in his suitcase to his friend Don Carlos. He instructs Don Carlos that if he dies, the box is to be opened and the contents destroyed. If he lives, Don Carlos is to do nothing. Suspicious that the contents might hold the answer to his quest, Don Carlos opens the box and reads the letters therein. From them he discovers that Don Fadrique is really Don Alvaro, his enemy. At that point Don Carlos vows to care for Don Alvaro until he is recovered from his injuries. Then he swears to exact judgment against Don Alvaro and thereby recover his family's honor. After Don Alvaro convalesces, Don Carlos reveals his true identity and challenges Don Alvaro to a duel. Despite his desire to avert a confrontation, Don

Alvaro is forced to defend his honor, prevails against Don Carlos, and disappears once again.

The final act of *Don Alvaro* opens in the convent of Los Angeles four years after the death of Don Carlos in Italy. After fending off beggars and others who had gathered at the portal of the convent, Father Melitón approaches Father Guardián to complain. During the course of the conversation, Father Melitón lodges a protest against Father Rafael who refuses to deal with the poor and infirm, preferring to lock himself away in his cell. Shortly after Father Guardián leaves, a young man by the name of Don Alfonso approaches Father Melitón. He makes several inquiries regarding Father Rafael and then demands to be taken to him. When Don Alfonso enters the priest's cell he immediately recognizes Father Rafael to be Don Alvaro. Don Alfonso locks the door behind him and denounces the friar as a fraud and as the murderer of his brother and father. The two of them soon leave the convent and continue their confrontation in the nearby mountains. As the conversation unfolds, Don Alvaro discovers that Leonor is alive. This knowledge revives his hope of forgiveness, but only for a moment. Quickly, Don Alfonso renews his attack on Don Alvaro. Finally, in the throes of anger and despair, Don Alvaro strikes Don Alfonso and mortally wounds him. The young nobleman escapes to a small dwelling where he pleads for help. Terrified, the occupant rings a warning bell that will summon the Fathers from the convent. When the hermit opens the door, Don Alvaro immediately recognizes the recluse to be Doña Leonor. As she approaches Don Alvaro, she recognizes yet another voice, that of her brother. As Doña Leonor reaches to embrace her sibling, she is denounced by him as a traitor and stabbed. Seeing the carnage around him, Don Alvaro climbs to a precipice and, in the presence of the convent Fathers, curses God and casts himself into the abyss.

For Rivas's the years 1840 and 1842 are among his most productive. In just two years he writes five new works. The first of these pieces is a comedy entitled *Solaces de un prisionero, o tres noches de Madrid* (1840). The work is an interesting story that follows the amorous adventures of Carlos V and Francis, the king of France. The next year Rivas writes *La morisca de Alajuar* (1841). Here we again encounter the conflict between Moors and Christians. Abdalla has incited Mulim-Abenzar to rebel against the Christians. As a result the entire city is obliged to condemn to death any Christian entering the city from that day forward. Don Fernando, a Christian, has entered the city on that fateful day. He is in love with María, the daughter of Mulim-Abenzar, who is a "Christian at heart" [cristiana de corazón]. Like so many of Rivas's works, this one also provides an unusual twist. The audience learns that María really is a Christian who was raised by the Moor after she was abandoned by her father. *El crisol de la lealtad* and *El parador de Bailén* are two more comedies that appear in 1842. The first of these two works ends in an uncommon fashion. Instead of marriage and happiness being the end result, the work concludes with a self-sacrificing act on the part of Don Pedro, who decides to render service to his queen instead of marrying Doña Isabel, the woman who loves him.

In *El parador de Bailén* (1842) Don Fernando, an Infantry captain, is in love with Doña Clara, the daughter of Don Luis. Though they have long corresponded, Don Fernando has not received permission to marry her. One day he receives a letter from Clara telling him that her father has promised her in marriage to Don Lesmes, her cousin. Hoping that he can persuade Clara to escape with him, Don Fernando arrives early on the morning that Clara is to meet Don Lesmes at "el parador de Bailén." While he is waiting, Don Lesmes arrives. Seizing the opportunity, Don Fernando pretends to be Clara's relative. Don Fernando lulls Don Lesmes into a false sense of security only to conspire with Marta, the innkeeper, to get Lesmes drunk and then lock him away. After Lesmes is drunk and locked away, Don Fernando meets with Don Luis, Clara's father, and his entourage. In this group is Doña Genoveva, an old woman, who falls in love with Don Fernando. While trying to avoid her advances, Don Fernando tries hard to prevent the discovery of his trickery. After Don Lesmes escapes from his "prison," Don Fernando decides to employ another ruse. That night, Fernando convinces Lesmes that Genoveva is a beautiful lady waiting for favors. Lesmes agrees to disguise himself as Fernando. Unable to see her clearly, he learns that she has money (the sole motive behind his willingness to marry Clara). After a raucous night of merriment he proposes marriage to Genoveva. In the end, Fernando marries Clara, Lesmes marries Genoveva, and all ends well.

Rivas's last work for the stage is *El desengaño en un sueño* (1842). Probably the most unusual of Rivas's works, *El desengaño* employs many of the props and trammels associated with the magical plays of the eighteenth century. The story opens on a distant island where the audience hears young Lisardo lamenting his isolation from the outside world. Marcolán, the boy's father, tells the youth that if he really wishes to leave, he may do so the next day. As the boy falls into a deep sleep, Marcolán, who is also a magician, invokes the spirits of both good and evil to enter his dreams. The audience is introduced to four spirits: The Spirit of Love, The Spirit of Opulence, The Spirit of Power, and The Spirit of Evil. From that point forward, the boy enters a world that to him is real but to the audience is only a vision of what could be.

First, Lisardo finds himself in a beautiful garden. There he meets Zora, a beautiful young woman. Lisardo is so overcome by her beauty that he pleads with her father that he might be allowed to take her as his wife. Soon after their marriage, Lisardo hears the voice of Evil tell him that there is more to life than the simple beauty around him. Quickly the eager youth begins to crave riches. Feeling neglected, Zora wonders if he still loves her. Lisardo responds in the affirmative, yet his actions betray him. He remains ever set upon gaining wealth and comfort for himself. While the two are engaged in this conversation, two richly dressed gentlemen approach. They take Lisardo and Zora to a magnificent palace. Lisardo is mesmerized by its beauty and splendor. The two gentlemen inform Lisardo that everything he sees belongs to him. Though he now has a loving, devoted wife and great riches, he remains dissatisfied.

Act II opens with Lisardo being hailed for a successful military campaign. As a General in the Royal Army he presents himself before the King and Queen. Again, the voice of Evil tempts him. Now instead of being enticed by wealth, he covets power and position by seducing the Queen. Meanwhile, Arbolán, one of the kingdom's finest warriors, approaches Lisardo and praises him for his prowess as a general. Lisardo is distracted by the beauty of the Queen, sensing a need to be near her. After Arbolán, Lisardo runs to the throne where he meets the Queen. During the ensuing conversation, the Queen expresses her admiration for Lisardo. She tells him that the throne was an inheritance from her father and belongs to her and to whomever she places thereon. At this point they plan the disposition of the King. Immediately after the Queen sets out to put her plan into action, Zora appears. She again questions Lisardo's love for her. When the voice of Evil insists that he must choose between Zora and the Queen, Lisardo chooses the latter.

Lisardo opens Act III with the declaration that he is King. With his Queen at his side he realizes his highest aspiration. However, there is a foreboding feeling when a witch comes to Lisardo to advise him. During their interview the witch gives a ring to him. He is informed that it can render him invisible. With this device Lisardo is empowered to move about the palace and among his subjects without detection. After he accepts the ring, Lisardo sets about to discover what the people think of him. Much to his chagrin he finds out that all are dissatisfied. Furious he returns to the throne room to find the Queen and Arbolán. While he is invisible Lisardo learns of their plan to poison him, thereby enabling Arbolán to assume the throne alongside the Queen. Lisardo feels compelled to remove the ring and surprise the conspirators but quickly changes his mind. He remembers that he too is a criminal and guilty of the murder of the King. When the day arrives that the plan to poison him will be put into action, Lisardo arrives prepared with an entourage of loyal captains and soldiers. As the festivities begin, Lisardo is offered a goblet of wine, which he refuses. With satisfaction he offers it instead to the Queen. When she refuses, he denounces her and calls for the support of his army. During the initial clash, Arbolán steps forward and reveals the truth behind the King's death. Lisardo places the ring on his hand, turns it, and disappears.

The final act represents the same garden where Lisardo first met Zora. While he laments his misfortunes, he sees a funeral procession coming toward him. Curious as to whom the deceased is, he approaches one of the pallbearers. He is told that it is the body of a beautiful maiden named Zora who was abandoned by her husband. Racked with pain, Lisardo pushes the mourners and bearers away from the body. While lamenting his loss, Liseo, Zora's father appears. Furious that the vain youth had broken his promise to care for and love Zora, Liseo sends him away. Alone, Lisardo contemplates his misfortune. Suddenly in a clap of thunder, the Devil appears with a host of demons. With a sword in hand, the foolish youth is willing to sell his soul for the chance to regain his power and fortune. At the moment that all seems lost, an Angel appears and disperses the Devil and his unholy host.

Alone in the garden, Lisardo hears the voices of Arbolán and the Queen's soldiers. As he attempts to evade them, he is confronted, first, by the murdered King and then by Zora. Both chasten him and rebuke him for his greed. Just as he is reminded by the voice of Evil that his fate is an eternity in Hell, Lisardo awakes. It is morning and Marcolán has come to bid farewell to the youth. When asked if he still wishes to leave, Lisardo answers with a resounding no. The scene closes with Marcolán embracing his son.

CRITICS' RESPONSE

The reception and criticism of Rivas's literary production are skewed toward his better-known piece *Don Alvaro o la fuerza del sino*. However, interesting and significant studies have been written on a few of his other works. This review of critical materials will briefly consider *Ataúlfo* (1814) and *El desengaño en un sueño* (1844) before considering selected articles critiquing and reviewing *Don Alvaro*.

Of Rivas's early tragedies, only two have received any critical attention. The first is *Ataúlfo* (1814). Donald Shaw and Rosalía Fernández Cabezón have suggested numerous interpretations and evaluations of the work. In "*Ataúlfo*: Rivas' First Drama," Shaw identifies García de la Huerta's *Raquel* (1778) as the model on which Rivas constructed his play and characters. Accordingly, Rivas places at the center of the play's plot the conflict between the monarch's love for and marriage to an unsuitable woman and the well-being of his people. Shaw comments that the primary critical difficulty with *Ataúlfo* and *Raquel* is that of "establishing how far the authors have succeeded in developing the basic situation in authentically tragic terms" (231). Based on this premise, Shaw outlines the tenets of tragedy and how they function or fail within the context of the play. Two observations are central to Shaw's thesis. First, he notes, "For part of the nature and function of tragedy is to call into question the cosmic harmony which representative mainstream intellectual opinion in the eighteenth century wished to take for granted. . . . It was this dilemma that confronted Rivas at the end of Act I of *Ataúlfo*. Navas Ruiz . . . and above all Cardwell have suggested that he was only able to resolve it twenty years later in *Don Alvaro* by resolutely abandoning any harmonious interpretation of the human condition" (233). Second, Shaw surmises that "Ataúlfo undergoes no tragic evolution of character and fails to convince us of his tragic stature" (233).

Based on these two premises, Shaw offers considerable evidence to support his thesis that Ataúlfo is not a tragic figure. He concludes that "Rivas' dependence on García de la Huerta's implicit formula provides a certain measure of pathos, yet fails to seriously question the existential confidence of the audience. The important feature of Rivas' subsequent evolution as a dramatist is his gradual realization of the inadequacy of such a formula and his eventual abandonment of it in *Don Alvaro*" (242).

Rosalía Fernández Cabezón presents a less analytical and more comparative view of *Ataúlfo*. The fundamental argument of her article is the differing viewpoint of a single event as seen by Agustín de Montiano y Luyando in his *Athaulpho* (1753) and Rivas. One of the more challenging premises of this article is the author's attempt to connect the work's plot to events from Rivas's own experience. Though the arguments seem implausible, they do proffer an interesting and unique perspective on the work.

Rivas's *El desengaño en un sueño* (1844) has received considerable attention in recent years. Each study offers widely diverging approaches to the work, ranging from psychoanalytic to deconstructive to structural analysis. One of the early considerations of this work comes in the form of a letter from Arturo Farinelli. In this epistle Farinelli attempts to connect Rivas's work to that of Grillparzer, *Der Traum ein Leben* (1834). Though apparently convincing, Farinelli fails to prove an absolute connection. To the contrary, Douglas Hilt shows several connections between the two works that prove more tenable. This critic argues that both Grillparzer and Rivas discuss similar ideas. However, this connection may be based more on the fact that the two dramatists relied heavily on the same secondary sources, including Shakespeare and Gracián. More conclusive is R. B. O'Connell's "Rivas' *El desengaño en un sueño* and Grillparzer's *Der Traum ein Leben*" where he carefully shows that Farinelli's conclusions were completely unfounded since it is doubtful that Rivas ever read or had access to Grillparzer's work. Rupert C. Allen's seminal piece "An Archetypal Analysis of Rivas' *El desengaño en un sueño*" addresses "the fundamental question of the relationship between myth and psychic structure, in a universal, or collective sense" (201). Allen emphasizes the psychological and physiological extremes represented by Lisardo and Marcolán. The latter represents the mother figure who shields the former from the dangers of the world. The author writes, "Marcolán, instead of helping the boy to see how his burgeoning masculinity can be constructively channelled, seems bent on demonstrating that youthful virility is a force which, when unleashed, must necessarily destroy, and not consolidate the citadel of ego-consciousness" (206). After discussing the basic principles on which he will base his arguments, Allen outlines the mythic structure in Lisardo's dream. Here he discusses the several archetypes and devices employed by Rivas. Allen shows how these dramatic effects work together to undermine the young man's masculinity and reinforce his dependence on Marcolán. The last section skillfully compares Lisardo to Don Alvaro.

Susan G. Polansky considers the structural qualities of Rivas's *El desengaño en un sueño* and the work's textual coherence. This she accomplishes by analyzing the Destiny theme. Polansky relies on speech act theory to support her argument—"A classification of the particular speech acts of protagonist Lisardo will establish the preponderance of references in which he asserts the existence of destiny or commits himself to performance reactive to its force" (3). After establishing the aforementioned premise, Polansky discusses the way that the element of destiny is woven into the play's discourse. In "Calderón in a Dream: The Duque de Rivas's *El desengaño en un sueño*" Charles Ganelin presents an interesting pharmacological analysis. Ganelin notes the essentiality of the *pharmakon* within the construct of the play, noting, "If the *pharmakon* functions both as a poison and remedy, its presence becomes clear: Marcolán wishes to purge his son from all desire for fame, wealth, and love, corrupt and corrupting as they are, in order to encourage him to continue a life of isolation away from the scourges of the world" (136). With this idea as the foundation of his arguments, Ganelin proceeds to identify other *pharmakons* that produce the desired effect in the protagonist. Interestingly, the author further suggests that by extension *El desengaño* is Rivas's attempt to recognize Calderón, yet leave in its wake his own imprint on poetic creation. Ganelin concludes, "Perhaps the Duke of Rivas sees the Romantic mind as poisoned. Perhaps his *pharmakon*—his act of writing—is an antidote or *palinodia* to Don Alvaro and to Segismundo" (144).

Of all Rivas's works, *Don Alvaro o la fuerza del sino* is the most popular and widely discussed among scholars. The work's position at the forefront of Spanish Romanticism has inspired considerable debate regarding its value. Carlos Feal has expressed this sentiment best: "The [work's] critical diversity has to do with distinct interpretations: for some *Don Alvaro* is an entanglement without meaning, while for others the depth and intensity of the drama stand out, in addition to its grand and expressive beauty" [la diversidad de criterios tiene que ver con distintas interpretaciones: para unos *Don Alvaro* es un embrollo sin sentido, mientras otros destacan la profundidad e intensidad del drama, además de sus grandes bellezas expresivas] (188).

Critics have addressed a broad spectrum of topics, including Satanism, musical structures, and periodic localization. The work has also been the subject of comparative investigations. Of particular interest are articles by Francisco Caravaca ("Mérimée y el Duque de Rivas") and Joaquín Hernández Serna ("*Les Solitaires de Murcie* de Jean François Marmontel y el *Don Alvaro o la fuerza del sino* del Duque de Rivas"), which draw important thematic corollaries between Rivas and his French contemporaries. Also, by way of comparison, B. Frank Sedwick, Zenia Sacks, and Paul A. M. Pinto have discussed the role of Rivas's *Don Alvaro* on Verdi's *La forza del destino*. These articles deal with the development of operatic characters, the influence of Spanish Romantic drama on the opera, and the textual differences between Rivas's work and Verdi's opera and the impact of these changes on the work's message. Because of the extensive commentary on this work, I will limit my discussion to a few milestone articles.

Carlos Feal provides an excellent discussion of love, honor, and liberty as they appear in *Don Alvaro*. It is significant to note that he sees these three entities as forming the primary motivational forces that lead Don Alvaro to his defeat. Feal surmises that "don Alvaro adapts to a traditional ideology where honor is overcome by love and Christian principles. Ironically, don Alvaro's defeat does not surface from his defiance of society but rather from his blind submission to its dictates" [don Alvaro se ajusta a un ideario tradicional, donde el honor se sobrepone al amor y a los principios cristianos. Irónicamente, pues, la ruina de don Alvaro no brota de un desafío a la sociedad sino de una ciega sumisión a sus dictados] (195). Walter Pattison also touches on the honor theme in *Don Alvaro*, but from the perspective of a young man who attempts to vindicate his worth as a nobleman. Pattison insists that Don Alvaro's "secret" becomes the impetus that drives the young man to seek acceptance from Leonor's father and brothers, thereby validating his "honor." However, the stigma associated with his *mestizaje*, or mixed race, only frustrates his plans. As a result he is led by "fate" to violent measures and ultimately to his own death.

Another interesting perspective on *Don Alvaro* comes from John Dowling, David Quinn, and George Mansour. All three discuss the time frame and setting of Rivas's work. Dowling postulates the date and year of each event based on Rivas's reference to the battle of Velletri, which took place on August 10, 1744. From this historically verifiable date Dowling speculates on the time frame between the time that Don Alvaro's misfortunes begin up to his death. Dowling concludes that "Saavedra's meticulous attention to time undergirds the action, inducing in the public a 'willing suspension of disbelief' and making the emotional impact of the drama more forceful" (361). Of equal interest are two articles, by Quinn and Mansour, respectively, that also deal with the localization of *Don Alvaro* in the eighteenth century. Contrary to the long-held assumption that the work takes place in the early part of the eighteenth century, Quinn asserts that the play occurs in the sixteenth century based on the sequence of kings referred to in the work. However, George Mansour effectively reaffirms the traditional contention that the setting of the work indeed occurs in the eighteenth century. He does this by providing indisputable evidence that disavows Quinn's assertions.

Angel Valbuena Prat reiterates the importance that love and destiny play in the tragic end to Don Alvaro and Doña Leonor. Significant to his study is Prat's comparison of *Don Alvaro* to Rivas's other works. The result is a clearer vision of the woman as an "angel from heaven" [angel del cielo] who is the victim of circumstance and destiny. Joaquín Casalduero treats the destiny theme in a similar fashion. His conclusion summarizes best the perspective of most critics regarding the interaction of love and fate in *Don Alvaro o la fuerza del sino*:

If destiny is a force whose sense escapes us, love moves us toward death. Romantic love does not flourish in a garden; its passion, its burning withers everything that it touches, converts the Eden into a desert—that wilderness where Doña Leonor and D. Alvaro have coexisted tormented and unaware of one another. It is the voice of the lover who calls the object of his love to her death.

[Si el destino es una fuerza cuyo sentido nos escapa, el amor llega hasta la muerte. El amor romántico no florece en el jardín; su pasión, su ardor agosta todo lo que toca, convierte el edén en un desierto—ese yermo en el cual han convivido atormentados e ignorándose Doña Leonor y D. Alvaro. Es la voz del amante quien llama a la amada a la muerte.] (49)

One of the most significant studies on *Don Alvaro* comes from Richard Cardwell, *"Don Alvaro* or the Force of Cosmic Injustice.*"* In this article Cardwell reviews briefly the plethora of articles (many which I have included here) that address the topic of destiny. He then presents the premise of his own study: *Don Alvaro* is more than a realistic representation; it is a deeply symbolic and philosophical analogy of man's contention with cosmic injustice. Cardwell supports his premise by analyzing the work in the context of its symbolic representation. He concludes, "The two dominant images of the play, the prison and the abyss, may be seen as symbols of divine injustice, symbols that underline the implications of the subtitle *la fuerza del sino*. It is this view of the world postulated in the play that clarifies and unifies what previously had been confused questions in the minds of its commentators" (579).

A review of the current criticism reveals the presence of a common thematic thread throughout Rivas's works: destiny. Though more benign in their treatment of destiny, Rivas's early works often emphasize the frustrating nature of existence when confronted with the unyielding forces of society, culture, and politics. Without a doubt the culmination of the poet's meditation of this topic surfaces in two distinct and significant productions, *Don Alvaro o la fuerza del sino* and *El desengaño en un sueño*. The fundamental dilemma in both of these works is whether the protagonist should act or be acted upon. This simple situation becomes the impetus behind a whole series of events that eventually lead to the protagonist's defeat or submission. Interestingly, Rivas touches upon a significant philosophical matter that would find its full development in Arthur Schopenhauer's study of human will.

Rivas addresses the unpredictable nature of destiny by allowing two forces to work against Don Alvaro and Lisardo. First, both individuals are subject to the whims and opinions of others. In the case of Don Alvaro, Leonor's brothers and even the dead Marquis maintain a stranglehold on the young nobleman by impugning his self-worth and status among the upper-class citizens of Seville. Even though he possesses the wealth, education, and "noble" background that would make him equal to the Marquis and those like him, his ethnicity and origin impede his social climb. Thus, Don Alvaro must suffer the fate of the marginalized class or social outcast. It is also noteworthy that Don Alvaro's behavior begins to reflect that of this marginalized class. Like others of this type, Don Alvaro experiences two opposing emotions: self-destruction and self-justification or forgiveness. These two forces, like destiny, are intangibles that push Don Alvaro forward in pursuit of them, yet provide little consolation for his soul. Unfortunately, when Don Alvaro attempts to redeem himself, he is pushed farther away from his goal. In the end, the forces that work against Don Alvaro disempower him and cause him to declare, "No, I am no more than a

reprobate, an unhappy prisoner of the devil!" [No, yo no soy más que un ré-
probo, presa infeliz del demonio!] (Act V:IX). Ironically, the force of destiny
that eventually destroys Don Alvaro is simultaneously the agent of his individuality and independence. When he curses God and commits suicide, Don Alvaro
breaks the bands of social conformity and declares his independence and individuality.

In a similar fashion, Lisardo is subject to a force that controls his actions: his
father Marcolán. Rupert Allen's discussion of archetypes provides important
clues regarding the psychological underpinnings of Lisardo's physical and emotional submission to his father. More important, Lisardo's submission becomes
symbolic of the struggle waged by the marginalized sector of society to conform
to the status quo. Like his counterpart Don Alvaro, Lisardo must accept what
fate and destiny have dealt him, or rebel. It is on this point that the two characters move in opposing directions. Where Don Alvaro rebels and defies social
restraints, Lisardo conforms and submits to them. As a result, Don Alvaro
pushes the limits of acceptable behavior and in the end breaks the bands of
conformity. His release from the physical world succeeds in redefining his individuality. On the other hand, Lisardo comes to symbolize those who have
surrendered their individuality. When he attempts to exert himself and thereby
realize his uniqueness as a person, he is constrained and tethered by another. It
becomes apparent that the linkage between Lisardo and Marcolán is mutually
beneficial. Within this relationship Lisardo can close himself off and ignore the
perils of the outside world. Thus, a confrontation with the more dominant entity
within this closed sphere is circumvented. For Marcolán the relationship em-
powers him and allows him to maintain his position of absolute authority. Thus,
Marcolán emasculates his son by depriving him of his independence and individuality.

As can be seen, Lisardo and Don Alvaro are diametric opposites. However,
a contrast and comparison of the two protagonists present a clearer image of
the Romantic self as it was perceived by Rivas. Fundamental to this liaison of
opposites is the fact that Don Alvaro and Lisardo are mirror images of each
other: the victim and the victor. In the first case, Lisardo is never allowed to
experience the pitfalls of life but rather is enveloped in the "loving" arms of his
domineering father. The link between Lisardo and Marcolán suggests a relationship in which the father neither loves nor cares for the child. To the contrary,
he relies on the existence of his child to vindicate his own existence. Thus,
Lisardo is coerced by his father, who possesses extraordinary powers of persuasion, into submitting to the status quo.

Even though Don Alvaro repeatedly manages to escape his foe's challenges,
and is always victorious in these encounters, he nonetheless remains a victim
to the ebb and flow of destiny. He is trapped both physically and emotionally
within a vicious circle; when he tries to "redeem" himself, the tables turn, and
he is thrust even deeper into the mental abyss of self-recrimination. Even in
death, destiny looms heavy over the fate of Don Alvaro. The audience is left to

consider the eternal reward that such a character might merit in the hereafter. In the end, the victory over the perils of mortality is circumvented by the hand of God and divine justice. Therefore, Rivas suggests that those who exist outside of society's acceptable boundaries are destined (or doomed) to surrender their self, either through physical submission or through rebellion and death. Thus, Don Alvaro, like Lisardo, has failed to change the status quo. In the end, both figures remain marginalized scapegoats of society and of humanity.

BIBLIOGRAPHY

Editions and Translations

Aliatar. Ed. Manuel Ruiz Lagos. Seville: Editoriales Andaluzas Unidas, 1989.

"*Ataúlfo,* tragedia inédita del Duque de Rivas." Ed. Juan Manuel Cacho Blecua. In *El Crotalón. Anuario de Filología Española* 1 (1984): 393–465.

Don Alvaro o la fuerza del sino. Ed. Alberto Blecua. Barcelona: Planeta, 1988.

Don Alvaro o la fuerza del sino. Ed. Alberto Sánchez. Madrid: Cátedra, 1992.

Don Alvaro o la fuerza del sino. Ed. Donald Shaw. Madrid: Clásicos Castalia, 1986.

Don Alvaro o la fuerza del sino; El desengaño en un sueño. Ed. Carlos Ruiz Silva. Madrid: Espasa Calpe, 1984.

Obras completas. Madrid: Imp. De la Biblioteca Nueva, 1854–1855.

Obras completas. Ed. Enrique Ruiz de la Serna. Madrid: Aguilar, 1945.

Critical Studies

Adams, Nicholson B. "The Extent of the Duke of Rivas' Romanticism." I:107 in *Homenaje a Rodríguez-Moñino. Estudios de Erudición que le ofrecen sus amigos o discípulos hispanistas norteamericanos.* Madrid: Castalia, 1966.

———. "A Note on Mme. Cottin and the Duke of Rivas." *Hispanic Review* 15 (1947): 218–221.

———. "El primer romanticismo del Duque de Rivas." *Boletín de la Academia de Ciencias, Bellas Letras y Nobles Artes de Córdoba* 87 (1965–1967): 41–54.

Alberich, José. "Rivas y Valle-Inclán: Otro pequeño 'plagio.' " *Bulletin of Hispanic Studies* 54 (1947): 9–12.

Allen, Rupert C. "An Archetypal Analysis of Rivas' *El desengaño en un sueño.*" *Bulletin of Hispanic Studies* 45 (1968): 201–205.

Andioc, René. "Sobre el estreno del *Don Alvaro.*" In *Homenaje a Juan López Morillas.* Madrid: Castalia, 1982. 63–86.

Azorín. *Rivas y Larra.* Madrid: Espasa-Calpe, 1973.

Barletta, Vincent. "Pearls Thrown before Romantics: Shakespeare, Milton and the *Don Alvaro o la fuerza del sino* of el duque de Rivas." *Mester* 23.2 (1994):17–30.

Billick, David J. "Angel de Saavedra, el Duque de Rivas: A Checklist of Criticism, 1927–1977." *Bulletin of Bibliography* 36 (1979): 113–118.

Blommers, Thomas J. "Rivas and Verdi: The Force of Destiny." *DAI* 39 (1978): 3617A.

Bordato, Elisa Esther. "Merimée y el Duque de Rivas." *Humanidades* 21 (1930): 233–246.

Busquets, Loreto. "Don Alvaro o la fuerza de la historia." *Cuadernos Hispanoamericanos: Revista Mensual de Cultura Hispánica* 547 (1996): 61–78.

———. "Estructuras musicales del *Don Alvaro.*" *RL* 51.102 (1989): 433–461.

Caldera, Ermanno. "La polémica sobre el Don Alvaro." *Crítica Hispánica* 17.1 (1995): 22–35.

Caravaca, Francisco. "Merimée y el Duque de Rivas: Ensayo de literatura comparada." *Revista de Literatura* 23 (1963): 5–48.

Cardwell, Richard A. "*Don Alvaro* or the force of Cosmic Injustice." *Studies in Romanticism* 12 (1973): 559–579.

Casalduero, Joaquín. "*Don Alvaro* o el destino como fuerza." *La Torre* 7.25 (1959): 11–49.

Cedeño, Aristofanes. "Don Alvaro o la carnavalización del heroe." *RLA: Romance Languages Annual* 9 (1997): 438–443.

———. "La transgresión femenina del código cultural: El caso de Leonor en *Don Alvaro o la fuerza del sino.*" *Letras Peninsulares* 11.3 (1998–1999): 763–774.

Cerny, Vaclav. "Quelques remarques sur les sentiments religieux chez Rivas et Espronceda." *Bulletin Hispanique* 36 (1934): 71–87.

Cruz Casado, Antonio. "Teatro y censura en el duque de Rivas: Una lectura polítia del *Ataulfo.*" In *Los románticos y Andalucía, I,* ed. Diego Martínez Torrón. Córdoba, Spain: Universidad de Córdoba, 1997. 43–53.

Dorado Dellmans, Valentín. "El Duque de Rivas, madrileño." *Revista de la Biblioteca, Archivo y Museo del Ayuntamiento de Madrid* 7 (1930): 305–308.

Dowling, John. "Time in *Don Alvaro.*" *Romance Notes* 18 (1978): 355–361.

Farinelli, Arturo. "El sueño maestro de la vida en dos dramas de Grillparzer y del Duque de Rivas. A. Allison Peers." In *Divagaciones hispánicas. Discursos y estudios críticos por Arturo Farinelli.* Barcelona: Bosch, n.d. I: 207–224.

Feal, Carlos. "Amor, honor y libertad en el *Don Alvaro* de Rivas." In *Estudios en homenaje a Enrique Ruiz-Fornells,* ed. Juan Fernández Jiménez, José J. Labrador Herraiz, and L. Teresa Valdivieso. Erie, PA: Asociación de Licenciados & Doctores Españoles en Estados Unidos, 1990. 189–196.

Fernández Cabezón, Rosalía. "Ataúlfo visto por dos trágicos: D. Agustín de Montiano y el Duque de Rivas." *Castilla* 8 (1984): 95–100.

Flitter, Derek. "The Romantic Theology of *Los amantes de Teruel.*" *Crítica Hispánica* 18.1 (1996): 25–34.

Gabriele, John P. "*Don Alvaro o la fuerza del sino*: ¿Contradicción u ortodoxia?" In *Estudios en homenaje a Enrique Ruiz-Fornells,* ed. Juan Fernández Jiménez, José J. Labrador Herraiz, and L. Teresa Valdivieso. Erie, PA: Asociación de Licenciados & Doctores Españoles en Estados Unidos, 1990. 226–232.

Gahete Jurado, Manuel. "Religión y mito en el drama romántico del duque de Rivas." In *Los románticos y Andalucía, I,* ed. Diego Martínez Torrón. Córdoba, Spain: Universidad de Córdoba, 1997. 71–92.

Ganelin, Charles. "Calderón in a Dream: The Duque de Rivas's *El desengaño en un sueño.*" In *The Prince in the Tower: Perceptions* of La vida es sueño, ed. Frederick A. de Armas. Lewisburg, PA: Bucknell University Press, 1993. 132–143.

Goenaga, Angel, and Juan P. Maguna. "El Duque de Rivas: *Don Alvaro o la fuerza del sino.*" In *Teatro español del siglo XIX. Análisis de obras.* New York: Las Americas, 1971. 95–120.

González Ruiz, Nicolás. *El Duque de Rivas o la fuerza del sino (El hombre y su época).* Madrid: Ediciones Aspas, S.A., 1943.

Grey, Ernest. "Satanism in *Don Alvaro.*" *Romanische Forschungen* 80 (1968): 292–302.

Hernández Serna, Joaquín. *"Les Solitaires de Murcie* de Jean François Marmontel y el *Don Alvaro o la fuerza del sino* del Duque de Rivas." In *Estudios literarios dedicados al profesor Mariano Baquero Goyanes,* ed. Vitorino Polo García. Murcia: Universidad de Murcia, 1974. 175–197.

Hilt, Douglas. "A. W. Schlegel and His Theories of Romanticism as Reflected in Parallel Plays of Grillparzer and Rivas." *DA* 28 (1967): 2248A.

———. "Grillparzer and Rivas: The Dreamer Awakened." In *From Pen to Performance: Drama as Conceived and Performed,* ed. Karelisa V. Hartigan. Lanham, MD: University Press of America, 1983. 51–65.

Impey, Olga Tudorica. "Apuntes sobre el estilo romanístico del Duque de Rivas." In *Actes du XIIIᵉ congrès international de linguistique et philologie romanes tenu à l'Université Laval (Québec, Canada) du 29 août au 5 septembre 1971,* ed. Marcel Boudreault and Frankwalt Möhren. 2 vols. Québec: P de l'U de Laval, 1976. 2: 895–904.

Knowlton, John F. "Don Alvaro: A Spanish Phaëton." *Romance Notes* 13 (1972): 460–462.

Larsen, Kevin S. *"Don Alvaro o la fuerza del sino* and *Oedipus Tyrannus*: The Duke of Rivas's Romantic Transcription of a Classical Theme." *Classical and Modern Literature: A Quarterly.* 16.3 (1996): 203–215.

Liñan y Heredia, N. J. de. "El Duque de Rivas al Conde de Ofalia." *Revista de Archivos, Bibliotecas y Museos* 53 (1947): 143–151.

López Anglada, Luis. *El Duque de Rivas.* Madrid: EPESA, 1972.

Lovett, Gabriel H. *The Duke of Rivas.* (TWAS 452.) Boston: Twayne, 1976.

———. *Romantic Spain.* New York: Peter Lang, 1990.

Mansour, George P. "Concerning 'Rivas' Unexplained Localization of *Don Alvaro* in the Eighteenth Century." *Romance Notes* 18 (1978): 349–354.

Materna, Linda. "Prodigal Sons and Patriarchal Authority in Three Plays by the Duque de Rivas: *Lanuza, Don Alvaro o la fuerza del sino* and *El desengaño en un sueño.*" *Letras Peninsulares* 11.2 (1998): 603–623.

Mathias, Julio. "Rivas, dramaturgo romántico." *La Estafeta Literaria* 326 (1965): 7–8.

Navas Ruiz, Ricardo. "Rivas a Ticknor: Una carta inédita." *Papales de Son Armandans* 83.248 (1976): 137–144.

Nougué, André. "La Violence dans *Don Alvaro o la fuerza del sino* du duc de Rivas." *Cahiers du Monde Hispanique et Luso-Brasilien Caravelle* 43 (1984): 109–124.

O'Connell, Richard B. "Rivas' *El desengaño en un sueño* and Grillparzer's *Der Traum ein Leben*: A Problem in Assessment of Influence." *Philological Quarterly* 40 (1961): 569–576.

Pattison, Walter T. "The Secret of Don Alvaro." *Symposium* 21 (1967): 67–81.

Pinto, Paul A. M. "Rivas' Operatic Characters: The Personages of Giuseppe Verdi's *La forza del destino.*" *Romance Notes* 21 (1980): 184–192.

Polansky, Susan G. "Textual Coherence in the Duke of Rivas' *El desengaño en un sueño*: The Dramaturgy of Destiny." *MLS* 18.3 (1988): 3–17.

Quinn, David. "Rivas' Unexplained Localization of *Don Alvaro* in the Eighteenth Century." *Romance Notes* 16 (1995): 483–485.

Ribbans, Geoffrey. "El regreso de Angel Saavedra de su destierro en 1834." *Revista de Filología Española* 47 (1964): 421–427.

Rivas, Josefa. "Don García y don Alvaro." *Duquesne Hispanic Review* 6.1 (1967): 15–19.

Rosales, Luis. "Vida y andanzas del Duque de Rivas." *Boletín de la Real Academia Española* 45 (1965): 395–406.

Ruiz Lagos, Manuel. "Método y diatriba política en la estructura dramática del Duque de Rivas." In *Historia y estructura de la obra literaria. Coloquios celebrados del 28 al 31 marzo de 1967.* Madrid: CSIC, 1971. 225–241.

Sacks, Zenia. "Verdi and Spanish Romantic Drama." *Hispania* 27 (1944): 451–465.

Sánchez, Roberto G. "On Staging *Don Alvaro* Today." In *Studies in Eighteenth-Century Spanish Literature and Romanticism in Honor of John Clarkson Dowling*, ed. Douglas Barnette and Linda Jane Barnette. Newark, DE: Juan de la Cuesta, 1985. 133–143.

Saro, Pilar de. "Algunos textos raros de y sobre el Duque de Rivas." *Revista de Literatura* 21 (1962): 82–85.

Schurlknight, Donald E. "Toward a Rereading of Don Alvaro." in *La Chispa '95: Selected Proceedings*, ed. Claire J. Paolini. New Orleans: Louisiana Conference on Hispanic Languages and Literatures, Tulane University, 1995. 337–346.

Sebold, Russell P. "Nuevos Cristos en el drama romántico español." *Cuadernos Hispanoamericanos: Revista Mensual de Cultura Hispánica* 431 (1986): 126–132.

Sedwick, B. Frank. "Rivas' *Don Alvaro* and Verdi's *La forza del destino.*" *Modern Language Quarterly* 16 (1955): 124–129.

Shaw, Donald L. "*Ataúlfo*: Rivas' First Drama." *Hispanic Review* 56.2 (1988): 231–242.

Shields, A. K. "Slidell MacKenzie and the Return of Rivas to Madrid." *Hispanic Review* 7 (1939): 145–150.

Valbuena Prat, Angel. "*Don Alvaro* o la problemática sin solución." *Anales de la Universidad de Murcia* 13 (1954–1955): 961–978.

Wentzlaff-Eggebert, Christian. "Angel de Saavedra, Duque de Rivas: *Don Alvaro, o la fuerza del sino.*" In *Das spanische Theater: Vom Mittelalter bis zur Gegenwart*, ed. Volker Roloff and Harald Wentzlaff-Eggebert. Düsseldorf: Schwann-Bagel, 1988. 241–249.

Williams, Margaret A. "Angel de Saavedra's Dealings with the French Government, 1830–1833." *Bulletin of Hispanic Studies* 37 (1960): 106–114.

JOSÉ MARÍA RODRÍGUEZ MÉNDEZ
(1925–)

Martha T. Halsey

BIOGRAPHY

José María Rodríguez Méndez, a member of Spain's "Realistic Generation" of the 1960s known for its critical realism, social commitment, and popular emphasis, was born on June 6, 1925, in the heart of Old Madrid, between the Plaza de la Cebada and the Plaza del Cascorro. This neighborhood, the setting of eighteenth-century *sainetes* or popular, one-act farces by Ramón de la Cruz depicting typical scenes of Madrid life and, later, in the second half of the nineteenth century, of *zarzuelas* or one-act operettas, by Ricardo de la Vega, is the inspiration for Rodríguez Méndez's *Historia de unos cuantos* [Story of a Few People] (1975).

As a schoolboy of twelve, Rodríguez Méndez recalls attending a theatrical revue in a theater on Madrid's Gran Vía Street, in 1937, when the city was under attack by Franco's Nationalists, who launched air raids and artillery bombardments on the city, which was defended only by Republican militias and the International Brigades. The theater was not far from the front lines, and the orchestra was full of combatants from the trenches. It was after one such performance to which he was taken by a neighborhood girl who had a minor role, and where he shared anchovies and comraderie with the cast, that he evidently decided on the theater as a career.[1]

At the end of the Civil War in 1939, Rodríguez Méndez and his family moved to Barcelona. There, the teenager experienced the pain of the immigrants who had flooded Catalonia from all parts of Spain, as well as a nostalgia for Old Madrid—factors reflected in such plays as *La vendimia de Francia* [The French Harvest] (1964) and *La batalla del Verdún* [The Battle of Verdun] (1965), about Andalusian émigrées in a working-class district of Barcelona forced to wage a daily battle for survival. Barcelona's Barrio Chino, or red-light district, also fascinated him and became the setting for *Flor de Otoño* [Autumn Flower] (1982), one of his most acclaimed plays.

In 1946, while studying law at the University of Barcelona, Rodríguez Méndez began to act in the TEU, or Teatro Español Universitario (Spanish University Theater), and, like other students of his generation, obtained through this experience a thorough knowledge and love of the Spanish classics—Cervantes, Lope de Vega, Tirso, and Calderón—and acquired a deep appreciation of the Castillian language. Problems with the university's central administration, whose members considered him a troublemaker, forced him to finish his studies at the University of Zaragoza.

Economic hardship in the difficult early years of the post–Civil War period soon led Rodríguez Méndez, who had taken officer training courses while a university student, to serve at a military post in Cadiz, where he came to love Andalusia, whose peasants and emigrants often appear in his plays. He subsequently received a grant from the Institute of Hispanic Culture that enabled him to eke out a Bohemian existence for a period in Madrid—difficult times that inspired his *Los inocentes de la Moncloa* [The Innocents of Moncloa] (1961), a play about the sordidness of student life in the capital. In 1954, he was clubbed and arrested by the national police while participating in a student demonstration, and *Alcalá*, the university cultural magazine for which he wrote, was banned. However, another grant enabled him to then travel with other postgraduates to Argentina for six months, where he served as a correspondent for Barcelona's *El Noticero Universal*, a paper on which he was to collaborate for many years. Upon returning to Madrid, increasing political repression and fear of arrest, as well as economic problems, led him to enlist in the regular army.

In 1956 Rodríguez Méndez was sent to Valladolid, then to Melilla, in Spanish North Africa, where he served as a lieutenant attached to the Spanish Foreign Legion. His love of Africa led him to make a subsequent trip to Morocco as a newspaper correspondent. Rodríguez Méndez's various experiences in the military are reflected in the large number of soldiers and officials appearing in his plays, especially *Bodas que fueron famosas del Pingajo y la Fandanga* [The Famous Nuptials of Pingajo and Fandanga] (1978), a work long censored because of passages ridiculing the army—an untouchable institution in the Franco era. Rodríguez Méndez's varied experiences in law, the military, and journalism as well as his travels and years as an immigrant in Barcelona all enrich his theater.

Upon his return to Barcelona in 1959, Rodríguez Méndez had his first play performed, *Vagones de madera* [Wooden Train Cars], which was premiered by the Spanish University Theater there; and from 1959 to 1966, it was acted and directed with La Pipironda, a theater group taking its name from an eighteenth-century popular dance and performing in Barcelona's working-class neighborhoods. The year 1961 marked Rodríguez Méndez's first major triumph as a playwright when *The Innocents of Moncloa*, now considered a key play of the "Realistic Generation," was performed at the Candilejas Theater in Barcelona and, later, in Madrid. Several of his subsequent plays in the 1960s and 1970s were performed by professional companies in Barcelona or by La Pipironda. However, he continued to earn his living primarily from his theater articles in newspapers, editorial work with Espasa-Calpe, and his books of essays. Recently the playwright returned to Castile, first to live for a few years in Ávila and then to settle in his native Madrid, where several of his plays long banned by government censors during the Franco era were performed in the first few years after the dictator's death. *The Famous Nuptials of Pingajo and Fandanga* was chosen to open Madrid's new Centro Dramático Nacional (National Theater Center) in the fall of 1978.

Rodríguez Méndez's theater provides an open or dialectical vision of Spanish society. Like other members of the Realistic Generation, he views the theater as an instrument of social change and emphasizes the need for genuinely popular plays representative of all of Spanish society, not merely a theatergoing middle class. Rodríguez Méndez uses the popular *sainete* as the basis for works in which the sketch of customs ceases to be an end in itself and becomes an instrument of exposition and implicit denunciation. Most of his plays chronicle the tragedy of the common people in Spain, presenting them as victims.

DRAMATURGY: MAJOR WORKS AND THEMES

Wooden Train Cars (1959) shows the fate of young soldiers carted off, in 1921, to serve as cannon fodder in the colonial war in North Africa. *The Innocents of Moncloa* (1961) depicts the sordid existence of embittered and anguished Spanish students of the 1950s, forced to compete for professional posts in a degrading, dehumanizing system. *The Battle of Verdún* (1965) portrays Andalusian peasants forced to emigrate to work in Barcelona's factories.

Several of Rodríguez Méndez's best works are popular chronicles in which the dramatist presents major events of Spain's history as seen through the eyes of the populace. Eschewing the use of well-known personages, he focuses on the masses: Events are seen "from below," from the viewpoint of the outcasts who are history's victims. These popular chronicles consist of a succession of sketches of everyday life, each of which is significant not only for what it contributes to the whole but in itself. The stage directions incorporate extensive descriptive and narrative passages usually associated with the novel.

Story of a Few People (1975) depicts the lives of two families throughout a half-century of Spain's history. The major characters came from two popular nineteenth-century *zarzuelas*, or one-act operettas. Felipe and Mari Pepa, who suffer both during the Bourbon Restoration of 1874 and the Republic of 1931–1936, represent the Spanish populace, who are the victims of history. Julian, the printer who prospers and becomes a Republican official, represents the opportunistic politician who abandons his ideals. When Mari Pepa appears at the end of the drama as a proud old woman reduced, after her husband's death, to selling contraband tobacco in a Madrid doorway, she represents the common people's power to endure. The chronicle dramatizes ten moments in Spanish history, including the royal wedding and festivities that accompanied it in 1906 while the populace went hungry and unemployment increased, the carnage in Melilla in 1921, the socialist and anarchist advances at the end of the 1920s, the beginning of the Second Republic in 1931 and the accompanying celebrations in a humble patio of old Madrid, and finally, the disintegration of the Republic in 1931 and the disillusionment of the 1940s. The play's theme is the oppression of the populace under various governments—monarchy, republic, and dictatorship—and the destruction of faith.

The Famous Nuptials of Pingajo and Fandanga (1978) is a tragicomedy set in the *arrabales*, or shantytowns, of Madrid. The time is 1898, the year of the "disaster" in which Spain lost the last part of what was her Empire. The play depicts Spain's moral and economic decadence, especially the disintegration of the illiterate and degraded masses. The Bourbon Restoration of 1874–1931, following the failure of the short-lived First Republic of 1873–1874, represented the survival, behind an updated facade, of a traditional ideology that survived from the past. Moreover, under the respectable surface of a parliamentary system, abuse and privilege were rampant; power rested with the large landholders, army, and Church; the alternation of Liberals and Conservatives had little meaning as elections were managed (thus nullifying the newly voted universal suffrage of 1890); and the new worker movement, which was severely fragmented, remained outside the political arena.

Impoverished and embittered masses of workers and peasants provided cannon fodder for the colonial wars in Cuba and Morocco and suffered the results of the economic depression that followed the defeat of 1898. The discredited oligarchy, which retained power only because its enemies were divided and which survived in the form of the Franco regime, evinced the contradictions and hypocrisy of a middle class that wanted a more democratic system but refused to abandon the rights of capital and property. In this period Rodríguez Méndez sees the roots of many of Spain's continuing problems. In fact the discrimination against, and alienation of, the masses during the Restoration is little different from the fate of the isolated and marginal outcasts he presents in many of his dramas depicting life in the 1960s.

The Famous Nuptials depicts the marriage of Pingajo, a draftee back from Cuba, who wins his thirteen-year-old virgin bride in a game with two rogues— Salamanca, a pickpocket, and Petate, an ex-convict. The protagonist is not a hero but an antihero, having received his nickname ("Rag") because he displayed such cowardliness in battle that he was stood up like a scarecrow to frighten off the enemy. Pingajo seems unable to realize or question his own degradation. With a bravado that conceals his timidity and fear, he apes the words and gestures of the powerful, even donning for his wedding the stolen dress uniform of a hussar lieutenant—all in an unconscious effort to feel part of a society that rejects him.

Pingajo's fear of a beating for having returned late to the barrack as well as an extreme naïveté makes him promise to hand over his future bride to his lieutenant so that the latter may have the pleasure of deflowering her. Nevertheless, the tenderness Pingajo feels for his fiancée—who appears sucking lollipops and looking at him with big dumb eyes like those of a carnival doll—prevents him from sacrificing her. When, instead, he holds up the Casino to pay for a splendid wedding feast—the only way he can command respect in a hostile world—he is shot, victim of a society of which he was never a part, in a ritual he does not understand.

The *sainete*, together with the nineteenth-century *zarzuela*, is the source of the characters that Rodríguez Méndez, eschewing unnecessary psychological analysis, presents in all their rich simplicity, of the popular language, and of the local color of the most picturesque of the eight sketches into which the chronicle is structured. The detailed descriptions that begin each sketch, which often seem designed especially for the reader, constitute frescos of popular turn-of-the-century Madrid.

In the animated sketch of the Retiro Park, where Pingajo takes Fandanga on a Sunday afternoon, a gallery of the types that characterized the Restoration parade before the audience's eyes—*barquilleros* or vendors of rolled wafers, soldiers and their girls, pensioned government workers dozing on benches, street musicians with violins, and organ grinders—as the notes of the music mingle in a rustic symphony.

In the sketch of the wedding feast, organ grinders play tunes from the *zarzuela* and bullring and a chorus of children makes music with pots and mortars, as they sing the popular song that inspired the play. The streets, gaily decorated with brightly colored paper chains and flowers, recreate a Goya fresco. A table with huge *paellas* and wine-skins, all bought with money from the robbery of the Casino, awaits the guests. According to the description in the stage directions, it is as if the Verbena of St. Isidro had moved its tents to the miserable shantytown or as if the famous Camacho, who gave a splendid wedding banquet in *Don Quixote*, had descended from the lands of La Mancha to invite its humble inhabitants to a sumptuous meal. Members of the wedding party, decked out in manila shawls and other finery given them by Pingajo, dance the popular *jerigonza*. However, the colorful scene soon darkens into a grotesque etching as police appear, fix the guests in their gunsights, and arrest Pingajo and his two accomplices.

The epilogue is reminiscent of Valle-Inclán's sarcastic distortion (as is the barrack scene in which Pingajo is mocked by the other soldiers, who spread his arms apart as if he were a scarecrow, dance around him like grotesque bats, and beat him over the head). Pingajo is shot after the lieutenant props him up lopsidedly to keep him from fainting with fear and sticks a limp cigarette in his mouth. Wrapped in a ragged Spanish flag—symbol of a debased nation—he is an esperpentic hero redeemed only by his refusal to sacrifice Fandanga.

Rodríguez Méndez approaches history with a high degree of ironic distancing. However, his irony in no way negates the humanity of his vision or the sympathy inspired by the characters. The play's themes are the moral and economic decadence of 1898 and the disintegration of the populace.

Autumn Flower (1982) was inspired by the picture from an old chronicle of a transvestite singer of Barcelona's red-light district who was also an anarchist gunman. This historical play effectively recreates Barcelona of the 1930s, from the respectable middle-class society to which the singer belongs, to the Barrio Chino where he performs under his alias, to the workers' cooperatives where the aborted anarchist revolution occurs. The play shows the subversion of values that typified the middle class at the conclusion of the dictatorship of Primo de Rivera with which the Bourbon Restoration ended, together with the problem of anarchist terrorism. Rodríguez Méndez makes the singer, Luiset, a labor lawyer belonging to a well-known Barcelona family. After assaulting the Fort of Ataranzanas to obtain arms, and acting as leader in an aborted revolution begun at the Workers' Cooperative of Poble Nou, Luiset and his companions are executed before the walls of the Military Prison of Montjuih, a death reminiscent of that of Pingajo in *The Famous Nuptials*.

Rodríguez Méndez's dramatic monologue, *Teresa de Ávila* (1985), which he subtitled a "dramatic oratory" and which was performed by the admired actress María Paz Ballesteros, in Madrid's Capilla del Arzobispo and various churches throughout the country, represents a new direction in his dramaturgy. In 1989, four years after Rodríguez Méndez's dramatic monologue honoring St. Teresa, his *El Cantar de los cantares* [The Song of Songs], a "Semitic Oratory for Peace," opened at the Albéniz Theater in Madrid. A single actress (Esperanza Alonso) played the role of two women representing Palestinians and Jews. As Part I ("Death") opens, the first woman, veiled in black, searches for her children amid desolation, as a Voice offstage documents recent struggles between the two peoples. As in all his history plays, past and present merge as Rodríguez Méndez speaks of his audience's own time. Part II ("Resurrection") is based on Spanish poet Luis de León's translation of the Song of Songs. As the Palestinian woman listens to the verses traditionally attributed to Salomon, the emphasis changes from death and destruction to love and resurrection. The actress removes her black shrouds to reveal the red and gold garments of the biblical Sulamita (the Shulammite)—the Jewish woman of peace in Rodríguez Méndez's oratory—and the tombstone seen in Part I becomes a banquet table prepared for a celebration. The set depicts Salomon's tent, and objects prominent in the Song of Songs figure as props: bread, wine, apples and grapes, rose petals, lilies, gold, and pearls. The focal point is an immense oval mirror in which the Jewish and Palestinian peoples—represented by the two women—finally meet in an embrace of peace. In addition to the one actress, the oratory features a female singer who renders songs in both Arabic and Sephardic.

Like *Teresa de Avila*, Rodríguez Mendez's *Literatura española* [Spanish Literatura], deals with a well-known figure from Spain's Golden Age. Premiered in Melilla, North Africa, in 1966 under the title *Con el pie en el estribo* [With his Foot Already in the Stirrup], the play is an homage to Cervantes. Rodríguez Méndez presents the writer as an old man ready for the final journey, as he gazes through the grill of the window in his last home in Madrid. Out in the street before Cervantes' eyes, well-known figures of his time as well as characters from his popular *entremeses* or interludes—Preciocilla, Rinconete, Cristinica, and others—appear and reenact lively scenes written by their creator. These stories are intertwined with new adventures invented by Rodríguez Méndez as the old man behind the grill watches with emotion on the day before his death.

CRITICS' RESPONSE

Government censorship of the theater prevented many of Rodríguez Méndez's major plays from being performed in the Franco period. His first major success came in 1964 when *The Innocents of Moncloa* opened at Madrid's Cómico Theater and won the Larra Award given by the Madrid critics.

In 1968 Taurus Publishers brought out a volume dedicated to Rodríguez Méndez and edited by José Monleón. The latter's extensive introduction underscored the popular nature of Rodríguez Méndez's plays and compared them to the *esperpentos*, or savage subversive farces, by Valle-Inclán of Spain's Generation of 1898, who attacked the conservative politics of Spain's Bourbon Restoration of 1974, the same epoch that Rodríguez Méndez portrays critically in *The Famous Nuptials of Pingajo and Fandanga* and where he sees as the origin of many of Spain's problems that continued in the 1960s and 1970s. The volume also included some of the playwright's own essays on theater. Monleón, a socially committed critic and the editor of *Primer Acto*, Spain's most important journal of contemporary theater, devoted considerable attention in its pages to the members of the "Realistic Generation" and helping popularize their theater.

In 1978 and 1979 César Oliva, a theater professor and director at the University of Murcia, published two books with extensive studies of Rodríguez Méndez's drama. *Cuatro dramaturgos "realistas" en la escena de hoy: Sus contradicciones estéticas* [Four "Realistic" Playwrights on Today's Stage:) Their Aestethic Contradictions] contains a chapter focusing on the evolution of Rodríguez Méndez's esthetics, from the early plays based on the *sainete* to the recent ones where the dominant note is the bitter caricature of Valle-Inclán. *Disidents de la generación realista* [Dissidents of the Realistic Generation], a general introduction to the same four playwrights considered in the former book (Olmo, Martín Recuerda, Muñiz, and Rodríguez Méndez), studies the plays of the group in the context of the theater of their times and concentrates more than the previous book on thematics.

The most complete study of Rodríguez Méndez's theater is *La tragedia de España en la obra dramática de José María Rodríguez Méndez: Desde la Restoración hasta la Dictdevea de Franco* [The Tragedy of Spain in the Dramatic Works of José María Rodríguez Méndez: *From the Restoration to the Dictatorship of Franco]* (1979) by fellow playwright Martín Recuerda. The book includes a detailed account of Rodríguez Méndez's life to date, readings of individual plays, and comments on the evolution of the playwright's language, dramatic structure, and thematics. In the United States, studies of his theater have been done by Martha Halsey and B. Antonio González. In his *Estreno* article the latter assesses the playwright's theater in the light of the theories the latter has published in his essays. Important collections of theater essays published by Rodríguez Méndez include his polemical *Comentarios impertinentes sobre el teatro español* [Impertinent Comments on the Spanish Theater] (Barcelona, 1972), *La incultura teatral en España* [The Lack of Theatrical Culture in Spain] (Barcelona, 1974), and *Los despojos del teatro* [The Plunder of the Theater] (Madrid, 1993).

AWARDS AND DISTINCTIONS

In 1994 Rodríguez Méndez was awarded Spain's Premio Nacional de Literatura Dramática (National Prize for Dramatic Literature) for his play *El pájaro solitario* [The Solitary Bird] about St. John of the Cross.

NOTE

1. José Martín Recuerda, *La tragedia de España en la obra dramática de José María Rodríguez Méndez* (Salamanca: Universidad de Salamanca, 1979), 18–19.

BIBLIOGRAPHY

Editions

La batalla del Verdún. Barcelona: Editorial Occitania, 1966.
Bodas que fueron famosas del Pingajo y la Fandanga. In *El teatro y su crítica*. Málaga: Instituto de cultura de la Diputación Provincial, 1975. 465–520. Madrid: Cátedra, 1979. Ed. José Martín Recuerda.
Flor de Otoño. *Primer Acto* 173 (1974): 22–47. Madrid: Cátedra, 1979. Ed. José Martín Recuerda. Madrid: Preyson, 1983.
Historia de unos cuantos. Murcia: Ed. Godoy, 1982.
Los inocentes de la Moncloa. *Primer Acto* 24 (1961): 24–43. J. M. Rodríguez Méndez, *Teatro*. Madrid: Taurus, 1968. 131–176. Salamanca: Ed. Almar, 1980. Ed. Martha T. Halsey.
Literatura española. Murcia: Universidad de Murcia, 1989.
El pájaro solitario. Ávila: Diputación Provincial de Ávila, 1993.
Los quinquis de Madriz. Murcia: Ed. Godoy, 1982.
Teresa de Ávila Murcia: Ed. Godoy, 1982.
Última batalla en el Pardo. Madrid: Centro de Documentación Teatral, 1991.
Vagones de madera. *Primer Acto* 45 (1963): 38–55.
La vendimia de Francia. Barcelona: Biblioteca Teatral Yorick, 1965.

Critical Studies

Balboa-Echeverría, Miriam. "Lenguaje teatral: Voz e imagen en *Los quinquis de Madriz* de José María Rodríguez Méndez." *Gestos* 2.3 (1987): 67–75.

Fernández Insuela, Antonio. *"Bodas que fueron famosas* . . . Degradación e ironía." *Archivum* (Universidad de Oviedo) 31–32 (1981–1982): 289–304.

González, B. Antonio. "Teatro nacional popular: sobre la teoria y practica de Jose Maria Rodriguez Mendez." *Estreno* 20.1 (1994): 29–34.

Halsey, Martha T. "Dramatic Patterns in Three History Plays of Contemporary Spain." *Hispania* 71.1 (1988): 20–30.

———. "History 'From Below': The Popular Chronicles of José María Rodríguez Méndez." *Revista de Estudios Hispánicos* 21.2 (1987): 39–58.

Jiménez Sánchez, Gonzalo. *El problema de España. Rodríguez Méndez: Una revisión dramática de los postulados del 98.* Salamanca: Universidad Pontificia de Salamanca, 1998.

Martín Recuerda, José. *La tragedia de España en la obra dramática de R. Méndez (Desde la Restauración hasta la Dictadura de Franco).* Salamanca: Universidad de Salamanca, 1979.

Monleón, José. "Rodríguez Méndez." In *Cuatro autores críticos.* Granada: Secretariado de Extension Universitaria, Universidad de Granada, 1976. 13–21.

———. "Teatro popular: La respuesta de Rodríguez Méndez." In *Teatro.* By J. M. Rodríguez Méndez. Madrid: Taurus, 1968. 21–55.

Oliva, Cesar. *Disidentes de la generación realista (Introducción a la obra de Carlos Muñiz, Lauro olmo, Rodríguez Méndez y Martín Recuerda).* Murcia: Universidad de Murcia, 1979.

———. "José María Rodríguez Méndez." In *Cuatro dramaturgos "realistas" en la escena de hoy: Sus contradicciones estéticas.* Murcia: Departamento de Literatura Española, Universidad de Murcia, 1978. 77–113.

———. "José María Rodríguez Méndez." In *El teatro desde 1936.* Madrid: Alhambra, 1989. 284–294.

Ruiz Ramón, Francisco. "Rodríguez Méndez." In *Historia del teatro español. Siglo XX.* Madrid: Cátedra, 1975. 509–516.

CONCHA ROMERO
(1945–)

Carolyn J. Harris

BIOGRAPHY

Born on January 1, 1945, in Puebla del Río, Seville, Concha Romero developed an interest in the theater at an early age. During the formative school years, she participated in many dramatic activities, and while studying at the University of Seville, she participated in a University Theater Group. After staging various works over a two-year period with this group, Romero left for the University of Salamanca, where she would study classical languages. Having completed this degree, which enabled her to later teach Latin at the high school level, the future playwright studied at the Madrid School of Cinematography and collaborated in the writing of screenplays for film and television. In the 1980s Romero began to write for the stage, publishing in 1983 her first play, *Un olor a ámbar* [A Scent of Amber]. Although only one of her dramatic works has been staged commercially to the present date, her full-length plays and two monologues have been produced by university and independent groups and have inspired much enthusiasm among Hispanists. Romero presently resides in Madrid, where she combines playwriting with scripting for movies and television and teaching classical studies at a secondary school.

DRAMATURGY: MAJOR WORKS AND THEMES

Beginning with plays based on historical or mythological events and characters and evolving into contemporary themes, Romero's dramatic production focuses on relationships of all kinds and the use and abuse of power, representing these topics from a feminine perspective. Female characters often take center stage to tell their own stories, questioning the official versions of history that have often silenced or misrepresented the feminine point of view. Through metatheater, intertextuality, and irony, Romero's works question traditional gender roles and present on stage women's search for their own identity and voice in a patriarchal society.

Set in sixteenth-century Spain, Romero's first dramatic work, *Un olor a ámbar*, recreates the events surrounding the death of Santa Teresa de Jesús and the conflict that arose over the possession of her mortal remains. The play traces the discovery, due to the pleasant odor to which the title refers, that Teresa's body has miraculously remained intact after its interment. While remaining faithful to historical documents, Romero places contemporary and colloquial language in the mouths of her characters to make them come alive on stage to comment on the grotesque and macabre situation that results from the presence of a saintly corpse that is disputed and mutilated. Combining humor with the representation of the abuse of authority and the silencing of the female voice, this play makes an important statement about power relationships and the situation of women in contemporary Spain and will be studied in more detail here.

Romero's second play and, in her own estimation, her most ambitious work to date, analyzes romantic love from many angles and perspectives, both masculine and feminine.[1] *Así aman los dioses* [How the Gods Love], published in 1991, re-presents classical mythology and discovers that little has changed in the arena of amorous conduct and sentiment in the many years that have passed since the conception of the mythological heroes and heroines of ancient Greece and Rome. Due perhaps to its length and many characters and subplots, *Así aman los dioses* has not been staged, nor has it received the critical attention enjoyed by Romero's other dramatic works. It has in common with her other plays, however, the presentation of female characters who are strong and rebellious women, struggling to establish their own identity and change their adverse circumstances in spite of the many obstacles placed in their paths by the masculine power structure, represented here by Jupiter.

Returning to Spanish history, Romero wrote in 1988 and 1989 two plays based on events in the lives of Isabel la Católica, her brother Enrique IV, and her daughter Juana la Loca. Like *Un olor a ámbar*, these works remain true to historical accounts of their fifteenth-century characters while focusing on their motives and inner lives. Through the creation of lively dialogue that includes current colloquialisms, the play's connection with contemporary Spain is evident. Both plays examine tensions that arise between individuals and power structures and the characters' divided consciousnesses that result from the conflicting demands of public and private lives.

Las bodas de una princesa [The Wedding of a Princess], published in 1988, portrays the struggles of a young Isabel to escape victimization at the hands of manipulative political forces and to achieve some degree of control over her own destiny. Having observed the way in which the nobles have controlled her brother, Enrique IV, suppressing his progressive views, Isabel learns at an early age that she must fight to defend herself and the interests of her nation. A naive adolescent as the play begins, circumstances have transformed Isabel by its conclusion into a strong woman capable of ruling a nation. She has resisted attempts by others to marry her off according to their wishes, and the play ends with her triumph through her marriage to Fernando, a choice that enables her to make compatible her desires for her private and public life. As desirable as this union is to her, Isabel marries only with Fernando's acceptance of the condition she has imposed: "In Castile and Aragón he and I will rule equally" [En Castilla y Aragón tanto debe mandar él como debo mandar yo] (72). The young Isabel has discovered the way to affirm her personal identity and assert her feminine point of view.

Juego de reinas o razón de estado [Queens Play or Reason of State], first staged in 1991, portrays a much older Isabel la Católica and focuses on her daughter Juana's path to madness and silence.[2] A dialogue between the two women, this play confronts Isabel's "masculine" reason, which gives primary importance to matters of state, with the much younger Juana's "feminine" sentiment, which wants to reconcile her personal needs with the demands of her public position. Unable to convince her daughter that duty to country must take precedence, Isabel is forced to have her daughter locked in her room for a time in order to prevent her from following her husband Felipe, a politically unacceptable choice for Spain. Left alone, Juana begins to imagine her husband's infidelity and exhibits signs of her future madness, understood here as the inability to transcend the limits of gender and a metaphor for her lack of voice. Although the mature Isabel is seen as a woman who has been successful in both public and private life, the play points to the tension and interior conflicts that she has endured through the years as a result of her simultaneous roles as mother and political leader.

In addition to these works based on historical or mythological characters, Romero has written one full-length play and two monologues that are set in contemporary Spain. *Un maldito beso* [One Damn Kiss], first published in *Gestos* in 1989, makes use of a variety of metatheatrical techniques to create a fascinating look at male-female relationships in the 1980s. The play revolves around the world of acting and theater, with María, a professional actress, married to Manolo, a successful director. The fateful kiss of the title is the result of María's witnessing and misinterpreting a theatrical improvisation in which her husband tests the abilities of an aspiring young actress. Through a series of plays within the play, both voluntary and involuntary, the couple examines their relationship. María discovers that Manolo has been unfaithful to her in spite of her efforts to assure equality in the marriage, which have included the signing of an official contract. Metatheater in this work provides interesting insights into male and female roles in contemporary society and sexist attitudes that persist in spite of legislative victories for gender equality.

The theme of marital problems in contemporary society is further examined in Romero's two monologues, which were written to be performed together.[3] "¿Tengo razón o no?" [Am I Right or Not?] gives voice to Carlos, an aging Don Juan, whose discovery that his wife has abandoned him for another man destroys his self-confidence and causes him to reject the reality of his situation by means of an alcohol-induced fantasy. The female protagonist of *Allá él* [That's His Loss], first published in *Estreno* in 1994, faces a similar dilemma, as a housewife who is cast aside by her husband of many years, but Pepa determines a very different course of action from that of Carlos. Through the help of a sister's phone call and the imagined visit of an old friend, Pepa comes to see her new situation as an opportunity to find her own identity. When her husband calls at the play's conclusion, she thanks him for leaving, explaining: "It's as if I had been paralyzed and all of a sudden a miracle occurred. As if a curtain had opened and you saw your past, full of indifference, of emptiness, of nothing, because I wasn't living my life but yours in disguise" [Es como si hubiera estado paralítica y de pronto ocurriera el milagro. Como si se descorriera una cortina y vieras tu pasado, lleno de desamor, de vacío, de nada, porque no estaba viviendo mi vida sino la tuya disfrazada] (14). Unlike Carlos, who clings to his donjuanesque role even after coming to see it as a charade, Pepa accepts the changes in her life and is willing, like so many of Romero's female characters, to accept the truth and to struggle to grow as a person while holding fast to her feminine values.

Un olor a ámbar

A closer study of Romero's first full-length play demonstrates the way in which her dramatic production as a whole re-presents on stage the lives of women from a feminine perspective and her historical works in particular rewrite the stories of female protagonists of Spain's past. In recent years feminist criticism has pointed to the need to reread literary and historical texts "like a woman" in order to discover the aspects of women's lives forgotten or silenced in masculine readings accepted as "universal." Annette Kolodny calls this new way of reading from a feminine perspective "revisionary rereading" and argues that "feminist appeals to revisionary rereading . . . offer us all a potential enhancing of our capacity to read the world, our literary texts, and even one another, anew" (465). Romero's rereading of history relates her understanding of feminine consciousness to past events in order to show how women have resisted or attempted to overcome the traditional limitations of their role in society. She examines personal and public aspects of her female protagonists, focusing on their inner worlds, in order to discover what traditional versions of women's lives have omitted. Romero's theater re-presents women who have become protagonists in a masculine world not by renouncing their feminine vision and values but by finding a way to subvert the masculine authority that limited their possibilities of action.

Through the dramatization of the historical fight for the remains of Santa Teresa in Un olor a ámbar, Romero brings to life on stage this important religious reformer and mystic writer of sixteenth-century Spain, shedding new light on the events of her life and death. By means of humor often tinged in black and contemporary dialogue, Romero rescues the historical figure from her inscription in masculine history through the process María Pilar Pérez-Stansfield has called the "desacralization of an historic and literary myth" [desacralización de un mito histórico y literario] (92). Teresa of Avila comes alive on stage through the memories of those who knew her well, and the fight for her body symbolizes women's resistance to repression and silencing by male authorities. The nuns of Alba de Tormes, under the leadership of the Prioress, fight to keep the saint's remains in their convent because they remember her life, her words, and the causes for which she relentlessly fought. The Provincial, representative of masculine authority, attempts to make use of Teresa's body, carrying it off to Avila, while expressing his desire to silence her ideas and teachings. Candyce Leonard has observed that "the prospect of canonization has made her body a trophy to be won," and the play's subtext is "the metaphorical masculine possession of the feminine as object, particularly when such possession includes the notion of control" "Women Writers" (247).

The theme of women who rebel against unjust authority and limitations imposed by traditional gender roles is present throughout Romero's work, even as the sweet scent of amber permeates the convent, making all aware of the presence of the saint, whose influence is too large to be contained and buried. Due to the mysterious scent that leads to the uncovering of Teresa's intact remains and the subsequent investigation that will bring about her canonization, the nuns of Alba de Tormes recount many events of her life and death. Through lively metatheatrical role-playing they rehearse the miracles they witnessed that will contribute to the case for her canonization. Teresa's friend and confessor Gracián recalls her humanity and her sense of humor. The image that all the characters relate is that of a woman who fought to defend her beliefs, traveled extensively in order to found new convents, and was constantly pursued by church authorities. The Prioress comments upon learning of the church leaders' plan to move her remains to Avila, "Not even in death will you allow her to rest!" [¡Ni muerta la dejaréis descansar!] (66).

After her death, Teresa's writings have been confiscated by the Inquisition, and church officials want to change the constitutions she wrote for her convents. Gracián is grateful for the miracle of her intact remains, which will make it more difficult to reverse her reforms and destroy her writings. Alone with the body at the close of the first act, he tells the saint: "You probably already know what they are plotting against the reforms. They want to change the constitutions, in nothing less than twenty points. You charged me not to allow them to take out one single comma!" [Ya estarás al tanto de lo que están tramando contra la reforma. Quieren cambiar las constituciones, y nada menos que en veinte puntos. ¡Tú me encargaste que no permitiera que quitaran ni una sola coma!] (40). At the play's conclusion the Prioress points out that the same masculine power structure that has fought to obtain Teresa's body is working to silence her voice and reverse her doctrine. "What a contradiction!" [¡Qué contradicción!] she tells the Provincial. "You want to take her body to exalt it and at the same time you put her doctrine to the sword and even try to change the constitution. After all the work she put into having it accepted, to the point of being careful of each period and comma!" [Quiere llevarse el cuerpo para ensalzarlo y en cambio tira a degüello contra su doctrina y hasta pretende cambiar la constitución. ¡Con el trabajo que le costó que la aceptaran, que hasta de los puntos y comas se cuidó!] (67).

Together with the sense of the presence of Teresa, achieved by intertextual references to her life and writings, additional stories of women who challenge or resist authority are interwoven with the central plot of *Un olor a ámbar* and have the effect of reinforcing the image of the historical figure's struggle with the confines of her sex. The play opens with a conversation between two lay sisters who are cleaning the sacristy. In order to hide from the Prioress her curiosity about the scent of amber in the convent, the first sister claims to have stopped work to look at spiders' webs in the ceiling. Left alone with her companion, she recounts a favorite story of a young girl of Arcadia whose tapestries were so skillfully woven that she dared to challenge Minerva, the goddess of the arts, to a competition. The lay sister's story follows closely Ovid's account of this myth in his *Metamorphoses* and so captivates her fellow worker as to make her forget her vow of silence and promise to give up her snack if she can only hear how it ends. The sisters' recognition that they have sinned in telling this secular story reminds the spectator of women's lack of access to literature in Teresa's time and the future writer's secret passion for chivalry novels as a young girl. The punishment of the girl who has dared to enter the forbidden world of the arts points to the difficulties of women writers through the ages as they attempt to participate in the masculine arena of intellectual creativity. The storytelling sister explains that the goddess decides the girl must be punished due to her pride and comments: "What a paradox, don't you think? For having dared being a poor mortal to challenge the art and wisdom of the goddess of Olympus" [Qué paradoja, ¿no crees? Por haberse atrevido siendo una pobre mortal a desafiar el arte y la sabiduría de la diosa del Olimpo] (20). Minerva's punishment, changing her competitor into a spider and condemning her to weave for all of time the same tapestry in the ceilings of houses, brings to mind the image of women's traditional confinement and lack of access to the world of the arts. The lay sisters go on to comment on the images portrayed in the girl's tapestry that depict other mythological abuses against women, including Jupiter's deception of Europa, a story that leads them to remember his unfaithfulness to his wife Juno.

In the play's second act, amid excitement over preparations for the expected canonization of Teresa, the nuns of the convent present a drama that they have prepared secretly in honor of the Prioress's birthday. This play within the play portrays the struggle of Coloma, a third-century Spanish martyr who refuses to renounce her Christian faith in spite of Roman Emperor Aurelian's threat to have her raped if she does not outwardly deny her beliefs. Coloma valiantly resists the soldier who is ordered to attack her, calling on her God, who sends a bear to protect her. Although she is later martyred, she dies a virgin and has seen the soldier who attempted to rape her converted to Christianity. The Prioress congratulates the nun who directed the play, telling her: "If God had not called you to his service and the century didn't prohibit this profession to women, you would have had great success in the theater world" [si Dios no la hubiera llamado a su servicio y el siglo no prohibiera este oficio a las mujeres, habría tenido un gran éxito en el mundo del espectáculo] (56–57).

Immediately following this metatheatrical representation of a powerless young woman's refusal to surrender her vision and values to those in power, the new Provincial, Nacianceno, arrives at the convent and reveals his plan to secretly transfer Teresa's remains to Avila. The Prioress, who is portrayed as a strong and resolute woman, confronts her superior without hesitation, arguing for the convent's right to keep the saint's body in Alba de Tormes. When Nacianceno argues that it was not God's will for Teresa to die in Alba but that of a friar who persuaded her to stop there, the Prioress responds: "As an argument it is all right. But it doesn't convince me. No one can choose the place and date of his death. It is God who chooses them" [Como argumento está bien. Pero no me convence. Nadie puede elegir lugar y fecha de su muerte. Es Dios quien las elige] (61). Nacianceno replies: "You reason well for a woman, but I don't think it is respectful for a nun, even if she is a prioress, to dare to call a friar a 'circumstance' " [Razona bien para ser mujer, pero no me parece respetuoso que una monja, por muy priora que sea, se atreva a llamarle a un fraile "circunstancia"] (61).

As the argument between the two becomes more heated, the Prioress exclaims: "With papers or without them, it [the body] will not leave here, because God willed that she would die here!" [¡Con papeles o sin ellos, de aquí no sale, porque aquí quiso Dios que muriera!] (63). When the Provincial threatens to take away the Prioress's position and even her habit, she does not retreat but tells him: "The position doesn't matter to me, it is yours to take. I didn't enter this convent to rule but to obey. But this isn't an act of obedience, this is an abuse and a robbery" [El cargo no me importa, está a su disposición. No entré en este convento para mandar, sino para obedecer. Pero esto no es un acto de obediencia, esto es un atropello y un robo] (64). To this, Nacianceno responds by threatening excommunication, forcing the Prioress to back down and turn over the key to the sepulchre.

Yet even as she accepts defeat, Romero's protagonist finds a way to negotiate with those in authority. Having aroused the town's curiosity by ringing the convent bells, the Prioress convinces the Provincial to leave Teresa's right arm with the nuns in return for settling the townspeople. At the play's conclusion she raises the arm in the air and tells the nuns: "My daughters, I promise you that I will not rest until that body, that now leaves hidden in the dark, returns to be reunited with this arm, in bright daylight and with all the bells in the tower ringing" [Hijas mías, os prometo que no descansaré hasta que ese cuerpo, que ahora sale a oscuras y a escondidas, vuelva a reunirse con este brazo a la luz del día y con todas las campanas del campanario al aire] (70). The Prioress has been forced to yield to the masculine power structure but has not given up her opposition to what she considers to be its injustice.

Throughout the work, the struggle for the possession of Teresa's remains symbolizes women's battle to repossess their bodies, which have been manipulated and controlled by a patriarchal society in the same way that their voice has been silenced. The grotesque presence of Teresa's corpse on stage creates a visual image of the objectification and dismemberment of women at the hands of patriarchy. When first uncovered, each body part is examined and referred to separately. Upon entering to see the body, Gracián and Cristóbal feel the flesh and comment on Teresa's ample figure. Left alone on stage, Gracián cuts off a hand and Cristóbal, a toe, to take with them. When Nacianceno finally carries the corpse off to Avila, it is in a sack thrown over his shoulder. The Prioress cries out in protest: "Oh, tremendous contempt! . . . Our mother in a sack, as if she were potatoes, acorns or carob beans!" [¡Oh, tremendo desacato! . . . ¡Nuestra madre en un saco, como si fuera patatas, bellotas o algarrobas!] (65). Her concern for Teresa's importance as spiritual mother to the nuns contrasts sharply with the church authorities', view of her remains as a source of material profit.

Un olor a ámbar re-presents the life and death of Spain's first recognized woman writer from a feminine perspective, portraying her as a subject whose struggle to break away from the confines of traditional gender roles serves as a model for men and women of her day and for centuries to come. In her first dramatic work, Concha Romero masterfully gives voice to an important historical female protagonist and points to the need to reexamine the past and the present with new eyes in order to better know ourselves and to change fundamental attitudes of our society.

CRITICS' RESPONSE

Although most of her works have not yet been staged commercially, *Un olor a ámbar* and Romero's theater in general have been treated in many conference papers, articles, and doctoral dissertations. Most critics have focused on the feminist inferences that can be drawn from her revisionary reading of the position and perspective of Spanish women throughout history. They study the way in which her works examine and challenge gender stereotypes, finding her female protagonists to be strong, determined women who strive to gain personal independence and the right to control their own lives.

María Pilar Pérez-Stansfield sees *Un olor a ámbar* as a satire on men's abuse of power and gender constructs in Spain and a denunciation of masculine discourse. Carolina Henriquez-Sanguineti points to the demythification of the masculine hero and his code of values with the substitution of a feminine hero in this play. Wilfried Floeck writes of an esperpentic deformation of reality in the work, with a feminist subtext in which the church symbolizes masculine power and oppression. Helen Roberts relates this underlying text to the contemporary debate over a woman's right to control her own body, pointing out that Santa Teresa's remains are objectified and dismembered on stage.

Teresa Anita San Pedro and Candyce Leonard among others have studied

Romero's dramatic technique and the use of intertextuality and metatheater in her theater. San Pedro draws a parallel between the nuns' struggle in *Un olor a ámbar* and the dilemma of the female playwright who must face the masculine power structure in her attempt to see her works and her perspective produced on stage for the public. These critics point to the role-playing that is an integral part of Romero's theater as a representation of women's search for an authentic personal identity apart from the restrictive gender roles prescribed by a patriarchal society.

NOTES

1. Concha Romero spoke of her works in a presentation entitled "Aporía" [Anxiety] on October 6, 1994, at the symposium "A Stage of Their Own," which took place at the University of Cincinnati.

2. *Juego de reinas* was originally entitled "Razón de estado" [Reason of State]. Romero stated in "Aporía" that the new title was considered by the play's director to be more commercial. It was published in 1997 with both titles.

3. Personal interview, July 1993.

BIBLIOGRAPHY

Dramatic Texts

"Abrázame, Rhin." [Unpublished play, 1995.]

Allá él. Estreno 20.2 (1994): 8–14. Also published in *Esencia de mujer: Ocho monólogos de mujeres para mujeres*, ed. Charo Solanas y Joaquín Solanas. Madrid: García Verdugo, 1995. 43–60.

Así aman los dioses. Madrid: Clásicas, 1991.

Las bodas de una princesa. Madrid: Lucerna, 1988.

Juego de reinas o Razón de estado. Madrid: García Verdugo, 1997.

Un maldito beso. Gestos 8 (1989): 109–144. Also published in Murcia: Universidad de Murcia, 1994.

Un olor a ámbar. Madrid: La Avispa, 1983.

¿Tengo razón o no? In *Esencia de mujer: Ocho monólogos de mujeres para mujeres*, ed. Charo Solanas y Joaquín Solanas. Madrid: García Verdugo, 1995. 29–42.

Interviews and Roundtable Discussions

"Encuesta: ¿Por qué no estrenan las mujeres en España?" *Estreno* 10.2 (1984): 23–24.

Harris, Carolyn J. "Concha Romero y Paloma Pedrero hablan de sus obras." *Estreno* 19.1 (1993): 29–35.

Johnson, Anita. "Dramaturgas españolas: Presencia y condición en la escena española contemporánea." *Estreno* 19.1 (1993): 17–20.

Ortiz, Lourdes. "Nuevas autoras españolas." *Primer Acto* 220 (1987): 10–21.

Romero, Concha. "Aporía." In *Un escenario propio/A Stage of Their Own*, Vol. 1, ed. Kirsten Nigro and Phyllis Zatlin. Ottawa: Girol, 1998. 71–77.

Critical Studies

Floeck, Wilfried. "Entre el drama histórico y la comedia actual: el subtexto femenino en el teatro de Concha Romero." *Estreno* 23.1 (1997): 33–38.

Gabriele, John P. "Concha Romero." In *Spanish Women Writers. A Bio-Bibliographical Source Book*, ed. Linda Gould Levine, Ellen Engelson Marson, and Gloria Feiman Waldman. Westport, CT: Greenwood Press, 1993. 441–450.

Harris, Carolyn J. "Isabel y Juana: Protagonistas históricas del teatro de Concha Romero." *Estreno* 19.1 (1993): 21–25.

———. "Love, Madness, and Silencing in Concha Romero's *Juego de reinas*." In *Entre Actos: Diálogos sobre teatro español entre siglos*, ed. Martha T. Halsey and Phyllis Zatlin. University Park, PA: Estreno, 1999. 79–86.

———. "La perspectiva femenina en escena: *Allá él* de Concha Romero." *Estreno* 20.2 (1994): 5–7.

———. "The Portrayal of Feminine Consciousness in Two Plays by Concha Romero: *Juego de reinas* and *Un maldito beso*." In *Continental, Latin-American and Francophone Women Writers*, Vol. IV, ed. Ginette Adamson and Eunice Myers. New York: University Press of America, 1997. 53–61.

Henriquez-Sanguineti, Carolina. "Drama histórico y feminismo en la dramaturgia de Concha Romero." In *Literatura femenina contemporánea de España*, ed. Juana Arancibia, Adrienne Mandel, and Yolanda Rosas. Westminster, CA: Instituto Literario y Cultural Hispánico, 1991. 129–137.

Johnson, Anita. "La apropiación y subversión del discurso teatral hegemónico en ¿*Tengo razón o no*? por Concha Romero." *Confluencia* 10.1 (1994): 125–129.

Kolodny, Annette. "A Map for Rereading: Or, Gender and the Interpretation of Literary Texts." *New Literary History* 11 (1980): 451–467.

Leonard, Candyce. "Los niveles de ficción en *Un maldito beso* de Concha Romero." In *De lo particular a lo universal: el teatro español del siglo XX y su contexto*, ed. John P. Gabriele. Frankfurt: Vervuert Verlag, 1994. 188–195.

———. "Role-Playing in Concha Romero's *Un maldito beso*." *Estreno* 20.2 (1994): 15–17.

———. "Women Writers and Their Characters in Spanish Drama." *Anales de la Literatura Española Contemporánea* 17.1–2 (1992): 243–256.

O'Connor, Patricia W. *Dramaturgas españolas de hoy: Una introducción*. Madrid: Fundamentos, 1988.

———. "Una nueva voz femenina para el teatro." *Un olor a ámbar*. By Concha Romero. Madrid: La Avispa, 1983. 7–13.

———. "¿Quiénes son las dramaturgas españolas contemporáneas y qué han escrito?" *Estreno* 10.2 (1984): 9–12.

Pérez-Stansfield, María Pilar. "La desacralización del mito y de la historia: Texto y subtexto en dos nuevas dramaturgas españolas." *Gestos* 4 (1987): 83–99.

Podol, Peter. "Three 'Stages' in the Life of Isabel: Plays by Alberto Miralles, Manuel Martínez Mediero and Concha Romero." *Estreno* 16.1 (1990): 28–31.

Roberts, Helen. "Female Power and Solidarity in *Un olor a ámbar* by Concha Romero, and *Humo de beleño* by Maribel Lázaro." In *Entre Actos: Diálogos sobre teatro español entre siglos*, ed. Martha T. Halsey and Phyllis Zatlin. University Park, PA: Estreno, 1999. 95–100.

San Pedro, Teresa Anta. "Intertextuality, Text and Metatext in Concha Romero's *Un olor a ámbar*: The Eternal Gender Struggle." *Readerly/Writerly Texts* 2 (1995): 113–129.

Serrano, Virtudes. "Hacia una dramaturgia femenina." *Anales de la Literatura Española Contemporánea* 19 (1994): 321–342.

———. Introduction. *Un maldito beso*. By Concha Romero. Murcia: Universidad de Murcia, 1994. 9–25.

———. "La pieza breve en la última dramaturgia femenina." *Art Teatral* 5 (1993): 93–97.

Sweetland, Karen K. "The Female Body as Symbol of Oppression and Means of Subversion in Concha Romero's *Un olor a ámbar*." In *Entre Actos: Diálogos sobre teatro español entre siglos*, ed. Martha T. Halsey and Phyllis Zatlin. University Park, PA: Estreno, 1999. 87–93.

Theses

Barkemeyer, Helga. "La reivindicación feminista de la historia en obras de Lourdes Ortiz y Concha Romero." Master's thesis, Montclair State University, 1996.

Henriquez-Sanguineti, Carolina. "La degradación del espacio sagrado en el teatro español actual." Ph.D. diss., University of California at Irvine, 1990.

Leonard, Candyce. "Theoretical Models for Reading Twentieth-Century Spanish Metadrama." Ph.D. diss., Indiana University, 1992.

Roberts, Helen. "Female Protagonists in Contemporary Spanish Drama by Women: Their Quest for Self-Authentication, Power and Independence." Ph.D. diss., University of Connecticut, 1996.

Tahiri, Tracy Clare. "Hacia una poética de la dramaturgia femenina española contemporánea." Master's thesis, Arizona State University, 1990.

PEDRO SALINAS
(1891–1951)

Susan G. Polansky

BIOGRAPHY

Best known as a poet and senior member of Spain's Poetic Generation of 1927, Salinas was described in 1951 by contemporary Dámaso Alonso as perhaps the Spanish writer of most facets and most varied talents of the present moment [quizá el literato español de más facetas y más aptitudes variadas del momento presente] (Alonso, *Poetas* 197). He authored fourteen plays, in addition to nine volumes of poetry seven volumes of essays, and literary criticism that include seminal studies of the poetry of Rubén Darío and Jorge Manrique and *Reality and the Poet in Spanish Poetry*, four volumes of critical editions, several volumes of translations of Proust and Musset, and three volumes of narrative prose. His dramatic works, written during the last fifteen years of his life, evidence the mature author expanding his artistry through the medium of drama. Jorge Guillén, poet, critic, and intimate friend of Salinas, divided Salinas's sixty years into thirty years of preparation and thirty years of production (*Reality and the Poet* ix; *Poesías completas* 11). The preparation began in the Madrid of his infancy and youth.

Born in Madrid on November 27, 1891, Pedro Salinas grew up an only child in the heart of the capital city, just off the Plaza Mayor. His early years were to engender in him a nostalgia for Spain that proved significant in his later life and literary production. His activities as a student, teacher, writer, and lover of life and literature were closely linked to the turbulent artistic, historical, and political currents of the first half of the twentieth century. By the time of his too early death of cancer in 1951, Salinas's personal and professional pursuits had led him into a cosmopolitan life beyond his neighborhood and homeland and, ultimately, into a fifteen-year exile from Spain that remained near and dear to his heart.

Across the street from his boyhood home, Salinas attended primary school at the Colegio Hispano-Francés, where he first studied French language. This early education prefigured his achievements as Lecturer at the Sorbonne, translator of three volumes of Proust, recipient of a French Legion of Honor medal, as well as his association with eminent French figures such as Marcel Auclair, Marcel Bataillon, Jean Casou, Ernest Mérimée, and Paul Valéry. He studied law at Madrid's Universidad Central but eventually followed his preference for literature. He formally completed his law degree and graduated with a Licentiate degree in Philosophy and Letters in 1913. It was during these student years that Salinas published his first poems and began to gain a reputation in literary circles. Salinas spent the next three years (1914–1917) in Paris, where he taught Spanish literature as a Lecturer while working on his doctoral dissertation, "The Illustrators of Don Quijote." Also during the Paris years, in 1915, he married Margarita Bonmatí, whose family, originally from Alicante, lived in Algiers.

As a young man in his early twenties, Salinas wrote some 600 letters to Margarita (104 of which were edited by their daughter Solita Salinas de Marichal in the collection *Cartas de amor a Margarita, 1912–1915*). They had met in 1911 while on summer vacation in Santa Pola, a little coastal town south of Alicante on the Mediterranean. Their intense correspondence began after they became engaged at the end of the following summer in September of 1912. Salinas remained an avid letter writer throughout his life, and his epistolary voices of poet and correspondent provide important insight into his personality, aesthetics, and preoccupations. Though he would turn more intently to the writing of drama some two decades later, his letters to Margarita from Paris in 1915 reveal an early attempt at playwriting (Salinas de Marichal, "Tradición y modernidad" 3) and make mention of his love of theater together with the nostalgia for his boyhood years:

My Margarita, today, Sunday afternoon, I have been at the theater. You do not know the charm these words "theater . . . Sunday afternoon" . . . have for me: it is a delight of my childhood, a string of memories of boyhood, thinking about that life of the sad and solitary boy who some Sundays would go to the theater with his aunts and uncles or grandparents. It is a whole period of my life!

[Margarita mía, hoy domingo, por la tarde he estado en el teatro. No sabes estas palabras "teatro . . . domingo por la tarde" . . . el encanto que tienen para mí: es un encanto de mi infancia, un rosario de recuerdos de niñez: mis diez años reviven, pensando en aquella vida de niño triste y solitario que algunos domingos iba al teatro con sus tíos o sus abuelos. ¡Es toda una época de mi vida!] (*Cartas* 232)

Upon returning from Paris, Salinas obtained a professorship of Spanish literature at the University of Seville. Among his students were the poet Luis Cernuda and Enrique Canito, the future director of *Insula*. During the Seville years, children Solita and Jaime were born. Also, Salinas accepted a one-year lectureship at Cambridge (1922–1923) and was involved in the summer language program with the University of Toulouse at Burgos (1924–1926), the first of many cross-cultural exchanges that were to mark his career as a gifted teacher.

In later years, he would direct the summer program sponsored by the Centro de Estudios Históricos in Madrid (1928–1931), serve as Secretary General of the International Summer University in Santander (1933–1936), and teach in summer programs in the United States at Middlebury College, Duke University, and the University of California at Los Angeles and Berkeley.

Through the 1920s, Salinas's poems continued to appear in a variety of newspapers and journals, both mainstream and vanguard, and his contacts with many important twentieth-century literary figures were expanding, with members of the Generation of 98 and others—Baroja, Juan Ramón Jiménez, Antonio Machado, Gabriel Miró, Ortega y Gasset, Guillermo de Torre, Unamuno, Valle-Inclán. Increasingly drawn to the literary hub of his country, Salinas eventually resigned from his position in Seville to return to his native city. For close to a decade (1928–1936), Salinas worked in the Spanish government's Centro de Estudios Históricos directed by Ramón Menéndez Pidal. His ties to the Residencia de Estudiantes drew him further into the literary scene and to close friendships with a number of writers who came to be known as the Generation of 1927.

Salinas was the eldest of this group that led a resurgence of interest in Spain's literary traditions, both classical and popular, and at the same time, touched by Vanguard currents of artistic experimentation of the early decades of their century, looked outward to Europe, especially France. The most prominent figures included Rafael Alberti, Vicente Aleixandre, Manuel Altolaguirre, Luis Cernuda, Federico García Lorca, Jorge Guillén, and Emilio Prados. According to Guillén, "There was no program, there was no manifesto attacking or defending fixed positions. There were dialogues, letters, dinners, walks, and friendship under the bright light of Madrid" (*Language and Poetry* 211). While representing a great diversity of intention, theme, technique, and language, the Generation's cohesion was in part tied to its marking of the three hundredth anniversary of the death of Spanish Golden Age poet Luis de Góngora in 1927. Salinas did not make the commemoration pilgrimage to Seville, but he did take part in a lecture series in Córdoba, Góngora's birthplace, and in the production of scholarly studies.

From the end of the 1920s until his departure from Spain in 1936, Salinas gained distinction as a scholar, educator, public figure, and poet and also turned to the genre of drama. As head of the modern literature section of the Centro de Estudios Históricos, he edited *Indice Literario* and *Cuadernos Monográficos*. He wrote the lead articles for each issue, which were later collected in his *Literatura española siglo XX* [Twentieth Century Spanish Literature] (México, 1941; Madrid, 1970). He published a modernized edition of the *Poem of the Cid*, translations of Proust, and four volumes of poetry, including *La voz a ti debida* [The Voice Owed to You], hailed as a work that provided a love rhetoric for a generation (Newman 143). In years of intensifying European nationalism and growing internal national conflict, Salinas worked idealistically to promote intellectual freedom. In 1929, he was one of some two dozen intellectuals who signed a document that upheld nonpartisan liberalism and modern, free thinking of the broadest nature. Moreover, Salinas devoted much energy to cultural projects of the Second Republic such as the Misiones pedagógicas, educational missions to Spanish villages to share presentations of creative artistic production. During these years, García Lorca was director of the similarly inspired traveling theater troupe La Barraca. Their ongoing friendship occasioned García Lorca's frequent readings of his own plays to Salinas before staging them. Also, his correspondence with Guillén indicates that he had completed his first dramatic work, *El director* [The Director] while still in Spain, by the end of January 1936. (In a letter dated April 11, 1930, to Guillén, Salinas mentioned that he had been working on his first play, "La cama de matrimonio" [The Marriage Bed] [*Pedro Salinas/Jorge Guillén Correspondencia* 108], but a manuscript of the work has not been found, and it is unclear that it was ever completed.)

In August 1936, one month after the outbreak of the Spanish Civil War, Salinas left Spain, never to return. His yearlong visiting professorship at Wellesley College in Massachusetts lengthened to several (1936–1940) and marked the beginning of life in exile. After Wellesley, Salinas accepted a professorship at Johns Hopkins University, where in 1937 he had delivered the Turnbull Lectures, later published as *Reality and the Poet in Spanish Poetry*. Eleanor Turnbull of the sponsoring family became a close friend, chief translator of his poetry, and promoter of his work in English. He lectured throughout the Americas and taught many summers at Middlebury College and other institutions. He lived comfortably and was warmly welcomed in exile. He marveled at the abundance of resources, library facilities, and inventions. His delight with many aspects of life in the United States is evidenced in numerous anecdotes about his love of gadgets and toys. Yet he struggled with his separation from Spain and was deeply troubled by current events and the threat of world devastation. His displacement made him acutely aware of the linguistic and cultural isolation of the writer in a foreign milieu. Salinas thus especially treasured the time he spent at the University of Puerto Rico at Río Piedras (1943–1946), which allowed him to reconnect with life in a Spanish-speaking environment and assuage somewhat his profound nostalgia for Spain. The last years of his life he continued writing, teaching, and traveling.

During Salinas's final months, what he thought to be arthritis was found to be a cancer that progressed rapidly. After his death on December 4, 1951, he was buried in Puerto Rico as he had requested, close to the Sea of San Juan that had inspired much of his later work and helped him find tranquillity during the difficulties of exile.

Salinas confronted his exile with enormous productive output. In addition to *Reality and the Poet*, he wrote numerous essays about the plight of the writer, language, and contemporary life that appeared in *El defensor* [The Defender] (1948) and posthumously in *La responsibilidad del escritor* [The Responsibility of the Writer] (1961). He published his studies of Manrique (1947) and Darío (1948), a novel, a collection of stories, composed four additional volumes of poetry, and wrote the rest of his dramatic works, all published after his death.

DRAMATURGY: MAJOR WORKS AND THEMES

Salinas's fourteen plays are fruit of his maturity. His letters to Guillén after the composition of *El director*, the only work he wrote prior to his exile, indicate the following chronology: *El parecido* [The Resemblance] (between December 1942 and August 1943), *Ella y sus fuentes* [She and Her Sources] (before November 1943), *La Bella Durmiente* [Sleeping Beauty] (1943), *La isla del tesoro* [Treasure Island] (January 1944), *La cabeza de Medusa* [The Head of Medusa] (before February 1945), *Sobre seguro* [The Insurance Envelope] (before February 1945), *Caín o una gloria científica* [Caín or the Glory of Science] (before February 1945), *Judit y el tirano* [Judith and the Tyrant] (May 1945), *La estratoesfera. Vinos y cervezas* [The Stratosphere. Wines and Beers] (May 1945), *La fuente del Arcángel* [The Fountain of the Archangel] (January 1946), *Los santos* [The Saints] (1946), *El precio* [The Price] (before June 1947), *El chantajista* [The Blackmailer] (June 1947), (Ruiz Ramón "Contexto y cronología" 197–198).

Salinas lived to see the production of just one of his plays, *La fuente del Arcángel*, at Columbia University, New York, on February 16, 1951. Dámaso Alonso's recollections of the evening, attended by distinguished colleagues and friends of Salinas, constitute a poignant tribute to Salinas the man and writer taking delight in a memorable event in his last year ("Con Pedro Salinas" 55–58). Salinas's illness prevented him from attending the premiere of *Judit y el tirano* in Cuba in May 1951. Since his death, other performances, staged primarily by university groups, have taken place in the United States, Spain, Cuba, and Puerto Rico. In July 1980, *Los santos* was performed in Madrid. On July 9, 1992, *Judit y el tirano* opened at the Teatro Español in Madrid.

Salinas firmly believed that drama was a performing art and considered unperformed theater imperfect, or only potentially theater: Solely in its representation could it achieve its full authenticity and meaning (Alonso, *Poetas* 197). Very reluctantly, shortly before his death, he acceded to requests to publish three of his plays in the hopes of facilitating their representation: *La cabeza de Medusa, La estratoesfera*, and *La isla del tesoro*. In 1957, for reasons of censorship, his so-called *Teatro completo* appeared without the inclusion of *Los santos*, a play that deals with the Spanish Civil War. Published separately in *Cuadernos Americanos* in 1954, and again in *Estreno* in 1981, *Los santos* finally appeared in a publication of his full *Teatro completo* in 1992.

Salinas's attention to language and communication from the perspective of poet gave strong impetus to his expansion of the expressive forces of language through drama. In the studies that explore the relationship between Salinas's life in exile and his turn to the theater, there is consensus that the theater permitted him to broaden his powers of expression and that his turn to writing plays during his last years manifested his search for a more concrete, yet multifaceted, representation of universal themes and viewpoints in a distinctly modern context (Baader 248–251; Crispin 14; Gullón 9; Helman 211–12; Maurín 1, 3; Ruiz

Ramón, *Historia* 282–284; Torres Nebrera, ed., Pedro Salinas, *Teatro* 23–26; Zuleta 147).

Salinas considered the theater a powerful agent for the poet's reinvigoration of everyday language. The dramatist could create dialogue close to ordinary conversational style, yet infuse this speech with unaccustomed expressive power. Writing plays thus became a vehicle for Salinas to maintain a hold on Spanish as a living language and an outlet for his nostalgia for Spain. Seeking to exercise his powers of the writer [poderes de escritor] and give more sound and social dimension to the poetic voice, Salinas the poet turned playwright. Ironically, Salinas's "amplified" voice as a dramatist was not really heard as he intended. Some believe that his plays did not attain wide popularity on stage in large measure because of his intense preoccupation with verbal communication that consequently led to downplaying other essential dimensions of the medium (Ruiz Ramón, *Historia* 284). The predominant force in his plays derives from the dramatic dialogue, which, although lauded in his essays as the preferred vehicle of social interaction, in practice at times overshadows other action and elements of scenic design.

While the length (twelve one-act and two three-act works), classificatory subtitles (drama, comedy, tavern scene, mystery, fantasy), and specific milieus of the individual plays differ, all represent modern settings (a department store boutique, hotel room, restaurant, park, garden, vacation retreats, country homes) and connect to his preoccupations with communication and the modern world. Three plays portray distinctly Spanish locales: *La estratoesfera* hearkens to Salinas's boyhood as a madrileño; *La fuente de Arcángel* is set in Andalusia; and *Los santos* takes place in Castille. In many pieces, Salinas addressed problems specific to the twentieth century that touched him profoundly: the Spanish Civil War, the dangers of nuclear war, modern tyranny, and the degeneration of modern society in the name of progress in the areas of business, advertising, and scientific research.

It could be said that all the leading figures in Salinas's theater works are poet figures inasmuch as they demonstrate exceptional creative abilities. Through the genre of drama, which permitted Salinas to develop an augmented system of voices of poets and receivers, he could project the personal voices of key poet characters into complex public, social realms. The inner monologue of the solitary poet contemplator in the poetry expanded and transformed in the drama to multivoiced speech action among dominating poet characters. He constructed primary poet liberators to lead certain proximate characters to enter new, redemptive milieus. Moreover, he portrayed the poet figures as highly conscious of their project and involved in reflection upon their speech and action. The single voice of his poetry, which examined with profundity various configurations of reality and their connection to the poet, evolved in his drama with continued creative introspection into more complex and developed interrelationships among characters facing the challenges of being bound in circumstances exacerbated by conditions of the modern world.

A basic plot design is discernible throughout the dramatic corpus. In each play the fundamental redemptive action begins when a primary poet figure successfully sets forth to a proximate poet figure a vision that involves self-identification and the desirability of a liberating redemption. The liberation process develops as the secondary poet character shows a predisposition to enter the orbit of the primary one. The redemption then occurs through a kind of union between these interacting figures: when the proximate poet character comes to define himself or herself in terms of the primary poet. The poet protagonists are idealists but not escapists; they do not avoid obstacles or challenges in the process of transformation. Their sometimes ambivalent attitude with respect to choosing and using words is an important reflection of their preoccupation with confinement and freedom. Fixated upon emancipation, the poet figures hold special worldviews that Salinas highlights in the dramatic discourse through an elaborate system of references to their visionary powers. The dramatic corpus is punctuated with perspicuous designations of seeing, blindness, eyes, windows, and mirrors. Seeking access to a liberating, extraordinary reality, the poet protagonists are in constant pursuit of a redefinition of their own social circumstances. This redefinition can be analyzed in terms of Salinas's intertextual weavings of Cervantine, mythical, and biblical traditions to create new milieus. Salinas's views of Don Quijote as a model of unity, of the modern individual as a divided soul, and of the desired ideal of unity aid exploration of the social force of the drama and enable a fuller appreciation of the mature writer's relationship to the powers of language, exile, and modernity.

Being neither in the mold of commercially successful, evasionist entertainment nor of the engaged theater of protest and bitter denunciation, Salinas's theater represents a unique blending of aspects of both of these types that were popular during his time. His work is warm and humorous but does not avoid issues that invite confrontation and painful consideration of change. His work is also serious but not acerbic or thesis ridden. His plays are rooted in the poet-turned-dramatist's adherence to a "tema vital," or all-encompassing theme that illuminates how immersed he was as an intellectual in his cultural tradition as well as in his immediate circumstances as citizen in the modern world. Salinas's dramatic works may be viewed as modern yet universal morality plays that provide models for human interactivity in the process through which individuals seek fulfillment, happiness, insight into shared relationships, and transcendence.

CRITICS' RESPONSE

For the most part, Salinas's plays have been integrated thematically into his total poetic production and, like his narrative prose, have received considerably less critical attention than his poetry. A dominant perspective considers the dramatic works primarily an extension of his poetic work and a continuation of his concern with the theme of illusion versus reality (Cowes, *Relación*; Helman 207; Martínez Moreno 457–458; Moraleda, *El teatro*; Rodríguez Richart; Torres

Nebrera, ed., Pedro Salinas, *Teatro* 33–99). Cowes classifies realms of reality ("fantastic," literary, everyday, economic, artistic) and the I-you (*yo-tú*) relationships central to the transformations that the characters undergo. Helman emphasizes the importance of language in the shift from reality to fantasy. Martínez Moreno traces the search for an Eden-like reality. Moraleda's studies typologize the plays according to various phases or stages of reality [fases de la realidad] and also examine specific plays in relation to geographical or literary influences ("Un pueblo andaluz," "Rasgos unamunianos"). Rodríguez Richart discusses two key themes that derive from Salinas's poetry: two unique kindred spirits who seek out each other ["los únicos dos"] and unfulfilled happiness [la víspera como gozo] (420–421). Torres Nebrera, in his critical edition of four of the plays, traces Salinas's trajectory from poet to dramatist and groups the dramatic corpus into theater of discovery [hallazgo], rupture [ruptura], and rebellion and confidence [rebelión y confianza] (33).

Productive research has provided information about the composition and chronology of the plays (Newman; Ruiz Ramón, "Contexto"; Salinas de Marichal, "Tradición"). A number of studies have highlighted fruitfully key aspects of the plays such as linguistic and structural elements (Materna, "Dialogue," "Ideology"), woman, the artist, Giraudoux (Maurín), Pirandellism (Newberry), comparisons with T.S. Eliot (Pérez Romero), and poet figures (Polansky, "Communication"). Others have underlined the Salinian themes of love (Escartín) and self-authentication (Orringer). *Los santos* has received the most individual study (Borrás; Cazorla; Cowes, "Realidad"; Crispin 153–155; Materna, "Ideology"; Ruiz Ramón, *Historia* 287–288; Salinas de Marichal, "Introducción"), and a variety of articles have analyzed other specific plays such as *El chantajista* (Gila; Polansky, "Mail and Blackmail"), and *La fuente del Arcángel* (Materna, "Dialogue").

While the plays do exhibit features familiar in the poetry, and may be said to represent the voice of the poet Salinas, the dramatic works constitute a thrust importantly different from the poetry. The poet's preoccupation with reality expands to acquire dimensions beyond the more purely private and aesthetic realms explored in the poetry. A powerful social dimension prevails in Salinas's body of theatrical works that Ruiz Ramón has appropriately deemed "teatro de salvación" [theater of salvation] (*Historia* 282). Many studies of Salinas's poetry have pointed to the significance of dialogue or to his preoccupations with modernity (Crispin 116–120; Debicki 113–117; Dehennin 194; Maurer 301–309; Soufas 63–101; Zubizarreta), but less attention has been directed to these aspects in the dramatic works, where Salinas focused more systematically upon human social interactions and circumstances. He grappled with a dialectic of confinement and liberation that can be viewed as a common thematic unity throughout the plays.

Salinas's portrayal of the poet figures in quests for harmonious, emancipatory alliances reflects his assimilation of a broad spectrum of intellectual and artistic currents. In his numerous essays devoted to Hispanic literature, Salinas demonstrated explicitly the breadth and depth of his rootedness in his native tradition while he searched for its universal nature. Salinas was not plagued by a narrow nationalism. Rather, he sought to illuminate the unity and the totality of an artistic process or production. In "Pedro Salinas and the Values of Hispanic Literature" [Pedro Salinas y los valores de la literatura hispánica], the introductory essay to Salinas's collection of essays on Hispanic literature (*Ensayos de literatura hispánica*). Marichal emphasized Salinas's constant preoccupation not only with visions of human values but also with how these representations inform the contemporary orientation toward existence: "Inseparable functions that carry the Spanish writer, to be able to appreciate adequately his literary heritage and to know how to link it with vital contemporary necessities, to transcend the limits of his national culture and to absorb the spirit of our time" [Funciones inseparables que llevan al escritor español, para poder estimar adecuadamente su patrimonio literario y para saber enlazarlo con las necesidades vitales contemporáneas, a trascender los límites de su cultura nacional y a absorber el espíritu de nuestro tiempo] (10).

Salinas aimed for compatibility, for a reconciliation of traditional and modern values, and for a harmony between the human being and his or her circumstances. His dramatic works, and particularly his creation of poet figures as social forces in relationship to their milieus, constitute the vivid manifestation of a powerful embrace of Spanish heritage and contemporaneousness, bound with a universal humanistic outlook. The poet characters, as they redefine and recreate milieu, enact this forging of perspectives and the consequential redemption. To overcome obstacles that impede liberating views and experiences, the poet characters take charge to broaden and deepen the scope of those with whom they interact.

There are undeniable echoes of Ortega's *Meditations on Quixote* in Salinas's accentuation of the significance of self and circumstance in the dramatic works. Inspired by the Cervantine world, Ortega's meditations on Spain bring together the notions of self and situation, tradition and modernity, and underline the universal importance of love and linkage. Advocate of the quixotic perspective for modernity, Salinas, as essayist, pointed to a consciousness of the social function and world vision of Don Quijote and, as playwright, translated it into his dramatic works through the visions of his poet characters. Salinas called the *Quijote* "the great drama of the individual facing society; the great drama of this man alone, with all the people of every class who surround him" [el gran drama de un individuo frente a la sociedad; el gran drama de este hombre solo, con todas las gentes de todas clases que le rodean] (*Ensayos de literatura hispánica* 93). Don Quijote functions in the world as an integral being true to his inner spirit, one who never deserts his soul and who holds a perfect harmony between thought and deed. He is "the knight of unity" [el caballero de la unidad] (*Ensayos de literatura hispánica* 84]. Contrasting Don Quijote with modern man, Salinas asserted that the typical individual in present-day society was a fragmented being with an underdeveloped sense of morality, a sufferer from the distractions of modern life. A superabundance of ideas and inventions moves modern existence, but according to Salinas, what was lacking was an operating force well guided by moral stimulus and profound spiritual orientation.

Salinas thus elevated Don Quijote as a model whose fusion of an internal sense of goodness and justice with many aspects of external reality represented an attractive means of societal salvation. Salinas's modern stage with its poet-character saviors and their sights set toward a redemptive realm beyond the confines of immediate circumstances (a "más allá") resounds with echoes of the *Quijote*. The poet heroes in the plays demonstrate this quixotic spiritual orientation in their quests to transform conditions. Furthermore, as they aspire toward a humanization of modernity, their impact upon surroundings is intensified through Salinas's blending of additional quest-oriented codifications of milieu derived from other literary sources, biblical elements, myth, and legend. In the most vivid examples, Salinas appropriates subjects and circumstances related not only to the *Quijote* but also to the myths of Eros (*La fuente del Arcángel*), Medusa (*La cabeza de Medusa*), and Pygmalion (*La estratoesfera, El precio, La fuente del Arcángel, El chantajista, El director*), to the legendary Don Juan (*La estratoesfera*), Sleeping Beauty (*La Bella Durmiente*), and Mariana Pineda (*Ella y sus fuentes*), and biblical accounts of Cain and Abel (*Caín o una gloria científica*), Judith of the Apocrypha (*Judit y el tirano*), the Archangel Michael (*La fuente del Arcángel*), and various other saints (*Los santos*). The intertextuality of the redefinitions of surroundings by poet characters points to the great literary sophistication of the dramatic works. Also, it highlights the view of milieu as spiritually and morally charged sphere as well as physical environs.

The visionary movement of the poet characters, their melding of the concrete with the abstract, might be considered reflective of Salinas's poetic generation's revaluation of Góngora and of Salinas's conception of metaphor. Góngora's fusion of the concrete with the abstract was found to create a new level of reality, a different way of viewing the world. The poet characters perform acts of metaphor in their searches for ideal realms. In their roles as interfaces between commonplace, explicit settings and Cervantine and other implicit domains, they pursue ideal milieus and effect unique recastings of circumstances.

Fundamentally, as the poet characters aim to inhabit ideal realms for human interaction, a deliverance from exile or separateness parallels a quest for fulfillment through a love connection. Many of the amorous relationships involve romantic pairings (*El director, El parecido, La Bella Durmiente, La isla del tesoro, La cabeza de Medusa, Judit y el tirano, El chantajista*); others portray maternal devotion (*Sobre seguro*), brotherly love (*Los santos, Caín o una gloria científica*), or passionate attachment to an artistic production (*El precio, Ella y sus fuentes*). Salinas often wove into these associations a pursuit of truth with ethical, social, and political dimensions.

In *Judit y el tirano*, for example, in the dehumanized world of a political dictatorship, the heroine of the title combats the possibility of her own spiritual nullification and occupies the sensibilities of the tyrant who has become resigned to his place. Judit's transformation of the tyrant's experience of milieu moves him beyond an existence circumscribed by loneliness and cruelty. Her quixotic social role is that of redeemer as well as destroyer of the tyrant in this adaptation of the biblical account of Judit and Holofernes. Judit's mission is to enter the enemy ruler's domain and kill him, but when she discovers that beneath the histrionics of the black cape, the mask, and the hollow voice of the Regent [Regente] exists Andrés the man, she agrees to forward his attempt to disassociate the inhumane tyrant from the sensitive man. Under Judit's guidance, after spending every evening with her for a month, the Regente learns to go out among people and to participate in many things closed to him in the position of tyrant. As part of the process of erasure of the barriers between the tyrant and his subjects, Judit and Andrés's seemingly commonplace frequenting of movies, theaters, and the streets of the city acquires intensely human dimensions and pushes him toward a definitive break with the oppressive milieu and into a promising life with Judit. Judit does not describe this future as an ordinary tomorrow. Rather, in an extremely refined expression of her idealism, she awaits the light of a new day and a new man. Judit's definition of a truly new day transcends the concrete significance of the rising of the sun in the physical world. In a rhythmic, evocative passage, she internalizes the notions of "light" and "new day," then reconnects them with another aspect of the external world, the swelling approach of the waves of the sea, which in turn suggest an impending fulfillment with the arrival of the Regente. Her reference to the bird again points to a tangible reality, but with spiritual significance and dramatic irony. The chirping, normally indicative of the beginning of a new day, here carries to Judit a message that she cannot decipher, but her words about the bird's song suggestively warn of approaching trouble and cast an appropriate shadow over the light of her idealism:

Now I feel you. . . . Now you are here, new day. . . . New days, all, just because every day there is a dawn. It is not like that. . . . They will be new for the sea, the trees, and the mountains, that wait only for the light. We wait for [what] the light brings us. . . . And the light arrives many times with empty hands. . . . No, those are not new days. . . . What you will bring me, light—now I feel you on my eyelids that resist you—no day ever brought me. You will be the new one among all, the newest of my life, and I feel you growing, each time more clear, wave after wave, like the sea that swells and approaches, until it arrives and puts before me the joy it brings me, that which its tide is pushing slowly toward me. . . . No, he couldn't come by night. . . . And the bird that does not tire of singing. . . . Perhaps it will sing when he arrives. . . . And perhaps he will understand what the bird is saying, like the girl wanted him to. . . . But what is this? . . . He is coming, he is here. . . . It had to be like this. . . . the light and you.

[Ya te siento. . . . Ya estás ahí, día nuevo . . . ¿Días nuevos, todos, sólo porque cada día hay un amanecer. No es así. . . . Nuevos serán para el mar, y los árboles, y las montañas, que no aguardan más que la luz. Nosotros esperamos lo que nos trae la luz. . . . Y la luz llega muchas veces con las manos vacías. . . . No, esos días no son días nuevos. . . . Lo que me vas a traer tú, luz—ya te siento en los párpados que te resisten—no me lo trajo nunca día alguno. Tú serás el nuevo entre todos, el más nuevo de la vida, y te siento crecer, cada vez más claro, onda tras onda, como el mar que se hincha y se acerca, hasta que llegue y me ponga delante la dicha que me trae, la que su marea está lentamente empujando hacia mí. . . . No, no podía venir de noche. . . . Y el pájaro que no se cansa de cantar. . . . Quizá cante cuando él llegue. . . . Y puede que él entienda lo que dice el pájaro, como quería la muchacha. . . . Pero ¿qué es esto? . . . Es que viene, es que está aquí . . . Así tenía que ser . . . la luz y tú.] (*Teatro completo*, ed. Moraleda, 409)

Judit's social function as instrument of the tyrannicide in Salinas's remolding of the biblical story constitutes a condemnation of tyranny and also provides a view of the nature of tyranny in the modern world. The socioethical romantic ideal of the poet impels her to save a tyrant who turns out not to be a tyrant; yet Andrés dies because the political structure obstructs any view of the ruler other than that publicly projected through a mass media that substitutes constraining messages for genuine communication. The real tyranny is in the system itself and in the forces it develops to keep itself alive. Fundamental to this structure is the prevention of open interaction between individuals, precisely the opposite of what the poet upholds. The faceless way in which the Regente relates to his people expresses this theory of government: The individual is nothing, the idea is everything [el individuo no es nada, todo es la idea] (369). The assassination of Andrés by his own secret police and Judit's weapon is the final proof of man's lack of worth within a tyrannical structure. He is captured by his own underlings and a corrupt system, and his death makes no difference. Indications are that the tyranny will continue, with another faceless creature acting as the "official" tyrant. The activity of the poet figures indicates that it is important to seek out the humanity of individuals under their masks, but even if it can be found, there is danger that the power of tyranny can be so strong that individual identity can be lost within its structure.

Infused with a certain Cervantine perspective, as social forces promoting liberation, Salinas's poet characters, whatever the ideal milieu that they set forth, make to others loud appeals to free themselves from oppressive circumstances. Of Cervantes's work Salinas wrote, "The *Quijote*, my friends, is an invitation to freedom" [El *Quijote*, amigos míos, es una invitación a la libertad] (*Ensayos de literatura hispánica* 104). Salinas believed that Cervantes lauded the social mission of Don Quijote but that Cervantes did not impose this perspective upon his readers. Rather, he asserted that Cervantes extended to his readers a constant choice of options among the many quixotic stances. By contrast, Salinas the dramatist's invitation to freedom does not encourage his audience to exercise this kind of choice and thereby possibly reject the world vision of his key figures. Instead, he upholds their idealism as itself a stance of freedom to assume in order to reinvigorate milieu in spiritual, moral, and artistic terms. It is telling that in ascribing contemporary significance to Don Quijote, Salinas criticizes with a theater metaphor the faulty, superficial vision of today and tomorrow held by many moderns:

And here is the meaning of Don Quijote, the current meaning. The world of tomorrow, that is, the door to our defeat, some imagine to be a huge theater set. Everything is erected, every machine in its place. The war will end, the curtain will rise, and we will enter the sphere of an electrified paradise. A poor illusion! We carry within us the world of tomorrow; out of us it must emerge, and that is our task now, today's task and tomorrow's.

[Y he aquí la significación de Don Quijote, el actual. El mundo del mañana, esto es, el puerto de nuestra derrota, se lo imaginan algunos como decoración magna de teatro; ya está todo montado, cada máquina en su lugar, cada felicidad en su sitio. Acabará la guerra, se alzará el telón, y nos entraremos en ese ámbito de una Jauja electrificada. ¡Pobre espejismo! El mundo del mañana lo llevamos dentro, de nosotros ha de salir, y es labor nuestra, de hoy ya, y de mañana.] (*Ensayos de literatura hispánica* 85)

Through his theater, Salinas offers the model for a better world defined not by static boundaries or imposing technology that divide and dissect humankind but by dynamic thinking and feeling that promote the fellowship and unification of individuals. In designing his characters to exercise freedom and forge connections as model spiritual and social forces, in urging their assemblage of the fragments of self and other, in reinforcing their linkages in the face of divisive constraints, Salinas demonstrates how as dramatist he committed to the poet's stewardship in the defining of self, society, and their ideal cohesion. The conditions of Salinas's exile and his cognizance of many modern ills generated powerful testimony in his plays about the loss of freedom and degeneration of communication. Salinas created a theater to exalt his poet heroes in opposition to that destruction, though it did not reach the public as he had hoped. Ironically, even before he wrote his first play, Salinas was to describe his own situation in 1933 with words about Unamuno, Valle-Inclán, and Azorín: writers who had achieved the height of circulation and possible success in genres other than drama but whose plays remained in the shadows ("se mueven . . . en cuanto a su labor dramática se refiere, en zona de sombra") (*Literatura española siglo XX* 69). Although shortcomings in Salinas's stagecraft may be discerned, the powerful literary quality of his work, together with its moral force, has challenged directors to bring to life the dramatic tension in his plays (Manuel Collado, telephone interview, July 20, 1995). His spiritually charged, penetrating, yet uplifting perspective on modernity at midcentury remains provocative today.

AWARDS AND DISTINCTIONS

Chevalier de la Legion d'Honneur, 1933

Percy Turnbull Memorial Lecturer, Johns Hopkins University, 1937

Doctor Honoris Causa, Middlebury College, 1937

Professor Honoris Causa, Colegio Mayor, Guanajuato, Mexico, 1940

BIBLIOGRAPHY

Editions of Dramatic Works

Ella y sus fuentes. Número (Montevideo) 4.18 (1952): 11–39.

Teatro. La cabeza de Medusa. La estratoesfera. La isla del tesoro. Madrid: *Insula*, 1952.

Los santos. Cuadernos Americanos 13.3 (mayo-junio 1954): 265–291.

El parecido. Número 7.8 (1955): 13–19.

Teatro completo. Ed. Juan Marichal. Madrid: Aguilar, 1957.

Teatro. La fuente del arcángel. La bella durmiente. El director. Caín o una gloria científica. Ed. Gregorio Torres Nebrera. Madrid: Narcea, 1979.

Los santos. Estreno 7.2 (1981): 13–19.

Judit y el tirano. Madrid: Teatro español, 1992.

Teatro completo. Edición crítica e introducción de Pilar Moraleda García. Sevilla: Alfar, 1992.

Plays

Dates given are completion dates.

El director. 1936.

El parecido. 1942–1943.

La Bella Durmiente. 1943.

Ella y sus fuentes. 1943.

La isla del tesoro. 1944.

La cabeza de Medusa. 1944–1945.

Caín o una gloria científica. 1944–1945.

Sobre seguro. 1944–1945.

La estratoesfera. Vinos y cervezas. 1945.

Judit y el tirano. 1945.

La fuente del Arcángel. 1946.

Los santos. 1946.

El precio. 1946–1947.

El chantajista. 1947.

Selected Editions of Other Works—Poetry

Presagios. Madrid: Biblioteca de Indice, 1923. (actually appeared in 1924)

Seguro Azar. Madrid: Revista de Occidente, 1929.

Fábula y signo. Madrid: Plutarco, 1931.

La voz a ti debida. Madrid: Signo, 1933.

Razón de amor. Madrid: Cruz y Raya, 1936.

Largo lamento. 1936–1939. (published in *Poesías completas,* 1975)

El contemplado. Mexico: Stylo, 1946.
Todo más claro. Buenos Aires: Losada, 1949.
Confianza. Ed. Juan Marichal. Madrid: Aguilar, 1955.
Poesías completas. Ed. Soledad Salinas de Marichal. 2d ed. Barcelona: Barral, 1975.

Narrative Prose

Víspero del gozo. Madrid: Revista de Occidente, 1926.
Es desnudo impecable y otras narraciones. México: Tezontle, 1951.
La bomba increíble. Fabulación. Buenos Aires: Sudamericana, 1950.
Narrativa completa. Ed. Solita Salinas de Marichal. Barcelona: Barral, 1976.

Essays, Literary Criticism, and Letters

Reality and the Poet in Spanish Poetry. Baltimore: Johns Hopkins University Press, 1940.
Literatura española siglo XX. Madrid: Séneca, 1941.
Mundo real y mundo poética y dos entrevistas alvidadas 1930–1933. Edición, prólogo y Fiotas de Christopher Maurer. Valencia: Pre-Textos, 1996.
La poesía de Rubén Darío. Madrid: Séneca, 1948.
Jorge Manrique, o tradición y originalidad. Buenos Aires: Sudamericana, 1947.
El defensor. Bogota: Universidad Mayor, 1948.
Ensayos de literatura hispánica. Ed. Juan Marichal. Madrid: Aguilar, 1958.
La responsabilidad del escritor. Barcelona: Seix Barral, 1961.
Ensayos completos. Ed. Soledad Salinas de Marichal. Madrid: Taurus, 1983.
Cartas de amor a Margarita, 1912–1915. Ed. Solita Salinas de Marichal. Madrid: Alianza, 1984.
Cartas de viaje [1912–1951]. Edición, prólogo y notas de Enric Bou. Valencia: Pre-Textos, 1996.
Pedro Salinas/Jorge Guillén, Correspondencia (1923–1951). Ed. Andrés Soria Olmedo. Barcelona: Tusquets, 1992.

Critical Studies

Alonso, Dámaso. "Con Pedro Salinas." In *Pedro Salinas*, ed. Andrew P. Debicki. Madrid: Taurus, 1976. 53–60.
———. *Poetas españoles contemporáneos.* Madrid: Gredos, 1958.
Anónimo. "Estreno en España de la obra *Los santos* de Pedro Salinas." *El País* (27 julio 1980): 29.
Anonymous. *Who Was Who in America.* Vol. 3. Chicago: The A. N. Marquis Company, 1960.
Baader, Horst. "Pedro Salinas Studien zu seinem dichterischen und kritischen Werk." Diss. Kolner romantische Arbeiten, 1956.
Borrás, A. A. "Twentieth Century Spanish Drama: In Defense of Liberty." In *The Theatre and Hispanic Life: Essays in Honour of Neale H. Taylor*, ed. Angelo Augusto Borras. Waterloo: Wilfrid Laurier University Press, 1982. 55–76.
Cano, J. L. *"La fuente del Arcángel* de Pedro Salinas." *Insula* 7.75 (1952): 12.

————. "El teatro de Pedro Salinas." In *La poesía de la Generación del 27*. Madrid: Guadarrama, 1973. 59–62.

Cazorla, Hazel. "Art Mobilized for War: Two Spanish Civil War Plays by Rafael Alberti and Pedro Salinas." *Estudios en Homenaje a Enrique Ruiz-Fornells* (1990): 92–98.

Collado, Manuel. Telephone interview. July 20, 1995.

Cowes, Hugo W. "Realidad y superrealidad en 'Los santos' de Pedro Salinas." *Cuadernos Americanos* 188 (1973): 262–277. Rpt. in *Pedro Salinas*. Ed. Andrew P. Debicki. Madrid: Taurus, 1976. 213–227.

————. *Relación yo-tú y trascendencia en la obra dramática de Pedro Salinas*. Buenos Aires: Universidad de Buenos Aires, Facultad de Filosofía y Letras, 1965.

Crispin, John. *Pedro Salinas*. New York: Twayne, 1974.

Debicki, Andrew P. "La metáfora en algunos poemas tempranos de Salinas." In *Pedro Salinas*, ed. Andrew P. Debicki. Madrid: Taurus, 1976. 113–117.

Dehennin, Elsa. *Passion d'absolu et tension expressive dans l'oeuvre poétique de Pedro Salinas*. Gent: Rijksunivte Gent, 1957.

Escartín Gual, Montserrat. "El sentimiento amoroso en la obra de Pedro Salinas." *DAI* 50/20c (1988): 173.

Fernández Almagro, M. "Teatro por Pedro Salinas." *ABC*, 31 julio 1962: 7.

Fernández Méndez, E. "Pedro Salinas. Teatro." *La Torre* 1.1 (1953): 188–189.

Gila, Antonio. "*El chantajista* y el teatro de Salinas." *Duquesne Hispanic Review* 6 (1968): 13.

Guillén, Jorge. *Language and Poetry; Some Poets of Spain*. Cambridge: Harvard University Press, 1961.

Gullón, Ricardo. "Salinas el intelectual." *Insula* 7.74 (1952):9.

Hartfield-Méndez, Vialla. *Woman and the Infinite. Epiphanic Moments in Pedro Salinas's Art*. Lewisburg: Bucknell University Press and London: Associated University Press, 1996.

Havard, Robert. "Guillén, Salinas, and Ortega: Circumstance and Perspective." *Bulletin of Hispanic Studies* 60 (1983): 305–318.

Helman, Edith F. "Verdad y fantasia en el 'teatro' de Pedro Salinas." *Buenos Aires Literaria* 13 (1953): 69–78. Rpt. in *Pedro Salinas*. Ed. Andrew P. Debicki. Madrid: Taurus, 1976. 207–212.

Marichal, Juan. *Tres voces de Pedro Salinas*. Madrid: Taller de Ediciones Josefina Betancor, 1976.

Martínez Moreno, Isabel. "La intuición del espacio edénico en el teatro de Pedro Salinas." *Revista de Literatura* 52. 104 (1990): 457–486.

Materna, Linda S. "The Dialogue of Pedro Salinas' *La fuente del arcángel*: A Dialectic of Poetry and Realism." *Hispanic Review* 54.3 (1986): 297–312.

————. "Ideology and Vivification of Art in Pedro Salinas' *Los santos* and Rafael Alberti's *Noche de guerra en el Museo del Prado.*" *Hispanófila* 34.100 (1990): 15–28.

————. "Poetry and Realism in Modern Spanish Theater: Pedro Salinas and Other Dramatists of the Generation of 1927." *DAI* 41.12 (1981): 5120–5121.

Maurer, Christopher. "Sobre 'joven literatura' y política: Cartas de Pedro Salinas y de Federico García Lorca (1930–1935)." In *Estelas, laberintos, nuevas sendas: Unamuno, Valle-Inclán, García Lorca, la Guerra Civil*, ed. Angel G. Loureiro. Barcelona: Anthropos, 1988. 297–319.

Maurer, Christopher, Efraín Kristal, Solita Salinas de Marichal, and Wadda Ríos Font. "Homenaje a Pedro Salinas." *Boletín de la Fundación Federico García Lorca* 2.3 (June 1988): 9–61.

Maurín, Mario. "Temas y variaciones en el teatro de Pedro Salinas." *Insula* 104 (1954): 1, 3.

Miras, Domingo. "Exilio: En torno a Salinas." *Primer Acto: Cuadernos de Investigación Teatral* 234 (1990): 123–129.

Moraleda, Pilar. "Pedro Salinas: el dramaturgo y las fases de la realidad." In *Signo y memoria: Ensayos sobre Pedro Salinas*, ed. Enric Bou y Elena Gascón Vera. Madrid: Pliegos, 1993. 161–174.

———. "Un pueblo andaluz llamado Alcorada." *Axerquía* 11 (1984): 271–291.

———. "Rasgos unamunianos en el teatro de Pedro Salinas." *Alfinge* 1 (1983): 113–120.

———. *El teatro de Pedro Salinas*. Madrid: Pegaso, 1985.

———. "La vocación dramática de Pedro Salinas." *Insula* 540 (1991): 22–23.

Morello Frosch, Marta. "Teatro y crítica de Pedro Salinas." *Revista Hispánica Moderna* 26.1–2 (1960): 116–117.

Morris, C. B. *A Generation of Spanish Poets. 1920–1936*. Cambridge: Cambridge University Press, 1969.

Nagel, Susan. *The Influence of the Novels of Jean Giraudoux on the Hispanic Vanguard Novels of the 1920s–1930s*. Lewisburg: Bucknell University Press; London and Toronto: Associated University Press, 1991.

Newberry, Wilma. "Pirandellism in the Plays of Pedro Salinas." *Symposium* 25 (1971): 59–69.

Newman, Jean Cross. *Salinas and His Circumstance*. San Juan: Inter American University Press, 1983.

Orringer, Stephanie. *Pedro Salinas' Theater of Self-Authentication*. New York: P. Lang, 1995.

Pérez Firmat, Gustavo. "Pedro Salinas' 'Mundo cerrado' and Hispanic Vanguard Fiction." In *La Chispa '81: Selected Proceedings, February 26–28, 1981*, ed. Gilbert Paolini. New Orleans: Tulane University Press, 1981. 261–267.

Pérez Romero, Carmen. *Ética y estética en las obras dramáticas de Pedro Salinas y T. S. Eliot*. Cáceres: Universidad de Extremadura, 1995.

Polansky, Susan G. " 'Aprecio y defensa del lenguaje' in the Dramatic Works of Pedro Salinas." *DAI* 45.4 (1984): 1128A.

———. "Communication and the 'Poet Heroes': The Essence of the Dramatic Works of Pedro Salinas." *Hispania* 70 (September 1987): 437–446.

———. "How Many Saints Are in Salinas's *Los santos?*" *Estreno* 9 (1983): 4.

———. "Irony, Allusion, and the Nature of Tyranny in Pedro Salinas's *Judit y el tirano.*" *Revista de Estudios Hispánicos* 17–18 (1990–1991): 99–104.

———. "Mail and Blackmail: Pedro Salinas's *Cartas de amor a Margarita* and *El chantajista.*" *Hispania* 78 (March 1995): 43–52.

Rodríguez Monegal, Emir. "La obra en prosa de Pedro Salinas." *Número* 9.18 (1952): 66–92. Rpt. in *Pedro Salinas*. Ed. Andrew P. Debicki. Madrid: Taurus, 1976. 229–248.

Rodríguez Richart, José. "Sobre el teatro de Pedro Salinas." *Boletín de la Biblioteca Menéndez y Pelayo* 26 (1960): 397–427.

Ruiz Ramón, Francisco. "Contexto y cronología del teatro de Pedro Salinas." In *Pedro*

Salinas: Estudios sobre su praxis y teoría de la escritura, ed. Ciriaco Morón Arroya and Manuel Revuelta Sañudo. Santander: Sociedad Menéndez y Pelayo, 1992. 173–198.

————. *Historia del teatro espanol. Siglo XX*. Madrid: Alianza, 1986. 2–282–293.

————. "Para la cronología del teatro de Pedro Salinas." *Insula* 540 (1991): 20–22.

————. "Salinas, dramaturgo: ¿Compromiso o evasión?" In *Estudios sobre literatura y arte dedicados al profesor Emilio Orozco Díaz*. Publicaciones de la Universidad de Granada, 1979. 189–201.

————. "Trágica ironía: Los santos fusilados." *Estreno* 7.2 (1981): 12.

Salinas de Marichal, Solita. "Introducción a *Los santos* de Pedro Salinas." *Estreno* 7.2 (1981): 10–11, 20.

————. "Tradición y modernidad en el teatro de Pedro Salinas." *El País* (2 agosto 1980): 3 (Suplemento "Artes").

Soufas, C. Christopher. *Conflict of Light and Wind The Spanish Generation of 1927 and the Ideology of Poetic Form*. Middletown, CT: Wesleyan University Press, 1989.

Torres Nebrera, Gregorio. "En el teatro." *ABC*, 27 noviembre 1991: 53.

————. "Teoría del teatro de Pedro Salinas." *Insula* 370 (1977): 10.

Zubizarreta, Alma de. *Pedro Salinas; El diálogo creador*. Prólogo de Guillén. Madrid: Gredos, 1969.

Zuleta, Emilia de. "Pedro Salinas en su poesía y en su teatro." *La Biblioteca* (Buenos Aires) IX, Segunda Epoca, 5 (1960): 136–150.

JAIME SALOM
(1925–   )

Phyllis Zatlin

BIOGRAPHY

Born and raised in Barcelona, Jaime Salom y Vidal is the contemporary Catalán playwright who has become most fully integrated into the theatrical life of Madrid. He began writing plays in the late 1940s during his medical school days at the University of Barcelona and continued to do so after establishing an ophthalmology practice in his native city. Nevertheless, he was to wait until 1955 for his first stage production and entered actively into the theater world in the 1960s; he has deliberately destroyed most of his youthful attempts at writing. He gained national recognition as an author for the prize-winning stagings of *El baúl de los disfraces* (1964) and *La casa de las Chivas* (1968). Starting in 1971, for over twenty years Salom divided his time between his two professions and the two cities, holding office hours in Barcelona on Tuesday through Thursday and spending long weekends in Spain's theater capital. Since his retirement as a doctor, he and his actress wife, Montse Clot, reside in Madrid.

Salom was born into a comfortable and relatively conservative middle-class family. He experienced the trauma of the Spanish Civil War (1936–1939) and subsequently received the rigid education dictated by Franco-era National Catholicism. Several of his early staged plays reflect a related moralistic bent, but gradually Salom developed a liberal stance that affected both his theater and his personal life. Married in 1952, he separated from his wife in the 1970s; following the death in 1975 of Generalísimo Francisco Franco, Salom became an outspoken champion for legalizing divorce and other social reforms.

Highlights of Salom's career include the record-breaking Madrid run of *La casa de las Chivas* (1,343 continuous performances in a single Madrid theater) and such other box-office hits as *La noche de los cien pájaros* and *Tiempo de espadas*, each of which ran for more than 400 performances in 1972, and *La piel del limón* (1976). More recently the two-character *Una hora sin televisión* (1987) remained on tour for four years.

Although he is principally a playwright, additionally Salom has written film scripts, adapted foreign plays, and published novels. His involvement in theater for a brief period included owning his own playhouse in Barcelona. He has long served as a dramatist representative on the council of the Sociedad General de Autores y Editores and is vice-president of an association of physician writers.

Salom is a bilingual speaker of Catalán but received his formal education in Castilian Spanish, the language in which he prefers to write. A number of his works have been translated to Catalán, German, French, English, Slovak, Portuguese, Arabic, and Italian. His plays have also been widely performed in their original versions in Spanish American and in the United States and have enjoyed frequent revivals in Spain. Several works have been televised or made into films.

DRAMATURGY: MAJOR WORKS AND THEMES

Salom first achieved national and international success with *Culpables* (1961), a thriller inspired by Agatha Christie and Alfred Hitchcock, but he considers *El baúl de los disfraces* to be the first work to bear his original stamp. A poetic fantasy that treats man's life stages and the eternal feminine, this anthology play calls for the doubling of three actors in all of the roles in several episodes; it thus introduces a theatricalist tendency that Salom was to repeat in his mature plays.

Although Salom's minor works include other mysteries and fanciful comedies, dominant among the staged plays of his first period were moralistic dramas, dealing with themes of guilt and remorse and written somewhat in the mold of J. B. Priestly. The most successful of these, the 1972 hit *La noche de los cien pájaros*, was a reworking of an earlier text. An expressionistic evocation of the past by a man who feels himself guilty of his wife's death, *La noche de los cien pájaros* enhances its ironic impact through temporal fluidity in the form of brief flashbacks. In that the exact cause of the woman's death—heart attack, suicide, or murder via an overdose of medicine—remains forever in doubt, the drama also has Pirandellian overtones.

La casa de las Chivas, whose action takes place behind the front lines in Catalonia, has the distinction of being the first Spanish play to portray the Civil War from the Republican side. In another respect, however, it is a psychological drama that represents the culmination of Salom's moralistic period. The play revolves around a prostitute, the younger sister she tries to protect, and Juan, a would-be priest who must conceal his religious vocation from his fellow soldiers. Ultimately Juan functions as a catalyst both for the older sister's salvation and for the younger one's self-destruction when she does not understand why he rejects her love.

Los delfines (1969) announced a new phase in Salom's theater: plays that raise political, social, and religious issues, albeit veiled by an allegorical or historical framework. On the surface, *Los delfines* reveals the decline of a patriarchal industrial family in Catalonia, but at a deeper level it provides an allegorical commentary on the impending end of the Franco regime. *Tiempo de espadas* is a provocative theological drama that presents the events leading up to the Last Supper; ostensibly a modernization of the Christ story, it likewise carries a contemporary political message. In his early, moralistic plays, the author had limited himself to individual guilt and responsibility, imposing solutions and judgments based on a narrow interpretation of Catholic doctrine. In his later works, he widens his sphere of interest to examine the collective concerns of humanity and calls into question the hypocrisy of the conservative, materialistic Spanish society whose values he had previously defended. *Nueve brindis por un rey* (1974), a satirical farce dealing with a significant event in Catalan history, further deepens Salom's immersion in the theater of denunciation.

With *Los delfines*, Salom also continued his experimentation with innovative, theatricalist kinds of theater by introducing psychological expressionism, a technique that links him to Arthur Miller and, in Spain, to Antonio Buero-Vallejo. The 1969 text is marked by spatial and temporal fluidity; much of the dialogue and action are not "real" but rather projections of the protagonist's thoughts. These same strategies, which contributed to the success of *La noche de los cien pájaros*, recur in *La piel del limón*, Salom's impassioned plea for divorce reform. Juan would like to leave his wife and their empty marriage but is torn between his love for Bárbara and for his teenaged daughter, Alejandra. To visualize Juan's inner conflict, the same actress doubles in these roles. The "real" action of the two acts takes place in the family home during Alejandra's thirteenth and sixteenth birthday parties; simultaneously Juan relives his ill-fated love story with Bárbara, who appears only on the imaginary plane of memory.

There are structural and thematic ties between *La piel del limón* and Salom's controversial historical play *El corto vuelo del gallo* (1980). The rooster of the title is Nicolás Franco, Francisco's outspoken, liberal, nonconformist, and libertine father whose image had been virtually erased from memory during the Generalísimo's long regime. Utilizing expressionistic and theatricalist techniques, *El corto vuelo del gallo* presents on the plane of reality episodes from the end of the Civil War in 1939 to Nicolás's death in 1942 while simultaneously evoking remembered and imaginary scenes from the past. In essence, it functions on the stage like stream of consciousness in the novel. It is Salom's thesis that Francisco Franco's repressive National Catholicism stemmed from siding with his conservative, intransigent, and frigid mother Pilar in the failure of her marriage with the fun-loving, charismatic Nicolás. At the heart of *El corto vuelo del gallo* is the love story of Nicolás and Agustina, the woman with whom he shared his life for almost forty years after leaving his wife and children.

Una hora sin televisión continues the exploration of marital conflict but breaks with the complex structure of Salom's episodic, expressionistic plays. The author has termed this work "intimate theater": a stage equivalent of television dramas that allow the audience to eavesdrop on private conversations. The realistic dialogue and critical portrait of a self-centered and machista middle-aged Spanish husband no doubt contributed to the play's enduring success. In *Historias íntimas del paraíso* (1978), Salom had presented a rollicking feminist version of the story of Adam and Eve. Continuing in this vein, in *Una hora sin televisión* he clearly sides with the wife and her desire for self-fulfillment.

Salom's mature theater has been characterized by constant experimentation. Among his most recent works are found such diversified texts as *Casí una diosa* (1993), an intense portrait of Gala, the woman who inspired Paul Eluard and Salvador Dalí; *Una noche con Clark Gable* (1994), a light, two-actor comedy that features one actress in the dual role of two sisters; and *El otro William*(1995), a history farce that attempts to identify the real author of Shakespeare's works. Salom's interest in historical theater has reappeared at intervals throughout his career, usually bearing strong ideological messages, and also includes two important texts that premiered in 1990: *El señor de las patrañas* and *Las Casas una hoguera al amanecer*.

El señor de la patrañas, the basis as well for the 1992 Catalán-language musical *La lluna de València*, is a metaplay centering on the Renaissance editor and actor-playwright Valencian Juan Timoneda. Employing the strategy of the play-within-the-play, the action begins with the rehearsal on an improvised stage in Timoneda's printshop of a joyful, erotic farce. The subversive potential of metatheater surfaces as the audience realizes the connections between the "fiction" and the "real life" of the actor-characters, whose amorous deceptions are mirrored in the farce they are performing. Nevertheless, the play's underlying theme is not carnal love but freedom of expression. Spain's happy, Mediterranean-inspired Renaissance draws to a conclusion as the repressive, moralistic forces of the Counter Reformation intervene. Timoneda and his acting company must choose between being "actors"—that is, playing the roles in society now demanded of them by those in power—or remaining true to themselves.

Paradoxically, while Salom's innovative dramatic treatment of Bartolomé de las Casas, the Dominican friar known as the Apostle of the Indians, has been performed internationally (Mexico, United States, France) and has attracted substantial scholarly attention, it has yet to be produced in Spain. In a number of ways, *Una hoguera al amanecer* incorporates Salom's characteristic theatrical techniques and themes and therefore is an appropriate choice for more detailed commentary as his representative work.

The historical Las Casas (1474–1566) made his first trip to the New World in 1502. Despite becoming in 1512 the first priest ordained in the Americas, he also had charge of an *encomienda*, a plantation operated with forced native labor and justified as a means of bringing Christianity to the alleged savages. Stirred by the inhumane treatment of the indigenous people, through his writings and his incessant lobbying of authorities in Spain, Las Casas fought for and achieved needed reform. He is credited with propagating both the Black Legend of the Conquistadors' cruelty and the myth of the Noble Savage. A polemical figure in his own time because of this ideological stance, which today might be related to Latin American Liberation Theology, Las Casas has been negatively viewed by more recent generations because of his support, later retracted, for the enslavement of Black Africans as a way of saving the Native Americans.

Probing beneath the facts and condensing historical persons and events, Salom develops a psychological drama that explores the contradictions in Las Casas's character and the motivation for his gradual conversion from privileged landowner to activist reformer, from proud priest to humble friar. The playwright's polemical thesis—coincidentally shared by some historians—is that Las Casas had experienced a homosexual attraction to a young Indian slave. Upon returning to Seville from Columbus's second voyage, Las Casas's father had given Bartolomé the slave—named Señor in the play—but the boy was sent back to the New World when Queen Isabella outlawed the slavery of all her people. Fearing his own inclinations, the fictional Bartolomé fails to prevent the deportation and hence their separation; Señor does not return to freedom but rather to death from forced labor in the mines. The protagonist's sense of guilt and personal loss, coupled with his repressed love for a particular Indian, ultimately leads him to champion the cause of Señor's people.

Salom's text utilizes a Brechtian episodic structure and requires in the lead role a skilled actor who can represent the evolution of Las Casas from an arrogant, passionate, and yet idealistic youth, tempted by power and the attractions of the flesh, to a self-effacing old man, who continues to fight for justice even as he judges his own efforts to be inadequate. To facilitate temporal and spatial fluidity, including simultaneous action, the stage is to be divided into two, connected levels.

The upper level variously suggests the ship on which Bartolomé travels to the Americas, the pulpit from which Fray Antonio Montesinos delivers his famous Advent sermon denouncing the Spanish colonists for their treatment of the natives, and the royal palace in Spain where Bartolomé will plead the Indians' cause, first to King Ferdinand and then to Emperor Charles V. On the lower level are enacted scenes from daily life—at the Las Casas family home in Seville, at Bartolomé's plantation in Hispaniola, in the old man's convent cell—as well as the impressionistic evocation, through lighting and sound effects, of two massacres: one by the Spanish of defenseless natives and the other, a decade later, an indigenous uprising against the model colony that Bartolomé stubbornly attempts to establish with the aid only of family and friends. In the final scene, the upper level shifts to a symbolic, poetic plane. Above and behind the dying old man is seen a map of the New World, with points of light to identify the countries affected by Bartolomé's humanitarian crusade. At his death, the map is to disappear and the lights remain, like stars watching over his body.

The fluidity of action in *Una hoguera al amanecer*, with shifts not only between the fictive present and a remembered past but also between Spain and various locations in the New World, is the most complex development of this technique in Salom's theater. His expressionistic use of doubling also reaches its culmination in this historical drama. For satirical purposes, the caricatured royal figures and their advisers are played by the same actors; the overt impact of the strategy is to emphasize how all ambitious powermongers tend to resemble one another like "drops of water." In the vein of psychological expressionism, doubling is likewise used to externalized the old man's consciousness: his memories of the seductive Petrilla, his confusion of a young friar with a long-deceased friend, his identification of a visiting mestizo poet with the martyred Señor.

Una hoguera al amanecer presents its impassioned defense of the indigenous people of the New World in part through its sympathetic portrayal both of the charming young Señor and of María, a gentle but valiant young woman whose family is slaughtered by the Spaniards. Through the voice of the second Señor, the mestizo who has written down the cultural heritage of his Indian ancestors, Salom verbalizes the future revolutionary spirit of Latin America: the desire for a day when a new race—a melding of Indian and Spanish, of pagan and Christian—will achieve independence from European rulers. Nor does Salom fail to present the case for women's equality, primarily through the character of the earthy Petrilla, who journeys from Seville to the Americas. There she discovers that her marriage to Bartolomé's Uncle Gabriel provides her with "respectability" but takes away her freedom, turning her into another kind of slave. Bartolomé's mother and sister also present a strong egalitarian voice. The former attempts to free the slave boy and speaks out against the materialistic exploitation of the Indians; the latter affirms that she can run the family business by herself, without the men who have gone off seeking adventure in the New World.

Salom's critical perspective on the conquest of the New World should not be interpreted as an attack on Spain and all Spaniards. With the exception of the greedy and lecherous Uncle Gabriel, none of the principal Spanish characters is treated unsympathetically. The action of the drama thus centers on the Spaniards whose heritage the mestizo Señor readily accepts as half of his own identity: the humanitarian Dominican missionaries and their allies, and his mother Petrilla, who conceived him in an act of defiant love, saved the newborn from Gabriel's wrath, and raised him with tender love and considerable personal sacrifice. *Una hoguera al amanecer* thus develops once again Salom's image of two Spains: the materialistic, hypocritical, and repressive one that he rejects and the liberal one that has fostered a spirit of freedom, love, and tolerance.

CRITICS' RESPONSE

In reviewing Salom's career from the perspective of the 1990s, José Monleón astutely observes that the playwright's theater long resisted classification into either of the two dominant currents of the Franco era: a politically committed theater that attacked contemporary Spanish reality and an escapist theater that avoided the subject. Because he fell into neither category, Salom was largely ignored by liberal critics, like Monleón himself and others associated with *Primer Acto*, the theater journal he edits.

This is not to say that Salom's theater failed to elicit enthusiastic praise from more conservative commentators, in spite of the increasingly controversial nature of his themes. Federico Carlos Sainz de Robles was so impressed by the poetic fantasy of *El baúl de los disfraces* that he included the work, based on its Barcelona production, in his annual anthology of the best plays of the Madrid stage. In 1973, the influential Alfredo Marqueríe dedicated a book-length study to Salom, but his superficial analysis of the texts and his grouping of them under Torres Naharro's sixteenth-century categories of comedy no doubt contributed to a tendency by other writers to pass Salom's plays off as trivial mysteries and light comedies aimed at a bourgeois audience. On the other hand, in his 1974 prologue to Salom's selected theater, Luis María Ansón correctly recognized the mature plays as a theater of denunciation.

While many of his plays were awarded major theater prizes and enjoyed long runs, a balanced assessment of Salom's theater came later in Spain than in the United States. This point is made clearly by Ricard Salvat, the noted Catalán theater director and scholar. In his prologue to Jesús Izquierdo Gómez's recent monograph, Salvat identifies Ansón's criticism as transitional between studies like Marqueríe's and the thorough analyses of Phyllis Zatlin-Boring (Twayne World Authors Series, 1982) and Izquierdo Gómez. Salvat affirms that Salom paid dearly for his nonconformity to the prevailing Spanish theater but that his works, like good wine, have improved over time. To be sure, the times, not the works, have changed. As fellow playwright Carlos Muñiz observed in 1978, when *La casa de las Chivas* was revived on Spanish television to great acclaim, Salom's plays have been of prophetic interest.

Izquierdo Gómez's painstaking project divides Salom's theater into nine categories, ranging from "mystery-love" and "humor with an ethical purpose" to "social-political." He finds in Salom's trajectory a progressive fight for freedom and individual authenticity in response to institutionalized power (*Obra teatral*).

AWARDS AND DISTINCTIONS

Salom's plays have won numerous awards over the years, ranging from a university theater prize in 1948 for *Mamá sonríe* to the prestigious Premio Nacional de Literatura in 1969 for *Los delfines*. *La casa de las Chivas* (1969) and *Tiempo de espadas* (1972) were selected for the annual El Espectador y la Crítica prize for the best Spanish play staged in Madrid, and three of his plays were granted awards by the Real Academia de la Lengua: *El baúl de los disfraces* (Premio Fastenrath, 1965), *La casa de las Chivas* (Premio Álvarez Quintero, 1972), and *La piel del limón* (Premio Espinosa y Cortina, 1977). Recipients of the Barcelona Critics Prize were *La gran aventura* (1961) and *Cita los sábados* (1967), while *Motor en marcha* was honored by the City of Barcelona Prize (1963). Other awards include the Premio de la Academia de Lérida for *El cuarto jugador* (1962), Premio Isaac Fraga for *Juegos de invierno* (1963), and a national prize to a humanist physician in 1990 for *La piel del limón.*

BIBLIOGRAPHY

Plays: Collections

Teatro selecto de Jaime Salom. Madrid: Escelicer, 1971. Includes: *Culpables, El baúl de los disfraces, La casa de las Chivas, Los delfines, La playa vacía, Viaje en un trapecio.*

Teatro/Jaime Salom. Madrid: G. del Toro, 1974. Includes: *Culpables, El baúl de los disfraces, Espejo para dos mujeres, Cita los sábados, La casa de las Chivas, Los delfines, La playa vacía, Viaje en un trapecio, La noche de los cien pájaros, Tiempo de espadas.*

Plays: Original Stage Works

These are listed in order of performance

El mensaje (produced Bilbao, 1955). Madrid: Escelicer, 1963.

El triángulo blanco (produced Barcelona, 1960). Unpublished.

Verde esmeralda (produced Madrid, 1960). Madrid: Escelicer, 1962.

Culpables (produced Madrid, 1961). Madrid: Escelicer, 1962; in *Teatro selecto*, 1971; in *Teatro/Jaime Salom*, 1973; Madrid: Preyson, 1985.

La gran aventura (in Catalán; produced Barcelona, 1961). Barcelona: Editorial Millà, 1963; *Estreno* 8.2 (1982): 23–44 (Castilian version).

El cuarto jugador (produced Lérida, 1962). Unpublished.

El baúl de los disfraces (produced Barcelona, 1964). Madrid: Escelicer, 1965; in *Teatro español, 1963–64*, ed. F. C. Sainz de Robles, 1965; Barcelona: Círculo de Lectores, 1966; in *Teatro selecto*, 1971; in *Teatro/Jaime Salom*, 1973; Madrid: Espasa-Calpe, 1973.

Juegos de invierno (produced Madrid, 1964). Madrid: Escelicer, 1964.

El hombre del violín (produced Palma de Mallorca, 1964). Unpublished.

Falta de pruebas (produced Barcelona, 1964). Madrid: Escelicer, 1968.

Espejo para dos mujeres (produced Barcelona, 1965). Madrid: Escelicer, 1966; in *Teatro/ Jaime Salom*, 1973.

Parchís party (produced Madrid, 1965). Madrid: Escelicer, 1966.

Cita los sábados (reworking of *Parchís party*; produced Barcelona, 1967). In *Teatro/ Jaime Salom*, 1973.

La casa de las Chivas (produced Barcelona, 1968). Madrid: Escelicer, 1969; in *Teatro español, 1967–68*, ed. F. C. Sainz de Robles, 1969; in *Teatro selecto*, 1971; in *Teatro representativo español*, Madrid: Escelicer, 1972; in *Teatro/Jaime Salom*, 1973; Madrid: Espasa-Calpe, 1973.

Los delfines (produced Barcelona, 1969). Madrid: Escelicer, 1969; in *Teatro español, 1968–69*, ed. F. C. Sainz de Robles, 1970; in *Teatro selecto*, 1971; in *Teatro/ Jaime Salom*, 1973; Madrid: Espasa-Calpe, 1973.

La playa vacía (produced Madrid, 1970). Madrid: Escelicer, 1971; in *Teatro selecto*,

1971; in *Teatro español, 1970–71*, ed. F. C. Sainz de Robles, 1972; in *Teatro/ Jaime Salom*, 1973; Madrid: Espasa-Calpe, 1975.

Viaje en un trapecio (produced Barcelona, 1970). Madrid: Escelicer, 1971; in *Teatro selecto*, 1971; in *Teatro/Jaime Salom*, 1973.

La noche de los cien pájaros (reworking of *Falta de pruebas*; produced Madrid, 1972). Madrid: Escelicer, 1972; in *Teatro/Jaime Salom*, 1973; Madrid: Espasa-Calpe, 1973; in *Teatro español, 1971–72*, ed. F. C. Sainz de Robles, 1973.

Tiempo de espadas (produced Madrid, 1972). Madrid: Escelicer, 1972; in *Teatro/Jaime Salom*, 1973; in *Teatro español, 1972–73*, ed. F. C. Sainz de Robles, 1974; Madrid: Espasa-Calpe, 1975.

Nueve brindis por un rey (produced Madrid, 1974). Madrid: Escelicer, 1975. With *Jerusalén hora cero*. Madrid: Fundamentos, 1996.

La piel del limón (produced Madrid, 1976). Madrid: Escelicer, 1976; Salamanca: Almar, 1980.

Historias íntimas del paraíso (produced Madrid, 1978). Madrid: Preyson, 1984; Madrid: Espiral/Fundamentos, 1993.

El corto vuelo del gallo (produced Madrid, 1980). Barcelona: Grijalbo, 1981; Madrid: Preyson, 1982; Madrid: Fundamentos, 1994.

Un hombre en la puerta (produced Madrid, 1984). Madrid: Preyson, 1985. Madrid: Espiral/Fundamentos, 1998.

Una hora sin televisión (produced Alicante, 1987). Madrid: Ediciones Antonio Machado, 1988.

El señor de las patrañas (produced Madrid, 1990). Madrid: Centro Cultural de la Villa, 1990; Madrid: Sociedad General de Autores de España, 1992.

Las Casas, una hoguera al amanecer (produced Mexico City, 1990). Original title: *Las Casas, una hoguera en el amanecer*. Madrid: Instituto de Cooperación Iberoamericana, 1986; Mexico City: Editorial Planeta Mexicana, 1990. Revised title: *Una hoguera al amanecer*, Madrid: Sociedad General de Autores de España, 1994; Madrid: Fundamentos, 1994.

La lluna de València (musical version, in Catalán, of *El señor de las patrañas*; produced Barcelona, 1992). Barcelona: Editorial Millà, 1992.

Casi una diosa (produced Madrid, 1993). Madrid: Fundamentos, 1993.

Mariposas negras (produced Alicante, 1994). Valencia: Ediciones Antonio Ruiz Negre, 1994; Madrid: SGAE, 1995.

Una noche con Clark Gable (original version staged in French, Avignon, 1994; Spanish premiere, New York, 1994). Madrid: SGAE, 1995; Estreno 22.2 (1996): 14–26.

La trama (reworking of *Culpables*; produced Segovia, 1996).

El otro William (produced Madrid, 1998). *Primer Acto* 271 (1997): 67–99. Madrid: Espiral/Fundamentos, 1998.

Más o menos amigas (reworking of *Una noche con Clark Gable*; produced Madrid, 1999).

Novels

La casa de las Chivas. Novelization by Elisabeth Szél and Cristóbal Zaragoza. Barcelona: Planeta, 1972.

Las rayas blancas. Barcelona: Planeta, 1985.

La danza de las horas. Barcelona: Planeta, 1990.

Translations

Almost a Goddess. Trans. Gwynne Edwards. London. In press.

Behind the Scenes in Eden (Historias íntimas del paraíso). Trans. Marion Peter Holt. Full text unpublished. Selected scenes in *The Literary Review* 36.3 (1993): 398–411.

Bitter Lemon (La piel del limón). Trans. Patricia W. O'Connor. In *Plays of the New Democratic Spain (1975–1990),* ed. Patricia W. O'Connor. Lanham, MD: University Press of America, 1992. 103–164.

Bonfire at Dawn (Las Casas: Una hoguera al amanecer). Trans. Phyllis Zatlin. University Park, PA: Estreno, 1992.

The Cock's Short Flight. Trans. Marion Peter Holt. In *Drama Contemporary: Spain,* ed. Marion Peter Holt. New York: Performing Arts Journal Publications, 1985. 139–190.

"One Hour Without Television." Trans. Jack Agueros. Unpublished. Staged New York City, 1996.

"Rigmarole" (*El señor de las patrañas*). Trans Gary Racz. Unpublished.

"The Empty Beaches" Trans. Jack Agueras. Unpublished. Staged New York City, 1998.

"The House of the 'Chivas.' " Trans. Barbara Carballal. Unpublished.

"Time of Swords." Trans. Marion Peter Holt. [Part of National Endowment for the Arts grant project. Unpublished.]

Critical Studies

Alvaro, Francisco. *El espectador y la crítica* (theater annual). Valladolid: Edición del autor, 1959–1970, 1978–1986; Madrid: Prensa Española, 1971–1977.

Ansón, Luis María. "Prólogo" to *Teatro/Jaime Salom.* Madrid: G. del Toro, 1974. 7–16.

Cazorla, Hazel. "Breve juego unamuniano: *Una noche con Clark Gable* de Jaime Salom." *Estreno* 22.2 (1996): 11–12.

Delgado, Jaime. "El teatro de Jaime Salom." In *Teatro selecto de Jaime Salom.* Madrid: Escelicer, 1971. vii–lxiii.

Estreno 8.2 (1982). Issue devoted to theater of Salom. (Includes articles by Hazel Cazorla, Francisco García Pavón, Marion P. Holt, Joan de Sagarra, Jaime Salom, and Phyllis Zatlin.)

Gómez, María Asunción. "Estrategias dramáticas para una reescritura de la historia: *Las Casas, Una hoguera en el amanecer* de Jaime Salom." *Explicación de Textos Literarios* 23.2 (1994–1995): 13–22.

Halsey, Martha T., and Phyllis Zatlin, eds. *The Contemporary Spanish Theater: A Collection of Critical Essays.* Lanham, MD: University Press of America, 1988.

Holt, Marion P. "Jaime Salom." In *The Contemporary Spanish Theater (1949–1972).* Boston: Twayne, 1975. 156–159.

Introduction to *El señor de las patrañas.* Madrid: Centro Cultural de la Villa, 1990. 5–57. (Includes articles by the author, producer, and director and by critics José Monleón, André Camp, Phyllis Zatlin, Irène Sadowska-Guillon, and Luis Reyes de la Maza.)

Izquierdo Gómez, Jesús. "Jaime Salom y su teatro: Panorama general." In *Homenaje al profesor Antonio Gallego Morell II.* Granada: University of Granada, 1989. 129–143.

————. *Obra teatral de Jaime Salom*. Prologue Ricard Salvat. Granada: Universidad de Granada, 1993.

————. *Conformación y éxito de un dramaturgo: Jaime Salom*. Granada: Universidad de Granada, 1997.

————. "La evolución teatral de Jaime Salom." *Primer Acto* 267 (1997): 15–28.

Klein, Dennis A. "Epic Theater of the Conquest: Jaime Salom's *Las Casas. Una hoguera en el amanecer* and Peter Shaffer's *The Royal Hunt of the Sun.*" *Estreno* 18.2 (1992): 34–36.

Margenot III, John B. "Metateatro en *El baúl de los disfraces* de Jaime Salom." *Estreno* 15.1 (1989): 25–28.

Marqueríe, Alfredo. *Realidad y fantasía en el teatro de Jaime Salom*. Madrid: Escelicer, 1973.

Molero Manglando, Luis. *Teatro español contemporáneo*. Madrid: Editora Nacional, 1974. P. 321–335.

Monleón, José. "Salom. La libertad paso a paso." *Primer Acto* separata del no. 238 (1991): 33–34.

Muñiz, Carlos. *"La casa de las Chivas."* *Tele/radio*, 22–28 mayo 1978: 14–16.

Ortega, José. "La figura heróica de Las Casas en *Las Casas. Una hoguera en el amanecer* de Salom." *Estreno* 18.2 (1992): 37–38.

Pascual, Itziar. "La intriga como trama, la trama como intriga." (On *La trama* by Jaime Salom.) *Primer Acto* 267 (1997): 29.

Sainz de Robles, Federico Carlos. "Prólogo" to *La casa de las Chivas/El baúl de los disfraces*. Madrid: Espasa-Calpe, 1973. 9–15.

————. *Teatro español* (annual anthology). Madrid: Aguilar, 1965–1974.

Zatlin, Phyllis. "Bartolomé de las Casas en el escenario contemporáneo: La perspectiva de Jaime Salom." In *España y América en sus literaturas*, ed. María Angeles Encinar. Madrid: Saint Louis University and Instituto de Cooperación Iberoamericana, 1993. 17–39.

————. "Two-Character Plays as 'Teatro íntimo': Examples from Díaz, Junyent, and Salom." *España Contemporánea* 4.1 (1991): 97–102.

Zatlin Boring, Phyllis. "Expressionism in the Contemporary Spanish Theatre." *Modern Drama* 26.4 (1983): 555–569.

————. *Jaime Salom*. Twayne's World Authors Series 588. Boston: G. K. Hall, 1982.

————. "Jaime Salom and the Use of Doubling." *American Hispanist* 4.34–35 (1979): 11–14.

————. "The Discovery of the New World and National Identity: Theatrical Perspectives of Gala and Salom." *España Contemporánea* 12.2 (1999): 95–102.

ALFONSO SASTRE
(1926–   )

Nancy Vogeley

BIOGRAPHY

Alfonso Sastre was born in Madrid on February 20, 1926; his life until the late 1970s was largely spent in that capital city. His boyhood memories are filled with the terror of the Civil War's bombing and killing. In the years studying for his *bachillerato* (school degree), he developed an enthusiasm for the theater and became close friends with several persons who shared that enthusiasm. In 1945, Sastre, Medardo Fraile, José Gordón, Alfonso Paso, José María Palacio, Carlos J. Costas, José Franco, and José María de Quinto founded an experimental theater company, Arte Nuevo (New Art). Sastre wrote two plays of his own in that period: *Uranio 235* [Uranium 235] (1946) and *Cargamento de sueños* [Cargo of Dreams] (1946). And Sastre and Fraile collaborated in the writing of two other plays: *Ha sonado la muerte* [Death Has Knocked] (1945) and *Comedia sonámbula* [Somnambule Comedy] (1947). The group's theoretical discussions, as well as their performances of new and old works such as the unknown play by García Lorca, *Así que pasen cinco años* [As Soon as Five Years Have Passed], were generally recognized in the Madrid press as profoundly innovative.

In 1950, still aiming to bring about theater reform, Sastre and Quinto published the manifesto of the Teatro de Agitación Social (Theater of Social Agitation) in the university student magazine *La hora* [The Hour]. They particularly wanted to introduce works and ideas of important contemporary dramatists of Europe and the United States into Spain. The group was never able to stage plays, however, because despite their claims that they did not want their theater to espouse a single party line, government officials were suspicious of their arguments that art should influence society and soon clamped down. Sastre had begun his university studies at the University of Madrid in 1945, in the area of philosophy; he then enrolled at the University of Murcia, but when he failed to appear for an important exam there, he did not receive the degree.

Sastre's dramatic career, until Francisco Franco's death in 1975, was a series of frustrated attempts to have his work published and performed. *Prólogo patético* [Pathetic Prologue], begun in 1950, was officially prohibited in 1954. *Escuadra hacia la muerte* [The Condemned Squad], probably Sastre's most famous work, was begun in 1951 at the invitation of a London theater director. When that opportunity did not materialize, the work was staged, however, at the María Guerrero Theater in Madrid by actors from the Teatro Popular Universitario [Popular University Theater]. Nevertheless, after three performances, censors closed the production down. General José Moscardó, one of Franco's generals, hero of the siege of the Alcázar in Toledo, had intervened, upset by what looked to him like the play's criticism of the military.

Other plays followed: *El cubo de la basura* [The Garbage Pail] (1951); *El pan de todos* [Community Bread] (1953); *La mordaza* [The Gag] (1954); *Tierra roja* [Red Earth] (1954); *Ana Kleiber* (1955); *La sangre de Dios* [The Blood of God] (1955); *Muerte en el barrio* [Death in the Neighborhood] (1955); *Guillermo Tell tiene los ojos tristes* [Sad Are the Eyes of William Tell] (1955); *El cuervo* [The Raven] (1956): *Asalto nocturno* [Nocturnal Assault] (1959); *En la red* [In the Net] (1959); *La cornada* [Death Thrust] (1959). The plays were variously performed in Madrid, Barcelona, and Valencia but also in Geneva, Athens, and Montevideo; and Sastre began to attract international attention as collections of his works were published abroad (importantly, Losada's 1960 Buenos Aires edition). In 1956 Sastre traveled to Paris on a six-month scholarship from UNESCO (United Nation's Educational Scientific and Cultural Organization) to study theater; in that same year, he was jailed for a short time for political activities.

In 1960 Sastre, together with Quinto, founded the Grupo de Teatro Realista [Group of Realist Theater]. Their efforts, both theoretical and performing, were designed to bring "realism" to the light, escapist entertainment mode, prevailing at that time in Spain. In 1960 Sastre also began his public discussion with Antonio Buero Vallejo on the social possibilities of art. Sastre became identified with the *imposibilista* position—that is, a dramatist should maintain his moral and artistic integrity and remain silent, if necessary, rather than try to force his thought onto the constraints imposed by censorship and official culture.

In the 1960s, 1970s, and throughout the 1980s Sastre continued to produce for the theater, although many of the plays remained unpublished and unperformed until years later. The long list demonstrates the fertility of his imagination: *Oficio de tinieblas* [Office of Darkness] (1967); *M.S.V. o La sangre y la ceniza* [M.S.V. or the Blood and the Ashes] (1962–1965); *El banquete* [The Banquet] (1965); *La taberna fantástica* [The Fantastic Tavern] (1966); *Crónicas romanas* [Roman Chronicles] (1968); *Melodrama* [Melodrama] (1969); *Ejercicios de terror* [Exercises in Terror] (1969–1970); *Las cintas magnéticas* [The Recording Tapes] (1971); *Askatasuna!* (1971); *El camarada oscuro* [The Dark Comrade] (1972); *Ahola no es de leil* [Now Is No Time to Laugh] (1975); *Análisis espectral de un Comando al servicio de la Revolución Proletaria* [Spectral Analysis of a Commado in the Service of the Proletarian Revolution] (1968);

El hijo único de Guillermo Tell [The Only Son of William Tell] (1980); *Aventura en Euskadi* [Adventure in Euskadi] (1982); *Los hombres y sus sombras (Terrores y miserias del IV Reich)* [Men and Their Spirits, Terrors and Miseries of the Fourth Reich] (1982); *El cuento de la reforma o ¿Qué demonios está pasando aquí?* [The Story of Reform or What the Devil Is Happening Here?] (1984) ; *Detrás de algunas puertas o La columna infame* [Behind Some Doors or the Infamous Column] (1986); *Revelaciones inesperadas sobre Moisés* [Unexpected Revelations about Moses] (1988); *Demasiado tarde para Filoctetes* [Too Late for Philoctetes] (1989).

Ahola no es de leil is an interesting example of Sastre's utilization of Chinese working-class culture in Cuba for theatrical inspiration. Sastre had traveled to Cuba several times to participate in cultural events sponsored by Fidel Castro's Casa de las Américas; and this theater piece, set in another cultural world yet with an obvious popular message for home audiences, was performed in a working-class district of Madrid in 1979. Still unperformed, however, were *El banquete, Melodrama, El camarada oscuro, Análisis espectral, Las quitarras, El hijo único, Aventura, El cuento de la reforma, Detrás de algunas puertas, Revelaciones, Demasiado tarde.*

During this time Sastre also sought inspiration in literary subjects from Spain's past: *Tragedia fantástica de la gitana Celestina* [Fantastic Tragedy of the Gypsy Celestina] (1977–1978), *Jenofa Juncal, la roja gitana del monte Jaizkibel* [Jenofa Juncal, The Red Gypsy from Mount Jaizkibel] (1983, based loosely on Vélez de Guevara's *La serrana de la vera* [Mountain Girl from the Border]), *El viaje infinito de Sancho Panza* [The Endless Journey of Sancho Panza] (1983–1984), *Asalto a una ciudad* [Assault on a City] (1992, based on Lope de Vega's *El asalto de Mastrique* [The Siege of Maastricht]). These intertextual rewritings of earlier works are important revisions of Spain's canon.

Similarly, Sastre's translations or free adaptations of several classical and modern works from other national traditions show an increasing curiosity about the process whereby cultures variously create their icons and channel their art. A children's play *El circulito de tiza o Historia de una muñeca abandonada* [The Chalk Circle or Story of an Abandoned Doll] (1962) and *Las guitarras de la vieja Izaskun* [The Guitars of Old Lady Izaskun] (1979) draw on pieces by Bertolt Brecht; *Los últimos días de Emmanuel Kant contados por Ernesto Teodor Amadeo Hoffmann* [The Last Days of Immanuel Kant Told by E.T.A. Hoffman] (1984–1985) refers to those German writers; *¿Dónde estás, Ulalume, dónde estás?* [Where Are You, Ulalume, Where Are You?] (1990) invokes the literary presence of Edgar Allan Poe. The list is long of Sastre's versions of works by Euripides, Lenormand, Ibsen, Strindberg, Langston Hughes, Weiss, Sartre, O'Casey, Pirandello, Büchner, and Wilde. And in his introduction to the Spanish translation of Erwin Piscator's *Political Theater* Sastre states his own approach to the topic (1976).

In those years Sastre also turned to other literary genres. Book-length essays explore ideas he had examined in *Drama y sociedad* [Drama and Society]

(1956). In *Anatomía del realismo* [Anatomy of Realism] (1965, 1974) he presses some of the questions of aesthetic distance that Aristotle, Brecht, and others had posed. In *La revolución y la crítica de la cultura* [Revolution and The Critique of Culture] (1970) he considers the role of art in transforming society. In *Crítica de la imaginación* [Critique of Imagination] (1978) he purses the personal ingredient of the artist's subjectivity in creating and representing a fictitious reality.

Short and long fiction also convey some of the concerns Sastre expressed theatrically. A principal theme is terror. In works like *Las noches lúgubres* [Lugubrious Nights] (1964, 1973), *El paralelo 38* [The 38th Parallel] (1965, 1992), *Flores rojas para Miguel Servet* [Red Flowers for Miguel Servet] (1967, 1982), *El lugar del crimen—Unheimlich* [The Scene of the Crime—Unheimlich] (1982), and *Necrópolis* [Burial Ground] (1993) he perhaps exteriorized some autobiographical experiences. In 1974 Sastre's wife, Eva Forest, was arrested and charged in the ETA (Euskadi Ta Askatasuna [Basque Nation and Freedom]) plot to assassinate Franco's chosen successor, Admiral Luis Carrero Blanco. She remained in jail for two years; and Sastre was also taken into custody, imprisoned for six months in Madrid.

Sastre's jail experience particularly affected his consciousness of the language varieties available to a Spanish writer. In meeting low-life criminal, marginalized types in prison, he saw similarities between their strategies of concealment and Baroque rhetoric. Much of Sastre's theatrical language, prior to that time, was deliberately generic, free of specific dialects; but his theater, written after that date, begins to explore the communicative richness a "realistic" writer might employ to reproduce Spain's verbal culture. Several books of poetry emerge during that period: *Balada de Carabanchel y otros poemas celulares* [Ballad of Carabanchel and Other Cellular Poems] (1976), *El español al alcance de todos* [Spanish within Reach of Everyone] (1978), and *TBO* (1978). And in a long picaresque novel, *Lumpen marginación y jerigonça* [Lumpen, Marginalization and Gibberish] (1980), Sastre plays with the notion of his transgression in bringing to the pages of a book many linguistic forms earlier writers (even Cervantes) claimed to be incorporating but really omitted.

Today Sastre and his wife live in the Basque country in northern Spain.

DRAMATURGY: MAJOR WORKS AND THEMES

Sastre, like Jean-Paul Sartre, is a thinking-man's dramatist. His plays generally take on a tough philosophical question, growing out of his, and his generation's, increasing dissatisfaction with traditional religious belief and ideological presuppositions. The plays' dramatic action, although violence sometimes intervenes, is often a function of the characters' debating of ideas. Over the years, his theatrical production has undergone constant revision as he adjusts his praxis to his changing theories. Yet he remains committed to the dramatist's moral obligation to represent reality in such a way that society is improved by his art.

Escuadra hacia la muerte tells the story of five soldiers and their commanding officer, who have been assigned to guard duty in a no-man's land. As the ordinary, unheroic men face enemy troops, each questions why he has been sent on this mission. When they then murder their commander, who has been harassing them with his taunts and strict discipline, they seal their own doom; they themselves by their action have cut off their one possibility for life since they will surely be court-martialed when their crime is found out. Damned, one commits suicide, another attempts to pass over to the enemy's side, and still another decides to try to survive as a fugitive. Even the commander, theater-viewers understand, has played a role in bringing about his own violent end and is simultaneously executioner and victim, like his soldiers.

Time and place are unspecified in the play so *that the soldiers' situation suggests the watchfulness and fearfulness of the Cold War decades as a nuclear World War Three threatened. The story is also intended to evoke the existential anguish of modern man, propelled into a hostile zone by some mysterious force, condemned for a sin of which he is unaware, and driven to commit actions that foreclose any possibility of salvation.

In *M.S.V. o La sangre y la ceniza*, representative of his middle period, Sastre dramatizes the story of Miguel Servet, an Aragonese physician and theological writer who, in the sixteenth century, was burned alive in John Calvin's Geneva for daring to question Church doctrine. It is historically accurate that both the Catholic Church's Inquisition officials and the Swiss Protestant Reformed churches cooperated to punish the thinker and destroy his books. The drama's main issue, freedom of thought, is at the heart of Sastre's own dilemma at that moment of extreme censorship in Francoist Spain. The play tells how printers and book sellers were forced to disguise a work's authorship, if they even dared to print the book at all.

The play is a carefully researched historical drama, involving one of Spain's intellectual sons who, like Luis Vives and Alfonso and Juan de Valdés, moved in international circles at a critical moment in Europe's development. But Sastre, as is clear from Magda Ruggeri Marchetti's edition, which emphasizes Sastre's sources in Marcelino Menéndez y Pelayo's history of heterodoxy in Spain, is taking on in the play's story the large question of Spain's religious orthodoxy.

In addition to Servet's personal story, long doctrinal discussion of adult baptism and the notion of the Trinity makes the play interesting for many, while alienating others. Technically, *Sangre y ceniza* shows departures from traditional dramaturgy in actors' asides and poetic interludes. In a prefatory note Sastre tells his readers that the work is a *tragicomedia* [tragicomedy] and Servet should not appear to be a hero (the play was unpublished for many years and only read until it came out in an edition after Franco's death). Sastre says he is aware of Brecht's theory of alienation, or distancing, but insists that he moves freely, experimentally, among Greek and modern tragedians to find his own dramatic version of tragedy.

The setting of *La taberna fantástica*, still another work from Sastre's middle period but one that was a long-running hit in Madrid, is a bar in a working-class section of Madrid. The choice of such a popular locale, and contemporaneous history, would seem to promise a more accessible story line and dialogue for Madrid theatergoers. But if *Sangre y ceniza* is exclusionary in its intellectualness, so also is *La taberna fantástica* because in this autobiographical play Sastre moves to documenting the low-life world of *quinquilleros*. Madrid audiences, unfamiliar with the reference, must first of all be made to understand just who these people are; *quinquilleros*, Sastre says in a program note, are those itinerant peddlers and fixers of household utensils who cluster in residential neighborhoods in makeshift dwellings and who are often petty thieves. Sastre sees in their hidden existence the exploitation prosperity is often secretly based on. He is intrigued by their speech for he sees in its inventiveness the same imaginative play that writers attempt. The play's language, then, is a series of obscure codes for respectable audiences who must be willing to tolerate the departure from their bourgeois world; and in fact, when the play was staged, Sastre had to rewrite much of this foreign, yet still Spanish, language so as to make the play acceptable.

Language, the medium by which a society communicates, is an important theme in *Taberna*. The usage that Sastre records—familiar slang, elliptical speech, an omnipresent concern with money and material matters, obscenities, anger, throwaway gossip, drunken talk—indicts earlier literature, which in its so-called realism claimed to represent the Spanish linguistic world fully and honestly. The *Dictionary* of the Royal Spanish Academy is challenged by this work, as well as by Sastre's *lumpen*, because much of their unauthorized vocabulary is absent in that official word list.

But it is the mood of the bar and its clientele that Sastre's play most significantly captures. The men and women are under constant surveillance by the police and civil guards, even as society relies on their labor. Many of them sell their blood in a vampiresque business. Families are broken. One man returns after years of work in Germany, unsure of his wife's faithfulness and, therefore, of the extent of his family; another is too drunk to attend his mother's funeral. Relationships are characterized by abuse. Two men fight and one is murdered. The terror, which the characters feel, blurs the line between reality and fantasy; and Sastre enhances this mood through the use of the allegorical figures of Hunger, Terror, Suffering, Sickness, and Cold, which move across the stage, suggesting their effect on these people's lives.

This view of the underclass is neither romantically nostalgic nor socialistically explicit. Sastre does not study that world so as to argue that individual's can heroically transcend their destiny; nor does he focus on it to find evidence of class solidarity or the promise of social struggle. Rather, the view of suffering at the most basic human level, without, on the one hand, sentimentalizing that life or, on the other hand, degrading it, is a corrective of ideology. The honest theatrical presentation of ugliness and baseness rewrites earlier naturalistic literature and signals a new direction for *vanguardista* art.

CRITICS' RESPONSE

Alfonso Sastre probably will be best remembered for *Escuadra hacia la muerte*. But Gerardo Malla in the edition of *Los hombres y sus sombras* prepared by the University of Murcia (1988) calls *La taberna fantástica* one of "the key texts of Spanish dramatic literature, one to which students and theater professionals will return in order to rediscover one of the most suggestive, profound and brilliant foundations of theater's developments recently: what Sastre calls 'complex tragedy' " [uno de los textos claves de la literature dramática española, sobre el que volverán estudiosos y profesionales del teatro para redescubrir en él los fundamentos de una de las corrientes teatrales más sugerents, profundas y brillantes de los últimos tiempos: la que Sastre denomina "tragedia compleja"] (11).

Sastre's theater, which looks increasingly like unperformable narrative in its self-reflective apparatus of prologues and long scenographic explanations, reflects the same breakdown of generic divisions that is visible in other contemporary literary forms such as the novel. Like Juan Goytisolo, whose bewildering sense of the novel borrows from the linguistic consciousness of the Spanish American BOOM novelists, Sastre attacks inherited linguistic and literary classifications. His later theater especially, perhaps meant for readers rather than viewers, looks like narrative and poetry; his narrative and poetry, written during periods when he was cut off from the possibility of having his theater performed and unrestricted as to performance demands, have theatrical elements.

Sastre's literary reputation, however, rests principally on his theater; and he must be considered in both the contexts of Spanish and world theater. He has acknowledged the influence on his work of the *esperpentos* of Ramón de Valle-Inclán. He has read appreciatively, yet also critically, the celebrated Golden Age dramatists and the *género chico* writers, Ramón de la Cruz and the Alvarez Quintero brothers. He has worked with, and engaged in dialogue with, others of his generation of Spanish playwrights, intellectuals, and academics. But his insistence that Spain participate in international theatrical developments—both theoretical and technical—has been a salutary force in that country's cultural development. Sastre is the only Spanish dramatist of the second half of the twentieth century whose plays are regularly included in anthologies of European and world drama.

Madrid's *literati* have accused Sastre of being too political; others, particularly some Latin American activist artists who often regard theater as *agitprop*, have found him not political enough. In the post-Franco era, which has interpreted liberalism to mean profitable silliness and hedonism, he has regularly been ignored. Although he has had several commercial successes in Madrid in recent years—*La taberna fantástica* (1985), *Los últimos días de Emmanuel Kant* (1990) *El Viaje infinito de Sancho Panza* (1992)—he has remained relatively isolated from official and academic circles, exerting his considerable influence through newspaper and magazine essays, academic contacts, jury work in film and theater festivals, and scriptwriting (his *Miguel Servet. La sangre y la ceniza* was broadcast in seven episodes by Spanish television in 1987–1988). *Ahola no es de leil* was performed in Bordeaux and in a working-class neighborhood of Madrid (1979); *Tragedia fantástica* in Rome (1979) and Barcelona (1985); *Jenofa Juncal* in Leeds (England) in 1988; *Muñeca 88* in Milan (1976) and Madrid (1989); *El viaje infinito* in Seville (1992); *¿Dónde estás, Ulalume* in Alicante (1994); *Los dioses y los cuernos* in Alicante (1995); and *La gitana Celestina* at the University of Burgos in 1999.

In addition to the translations and adaptations of foreign works, which are listed below in their published form, Sastre has written the following unpublished and mostly unperformed plays: *El cobarde* (Lenormand, 1950); *El tiempo es un sueño* (Lenormand, 1951); *La p . . . respectuosa* (Sartre, 1968); *A puerta cerrada* (Sartre, 1968); *Muertos sin sepultura* (Sartre, 1968); *Las troyanas* (Sartre, 1968); *Trotsky en el exilio* (Weiss, 1969); *El seguro* (Weiss, 1970); *Liolá* (Pirandello, 1970); *Las moscas* (Sartre, 1970); *Los secuestrados de Altona* (Sartre, 1972); and *Hölderlin* (Weiss, 1972).

Time and time again Sastre has been passed over by the Royal Spanish Academy for membership in that body. Nevertheless, he is widely recognized and admired internationally; and it is probable that future generations of Spaniards will come to recognize the breath and depth of his literary production and that, along with Valle-Inclán and García Lorca, Sastre will be remembered as one of the major Spanish dramatic writers of the twentieth century.

AWARDS AND DISTINCTIONS

In 1985 Sastre was awarded the Premio Nacional de Teatro [National Theater Prize] for *La taberna fantástica*; he won it again in 1993 for his unperformed play *Jenofa Juncal*. In 1986 he was awarded the prize "El espectador y la crítica" (The Spectator and the Critic) for *La taberna fantástica*.

BIBLIOGRAPHY

Editions and Translations

Sastre's works are partially available in his *Obras completas.* Vol. I. Madrid: Aguilar, 1967. Editorial Hiru (Hondarribia) is presently dedicated to publishing all of Sastre's works.

Anna Kleiber. Trans. Leonard C. Pronko. In *The New Theatre of Europe*, ed. Robert W. Corrigan. New York: Dell, 1962.
Anna Kleiber (selections) and *Drama and Society* (selections). Trans. Leonard C. Pronko. In *The Modern Theatre*, ed. Robert W. Corrigan. New York: Macmillan, 1964.
Death Thrust and *Drama and Society* (selections). Trans. Leonard C. Pronko. In *Masterpieces of the Modern Spanish Theatre*, ed. Robert W. Corrigan. New York: Collier Books, 1964.

Pathetic Prologue. Trans. Leonard C. Pronko. *Modern International Drama* I.2 (March 1968): 195–215.

Sad Are the Eyes of William Tell. Trans. Leonard C. Pronko. In *The New Wave of Spanish Drama*, ed. George Wellswarth. New York: New York University Press, 1970. 165–321.

Le notti logubri. Rome: Editori Riuniti, 1976.

The Abandoned Doll, Young Billy Tell. Trans. Carys Evans-Corrales. University Park, PA: Estreno. Collection Contemporary Plays, 10, 1996.

Theater

Teatro español. Ed. F. C. Sainz de Robles. Madrid: Aguilar, 1956, 1961, 1962, 1968. Volumes for 1954–1955, 1959–1960, 1960–1961, 1966–1967. Includes texts and critical reviews of *La mordaza, Escuadra hacia la muerte, En la red*, and *Oficio de tinieblas.*

Teatro (Escuadra hacia la muerte, Tierra roja, Ana Kleiber, Muerte en el barrio, Guillermo Tell tiene los ojos tristes, El cuervo). Buenos Aires: Losada, 1960.

Cargamento de sueños, Prólogo patético, Asalto nocturno. Madrid: Taurus, 1964.

Guillermo Tell tiene los ojos tristes, Muerte en el barrio, Asalto nocturno. Madrid: E.M.E.S.A., 1967.

Escuadra hacia la muerte y La mordaza. Ed. Farris Anderson. Madrid: Castalia, 1975.

La sangre y la ceniza y Crónicas romanas. Ed. Magda Ruggeri Marchetti. Madrid: Cátedra, 1979.

Teatro político (Askatasuna!, El camarada oscuro, Análisis espectral de un Comando al servicio de la Revolución Proletaria). Donostia: Hordago, 1979.

Ahola no es de leil. Madrid: Ed. Vox, 1980.

Tragedia fantástica de la gitana Celestina o Historia de amor y de magia con algunas citas de la famosa tragico-media de Calixto y Melibea. Primer Acto 192 (1982): 63–102.

El hijo único de Guillermo Tell. Estreno 9 (1983): T3–T8.

Asalto a una ciudad. Junta de Castilla y León: Consejería de Cultura y Bienestar Social, 1988.

Los hombres y sus sombras. Intro. Gerardo Malla. Murcia: Universidad de Murcia, 1988.

Los últimos días de Emmanuel Kant contados por Ernesto Teodoro Amadeo Hoffmann. Madrid: Centro de Documentación Teatral, 1989.

La taberna fantástica y Tragedia fantástica de la gitana Celestina. Ed. Mariano de Paco. Madrid: Cátedra, 1990.

Revelaciones inesperadas sobre Moisés: a propósito de algunos aspectos de su vida privada. Hondarribia: Hiru, 1991.

El viaje infinito de Sancho Panza. Bilbao: Hiru, 1991.

El banquete. Bilbao: Hiru, 1991.

Muñeca 88. Con citas textuales y referencia de fondo a "El círculo de tiza caucasiano" de Bertolt Brecht. Hondarribia: Hiru, 1991.

Teatro de vanguardia (Comedia sonámbula, Uranio 235, Cargamento de sueños). Hondarribia: Hiru, 1992.

Análisis de un comando. Hondarribia: Hiru, 1993.

Cuatro dramas vascos (Askatasuna!, Las quitarras de la Vieja Izaskun, Aventura en Euskadi, La columna infame). Hondarribia: Hiru, 1993.

El viaje infinito de Sancho Panza. Madrid: Sociedad General.

Dioses y los cuernos (sobre "Anfitrión" de Tito Maccio Plauto). Hondarribia: Hiru, 1995.

Melodrama (El cuento de la reforma). Hondarribia: Hiru, 1995.

Teoría de las catástrofes. Lluvia de ángeles sobre París: una sinfonía tonta: comedia en siete cuadros y un epílogo. Hondarribia: Hiru, 1995.

Asesinato de la luna llena: drama policíaco-psicológico. Hondarribia: Hiru, 1996.

Crimen al otro lado del espejo. Hondarribia, Hiru, 1996.

Han matado a Prokopius. Hondarribia: Hiru, 1996.

Evangelio de Drácula. Hondarribia: Hiru, 1997. Published originally as "El *Evangelio de Drácula*" horror y poesía, un capricho. Lo escribió Alfonso Sastre en la prisión de Caravanchel desde el 14 al 19 de mayo de 1975. Evasión. . . . de la cárcel. ¡Fuga ay imaginaria! In *Camp de l'arpa*. Barcelona, no. 33 (1976).

Adaptations

Asalto a una ciudad, de Lope de Vega. Versión de Sastre. Hondarribia: Hiru, n.d.

Búnbury, Opereta de Sastre sobre "La importancia de llamarse Ernesto" de Oscar Wilde. Hondarribia: Hiru, n.d.

¿Dónde estás, Ulalume, dónde estás? Fantástica reconstrucción de los últimos días de Edgar Alan Poe. Hondarribia: Hiru, n.d.

Ejercicios de terror. Hondarribia: Hiru, n.d.

El cuento de la reforma y Melodrama. Hondarribia: Hiru, n.d.

Historia de Woyzeck de Georg Büchner. Versión de Sastre y Pablo Sorozábal. Hondarribia: Hiru, n.d.

¡Irlanda, Irlanda! de Sean O'Casey. Versión de Sastre. Hondarribia: Hiru, n.d.

Jenofa Juncal, la roja gitana del monte Jaizkibel. Bilbao: Hiru, 1992.

La dama del mar, de Henrik Ibsen. Versión de Sastre. Hondarribia: Hiru, n.d.

La gitana Celestina. Hondarribia: Hiru, n.d.

La persecución y asesinato de Jean Paul Marat, de Peter Weiss. Versión de Sastre. Hondarribia: Hiru, n.d.

Los acreedores, de August Strindberg. Versión de Sastre. Hondarribia: Hiru, n.d.

Los hombres y sus sombras. Hondarribia: Hiru, n.d.

Medea de Eurípedes; versión para un teatro popular del siglo XX. Hondarribia: Hiru, 1992.

Mulato: drama de Langston Hughes, versión libre. Hondarribia: Hiru, 1992.

Noche de huéspedes y Mockinpott, de Peter Weiss. Versiones de Sastre sobre la traducción de Pablo Sorozábal. Hondarribia: Hiru, n.d.

Rosas rojas para mí, de Sean O'Casey. Versión de Sastre. Hondarribia: n.d.

Narrative

El paralelo 38. Madrid: LNP, 1965.

El paralelo 38. Madrid: Alfaguara, 1965.

Flores rojas para Miguel Servet. Madrid: Rivadeneyra, 1967: 2d ed. Barcelona: Argos Vergara, 1982.

Las noches lúgubres. Pról. Aurora de Albornoz. Madrid: Biblioteca Júcar, 1973.

Lumpen, marginación y jerigonça. Madrid: Legasa, 1980.

El lugar del crimen—Unheimlich. Barcelona: Argos Vergara, 1982.
Noches lúgubres. Madrid: Emiliano Escolar, 1982.
Las noches lúgubres. I. Las noches del Espíritu Santo. Madrid: Valdemar, 1989.
Necrópolis. Madrid: Grupo Libro 88, 1993.
Necrópolis, o Los amigos de Bram Stoker: novela. Madrid: Grupo 88, 1994.
Historias de California. Hondarribia: Hiru, 1996. (Primera edición en gallego. Santiago
   de Compostela: Ed. Laioventu, 1994).

Essays

Drama y sociedad. Madrid: Taurus, 1956.
Anatomía del realismo. Barcelona: Seix Barral, 1965; 2d ed. 1974.
La revolución y la crítica de la cultura. Barcelona: Grijalbo, 1970.
"Prólogo" to *Teatro político* by Erwin Piscator, trans. Salvador Vila. Madrid: Ed. Ayuso,
   1976. vii–xxi.
Crítica de la imaginación. Barcelona: Grijalbo, 1978.
"El lugar paradójico de la escritura teatral." In *Hispanismen omkring Sven Skydsgaard:
   Studieri i spansk og portugisisk sprog, litteratur og kultur til minde om Sven
   Skydsgaard*, ed. John Kuhlmann Madsen. Copenhagen: Romansk Inst., 1981.
   391–394.
Escrito en Euskadi. Madrid: Revolución, 1982.
"El éxito en el teatro: ¿Un incidente?" *Gestos* 2.3 (1987) : 132.
"Reflexiones sobre un teatro que no existe." *Confluencia* 2 (1987): 3–10.
"Teoría del teatro: El estado de la cuestión." *Gestos* 2.4 (1987): 37–46.
"Modesta aportación a la crítica de una verbena." *Hispania* 75 (1992): 852–855.
Prolegómenos a un teatro del porvenir. Bilbao: Hiru, 1992.
¿Dónde estoy yo? Hondarribia: Hiru, 1994.
"Unas conversaciones—memorables? Sobre la ilusión trágica." *Primer Acto* 267 (Janu-
   ary–February 1997): 7–10.

Poetry

Balada de Carabanchel y otros poemas celulares. Paris: Ruedo Ibérico, 1976.
El español al alcance de todos. Madrid: Sensemayá Chororó, 1978.
TBO. Madrid: Zero-Zyx, 1978.
Antología de la Libertad. Madrid: Ed. Revolutiôn, 1983. 137–152.
Alfonso Sastre (cassette with script). Donostia: Garabaketak Argitaratzaile Banatzaile,
   n.d.
Vida del hombre invisible por él mismo. Madrid: Ediciones Endymion, 1994.

Critical Studies

AA.VV. *Alfonso Sastre. Teatro*. Madrid: Taurus, El mirlo blanco, 1964.
Anderson, Farris. *Alfonso Sastre*. New York: Twayne, 1971.
Anthropos 126 (November 1991). Monograph Issue, "Alfonso Sastre. Tragedia y realismo
   social."
Ascunce, José Angel, ed. *Once ensayos en busca de un autor: Alfonso Sastre*. Hondar-
   ribia: Hiru, 1999.

Bryan, T. Avril. *Censorship and Social Conflict in the Spanish Theatre: The Case of Alfonso Sastre*. Washington, DC: University Press of America, 1982.

Caudet, Francisco. *Crônica de una marginación. Conversaciones con Alfonso Sastre.* Madrid: Ediciones de la Torre, 1984.

Cramsie, Hilde F. *Teatro y censura en la España franguista: Sastre, Muñiz y Ruibal.* New York: Peter Lang, 1984.

Cuadernos El Público 38 (December 1988). Monograph Issue, "Alfonso Sastre. Noticia de una ausencia."

Doll, Eileen J. "Hacia el tiempo y el espacio míticos: El Retablo de Valle-Inclán y Las cintas magnéticas de Sastre." In *De lo particular a lo uníversal: El teatro español del siglo XX y su contexto*, ed. John P. Gabriele. Frankfurt, Madrid: Vervuert, Iberoamerica, 1994. 68–75.

Donahue, Francis. *Alfonso Sastre, dramaturgo y preceptista.* Buenos Aires: Plus Ultra, 1973.

Estruch, Joan. *Edición, estudio preliminar y notas de* Escuadra hacia la muerte. Madrid: Alhambra, 1986.

Forest, Eva, ed. *Alfonso Sastre o la ilusión trágica.* Hondarribia: Hiru, 1997.

Forys, Marsha. *Antonio Buero Vallejo and Alfonso Sastre. An Annotated Bibliography.* London: Scarecrow Press, 1988.

Giuliano, William. *Buero Vallejo, Sastre y el teatro de su tiempo.* New York: Las Américas, 1971.

Hardison Londré, Felicia. "The Theatrical Gap between Alfonso Sastre's Criticism and His Later Plays." In *The Contemporary Spanish Theater*, ed. Martha T. Halsey and Phyllis Zatlin. Lanham, MD: University Press of America, 1988. 49–61.

Harper, Sandra N. "The Problematics of Identity in *Jenofa Juncal, La roja gitana del Monte Jaizkibel* by Alfonso Sastre." In *Entre Actos: Diálogos sobre Teatro Español entre siglos*, ed. Martha T. Halsey and Phyllis Zatlin. University Park, PA: *Estreno*, 1999. 247–258.

Isasi Angulo, Amando C. *Diâlogos del teatro español de la posguerra.* Madrid: Ayuso, 1974.

Johnson, Anita L. "El mito en el teatro último de Alfonso Sastre: Metateatro, intertextualidad, y parodia." In *Entre Actos: Diálogos sobre Teatro Español entre siglos*, ed. Martha T. Halsey and Phyllis Zatlin. University Park, PA: *Estreno*, 1999. 259–263.

Menchacatorre, Félix. "La taberna fantástica de Alfonso Sastre. Del simple sainete a la tragedia compleja." In *Actas del X Congreso de la Asociación de Hispanistas*, ed. Antonio Vilanova. Barcelona: Promociones y Pubs. Universitarias, 1992. 105–110.

Naald, Anje C. Van der. *Alfonso Sastre, dramaturgo de la revolución.* New York: Anaya, Las Américas, 1973.

Paco, Mariano de. *Alfonso Sastre.* Murcia: Universidad de Murcia, 1993.

———. "El teatro de Alfonso Sastre." In *Teatro español contemporáneo: Autores y tendencias*, ed. Alfonso de Toro and Wilfried Floeck. Kassel: Reichenberger, 1995. 147–166.

———. "El teatro de Alfonso Sastre en la sociedad española." *Boletín de la Fundación Federico García Lorca.* 19–20 (1996): 271–283.

Pallottini, Michele. *La saggistica di Alfonso Sastre. Teoria letteraria e materialismo dialettico (1950–1980).* Milan: Franco Angeli, 1983.

Pasquariello, Anthony M. "Alfonso Sastre y *Escuadra hacia la muerte.*" *Hispanófila* 15 (1962): 57–63.

Primer Acto 242 (January–February 1992). Monograph Issue, "Alfonso Sastre frente a la tradición teatral española."

Ruggeri Marchetti, Magda. *Il teatro di Alfonso Sastre*. Roma: Bulzoni, 1975.

Schwartz, Kessel. "Posibilismo and imposibilismo. The Buero Vallejo-Sastre Polemic." *Revista Hispánica Moderna* 34 (1968): 436–445.

Scialdone, Pierluigi. *Caratteri e figure miliebri nel teatro di Alfonso Sastre*. Florence: Università degli Studi, 1984.

Seator, Lynette. "Alfonso Sastre's Homenaje a Kierkegaard: *La sangre de Dios.*" *Romance Notes* 15 (1974): 546–555.

"Sobre Sastre (six accounts of the arrest and imprisonment of Sastre and Forest)." *Estreno* 1 (1975): 41–49.

Soto, Isabel. "Translation as Understanding: Alfonso Sastre's Adaptation of Mulatto." *Langston Hughes Review* 15 (1997): 1, 13–23.

Spang, Kurt. "Alfonso Sastre y el teatro épico de Bertolt Brecht." In *Europa en España-España en Europa (Simposio Internacional de Literatura Comparada*, by AA.VV. Barcelona: PPU-Universidad de Aquisgrán–Universidad de Navarra, 1990. 255–271.

Suplementos Anthropos 30 (January 1992). Monograph Issue; "Alfonso Sastre. De la polémica al ensayo."

Villegas, Juan. "Alfonso Sastre y la modernización del teatro español." *Anales de la Universidad de Chile* 125 (1967): 27–47.

———. "La sustancia metafísica de la tragedia y su función social: *Escuadra hacia la muerte* de Alfonso Sastre." *Symposium* 21 (1967): 253–263.

Vogeley, Nancy. "Alfonso Sastre on Alfonso Sastre" [Interview]. *Hispania* 64 (1981): 459–466.

MIGUEL DE UNAMUNO
(1864–1936)

Robert L. Nicholas

BIOGRAPHY

Miguel de Unamuno is, arguably, the dominant talent of Spanish letters of the twentieth century. Born in the Basque Country in 1864, he finished his doctorate in Madrid in 1888 and won a chair at the venerable University of Salamanca in 1891. This ancient Castilian city was to be his home for nearly a half century, whether as professor of Greek, president of the university, political persona, or famous writer. Indeed, it was there he died on New Year's Eve in 1936, under house arrest by the Nationalists.

This final travail was hardly the first for don Miguel. He had been fired from the presidency of the university on two occasions and even exiled from Spain by the dictator Primo de Rivera. It was this latter event that placed the public mantel once and for all on this aging professor of Greek. Deposed by the regime to the Island of Fuerteventura in 1923, Unamuno was shortly flown from there to France by an English pilot. After several months in Paris, the exiled writer moved to Hendaye, to be closer to his homeland. Although by that time he was free to return home, Unamuno vowed not to touch Spanish soil again until the dictator was gone. After his return to Spain in 1930, he was reinstated as president of the University of Salamanca and hailed as a national hero by the Republican regime. By 1936, however, the political situation had so deteriorated that when Francisco Franco and three other generals rebelled that summer, Unamuno lent them his support. It was a short-lived alliance, for the Nationalists' repression soon provoked his vociferous denunciation, which, in turn, resulted in his house arrest.

When he died at the age of seventy-two, Unamuno left an immense literary legacy, having authored dozens of books and literally thousands of pages of articles and commentaries on a myriad of topics. A voracious reader and writer, his interests ranged from Kierkegaard to Ibsen, from Pirandello to Japanese origami, from Schopenhauer and Nietzsche to Freud and Jung. He cultivated every literary genre: novels, plays, poetry, short stories, essays, journalistic articles, prose poems, critical commentaries, personal observations. The topics that captivated him sprang from every aspect of living but centered on the essential definition of the human personality as it struggles to transcend its historical and cultural context. Indeed, the dialectical relationship between the I and the Other became the fundamental vehicle for his exploration of the existential self.

DRAMATURGY: MAJOR WORKS AND THEMES

Although Unamuno's novels, beginning with his first so-called *nivola* in 1902, became the major stage for his experimental probing of the human creative psyche, the literal stage held a keen interest for him throughout his entire career.[1] He wrote thirteen plays, often in pairs and generally every few years. Consider the following chronology:

1880: *The Question of Galabasa* [El custión de Galabasa], (a short but incomplete popular farce)

1898–1899: *The Sphinx* [La esfinge] and *The Blindfold* [La venda]

1909: *Princess Donna Lambra* [La princesa doña Lambra] (farce) and *The Deceased Woman* [La difunta] (short popular realistic play)

1910: *The Past that Returns* [El pasado que vuelve] and *Phaedra* [Fedra]

1921–1922: *Solitude* [Soledad] and *Rachel Enchained* [Raquel encadenada]

1926: *Shadows of Sleep* [Sombras de sueño] and *The Other* [El otro]

1929: *Brother John or the World Is a Stage* [El hermano Juan o el mundo es teatro]

1933: A version of Seneca's *Medea*

Don Miguel's interest in theater was not the result of success in staging his plays, for they were not usually favored by critics, entrepreneurs, or the public. He belonged to no theatrical "in" group; quite the contrary, he purposely distanced himself from stage professionals who, according to him, wasted time in salons fawning over each other for favors. Moreover, he refused to create roles for particular actors and actresses. Audiences were also problematic for him since their taste was rarely uplifted by the customary theatrical fare then in vogue. Unamuno insisted that it was necessary "to educate the public so it [would] like bare tragedy" [educar al público para que guste del desnudo trágico] ("Exordio a *Fedra*" 401).

The "naked" quality of Unamuno's plays is manifested in the following ways, according to Spanish critic Francisco Ruiz Ramón (1) the suppression of scenic ornamentation, (2) the suppression of rhetorical oratory, (3) a minimum number of characters, (4) the presentation of essential "passions," (5) schematic action (Ruiz Ramón 82). Through this "phenomenon of esthetic reduction" Unamuno attempts to return to the essence of theater: the spoken word, not in a rhetorical, florid sense but with poignant meanings that emerge from simple repetitions and heartfelt utterances.

Ruiz Ramón attributes the failure of Unamuno's plays to their excessive nakedness, that is, the very schematic nature of their plots. He may well be correct; certainly no one can dispute the fact that most of Unamuno's plays were "failures," at least in the conventional sense. And yet I get the sense that don Miguel was tinkering with something so fundamental in his plays—so radically new—that we may have missed it. I am referring to his use of dialogue.

It has long been known, of course, that his novels eschewed realism's emphasis on external detail and historical reference in favor of symbolical systems and dialectical structures. In his eagerness to plunge deeply within the human personality, he turned to dialogue. This is not surprising, for dialogue provides a propitious "stage" for provoking and probing the clash of human personalities.[2]

The word *dialogue* suggests, of course, a philosophical and literary tradition dating from the *Dialogues* of Plato to medieval debates, from the colloquia of the Renaissance to the "dialogical" studies of recent critics. Philosophically it points toward the rational principle according to which the universe is developed and governed; theologically it underscores the divine "Word," incarnated in Jesus Christ; and artistically it evokes, among other examples, the Cervantine literary model. In *Mist* [Niebla] and other novels such as *Abel Sánchez, Three Exemplary Novels and a Prologue* [Tres novelas ejemplares y un prólogo], *Aunt Tula* [La tía Tula], and *How to Make a Novel* [Cómo se hace una novela] Unamuno not only juxtaposes two interlocutors but, also, contrary ideologies, postures, and images from the traditions cited. There is his opposition of protagonists and antagonists (Augusto-Eugenia, Joaquin-Abel, Raquel-Berta, Gertrudis-Rosa), of themes (being-knowing, dying-"being unborn," I-other, art-science), of symbols and images (lake-mountain, surface-depths, sea-fountain head), of titles (*Nothing Less Than All of a Man* [Nada menos que todo un hombre], *Saint Emmanuel Good, Martyr* [San Manuel Bueno, mártir]). Absolutely everything in Unamuno's works is presented in terms of its otherness. In a figurative sense, the structural essence of dialogue permeates all his themes and techniques. And in a literal sense, one character always speaks and another listens.

Such continuous dialogue assures that ideas never become disconnected from flesh and blood individuals who are, in fact, creating themselves as they speak. As the living word enters their mouths, they are filled with the mythical breath of life. In a sense, dialogue creates the present, all at once, without need for historical antecedents or referents—hence, its existential importance.

In Unamuno's works a character's struggle to form and to exceed himself always develops on the basis of the creative word; thus, what a character says in a given moment suggests what has been, what will be, and in the tension created by these two implicit constants, what *is*, that dynamically and creatively is being forged with every syllable spoken. For Unamuno, therefore, dialogue is never utilitarian, comic, or ironic; it is never merely functional in order to advance some intrigue, make a transition, or fulfill this or that social formula. It represents in itself the drama of living and of surviving. In the *nivola* history is born from the present and not the reverse. This is the true secret of "nivol-esque" dialogue. The past and the future become actualized in the drama that unfolds before our eyes, seemingly at the very instant it is being created. Una-muno seeks to immerse the reader in his own existential drama, to converse with himself, to become enmeshed in a trajectory between his I (subject) and the other (object) as he discovers and defines himself through his literary "liv-ing" (i.e., his reading).[3]

Unamuno's lifelong attraction to theater is based in part, I would suggest, on his desire to engage, totally and unconditionally, the individual spectator in the drama of being that is central to his other writings. Indeed, by the mediation of flesh and blood actors, don Miguel surely hoped to make this human "drama" even more compelling in his plays than in his novels.

Certainly such fundamental questioning of human identities and motives also lies at the core of all his theatrical probing. The debate underlying the action of *The Blindfold* [La venda] juxtaposes "truth that is life" and "life that is truth." Faith and reason are the means advanced by opposing characters for achieving one or the other. In *The Past That Returns* [El pasado que vuelve] revolutionary, utopian goals contrast with reactionary, practical outlooks, an opposition that becomes personalized by its identification with alternating generations of one family. Both *Phaedra* [Fedra] and *Rachel Enchained* [Raquel encadenada] fea-ture heroines who "save" themselves by death and rebellion. After her suicide Phaedra is viewed by her stepson as a "martyred saint" because she "knew how to die." Love, impossible in life, became at least admiration in death. Rachel experiences an existential "lack of being" because her husband denies her the essential achievement of her womanhood, childbirth. To free herself she must break the social "chains" that bind her to her husband. *The Sphinx* [La esfinge] and *Solitude* [Soledad] both offer a series of essential oppositions: public versus private life, glory and solitude, struggle (and death) versus calm (and life), and so on. The protagonists of both plays internalize this conflict as they struggle to fulfill themselves. The tragedy of their situations springs from the impossi-bility of making such a selection, because the moment a choice is made, an inherent part of the ego is irrevocably lost. The protagonist of *The Sphinx* wants to believe but cannot; he is obsessed by the idea of death and tormented by the possibility of nothingness after death.

All Unamuno's dramatic experiments develop along structural lines implicit in the dialectical process described above. Character oppositions are reflected in symbolic actions, and images replicate, in turn, the essential thematic dichoto-mies. In a sense, plots build incrementally, one oppositional construct subsuming its predecessor in a manner reminiscent of the Chinese boxes that so fascinated the author. In this way, outer realities cede continually to inner realms where, Unamuno would insist, the true drama of existence always transpires.

The Other [El otro], first written in 1926 but revised at least twice before its final version appeared in 1932, is considered one of Unamuno's best plays. It was also one of his favorites. And unlike his other plays, it was performed numerous times: in Berlin in 1928 or 1929, in Madrid in 1932 (at least twenty performances), and in Buenos Aires in 1934 (more than fifty performances) (Paraíso de Leal 188). I shall examine it in some depth here in order to illustrate many of the thematic and technical concerns typical of his other theatrical offerings and also to appreciate its innovations for themselves.

The play's plot is simple enough: One brother killed his identical twin because they both loved the same woman. However, along the way there may have been a change of identities: Which brother killed which? The remaining twin, overcome with remorse, has "internalized" his dead brother (i.e., subsumed in his own being the victim's essence). In the process he has lost any sense of self; consequently, he insists on referring to himself only as the Other.

Stripped of all self-awareness and plunged into a labyrinth of despair, the Other attempts to avoid other men since they mirror for him the human essence he wishes to forget. His madness has far-reaching repercussions, for carrying a "corpse" within casts him as victim and executioner at once and also underscores his "death in life" in contrast to his brother's "death in death." Murder is viewed as self-defense, the murderer is the victim, and being a victim is a way to gain vengeance. When confronted with Laura and Damiana, the respective wives of the twins Cosme and Damián, the Other is unable or unwilling to say which is his wife. Unlike the mythological Furies, the two women are not so intent on punishing this crime at the instigation of the victim, whoever that is, as they are in protecting their own vested interests. Laura expresses a death wish; whether homicide or suicide, she would die for the Other since he killed for her; but Damiana opts for life; she is expecting twins.[4] However, the double birth will perpetuate not just hate but also self-hate. As a consequence, the permanence of death in life is assured.

To know oneself is the necessary antecedent to being known by others. Thus spiritual envy, the abiding desire *not* to be forgotten by the Other (God), is also related, in a fundamental way, to one's attitude toward self. Hatred of the other is irrevocably tied up with hatred of self. The problem here, as in all of Unamuno's plays, is distinctly human, never abstract. And in a human sense, who introduces death into life? Who continues introducing it? Is God the Other who kills us and, for that very reason, also kills Himself? In this play the Other finally ends his agonized soul searching by suicide, an act that he externalizes by claiming that "the Other is killing me." Madness thus gives way to what might be called a "mystery," a sublime mystery since it fuses the Other's total human awareness with destiny and fate, the two names of God, in the words of the playwright (830).[5]

Notwithstanding the use of biblical symbols, the basic problem is actual—here and now, vital and essential. It lacks a historical sense—"it is not something for reading" [no es cosa de lecturas], insists Laura (806). In the epilogue the male doctor (representing knowledge) desires to know the story; he seeks a collective solution, while the female Ama (representing being, existence) intuits the individual mystery and insists on not disturbing it.

The dialogue in *The Other* is at once narrative, dramatic, and lyric. There are few stage directions, so there is not even the traditional outlet for discursive (narrative) commentary. Moreover, the essence of most of the dramatic encounters in this play are fundamentally narrative, as one character relates past events to another: In the play's first scene the doctor don Juan sketches the basic mystery of the Other's madness for Ernesto; in scene II Laura reveals more details of her husband's obsession to her brother; in scene III the Other agrees to relate his secret to his brother-in-law and, in scene IV, tells of the corpse in the basement. The resulting feel is that of a whirlpool. We are pulled more downward than forward, it seems, by the multiple versions of the Other's story, augmented in the repeated variations that successively constitute this dramatic unfolding. And, yet, rather than revealing character, baring motives, and stripping away successive layers of intentions and motives, such an "unfolding" actually complicates and intensifies the drama's essential mystery.

Indeed, as it proceeds, the play acquires additional layers of meaning through the following techniques (1) the "circular" structure arising from the repetition of stories and conversations, (2) the doubling of the central characters, (3) the ontological repercussions of the I/Other opposition, (4) the shifting of blame away from the perpetrator of the crime to those with ultimate responsibility (i.e., the Father who created them in the first place, the women who nurtured them, and those who demand from him/them the inevitable son). Underlying all of this, of course, is the allegorical echo of the biblical Jacob and Esau but also Cain and Abel. The story ceases being a "murder mystery" as the intrigue increasingly becomes an "existential mystery."

Because of its incessant sameness, the story acquires a peculiar movement— not entirely dramatic or narrative. Whatever linear movement it has seems illusory as it doubles back on itself time and again, pulling us downward while also seeming to push us upward. The Other examines himself from within as others scrutinize him from without. It is as if the vortex in which he is trapped were simultaneously concave and convex. In one he is the subject probing ever more deeply the concealed recesses of his soul, while in the other he is the examined object, flung ever outward from the ontological center of his existence.[6]

This kind of "vertical" development works for Unamuno as symbolic structure. Moreover, it is a radically innovative approach to theater. However, it may be too subtle for its own theatrical good. The repetition required to pull off the "feel" I have just described ends up seeming more narrative than dramatic, more discursive than poetic.

Like the human personality, every instant of this unfolding means to feel proactive and reactive, forward looking, and retrospective. This is intended to be a uniquely existential play, for its dramatic "ground of being"—its quintessential focus on the present—embodies, at every instant, both the past and the future. Such an experiment is probably destined to fail from the moment of its conception. Most theatergoers—certainly those of the 1920s in Spain—were ill prepared for such demanding experimentation. Indeed, the ideal audience for such a symbolic, cathartic journey might be only a professor of Greek literature. And this brings up, perhaps, the most telling characteristic of this dramatic undertaking: More than a drama for an audience, *The Other*, like so many Unamunian experiments, is a vehicle for self-exploration and expression. In this sense, it is a lyric poem, a haunting and obsessive work that hammers out its theme like a heart that, from one perspective at least, could be viewed as little more than a monotonous piece of machinery. More than a work for seeing or reading, *The Other* seems most appropriate for reflection. Once viewed or read, this play unleashes a torrent of thoughts. Even in this its circular structure is at work, forcing the spectator or reader to expand beyond (forwards and backwards) from the initial impression. Frankly, this is the most exciting dimension of this creative venture. And yet one must first get by that requisite viewing or reading! And that may well be the reason why Unamuno's theater has remained from inception until now curious museum pieces, at once behind their time and ahead of it. They leaped over their many predecessors (realistic, romantic, etc.) to embrace the essentials of Greek tragedy. But in so doing they also jumped ahead, daringly close to the nihilistic repetitions of what we now know as the theater of the absurd. Consider the obsessive, circular behavior and speech of a character from Thomas Beckett or Fernando Arrabal. Both these authors would seem Unamunian, to some extent, if placed two or three generations earlier. In a sense, this work allows us to witness Unamuno's basic artistic intuition as he struggles with form and content; he delves into the past for the legends and myths that make us what we are while, at the same time, anticipating forms that will not be accepted for years.

CRITICS' RESPONSE

Unamuno did not like to publish his plays before they were performed. But since performances for them were often rare, their publication was also irregular, hence the relatively scarce criticism of his works during the early decades of the century. Manuel García Blanco did the most to publish and preserve Unamuno's theatrical works; a 1954 anthology edited by him contained *Phaedra, Solitude, Rachel Enchained*, and *Medea* (the latter three had never been published previously). In 1959 he collected all of Unamuno's plays into one volume. In the accompanying introduction he probes the genesis of each play, details attempts to perform them, summarizes key critical responses (often revealed in Unamuno's correspondence), and offers pertinent quotes from numerous journalistic reviews and articles.

Perhaps the most conclusive analyses of Unamuno's plays, in placing them in the Spanish theatrical tradition and exploring them individually as dramatic experiments, were carried out in the 1970s by the noted theatrical critic Francisco Ruiz Ramón. He suggested that the real importance of Unamuno's dramas resides in their gaining access to the inner "theater" of each spectator's conscience.

In that way the spectator ceases being [a spectator] in order to become something like a co-protagonist or co-agonist of the drama, of his own. In effect, Unamuno conceives his theater in such a way and constitutes it in such a form that the persona of the character and that of the spectator are not separated, but centered in the same dramatic unity. The stage setting does not exist, rigorously, as a physical space, but as a metaphysical space where character and spectator are included. The character gives himself over to death or to dreams without having overcome the internal division, and it is the spectator who must carry out the synthesis.

[De esa manera el espectador deja de serlo para convertirse en algo así como co-protagonista o co-agonista del drama, del drama suyo propio. En efecto, Unamuno concibe de tal manera su teatro y lo constituye de tal forma que la persona del personaje y la del espectador no están separadas, sino radicadas en la misma unidad dramática. El escenario no existe, en rigor, como lugar físico, sino como espacio metafísico donde personaje y espectador estám incluídos. El personaje se entrega a la muerte o al sueño sin haber superado la división interior, y es el espectador quien debe realizar la síntesis.] (Ruiz Ramón 93)

In his 1993 edition of *The Other*, Ricardo de la Fuente Ballesteros offers a succinct but thorough account of Unamuno's biography as it develops in conjunction with his published works. This critic intersperses fascinating anecdotal material into his summaries and analyses: don Miguel's contacts with Pérez Galdós, his support of the allied cause in World War I, a previously unpublished letter regarding the dictator Primo de Rivera, and so on. His bibliography (general, theatrical, and specific to *The Other*) is very complete and up-to-date. In his analysis of this work de la Fuente compares the various extant manuscripts and editions of the play as he traces its philosophical roots and design to Schopenhauer.

AWARDS AND DISTINCTIONS

Unamuno was one of the most controversial figures in Spanish history. He was proud not to belong to any political party and continually felt the need to disagree, to follow his own paradoxical course. Surely for this reason he received few official honors during his long career. In fact, he undoubtedly achieved more negative than positive recognition in official circles. His six-year political exile is a case in point.

Nonetheless, his intellectual achievements placed him head and shoulders above most of his contemporaries. Unamuno read sixteen modern languages, besides Latin and Greek; he learned Danish in order to read Kierkegaard in the original. His attendance at literary and political gatherings in Madrid always heightened the public's interest in such events. By 1914 he had become the undisputed mentor of many young Spaniards, and in the ensuing years his fame spread throughout Europe. He was a favorite in France; two of his books were first published in French. In Italy and Portugal many looked upon him as a spokesman for the Latin countries of Catholic tradition. And his influence in the Spanish-speaking countries of the New World was enormous.

Unamuno's return from exile on February 9, 1930, was wildly cheered by many who perceived him as the principal democratic standard-bearer in the entire country. At a magnificent celebration in his honor in 1934, he was appointed "Rector for Life" at the University of Salamanca. In 1935 he was proclaimed an honorary citizen of the Spanish Republic. Despite this latter honor, he later withdrew his support of the Republican cause in favor of the Nationalists, whom subsequently he also rejected. At once revered and reviled, Unamuno was received in his time in a way that reflected his own paradoxical pattern of life and thought.

A similar pattern greeted his theater. Though not viewed during his lifetime as an important playwright, Unamuno has, in recent years, received the highest accolades for his dramatic experiments. José Monleón groups him with Strindberg, Ibsen, Lenormand, or Pirandello for his probing of the crisis of Western man (Monleón 27). Antonio Buero Vallejo, Spain's great playwright of the second half of the twentieth century, affirmed, simply, that Unamuno was "one of the greatest tragedians that we have had" [uno de los más grandes trágicos que hemos tenido] (Buero Vallejo 20).

NOTES

1. Jose María Lasagabaster describes Unamuno's theater as a *project* extending through his entire career (Lasagabaster 9).

2. The author also attributes the prevalence of dialogue in his novels to the characters' own esthetic pleasure. In *Mist* [Niebla] (1914) Victor Goti, his character-prologuist, insists that the characters must talk above all because "people like conversation for conversation's sake" [a la gente le gusta la conversación por la conversación misma] and because the author "won't bother us with his personality, with his Satanic I" [no nos molesta con su personalidad, con su yo satánico] (*Obras completas* II: 776, 777). It is clear in this theoretical formulation of the *nivola*, the most important in Unamuno's fiction, that this new genre was based on a fundamental dichotomy: the autonomy of the character's esthetic pleasure and, as a direct consequence of such artistic freedom, autonomous existence itself (i.e., the character's right to exist independently of the author). This dichotomy, then, motivates the metamorphosis of the creature into the creator, a transformation that becomes the artistic and ontological basis for most of Unamuno's creative endeavors.

3. On the basis of his discussion with Víctor Goti in chapter XVII on the *nivola* that he is writing, Augusto asks himself: "And my life, is it a novel, a nivola, or what is it? Everything that happens to me and that happens to those that surround me, is it reality or is it fiction?" [Y esta mi vida, ¿es novela, es nivola o qué es? Todo esto que me pasa y que les pasa a los que me rodean, ¿es realidad o es ficción?] (777; all translations are mine).

4. Isabel Paraíso de Leal considers Laura, like Petrarch's beloved, the prototype of femininity and the object of love for the two twins. Damiana is the "other" of Damián; her role is to provide him with the other (i.e., a son). See Paraíso de Leal 176.

5. In the original Spanish, *destiny* [el destino] and *fate* [la fatalidad] can be considered, respectively, as male and female, perhaps another of Unamuno's many subtle doublings (Paraíso de Leal 177–178).

6. Unamuno himself used these very words to characterize his method:

I don't want to be, reader, anything but the mirror in which you see yourself. So the mirror is concave or convex and of a kind of concaveness or convexedness that you don't recognize yourself and it hurts to see yourself that way? Well, you should see yourself every way possible. It's the only way to know yourself in depth.

[Yo no quiero ser, lector, sino el espejo en que te veas tú a ti mismo. ¿Que el espejo es concavo o convexo y de tal especie de concavidad o convexidad, que no te reconoces y te duele verte así? Pues conviene que te veas de todos los modos posibles. Es la única manera de que llegues a conocerte de veras.]

Unamuno, "El dolor de pensar," *Mi vida y otros recuerdos personales. Obras completas*, I: 166, cited in Stevens (280).

BIBLIOGRAPHY

Editions and Translations

La esfinge. Madrid: Alfil, 1960.

La esfinge. La venda. La Princesa Doña Lambra. La difunta. Fedra. El pasado que vuelve. Soledad. Raquel encadenada. Sombras de sueño. El otro. El hermano Juan o El mundo es teatro. Medea. Published in *Miguel de Unamuno: Teatro completo*. Ed. Manuel García Blanco. Madrid: Aguilar, 1959.

Fedra. Soledad. El otro. Published in *Miguel de Unamuno: Teatro*. Buenos Aires: Editorial Losada, 1964.

Fedra. Soledad. Raquel Encadenada. Medea. Published in *Miguel de Unamuno: Teatro*. Ed. Manuel García Blanco. Barcelona: Editorial Juventud, 1964.

El hermano Juan, o El mundo es teatro. Madrid: Espasa-Calpe, 1934.

El otro. Madrid: Espasa-Calpe, 1932.

El otro. Published in *Miguel de Unamuno: Obras selectas*. Ed. Julián Marías. Madrid: Editorial Plenitud, 1950. The 3rd edition (Madrid, 1956) contains *El otro* and *Soledad*.

El otro. Barcelona: Aymá, 1964.

El otro y El hermano Juan. Madrid: Espasa-Calpe, 1946.

The Other. Ed. Ricardo de la Fuente Ballesteros. Salamanca: Ediciones Colegio de España, 1993.

The Other. A Mystery in Three Acts and an Epilogue. Poet Lore. Vol. XIII. Boston: Poet Lore, Inc., 1947. 3–35. (translated by H. Alpern)

The Other. Selected Works of Miguel de Unamuno. Bollingen Series LXXXV. Princeton, NJ: University Press, 1976. (translated by Anthony Kerrigan)

The Other One. A Mistery (sic) in three acts and epilogue, by Miguel de Unamuno. Played in the Teatro Español, in Madrid, the night of December 14, 1932 (a typewritten English version preserved in Unamuno's Library in Salamanca; no author is noted).

Critical Studies

Aszyk, Ursula. "Miguel de Unamuno Teórico del Teatro." In *El teatro de Miguel de Unamuno*. San Sebastián: University of Deusto, 1987. 27–45.

Buero Vallejo, Antonio. "Antonio Buero Vallejo habla de Unamuno." *Primer Acto* 58 (November 1964): 19–21.

Elizalde, Ignacio. "Características del Teatro de Unamuno." In *El teatro de Miguel de Unamuno*. San Sebastián: University of Deusto, 1987. 46–65.

Gullón, Ricardo. "Unamuno en su teatro." In *El teatro de Miguel de Unamuno*. San Sebastián: University of Deusto, 1987. 227–241.

Hermenegildo, Alfredo. "La imposible ruptura de la Germinación: *El otro* de Unamuno." In *El teatro de Miguel de Unamuno*. San Sebastián: University of Deusto, 1987. 189–211.

Lasagabaster, Jose María. "Prólogo." In *El teatro de Miguel de Unamuno*. San Sebastián: University of Deusto, 1987. 9–11.

Marías, Julián. *Filosofía actual y existencialismo en España*. Madrid: *Revista de Occidente*, 1955.

Monleón, José. "Unamuno y el teatro de su tiempo." *Primer Acto* 58 (November 1964): 22–32.

Paraíso de Leal, Isabel. "Yo, el otro." In *El teatro de Miguel de Unamuno*. San Sebastián: University of Deusto, 1987, 153–188.

Ruiz Ramón, Francisco. *Historia del teatro español: Siglo XX*. Madrid: Alianza Editorial, 1971.

———. "Tres dramaturgos en busca de espacio: Valle-Inclán, Unamuno, Lorca." In *Selected Proceedings of the Singularidad y Trascendencia Conference*, ed. Nora de Marval-McNair. Boulder, CO: Publications of the Society of Spanish and Spanish-American Studies, 1990, 27–39.

Stevens, Harriet. "El Unamuno múltiple." *Papeles de Son Armadans* XXXIV, no. CII, IX (1964): 253–284.

Unamuno, Miguel de. "Exordio a *Fedra*." In *Obras completas*. Vol. XII. Madrid: Afrodisio Aguado, 1958.

———. *Niebla* (*Mist*). In *Obras completas*. Vol. II. Madrid: Afrodisio Aguado, 1951.

———. *El otro*. Edición de Ricardo de la Fuente Ballesteros. Salamanca: Ediciones Colegio de España, 1993.

———. *El otro* (*The Other*). In *Obras completas*. Vol. II. Madrid: Afrodisio Aguado, 1951.

Zavala, Iris M. "La dialogía del teatro unamuniano: Género interno." In *El teatro de Miguel de Unamuno*. San Sebastián: University of Deusto, 1987, 1987. 13–26.

———. "Unamuno: Palabra a dos voces." In *Selected Proceedings of the Singularidad y Trascendencia Conference*, ed. Nora de Marval-McNair. Boulder, CO: Publications of the Society of Spanish and Spanish-American Studies, 1990. 43–59.

RAMÓN DEL VALLE-INCLÁN
(1866–1936)

Felicia Londré

BIOGRAPHY

The writer known as Don Ramón María del Valle-Inclán y Montenegro was born Ramón José Simón Valle y Peña, the son of Ramón del Valle Inclán y Bermúdez and Dolores de la Peña Montenegro Cardecid y Saco Bolaño, in the Galician village of Villanueva de Arosa, near Pontevedra, on October 28, 1866. Although proud of their aristocratic lineage, the impoverished family (which included Valle-Inclán's two brothers, a sister, and a half-sister) lived modestly in the ancient stone house of the Peñas on Calle del Priorato. Young Valle-Inclán relished the Galician folktales and legends of goblins and saints told by the servants, and he devoured his father's library. He studied Latin with a local cleric and completed secondary school in 1885 at the Instituto de Pontevedra.

At nineteen Valle-Inclán began preparatory studies in law at the University of Santiago de Compostela. During his three years there, he began writing stories and poems as well as participating in various literary gatherings. The political career that his father had envisioned for him no longer seemed inevitable after his father died on January 14, 1890; and changes in the government further discouraged him. Abandoning his legal studies, he moved to Madrid, where he lived in the bohemian quarter and attempted to earn a living as a journalist.

In 1892 Valle-Inclán sailed for Mexico. He landed at Veracruz, then went on to Mexico City, where he wrote for two newspapers, *El Correo Español* and *El Universal*, and began using the name by which he has thenceforth been known. The choice of a pen name with old-fashioned chivalric overtones suited his developing persona as well as the modernist aesthetic with an element of mysticism that characterized his literary writing before World War I.

Returning to Spain in the spring of 1893, Valle-Inclán settled in Pontevedra and wrote his first book, *Femeninas. Seis historias amorosas* (1895). In 1896 he moved to Madrid where he lived penuriously, having rejected journalism in favor of devoting himself to an artistic ideal. Despite the critical disfavor that greeted his second book, *Epitalamio* (1897), he continued writing stories and supplemented that meager income by translating novels and plays from Portuguese and French. Often too poor to eat, he justified fasting as a spiritual exercise. Twice (in 1898 and 1899) he acted minor roles in stage productions. His eccentric appearance—a tall, gaunt figure with a long beard and large owlish glasses—gave impetus to the many anecdotes that circulated about him. He was a very vocal habitué of the *tertulias* at the Café de Madrid, and later the Café de Levante and the Café de la Montaña. The latter was the scene of an argument between him and Manuel Bueno in July 1899. Valle-Inclán reportedly threw a jug of water at Bueno, who retaliated by striking Valle-Inclán with his cane. The blow drove Valle-Inclán's cufflink into his wrist, which led to an infection and the amputation of his left arm. Pursuing his interest in theater, Valle-Inclán served as artistic director for a production of Shakespeare's *The Taming of the Shrew* by a company called the Teatro Artístico. As a benefit to buy Valle-Inclán an artificial arm, that company also produced his first play *Cenizas* (1899), which was published that year.

Valle-Inclán's first serious literary recognition came with the 1902 publication of his novel *Sonata de otoño. Memorias del Marqués de Bradomín*; many detected autobiographical elements in the larger-than-life title character. The year 1903 brought the publication of two collections of short stories, *Jardín umbrio* and *Corte de amor*. Valle-Inclán continued the amorous adventures of the Marqués de Bradomin in three sequels: *Sonata de estío* (1903), *Sonata de primavera* (1904), and *Sonata de invierno* (1905). Other books published during this period were a novel, *Flor de santidad* (1904), two additional collections of stories, *Jardín novelesco* (1905) and *Historias perversas* (1907), and a book of poetry, *Aromas de leyendo* (1907). The Carlist movement in Spain inspired his historical novels in a series called *La guerra carlista: Los cruzados de la causa* (1908), *El resplendor de la hoguera* (1909), and *Gerifaltes de antaño* (1909). It should be noted that Valle-Inclán frequently revised his works and published them in collections of works from various periods. The dates given here are those of composition or earliest publication.

In 1907 Valle-Inclán married actress Josefina Blanco; they would have six children before divorcing in 1932. Their marriage began with a theatrical tour, Josefina as leading actress and Valle-Inclán as artistic director of the Ricardo Calvo company. Later, in 1910, they toured South America together. Meanwhile, Valle-Inclán turned increasingly to writing for the theater: *El Marqués de Bradomín* (1906), *Aguila de blasón* (1907), *Romance de lobos* (1908), *La cabeza del dragón* (1909), *Cuento de abril* (1910), *Voces de gesta* (1911), *La marquesa Rosalinda* (1912), and *El embrujado* (1913). Then followed a hiatus in his dramatic endeavors until the 1920s.

In 1912 Valle-Inclán moved his family to Galicia and attempted without success to run a farm, but his health was poor and he was frequently drawn back to Madrid. One of Valle-Inclán's most important nondramatic works was published in 1916: *La lámpara maravillosa*, an aesthetic treatise that he subtitled "spiritual exercises." In May 1916 Valle-Inclán was invited by the French government to visit the front; he went as special war correspondent for two Madrid newspapers, and his observations were later collected in a book, *La media noche* (1917). He was even flown over the battlefield at Alsace. The war marked a shift in Valle-Inclán's outlook as expressed in his writing: away from the romantic decadence of modernism and toward a more socially committed art in keeping with the attitudes of the Generation of '98. In 1921 he accepted an invitation from the Mexican government to participate in the Independence Day celebrations there. He gave several lectures in Mexico, then visited Cuba and New York. In 1926 he published his most successful novel, *Tirano Banderas*. During Spain's period of political unrest in 1929, Valle-Inclán was twice jailed for his outspokenness.

Two volumes of poetry, *La pipa de kif* (1919) and *El pasajero* (1920), preceded a return to writing for the theater. Among a number of plays published in magazines and collected in books in the early 1920s were *Divinas palabras* (1920), *Luces de bohemia* (1920), *Los cuernos de don Friolera* (1921), and *Cara de Plata* (1922). *Cara de Plata* became the first play in a trilogy that included two earlier plays, *Aguila de blasón* and *Romance de lobos* under the umbrella title *Comedias bárbaras*. With *Luces de bohemia*, Valle-Inclán invented a new dramaturgical aesthetic that he called *esperpento*. It is characterized by a distortion of some aspects of reality, throwing events and characters into grotesque proportions, along with a mingling of elements of farce, horror, satire, mystery, violence, and parody. Valle-Inclán applied this term also to the three plays collected under the title *Martes de carnaval* (1930): *Las galas del difunto, Los cuernos de don Friolera*, and *La hija del capitán*.

In April 1933 Valle-Inclán traveled to Rome to take up the position of director of the Spanish Academy of Fine Arts there. However, he was already seriously ill and relinquished his duties in 1935. He died in a hospital in Santiago de Compostela on January 5, 1936.

DRAMATURGY: MAJOR WORKS AND THEMES

Although Valle-Inclán's dramatic writing evolved considerably over the years, certain characteristics are found throughout his works for the stage: a strong visual orientation, episodic construction, nostalgia for a chivalric ideal, atmospherically evocative and mystical elements, highly descriptive and often poetic stage directions, and characters less psychologically developed than representative of their social spectrum.

The plays Valle-Inclán wrote before World War I include tragedies, farces, and historical dramas. Most show the influences of *modernismo* (verbal preciosity, fairytale images, pursuit of an ideal of beauty) and Symbolism. The Symbolist aspects, according to John Lyon, derive from Richard Wagner's synthesis of all the arts as well as from Maurice Maeterlinck's spiritualism (13–19). Valle-Inclán learned his craft quickly, as evident in the clumsiness of his first play and the emergence of some of his characteristic techniques in the second. *Cen-*

izas, later revised as *El yermo de las almas. Episodios de la vida íntima*, is a journeyman piece, an adultery melodrama in a realistic vein. *El Marqués de Bradomín*, which Lyon calls "a rehash in dialogue form of material already published" (34), also deals with adultery but takes a more innovative dramatic approach with its background of Galician folklife.

According to Juan Bautista Avalle-Arce, the historical dramas are not so much rooted in historical fact as employing historicity to generate aesthetic evocations (353). In the *Comedias bárbaras* [Barbaric Comedies] trilogy, the male members of the aristocratic Montenegro family behave with a feudalistic arrogance that gives them a medieval aura in their interactions with a host of minor characters representative of the nineteenth-century rural Galicia in which the plays are set. The central character is Don Juan Manuel de Montenegro, a vigorous and charismatic man whose advancing age does not curtail his enormous sensual appetites. Lyon sees the two main narrative threads of the trilogy as Montenegro's conflict with his six grown sons and his spiritual conflict within himself (39). Of the sons, only Cara de Plata has inherited the sense of *noblesse oblige* that mitigates his father's cruelty and violence. The theme is the moral degeneration of the nobility. The stage directions describe settings and actions so varied and imaginative that Valle-Inclán could not have intended the plays for production by any standard of theatrical convention in his lifetime. However, a 1991 production of the trilogy (nearly seven hours' running time) at Madrid's Centro Dramático Nacional (with Jose Luis Pellicena as Montenegro) demonstrated the exciting theatricality of the work. Also in 1991 a French production of the trilogy directed by Jorge Lavelli premiered at the Festival of Avignon.

A consideration of the plot of the trilogy must begin with *Cara de Plata* even though it was written fifteen years after *Aguila de blasón* and *Romance de lobos*, the two plays that follow it in terms of narrative. *Cara de Plata* opens with an angry group of tenant farmers demanding passage for their cattle across Montenegro's land. These peasants and later some beggars function in choral counterpoint to the bigger-than-life Montenegros. The handsome Cara de Plata, on horseback, allows the women to pass. He loves the angelic young Sabelita, who was raised in the household, but she is helplessly attracted to his father, her godfather Montenegro. Cara de Plata brawls in a tavern and halfheartedly takes up with Pichona. When he learns that Sabelita has become his father's mistress, he goes to kill him. That act might also signal the peasants' awaited change in the social order. However, Cara de Plata cannot bring himself to do the deed. The play ends in a gesture of profanation: Montenegro seizes the chalice borne by the abbot and scatters the consecrated hosts. Women scream in horror as Montenegro laughs and wonders aloud whether he might be the devil incarnate.

In *Aguila de blasón* [Emblematic Eagle], Sabelita is villified by the people and maltreated by Montenegro; though conscience-stricken, she loves him still. When Montenegro's wife, the deeply religious Doña María, returns to the castle after a long absence, the two women are reconciled. Don Pedrito (Montenegro's wayward eldest son) goes to the miller seeking to extort money but rapes the miller's pregnant wife Liberata. Later, Montenegro takes Liberata into his castle as his mistress, and she enlists his buffoon and alter ego, Don Galán, to help her consolidate her position there. Sabelita leaves the castle, has a brief encounter on the road with Cara de Plata, and hurries on. Knowing he has lost her, Cara de Plata decides to go to war. He bids his mother farewell; she then has a surrealist dream of baby Jesus. Don Farruquiño, another of Montenegro's sons, is a seminarian who supports himself by grave-robbing and selling the skeletons. While Cara de Plata spends a last night with Pichona, Farruquiño simultaneously, in the next room, places the cadaver in a boiling cauldron to dissolve the flesh. The scene is a grotesque and sensational juxtaposition of love and death. Liberata has firmly ensconced herself as Montenegro's mistress (a comedic and pathetic parody of Sabelita) when Doña María returns to report Sabelita's attempted suicide and to order her husband out. He leaves, howling that he is a wolf.

Romance de lobos [Ballad of Wolves] completes the saga of the Montenegro family's decline and fall. Encountering a funeral procession on the road, Montenegro learns of Doña María's death. Meanwhile, back at the castle, his rapacious sons are looting the death chamber. In a violent thunderstorm and surrounded by beggars, Montenegro has a King Lear–like epiphany. He invites a leper to journey with him. Having found little of value in their father's house, Farruquiño and Pedrito rob a chapel. Pursued by the shadow of his mother, Pedrito encounters his father on the road. Montenegro taunts him, but Pedrito— like Cara de Plata before him—is unable to kill his father. Surrounded by the beggars and the leper, Montenegro seems to be either going mad or finding spiritual redemption. In the final scene, he is killed by four of his six wolfish sons (Cara de Plata and Pedrito being absent).

Cuento de abril. Escenas rimadas en una manaera extravagante [April Tale] is a medieval fantasy that pits a courtly, luxuriant, poetic Provençal aesthetic against an austere, disciplined, warrior, and huntsman-centered Castilian manner. The author's sympathies clearly lean toward the Provençals, represented by a graceful troubadour and his princess. Set during the Carlist wars, *Voces de gesta. Tragedia pastoríl* [Epic Voices] celebrates devotion to a traditional cause despite even when one has been victimized for one's beliefs and even in ultimate defeat. *El embrujado. Tragedia de tierra de Salnés* [The Bewitched] centers on Rosa la Galana's attempt to use her child for material advancement, a course of action that leads to the death of the child. In Lyon's view of this play, "the characters are the puppets of blind collective forces and the situations are consciously pushed beyond tragedy to grotesque farce" (77).

Modernist elements reappear alongside marionette-theater approaches to plot and character in two early plays labeled "farces." Set in an eighteenth-century garden with swans and roses, *La Marquesa Rosalinda. Farsa sentimental y grotesca* [Marquesa Rosalinda] is a lyrical fantasy with comedic by-play in which the aging Marquesa is attracted to the pleasure-seeking Arlequín. However, their elopement is thwarted, and she finds fulfillment in religion. *La cabeza del dragón* [The Dragon's Head] is called a *"farsa infantil"* and has traditionally been produced as a children's fairytale play, yet it abounds with satirical references to Spanish politics and social issues. The sly digs begin in the stage directions of the opening scene: Three young princes play football in the courtyard of the kind of fantasy castle a child would imagine; its ivy-covered walls "have not been restored by the King's architects. Praise God!" Scene 2 follows Prince Verdemar to a roadside inn, where he meets an ex-Court Jester and a Blindman and learns that the local Princess is scheduled to be sacrificed to a terrible dragon. Changing clothes with the Jester, the Prince goes to the palace of King Micromicón. There, in a garden that reeks of *modernismo*—with roses and marble staircases, royal peacocks spreading their tails, a lake on which two swans glide in unison, a labyrinthe of myrtles—the disguised Prince finds the Princess weeping by the fountain. He gives her hope in return for her promise to give him a rose if she should survive to return to the garden. After she leaves, the Prince calls upon his Duende, who promises him a diamond sword. In Scene 4, a Master of Ceremonies explains the etiquette of the sacrifice. The King contemplates giving up his throne and taking his daughter to a faraway land "where there are no monsters." But she refuses to abandon King Micromicón's loyal subjects to the dragon's wrath. Just then, Prince Verdemar appears in shining armor, like an Archangel. He fights the dragon and kills it. Surreptitiously, the Duende appears and cuts out the dragon's tongue. Scene 5 returns to the garden setting, where the Princess longs to see her rescuer again and shuns the Jester whom she had promised a rose. A well-dressed thug arrives, claiming to be the dragonslayer and producing the dragon's head as proof. The King is insistent that his daughter marry the supposed hero, even after the former Court Jester arrives and says that the pretender had stolen those clothes from the Jester, who had in turn obtained them from a Prince. With a doddering old general called in to testify that all creatures have tongues, the disguised Prince offers his own proof: He knows that the dragon's head has no tongue. The Princess recognizes his voice as that of the knight in shining armor. Against the King's objection to her marrying a Jester, Prince Verdemar reveals his identity. At the wedding in the final scene, the Duende plays a trick on the Prince's father that almost brings the two Kings to blows with each other. But all ends happily with the reminder that "constitutional monarchs are required to be vegetarians."

When Valle-Inclán returned to the drama in 1920 after a seven-year hiatus, his romantic and decadent aestheticism had been mitigated by a more cynical view of the human condition. He wrote two farces, *Farsa italiana de la enamorada del rey* [Italian Farce of the Woman in Love with the King] and *Farsa y licencia de la reina castiza* [Farce and Licentiousness of the Unsullied Queen], which he brought together with *La cabeza del dragón* under the umbrella title *Tablado de marionetas para educación de príncipes*. Several short plays were collected along with *El embrujado* under the title *Retablo de la avaricia, la lujuria y la muerte*; these are *Ligazón* [Blood Pact], *La Rosa de papél* [The Paper Rose], *La cabeza del Bautista* [The Head of the Baptist], and *Sacrilegio*

[Sacrilege]. Of the short pieces, "dances of death for marionettes or silhouettes," Roger Cornish notes that "each play climaxes in the same way: violent death is paired with sexual release—love-death" (viii). A final collection, *Martes de carnaval* brings together three of the plays that Valle-Inclán labeled *esperpentos: Las galas del difunto* [The Dead Man's Dress Suit], *Los cuernos de don Friolera* [Don Friolera's Horns], and *La hija del capitán* [The Captain's Daughter].

Although written before he coined the term *esperpento*, Valle-Inclán's rural drama *Divinas palabras. Tragicomedia de aldea* [Divine Words] contains elements of *esperpentismo*. The concept is explained in the dialogue of the play that is usually signaled as his masterpiece, *Luces de bohemia* [Bohemian Lights] (discussed in the next section). In Scene 12 of that play, the poet Max Estrella says: "Esperpentismo was invented by Goya. . . . Classical heroes reflected in concave mirrors, that's what the Esperpento is. The tragic sense of Spanish life can be known only through a systematically deformed aesthetic . . . In a concave mirror, even the most beautiful images are absurd . . . Deformation ceases to be so when it is subjected to a perfect mathematical law. My current aesthetic is to transform classical norms through the mathematics of a concave mirror." As manifested in the late plays, *esperpentismo* might be seen as a realism in which grotesque aspects of life are magnified, in which the horrible and the humorous are superimposed. The gallery of colorful characters in *Divinas palabras* might be described as amoral, uninhibited, cruel, hypocritical, displaying a full range of human vices. A hydrocephalic dwarf is used as an accessory for begging and thoughtlessly killed. A sexton rapes his daughter. When his wife, Mari-Gaila, is discovered as an adultress, the low-life mob strips her naked, ties her to a cart, and is about to stone her. She is saved only when the sexton reads a biblical injunction in Latin. The words have a mystical effect: The crowd dissipates and the naked woman serenely crosses the courtyard to enter the church beneath a vision of the dwarf's head crowned with flowers.

CRITICS' RESPONSE

Besides his conception of *esperpentismo*, Valle-Inclán's major contributions to dramatic literature are *Divinas palabras, Luces de bohemia*, and the three *Comedias bárbaras*. Most critics signal *Luces de bohemia* as his masterpiece.

Luces de bohemia was originally published as a weekly serial in *España* (July 31 to October 23, 1920) and, in a revised version, in *Opera Ominia* 19 (Madrid, 1924). It was not produced until 1963, when the Théâtre National Populaire in Paris presented it in French for the International Theatre Festival. Its Spanish premiere came in 1972 at Madrid's Teatro Bellas Artes, under the direction of José Tamayo. In his preface to the bilingual edition, Anthony N. Zahareas notes that the play is "an accurate documentary" of Bohemian Madrid after World War I and that "Valle-Inclán strove to include the smallest details of happenings, meetings, newspaper headlines, popular topics, political debates, common phrases, clichés, current slang, and, above all, of the physical aspects of the city" (x). It is not only Valle-Inclán's first *esperpento*, but it is also his first play in a contemporary setting. Given Valle-Inclán's previous focus on a stylized, mythic past as a means of evoking an essence or ideal, John Lyon sees this play as "a descent into hell" for the self-consciously aristocratic author. It is a criticism of "the anti-heroic, life-reducing aspects of modern existence which trivialize even what is noble and generous" (108). Alonso Zamora Vicente claims that *Luces de bohemia* is the first work of Spanish literature in which the traditional hero journeys toward self-effacement (or so one might interpret Max Estrella's Dante-esque pilgrimage toward death) in order to give way to a collective as central character (*La realidad esperpéntica* 8).

The play's protagonist, the blind poet Máximo Estrella, is perhaps Valle-Inclán's most autobiographical character, although critics have also pointed out close, intentional resemblances between the character and writer Alejandro Sawa. Max Estrella is described as the premiere poet in Spain, though ignored by the Academy and scorned by the press. He is a compelling figure, despite what most critics see as an absence of psychological development. John P. Gabriele, however, finds a basis for psychological analysis of the character beyond his archetypal qualities "Estructura" 659–60.

The opening scene introduces Max, his wife, and daughter, all starving in a garret, his writing unappreciated by publishers. His friend Don Latino was to have sold some books for him but could not get a decent price, so he asks Max to go with him. At the bookseller's shop, they discuss Spain's problems but get nothing more for the books. Max and Latino head for the tavern. Max pawns his cloak to buy drinks. The sounds of rioting workers are heard from the street. Later that night Max and Latino stagger drunkenly under the broken street lamps seeking the streetwalker who appropriated Max's lottery ticket. A police patrol takes Max for an anarchist and they arrest him. Latino and the habitués of the Modernist Café accompany him to police headquarters where Max's irreverent jibes antagonize the officer. He is placed in a cell with a Catalán political prisoner, and the two commiserate about social conditions until the prisoner is taken out, presumably to be killed. Scene 7 is set in the office of a populist newspaper; Latino has come to stir up a protest against Max's arrest, but the scene is largely an excuse for satiric commentary on the press and the government as well as artistic and proletarian movements. Having been set free, Max goes to the Minister of Internal Affairs, an old friend, to call attention to the injustice of his unprovoked arrest. The Minister offers him a pension, which the starving Max realizes he must accept. There is a grotesque quality to the embrace of the ragged and blind but dignified poet by the overweight, foppish Minister who presses money into his hand.

Latino leads Max to an expensive café, where Max treats him and poet Rubén Darío to dinner; their drinking yields them a shared vision of Paris. Later, in a moonlit park Max and Latino encounter two streetwalkers. In the next scene they reach a street where broken glass, bullet marks, and a mother carrying a dead child give evidence of a recent riot. Overcome by the senselessness and futility of such conditions, Max asks Latino to lead him home. They arrive at Max's doorstep at daybreak, and here it is that Max describes Spain as an *esperpento*. Max dies, and Latino relieves him of his wallet. Latino shows up soddenly drunk for the funeral gathering in the garret where Max's wife and daughter live. Other grotesque figures arrive until finally all are convinced—in a sequence that is both farcical and poignant—that Max Estrella is truly dead. A scene at the cemetery provides opportunity for a discussion by the gravediggers of conditions in Spain, but Rubén Darío and the Marqués de Bradomín become ego-involved in talking of their own writing. At the tavern Don Latino spends extravagantly, having won a great deal of money with the lottery ticket that was in Max's wallet. News arrives that Max's wife and daughter have committed suicide. The tavernkeeper notes that Don Latino with his lottery ticket could have saved them from starvation. Boasting of his great-heartedness, Latino asserts that of course he would have helped them. But alas, the world is skewed. It's all an *esperpento*.

There are numerous analyses of the play in the context of *esperpentismo*, including Alonso Zamora Vicente's book-length study, chapters on the play in Cardona and Zahareas's examination of the *esperpento* in theory and practice, and a chapter in Emilio González López's book on Valle-Inclán's drama. Other critics have explored the play's topical, literary, historical, and site-specific references. Among these are Allen W. Phillips's study of the literary context, Zamora Vicente's tracking of personalities on which the characters are based (*La realidad esperpéntica* 30–56) and his comments on the mirrors of Cat Alley that figure in Max's formulation of *esperpentismo* ("En torno" 310–313). Various studies trace the literary influences of writers such as Cervantes, Shakespeare, and Maeterlink. Fernando Ponce offers specific examples of social protest in the play.

John Lyon interprets *Luces de bohemia* as a study of "the relationship between society and the artist, specifically the metamorphosis of the heroic into the absurd under the influence of a trivialized and grotesque social context" (109). Similarly, Sumner M. Greenfield sees the play as "a confrontation between the Bohemian poet and the institutionalized world" (*Anatomía* 229). Zahareas finds the ideal of tragic heroism exposed as a "sham—both on the personal and the national level"—transmuting noble values "into the grotesque gestures of puppets" (Introduction 262). Domingo Ynduráin signals two defining moments in Max's progressive rejection of the heroic stance, both moments of hallucination. The first is in Scene 1 when he tells his wife that he has suddenly recovered his eyesight, and the other is the vision of Paris at the end of Scene 9. In both cases, the momentary enjoyment of beauty and plenitude is fleeting (351–353). For Juan Antonio Hormingón, the play is a deromanticization of Bohemian life; its narrative line is a coming to awareness that culminates not in social action but in death (363–364).

During the first eleven scenes Max wanders from place to place, observing his surroundings. At first he seems to be semidetached, but gradually he begins to absorb and identify with the senselessness of it all. Thus, he evolves from the supreme poet standing upon his own dignity to a bemused extra on the great stage of life, reduced to staging his own death in a manner that Lyon sees as a conscious choice of farce over tragedy (119). Although he is alluded to as having a classical heroic stature, his behavior—contrary to that of any hero of tragedy—is strangely passive. He rarely initiates an action but allows Don Latino to take the lead, or merely reacts to people he meets and events that unfold. In this apparently aimless trajectory, it is surprising that Max so fully commands the reader's or theatergoer's attention. It is possible to see the play as an expressionistic projection of Max's experience of reality. His blindness would thus account for the apparent deformities in that reality, as well as allowing a symbolist reading of blindness as a kind of superior vision. Shakespearean echoes are evident in the gravedigger scene, and—as in *King Lear*—there is a postapocalyptic quality about Max's nighttime urban excursions over broken glass while the sounds of police sirens and rioting mobs are heard not far away. If this illustrates a society that does not revere its artists and geniuses, then *Luces de bohemia*, despite its 1920s Madrid topicality, has much to say to Americans in a decade that has seen the arts under siege.

AWARDS AND DISTINCTIONS

In accordance with the Spanish custom of fêting artists, many banquets were given in Valle-Inclán's honor: January 1907 in Las Palmas; June 24, 1910, in Buenos Aires; March 29, 1913, in Santiago de Compostela; April 1, 1922, in Madrid; March 23, 1925, in Barcelona; June 7, 1932, in Madrid.

José Ortega y Gasset dedicated his "Glosa" (1902) to Valle-Inclán in honor of the writer and his native Galicia.

Valle-Inclán's story "Malpocado!" won second prize (250 pesetas) in a 1902 literary competition sponsored by *El Liberal*; no first prize was awarded.

He was invited to speak at the prestigious Ateneo in Madrid and presented his very successful lecture there on May 2, 1907.

He was the recipient of the Carlists' highest medal, the Cruz de la Legitimidad Pospuesta. He was later named Cabellero de la Orden de la Legitimidad Proscrita.

He briefly held the Chair of Esthetics, created especially for him in 1916, at the Madrid School of Painting, Sculpture, and Engraving.

The January 1923 issue of *La Pluma* was devoted entirely to Valle-Inclán and his work, with articles by many leading writers as well as portraits by various artists. Other (posthumous) special issues of journals in his honor are included in the bibliography.

He was appointed Conservador General del Patrimonio Artístico Nacional by Spain's Republican government in 1931 (but held the post only a few months before resigning).

In 1932 he was elected president of the Ateneo de Madrid and nominated as the only Spaniard to serve on an international committee to prepare an agenda for a Grand Congrès Mondial contre la Guerre. The following year he was elected president of the Asociación de Amigos de la Unión Soviética. In 1935 he headed the Spanish section of the Asociación Internacional de Escritores, became Honorary President of a national campaign against capital punishment, and joined the presidium of the Association Internationale des Ecrivains pour la Défense de la Culture.

January 6, 1936 (the day after Valle-Inclán's death), was declared a day of mourning in Santiago de Compostela. The Ateneo of Madrid held a memorial tribute to him on February 14, 1936.

BIBLIOGRAPHY

Editions and Translations

Editions

Aguila de blasón: Comedia bárbara. Madrid: Imprenta Sáez Hermanos, 1922.

Cara de plata: Comedia bárbara. Madrid: Imprenta Cervantina, 1923.

————. Edición crítica de Antón Risco. Madrid: Espasa-Calpe, 1992.

Divinas palabras: Tragicomedia de aldea. Edición crítica de Luis Iglesias Feijoo. Madrid: Espasa-Calpe, 1991.

———— and *Luces de Bohemia.* Introduction and notes by Anthony Zahareas and Sumner Greenfield. Long Island City: Las Américas (Colección la Noria), 1972.

Luces de Bohemia. Madrid: Espasa-Calpe, 1961.

————. Edición, prólogo y notas de Alonso Zamora Vicente. Madrid: Espasa-Calpe, 1973.

La Marquesa Rosalinda: Farsa sentimental y grotesca. Edición César Oliva. Madrid: Espasa Calpe (Colección Austral), 1990.

————. Edición crítica de Leda Schiavo. Madrid: Espasa-Calpe, 1992.

Martes de carnavál. Madrid: Espasa-Calpe, 1930. Contains *Las galas del difunto, Los cuernos de Don Friolera, La hija del capitán.*

————. Edición crítica de Ricardo Senabre. Madrid: Espasa-Calpe, 1990.

Retablo de la avaricia, lu lujuria y la muerte. Madrid: Espasa-Calpe, 1961. Contains *Ligazón, La rosa de papél, El embrujado, La cabeza del Bautista,* and *Sacrilegio.*

Romance de lobos. Madrid: Espasa-Calpe, 1947.

Tablado de marionetas para educación de príncipes. Madrid. Espasa-Calpe, 1961. Contains *Farsa italiana de la enamorada del rey, Farsa infántil de la cabeza del dragón, Farsa y licencia de la reina castiza.*

Teatro selecto. Madrid: Las Americas Publishing Co., 1969. Contains *Romance de lobos, Tablado de marionetas, Divinas palabras.*

El yermo de las almas: Episodios de la vida intima. Madrid: Alianza Editorial, 1970 [with "Una tertulia de antaño"].

Translations

Comédies barbares. Texte français et adaptation de Armando Llamas. Paris: Editions Actes Sud-Papiers, 1991.

Divine Words. Trans. Edwin Williams. In *Modern Spanish Theatre*, ed. by Michael
   Benedikt and George E. Wellwarth. New York: E. P. Dutton, 1969.
Divine Words. Trans. T. Faulkner. London: Heinemann, 1977.
The Grotesque Farce of Mr. Punch the Cuckold [Los cuernos de Don Friolera]. Trans.
   Robin Warner and Dominic Keown. Warminster, England: Aris & Phillips, Ltd.,
   1991.
Luces de Bohemia. [Spanish/English parallel texts] Ed. and trans. Anthony N. Zahareas
   and Gerald Gillespie. Austin: University of Texas Press (Edinburgh Bilingual
   Library 10), 1976.
Savage Acts: Four Plays. Trans. Robert Lima. University Park, PA: Estreno (Contem-
   porary Spanish Plays 3), 1993. [*Blood Pact, The Paper Rose, The Head of the
   Baptist, Sacrilege*]
Valle-Inclán Plays: One. Trans. and introduced Maria Delgado. London: Methuen Drama,
   1993. [*Divine Words, Bohemian Lights, Silver Face*]
Wolves! Wolves! A Play of Savagery in Three Acts [Romance de lobos]. Trans. Cyril
   Bertram Lander. Birmingham: C. B. Lander, 1957.

Critical Studies

Books and articles on Valle-Inclán and his work are so numerous that the following
can serve only as a tiny sampling. The listing below includes bibliographies by Robert
Lima and J. Rubia Barcia. The books edited by Ricardo Domeinech and John P. Gabriele
also contain substantial bibliographies.

Avalle-Arce, Juan Bautista. "*Cuento de abril*: Literary Reminiscences and Common-
   places." In *Ramón del Valle-Inclán: An Appraisal of His Life and Works*, ed.
   Anthony N. Zahareas. New York: Las Americas Publishing Co., 1968. 355–373.
Bermejo Marcos, Manuel. *Valle-Inclán: Introducción a su obra.* Salamanca: Ediciones
   Anaya (Temas y estudios), 1971.
Canoa, Joaquina. *Semiología de las "Comedias bárbaras."* Madrid: Cupsa Editorial (Pla-
   neta/Universidad de Oviedo), 1977.
Cardona, Rodolfo, and Anthony N. Zahareas. *Visión del esperpento: Teoría y práctica
   en los esperpentos de Valle-Inclán.* Madrid: Editorial Castalia, 1970.
Carmen Porrúa, María del. *La Galicia decimonónica en las Comedias Bárbaras de Valle
   Inclán.* Coruña: Ediciós do Castro, 1983.
Cornish, Roger. Introduction to Valle-Inclán: *Savage Acts: Four Plays.* Trans. by Robert
   Lima. University Park: Estreno (Contemporary Spanish Plays 3), 1993.
Cowes, Hugo W. "Indicaciones sobre estructura de *Luces de Bohemia* de Valle-Inclán."
   Razón y fábula 10 (1968): 35–46.
Cuadernos Hispanoamericanos (Madrid) LXVII, nos. 199–200 (July–August 1966). In-
   cludes articles on *Luces de Bohemia* by Andrés Amorós and Alonso Zamora
   Vicente and many other theater-related essays.
Doménech, Ricardo, ed. *Ramón del Valle Inclán.* Madrid: Taurus, 1988.
Dougherty, Dru. "*Luces de Bohemia* and Valle-Inclán's Search for Artistic Adequacy."
   Journal of Spanish Studies 2 (1974): 61–75.
Edwards, Gwynne. *Dramatists in Perspective: Spanish Theatre in the Twentieth Century.*
   New York: St. Martin's Press, 1985. 36–74.

Fernandez, Angel R. "La literatura, signo teatral: El problema significativo de las acotaciones dramáticas: Valle-Inclán y *Luces de Bohemia*." In *La literatura como
signo*, ed. by José Romera Castillo. Madrid: Editorial Playor, 1981.

Freund, Markéta L. "La universalidad de *Luces de Bohemia*." *Hispanófila* 56 (1976):
63–78.

Gabriele, John P. "Estructura mítica y psique en *Luces de bohemia*." In *Suma valleinclaniana*, ed. John P. Gabriele. Barcelona: Anthropos, 1992. 655–671.

———. "Scene VI of *Luces de Bohemia* and the *Quijote* Connection." *Romance Notes*
30.3 (1990) 259–263.

———, ed. *Suma valleinclaniana*. Barcelona: Anthropos, 1992.

González López, Emilio. *El arte dramático de Valle-Inclán*. New York: Las Américas
Publishing Co., 1967.

Greenfield, Sumner M. *Anatomía de un teatro problemático*. Madrid: Editorial Fundamentos, 1972. 226–242.

———. *Valle-Inclán: Anatomía de un teatro problemático*. Madrid: Editorial Fundamentos, 1972.

Gullón, Ricardo, ed. *Valle-Inclán Centennial Studies*. Austin: University of Texas, 1968.

Hormigón, Juan Antonio. *Valle-Inclán: La política, la cultura, el realismo y el pueblo*.
Madrid: Communicación Serie B, 1972.

Insula (Madrid) XXI, nos. 236–237 (July–August 1966). Includes essays on *Luces de
Bohemia* by Allen W. Phillips and Lesley Lee Zimic, as well as other theater-
related essays.

Lima, Robert. *An Annotated Bibliography of Ramón del Valle-Inclán*. University Park:
Pennsylvania State University Libraries (Bibliographical Series No. 4), 1972.

———. *Ramón del Valle-Inclán*. New York: Columbia University Press, 1972.

———. *Valle-Inclán: The Theatre of His Life*. Columbia: University of Missouri Press,
1988.

Lyon, John. *The Theatre of Valle-Inclán*. Cambridge: Cambridge University Press, 1983.

Maier, Carol, and Roberta L. Salper, eds. *Ramón del Valle-Inclán: Questions of Gender*.
Lewisburg: Bucknell University Press, 1994.

March, María Eugenia. *Forma e idea de los Esperpentos de Valle-Inclán*. Madrid: Editorial Castalia (Estudios de Hispanófila 10), 1969.

Matilla Rivas, Alfredo. *Las "Comedias Bárbaras": Historicismo y expresionismo dramático*. New York: Anaya, 1972.

Palenque, Marta. "Los acotaciones de Valle-Inclán: *Luces de Bohemia*." *Segismundo* 37–
38 (1983): 131–157.

Phillips, Allen W. "Sobre *Luces de bohemia* y su realidad literaria." In *Ramón del Valle-
Inclán: An Appraisal of His Life and Works*, ed. Anthony N. Zahareas. New York:
Las Americas Publishing Co., 1968. 601–614.

Ponce, Fernando. *Aventura y destino de Valle Inclán*. Barcelona: Ediciones Marte, 1969.
141–150.

Primer Acto (Madrid) no. 28 (November 1961). Special issue on the theatre of Valle-
Inclán. See also issue 46 (1963) and 83 (1967).

Rubia Barcia, J. *A Bibliography and Iconography of Valle Inclán (1866–1936)*. Berkeley
and Los Angeles: University of California Press (University of California
Publications in Modern Philology, Vol. 59), 1960.

Servera Bañó, José. *Ramón del Valle-Inclán*. Madrid: Ediciones Jucar, 1983.

Smith, Verity. *Ramón del Valle-Inclán*. New York: Twayne Publishers, 1973.

Trapero Llobera, Ana P., and José Servera Baño. "Algunas consideraciones sobre el espacio en el montaje de *Luces de bohemia* del Centro Dramático Nacional (C.D.N.). Ramón del." *Caligrama* 2, nos. 3–4 (1985).

Valle Inclán, *Comedias bárbaras: Cuadernos de trabajo*. Madrid: Centro Dramático Nacional, 1991.

Vila, Xavier. *Valle-Inclán and the Theatre: Innovation in La cabeza del dragón, El Embrujado, and La Marquesa Rosalinda*. Lewisburg: Bucknell University Press, 1994.

Weber, Frances W. "*Luces de Bohemia* and the Impossibility of Art." *Modern Language Notes* 82 (1967): 575–589.

Weiss, Rosemary Shevlin. *Valle-Inclán in 1920: Disruption, Dehumanization, Demystification*. Ph.D. diss., City University of New York, 1985. (University Microfilms #DA8508746).

Ynduráin, Domingo. "Luces." In *Ramón de Valle Inclán*, ed. Ricardo Doménech. Madrid: Taurus, 1988. 349–363.

———. "*Luces de Bohemia*: variaciones: ironía y compromiso." *Cuadernos Hispanoamericanos* 94 (1973): 588–597.

Zahareas, Anthony N. Introduction and Commentary. *Luces de bohemia/Bohemian Lights*. Trans. Anthony N. Zahareas and Gerald Gillespie. Austin: University of Texas Press (Edinburgh Bilingual Library 10), 1976. 1–81, 222–262.

———, ed. *Ramón del Valle-Inclán: An Appraisal of His Life and Works*. New York: Las Americas Publishing Co., 1968.

Zamora Vicente, Alonso. "En torno a *Luces de bohemia*." In *Ramón de Valle Inclán*, ed. Ricardo Domenech. Madrid: Taurus, 1988. 310–336.

———. *La realidad esperpéntica (Aproximación a "Luces de Bohemia")*. Madrid: Editorial Gredos (Biblioteca Románica Hispánica), 1974.

JOSÉ ZORRILLA Y MORAL
(1817–1893)

Salvador García Castañeda

BIOGRAPHY

José Zorrilla y Moral was born in Valladolid on February 21, 1817. The future poet was educated in Madrid at the Seminario de Nobles and studied law for two years at the universities of Toledo and Valladolid. In the summer of 1836, he fled to Madrid unbeknownst to his parents, and there lived in freedom and poverty in the company of Miguel de los Santos Alvarez, his compatriot and lifelong friend, who would later introduce him to Espronceda.

At the funeral the day after Larra's suicide, Zorrilla read an elegy that immediately made him famous. He began to contribute to periodicals, made powerful friends, and his literary career skyrocketed. Nonetheless, his father, José Zorrilla Caballero, an intransigent man of absolutist ideas and superintendent of police under Fernando VII, would never forgive him for abandoning his studies. He disdained his son's literary success. The poet continually and dauntlessly sought his father's pardon throughout his life, a preoccupation that is reflected in his work.

Zorrilla's first book, *Poesías*, appeared in 1837, and between then and 1840 he published eight volumes of verse with the same title, in which he revealed his delicate lyrical talent. *Cantos del trovador* (1840–1841) was acclaimed by critics and the public alike, and Zorrilla was enshrined as the bard of tradition and national glory.

He was twenty-two years old when he married Da. Florentina O'Reilly, ten years his senior and so jealous that Zorrilla was forced to flee to France and England, and later to Mexico, where he lived for twelve years. The Emperor Maximilian named him director of the Teatro Nacional, but while Zorrilla was visiting Spain the political situation changed. The emperor's army was defeated, and Benito Juárez had the emperor shot.

Despite changes in literary taste during his absence, Zorrilla was enthusiastically welcomed when he returned to Spain. Da. Florentina had died, and Zorrilla married the young Da. Juana Pacheco (1869). Due to a chronic lack of foresight, he lived his entire life in a state of financial distress. He obtained a government commission in Rome (1871–1876), rewrote his *Tenorio* as a *zarzuela*, and finally was forced to tour Spanish cities giving poetry readings in order to make a living. In 1885 he occupied the seat in the Academy, to which he had been elected in 1848, and he was named national poet in Granada in a solemn ceremony in 1889. By that time Zorrilla was ill and disillusioned by the constant poverty that surrounded him. He died four years later in Madrid. Enormous crowds attended his funeral, a sign of the admiration and popularity he had always enjoyed.

DRAMATURGY: MAJOR WORKS AND THEMES

When Zorrilla appeared on the Spanish literary scene, García Gutiérrez, Hartzenbusch, Bretón de los Herreros, and Rodríguez Rubí were the major dramatists. At the age of twenty-two, he wrote his first play, *Juan Dandolo* (1839), in collaboration with García Gutiérrez; a few weeks later he wrote *Cada cual con su razón* and, in the same year, *Ganar perdiendo*. In 1840 his first success was produced, part one of *El zapatero y el rey*. In this drama, the priest don Juan de Colmenares kills a cobbler, but Blas Perez, the cobbler's son, avenges his father's death by murdering the priest. Since the court has punished the priest by prohibiting his presence in church for a year, the king, in an exemplary manifestation of justice, forbids the youth from making shoes for the same period of time. The intrigue is complicated by the love affairs of Colmenares and of the king, by conjurations and secret rendezvous, and by duels and nocturnal apparitions. Considered one of Zorrilla's best works, it launched his theatrical career.

The second part of *El zapatero y el rey*, which premiered on January 5, 1842, dramatizes the final hours of King Pedro in Montiel. Blas Pérez is now a captain and confidant of the king. He falls in love with the daughter of the crown prince Enrique, Inés, who is with them as a hostage. When don Pedro is assassinated, Blas places his loyalty to the king before his love for Inés and has her killed. The play was enormously popular for its great dramatic effect and its strong characters. Contrary to the image given by most historians that portrayed the monarch as cruel, the dramatist depicted him as a charismatic and anarchical character who was as great in revenge as in generosity. In reality, he sought to reclaim the monarch's memory in various works. Picoche asserts that in these dramas, Zorrilla exalts a king and a people who, united against the nobility, represent the essence of Spanish virtues.[1]

Early in his theatrical career, the Romantic Zorrilla became interested in tragedy. In 1842 he wrote his own version of *Sancho García*, based on the legend of Count Sancho García of Castile, as it is told in the *Crónica general*, a theme that previously had also interested Cadalso and Cienfuegos. He called this great play a "composición trágica" [a tragic composition] in which he provided what basically would have been a Romantic drama with elements pertaining to tragedy, such as scenes written in eleven-syllable "romance" verses. Sancho García is an energetic, well-rounded character. His mother, the Countess, embodies the power of a late-blooming passion in a mature woman as well as the conflict between the love she has for her son and the love for her Moorish lover. Although in the legend *El montero de Espinosa* Don Sancho kills his mother and the Moor, Zorrilla gave his tragedy a less violent ending: The Countess enters a monastery, and the Moor is forced to drink poison. This play was followed by *Sofronia* (1843), a one-act tragedy in which Zorrilla modified Sofronia's ending. To avoid her commiting suicide to save her honor from Emperor Majencio's advances, Zorrilla has her become a Christian martyr who is subsequently murdered. Zorrilla subtitled *La copa de marfil* (1844) "a tragic show in three parts." It takes place in Verona in the sixth century and tells the story of Rosamunda, King Alboino's wife and her revenge.

El puñal del godo (1848), a drama in one act, was written by Zorrilla in one day. Based on the legend that King Don Rodrigo, the last of the Goths, died in Portugal, this play takes liberties with history. Count Julián meets King Rodrigo in the cabin of a hermit; after a heated argument, the King's faithful retainer Teudia kills don Julián when the latter attacks the King. The drama exemplifies the creative genius of the author who makes Don Rodrigo a high dramatic character, presents the theme with great simplicity in an original manner, and brings it to a masterful conclusion.

March 18, 1844, saw the debut in Madrid's Teatro de la Cruz of what is undoubtedly the most popular production of the Spanish stage, *Don Juan Tenorio*. It is not easy to determine Zorrilla's sources in writing this work, since not even his own words on the subject are reliable. The issue has been studied widely by scholars such as José Luis Varela (1975), García Castañeda (1975), Picoche (1986), and Fernández Cifuentes (1993) in their respective editions of the play. Regardless of which sources might have inspired him, Zorrilla maintained the setting and the characters created by Tirso. He added many new situations, created the character don Luis Mejia, Don Juan's antagonist, and introduced Brígida, who combines the role of *"graciosa"* with that of *go-between* in the tradition of Celestina. The servant Ciutti is not his master's conscience, like Tirso's Catalinón, but rather the executor of his wishes. However, the principal theme of the play is Zorrilla's main innovation: the redeeming power of pure love, a purpose that voids the Counter-Reformation character of Tirso's play.

Don Juan Tenorio is a Romantic drama devoid of any theological, moralizing, or didactic value. The supernatural intervention of Don Gonzalo and Doña Inés's offer to God to make her salvation contingent upon that of Don Juan, lack any religious meaning, belonging to the realm of fantasy.

The melodious fluidity of the rich verse, the liveliness of the action, the brilliancy of the spectacle, and the impact of the plot made *Don Juan Tenorio* the greatest creation of the Spanish Romantic theater.

The figure of the seducer appears more than once within Zorrilla's literary production: as the protagonist of "El capitán Montoya," "Margarita la tornera," "A buen juez, mejor testigo," and "Vivir loco y morir más," besides the popular don Juan in dramatic and *zarzuela* versions. The character Mr. La Bourdonnais of *El Tenorio bordelés* is also a depraved emulation of the Sevillian. Zorrilla wanted to adapt the traditional myth to a context and perspective different from those that had prevailed until then. For Torrente Ballester, the *Tenorio* is "perhaps the most discussed, the most praised and the most reviled of modern theatrical works, but the only popular one" [la más discutida, quizá, de las obras teatrales modernas, la más alabada y denostada, pero la únicamente popular].[2] As Fernández Cifuentes notes, contributing to the play's popularity are its numerous parodies, which can be seen as both attacks and signs of its vitality and of the admiration it has always inspired.[3]

Nevertheless, both Zorrilla and his critics considered *Traidor, inconfeso y mártir* (1847) to be his greatest achievement. After the death of King Sebastian of Portugal in the battle of Alcazarquivir, Portugal was annexed to the Spanish crown by Sebastian's uncle Phillip II. "Sebastianism" was born, a legendary belief that Don Sebastian was still alive and would return one day to claim his throne. Moved either by patriotic or by opportunistic reasons, several impostors aspired to the throne of Portugal. The last one was the pastry-cook of Madrigal, Gabriel Espinosa, who was sentenced to death. In his play, Zorrilla portrays Espinosa as the king, who hides his true identity for reasons that are unexplained. As Portugal is annexed to Spain, the king renounces the throne to avoid war. Refusing to break his silence, he is executed as an impostor, and only after his death is it revealed that he was indeed don Sebastian. Here Zorrilla's felicitous interpretation and modification of a dark and legendary historical event is not only original but also replete with dramatic possibilities. The identity of the character is uncertain until the denouement, and the mystery—why Espinosa cannot reveal the reasons for his heroical behavior—is skillfully and theatrically maintained. Espinosa is a proud, severe, and indomitable character and, as a true Romantic hero, appears to us surrounded by an aura of mystery. His figure is human, full of the nuances necessary for a dramatic creation of the highest caliber. The play is somber, solemn, devoid of distracting episodes. The action takes place in the same location for the first two acts and changes only in the third. The secondary actions are masterfully combined with the central plot, and serve to intensify the action. It is written in sonorous and beautiful verse, and Zorrilla was always proud of it.

Zorrilla was a great narrative poet with nostalgia for the past. The plots of his legends are taken from history, popular religiuous tradition, or his own fertile imagination. In his poems, as well as in his dramas, we find proud and enamored gallants ready to fight for their honor and their king, fathers who govern the future of their daughters, and modest and prudent ladies caught up in complicated amorous adventures Both legends and dramas also tell of miraculous events and exemplary punishments that manifest the fate reserved to sinners and the power of divine justice. Among the best known is "Margarita la tornera," the story of a nun who leaves her convent for a lover, and upon her return, repentant, finds out that the Holy Virgin, to whom she was very devout, had been taking her place and nobody had noticed her absence. In "A buen juez, mejor testigo," Diego promised Inés to marry her, but upon returning to Toledo from the wars, already a captain, he denies his pledge. Inés requests the testimony of the Christ on the cross, at whose feet the pledge was made, and, miraculously, the image speaks on her behalf and lays a wooden hand on the Gospels.[4]

There is a close relationship between Zorrilla's plays and his *leyendas*, or narrative poems of a legendary or historical theme. Many of these poems use dialogue extensively, with the characters' names printed before each speech in a way similar to how they appear in a drama. Each action is contained within a frame and forms an independent scene within the *leyenda*. Zorrilla was well aware of the theatrical quality of his *leyendas* and, on one ocasion, wrote that the dialogues appearing in *Las dos rosas* (1839) "change this legend into a drama." Also, fending off the critics who accused him of mixing the genres of theater and narrative poetry, he stated in *La leyenda del Cid* (1882–1883) that there was room in his legends for all literary genres. It is significant that his drama *El eco del torrente* (1842) has the same theme as the legend *Historia de un español y dos francesas* (1840–1841); *Sancho García* has its counterpart in the legend *El montero de Espinosa* (1842); the early *leyenda Recuerdos de Valladolid* (1839) reappears as the drama *El Alcalde Ronquillo o El diablo en Valladolid* (1845); and quite a few verses of *Margarita la tornera* are included in *Don Juan Tenorio*.

In the first days of October 1893 in the Madrid newspaper *El Imparcial*, Zorrilla began to publish his memoirs, *Recuerdos del tiempo viejo* ["Memories from the old times"]. Several parts hold special interest for us, particularly chapters XI to XX, "De cómo se escribieron y representaron algunas de mis obras dramáticas" [How some of my dramatic works were written and performed]. These memoirs are not always a reliable source of information, for Zorrilla at times forgets or prefers to modify his data. Yet, they provide us with precious information about the theatrical scene in Madrid in the nineteenth century. They also reveal that their author was a skilled playwright who knew well the secrets of his craft and how to please his public.

Zorrilla was an innovator of the historical drama that flourished in the 1840s. Both in his plays and in his legends he carried on the national tradition, and his verses evoke those of Spain's classical theater. Like other contemporary authors of historical plays, Zorrilla modified history. He also complicated his plots with elements of intrigue that maintain suspense until the end of each play. In his dramas, there is always a mysterious character, intelligent and powerful, who is in possession of a secret that will change the course of events. This character embodies justice and always prevails over the villains. The protagonist of Zorrilla's dramas is usually a charismatic character taken from Spanish history or legendary lore, and the author places him in the center of a plot full of action.

In his plays we find elements characteristic of Romantic drama, such as deadlines to be met, settings in cemeteries, dungeons, castles or hermitages, characters believed to be dead that unexpectedly reappear, anagnorises, intrigues, *coups de théâtre*, and a wide diversity of secondary characters that add a picturesque touch. Zorrilla's plays give a sentimental version of love and patriotism and invariably end with Good triumphing over Evil.

Although the majority of Spanish Romantics had a Neoclassical formation, with models such as Lista and Quintana, young Zorrilla read the Duque de Rivas and Espronceda. His work lacks intimacy and does not present ideological problems; instead, it depicts a conventional chivalric Spain of the past, populated with valiant cavaliers and noble ladies. His literary Catholicism manifests itself in great sins, great repentances, and exemplary miracles. He wrote more than thirty plays and in them, he restored traditionalism to a theater adulterated by French influence. He was responsible for extending the Romantic drama until well into Galdós's times.

CRITICS' RESPONSE

Zorrilla's verses were enthusiastically received by critics and public alike, and, between 1839 and 1847 when his first and last dramas were performed, he wrote more than thirty plays. Many writers of the new generation, such as Valera, Pereda, "Clarín" and Pardo Bazán, were his friends and appreciated his work. The young Rubén Darío admired him. Yet, literary tastes changed, and the critics eventually saw Zorrilla more and more as a surviving relic of Romanticism.

Although Zorrilla was a talented poet and was able to express in verse what the majority of playwrights put in prose, persistent economic necessities throughout his life forced him to become a "professional poet" who wrote for a living. According to Ramón Pérez de Ayala, Zorrilla had received poetry as a gift and he converted it into a trade.[5] Both his poverty and his creative facility are reflected in his work, in which great poetic achievements of musicality and fantasy come perilously close to carelessness in innumerable superfluous verses.

To date, the most enthusiastic biographer of Zorrilla and critic of his work has been Narciso Alonso Cortés, author of two works that are still indispensable today: *Zorrilla: Su vida y su obra* (Valladolid: Librería Santarén, 1943) and a critical edition of the *Obras Completas* of Zorrilla, also published by Librería Santarén in the same year.

For Allison Peers, the author's dramas were indebted to Golden Age theater for much of their versification and theatrical techniques.[6] In his recent *Panorama crítico del romanticismo español*,[7] Leonardo Romero Tobar disagrees with this opinion and points out that Zorrilla incorporated into his works many traditional elements that were alive in his time. Zorrilla owed his success to the rhythm and beauty of his verses and to the flattering way he presented history to the Spanish public.

With the exception of his *Tenorio*, Zorrilla's plays and verses are all but forgotten, both because of the persistent belief that he was a superficial poet and because of his conservatism and nostalgic approach to history. Although he was conscious of his country's ills, Zorrilla never dealt with themes related to contemporary problems. Turning his back on the present, he provided his public with a nationalistic theater of evasion, full of the color and dynamism that they sought.

Vicente Llorens considered Zorrilla a traditionalist, although he pointed out that the poet's personal opinion did not coincide with the exalted vision of Spain he gave in his work.[8] Yet certain passages in his poetry and in *Recuerdos del tiempo viejo* reveal Zorrilla's liberal ideology and a lyrical vision of Castile. These, according to Navas Ruiz, would rank him among the predecessors of the Generation of 1898.[9]

Although Zorrilla left an extensive body of work, critical attention has focused almost exclusively on the *Tenorio*, of which nine critical editions have appeared in the last ten years. In his own edition of this work, Fernández Cifuentes wrote an excellent review of the critical interpretations of the drama offered by contemporary scholarship.[10]

Though forgotten today, no poet or playwright of Zorrilla's time attained greater popularity or fame. As in the case of Tennyson, poet of Victorian England, Zorrilla incarnated the spirit of traditionalist Romanticism, and in his day he was regarded as the great national poet of Spain. It must be remembered that he was a man of his times and that our sensibilities have distanced us from his poetic conception. As poet and as playwright, he had a profound influence on those of his generation and of generations to come.

AWARDS AND DISTINCTIONS

The centenary anniversary of Zorrilla's death seems to have renewed interest in his work in general. The University of Salamanca organized a course devoted to his work (August 1993), and the University of Valladolid held a symposium, Congreso Internacional José Zorrilla: Una nueva lectura, in December of the same year. Number 564 of *Insula* (1993) was dedicated in part to Zorrilla. In March 1994, Michigan State University celebrated the Sesquicentennial Conference on *Don Juan Tenorio*, 1844–1994: The Play, Spanish Romanticism, the Legacy and Its Presence in Hispanic Cultures. In the following year Ricardo Navas Ruiz's *La poesía de José Zorrilla. Nueva lectura histórico-crítica* (Madrid: Gredos, 1995) appeared; in 1998 Ana-Sofía Pérez-Bustamante edited a volume of essays on *Don Juan Tenorio en la España del siglo XX. Literatura y cine* (Madrid: Cátedra, 1998); and in 2000, a critical edition of a selection of Zorrilla's *Leyendas* (Madrid: Cátedra, 2000) by Salvador Garcia Castañeda was published. Besides the stage, Don Juan is present today in cinema and TV: in 1990, *Don Juan, mi querido fantasma*, directed by Antonio Mercero (the subtitled English version is under the title *Don Juan, my love*); in 1991, *Don Juan en los infiernos*, directed by Gonzalo Suárez; and in 1997, *Don Juan*, directed by José Luis García Berlanga.

NOTES

1. José Zorrilla, *El zapatero y el rey*, Primera y segunda parte, ed. Jean-Louis Picoche (Madrid: Castalia, 1980), 46–47.

2. Gonzalo Torrente Ballester, "Zorrilla," in *Panorama de la literatura española contemporánea* (Madrid: Guadarrama, 1965), 45. Quoted by Fernández Cifuentes, 1993, 23.

3. José Zorrilla, *Don Juan Tenorio*, ed. Luis Fernández Cifuentes, with preliminary study by Ricardo Navas Ruiz. (Barcelona: Critica, 1993), 33.

4. Concerning Zorrilla as a poet, see Narciso Alonso Cortes's traditional study, *Zorrilla, Su vida y sus obras* (Valladolid: Santarén, 1943), Ricardo Navas Ruiz, *La poesía de José Zorrilla, Nueva lectura histórico-crítica* (Madrid: Gredos, 1995), and Salvador García Castañeda's critical edition of Zorrilla's *Leyendas* (Madrid: Cátedra, 2000).

5. Ramón Pérez, de Ayala, *El centenario de Zorrilla*, in *Obras completas*, ed. J. García Mercadal (Madrid, 1963), 4: 485–487. Quoted by J. L. Alborg, *Historia de la literatura española* (Madrid: Gredos, 1980), 4: 562–563.

6. E. Allison Peers, *Historia del movimiento romántico español*, 2 vols. (Madrid: Gredos, 1967), 216–231.

7. Leonardo Romero Tobar, *Panorama crítico del romanticismo* (Madrid: Castalia, 1994), 323.

8. Vicente Llorens, *El Romanticismo español* (Madrid: Fundación Juan March/Editorial Castalia, 1979), 438.

9. Ricardo Navas Ruiz, *El Romanticismo español* (Salamanca: Anaya, 1974), 238.

10. See Fernández Cifuentes in Zorrilla, *Don Juan Tenorio*, "Reception," in "Prólogo," 23–24.

BIBLIOGRAPHY

Main Plays: Editions in the Last Decade

Don Juan Tenorio. Ed. José Luis Varila, Madrid: Real Academia Española, 1974.

Don Juan Tenorio. Ed. Salvador García Castañeda. Barcelona: Labor, 1975.

Don Juan Tenorio. With *Traidor, inconfeso y mártir*. Ed. José Luis Gómez. Barcelona: Planeta, 1984.

Don Juan Tenorio. Ed. Jorge Campos. Madrid: Alianza Editorial, 1985.

Don Juan Tenorio. Ed. Aniano Peña. Madrid: Cátedra, 1986.

Don Juan Tenorio. With *Un testigo de bronce*. Ed. Jean-Louis Picoche. Madrid: Taurus, 1986.

Don Juan Tenorio. Ed. Francisco Nieva. Madrid: Espasa-Calpe, 1990.

Don Juan Tenorio. Ed. Luis Fernández Cifuentes, with preliminary study by Ricardo Navas Ruiz. Barcelona: Crítica, 1993.

Don Juan Tenorio. Ed. Gies, David T. Madrid: Castalia, 1994.

Translations of Plays

English

The Dagger of the Goth. Trans. Willis Knapp Jones. In *Poet Lore.* Boston: 1929.
The Fever (La Calentura). Trans. Albert K. Stevens and Willis Knapp Jones. N.p.,
    1930.
Don Juan Tenorio. Adapted from the Spanish and rendered into English verse by Walter
    Owen, with drawings by Carlos Vergottini. Buenos Aires: W. Owen, 1944.

French

Don Juan Tenorio. Traduction nouvelle par Henri de Curzon. Paris [1899].

German

Religios-phantastiches Drang in Zwei Abteilungen von *Don Juan Tenorio.* Aus dem
    Spanischen ubertraugen durch G. H. Wilde. Leipzig: Brockhaus, 1850.
Religios-phantastisches Drang in Zwei Abteilungen von *Don Juan Tenorio.* Aus dem
    Spanischen ubertraugen von Johannes Fastenrath. Dresden und Leipzig: C. Reis-
    ner, 1898.

Italian

Don Giovanni Tenorio: dramma religioso frantastico in due parti/Jose Zorrilla/nella ver-
    sione di Luigi Chiarelli. Roma: Atlantica editirice, 1946.

Portuguese

D. Joao Tenorio. Versao liberrima da peca de Zorrilla. 2a. edicao. Lisboa, Portugal-
    Brasil; por Julio Dantas [1920]; por Julio Dantas [1922].

Critical Studies

Alberich, José. *La popularidad de Don Juan Tenorio y otros estudios de literatura es-
    pañola moderna.* Zaragoza: Cometa, 1982.
Arias, Judith. "The Devil at Heaven's Door: Metaphysical Desire in *Don Juan Tenorio.*"
    Hispanic Review 81 (1993): 15–34.
———. "The Don Juan Myth: A Girardian Perspective." In *Modern Myths*, ed. David
    Bevan. Amsterdam: Rodopi, 1993. 23–59.
Becerra, Carmen. *Mito y literatura. Estudio Comparado de Don Juan.* Vigo: University
    Press, 1997.
Egido, Aurora. "Sobre la demonología de los burladores (de Tirso a Zorrilla)." *Cuadernos
    de Teatro Clásico* 2 (1988): 37–54.
Feal Deibe, Carlos. "Conflicting Names, Conflicting Laws: Zorrilla's *Don Juan Tenorio.*"
    PMLA 96.3 (1981): 375–387.
———. "Entre el amor y el honor: El *Don Juan Tenorio* de Zorrilla." In *En nombre de
    Don Juan (Estructura de un mito literario).* Amsterdam: John Benjamins, 1984.
    35–48.
Fernández, Luis Miguel. *Don Juan en el cine español. Haia una tearíg de la recressión
    Pilmica.* Santiago de Compostela: Publicacións, 2000.

Fernández Cifuentes, Luis. "Don Juan y las palabras." *Revista de Estudios Hispánicos* 25 (1991): 77–101.

Fuente, Ricardo de la, and Fabián Gutiérrez. "La 'teatralidad' en el *Don Juan Tenorio* de Zorrilla." *Crítica Hispánica. El teatro español en el siglo XIX.* 1995. 65–80.

López, Ignacio Javier. *Caballero de novela. Ensayo sobre el donjuanismo en la novela española moderna, 1880–1930.* Barcelona: Puvill Libros, 1986.

Marías, Julian. "Dos dramas románticos: *Don Juan Tenorio* y *Traidor, inconfeso y mártir.*" In *Estudios románticos.* Valladolid: Casa-Museo de Zorrilla, 1975. 181–197.

Marín, Diego. "La versatilidad del mito de Don Juan." *Revista Canadiense de Estudios Hispánicos* 6 (1982): 389–403.

Menaríni, Piero. "Don Juan contra Don Juan." *Cahiers d'Etudes Romanes* 11 (1986): 49–74.

Mitchell, Timothy. "Don Juan Tenorio as Collective Culture." In *Violence and Piety in Spanish Folklore.* Philadelphia, PA: Philadelphia University Press, 1988, 169–189.

Molho, Maurice. *Mitologías. Don Juan. Segismundo.* Madrid: Siglo XXI, 1993.

Oliva, César. "Trayectoria escénica del Tenorio." In *Anuario de "Literatura y cine."* A.S. Perez Bustamante, ed. Madrid: Cátedra, 1988, 27–38.

Pérez-Bustamante, Ana-Sofía, ed. *Don Juan Tenorio en la España del siglo XX. Literatura y cine.* Madrid: Cátedra, 1998.

———. "Saga y fugas de Don Juan." In *Anuario de "Literatura y cine."* A.S. Perez Bustamante, ed. Madrid: Cátedra, 1988, 11–24.

Pérez Firmat, Gustavo. "Carnival in Don Juan Tenorio." Hispanic Review 51 (1983): 269–281.

Rubio Jiménez, Jesús. "*Don Juan Tenorio*, drama de espectáculo: Plasticidad y fantasía." *Cuadernos de Investigación Filológica* 15 (1989): 5–24.

Serrano, Carlos. *Carnaval en Noviembre. Parodias teatrales españolas de "Don Juan Tenorio."* Alicante: Instituto Juan Gil Albert, 1996.

Singer, Armand E. *The Don Juan Theme. Versions and Criticism. A Bibliography.* Morgantown: West Virginia University Press, 1966. (With supplements for 1966, 1970, 1973, 1975, 1980)

Smeed, John William. *Don Juan. Variations on a Theme.* London and New York: Routledge, 1990.

GENERAL BIBLIOGRAPHY

EIGHTEENTH CENTURY

AA. VV. (Abreviatura de Autures Varios V.) "Literatura popular: Conceptos, argumentos y temas." *Anthropos. Revista de documentación científica de la cultura* (mayo-agosto 1995): 166–167.

Abellán, Manuel L. "La censura teatral. Espectáculos públicos." In *Censura y creación literaria en España.* 4 vols. Madrid: 1980. 3:31–36; 4:37–45.

Abril, Manuel. "La escenografía, moderna." In *La Ilustración Española y Americana.* Madrid: 1915. 7–8. (7 studies)

Aguilar Piñal, Francisco. *Bibliografía de autores españoles del siglo XVIII.* Madrid: Consejo Superior de Investigaciones Científicas/CSIC, 1983.

Alborg, Juan L. *Historia de la literatura española.* 3 vols. Vol. 3, *Eighteenth Century.* Madrid: Gredos, 1970.

Albrerich, J. M., et al. *Historia de la literatura española.* 2 vols. Vol. 2, *Desde el siglo XVIII hasta nuestros días.* Trans. Cristina Estévez et al. Madrid: Cátedra, 1990.

Alcalá Galiano, Alvaro. *Impresiones de arte.* Madrid: 1910.

Alenda y Mira. *Relaciones de solemnidades y fiestas públicas de España.* Madrid: 1903.

Alvarez, Emilio, ed. La vuelta del puente de Alcolea *de Guillermo Morera*; Los mártires de Arahal, *de Francisco Macaría*; ¡Abajo los Borbones!. A propósito, En un acto y en verso *y otras obras.* N.p., n.d.

Andioc, René. *Sur la querelle du théâtre au temps de Leandro Fernández de Moratín.* Tarbes: Imprenta Saint Joseph, 1970.

———. *Teatro y sociedad en el Madrid del siglo XVIII.* Madrid: Castalia, 1976.

———. *Teatro y sociedad en el Madrid del siglo XVIII.* Rev. 2d ed. Madrid: Castalia, [1988].

Arco y Garay, A. *La idea de imperio en la política y la literatura españolas.* Madrid: 1944.

Autoras en la historia del teatro español (1600–1994). Vol 1. Project Research Director, Juan Antonio Hormigón. Serie Teoría y práctica del teatro. No. 10. Madrid: Equipo de investigación, Publicaciones de la Asociación de Directores de Escena, 1996.

Azpitarte, J. M. "La ilusión escénica en el siglo XVIII." *Cuadernos Hispanoamericanos* (1975): 303.

Campos, Jorge. *Teatro y sociedad en España (1780–1820)*. Madrid: Moneda y Crédito, 1969.

Canas Murillo, Jesús. *La comedia sentimental: Género español del siglo XVIII*. Cáseres: Universidad de Extremadura, 1994.

Carnero, Guillermo. *Estudios sobre el teatro español del siglo XVIII*. Zaragoza: University of Saragossa Press, 1997.

Caro Baroja, Julio. *Teatro popular y magia*. Madrid: Publs., de la Revista de Occidente, 1974.

———. "Los najos." *Cuadernos Hispanoamericanos* 299 (May 1975): 281–349.

Chaussée, N. de la. *La razón contra la moda*, [French] *comedia*. Trans. Igancio de Luzán. Madrid, 1751.

Ciges Aparicio, Manuel. *España bajo la dinastía de los Borbones*. Madrid: Aguilar, 1932.

Cook, John A. *Neoclassic Drama in Spain: Theory and Practice*. Dallas: Southern Methodist University Press, 1974.

Cotarelo y Mori, E. *Bibliogrfía de las controversias sobre la licitud del teatro en España*. Madrid: 1904.

Díez Borque, José María. *Historia del teatro en España*. 4 vols. Vol. 2, *Siglo XVIII, Siglo XIX*. Madrid: Taurus, 1988.

Doménech Rico, Fernando, ed. *Antología del Teatro Breve del siglo XVIII*. Madrid: Biblioteca Nueva, 1997.

Falk, Heinrich Richard. "Enlightment Ideas, Attitudes, and Values in the Teatro menor of Luis Moncín." In *Studies in Eighteenth-Century Spanish Literature and Romanticism in Honor of John Clarkson Dowling*, ed. Douglas Barnette and Linda Jane Barnette. Newark, DE: Juan de la Cuesta Hispanic Monographs, 1985. 77–88.

Fernández de Moratín, Nicolás. *Desengaño al theatro español, respuesta al Romance liso y llano y defensa del Pensador*. 3 vols. Madrid, 1762–1763.

García Garrosa, María Jesús. *La retórica de las lágrimas: La comedia sentimental española. 1751–1802*. Office of Publications [Valladolid]: Universidad de Valladolid, Caja Salamanca, 1990.

Hazard, Paul. *La Pensée européenne au XVIIIème: De Montesquieu à Lessing*. Paris: Boivin, 1946.

Herrera Navarro, Jerónimo. *Catálogo de autores Teatrales del Siglo XVIII* [Catalog of Eighteenth Century Authors]. Madrid: Fundación Universitaria Española. Monografies 58. Alcalá: Gráficas, 1993.

Huerta Calvo, Javier. "Pervivencia de los géneros chicos en el teatro español del siglo XX." *Primer Acto* 187 (1981): 122–127.

Johnson, Colin B. "Madrid's Third 'Public' Theater." In *Studies in Eighteenth-Century Spanish Literature and Romanticism in Honor of John Clarkson Dowling*, ed. Douglas Barnette and Linda Jane Barnette. Newark, DE: Juan de la Cuesta Hispanic Monographs, 1985. 99–112.

Lucea García, Javier. *La poesía y el teatro en el siglo XVIII*. Madrid: Editorial Playor, 1984.

Luzan, Ignacío de. *Memorias literarias de Paris*. Madrid, 1751.

———. *La poética o Reglas de la poesía en general y de sus principales especies*. [texts of 1737 and 1789]. Ed. Prologue and glossary by Russell P. Sebold. Barcelona: Editorial Labor, 1977.

Martín Gaité, Carmen. *Love Customs in Eighteenth Century Spain*. Trans. María C. Tomsich. Berkeley: University of California Press, 1991.

————. *Usos amorosos del XVIII en España*. Madrid: Lumen, 1981.

McClelland, Ivy Lilian. *The Origins of the Romantic Movement in Spain: A Survey of Aesthetic Uncertainties in the Age of Reason*. 2d ed., 1957. Rpt. New York: Barnes and Noble, 1975.

————. *Spanish Drama of Pathos, 1750–1808*. Vol. 2. Toronto: University of Toronto Press, 1970.

————. *Spanish Drama of Pathos, 1750–1808. "Pathos" dramático en el teatro español de 1750 a 1808*. By I[vy] L[ilian] McClellan. Trans. Fernando Huerta Vinas and Guillermina Cenoz del Aguila. Liverpool: University of Liverpool Press, 1998.

Palacios Fernández, Emilio. "La descalificación moral del sainete dieciochesco." In *El teatro menor en España a partir del siglo XVI*. Ed. Grupo de investigación sobre teatro español. Madrid: CSIC, 1983.

————. *El teatro popular español del siglo XVIII*. Lleida: Editorial Milenio, 1998.

Palacios Fernández, Emilio, Ermanno Caldera, Antonietta Calderone, and Jesús Rubio Jiménez. *Historia del teatro en España. Siglo XVIII. Siglo XIX*. Vol. 2. Ed. José María Díaz Borque. Madrid: Taurus, 1988.

Pérez Teijón, Josephina. *Literatura popular y burlesca del siglo XVIII*. Salamanca: Universidad de Salamanca Press, 1990.

Rull Fernández, Enrique. *La poesía y el teatro en el siglo XVIII (neoclasicismo)*. Madrid: Taurus, 1987.

Sainz de Robles, Federico, ed. *Teatro español, historia y antología*. Vol. 5. (eighteenth century). Madrid: Aguilar, 1942–1943.

Sala-Valldaura, J. M. [Josep María]. *El sainete en la segunda mitad del siglo XVIII: La mueca de la Talía*. Lleida: Universitate de Lleida, 1994.

Sánchez, Roberto G. "On Staging *Don Alvaro* Today." In *Studies in Eighteenth-Century Spanish Literature and Romanticism in Honor of John Clarkson Dowling*, ed. Douglas Barnette and Linda Jane Barnette. Newark, DE: Juan de la Cuesta Hispanic Monographs, 1985. 133–143.

Santullano, Luis, ed. Prólogo. *Teatro y poesía del siglo XVIII*. Mexico City, Mexico: Editorial Orion, 1950.

Serrailh, Jean. *La España ilustrada de la segunda mitad del S. XVIII*. Mexico City: Fondo de Cultura Económica, 1957.

Shergold, N. D., and J. E. Varey. *Teatros y comedias en Madrid, 1699–1719: Estudio y documentos* [Study and Documentation]. London: Tamesis Books, 1986.

Varey, J. E. *Historia de los títeres en España desde sus orígenes hasta mediados del siglo XVIII*. Madrid: Revista de Occidente, 1957.

Varey, J. E., N. D. Shergold, and Charles Davis. *Fuentes para la historia del teatro en España*: XII–12. *Teatros y comedias en Madrid: 1719–1745. Estudio y documentos*. Madrid: Tamesis, 1994.

NINETEENTH CENTURY

Alvarez, Barrientos, Joaquín. "Enrique Rambal (1889–1956)." In *Teatro de Magia*, ed. Ermanno Caldera. 2 vols. Rome: Bulzoni, 1991.

Araujo Costa, Luis. *Ventura de la Vega, estudio biográfico-critico*. Madrid: Pérez Dubrull, 1904.

Avrett, Robert. "A Brief Examination into the Historical Background of Martínez de la

Rosa's *La conjuración de Venecia.*" In *Teatro Cuadernos para el diálogo.* Madrid: 1973. *Romantic Review* 21 (1930): 132–137.

Barbier, J. C. *Les deux arts poétiques d'Horace et de Boileau.* Ed. Ernest Thorin. Paris: Librairie du Collège de France et de l'Ecole Normale Supérieure, 1874.

Beccaria, Cesare. *Dei delitti e delle pene.* Torino: Unione Tipografico-Editrice Torinese, 1911.

Benitez Claros, Rafael. "Variaciones sobre el sentimentalismo neoclásico." In *Visión de la literatura española.* Madrid: Ediciones Rialp, 1963. 199–208.

Bernbaum, Ernest. *The Drama of Sensibility: A Sketch of the History of English Sentimental Comedy and Domestic Tragedy (1695–1789).* Cambridge, MA: Harvard University Press, 1925.

———. "The Romantic Movement." In *The English Romantic Poets: A Review of Research,* ed. Thomas M. Raysor. New York: Modern Language Association of America, 1950. 1–37.

Caldera, Ermanno. *Il dramma romantico in Spagna.* Instituto di litteratura spagnola e ispano-americana, no. 26/26. Pisa: Universita di Pisa, 1974.

Caldera, Ermanno, and Antonietta Calderone. *La commedia romantica in Spagna.* Pisa: Giardini, 1970.

———. "El teatro en el siglo XIX (1808–1844)." In *Historia del teatro en España.* 4 vols. Vol. 2, *Siglo XIX.* Ed. José María Díez Borque. Madrid: Taurus, 1988. 377–624.

Calvo Asensio, Gonzalo. *El teatro hispano-lusitano en el siglo XIX.* Madrid: Imprenta de los señores Rojas, 1875.

Campos, Jorge. *Teatro y sociedad en España (1780–1820).* Madrid: Editorial Moneda y Crédito, 1969.

Canáls, Salvador. *El año teatral (1895–1896). Crónicas y documentos.* Madrid, 1896.

Casalduero, Joaquín. *Estudios sobre el teatro español.* 2d ed. Madrid: Gredos, 1967.

Caso Gonzáles, José M. *"El delincuente honrado, drama sentimental": La poética de Jovellanos.* Madrid: Prensa Española, 1972. 193–234.

Cavalle, A. "Memorias y autobiografias en España (siglos XIX y XX)." *Supplements Anthropos* 29 (1991): 143–169. (Número monográfico sobre La autobiografía y sus problemas teóricos. Estudios e investigación documental [monographic volume, dedicated to Autobiography and Its Theoretical Problems. Document Study and Research])

Chicharro Chamorro, Dámaso, and Julio López. *Teatro y Poesía en el Romanticismo.* Madrid: Cincel, 1981.

Cobb, Christopher H. "Mundo obrero y la elaboración de una política popular (1931–1938)." In *La prensa de los siglos XIX y XX,* ed. M. Tuñón de Lara and C. Garitaonondia. Bilbao: Universidad del País Vasco, 1986. 277–290.

Correa Calderón, Evaristo. "Larra, crítico de teatro." *RIE/Revista de Investigación de España* 33 (1974): 191–212.

Cotarelo y Mori, Emilio. *Bibliografia de las controversias sobre la licitud del teatro en España.* Madrid: Archivos, Bibliotecas y Museos, 1904.

———. "Ensayo histórico sobre la zarzuela o el drama lírico español desde su origen a fines del siglo XIX." *Boletín de la Real Academia Española* 19 (1932): 625; 20 (1933): 97; 21 (1934): 113.

———. *Isidoro Máiquez y el teatro de su tiempo.* Madrid: José Perales y Martínez, 1902.

Deleito y Piñuela, José. *Origen y apogeo del género chico.* Madrid: Revista de Occidente, 1949.

Díaz de Escovar, Narciso. *Intimidades de la farándula: Colección de artículos referentes a la escena, comediantes y escritores dramáticos desde el siglo XVI hasta el día.* Cadiz: España y América, 1916.

Diez Borque, José María, ed. *Historia de la literatura española.* 2 vols. Madrid: Taurus, 1988.

Equipo de Investigación sobre el teatro español. Instituto "Miguel de Cervantes" del Consejo Superior de Investigaciones Científicas (CSIC), ed. *El teatro menor de España a partir del siglo XVI.* Madrid: Consejo Superior de Investigaciones Científicas, 1963.

Escritoras españolas del siglo XIX. Manual bio-bibliográfico. Nueva Biblioteca de erudición y crítica. Madrid: Editorial Castalia, 1991.

Esgueva, Martínez Manuel. *La colección teatral La farsa. Bibliografía descriptiva* [Descriptive Bibliography] [nineteenth and twentieth centuries]. Madrid: Consejo Superior de Investigaciones Científicas/CSIC, Instituto Miguel de Cervantes, 1971.

Espin Templado, María del Pilar. *El sainete del último tercio del siglo XIX, culminación de un género dramático en el teatro español.* Madrid: *Espos* 3, 1987.

Esquer Torres, Ramón. "Tamayo y Baús y la política del siglo XIX." *Segismundo* 1 (1965): 71–91.

———. *El teatro de Tamayo y Baús.* Madrid: Consejo Superior de Investigaciones Científicas/CSIC, 1965.

Fábregas, Xavier, ed. *Sainets del sigle XIX.* Barcelona: Millà, 1979.

Falconieri J. "Historia de *la Commedia dell' Arte* en España." *Revista de Literatura* 11 (1957): 3–37; 12 (1957): 69–90.

Fernández de Moratín, Leandro. *Obras de Don Nicolás Fernández de Moratín.* Biblioteca de Autores Españoles (BAE). Madrid: Real Academia, 1944.

———. *Teatro completo. Textos Hispánicos modernos.* Biblioteca de la literatura y el pensamiento hispánicos, 19. Madrid: Editorial Nacional, [1977].

Ferreras, Juan Ignacio, and A. Franco. *El teatro en el siglo XIX.* Madrid: Taurus, 1989.

Fitz-Gerald, J. D. "*Un drama nuevo* on the American Stage." *Hispania* 7 (1924): 22–34.

Flynn, Gerald. *Una bibliografia anotada sobre Manuel Bretón de los Herreros.* Paris: La Beher. 1976.

———. *Manuel Bretón de los Herreros.* Boston: G. K. Hall, 1978.

———. *Manuel Tamayo y Baus.* New York: Twayne, 1973.

Ganelín, Charles. *Rewriting Theatre: The Comedia and the Nineteenth-Century "Refundiciones"* [Adaptations]. Lewisburg, PA: Bucknell University Press, 1994.

García Castañeda, Salvador, ed. *El teatro español en el siglo XIX.* Vol. XVII. No. 1. Madrid: Crítica Hispánica, 1995.

Gies, David Thatcher. "Don Juan Tenorio y la tradicíon de la comedia de magia." *Hispanic Review* 58 (1990): 1–17.

———. "Hacia un mito anti-napoleónico en el teatro español de los primeros años del siglo XIX." In *Teatro politico spagnolo del primo ottocento,* ed. Ermano Caldera. Rome: Bulzoni, 1991. 43–62.

———. *Theater and Politics in Nineteenth Century Spain: Juan Grimaldi as Impresario and Government Agent.* Cambridge: Cambridge University Press, 1988.

———. *The Theater in Nineteenth-Century Spain.* Cambridge: Cambridge University Press, 1994.

Goenaga, Angel, and Juan P. Maguna. *Teatro español del siglo XIX*. New York: Las Americas, 1971.

González López, Emilio. *Historia de la civilización española*. Vol. II of 2 vols. New York: Las Americas, 1959.

Gregersen, Halfdadan. *Ibsen and Spain: A Study in Comparative Drama*. Cambridge, MA: Harvard University Press, 1936.

Hazard, Paul. *La crise de la concience européenne*. Paris: Boivin, 1935.

Juliá Martínez, Eduardo, ed. *Teatro moderno* [nineteenth-century], *selección, observaciones preliminares y notas*. Madrid: Instituto Antonio de Nebrija, 1947, Consejo Superior de Investigaciones Científicas/CSIC, 1947. [Selection, Introduction, and Notes by him].

Juretschke, H. *Vida, obra y pensamiento de A[lberto] Lista*. Madrid: Consejo Superior de Investigaciones Científicas/CSIC, 1951.

La Cecilia, Giovanni, ed. and trans. *Teatro scelto Spagnuolo antico e moderno raccolta dei migliori drammi*. Nuova Biblioteca Populare. 6 vols. Torino, 1857–1859.

Larra, Mariano José. *Artículos literarios*. Ed. Juan José Ortiz de Mendivil. Barcelona: Plaza and Janés, 1985.

Leslie, John Kenneth. *Ventura de la Vega and the Spanish Theater, 1820–1865*. Princeton, NJ: Princeton University Press, 1940.

Liverani, Elena. *Un personaggio tra storia e letteratura: Don Carlos* [Prince of Asturias] *nel teatro spagnolo del XIX secolo*. Firenze: La Nuova Italia, 1995.

Lloréns, Vicente. *Liberales y románticos*. Mexico City, Mexico: Fondo de Cultura, 1954.

Loftis, John Clyde. "The Duchess of Malfi on the Spanish and English Stages." *Research Opportunities in Renaissance Drama* XII (1969): 25–31.

Lomba y Pedraja, José Ramón. *Mariano José de Larra (Figaro)* [as a writer of folklore, political writer, literary critic, and dramatist] *cuatro estudios . . .* Madrid: Tipografía de Archivos, 1936.

Lope, Hans-Joachim. "La imagen de los franceses en el teatro español de propaganda durante la Guerra de Independencia (1808–1813)." *Bulletin of Hispanic Studies* 68 (1991): 219–229.

López de Ayala, Adelardo. *Obras/Works*. 6 vols. Madrid: Imprenta Nacional, 1881–1883.

López Soler, R. *Análisis de la cuestión agitada entre románticos y clasicistas, in El Europeo*. Consejo Superior de Investigaciones Científicas/CSIC. Madrid: Guarner, 1954.

Lorenz, Charlotte M. "Seventeenth Century Plays in Madrid from 1801–1818." *Hispanic Review* 6 (1938): 324–331.

Lott, Robert E. "On Mannerism and Mannered Approaches to Realism: *Un drama nuevo, Consuelo*, and Earlier Nineteenth Century Spanish Plays." *Hispania* 54 (1971): 844–855.

Maravall, José Antonio. *Antiguos y modernos: La idea de progreso en el desarrollo inicial de una sociedad*. Madrid: Sociedad de Estudios y Publicaciones, 1966.

Marichal, Carlos. *Spain (1834–1844): A New Society*, London: Tamesis, 1977.

Marrast, Robert. *José de Espronceda et son temps. Littérature, société, politique au temps du Romantisme*. Paris: Editions Centre National du Rechercé Scientifique/CNRS, 1974.

Martín, Gregorio C. "Querer y no poder, o el teatro español de 1825 a 1836." In *Studies in Eighteenth-Century Spanish Literature and Romanticism in Honor of John*

Clarkson Dowling, ed. Douglas Barnette and Linda Jane Barnette. Newark, DE: Juan de la Cuesta Hispanic Monographs, 1985. 123–132.

Martínez Espada, Manuel. *Teatro contemporáneo*: [The 1898–1900 Theatrical Season] *Apuntes para un libro de crítica* [Notes for a Book of Criticism]. Madrid: Imprenta-Ducazcal, 1900.

Martínez Ruiz, José [Azorin]. *Historia y anecdotario del Teatro Real* [from the second half of the nineteenth century]. Madrid, 1997. Rpt. from the Madrid: Plus Ultra, 1949, J. Subirá's edition.

Martínez Torrón, Diego, ed. *El alba del romanticismo español: With a collection of Unpublished Works by Lista, Quintana, y Gallego*. Sevilla: Ediciones Alfar, Servicio de Publicaciones de la Universidad de Córdoba, 1993.

Mas Ferrer, Jaime. *Vida, teatro y mito de Joaquín Dicenta*. Alicante: Secretaría Provincial de Alicante, 1978.

McClelland, I. L. *The Origins of the Romantic Movement in Spain*. Liverpool: University of Liverpool Press, 1937.

———. *Spanish Drama of Pathos, 1750–1808*. 2 vols. Toronto: University of Toronto Press, 1970.

Menéndez Onrubia, Carmen. "El teatro clásico durante la Restauración y la Regencia (1875–1900)." *Cuadernos de Teatro Clásico* 5 (1990): 187–207.

Meranini, Piero, et al. *El teatro romántico español (1830–1850): Autores, obras, bibliografía*. Bologna: Atesa, 1982.

Mesonero Romanos, Ramón. *Memorias de un setentón*. Illustrated ed. Madrid: España y America, 1881.

Monleón, José. *El teatro del 98 frente a la sociedad española*. Madrid: Cátedra, 1975.

Montero Alonso, José. *Ventura de la Vega, su vida y su tiempo*. Madrid: Editorial Nacional, 1951.

Navas Ruiz, Ricardo. *Imágenes liberales. Rivas—Larra—Galdós*. Salamanca: Almar, 1979.

———. *El romanticismo español: Documentos*. Madrid: Anaya, 1971.

———. *El romanticismo español. Historia y crítica*. Madrid: Anaya 1970.

Oenslager, Donald. *Stage Design: Four Centuries of Scenic Invention*. New York: 1975.

Ossorio y Bernard, Manuel. *Ensayo de un catálogo de periodistas españoles del siglo XIX*. Madrid: J. Palacios, 1903–1904.

Parker, A., and Edgar Allison Peers. "The influence of Victor Hugo on Spanish Drama." *Modern Language Review* 28 (1933): 205–216.

Pataky Kossove, Joan Lynne. *The "Comedia lacrimosa" and Spanish Romantic Drama (1773–1865)*. London: Tamesis, 1997.

Paz y Meliá, Antonio. *Catálogo de las piezas de teatro que se conservan en el departamento de manuscritos de la Biblioteca Nacional*. 2d ed. 1899. Rpt. Vol. 1. Madrid: Colegio Nacional de Sordomudos y de Ciegos, 1934.

Peak, J. Hunter. *Social Drama in Nineteenth Century Spain*. Chapel Hill: University of North Carolina Press, 1964.

Peers, E. Alison. *Historia del movimiento romántico español*. 2 vols. Madrid: Gredos, 1967.

Pellicer, Cassiano. *Tratado histórico sobre el origen y progresos de la comedia y del histrionismo en España*. Ed. José María Díez Borque. 2 vols. Madrid, 1804. Barcelona: Labor, 1975.

Pérez Pastor, Cristóbal. *Noticias y documentos relativos a la historia y literatura españolas. Memorias.* Vols. 10–13. Madrid: Real Academia Española, 1910–1926.

Pérez Teijón, Josephina. *Aportación al estudio de la literatura popular y burlesca del siglo XVIII.* Salamanca: Gráficos Cervantes, 1991.

Polt, John H. R. "El delincuente honrado." *Romance Review* 50 (1959): 170–190.

————. *Gaspar Melchor de Jovellanos.* New York: Twayne Publishers, 1971.

Puppo, M. *Poética e cultura del romanticicismo.* Roma, Editorial Canesi, 1982

Reynaud, Louis. *Le Romantisme: Les origines anglo-germaniques.* Paris: Librairie Armand Colin, 1926.

Río, Angel del. "Present Trends in the Conception and Criticism of Spanish Romanticism." *Romanic Review* 39 (1948): 229–248.

Ríos-Font, Wadda C. *Rewriting Melodrama: The Hidden Paradigm in Modern Spanish Theater.* Lewisburg, PA: Bucknell University Press, 1996.

Rodríguez Rubi, Tomás. "Excelencia, importancia y estado presente del teatro." *Discursos leídos ante la Real Academia Española.* Madrid: Matute, 1860. 1–39.

Rodríguez-Sánchez, Tomas. *Catálogo de Dramaturgos españoles del siglo XIX.* Monographs 61. Instituto Nacional de Artes. Madrid: Fundación Universitaria, 1994.

Romero Ferrer, Alberto. *El género chico: Introducción al estudio del teatro corto. Fin de siglo: De su incidencia gaditana* [Short Theater: Introduction to the Study of Short Theater. End of the Century: Its incidence in Cadiz]. Cadiz: Universidad de Cadiz, Servicio de Publicaciones, 1993.

Rubina, E. Henry, and Enrique Ruiz Fornells, eds. "Introducción." *La muralla.* By José Calvo Sotelo. New York: Appleton Century Crofts, 1962.

Rubio, A. *La crítica del galicismo en España (1726–1832).* Mexico City: 1937.

Rubio Jiménez, Jesús. *El teatro en el siglo XIX.* Madrid: Editorial Playor, 1983.

Ruiz Silva, Adolfo. "Motivos románticos europeos en *El Trovador* de García Gutiérrez." *Revista de Literatura Moderna/RLM* 13 (1973): 151–190.

————. "*El Trovador*, de García Gutiérrez, drama y melodrama." *Cuadernos Hispanoamericanos* 335 (1978): 251–272.

Sainz de Robles, Federico, ed. *Teatro español, historia y antologia.* Vols. 6 and 7 [nineteenth century]. Madrid: Aguilar, 1943.

Salerno, Henry F., trans. *Scenarios of the "Commedia dell'Arte": Flaminio Scolá's 'Il Theatro delle favole rappresentative.* New York: New York University Press, 1967.

Sánchez Pérez, A. *El teatro español en fin de siglo* [Nineteenth]. Ed. Juan Valerno de Tornos. Madrid: Sucesores de Rivadeneyra, 1895.

Sebold, Russell P. "Enlightenment Philosophy and the Emergence of Spanish Romanticism." In *The Ibero-American Enlightenment.* Urbana: University of Illinois Press, 1971. 111–140.

————. "El incesto, el suicidio y el primer romanticismo español." *Hispanic Review* 41.4 (Autumn 1973): 669–692.

————. "Sobre el nombre español del dolor romántico." *Insula* 264 (November 1968): 1, 4–5.

Shaw, Donald Leslie. "The Anti-Romantic Reaction in Spain." *Modern Language Review* 63 (1968): 606ss.

————. *Historia de la literatura española. El siglo XIX.* Barcelona: Ariel, 1986–1987.

Shaw, G. B. "The Echegaray Matineés." In *Dramatic Opinions and Essays II.* New York: 1907.

———. "Spanish Tragedy and English Farce." In *Dramatic Opinions and Essays I*. New York: 1906.

Simón Palmer, María del Carmen. "Construcción y apertura de teatros Madrileños en el siglo XIX." *Segismundo* 11 (1975): 85–137.

———. *Escritoras españolas del siglo XIX. Manual bio-bibliográfico*. Madrid: Castalia, 1991.

———. "Mil escritoras españolas del siglo XIX." In *Crítica y ficción literaria: Mujeres españolas contemporáneas*, ed. Aurora López and María Angeles Pastor. Granada, 1989. 39–59.

Smith, W. F. "Contributions of Rodríguez Rubí to the Development of the *alta comedia.*" *Hispanic Review* 10 (1942): 53–63.

———. "The Historical Plays in the Theater of Tomás Rodríguez Rubí." *Bulletin of Hispanic Studies* 28 (1950): 221–228.

Sobejano, Gonzalo. "Echegaray, Galdós y el melodrama." *Anales Galdosianos (Supplement)* 13 (1978): 91–117.

———. "Razón y suceso de la dramática Galdosiana." *Anales Galdosianos* 5 (1970): 39–54.

Spell Jefferson, Rea. *Rousseau in the Spanish World before 1833: A Study in Franco-Spanish Literary Relations*. Austin: University of Texas Press, 1938.

Stoudemire, S. A. *The Dramatic Works of Gil y Zárate*. Chapel Hill: University of North Carolina Press, 1930.

Subirá, José. "Estudios sobre el teatro madrileño. Los 'melólogos' de Russeau, Iriarte y otros autores." *Revista de la Biblioteca. Archivos y Museos* 5 (1928): 360–364.

———. *Historia de la música teatral de España*. Barcelona: Labor, 1945.

———. *Historia y anecdotario del Teatro Real*. Madrid: Plus Ultra, 1949.

———. *Tamayo y Baus. Obras*. "Introduction" by Alejandro Pidal. 4 vols. Madrid, 1898–1900.

Tayler, Neale H. *Las fuentes del teatro de Tamayo y Baus: Originalidad e influencias*. Madrid: Gráficas Uguina, 1959. Rpt. Madrid, 1965.

Thompson, John Archie. *Alexander Dumas pere and Spanish Romantic Drama*. Louisiana State University Studies. No. 37. Baton Rouge: Louisiana State University Press, 1938.

Traubner, Richard. *Operetta: A Theatrical History*. Garden City, NY: Doubleday, 1983.

Valbuena Prat, Angel. *Historia del teatro español*. Barcelona: Noguer, 1965.

Van Tieghem, Paul. *Le Romantisme dans la litèrature européenne*. Paris: Editions Albin Michel, 1948. Spanish trans: *El Romanticismo en la literatura europea*. México, 1958.

Varey, E. J. *Fuentes para la historia del teatro en España*. Vol. 8, *Cartelera de los títeres* [Puppets Shows] *y otras diversiones populares de Madrid: 1758–1840. Estudio y documentos* [Study and Documentation]. Madrid: Tamesis, 1995.

Vico, Antonio. "Isidoro Máiquez, Carlos Latorre y Julián Romea. La escena española desde comienzos del siglo. La declamación en la tragedia, en el drama y en la comedia de costumbres." In *La España del siglo XIX*. Madrid: Ateneo, 1886.

Villalón, Cristóbal, de. *Ingeniosa comparación entre lo antiguo y lo presente*. Ed. M. Serrano y Sánz. Madrid, 1898.

Zavala, Iris. *Ideología y política en la novela española del siglo XIX*. Salamanca: Anaya, 1971.

———. "La realidad del folletín." In *Historia y crítica de la literatura española*, ed. Francisco Rico. Vol. 5. Barcelona: Editorial Crítica, 1983.

———. *Románticos y socialistas*. Madrid: Siglo 21, 1972.

TWENTIETH CENTURY

Abel, Lionel. *Metatheater. A New View of Dramatic Form*. New York: Hill and Wang, 1963.

Abellán, Manuel L. "La censura teatral durante el franquismo." *Estreno* 15. 1 (Spring 1989): 20–23.

———. *Censura y creación literaria en España (1939–1976)*. Temas de historia y política contemporánea 9. Barcelona: Península, 1980.

———. "Literatura censura y moral en el primer franquismo." *Papers* 21 (1984): 153–172.

———, ed. *Censura y literatura peninsulares. Diálogos hispánicos de Amsterdam* 5. Amsterdam: Rodopi, 1987.

Abrams, Dianne. "The Short Play in the United States and Spain" (Review). *Estreno* 23.2 (Fall 1997): 5.

Abril, Manuel. "La escenografía moderna." *La ilustración Española y Americana*. Madrid 1915. 7–8.

———. "Los pintores de Eslava." In *Un teatro de arte en España, 1917–1925*, ed. Gregorio Martínez Sierra. Madrid: La Esfinge, 1925. 19–36.

Acción Católica de la mujer. *De teatros. ¿Qué obras podré ver yo?* Oviedo: Editorial Gráfica Asturiana, 1925.

Adams, Mildred. "The Theatre in the Spanish Republic." *Theatre Arts Monthly* 3 (1932).

Adamson, Ginette, and Eunice Myers, eds. *Continental, Latin-American and Francophone Women Writers*. New York: United Press of America, 1997.

Aguilera Sastre, Juan. "Del teatro comercial a una escuela integral del arte escénico (1929–1936)." *Cuadernos de El Público* 42 (December 1969): 21–25. (Monographic volume dedicated to Cipriano Rivas Sherif)

Alás-Brun, María Montserrat. *De la comedia del disparate al teatro del absurdo (1939–1946)*. Barcelona: Promociones y Publicaciones Universitarias (PPU), 1995.

Alberich, J. M., et al. *Historia de la literatura española*. 2 vols. Vol. 2, *Desde el siglo XVIII hasta nuestros días* Trans. Cristina Estévez et al. Madrid: Cátedra, 1990.

Alonso, Alejandro. "Los nuevos espacios teatrales de Barcelona: El Milenio que viene." *Teatro* 60–61 (1997): 132–139.

Alonso, José Luis. "Teatro de cada día: Escritos sobre teatro." In *Teoría y práctica del teatro*, ed. Juan Antonio Hormigón. Vol. 4. Madrid: Publicaciones de la Assn. de Directores de Escena, 1991.

Alsina, José. "Crónica: El encanto de la opereta." *Comedias y Comediantes* 31 (May 1911): 4.

Altoagruirre, Manuel. "Nuestro teatro." *Hora de España* 9 (1937): 29–37.

Alvarez Barrientos, Joaquín. "Enrique Rambal (1889–1956)." In *Teatro de magia*, ed. Ermanno Caldera. 2 vols. Rome: Bulzoni, 1991.

Alvarez de Miranda, Angel. *La metáfora y el mito*. Madrid: Taurus, 1963.

Alvaro, Franco. *El espectador y la crítica. (El teatro en España en 1958)*. Valladolid, Spain: Sever Cuesta, 1959.

————. *El espectador y la crítica. (El teatro en España en 1959)*. Valla: Author, 1960.

————. *El espectador y la crítica. (El teatro en España en 1960)*. Valla: Author, 1961.

————. *El espectador y la crítica. (El teatro en España en 1961)*. Valla: Author, 1962.

————. *El espectador y la crítica. (El teatro en España en 1962)*. Valla: Author, 1963.

————. *El espectador y la crítica. (El teatro en España en 1963)*. Valla: Author, 1964.

Amestoy Egiguren, Ignacio. "La literatura dramática española en la encrucijada de la posmodernidad." *Insula* 601–602 (1997): 2–5.

Amorós, Andrés. *Luces de candilejas: Los espectáculos en España (1898–1939)*. Madrid: Espasa-Calpe, 1991.

————. ¿Nuevas dramaturgias? Asociación de Directores de Escena." *Teatro* 50–51 (1996): 96–97.

Amorós, Andrés, Marina Mayoral, and Francisco Nieva. *Análisis de cinco comedias (teatro español del postguerra)*. Madrid: Editorial Castalia, 1977.

Anaya, Ruiz, Francisco. "El Teatro Lírico Nacional. Laboremos por la ópera española." *Nuevo Mundo*, February 3, 1928.

Anderson, Andrew A. "Bewitched, Bothered and Bewildered: Spanish Dramatists and Surrealism, 1924–1936." In *The Surrealist Adventure in Spain*, ed. C. Brien Morris. Ottawa: Dovenhouse Editions, 1991. 240–281.

Anderson, Andrew W. "Una desorientación absoluta: 'Juliet' and the Shifting Sands in García Lorca's *El Público*." *Revista Hispánica Moderna* 50.1 (1997): 67–85.

Anderson, Farris. "Sastre on Brecht: The Dialectics of Revolutionary Theatre." *Comparative Drama* 3.4 (1969–1970): 282–296.

Angélico, Halma. "La revolución de la escena." *Técnicos*, August 5, 1937: 53–74.

Araquistain, Luis. "¿Qué es teatro?: El caso de Luigi Pirandello." *La Voz*, December 26, 1923: 1.

————. "La vida y el arte. Una teoría del humorismo." *La Voz*, January 24, 1924: 1.

Arias de Cossio, Ana María. *Dos siglos de escenografía en Madrid*. Madrid: Mondadori, 1991.

Armstrong, Paul G. *Conflicting Readings: Variety and Validity in Interpretation*. Chapel Hill: University of North Carolina Press, 1990.

Artaud, Antonin. *The Spurt of Blood. Antonin Artaud, Selected Writings*. Ed. and intro. Susan Sontag. New York: Ferrar, Straus and Giroux, 1976.

————. *The Theater and Its Double*. Spanish trans. *El teatro y su doble* by Mary Caroline Richards. New York: Grove Press, 1958. Barcelona: Edhasa, 1978.

Ascoaga, Enrique. "Las misiones pedagógicas." *Revista de Occidente* 7–8 (November 1981): 222–232.

Asenjo, Antonio. "Crónica: La decadencia del género chico." *Comedias y Comediantes* 15 (May 1910): 10.

Aszyk, Ursula. "Das spanische Theater und die Avantgardebewegungen in 20 Jahrhundert." In *Spanishes Theater in 20. Jahrhundert. Gestalten and Tendenzen*, ed. Wilfred Floeck. Tübingen: Francke, 1980.

————. "En torno a la cuestión del teatro surrealista español anterior a la guerra civil." *Acta Universitatis Wraatislaviensis*. Serie *Estudios Hispánicos* 1875.5 (1997): 23.

Aub, Max. "Piscator y una nueva valoración del teatro." *Nueva Cultura*, 3 (March 1935): 6–7.

————. *Proyecto de estructura para un Teatro Nacional y Escuela Nacional de Baile, addressed to His Excellence the President, Don Manuel Azaña y Díaz, writer.* Valencia: Tipografía. Moderna, 1936.

Aubrun, Charles V. "La fortune du téâtre de García Lorca en Espagne et en France." In *Le Téâtre moderne: Hommes et tendances*, ed. Jean Jacquot. Paris: Éditions du Centre National de la Recherche Scientifique, 1958. 299–307.

Autoras en la historia del teatro español (1500–1994). Teoría y práctica del Teatro. Vol. 2, *Siglo XX (1900–1975)*. Project Research Director, Juan Antonio Hormigón. Madrid: Asociación de Directores de Escena de España, 1997.

Aúz Castro, Víctor. "Panorama of the Spanish Theatre Today/Panorama du théâtre espagnol contemporain." *Le Théâtre dans le Monde/World Theatre* 12 (1963): 191–228.

Aznar Soler, Manuel. "José María de Quinto." In *Critico teatral de los sesenta*. Murcia: Publicaciones de la Universidad de Murcia, 1997. Earlier as "José María de Quinto, crítico teatral del realismo social." *Ciel* 4.1 (1993): 207–232.

———. *Literatura española y antifascismo (1927–1939)*. Valencia: Conselleria de Cultura, Educació i Ciencia, 1987.

———. " 'Presentación' de Rafael Dieste." In *Teatro*. 2 vols. Barcelona: Laia, 1981.

———. "El teatro durante la II República (1931–1939)." *Monteagudo* 2 (1997): 45–57.

———, ed. *Veinte años de teatro y democracia en España (1975–1995)*. Madrid: Compañia Investigadora de Teatro Español Contemporáneo, 1996.

Baeza, Ricardo. "En torno al problema del teatro. Campo en barbecho." *El Sol*, January 13, 1921: 1.

———. "En torno al problema del teatro. Necesidad de una acción pública." *El Sol*, January 22, 1921: 1.

Barish, Jonas. *The Anti-Theatrical Prejudice*. Berkeley: University of California Press, 1981.

Barlow, John D. *German Expressionist Film*. Boston: Twayne, 1982.

Baroja, Ricardo. "Amargas reflexiones de un autor fracasado acerca del teatro español moderno, de los autores cómicos, de los empresarios, de los críticos y del público." *La Farsa* 2 (1926): 19.

Basalisco, Lucio. *Due studi sull' Auto degli anni trenta*. Verona: Libreria Universitaria, 1983.

Baudrillard, Jean. *The Mirror of Production*. Trans. and "Introduction" by Mark Poster. St. Louis, MO: Telos Press, 1975.

Bayo Manuel. "Alberti por Alberti." *Primer Acto*. 150 (November 1972): 6–12.

Bearsley, Theodore S., Jr. "El sacramento desautorizado. *El hombre deshabitado* de Alberti y los autos sacramentales de Calderón." In *Studia Iberica. Festchrift für Hans Flasche*. Berna-Munich: Francke, 1973.

Belfiore, Elizabeth S. *Tragic Pleasures: Aristotle on Plot and Emotion*. Princeton, NJ: Princeton University Press, 1992.

Bello, Luis. "Leo Fall y las viejas operetas austriacas." *Nuevo Mundo*, November 20, 1925: 12.

Bellveser, Ricardo. *Teatro en la encrucijada*. Valencia: Ajuntament de Valencia, 1987.

Benamou, Michel, and Charles Caramello. *Performance in Postmodern Culture*. Madison, WI: Coda Press, 1977.

Best, Steven, and Douglas Kellner. *Postmodern Theory: Critical Interrogations*. New York: Guilford Press, 1991.

Bilbatua, Miguel. Prologo. *Teatro de agitación politica. 1933–1939*. Madrid: Edicusa, 1976.

Blasco, Ricard. *El teatre al País Valencià durant la guerra civil (1936–1939)*. Barcelona: Curial, 1986.

Bobes, María del Carmen. *Semiología de la obra dramática*. Madrid: Taurus, 1987.

Block, Haskell M. *Mallarmé and the Symbolist Drama*. Detroit, MI: Wayne State University Press, 1963.

Bolton, Richard. *Culture Wars*. New York: New Press, 1992.

Borel, Jean-Paul. *Théâtre de l'impossible. El teatro de lo imposible: Ensayo sobre una de las dimensiones fundamentales del teatro español contemporáneo*. Trans. Gonzalo Torrente Ballester. Colección de Crítica y Ensayo 46. Madrid: Guadarrama, 1966.

Borja, Margarita. *Helénica. Poema para "El Público." Una pieza teatral*. Barcelona: Antrops, 1996.

Borrás Tomás. "Un acontecimiento artístico. La españolización del teatro Real." *Nuevo Mundo*, December 14, 1923: 1.

———. "¿Cómo debe ser el teatro falangista?" *Revista Nacional de Educación*, no. 35 (November 1943): 71–84.

———. "Un teatro de arte en España." In *Un teatro de arte en España, 1917–1925*, ed. Gregorio Martínez Sierra. Madrid: La Esfinge, 1926. 9–16.

Brandes, George. *Friedrich Nietzsche*. New York: Haskell House Publishers, 1972.

Brecht, Bertolt. *Breckt on Theater: The Development of an Æsthetic*. Ed. John Willet. New York: Hill and Wang, 1964.

Brenan, Gerald. *The Face of Spain*. London: Turnstile Press, 1950.

Brown, G. "The Twentieth Century." *In A Literary History of Spain*, ed. R. O. Jones. 8 vols. London: Ernest Benn; New York: Barnes and Noble, 1971–1973. Vol. 6, 1972.

Brown, J. *Women Writers of Contemporary Spain*. NJ: Associated University Press, 1991.

Brown, Sharon. *Modern Drama Studies: An Annual Bibliography. Modern Drama* 37.2 (1994): 302–313.

Brunetta, Gean Piero. *Letteratura e cinema*. Bologna: Zanichelli, 1976.

Bryan, T. Avril. *Censorship and Social Conflict in the Spanish Theater: The Case of Alfonso Sastre*. Washington, DC: University Press of America, 1982.

Bueno, Javier. *Vicios de París*. Barcelona: Pauzá, [1914].

Bueno, Manuel. *Teatro español contemporáneo*. Madrid: Biblioteca Renacimiento, 1909.

Buero Vallejo, Antonio. "García Lorca ante el esperpento." In *Tres maestros ante el público*. Madrid: Alianza Editorial, 1973.

Buero Vallejo, Antonio, et al. *El teatro español actual*. Madrid: Fundación Juan March/ Edns. Cátedra, 1977.

Buñuel, Luis. "Tragedias inadvertidas como temas de un teatro novísimo." Alfan 26 (February 1923). Rpt. *Obra literaria*. Ed. A. Sánchez Vidal. Zaragoza: Heraldo de Aragón, 1983. 83–84.

Bürger, Peter. *Theorie der Avantgarde*. Frankfurt: Suhrkamp, 1974.

Butt, John. *Writers and Politics in Modern Spain*. London: Hodder and Stoughton, 1978.

Cabal, Fermín. *La situación del teatro en España*. Madrid: Asociación de Autores de Teatro, 1994.

Cabello Lapiedra, Xavier. "El homenaje a los Quintero. Los insignificantes. El teatro Nacional." *La Epoca*, February, 14, 1928: 1.

———. "Seamos españoles." *Nuevo Mundo*, May 5, 1916: 31.

———. "El teatro nacional debe instalarse en el teatro Real." *La Epoca*, March 10, 1928: 4.

Callahan, David. "Harley Granville-Barker and the Response to Spanish Theater, 1920–1932." *Comparative Drama* 25.2 (1991): 129–146.

Calvo, Luis. "El surrealismo en el teatro." *ABC*, March 31, 1931: 10–11.

Calvo Sotelo, Joaquín. *Teatro*. Madrid: G. Del Toro, 1974.

Campbell, Colin. *The Romantic Ethic and the Spirit of Modern Consumerism*. London: Basil Blackwell, 1987.

Canavaggio, Jean. "García Lorca ante el entremés cervantino: El telar de *La zapatera prodigiosa*." In *El teatro menor en España a partir del siglo XVI*. Equipo de Investigación sobre el teatro español. Instituto "Miguel de Cervantes" del Consejo Superior de Investigaciones Científicas (CSIC). Madrid: CSIC, 1983. 141–152.

Canavaggío, Jean, and [the] Muñoz Seca [Playhouse]. *"El embrujado"* (Performance Review). *El Imparcial*, December 12, 1931: 6.

Cantalapiedra, Fernando. *El teatro español de 1960 a 1975: Estudio socio-económico. Problemata Literaria* 5. Kassel: Reichenberger, 1991.

Cardwell, R. A. "The Persistence of Romantic Thought in Spain." *Modern Language Review* 65 (1970): 803–812.

Caro Baroja, Julio. *Teatro popular y magia*. Madrid: Editions of the Revista de Occidente, 1974.

Carr, Raymond. *Modern Spain: 1875–1980*. Oxford: Oxford University Press, 1980.

———. *Spain: 1808–1975*. 2d ed. Oxford: Clarendon Press, 1982.

Carrere, Emilio. "La zarzuela y la revista." *Nuevo Mundo*, July 19, 1928: 5; and August 21, 1928: 3.

Cases, Antonio. Prólogo. Antonio Mori's *El teatro. Impresiones críticas en un momento de transición (1919–1920)*. Madrid: Reus, 1920.

Castro, Cristóbal de. "La evolución escénica. Las cuatro escuelas del Conservatorio: Música, Declamación, Canto y Cine." *Nuevo Mundo*, June 7, 1929: n.p.

———. *"Teatro de mujeres." Tres autoras españolas*. Madrid: Aguilar, 1934.

Castrovido, Roberto. "El teatro y la política." *El Liberal*, March 3, 1935: 1–2.

Caudet, Francisco. "La hora (1948–1950) y la renovación del teatro español de posguerra." In *Entre la Cruz y la espada: En torno a la España de posguerra: Homenaje a Eugenio de Nora*, ed. José Manuel López de Abiada. Madrid: Gredos, 1984. 109–126.

Cavalle, A. "Memorias y autobiografías en España (siglos XIX y XX)." *Supplements Anthropos* 29 (1991): 143–169.

Centeno, Enrique. *La escena española actual. Crónica de una década: 1984–1994*. Madrid: Marco Gráfico, 1996.

———. "Una Historia del Teatro Representado." *Insula* 601–602 [Monographic volume] *Teatro* [español]: *Género y espectáculo* (enero, febrero 1997): 5–7.

Cervera, Juan. *Historia crítica del teatro infantil español*. Madrid: Editorial Nacional, 1980.

[Cincuenta] *50 años de teatro: José Tamayo (1941–1991)*. Madrid: Ministerio de Cultura, 1991.

Clurman, Harold. *The Divine Pasttime: Theatre Essays*. New York: Macmillan, 1974.

Cobb, Christopher H. "El agit-prop cultural en la guerra civil." *Studia Histórica–Historia Contemporánea* 10–11 (1992–1993): 237–249.

———. "Mundo obrero y la elaboración de una política popular (1931–1938)." In *La prensa de los siglos XIX y XX*, ed. M. Tuñón de Lara and C. Garitaonondia. Bilbao: Universidad del País Vasco, 1986. 277–290.

Coca, Jordi. *Qüestions de teatre: Monografies de Teatre*. 18. Barcelona: Editions 62, Institut del Teatre, 1985.

Coca, Jordi, Eric Gallen, and Ana Vazquez. *La Generalitat Republicana i el Teatre (1931–1939)*. *Legislació*. Barcelona: Institut del Teatre de la Diputació de Barcelona, 1962.

Conde Guerri, María José. *Panorámica del teatro español de la posguerra a la transición (1940–1980)*. *Damos la palabra: Ensayo breve*. Madrid: Asociación de Autores de Teatro, 1994.

Cotarelo y Mori, Emilio. *Proyecto de organización del Teatro Clásico Español*. Madrid: 1935.

Crescioni Neggera, Gladis. "Miguel Mihura: Iniciador del teatro del absurdo." *La estafeta literaria*, no. 572 (September 15, 1975): 9–11.

Crespo Matellán, S. *La parodia dramática en la literatura española*. Salamanca: University of Salamanca Press, 1979.

[Cuarenta y cuatro] *44 autores de teatro en activo*. Madrid: Asociación de Autores de Teatro, 1996.

Cueva, Jorge de la. *"La reina castiza."* *El Debate*, June 4, 1931: 5.

Culler, Jonathan. *The Pursuit of Signs. Semiotics, Literature, Deconstruction*. Ithaca, NY: Cornell University Press, 1981.

Deleito y Piñuela, José. *Origen y apogeo del "género Chico."* Madrid: Publicaciones de la Revista de Occidente, 1949.

Delgado, María, *Spanish Theatre 1920–1955. Strategies in Protest and Imagination*. London: Hardwood Academic Publishers The Gordon and Breach Publishing Group. *Contemporary Drama Review* 7: 2–4 (1998).

Derrida, Jacques. "Freud and the Scene of Writing." In *Writing and Difference*, trans. Alan Bass. Chicago: University of Chicago, Press, 1978.

Díaz-Canedo, Enríque. "Calderón en Salzburgo." *España* 344 (1922): 10–11; 347 (1922): 12–13; 348 (1922): 9–10.

———. "Panorama del teatro español desde 1914 hasta 1936." *Hora de España* 16 (April 1935): 13–52. Reprinted in: *Articulos de critica teatral. El teatro español de 1914 a 1936*. Vol. 1. Mexico: Joaquín Mortiz, 1968.

———. (Critilo). "Teatro de anteayer, de ayer, de hoy de mañana." *España* 260 (April, 24, 1920): 9–11.

———. "Los teatros: Muñoz Seca 'Entre la cruz y el diablo' " [Halma Angélico]. *El Sol*, June, 12, 1932: 12.

Díaz-Plaja, Guillermo. *Vanguardismo y protesta en la España de hace medio siglo*. Barcelona: Asenet, 1975.

———, ed. *El teatro: Enciclopedia del arte escénico*. Barcelona: Noguer, 1958.

Diez Taboada, Juan María. *Das Spanische Theatre des 19-Jahrhunderts. Darmstadt*. Wissenschaftliche: Buchgesellschaft, 1985.

Dolan, Jill. *The Feminist Spectator as Critic*. Ann Arbor: University of Michigan Research Press, 1988.

Doménech, Ricardo. "Aproximación al teatro del exilio." In *El exilio español de 1939: Cultura y literatura*. Madrid: Taurus, 1977. 183–246.

———. "Azorín dramaturgo." *Cuadernos Hispanoamericanos* 226–227 (1968).

———. "Doble lectura de *Así que pasen cinco años."* *Boletín de la Fundación Federico Garcia Lorca* 7–8 (December 1990): 233–254.

———. "Encuesta sobre la censura." *Primer Acto* 165–166 (1974): 4–14.

――――. "La muralla treinta años después." *Cuadernos para el diálogo. La cultura de hoy*, número monográfico [monographic number] (July 1967).

――――. "Simbolo, mito y rito en *La casa de Bernarda Alva.*" In *"La casa de Bernarda Alva" y el teatro de Garcia Lorca*, ed. Ricardo Doménech. Madrid: Cátedra, 1985. 187–209.

――――. *El teatro de Buero Vallejo: Una meditación española.* 2d ed. Madrid: Gredos, 1993.

――――. "El teatro de Lauro Olmo." *Cuadernos Hispanoamericanos* 229 (1969).

Dougherty, Dru. "La escena madrileña entre 1900–1936. Apuntes para una historia del teatro." *Anales de la literatura Española Contemporánea/ALEC* (1992).

――――. "The Semiosis of Stage Decor in Jacinto Grau's *El señor de Pigmalión.*" *Hispania* 47 (1984): 351–357.

――――. "Talía convulsa: La crisis teatral de los años 20." In *Dos ensayos sobre teatro español de los [años] 20*, ed. Robert Lima and Dru Dougherty. Murcia (Spain): *Cuadernos de la Cátedra de Teatro de la Universidad de Murcia* 11 (1984): 85–155.

――――. "Valle-Inclán ante el cine." In *Valle-Inclán y el cine. Catálogo de la retrospectiva organizada por la Filmoteca Española* [Catalog of the Retrospective Organized by the Film Library of Spain]. Madrid: Ministerio de Cultura, 1986.

――――. *Un Valle-Inclán olvidado: Entrevistas y conferencias.* Madrid: Fundamentos, 1983.

――――. *Valle-Inclán y la Segunda República.* Valencia: Pre-Textos, 1986.

――――. *Valle-Inclán y su tiempo.* Madrid: Ministerio de Cultura, 1986.

Dougherty, Dru, and María Francisca Vilches de Frutos, eds. *La escena madrileña entre 1918 y 1926: Análisis y documentación.* Madrid: Fundamentos, 1990.

――――. *La escena madrileña entre 1926 y 1931. Un lustro de transición.* Madrid: Fundamentos, 1997.

――――. *El teatro en España. Entre la tradición y la vanguardia (1918–1939).* Madrid: CSIC/Group Tabacalera, Fundación Federico García Lorca, 1992.

Durán, Manuel, and Francesca Colecchia, eds. *Lorca's Legacy. Essays on Lorca's Life, Poetry, and Theatre.* New York: Peter Lang, 1991.

Eco, Humberto. "Semiotics of Theatrical Performance." *The Drama Review* 21.1 (1977): 107–117.

Edwards, Gwynne. *Dramatists in Perspective: Spanish Theater in the Twentieth Century.* New York: St. Martin's Press, 1985.

――――. "Spain." In *European Theatre: 1960–1990: Cross Cultural Perspectives*, ed. Ralph Yarrow. London: Routledge, 1992. 138–159.

Elam, Keir. *The Semiotics of Theatre and Drama.* London and New York: Methuen, 1980.

Equipo [Group] Multitud, ed. *Escenografí a teatral española.* Catalogue. Madrid: Galería Multitud, 1975.

Escrivá, Pellicer. M. *El desafío yanqui y España. Colección Mundo Nuevo 25* Santander: Editorial Sal Terrae, 1974.

Esgueva, Martínez Manuel. *La colección teatral La farsa. Bibliografia descriptiva* [Descriptive Bibliography (nineteenth and twentieth centuries)]. Madrid: Consejo Superior de Investigaciones Científicas, Instituto Miguel de Cervantes, 1971.

Espina, Antonio. "Las dramáticas del momento." *Revista de Occidente* 30 (1925): 318–329.

Esquer Torres, Ramón. *La colección dramática "El teatro Moderno."* Madrid: Consejo Superior de Investigaciones Científicas, 1969.

Esslin, Martín. *El teatro del absurdo.* Barcelona: Seix Barral, 1966.

Estreno Cuadernos del teatro español contemporáneo. Modern Spanish Drama on the Professional English Speaking Stage. Monographic Vol. 14, no. 2 (1988); *Teatro español en Inglaterra, Estados Unidos y Francia.* Monographic Vol. 16, no. 2 (1990).

Esturo, Juan Carlos. "La problemática del teatro del absurdo en España a partir de 1960." *Estudios Escénicos*, no. 21 (September 1976): 85–93.

Fábregas, Xavier. *Historia del teatre cataá. Catalynya Teatral: Estudis.* Vol. 1. Barcelona: Editorial Millá, 1978.

———. *Teatre Català d'agitació política.* Libres a l'Abast, 74. Barcelona: Edicions 62, 1969.

———. "El teatre edificant dels anys 50: El melodrama religiós pre-conciliar." *Siglo de Oro*, no. 199 (April 15, 1976): 95–98.

Feldman, Sharon. "Agustín Gómez-Acros's *Diálogos de la herejía* and the Deconstruction of History." *Gestos* 18 (1994): 61–80.

Fernández Cid, Antonio. *Cien años de teatro musical.* Madrid: Real Musical Editores, 1975.

Fernández Cifuentes, Luis. *García Lorca en el teatro: La norma y la diferencia.* Zaragoza: Universidad de Zaragoza, 1986.

———. "Poder y resistencia en el teatro de García Lorca." *Crítica Hispánica* 16.1 (1994): 157–168.

Fernández Insuela, Antonio. "Sobre la recepcíon de Brecht en revistas culturales españolas de posguerra." *Anuario de estudios filosóficos* 16 (1993): 126–138.

Fernández Santos, Angel. "García Pintado y las dificultades de la farsa." *Primer Acto* 123–124 (1970): 84–85.

Fernández-Shaw, Guillermo. *La larga historia de "La vida Breve."* Madrid: Publications of the Revista de Occidente, 1972.

Ferreras, Juan Ignacio. *El teatro del siglo XX (desde 1939).* Historia crítica de la Literatura Hispánica 25. Madrid: Taurus, 1988.

Filippo, Luigi De. "Pirandello in Spagna." *Nuova Antología* 99.2 (1964): 197–206.

Fletcher, Angus. *Allegory: The Theory of a Symbolic Mode.* New York. Cornell University Press, 1964.

Floeck, Wilfried. "Escritura dramática y posmodernidad: El teatro actual entre realismo y vanguardia." *Insula* 601–602 (1997): 12–14.

———, ed. *Spanishches Theatre in 20. Jahrhundert: Gestalten und Tendenzen.* Mainzer Forschungen zu Drama und Theater 6. Tübingen: Francke, 1990.

Forgacs, David, ed. *Rethinking Italian Fascism: Capitalism, Populism and Culture.* London: Lawrence and Wishart, 1986.

Foucault, Michel. *The Archeology of Knowledge.* Trans. A. M. Sheridan Smith. New York: Pantheon Books, 1972.

Fraile, Medardo, ed. *Teatro español en un acto (1940–52).* Letras Hispánicas 303. Madrid: Cátedra, 1989.

Frenzel, Elizabeth. *Diccionario de motivos de la literatura universal.* Madrid: Gredos, 1980.

Fuchs, Elinor. "The Death of Character. Reflections on Theater after Modernism." Ph.D.

diss., Graduater Center and University Center of The City University of New York, 1995.

Fuentes Victor. *La marcha al pueblo en las letras españolas.* Madrid: De la Torre, 1980.

Gabriele, John P. "Interview with Alberto Miralles: From the Independent Theater to the Theater of Democratic Spain." *Western European Stages* 9.1 (1997): 27–32.

———, ed. *De lo particular a lo universal: El teatro español del siglo XX y su contexto.* Frankfurt am Main: Vervuert Verlag, 1994.

Gabriele, John P., and Andreina Bianchini, eds. *Perspectivas sobre la cultura hispánica: XV aniversario de una colaboración interuniversitaria.* Córdoba: Servicios de Publicación–Universadad de Córdoba, 1997.

Gagen, Derek. "Traditional Imagery and Avant-garde Staging. Rafael Alberti's *"El hombre deshabitado."* In *Staging in the Spanish Theatre*, ed. Margaret Rees. Leeds: Modern Humanities Research Association, 1984. 55–86.

Gagen, Derek, and David George, eds. *La guerra civil española: Arte y violencia.* Colección Maior 20. Murcia: Universidad de Murcia, 1990.

Galán, Eduardo. *Reflexiones en torno a una politica teatral.* Madrid: Fundación para el Análisis de los Estudios Sociales, 1995.

———, ed. *Teatro realista de hoy.* Clásicos Edelvives, 26. Zaragoza/Madrid: Luis Vives, 1993.

Galerstein, Carolyn, ed *Women Writers of Spain. An Annotated Bio-Bibliographical Guide.* Westport, CT: Greenwood Press, 1986.

Gallego Morell, Antonio. "Resurrección de los Autos Sacramentales en Granada en 1927." In *Proceedings of the Third International Congress on Calderón*, ed. Luciano García Lorenzo. Madrid: Consejo Superior de Investigaciones Científicas (CSIC), 1983. 1411–1420.

Gallén, Enric. "Notes sobre la introducció de l'existencialisme: Sartre i el teatre a Barcelona (1948–1950)." *Els Marges*, no. 26 (September 1982): 120–126.

Gallina, Ana María. "Pirandello in Catalogna." In *Atti del Congresso Internationale de Studi Pirandelliani. Proceedings of the International Congress on Pirandello.* Firenze: Mounier, 1967. 201–208.

García Crisógono. *Estrenos teatrales en el Madrid de las últimas décadas.* Madrid: Grupo Libro, 1992.

García de la Concha, Victor. *La poesia española de posguerra: Teoría e historia de sus movimientos.* Estudios de Critica y Filología 22. Madrid: Prensa Española, 1973.

García Lorenzo, Luciano. "De Jacinto Grau a Antonio Buero Vallejo: Variaciones sobre un mismo tema." *Cuadernos Hispanoamericanos* 244 (1970): 169–178.

———. Introducción. *Jacinto Grau. Teatro selecto.* Madrid: Escélicer, 1971.

———. "La puesta en escena del teatro clásico." *Insula* 601–602 (enero–febrero 1997): 14–16.

———. *El teatro español hoy.* Biblioteca Cultural 6. Barcelona: Editorial Planeta/Editorial Nacional, 1975.

———, ed. *Documentos sobre el teatro español contemporáneo.* Colección Temas 17. Madrid: Sociedad General Española de Librería, 1980.

García Pavón, F. *El teatro social de España (1895–1962).* Madrid: Taurus, 1962.

———. *Textos y escenarios.* Barcelona: Plaza y Janés, 1971.

García Ruíz, Victor. "Teatro español de preguerra y de posguerra: Ruptura y continuidad." *Journal of Hispanic Research* 1 (1992–1993): 371–382.

Gassner, John. *The Theatre in Our Times.* New York: Crown Publishers, 1954.

George, David. "The Commedia dell'arte and the Circus in the Works of Jacinto Benavente." *Theatre Research International* 6.2 (1981): 92–109.

————. *The History of the Commedia dell'Arte in Modern Hispanic Literature with Special Attention to the Work of García Lorca*. Lewiston, NY: Edward Mellen Press, 1995.

Gerould, Daniel, ed. *Doubles, Demons, and Dreamers: An Anthology of Symbolist Drama*. New York: Performance Arts Journal Publications, 1985.

Gies, David Thatcher. *Theater and Politics in Nineteenth-Century Spain: Juan de Grimaldi as Impresario and Government Agent*. Cambridge: Cambridge University Press, 1988.

————. *The Theater in Nineteenth-Century Spain*. Cambridge: Cambridge University Press, 1994.

Gómez, José Luis. "La guerra de los teatros y la cultura." *El Pais. Sección Madrid*, November 14, 1993: 4.

Gómez de Baquero, Eduardo (Andrenio). *Pirandello y compañía*. Madrid: Mundo Latino, n.d.

Gómez-García, Manuel. *El teatro de autor en España (1901–2000)*. Madrid: Asociación de Autores de Teatro, 1996.

Gómez García, Miguel. *Diccionario del teatro*. Madrid: Ediciones Akal, 1997. Madrid: Grefal, S.A., 1998.

Gómez Torres, Ana María. *Una tearía teatral de la ruptura: Lorca y España de anteguerra*. Málaga: Universidad de Málaga, 1997.

Gómez Valera, José Antonio. "Coval." In *Historia visual del escenario*. Madrid: La Avispa, 1997.

Gómez Yebra, Antonio. "El teatro de humor como escape social: El éxito de Jardiel Poncela." *Boletín de la Fundación Federico García Lorca*, nos. 19–20 (December 1996): 285–298.

González-Blanco, Andrés. *Los dramaturgos españoles contemporáneos. First Serie*. Valencia: Cervantes, 1917.

González del Valle, Luis T. *El canon: Reflexiones sobre la recepción literaria-teatral (Pérez de Ayala ante Benavente)*. Madrid: Huerga and Fierro, 1993.

————. *Teatro español e iberoamericano en Madrid 1962–1991. [Juan Mollá]*. Boulder, CO: Society of Spain and Spanish American Studies, 1993.

Gordón, José. *Teatro experimental en España (antologia e historia)*. Colección 21, no. 39. Madrid: Escelicer, 1965.

Grau, Jacinto. "El Teatro Nacional. Al margen de un artículo." *Informaciones*, March 3, 1928: 1.

Gregersen, Halfdan. *Ibsen and Spain* Cambridge, MA: Harvard University Press, 1936. Rpt. New York: Kraus, 1966.

Guerrero Zamora, Juan. *Historia del teatro contemporáneo*. 4 vols. Barcelona: Juan Flors, 1961–1967.

Guillén, Claudio. "El misterio evidente en torno a *Asi que pasen cinco años*." *Boletin de la Fundación García Lorca* 7–8 (1990): 215–232.

Gutiérrez, Cuadrado, Juan. "Crónica de una recepción: Pirandello en Madrid." *Cuadernos Hispanoamericanos* 333 (1978): 347–386.

Halsey, Martha T. *From Dictatorship to Democracy: The Recent Plays of Buero Vallejo*. Ottawa Hispanic Studies 17. Ottawa: Dovehouse Editions Canada, 1994.

————. "Vigencia y universalidad de Antonio Buero Vallejo y su generación." *Insula* 601–602 (enero–febrero 1997): 26–28.

Halsey, Martha T., and Phyllis Zatlin, eds. *The Contemporary Spanish Theater: A Collection of Critical Essays.* Lanham, MD: University Press of America, 1988.

Häringer, Heribert. *Oppositionstheater in der Diktadur. Spanienkritik im Werk des Dramatikers Antonio Buero Vallejo von dem Hintergrund der franquistischen Zensur.* Wilhelmsfeld: Gottfried Egert, 1997.

Hartnoll, Phyllis, ed. *The Oxford Companion of the Theatre.* 4th ed. Oxford: Oxford University Press, 1983.

Hawkins Dady, Mark, ed. *International Dictionary of the Theater.* Chicago and London: St. James Press, 1992.

Hayes, Carlton J. H. *The United States and Spain: An Interpretation.* New York: Sheed and Ward, 1951.

Hendersen, John A. *The First Avant-Garde, 1887–1894.* London: George G. Harrap & Co., 1971.

Hernández, Mario, ed. *El libro de los dibujos de Federico Garcia Lorca.* Madrid: Tabapress, 1990.

Herrero García, Miguel. *Madrid en el teatro.* Madrid: Consejo Superior de Investigaciones Científicas/CSIC, 1963.

Holderness, Graham. *The Politics of Theatre and Drama.* London: Macmillan, 1992.

Holloway, Vance R. "La página teatral del *ABC*: Actualidad y renovación del teatro madrileño (1927–1936)." *Siglo XX* 7 (1989–1990): 1–6.

Holt, Marion Peter. "Artaudian Affinities in the Theater of Antonio Buero Vallejo." In *Antonin Artaud and the Modern Theater*, ed. Gene Plunka. Madison: Fairleigh Dickinson University Press, 1994. 252–262.

————. *The Contemporary Spanish Theater (1949–1972).* Boston: Twayne, 1975.

————. "Staging *The Sleep of Reason* on the English Speaking Stage: In Search of the Buerian Mode." In *Homenaje/A Tribute to Martha T. Halsey*, ed. Robert E. Lima and Phyllis Zatlin. University Park, PA: *Estreno*, 1995.

————. "Twentieth Century Spanish Theater and the Canon(s)." *AEC/Anales de la Literatura Española Contemporánea* 17 (1992): 47–54.

————, ed. and trans. *Modern Spanish Stage: Four Plays.* New York: Hill and Wang, 1970.

Homby, Richard. *Drama, Metadrama, and Perception.* Lewisburg: Bucknell University Press, 1986.

Hormigón, Juan Antonio. *Teatro, realismo y cultura de masas.* Madrid: *Edicusa/Cuadernos para el Diálogo*, 1974.

Hornedo, Rafael María de. "*La Muralla* y el drama católico." *Razón y Fe*, no. 686 (March 1955): 297–304.

Hoz, Enrique de la, ed. *Panorámica del teatro en España.* Madrid: Editora Nacional, 1973.

Huelamo Kosma, Julio. "La influencia de Freud en el teatro de García Lorca." *Boletín de la Fundación García Lorca* 6 (1989): 59–83.

Huerta Calvo, Javier. "Arniches en la tradición del teatro cómico breve." In *Arniches*, ed. A. Ríos Carratalá. Alicante: Caja de ahorros Provincial de Alicante, 1990. 182–201.

————. "Pervivencia de los géneros chicos en el teatro español del siglo XX." *Primer Acto* 187 (1981): 122–127.

———. *El teatro del siglo XX* Lectura Crítica de la Literatura Española 21. Madrid: Playor, 1985.

Isasi Angulo, Armando C. *Diálogos del teatro español de la posguerra*. Madrid: Ayuso, 1976.

Jencks, Charles. *What Is Post-Modernism?* London and New York: Academy Editions and St. Martin's Press, 1986.

Jerrez-Farran, Carlos. "La estética expresionista en *El público* de García Lorca." *Anales de la Literatura Española Contemporánea/ALEC* 11 (1986): 111–127.

Jiménez, José Olivio, ed. *El simbolismo*. Madrid: Taurus, 1979.

Jordan, Barry.*Writing and Politics in Franco Spain*. London: Routledge, 1990.

Jurkowski, Henryk. *Ecrivains et marionnettes. Quatre siècles de littérature dramatique*. Charleville-Mézières: Institut International de la Marionnette, 1991.

———. "La marioneta literaria. De Maeterlinck a Ghelderode." *Puck* 1 (1988): 4–7.

Kaiser Lenoir, Claudine. "*El señor Pigmalión*, de Jacinto Grau: Una subversión doble." *Insula* 432 (1994): 15, 16.

Kristeva, Julia. *Semiótica*. Trans. José María Arancibia. 2d ed. Vol. 1. Madrid: Fundamentos, 1981.

Kulenkampff, Barbara-Sabine. *Theater in der Diktatur: Spanishches Experimentiertheatre unter Franco*. Münchener Universítätsschriften: Münchener Beiträge zur Theaterwissenschaft 12. Munich: J. Kitzinger, 1979.

Lafora, Gonzalo R. "Estudio psicológico del cubismo y expresionismo." In *Don Juan, los milagros y otros ensayos*. Madrid: Biblioteca Nueva, 1927. 187–259.

Lafranque, Marie. "Estudio preliminar." In *Federico García Lorca: Teatro inconcluso, fragmentos y proyectos inacabados*. Granada: University of Granada Press, 1987.

Larraz, Emmanuel. *Teatro español contemporáneo*. Paris: Mason et Cie, 1973.

Lavaud, Jean Marie. "Con M de marioneta y M de militar: En torno a *Los cuernos de don Friolera*." In *Homage to José Antonio Maravall*. Madrid: Centro de Investigaciones Sociológicas, 1985. 427–441.

Lázaro Carreter, Fernando. "*El público*, de García Lorca." *Blanco y Negro*, July 24, 1988: 12.

Lenormand, Henry-René. *Confessions d'un auteur dramatique*. Vol. 2. Paris: Albin Michel, 1953.

Leonard, Candyce, and John Gabriele. *Panorámica del teatro español actual*. Madrid: Espinal/Fundamentos, 1996.

———. *El teatro de la España democrática: Los noventa*. Madrid: Editorial Fundamentos, 1996.

Lezcano García, Sylvia. "Pequeña historia del teatro insular de cámara (Gran Canaria)." *Gestos*, no. 4 (November 1987): 137–142.

Liana, Luis. "Escenografía." *Cuadernos del Teatro Universitario* 1 (May 1937): 35.

Lima, Robert. *Valle-Inclán: The Theatre of His Life*. Columbia: University of Missouri Press, 1988.

Linares Rivas, Manuel. "La crisis del teatro." *La Esfera* 76 (June 12, 1915): 9.

Lista, Giovanni. "El espacio marionetizado o el teatro máquina del futurismo." *Puck* 1 (1988): 22–26.

London, John. "Miguel Mihura's Place in the Theater of the Absurd: Possible Reasons for and Objections to a Generic Approach." *ALEC/Anales de la Literatura Española Contemporánea* 14 (1989): 79–95.

————. *Reception and Renewal in Modern Spanish Theatre, 1939–1963*. Vol. 45. Leeds: W. S. Maney and Sons, for the Modern Humanities Research Association, 1996.

————, ed. and trans. *The Unknown Federico García Lorca: Dialogues, Dramatic Projects, Unfinished Plays and a Filmscript*. London: Atlas Press, 1996.

Lopez Mozo, Jeróniimo. "¿Dónde está el Nuevo Teatro Español?" *Estreno* 12.1 (1986): 35–39.

López Prudencio, J. "Notas de lector: Angelita, por Azorín." *ABC*, August 13, 1930: 10.

Lukács, George. *The Meaning of Contemporary Realism*. Trans. John and Neke Mander. London: Merlin Press, 1963.

Lyonette, Henry. *Le Théâtre en España, Le Théâtre hors de France*. Paris: Paul Ollendorff, 1897.

Machado, Manuel. *La guerra literaria (1898–1914)*. Madrid: Imprenta Hispano-Alemana, 1913.

Macksey, Richard, and Eugenio Donato, eds. *The Structuralist Controversy*. Baltimore, MD: Johns Hopkins University Press, 1972.

Madarriaga, Salvador de. *Las tres caravelas en el teatro, en prosa y verso*. Madrid: Espasa-Calpe, 1983.

Maeterlinck, Maurice. "The Tragical in Daily Life." In *The Treasure of the Humble*, trans. Alfred Sutro. New York: Dodd, Mead and Co.; London: George Allen, Ruskin House, 1905.

Mainer, José-Carlos. "La evolución del naturalismo en la novela y el teatro." In *Modernismo y 98. Historia y crítica de la literatura española*, ed. Francisco Rico. Barcelona: Crítica, 1980.

————. *Literatura y pequeña burguesía en España*. Madrid: Edicusa, 1972.

Mallo, Jerónimo. "*La muralla* y su éxito en el teatro español contemporáneo." *Hispania* 45 (1962): 383–388.

Marinetti, Filippo Tommaso, et al. *Il teatro futurista sintético*. Biblioteca Teatrale 10. Piacenza: Ghelfi Constantino, 1919.

Mariscal, Ana. *Cincuenta años de teatro en Madrid*. Madrid: Avapiés, 1984.

Marqueríe, Alfredo. *Desde la silla eléctrica, crítica teatral; con un diálogo de Tomás Borrás*. Madrid: Editorial Nacional, 1942.

————. *Novedad en el teatro de Jardiel. El teatro de humor en España*. Madrid: Editorial Nacional, 1966.

————. *El teatro de Jardiel Poncela*. Bilbao: Hispano Americana, 1945.

————. *Veinte años de teatro en España*. Madrid: Editorial Nacional, 1959.

Marquina, Rafael. "La batalla de Alberti." *La Gaceta Literaria* 101–102 (March 15, 1931): 5–6.

Marrast, Robert. *El teatre durant la guerra civil española*. Barcelona: Publicacions de l'Institut del Teatre/Edicions No. 62, 1978.

Martín, Eutimio. "Pemán, poeta del nacional-catolicismo español." *Cahiers d'Etudes Romanes* (Paris) 5 (1979): 57–65.

Martínez Espada, M. *Teatro contemporáneo* [The 1898–1900 Theatrical Season]. *Apuntes para un estudio crítico*. Madrid: Imprenta Ducal, 1900.

Martínez Olmedilla, Augusto. *Arriba el telón. Colección panorama de un siglo*. Madrid: Aguilar, 1961.

————. *Los teatros de Madrid*. Madrid: Editorial J. Ruiz Alonso, 1947.

Martínez Ruiz, (Azorín). "*Dos autos sacramentales.*" In *Ante las candilejas: obras Completas XI*. Madrid: Aguilar, 1954; *ABC*, May 15, 1936.

————. *Historia y amecdotario del Teatro Real* [from the second half of the nineteenth century]. Madrid: 1997. Rpt. from the J. Subirá ed. Madrid: Plus Ultra, 1949.

————. "Teatros" [Teatro Nacional]. *Luz*, June 8, 1932: 3.

Martínez Sierra, Gregorio, ed. *Un Teatro de Arte en España, 1917–1925*. Madrid: La Esfinge, 1926.

Martínez Sierra, María. *Gregorio y yo. Medio siglo de colaboración*. Mexico: Biografía Gandesa, 1933.

Martínez Trives, Trino. *Ionesco en Espagne*. Trans. Marcel Schneider. *Cahiers des Saisons* 15 (1959): 279–281.

Materna, Linda. "Los códigos sexuales y la presentación de la mujer en el teatro de García Lorca." In *Estelas, laberintos, nuevas sendas*, ed. Angel García Lorenzo. Barcelona: Antropos, 1987. 263–277.

McGaha, Michael D. "El teatro. Esplendores y miserias del astracán." *La Libertad*, September 17, 1926: 4.

————. "El teatro. La crisis teatral: Los empresarios. El director. La crítica." *La Libertad*, September 17, 1926: 4.

————. "Los teatros. *La bondad*, comedia en tres actos por D. Pedro Muñoz Seca." *La Libertad*, August 1, 1925: 5.

————. *The Theatre in Madrid during the Second Republic*. London: Grand and Cutler, 1976.

McKay, Douglas R. "Forty Years of Titillation: The Absurdist Trend in Spanish Theater. Humor." *Estreno*, no. 7 (Spring 1981): 11–13.

————. *Miguel Mihura*. Twayne's World Authors Series, 436. Boston, MA: Twayne, 1977.

Membrez, Nancy, and J. Hartley. "The Bureaucratization of the Madrid Theater: Government Censorship, Curfews and Taxation (1868–1925)." *Anales de la Literatura Española Contemporánea / ALEC* 17 (1992): 99–103.

————. "The Teatro por horas. History, Dynamics, Comprehensive Bibliography of a Madrid Industry (1867–1922)." Ph.D. diss., University of California, Santa Barbara, 1987.

Mermall, Tomás. "Æsthetics and Politics in Falangist Culture (1935–45)." *Bulletin of Hispanic Studies/BHS* 50.1 (1973): 45–55.

Miguel Martínez, Emilio de. *El teatro de Miguel Mihura*. Rev. 2d ed. Salamanca: Universidad de Salamanca (Estudios Filológicos), 1997.

Milla, Fernando de la. "Diálogos actuales. Eduardo Marquina, el teatro internacional de París y los autores nuevos. Impresiones, proyectos, sugestiones." *La Esfera*, July 31, 1935: 4–5.

Miralles, Alberto. *Aproximación al teatro alternativo*. Madrid: Asociación de Autores de Teatro, 1994.

————. "El nuevo teatro español ha muerto, ¡mueran sus asesinos!" *Estreno* 12.2 (1986): 21–24.

————. *Nuevo teatro español: Una alternative social*. Colección Hoy es siempre todavía, 2. Madrid: Editorial Villalar, 1977.

Mira Nouselles, Alberto. *De silencio y espejos. Hacia una estética del teatro español contemporáneo*. Series Teatro Siglo XX. Valencia: Universidad de Valencia Press, 1966.

Moi, Toril. *Sexual/Textual Politics: Feminist Literary Theory*. London: Routledge, 1988.

Monleón, José. *La cultura bajo el Franquismo*. Barcelona: Ediciones de Bolsillo, 1977.

————. *Larra. Escritos sobre teatro*. Madrid: Cátedra, 1976.

————. *Miguel Mihura. Teatro*. Madrid: Taurus, 1965.

————. *El mono azul. Teatro de urgencia y Romancero de la guerra civil. Alianza de Intelectuales Antifascistas para la defensa de la cultura*. Madrid: Ayuso, 1979.

————. *El teatro del 98 frente a la sociedad española*. Madrid: Cátedra, 1975.

————. *Treinta años de teatro a la derecha*. Barcelona: Tusquets, 1971.

————, ed. *Seis dramaturgos españoles del siglo XX*. Madrid: *Primer Acto* [Ottawa, CA]: Girol Books, 1989.

Morales, José-Ricardo. *La Barraca, El Buho y El Teatro Experimental*. Madrid: *Primer Acto* 240, 1991.

Morales y Marín, José. *Diccionario de iconología y simbología*. Madrid: Taurus, 1984.

Moreno Baez, Enrique. "*La Barraca*. Revista de la Universidad Internacional de Santander 1 (1993)." In *Treinta entrevistas a Federico García Lorca*, ed. Andrés Soria Olmedo. Madrid: Aguilar, 1988.

Mori, Arturo. "El teatro Lírico Nacional. Razonemos como españoles: Con entusiasmo y prudencia. *Boletín Musical* 5 (July 1928): 6–7.

————. "El teatro Lírico Nacional. Un tema que no se agota pero que acabará por no interesar." *Boletín Musical* 6 (August 1928): 8–11.

Morris, C. Brian. *Surrealism and Spain, 1920–1936*. Cambridge: Cambridge University Press, 1972.

————. *This Loving Darkness. The Cinema and Spanish Writers 1920–1936*. Oxford: Oxford University Press, 1980.

————, ed. *The Surrealist Adventure in Spain*. Ottawa, Canada: Doven House, 1991.

Mundi, Pedret F. *El teatro de la Guerra Civil*. Barcelona: *(PPU) Promociones y Publicaciones Universitarias*, [1987].

Muñoz-Alonso-López, Agustín. *Ramón y el teatro. (La obra dramática de Ramón Gómez de la Serna)*. Cuenca: Ediciones de la Universidad de Castilla–La Mancha, 1993.

Navas, Federico. *Las esfinges de Talía. Encuesta sobre la crisis del teatro*. El Escorial: Imprenta del Real Monasterio, 1928.

Neuschäfer, Hans Jörg. *Macht und Ohnmcht der Zensur: Literature, Theater und Film in Spanien (1933–1976)*. Stuttgart: J. B. Metzler, 1991.

Newberry, Wilma. *The Pirandellian Mode in Spanish Literature from Cervantes to Sastre*. New York: New York University Press, 1973.

Nicholas, Robert. *El sainete serio*. Murcia: *Cuadernos del Teatro Universitario de Murcia*, 1992.

Nieva, Francisco. "García Lorca, metteur en scène les intermedes de Cervantes." In *La mise en scène des oeuvres du passé*. Paris: Editions Centre National du Recherché Scientifique/CNRS, 1957. 81–90.

Nieva de la Paz, Pilar. *Autoras dramáticas españolas entre 1928 y 1936 (texto y representación)*. Madrid: Consejo Superior de Investigaciones Científicas/CSIC, 1993.

O'Connor, Patricia. *Antonio Buero Vallejo en sus espejos*. Madrid: Editorial Fundamentos, 1996.

————. *Dramaturgos españoles de hoy*. Madrid: Fundamentos, 1988.

————. "Post-Franco Theater: From Limitation, to Liberty to License." *Hispanic Journal* 5.2 (1984): 55–73.

————. ¿Quiénes son los dramaturgos españoles contemporáneos y qué han escrito?" *Estreno* 10.2 (1984): 9–12.

————, ed. *Plays of the New Democratic Spain (1975–1990)*. Lanham, MD: University Press of America, 1992.

Oliva, César. *Cuatro dramaturgos "Realistas" en la escena de hoy: Sus contradiciones estéticas*. Murcia: University of Murcia Press, 1978.

————. *Historia de la literatura española actual*. Vol. 3, *El teatro desde 1936*. Madrid: Alhambra, 1989.

————. *Ocho años de teatro universitario*. Murcia: Murcia University of Murcia Press, 1975.

Oliva, César, and Francisco Torres Monreal. *Historia básica del arte escénico*. Madrid: Cátedra, 1990.

Oliver, William I. "The Trouble with Lorca." *Modern Drama* 7 (1964): 2–15.

"Organisation du téâtre dans le monde: Espagne: Le téâtre en Espagne." *La Gazette Officiale du Spectable* 173.1: xi.

Orozco Díaz, Emilio. "Invención teatral y realidad histórica: '*Las arrecogías del Beataio de Santa María Egipcíaca.*' " *Pipirijaina* 4 (1977).

Orrey, Leslie. "Operetta, Comedy and the Musical." In *Concise History of Opera*. London: Thames and Hudson, 1972.

Ortega y Gasset, José. *La deshumanización del arte y otros ensayos estéticos*. 8th ed. Madrid: Publicaciones de la Revista de Occidente, 1964.

————. *La idea del teatro*. El Arquero 16. 3d ed. Madrid: Revista de Occidente, 1977.

Otero Ortaza, Eugenio. *Las misiones Pedagógicas: Una experiencia de educación popular*. Coruña: Ediciós do Castro, 1982.

Oteyza, Luis de. *López de Ayala o el figurón político-literarío*. Madrid: 1932.

Paco Moya, Mariano de. "Teatro: Crisis y renovación." *Insula* 529 (1991): 35–36.

Pascual, Itziar. "Teatro alternativo: Un intento de panorámica." *Insula* 601–602 (1997): 32–33.

Pascuariello, Anthony M. "*La Muralla*: The Story of the Play and a Polemic." *Kentucky Foreign Language Quarterly* 4 (1957): 153–199.

Pavis, Patrice. "Production et réception du téâtre: La concrétisation du texte dramatique et spectaculaire." *Revue des Sciences Humaines* 189 (January–March 1983): 51–88.

Pedraza Jiménez, Felipe B., and Milagros Rodríguez Cáseres. *Manual de literatura española*. Vol. 14, *Posguerra: Dramaturgos y ensayistas*. 2d ed. Pamplona: Cénit, 1995.

Peláez, Andrés, ed. *Historia de los teatros nacionales 1939–1985*. 2 vols. Vol. 1. Madrid: Instituto Nacional de las Artes Escénicas y la Música, Ministerio de Cultura, Centro de Documentación Teatral. (List of most of the operas staged during these years, notes on authors, stage directions and so on.) n.d.

————. *Historia de los teatros nacionales, 1960–1985*. Madrid: Instituto Nacional de las Artes Escénicas y la Música, Ministerio de Cultura, Centro de Documentación Teatral, n.d.

Pereira, Aureliano. "La decadencia del teatro español contemporáneo." *Revista Europea* 1 (April 1977).

Pérez, Janet. *Contemporary Women Writers of Spain*. Boston: Twayne, 1988.

Pérez Coterillo, Moisés. Introduction to *Teatro furioso* by Francisco Nieva. Madrid: Akal, 1975.

————, ed. *Escenarios de dos mundos: Inventario teatral de Iberoamérica.* 4 vols. Madrid: Centro de Documentación Teatral, 1988. 2: 187–297.

Pérez de Ayala, Ramón. *Las máscaras. La reteatralización. Obras completas.* Madrid: Aguilar, 1966. Rpt. from *España* 44 (November 25, 1945).

Pérez Minik, Domingo. "Jacinto Grau o el retablo de las maravillas." In *Debates sobre el teatro español contemporáneo.* Santa Cruz de Tenerife: Goya, 1953: 141–159.

————. *El teatro europeo contemporáneo.* Madrid: Guadarrama, 1961.

Pérez-Razilla, Eduardo. "La escritura teatral hoy." *Insula* 601–602 (enero–febrero 1997): 33–35.

————. "No hay teatro sin conflicto." *Insula* 625–626 (enero–febrero 1999): 35–37.

————. "Panorámica de la literatura dramática española de los últimos 25 años." In *Actas del Seminario sobre Literatura dramática española contemporánea* [at Castillo de la Mota, University Carlos III, on June 28, 1996]. Madrid: Asociación de Directores de Escena/ADE, 1996.

Pérez-Stansfield, María Pílar. "La desacramentalización del mito y de la historia: Texto y contexto en dos nuevas dramaturgas españolas." *Gestos* 2 (1987): 83–99.

————. *Direcciones de teatro español de posguerra: Ruptura con el teatro burgués y radicalismo contestario.* Madrid: José Porrúa Turanzas, 1983.

Picón, Jacinto Octavio. " 'Prólogo.' Historia del Sainete." *La Novela Cómica* 18 (1917).

Pillement, Georges. *Le Theatre d'aujourd'hui de Jean Paul Sartre à Arrabal.* Paris: Le Beher, 1970.

Pirraglia, Elvira. "Parodia y discurso subversivo en las obras de Valle-Inclán." Ph.D. diss., Graduate Center of the City University of New York, 1997.

Plunka, Gene A. *Peter Schaefer: Roles Rites and Rituals in the Theater.* Rutherford, NJ: Fairleigh Dickinson University Press, 1988.

Poglioli, Renato. *Teoria dell'arte d'avanguardia.* Bologna: Il Mulino, 1962.

Porset, Fernando. *De telón adentro.* Madrid: Imprenta de Hijos de R. Alvarez, 1912.

Poutet, Jean, and Pedro Páramo. *Le Têâtre en Espagne.* Notes et Études Documentaries 361. Paris: Secrétariat Général du Gouvement, 1970.

Poyán Diaz, Daniel. *Enrique Gaspar. Medio siglo de teatro español.* Madrid: 1957.

Prego, Adolfo. Introduction. *Itenerario temático y estilístico del teatro contemporáneo español: scripts . . . Radio Nacl., de España 1975–1976.* Ed. Miguel Suárez Radillo. Madrid: Playor, [1976].

Puente Samaniego, Pilar de la. *Antonio Buero Vallejo, proceso a la historia de España.* Acta Salmantina. Estudios Filológicos 206. Salamanca: University of Salamanca Press, 1988.

Quinto, José María de. *La tragedia y el hombre (notas estético-sociológicas).* Barcelona: Seix Barral, 1962.

Ragué-Arias, María-José. "Los personajes femeninos de la tragedia griega en el teatro español del siglo XX." Ph.D. diss., Universidad de Barcelona, 1986.

————. *El teatro de fin de milenio en España (de 1975 hasta hoy).* Barcelona: Ariel, 1996.

Ramírez, O. "Teatro para el pueblo [García Lorca]." *La Nación,* January 28, 1934.

Ramoneda Salas, Arturo. "Valle-Inclán: Un estreno frustrado." *Insula* 433 (1982): 1, 12, 13; 434 (1983): 3–4.

Rebello, Luis Francisco. *Combate por un teatro de combate.* Lisbon: Seara Nuova, 1977.

Rees, Margaret A., ed. *Staging in Spanish Theater.* Leeds: Trinity and All Saints College, 1984.

Rehder, Ernest C. "Reformist Tendencies in the Later *Thesis Dramas* of Joaquín Calvo Sotelo." *Estreno* 3.1 (1977): 19–22.

Requelme, J. *El auto sacramental de Miguel Hernández.* Alicante: Técnica Gráfica Industrial, 1990.

Reyero Hermosilla, C. *Gregorio Martínez Sierra y su Teatro de Arte.* Madrid: Fundación Juan March, 1980.

Ríos, Blanca de los. "Calderón, precursor de Wagner y del teatro moderno." *ABC*, June 2, June 9, June 20, August 25, September 22, 1927.

Ríos, Juan Antonio. *Arniches y el cine.* Alicante: Caja de ahorros, Caja Provincial de Alicante, 1986.

Ríos-Carratalá, Juan Antonio, ed. *Estudios sobre Carlos Arniches.* Alicante: Diputación de Alicante, 1994.

Ríos-Font, Wadda C. *Rewriting Melodrama: The Hidden Paradigm in Modern Spanish Theater.* Lewisburg, PA: Bucknell University Press, 1997.

Rivas Cherif, Cipriano. *Cómo hacer teatro. Apuntes de orientación profesional en las artes y oficios del teatro español.* Ed. Enrique Rivas. Valencia: Pre-Textos, 1991.

———. "La obra de Benavente al fulgor del premio Nobel." *La Pluma* 3 (1922): 439.

———. "Propósitos incumplidos del Teatro Intimo en Madrid, con otros atisbos de esperanza." *Teatrón* 1 (1926): 2.

———. "Teatro crítico." *Heraldo de Madrid*, October 16, 1926: 4.

———. "Temas con variaciones. Veintisiete mil, una" [Teatro Nacional]. *El Sol*, July 14, 1931: 1.

Rodrígo, Antonina. "Don Ramón del Valle-Inclán y Margarita Xirgu." In *Homenaje del Ateneo de Madrid.* Madrid: Ateneo, 1991. 287–305.

———. *Margarita Xirgu y su teatro.* Barcelona: Planeta, 1974.

Rodríguez Acasuso, Luis. *Del teatro al libro* [Benavente]. Buenos Aires: Cooperativa Editorial, 1920.

Rodríguez Celada, Antonio. "Buero/Miller: Anverso y reverso de una misma realidad." *Segismundo* 33–34 (1981): 267–282.

———. "Buero, Miller y el 'common man.' " *Estreno* 10.1 (Spring 1984): 23–28.

Rodríguez Méndez, José María. *Benavente, un autor para una sociedad. Pubcs. de la Revista de Occidente* 4 (1966).

———. *Los despojos del teatro.* Madrid: Ediciones J. García Verdugo, 1993.

———. *La generación realista y la cultura teatral en España.* Occasional Lectures. Series 3. Bristol: Department of Hispanic, Portuguese and Latin American Studies, University of Bristol, 1987.

———. *La incultura teatral en España.* Barcelona: Laia, 1974.

Rodríguez Puértolas, Julio. *Literatura fascista española.* 2 vols. Madrid: Ediciones Alcalá, 1986–1987.

———. "Tres aspectos de una misma realidad: Buero, Sastre, Olmo." *Hispanófila*, no. 31 (September 1967): 43–58.

Rodríguez Richat, José. "Das junge spanische Theatre." *Die Neueren Sprachen* 65 (1966): 318–323.

Rodríguez-Seda de Laguna, Asela. *Shaw en el mundo hispánico.* Colección Mente y Palabra. Río Piedras: Universidad de Puerto Rico, 1981.

Rubio Jiménez, Jesús. *Ideología y teatro en España: 1890–1900.* Zaragoza [Saragossa]: Libro Pórtico, 1982.

———. *Modernismo y teatro poético en España (1900–1914): Una renovación nece-*

saria. Cien Años de Azul (1888–1988). Granada: Universidad de Granada Press, 1992.

———. "El 'Teatro de Arte' (1908–1911): Un eslabón necesario entre el modernismo y las vanguardias." *Siglo XX/20th Century* 5.1–2 (1987–1988): 25–33.

———. "Teatro y política: Las aleluyas vivientes de José María de Alba." *Crítica Hispánica* 17.1 (1995): 127–141.

Ruggeri Marchetti, Magda. "Texto y representación en dos obras contemporáneas [Nieva]." *Teatro* 11 (1997): 211–217.

Ruibal, José. *Teatro sobre teatro.* Madrid: Cátedra, 1975.

Ruiz, David. "España 1902–1923: Vida política, social y cultural." In *Revolución burguesa, oligarquía y constitucionalismo (1834–1923),* ed. Manuel Tuñón de Lara. Historia de España, Vol. 8. Barcelona: Labor, 1981. 492–497.

Ruiz Albeniz, Víctor. *Historia del Teatro Apolo.* Madrid: Prensa Castellana, 1953.

Ruiz-Fornells, Enrique. "Twenty-five Years of Spanish Theater." *Drama Critique* 9 (1966): 50–58.

Ruiz Ramón, Francisco. *Estudios de teatro español clásico y contemporáneo.* Madrid: Fundación Juan March/Cátedra, 1978.

———. *Historia del teatro español del siglo XX.* 5th ed. Madrid: Ediciones Cátedra, 1975.

———. "Valle-Inclán y el teatro público de su tiempo: Los signos de la diferencia." *Bulletin Hispanique* 91 (1989): 127–146.

Sáenz de la Calzada, Luis. *La Barraca," teatro universitario.* Madrid: Publicacíones de la Revista de Occidente, 1976.

Sainz de Robles, Federico. *El espíritu y la letra; cien años de literatura española: 1860–1960.* Series Evocaciones y Memorias. Madrid: Aguilar, 1966.

———, ed. *Teatro español, historia y antología: 1949–1950.* 3rd ed. Madrid: Aguilar, 1959.

———. *Teatro español: 1950–1951.* 2d ed. Madrid: Aguilar, 1957.

———. *Teatro español: 1951–1952.* 2d ed. Madrid: Aguilar, 1962.

———. *Teatro español: 1952–1953.* 2d ed. Madrid: Aguilar, 1958.

———. *Teatro español: 1953–1954.* Madrid: Aguilar, 1955.

———. *Teatro español: 1954–1955.* Madrid: Aguilar, 1956.

———. *Teatro español: 1955–1956.* Madrid: Aguilar, 1957.

———. *Teatro español: 1956–1957.* Madrid: Aguilar, 1958.

———. *Teatro español: 1957–1958.* Madrid: Aguilar, 1959.

———. *Teatro español: 1958–1959.* Madrid: Aguilar, 1960.

———. *Teatro español: 1959–1960.* Madrid: Aguilar, 1961.

———. *Teatro español: 1960–1961.* Madrid: Aguilar, 1962.

———. *Teatro español: 1961–1962.* Madrid: Aguilar, 1963.

———. *Teatro español: 1962–1963.* Madrid: Aguilar, 1964.

———. *Teatro español: 1963–1964.* Madrid: Aguilar, 1965.

Salaún, Serge. "El género chico o los mecanismos de un pacto cultural." In *Teatro menor de España a partir del siglo XVI.* Ed. Equipo de Investigación sobre el Teatro español. Madrid: Instituto "Miguel de Cervantes," Consejo Superior de Investigaciones Científicas/CSIC, 1983. 251–260.

Salinas, Pedro. "Del género chico a la tragedia grotesca: Carlos Arniches." In *Literatura española del siglo XX.* Madrid: Alianza Editorial, 1970. 126–131.

———. *Ensayos de literatura hispánica.* Madrid: 1958.

Salvat, Ricard. "Cunqueiro y el teatro europeo de su tiempo." *Primer Acto* 241 (1991): 25–53.

———. "Esencia de una nueva generación." *Primer Acto* 133 (1971): 17–18.

———. Introducción. *Noche de Guerra en el Museo del Prado*. By Rafael Alberti. Madrid: Edicusa, 1975.

———. *Teatre contemporani*. Collecció a l'Abast. 2 vols. 39–40. Barcelona: Ediciones, 1962. Rpt., 1966.

Sánchez, Roberto. "Gordon Craig y Valle Inclán." *Revista de Occidente* 4 (1976): 27–37.

Sánchez-Biosca, Vicente. *El expresionismo: Hacia una relectura de las vanguardias*. Vol. 2, *Ideologies and Literature*. Madrid: 1987.

Sánchez de Horcajo, Juan José. *Los teatros madrileños y su público*. 2 vols. Madrid: Autoedición, 1997.

Sánchez Esteván, Ismael. *María Guerrero*. Barcelona: Iberia (Joaquín Gil), 1946.

Sánchez Morales, Narciso. "Das moderne spanische Theater." *Brempunkte* 12 (1976): 107–121.

Sánchez Vidal, Agustín. *Buñuel, Lorca, Dalí: El enigma sin fin*. Barcelona: Planeta, 1988.

Santos Deulofeu, Elena. "La Farsa: Una revista teatral de vanguardia (1925–26)." *Siglo XX/20th Century* 6 (1988–1989): 57–65.

Sanz Villanueva, Santos. *El siglo XX: Literatura actual*. 6 vols. *Historia de la literatura española*. 2d ed. 6.2. Barcelona: Ariel, 1985.

Sassone, Felipe. "Para el teatro español. Admonición, esperanza y augurio." *ABC*, August 22, 1929: 11, 13.

———. *El teatro, espectáculo literario*. Madrid: 1930.

Sastre, Alfonso. *Anatomía del realismo*. Barcelona: Seix Barral, 1965.

———. "Del teatro Católico." *Cuadernos Hispanoamericanos*, no. 21 (May–June 1951): 484–485.

———. *Drama y sociedad*. Madrid: Taurus, 1956.

———. "Reaparición del teatro como tema. Estado de la cuestión teórica en 1966." In *La revolución y la crítica de la cultura*. Mexico: Grijalbo, 1970.

———. "Reflexiones después de Brecht." *Lateral* 3.17 (1996): 16.

Sastre, Alfonso, et al. *Alfonso Sastre: Noticia de una ausencia*. Cuadernos El Público 38. Madrid: Centro de Documentación Teatral, 1988.

Savater, Fernando. "El héroe como proyecto moral." *Revista de Occidente* 46 (1985): 61.

Schechner, Richard. *Pornography and the New Expression. The Perverse Imagination*. Ed. Irving Buchen. New York: New York University Press, 1970.

Schneider, Marshall J. *A Library of Literary Criticism*. New York: Ungar Publishing Co., 1984. 316–369.

Schober, Rita. "Réception et historicité de la littérature." *Revue des Sciences Humaines*, no. 189 (1983): 7–20.

Scholnicov, Hanna, and Peter Holland, eds. *The Play out of Context: Transferring Plays from Culture to Culture*. Cambridge: Cambridge University Press, 1989.

Schueter, Jane. *Metafictional Characters in Modern Drama*. New York: Columbia University Press, 1979.

Schwartz, Kessel. "Tragedy and the Criticism of Alfonso Sastre." In *The Meaning of Existence in Contemporary Hispanic Literature*, ed. Kessel Schwartz. Hispanic-

American Studies 23. Coral Gables, FL: University of Miami Press, 1969. 162–170; *Symposium* 21 (1967): 338–346.

Sender, Ramón. *Teatro de masas.* Valencia: Orto, 1932.

———. "El teatro nuevo." *Leviatán* 25 (June 1936).

Serreau, Geneviéve. *Histoire du "nouveau téâtre."* Paris: Gallimard, 1966.

Shapiro, Karl. *Beyond Criticism.* Lincoln: University of Nebraska Press, 1953.

Shaw, D. L. "The Anti-Romantic Reaction in Spain." *Modern Language Review* 63 (1968): 606–611.

Shaw, George Bernard. *The Quintessence of Ibsenism.* London: Constable, 1913.

Sheehan, Robert Louis. *Benavente and the Spanish Panorama, 1894–1954. Hispanófila* 37. Chapel Hill: University of North Carolina Press, 1975.

Siguán, Marisa. *La recepción de Ibsen and Hauptmann en el modernismo catalán.* Estudios de Literatura española y Comparada 5. Barcelona: Promociones y Publicaciones Universitarias, 1990.

Silva, Ernesto. "La reutilización de la tragedia griega: *Elektra* del grupo Atalaya." In *Del escenario a la mesa de la crítica,* ed. Juan Villegas. Irvine, CA: Ediciones Gestos, 1997. 127–136.

Silva Melo, Jorge. *El fin.* Asociación de Escritores Españoles. *Teatro* 62–63 (1997): 105–143.

Sinclair, Alison. "Elitism and the Cult of the Popular in Spain." In *Visions and Blueprints: Avant-Garde Culture and Radical Politics in Early Twentieth-Century Europe,* ed. Edward Timms and Peter Collier. Manchester: University of Manchester Press, 1988. 221–223.

Sito Alba, Manuel. *Análisis de la semiótica teatral.* Madrid: Universidad Nacional de Educación a Distancia, 1987.

Sobel, Alan. *Pornography, Marxism, Feminism and the Future of Sexuality.* New Haven, CT: Yale University Press, 1989.

Soldevila Durante, Ignacio. "Sobre el teatro español de los últimos veinticinco años." *Cuadernos Hispanoamericanos* 22. 1 (January–February 1963): 256–289.

Soler Marcel, María-Lourdes. "Dramaturgia hispana en tablas germánicas en la década de los ochenta." *Estreno* 18.1 (Spring 1992): 33–36.

Soria Olmedo, Andrés, ed. *Treinta entrevistas a Federico Garcia Lorca.* Madrid: Aguilar, 1988.

Soufas, Christopher C. *Audience and Authority in the Modernist Theater of Garcia Lorca.* Tuscaloosa: University of Alabama Press, 1996.

Souriau, Etiènne. *Les deux cent mille situations dramatiques.* Paris: Flammarion, 1950.

Standish, Peter. "Pirandello, Pygmalion and Spain." *Revue de Littérature Comprarée* 47 (1973): 327–337.

Styan, J. L. *Modern Drama in Theory and Practice.* Vol. 3, *Expressionism and Epic Theater.* Cambridge: Cambridge University Press, 1983.

Suarez, Manuel Laurentino. *Teatro en verso del siglo XX: Un estudio crítico.* Miami, FL: Universal, 1975.

Subirá, José. *Historia de la música teatral de España.* Barcelona: Labor, 1945.

———. *Historia y anecdotario del Teatro Real.* Madrid: Plus Ultra, 1949.

Suleiman, Susan Rubin. "Pornography and the Avant-Garde." In *The Poetics of Gender,* ed. Nancy K. Miller. New York: Columbia University Press, 1990.

Tamames, Ramón. *La República. La era de Franco.* Historia de España 7. 4th ed. Madrid: Aliansa Editorial, 1975.

Taylor, John R. *The Penguin Dictionary of the Theater.* Harmondsworth: Penguin, 1966.

————. *The Rise and Fall of the Well-Made Play.* London: Methuen, 1967.

Thompson, Anne. *The Generation of 'ninety-eight: Intellectual Politicians.* Potomac, MD: Scripta Humanística 55, 1990.

Tomachevsky, Boris. "Temática." In *Teoría de la literatura de los formalistas rusos*, ed. T. Tudorov. Buenos Aires: Signos, 1970.

Torre, Guillermo de. *Historia de las literaturas de vanguardia.* Madrid: Guadarrama, 1965.

————. *Literaturas europeas de vanguardia.* Madrid: Caro Baggio, 1925.

————. *Las metamorfosis de Proteo.* Madrid: Publicaciones de la Revista de Occidente, 1967.

————. "Revisión de Benavente." In *Vigencia de Rubén Darío y otras páginas.* Madrid: Guadarrama, 1969.

Torrente Ballester, Gonzalo. *Teatro español contemporáneo.* 2nd ed. Madrid: Guadarrama, 1957.

Torres Monreal, Francisco. "*Guernica* y después (variación escénica sobre temas de Picasso)." *Arrecife*, no. 3 (May–June 1982): 67–76.

Torres Nebreba, Gregorio. "La obra literaria de María Teresa León (cuentos [short stories] y teatro)." *Anuario de Estudios Filológicos* 7 (1984): 361–384.

————. "La revista *Teatro: Una crónica del teatro español de los años cincuenta,*" *Anales de la Literatura Española Contemporánea/ALEC* 19 (1995): 383–440.

————. "Teoría del teatro en Pedro Salinas." *Insula* 370 (1977): 31.

Traubner, Richard. *Operetta: A Theatrical History.* Garden City, NY: Doubleday, 1983.

Tuñón de Lara, Manuel. *Medio siglo de cultura española.* Madrid: 1973.

Ubersfeld, Anne. *Semiótica teatral* [Francisco Nieva]. Trans. Francisco Torres Monreal. Madrid: Universidad de Murcia, 1989.

Ucelay, Margarita. "La problemática teatral: Testimonios directos de Federico García Lorca." *Boletín de la Fundación Federico García Lorca* 6 (1989).

Underhill, John Garrett. "Introduction." *Plays by Jacinto Benavente.* New York: Charles Scribner's Sons, 1920.

Urbano, Victoria. *El teatro español y sus directrices contemporáneas.* Madrid: Editora Nacional, 1972.

Urrutia, Jorge. *Imago litterae, cine, literatura.* Sevilla: Alfar, 1984.

————. *Semió(p)tica.* Valencia/Madrid: Fundación Instituto Shakespeare/Hiperión, 1985.

Ursic, Giorgio Ursini, ed. *Teatro e società nella spagna d'oggi.* Venice: La Biennale di Venezia, 1978.

Uterera, Jorge. *Literatura cinematográfica. Cinematografia literaria.* Sevilla: Alfar, 1987.

————. *Modernismo y 98 frente al cinematógrafo.* Sevilla: Universidad de Sevilla Press, 1981.

Valbuena Prat, Angel. *Historia del teatro español.* Barcelona: Editorial Noguer, 1956.

Valdivieso, L. Teresa. *España: Bibliografia de un teatro "silenciado."* Manhattan, KS: Society of Spanish and Spanish-American Studies, 1979.

Valenbois, Víctor. "El teatro de cámara en la posguerra española." *Segismundo* 23–24 (1976): 173–199.

Van der Naald, Anje C. *Nuevas tendencias en el teatro español: Matilla, Nieva, Ruibal.* Miami, FL: Ediciones Universal, 1981.

Vicente, Arie. *Lo judío en el teatro español contemporáneo.* Madrid: Editorial Pliegos, 1991.

516   General Bibliography

Videla, Gloria. *El ultraísmo. Estudio sobre movimientos poéticos de vanguardia en España*. 2d ed. Madrid: Gredos, 1971.

Vilaregut, Salvador. "Emile Fabre i la nova orientació de la 'Comèdia-Francesa' [Musset]." *Teatron* 1 (1926): 3.

Vilches de Frutos, María Francisca. "La temporada teatral española, 1994–1995." *Anales de la Literatura Española Contemporánea/ALEC* 22.3 (1997): 565–610.

———, ed. *La escena madrileña entre 1926–1931. Un lustro de transición*. Madrid: Fundamentos, 1997.

Vilches de Frutos, María Francisca, and Dru Hougherty. "La escena madrileña entre 1900–1936. Apuntes para una historia del teatro representado." *Anales de la Literatura Española Contemporánea/ALEC* (1992):

———. *El teatro en España entre la tradición y la vanguardia 1918–1939*. Madrid: Consejo Superior de Investigaciones Científicas/CSIC/Fundación Federico García Lorca, Grupo Tabacalera, S.A., 1992.

———. eds. *La escena madrileña entre 1918–1926: Análisis y documentación*. Colección Arte. Serie Teatro 109. Madrid: Fundamentos, 1990.

Villegas, Juan. *Nueva interpretación y análisis del texto dramático*. Ottawa, CA: Girol Books, 1991.

———. *Para un modelo de historia del teatro*. Irvine, CA: Ediciones Gestos, 1997.

———. "La sustancia metafísica de la tragedia y su función social: *Escuadra hacia la muerte* de Alfonso Sastre." *Symposium* 21 (1967): 255–263.

Villegas-Silva, Claudia. "España fragmentada, apocalíptica y posmoderna: Híbrid de Sémola Teatre." In *Del escenario a la mesa de la crítica*, ed. Juan Villegas. Irvine, CA: Ediciones Gestos, 1997. 115–125.

Walls, Vivian R. V. "Arrabal and Ionesco: A Study in the Theatre of the Absurd." In *Proceedings, Pacific Northwest Conference on Foreign Languages: 21st Annual Meetings*, ed. Ralph Baldner. Victoria, British Columbia: University of Victoria, 1969.

Weiss, Rosemary Shevlin. "Benavente and Martínez Sierra on Broadway." *Estreno* 14.2 (1988): 30–33.

Wellwarth, George E. *Spanish Underground Drama: Teatro Español Underground*. Ed. Alberto Miralles. Trans. Carmen Hierro. Colección hoy es siempre todavía 4. Madrid: Editorial Villalar, 1978.

———. ed. "Introduction." *The New Wave Spanish Drama*. New York: New York University Press, 1970.

Whitaker, Thomas R. *Fields of Play in Modern Drama*. Princeton, NJ: Princeton University Press, 1977.

White, Ann. *Guiding the Plot: Politics and Feminism in the Work of Women Playwrights from Spain and Argentina, 1960–1990*. New York: Peter Lang, 1996.

Wilder, Thorton. *Nuestra ciudad* (Spanish adaptation by José Juan Cadenas). Madrid, 1951.

———. "Some Thoughts on Playwriting." In *The Intent of the Artist*, ed. Augusto Centeno. Princeton, NJ: Princeton University Press, 1941.

Wofsy, Samuel A. "La calidad literaria del teatro de Miguel Mihura." *Hispania* 43 (1960): 214.

Yarmis, Marcia D. "New York City Production of Federico García Lorca's Tragedies: *Blood Wedding, Yerma, and The House of Bernarda Alba*." *Estreno* 14.2 (1988): 38–42.

Yates, Frances. *Theater of the World*. Chicago: University of Chicago Press, 1969.

Yin, Philippa. "El realismo, la esperanza, las relaciones en *Historia de una escalera* de Antonio Buero Vallejo y *Clash by Night* de Clifford Odets." In *De lo particular a lo universal en el teatro español del siglo xx y su contexto*, ed. John P. Gabriele. Teoría y Práctica del Teatro 2. Madrid: Iberoamericana, 1994. 101–111.

Yxar, José. *El arte escénico en España*. 2 vol. Barcelona: La Vanguardia, 1987. Rpt. from the 1894–1896 ed.

Zamacois, Eduardo. *Desde mi butaca*. Barcelona: 1911.

———. "Socialismo en el teatro." *España Artística* 55 (February 1, 1898).

Zatlin-Boríng, Phyllis. "Brecht in Spain." *Theater History Studies* 10 (1990): 57–66.

———. *Cross-Cultural Approaches to Theatre: The Spanish-French Connection*. Metuchen, NJ: Scarecrow Press, 1994.

———. "Homosexuality on the Spanish Stage: Barometer of Sexual Change." *España Contemporánea* 1.2 (1988): 7–20.

———. "Josefina Molina's Esquilache: Filmic Transformation of Theatre." *Anuario de cine y literatura en español* 3 (1997): 173–179.

———. "El teatro español contemporáneo en los escenarios norteamericanos." *Insula* 601–602 (1997): 39–40.

Zavala, Iris. "El arte por el arte y el realismo." In *Ideología y política en la novela española del siglo XIX*. Salamanca: Anaya, 1971. 167–209.

———. *Románticos y socialistas*. Madrid: Siglo 21, 1972.

Zita, Jacquelyn N. "Pornography and the Male Imaginary." *Enclitic* 9 (1987): 1–2.

Zurita, Marciano. *Historia del género chico*. Madrid: Prensa Popular, 1920.

INDEX

ABOUT THE CONTRIBUTORS

HAZEL CAZORLA is Professor of Spanish at the University of Dallas and Director of the Program in Spanish there. Born and educated in England, she received her degrees in Modern Languages from Oxford University, where she also gained experience in the theater. She worked as a translator of Spanish in London before moving to Spain to teach for the British Council at the Instituto Británico in Seville. Later, she and her husband moved to Texas, where she joined the faculty of the University of Dallas, becoming the Chair of the Department of Foreign Languages and Literatures and pioneering the production of plays in Spanish for the University community. Hazel Cazorla has published widely in English and in Spanish on the contemporary Spanish theater in journals including *Modern Drama*, *Revista de Estudios Hispánicos*, *Romance Quarterly*, *Estreno*, *Letras Péninsulares*, and *Pipirijaina* and edited Gala's *Los verdes campos del Edén*. Her English translation of Buero Vallejo's *Lázaro en el laberinto* [Lazarus in the Labyrinth] appeared in 1991 and that of *Juana del amor hermoso* [A Love Too Beautiful], by Manuel Martínez Mediero, in 1995. She is a member of the Editorial Board of *Estreno* and is currently working on a book on the theater of Antonio Gala.

LISA PAULINE CONDÉ is Senior Lecturer in the Department of Hispanic Studies, University of Wales, Swansea. She graduated from the University of Birmingham and obtained both her Master's and Doctor of Philosophy degrees from the University of Sheffield, on the novels and plays of Galdós, respectively. Her major publications include *Women in the Theatre of Galdós* (1990), *Stages in the Development of a Feminist Consciousness in Pérez Galdós* (1990), *Feminist Readings on Spanish and Latin American Literature* (coeditor with Stephen Hart) (1991), *The Theatre of Galdós: Realidad* (1993), *The Theatre of Galdós: La loca de la casa* (1995), *The Theatre of Galdós: Voluntad* (2000), and *Pérez Galdós: Tristana*, Critical Guides to Spanish Texts (2000).

MARÍA M. DELGADO is a Senior Lecturer in Drama at Queen Mary and Westfield College, the University of London. She is coeditor of the recent *In*

Contact with the Gods?: Directors Talk Theatre (1996), guest editor of the 1998 edition of *Contemporary Theatre Review* entitled "Spanish Theatre 1920–1995: Strategies in Protest and Imagination," and editor of *Valle-Inclán Plays: One* (1993, 1997). She is author of numerous articles on Hispanic performance and film, an adviser to the London Film Festival, and editor of a forthcoming collection of writings, lectures, and interviews by the American director Peter Sellars.

JOHN DOWLING, Alumni Foundation Distinguished Professor Emeritus of Romance Languages and Dean Emeritus of the Graduate School at the University of Georgia, has specialized in Spanish theater from the Golden Age to the present. He is the author of books and articles on the dramatist Moratín and the opera composer José Melchor Gomis, among others, and has edited numerous editions of dramatic texts.

SHARON G. FELDMAN, Assistant Professor of Spanish Literature at the University of Kansas, specializes in modern Spanish theater. She has published articles on Fermín Cabal, Federico García Lorca, and Agustín Gómez-Arcos. She is presently completing a book on the theater of Gómez-Arcos and is engaged in research on the Catalán theater of images.

JOHN P. GABRIELE is Professor of Spanish and Comparative Literature at the College of Wooster. He is the author of articles on el Duque de Rivas, Unamuno, Valle-Inclán, García Lorca, Buero Vallejo, Martínez Mediero, Lidia Falcón, Carmen Resino, Concha Romero, Juan Mayorga, and Florencio Sánchez, among others. He is the editor of several collections of essays, among them, *Suma valleinclaniana*, *El teatro español y su contexto*, and *Nuevas perspectivas sobre el 98*, and the author of *El teatro breve de Lidia Falcón* and *Manuel Martínez Mediero: Deslindes de un teatro de urgencia social*. He is currently working on a critical edition of the theater of Luis Araújo.

SALVADOR GARCÍA CASTAÑEDA received his doctorate in Romance Languages from the University of California at Berkeley. He is presently Professor of Spanish at the Ohio State University. He is a distinguished specialist in nineteenth-century studies in Spain and has authored numerous publications, including *Las ideas literarias en España entre 1840 y 1850* (1971), *Don Telesforo de Trueba y Cosío (1799–1835): Su tiempo, su vida, su obra* (1978), and *Los montañeses pintados por sí mismos. Un panorama del costumbrismo en Cantabria* (1991). In the field of theater, in addition to numerous articles, he has published critical editions of Hartzenbusch's *Los amantes de Teruel* (1971), Zorrilla's *Don Juan Tenorio*, and Muñoz Seca's *La venganza de Don Mendo* (1984).

DAVID GEORGE is Senior Lecturer in Hispanic Studies at the University of Wales, Swansea. He has published mainly on modern Spanish and Catalán drama, including a recent article on Sergi Belbel's production of Guimerà's *La filla del mar.* He has published a book on the *commedia dell' arte* in modern Hispanic literature and has coedited a book on contemporary Catalán drama. He is one of the translators of Belbel's *Després de la pluja.*

REBECCA HAIDT is Associate Professor of Spanish at the Ohio State University. She has published various studies of eighteenth-century Spanish texts, including *Embodying Enlightenment: Knowing the Body in Eighteenth-Century Spanish Literature and Culture* (1998). She is also a winner of the Modern Language Association of America's Katherine Singer Kovacs Prize for Outstanding Books Published in English in the field of Latin American and Spanish Literatures and Cultures.

MARTHA T. HALSEY is Professor of Spanish at the Pennsylvania State University. She has prepared editions of plays by Buero Vallejo, Rodríguez Méndez, and Martín Recuerda and is author of the recent *From Dictatorship to Democracy: The Recent Plays of Antonio Buero Vallejo (From "La Fundación" to "Música cercana").* In 1980 she organized an international symposium on contemporary Spanish theater. She has been editor of *Estreno* and of *Estreno*: Contemporary Spanish Plays Series since 1992.

CAROLYN J. HARRIS has taught Spanish at Western Michigan University since 1985. Her field of specialization is contemporary Spanish drama. She has published a book-length study of Antonio Gala's theater and articles on the dramatic works of Antonio Buero Vallejo, Concha Romero, Paloma Pedrero, and Carmen Resino.

MARION PETER HOLT is Professor Emeritus of Theatre at the Graduate Center of the City University of New York and of Modern Languages at CUNY's College of Staten Island. In 1986 he was elected a corresponding member of Spain's Real Academia Española. His translations of contemporary Spanish and Catalán plays have been performed in New York and London, as well as at leading regional theaters.

IRIDE LAMARTINA-LENS is Professor of Spanish and Italian and Chair of the Department of Modern Languages at Pace University (Manhattan campus) in New York. She has published extensively on contemporary Spanish theater, with a particular focus on women dramatists. She is the coeditor of a two-volume anthology on Spanish women playwrights of the 1990s entitled *Nuevos manantiales: Dramaturgas españolas de los noventa.* She is presently coediting a three-volume anthology on Spanish theater of the last fifty years entitled *Testimonios: Teatro español del siglo XX (1950–2000).*

CANDYCE LEONARD is on the faculty at Wake Forest University. She has coedited two collections of contemporary Spanish plays (1996) and in addition has published extensively in the field of contemporary Spanish theater of the Democratic period. Dr. Leonard has just completed coediting a new collection of plays by women, *Nuevos manantiales*, and has begun collaboration on a series of anthologies that embrace the last fifty years of Spanish theater.

FELICIA LONDRÉ is Curators' Professor of Theatre at the University of Missouri-Kansas City and dramaturg for Heart of America Shakespeare Festival and Nebraska Shakespeare Festival. She has been Visiting Foreign Professor at Hosei University, Tokyo (1993) and Women's Chair in Humanistic Studies at Marquette University, Milwaukee (1995). Among her ten books are *Federico García Lorca* (1984); *Shakespeare Around the Globe*, under general editor Samuel Leiter (Greenwood, 1986); *Shakespeare Companies and Festivals: An International Guide*, coedited with Ron Engle and Daniel J. Watermeier (Greenwood, 1995); and *The History of North American Theater: The United States, Canada, and Mexico from Pre-Columbian Times to the Present*, with Daniel J. Watermeier (1998, 2000). Twelve of Felicia Londré's plays have had academic or professional productions.

DOUGLAS MCKAY is Professor of Spanish in the Department of Languages and Cultures, University of Colorado, Colorado Springs. His area of specialization is nineteenth- and twentieth-century Spanish Peninsular literature. His publications include three Twayne studies in Spanish drama (*Carlos Arniches, Jardiel Poncela, Miguel Mihura*); four language texts (*Misterio y Pavor: Trece Cuentos, Understanding the Spanish Subjunctive, Dígalo Bien,* and *El habla vital: Creative Activities for Spanish Conversation*); and two works of regional Colorado history (*Asylum of the Gilded Pill: A History of the Cragmor Sanatorium* and *A Selective History of UCCS*).

GEORGE P. MANSOUR is Professor of Spanish at Michigan State University where he teaches courses in the Spanish literature and culture of the eighteenth and nineteenth centuries. His scholarly activities include coediting Larra's *Macías* for Espasa-Calpe, editing a special issue of *Crítica Hispánica* devoted to *Don Juan Tenorio*, and studies on Romantic drama and poetry, the *zarzuela*, Don Juan, and such authors as Martínez de la Rosa, Rivas, Zorrilla, and Echegaray, published in *Hispania, Romance Quarterly, Hispanic Journal,* and *Romance Notes*.

LINDA S. MATERNA is Professor of Spanish and Director of the Study Abroad Program at Rider University. She is a specialist in romantic and contemporary theater and has written articles on Rivas, Hartzenbusch, Larra, García Lorca, Salinas, and Alberti, and on the poetry of Ana Rossetti and the cinema of Pedro Almodóvar. She is working on a monograph on the theater of Andres Ruiz López.

ROBERT MAYBERRY and NANCY MAYBERRY are the authors of the book *Francisco Martínez de la Rosa* published in the Twayne World Authors Series in 1988. They received their Ph.D. degrees from the University of North Carolina at Chapel Hill.

NANCY J. MEMBREZ, Assistant Professor of Spanish at the University of Texas at San Antonio, received her Ph.D. from the University of California at Santa Barbara in 1987. She teaches and publishes in the areas of Modern Peninsular literature (especially theater) and culture, Peninsular and Latin American film, and Peninsular and Latin American women's literature. She has published articles in the University of Minnestota's *Hispanic Issues* series, *Siglo XX*, *ALEC*, *Purdue Romance Languages Annual*, *Letras peninsulares*, and *Cine-Lit* I and II. She is probably best known for her Ph.D. dissertation on *The Teatro por horas*. She is currently finishing *Mujeres: Bibliografía de la mujer en la revista ilustrada española 1857–1938/A Bibliography of Women in Illustrated Spanish Weeklies 1857–1938.*

DENISE G. MILLS is Associate Professor of Spanish at Daemen College in Amherst, NY. Her literary interests are Contemporary Spanish Drama and Contemporary Latin American Narrative.

ROBERT L. NICHOLAS is Professor of Spanish and the current Chair of the Department of Spanish and Portuguese at the University of Wisconsin-Madison. His specialties include the Generation of 1898 and contemporary Spanish theater. He has written extensively on Unamuno, Antonio Buero Vallejo, Lauro Olmo, Fernando Fernán-Gómez, and others. His books include *The Tragic Stages of Antonio Buero Vallejo* (1972), *Unamuno, narrador* (1987), and *El sainete serio* (1992). He has completed *Ficción y metaficción, realidad y metarealidad*, a work that examines the process of subjectification in the twentieth-century Spanish novel, and is currently at work on *El teatro, museo del vivir*, a retrospective on twentieth-century Spanish theater.

ADA ORTÚZAR-YOUNG is Professor of Spanish at Drew Univesity. She is the author of *Tres representaciones literarias de la vida política cubana*. She publishes and presents papers regularly at conferences on contemporary Hispanic literatures and cinematic adaptations of literary texts. She is particularly interested in the study of autobiographical and other forms of personal writings as life-texts, and as manifestations of class, gender, and cultural issues.

MARY PARKER is an independent scholar. Previously she was Assistant Professor of Modern Languages at St. John's University. Her specialty is Theater/ Spanish Golden Age Literature. She is the author of *Santas, Reinas, Mártires y Cortesanas*, "A Bibliography of Diamante's Primary Sources," in *Bulletin of Bibliography*, and editor of *Spanish Dramatists of the Golden Age*.

PETER L. PODOL is Professor of Spanish and Chair of the Foreign Languages Department at Lock Haven University, where he has taught since 1973. He is an authority in the field of contemporary Spanish theater. A member of the editorial board of *Estreno*, the only journal in the United States devoted to the contemporary theater of Spain, he has authored the Twayne book on Fernando Arrabal, the only extant edition of Arrabal's *And They Will Put Handcuffs on the Flowers* in Spanish, essays in several books devoted to the contemporary theater of Spain and to Antonin Artaud, and numerous articles and reviews in scholarly journals. Dr. Podol has also written on such contemporary playwrights as Athol Fugard, Sam Shepard, and Peter Shaffer.

SUSAN G. POLANSKY is Principal Lecturer in Spanish and Associate Head of the Department of Modern Languages at Carnegie Mellon. Her articles on Salinas and other nineteenth- and twentieth-century Spanish writers have appeared in *Hispania, Revista de Estudios Hispánicos, Letras Peninsulares, Hispanic Journal*, and *Modern Language Studies*. She is author of *Puntos de vista Lectura* (1994), *Exploraciones* (2001), *Eso es* (2001), and is currently working on a manuscript on the dramatic works of Salinas.

DAVID PRICE-UDEN is a part-time tutor in the Department of English and History at the Manchester Metropolitan University, where he is undertaking doctoral research on contemporary American theater.

WADDA C. RÍOS-FONT is Associate Professor in the Department of Hispanic Studies at Brown University. She is the author of a book entitled *Rewriting Melodrama: The Hidden Paradigm in Modern Spanish Theater*, as well as many articles dealing with nineteenth- and twentieth-century Spanish theater, the nineteenth-century romantic novel, and the relationship between "high" and "popular" literture in modern Spain.

ALVIN F. SHERMAN, JR. is an Associate Professor of Spanish at Idaho State University. He received his B.A. (1985) and M.A. (1987) in Spanish from Brigham Young University and his Ph.D. (1990) from the University of Virginia. Dr. Sherman has published several articles on topics ranging from early eighteenth-century mystic poetry to romantic theater. His book, *Mariano José de Larra: A Directory of Historical Personages*, is an encyclopedic work that identifies and defines the historical and literary figures that appear in Larra's numerous newspaper articles.

NÚRIA TRIANA TORIBIO is a Lecturer at Salford University. She obtained a Ph.D. from the University of Newcastle upon Tyne for her work on Subculture and Popular Culture in the Films of Pedro Almodóvar. She has taught cinema and Contemporary Spanish Culture and Society. She collaborated on the *Encyclopedia of European Cinema* (edited by G. Vincendeau, University of Warwick) and is currently preparing material for the *Encyclopedia of Women Film-makers* (to be published by Routledge). Her area of research is film studies and the popular culture of Spain.

ARIE VICENTE is presently the Director of the Graduate program in Foreign Languages at the University of Southern Mississippi.

NANCY VOGELEY is Professor Emerita of Spanish and Spanish American literatures from the University of San Francisco. She has had an interest in (and a friendship with) Alfonso Sastre over the last forty years.

PHYLLIS ZATLIN is Professor of Spanish at Rutgers, The State University. Her areas of specialization include contemporary Spanish theater, contemporary Spanish narrative by women writers, and translation studies. She is author of a monograph on Jaime Salom and numerous books, editions, articles, and translations related to the contemporary Spanish stage. Her published play translations include Salom's *Bonfire at Dawn*. Her most recent books are *Cross-Cultural Approaches to Theatre: The Spanish-French Connection* and *The Novels and Plays of Eduardo Manet: An Adventure in Multiculturalism*.